This volume may be ordered from:

Netti Schreiner-Yantis
6818 Lois Drive
Springfield, Virginia 22150

Price: $5.95

This volume of GENEALOGICAL AND LOCAL HISTORY BOOKS IN PRINT will be
available until approximately August 1978. A new catalogue will be issued in
1978. If you would like to be notified when the new catalogue is released, please
send your indication to the above address. [Individuals who have ordered this
catalogue will automatically be informed of the availability of new issues. They
need comply with the above only if they have changes of address.]

Preface

When the first volume of this series went to press in 1975 it was stated that there would be a supplement in 1976 if demand warranted. This book – with almost one hundred more pages than the work to which it is a supplement – is proof of such demand. Because of the size of the work, it was decided to call it Volume II, rather than a supplement. It is, however, a supplement in that (except for less than 50 titles out of almost 6,000) it contains all new material.

A large percentage of the research sources used by genealogists falls into the category of local history. The two fields are so closely related that many libraries, including the Library of Congress, combine the two departments. Genealogists are familiar with this relationship. However, it was brought to my attention that non-genealogists might not be. Accordingly, I have decided to change the name of the series to GENEALOGICAL & LOCAL HISTORY BOOKS IN PRINT, rather than retain the original title of GENEALOGICAL BOOKS IN PRINT. The change of title does not indicate a change in the scope of the material presented, but merely identifies the contents more clearly.

I wish to express my appreciation to Donna Hotaling who has encouraged and assisted me in many ways, but specifically for encouragement at the time this series was conceived. I am grateful to Jean D. Strahan, librarian at the National Genealogical Society, for suggestions concerning format of this work and for providing me with information concerning new genealogical titles. I am especially indebted to my typist-consultant, Florene Love, who, despite an injury received in an automobile accident, worked long hours to speed the completion of this volume.

Netti Schreiner-Yantis

Table of Contents

Names & Addresses of Vendors

[1] AHM Publishing Corporation, 1500 Skokie Boulevard, Northbrook, IL 60062

[2] AMS Press, Incorporated, 56 East 13th Street, New York, NY 10003

[3] A.R.B.O.R. Committee, P.O. Box 1776, Ironia, NJ 07845

[4] Academic Press, Incorporated, 111 Fifth Avenue, New York, NY 10003

[5] Academy of American Franciscan History, P.O. Box 34440, Washington, DC 20034

[6] Acadian Genealogy Exchange, 863 Wayman Branch Road, Covington, KY 41015

[7] ACETO Bookmen, RFD #3, Box 120A, Middleboro, MA 02346

[8] Adams, Golden V., Jr., Accredited Genealogist, 961 West 100 South, Provo, UT 84601

[9] Addison-Wesley Publishing Company, Incorporated, Jacob Way, Reading MA 01867

[10] Agathon Press, Incorporated, 150 Fifth Avenue, New York, NY 10011

[11] Alabama Press, University of, Drawer 2877, University, AL 35486

[12] Aldine Publishing Company, 529 South Wabash Avenue, Chicago, IL 60605

[13] Aldridge, E.T. & A.M., 368 South Gordon Way, Los Altos, CA 94022

[14] ALFCO Publications, P.O. Box 66, Corydon, IN 47112

[15] Allyn & Bacon, Incorporated, 470 Atlantic Avenue, Boston, MA 02210

[16] American Antiquarian Society, Distributed by University Press of Virginia, P.O. Box 3608 University Station, Charlottesville, VA 22903

[17] American Archivists, Society of, P.O. Box 8198, University of Illinois, Circle Campus, Chicago, Il. 60680

[18] American Association for State and Local History, 1315 Eighth Avenue, South, Nashville, TN 37203

[19] American Baptist Historical Society, 1106 South Goodman Street, Rochester, NY 14620

[20] American Bibliographic Center-CLIO Press, Riviera Campus, 2040 Alameda Padre Serra, Santa Barbara, CA 93103

[21] American Hungarian Review, 5410 Kerth Road, St. Louis, MO 63128

[22] American Library Association, 50 East Huron, Chicago, IL 60611

[23] American Map Company, Incorporated, 1926 Broadway, New York, NY 10023

[24] American Philosophical Society, 104 South Fifth Street, Philadelphia, PA 19106

[25] American Printing Company, The, 1597 1/2 Wadsworth Boulevard, Lakewood, CO 80215

[26] Ancestor's Attic, 4041 Pedley Road, #18, Riverside, CA 92509

[27] Anderson, Mrs. Alloa C., 1120 Lincoln Avenue, Ann Arbor, MI 48104

[28] Anderson, Alvin L., 6084 Leyton Avenue, Northeast, Canton, Ohio 44721

[29] Anderson, Doris, 2910 East Church Street, Eden, NY 14057

[30] Appalachian Studies Center, Pikeville College, Pikeville, KY 41501

[31] Appel (Paul P.), Publisher, Distributed by Gordian Press, Incorporated, 85 Tompkins Street, Staten Island, NY 10304

[32] ARCO Publishing Company, Incorporated, 219 Park Avenue, South, New York, NY 10003

[33] Arizona Press, University of, P.O. Box 3398, Tucson, AZ 85722

[34] Arizona State Genealogical Society, P.O. Box 6027, Tucson, AZ 85733

[35] Ares Publishers, Incorporated, 150 East Huron Street, Suite 1103, Chicago, IL 60611

[36] Argosy-Antiquarian, Limited, 116 East 59th Street, New York, NY 10022

[37] Arkansas Genealogical Society, 4200 "A" Street, Little Rock, AR 72205

[38] Arno Press, 330 Madison Avenue, New York, NY 10017

[39] Ashtabula County Genealogical Society, The, P.O. Box 885, Ashtabula, OH 44004

[40] Atheneum Publishers, Distributed by Book Warehouse, Incorporated, Vreeland Avenue, Boro of Totowa, Paterson, NJ 07512

[41] Attic Press, Stony Point, Route 2, Greenwood, SC 29646

[42] Augsburg Publishing House, 426 South Fifth Street, Minneapolis, MN 55415

[43] Augusta County Historical Society, Box 686, Staunton, VA 24401

[44] Augustana College Library, Rock Island, IL 61201

[45] Aurora Publishers, Incorporated, 170 Fourth Avenue, North, Room 619, Nashville, TN 37219

[46] Babcock, C. Merton, 1252 Ivanhoe Drive, East Lansing, MI 48823

[47] Baird, Josie, 909 East Johnston, Rotan, TX 79546

[48] Baker, John Milnes, 342 Madison Avenue, New York, NY 10017

[49] Ball, Bonnie S., 606 Wood Avenue, Big Stone Gap, VA 24219

[50] Ballantine Books, Incorporated, Division of Random House, Incorporated, Distributed by Random House, Incorporated - Order Department, Westminster, MD 21157

[51] Bancroft Press, 27 McNear Drive, San Rafael, CA 94901

[52] Barnes & Noble, Incorporated, Division of Harper & Row Publishers, Incorporated, Keystone Industrial Park, Scranton, PA 18512

[53] Barnes (A.S.) & Company, Incorporated, P.O. Box 421, Cranbury, NJ 08512

[54] Barry, Mrs. Elizabeth, 1117 South 22nd Street, Fort Smith, AR 72901

[55] Bauer, Armand, 305 26th Avenue North, Fargo, ND 58102

[56] Bauhan (William L.), Publisher, Dublin, NH 03444

[57] Beaman, Alden G., P.O. Box 585, East Princeton, MA 01517

[58] Beatty (R.W.), Limited, P.O. Box 26, Arlington, VA 22210

[59] Beaufort Book Company, Incorporated, 808 Bay Street, Box 1127, Beaufort, SC 29902

[60] Beebe, Ms. Elaine Elliott, 6209 East Lane Avenue, Fresno, CA 93727

[61] Bell, Raymond M., 413 Burton Avenue, Washington, PA 15301

[62] Bennett, James D., 102 Glenview Court, Battle Creek, MI 49017

[63] Bennington, Mrs. Charles D., Star Route (Lake of the Woods), Frazier Park, CA 93225

[64] Berkshire Traveller Press, Stockbridge, MA 01262

[65] Berndt, Mrs. Betty (Davis), 4663 North East Kelsey Road, Kansas City, MO 64116

[66] Bicha, Mrs. Frank, Jr., 712 Illinois Street, Racine, WI 53405

[67] Billingsley, Zora P., 1003 West 48th, Amarillo, TX 79110

[68] Binford & Mort, Publishers, 2536 Southeast 11th Avenue, Portland, OR 97202

[69] BIO Books, 515 Weldon Avenue, Oakland, CA 94610

[70] Birdsall, George A., Box 449, Annandale, VA 22003

[71] Black Letter Press, 663 Bridge Street, North West, Grand Rapids, MI 49504

[72] Blair, John F., Publisher, 1406 Plaza Drive, Southwest, Winston-Salem, NC 27103

[73] Bland Books, 401 Northwest, 10th Street, Fairfield, IL 62837

[74] Bloch and Company, P.O. Box 77, Fairfax Station, VA 22039

[75] Bloch Publishing Company, 915 Broadway, New York, NY 10010

[76] Blue & Gray Press, Incorporated, 605 Merrit Street, Nashville, TN 37203

[77] Bobbs-Merrill Company, Incorporated, Subsidiary of Howard W. Sams & Company 4300 West 62nd Street, Indianapolis, IN 46268

[78] Bonanza Press, 3350 el Camino Real, Santa Cruz, CA 95051

[79] Bond Wheelwright Publishing Company, Porter's Landing, Freeport, ME 04032

[80] Bookmark, The, P.O. Box 74, Knightstown, IN 46148

[81] Books for Libraries, Incorporated, 1 Dupont Street, Plainview, NY 11803

[82] Boone Family Research Association, Mrs. Samuel B. Ingels, Treasurer, 7130 Virginia Avenue, Kansas City, MO 64131

[83] Bordner, Howard W., (Author), 6500 Barnaby Street, Northwest, Washington DC 20015

[84] Bowie County Historical Commission, H.E. Fagan, Treasurer, P.O. Box 201, Redwater, TX 75573

[85] Bowker (R.R.) Company, Order Department, P.O. Box 1807, Ann Arbor, MI 48106

[86] Bowman, Mrs. Myreline, Route 1, Box 183 A., Atlanta, TX 75551

[87] Boyd, Mrs. Frank E., 296 Chewacla Drive, Auburn, AL 38830

[88] Boyer, Carl, 3rd, 24355 West La Glorita Circle, Newhall, CA 91321

[89] Brace, Mr. and Mrs. E.T., 2919 Meadow Lane, El Campo, TX 77437

[90] Branden Press, Incorporated, 221 Columbus Avenue, Boston, MA 02116

[91] Brethren Press, 1451 Dundee Avenue, Elgin, IL 60120

[92] Brigham Young University Press, Business 268 UPB, Provo, UT 84602

[93] British Book Center, 996 Lexington Avenue, New York, NY 10021

[94] Brooks-Sterling Company, 815 East 14th Street, Oakland, CA 94603

[95] Brouse, Gwendolyn I., 3762 Elmwood Court, Riverside, CA 92506

[96] Brown, Mr. Homer, 909 Fair Oaks, Oak Park, IL 60302

[97] Brown, Jean C., 1330 East Thompson, Sapulpa, OK 74066

[98] Brown, Mrs. L. F., 3306 Huron, Kalamazoo, MI 49007

[99] Brown University Press, 71 George Street, Box 1881, Providence, RI 02912

[100] Brown (William C.) Company, Publishers, 2460 Kerper Boulevard, Dubuque, IA 52001

[101] Brownell, Daphne M., P.O. Box 163, DeLand, FL 32720

[102] Brubaker, Joan Bake, RR 3, Box 159, West Alexandria, OH 45381

[103] Brunswick County Bicentennial Committee, P.O. Box 1776, Lawrenceville, VA 23868

[104] Bucknell University Press, P.O. Box 421, Cranbury, NJ 08512

[105] Bucks County Historical Society, Attention: Publications Department, Doylestown, PA 18901

[106] Burgess, Jo Ann, 913 - 7th Avenue North, Clear Lake, IA 50428

[107] Burton, Charles T., R # 2, Box # 191, Troutville, VA 24175

[108] Busby, Miss Rosa Lee, 2024 - 21st Avenue South, Birmingham, AL 35209

[109] Bushman, Leola Grant, 6641 Golden West, Arcadia, CA 91006

[110] Buys, Barbara Smith, B.A., M.A., C.A.L.S., R.D. #1, Sunset Hill, Fishkill, NY 12524

[111] California Historical Society, 2090 Jackson Street, San Francisco, CA 94109

[112] California Press, University of, Order Department, 2223 Fulton Street, Berkeley, CA 04720

[113] Callaway Family Association, The, Incorporated, c/o Mrs. Charles H. Sleight, Secretary, 7413 Sportsman Drive, Falls Church, VA 22043

[114] Cambridge University Press, 32 East 57th Street, New York, NY 10022

[115] Campus Publishers, 711 North University Avenue, Ann Arbor, MI 48108

[116] Canfield, Clifford R., Frankfurt Elementary School #2, Box #32, APO NY 09710

[117] Canner (J.S.) & Company, 49-65 Lansdowne Street, Boston, MA 02215

[118] Carlton Press, 84 Fifth Avenue, New York, NY 10011

[119] Carman, Clarice Eland, 209 Egan Drive, Streamwood, IL 60103

[120] Carnation Press, P.O. Box 101, State College, PA 16801

[121] Carolina Art Association, 135 Meeting Street, Charleston, SC 29401

[122] Carothers, Bettie, 1510 Cranwell Road, Lutherville, MD 21093

[123] Carpenter, Rear Admiral Charles L., 642 Foss Avenue, Drexel Hill, PA 19026

[124] Carrier, C.J. Company, P.O. Box 1114, Harrisonburg, VA 22801

[125] Cartwright, Lloyd, J., 2225 Mershon Street, Saginaw, MI 48602

[126] Cason, William R., Editor, The Cason Quarterly, P.O. Box 88393, Atlanta, GA 30338

[127] Caxton Printers, Limited, 312 Main Street, Caldwell, ID 83605

[128] Center for Migration Studies, Distributed by Jerome S. Ozer, Publisher, Incorporated, 475 Fifth Avenue, New York, NY 10017

[129] Chadwick, Naomi (Giles), 3375 Celeste Drive, Riverside, CA 92507

[130] Chalfant Press, Incorporated, P.O. Box 787, Bishop, CA 93514

[131] Chamberlain, Glenn J., Treasurer, Robert Bardwell Descendants' American Ancestry Association, 571 Gabilan Street, Los Altos, CA 94022

[132] Charlton Press, Incorporated, 84 Fifth Avenue, New York, NY 10011

[133] Chatham Press, Incorporated, Distributed by E. P. Dutton & Company, Incorporated, 201 Park Avenue, South, New York, NY 10003

[134] Chedwato Service, RFD #3, Box 120A, Middleboro, MA 02346

[135] Cherokee Publishing Company, P.O. Box 1081, Covington, GA 30209

[136] Cherokee Strip Volunteer League, Drawer G, Alva, OK 73717

[137] Chicago Press, University of, 5801 Ellis Avenue, Chicago, IL 60637

[138] Chicorel Library Publishing Company, 275 Central Park, West, New York, NY 10024

[139] Chilton, Harriett A., 3108 Annandale Road, Falls Church, VA 22042

[140] Christopher Publishing House, 53 Billings Road, North Quincy, MA 02171

[141] Citadel Press, Subsidiary of Lyle Stuart, Incorporated, 120 Enterprise Avenue Secaucus, NJ 07094

[142] Clagett, Brice M., Holly Hill, Friendship, MD 20758

[143] Clark, A.H., P.O. Box 401, Waycross, GA 31501

[144] Clark (Arthur H.) Company, 1264 South Central Avenue, Glendale, CA 91204

[145] Clark, Mrs. Larry P., 1211 Biscayne Drive, Little Rock, AR 72207

[146] Clark, Mrs. Neva Sturgill, P.O. Box 428, Welaka, FL 32093

[147] Clay County Historical Society, c/o Gordon L. Hadden, 325 North Water, Liberty, MO 64068

[148] Clay (Henry) Press, P.O. Box 116, Lexington, KY 40501

[149] Clearwater Publishing Company, 792 Columbus Avenue, New York, NY 10025

[150] Climo, Percy L., 526 Geneva Street, St. Catharines, Ontario, CANADA L2N 2H6

[151] Coke, Ben H., 346 Mayfair Boulevard, Columbus, OH 43213 (or) Route 1, Calhoun, KY 42327

[152] College and University Press, 263 Chapel Street, New Haven, CT 06513

[153] Collins (William) & World Publishing Company, Incorporated, 2080 West 117th Street, Cleveland, OH 44111

[154] Colonial Dames of America in the Commonwealth of Massachusetts, National Society, 55 Beacon Street, Boston, MA 02108

[155] Columbia University Press, 136 South Broadway, Irvington, NY 10533

[156] Cooke, Velma M., P.O. Box 813, Hempstead, TX 77445

[157] Coolidge, LtCol Lyle C., USA (Ret), 2431 West Wagon Wheel Drive, Tucson, AZ 85705

[158] Cooper, Mary Lester, 2621 Sweetbrier Avenue, Southwest, Roanoke, VA 24015

[159] Cooper Square Publishers, Incorporated, 59 Fourth Avenue, New York NY 10003

[160] Cordell, Donald L., 8932 Haddon Avenue, Sun Valley, CA 91352

[161] Corinth Books, Distributed by Book Organization, Elm Street, Millerton, NY 12546

[162] Cornell Maritime, Press, Incorporated, P.O. Box 109, Cambridge, MD 21613

[163] Cornell University Press, 124 Roberts Place, Ithaca, NY 14850

[164] Corner House Publishers, Green River Road, Williamstown, MA 01267

[165] Country Beautiful Corporation, Marketing Department, 24198 West Bluemound Road, Waukesha, WI 53186

[166] Covington, Elbert E., Route 1, Box 166, Desoto, IL 62924

[167] Craig, Marion Stark, M.D., 307 Doctors Building, 500 South University Avenue, Little Rock, AR 72205

[168] Crickard, Mrs. Madeline W., Route 1, Box 218, Beverly, WV 26253

[169] Crook, John A., Jr., M.D., 406 Piedmont Street, Reidsville, NC 27320

[170] Cross County Historical Society, Incorporated, Box 943, Wynne, AR 72396

[171] Crowell (Thomas Y.) Company, 666 Fifth Avenue, New York, NY 10003

[172] Crown Publishers, Incorporated, 419 Park Avenue, South, New York, NY 10016

[173] Cumming, Ross, Box 23, Stratford, Ontario, CANADA N5A 6S8

[174] Curfman, Margaret B., 122 North Pershing, Wichita, KS 67208

[175] Curtis, Janet Austin, C.G., 3329 Santa Clara, Southeast, Albuquerque, NM 87106

[176] Da Capo Press, Incorporated, 227 West 17th Street, New York, NY 10022

[177] Dade County Missouri Historical Society, 207 McPherson Street, Greenfield, MO 65661

[178] Dafft, P. R., 2557 Brandywine Drive, Dallas, TX 75234

[179] Danubian Press, Incorporated, Route 1, Box 59, Astor, FL 32002

[180] Daugherty, Joyce M., P.O. Box 512, Coronado, CA 92118

[181] David & Charles, Incorporated, Trafalgar Square, North Pomfret, VT 05053

[182] Davidson Books, 309 East 9th Street, West Point, GA 31833

[183] Davis, Mrs. William J., 1850-140th Place, Southeast, Bellevue, WA 98005

[184] Dawson's Book Shop, 535 North Larchmont Boulevard, Los Angeles, CA 90004

[185] Day, Leonard F., Sr., (compiler and publisher), 68 Matthews Street, Pontiac, MI 48058

[186] DeAngelis, Priscilla G., 8809 Brierly Road, Chevy Chase, MD 20015

[187] Decatur Genealogical Society, P.O. Box 2068, Decatur, IL 62526

[188] De Gruyter (Walter), Incorporated, 162 Fifth Avenue, New York, NY 10010

[189] Dennis, Barbara M., 207 - Southwest Normandy Road, Seattle, WA 98166

[190] Deseret Book Company, P.O. Box 659, Salt Lake City, UT 84110

[191] Dhonau, Robert W., 4410 Lee Avenue, Little Rock, AR 72205

[192] Dial Press, 1 Dag Hammarskjold Plaza, 245 East 47th Street, New York, NY 10017

[193] Dickenson Publishing Company, 16561 Ventura Boulevard, Encinco, CA 91316

[194] Dickson Genealogy, 1100 Republic Bank Building, Dallas, TX 75201

[195] Dietz Press, 109 East Carey, Richmond, VA 23219

[196] Dillon/Liderbach, Incorporated, 14567 Madison Avenue, Cleveland OH 44107

[197] Dillon Press, Incorporated, 500 South Third Street, Minneapolis, MN 55415

[198] Domonoske, Mrs. A. B., 207 East 8th Street, Davis, CA 95616

[199] Donnelly, Sister Louise, 9525 Lyra Court, Burke, VA 22015

[200] Donnelly, Ralph W., 913 Market Street, Washington, NC 27889

[201] Dorman, John Frederick, 2022 Columbia Road, Northwest, Washington DC 20009

[202] Dorrance & Company, 1617 J.F. Kennedy Boulevard, Philadelphia, PA 19103

[203] Doubleday & Company, Incorporated, 501 Franklin Avenue, Garden City, NY 11530

[204] Dover Publications, Incorporated, 180 Varick Street, New York, NY 10014

[205] Dreher, Mrs. Jean Opdycke, 2334 Kenwood Avenue, Fort Wayne, IN 46805

[206] Drotts, Mrs. Jane Vernon, 1011 Sanford, Richland, WA 99352

[207] Dufour Editions, Incorporated, Chester Springs, PA 19425

[208] Duke University Press, 6697 College Station, Durham, NC 27708

[209] Durrell Publications, Incorporated, Orders to: Stephen Green, Box 1000, Fessenden Road, Brattleboro, VT 05301

[210] Dutton (E.P.) & Company, Incorporated, 201 Park Avenue, South, New York, NY 10003

[211] Eastern Nebraska Genealogical Society, P.O. Box 541, Fremont, NE 68025

[212] Eastern Washington Genealogical Society, Box 1826, Spokane, WA 99210

[213] Eastwood, Mrs. R. L., 2 Bratenahl Place, Cleveland, OH 44108

[214] Edmondson, Eleanor Rogers, 2803 Byron Avenue, Odessa, TX 79762

[215] Eerdmans (William B.) Publishing Company, 255 Jefferson Avenue, Southeast, Grand Rapids, MI 49502

[216] Eller, Lynda S., P.O. Box 249, Lanett, AL 36863

[217] Emory & Henry College Bookstore, P.O. Drawer O, Emory, VA 24327

[218] Encino Press, 510 Baylor Street, Austin, TX 78703

[219] Engel, Beth B., 825 Egmont Street, Brunswick, GA 31520

[220] England, C. Walter, 2030 Forest Hill Drive, Silver Spring, MD 20903

[221] Enquist, Anita C. Clendinen, Box 246, Warm Springs, GA 31830

[222] Ericson, Carolyn Reeves, 1614 Redbud Street, Nacogdoches, TX 75961

[223] Essex Institute, 132 Essex Street, Salem, MA 01970

[224] Exposition Press, Incorporated, Hicksville, NY 11801

[225] Fader, Edythe, 1814 Douglas Street, Mount Vernon, WA 98273

[226] Fairfax County Administrative Services, Fairfax Building, 10555 Main Street, Fairfax, VA 22030

[227] Fairleigh Dickinson University Press, P. O. Box 421, Cranbury, NJ 08512

[228] Faith and Life Press, 724 Main Street, Box 347, Newton, KS 67114

[229] Farmer, Michal Martin, Farmer Genealogy Company, 8755 Rexford Drive, Dallas, TX 75209

[230] Farrar, Straus and Giroux, Incorporated, 19 Union Square, West, New York, NY 10003

[231] Favretti, Rudy J., Box 403, Storrs, CT 06268

[232] Featon Press, The, P. O. Box 7661, Birmingham, AI 35223

[233] Fernhill House, Limited, Distributed by: Humanities Press, Incorporated, Atlantic Highland, NJ 07716

[234] Fewell, Mildred M., 3730 North Versailles, Dallas, TX 75209

[235] Fieber, Dora Reid, 5631 Biscayne Boulevard, Miami, FL 33137, or (in summer) Albion, IL 62806

[236] Filson Club, The, 118 West Breckinridge Street, Louisville, KY 40203

[237] Finch Press, 220 East Huron Street, Ann Arbor, MI 48108

[238] Fiske, Mrs. John W., Stonecleave Road, Boxford, MA 01921

[239] Flavell, Carol Willsey, C.G., 4649 Yarmouth Lane, Youngstown, OH 44512

[240] Flayderman (N.) and Company, Incorporated, Kent Road, New Milford, CT 06776

[241] Flint Genealogical Society, The, 325 Cloverdale Place, Flint, MI 48503

[242] Florida Press, University of, 15 Northwest 15th Street, Gainesville, FL 32601

[243] Florida State University Press, 15 Northwest 15th Street, Gainesville, FL 32601

[244] Foglesong, Elizabeth C., Box 366, 407 North Gary Avenue, Wheaton, IL 60187

[245] Folcroft Library Editions, P. O. Box 182, Folcroft, PA 19032

[246] Foley, Louise Pledge Heath, 12 Dahlgren Road, Richmond, VA 23233

[247] Founders Project, P. O. Box 1810, Cleveland, OH 44106

[248] Franklin (Burt), Publisher, Distributed by Lenox Hill Publisher & Distributing Corporation, 235 East 44th Street, New York, NY 10017

[249] Frederick County Historical Society, 610 Tennyson Avenue, Winchester, VA 22601

[250] Freneau (Philip) Press, P. O. Box 116, Monmouth Beach, NJ 07750

[251] Freshwater Press, Incorporated, 446 The Arcade, Cleveland, OH 44114

[252] Fresno Genealogical Society, P. O. Box 2042, Fresno, CA 93718

[253] Friedman (Ira J.) Incorporated, Division of Kennikat Press, Incorporated, 90 South Bayles Avenue, Port Washington, NY 11050

[254] Friends of the Paris-Henry County Library, P. O. Box 456, Paris, TN 38242

[255] Friends United Press, 101 Quaker Hill Drive, Richmond, IN 47374

[256] Fritchey, John A., II, 106 November Drive, Camp Hill, PA 17011

[257] Frontier Book Company, P. O. Box 805, Fort Davis, TX 79734

[258] Frye, George W., 8108 Frontaine Court, Cincinnati, OH 45236

[259] Fulton County Historical and Genealogical Society, c/o Mr. Charles V. Petrovich, 1040 North Main Street, Canton, IL 61520

[260] Fulton County Historical Society, c/o Shirley Willard, Route #1, Box 130, Rochester, IN 46975

[261] Fulton Genealogical Society, P. O. Box 31, Fulton, KY 42041

[262] Furlong, Roland Dulany, Holly Hill, Mathews, VA 23109

[263] G. L. A. Press, 524 Southland Center, Dallas, TX 75201

[264] Gadbury, Mrs. Ruth, Route 1, Box 214, Lometa, TX 76853

[265] Galbreath, J. W., 14 Bonanza, Centralia, IL 62801

[266] Gale Research Company, Book Tower, Detroit, MI 48226

[267] Gannett, Michael R., 7310 Meadow Lane, Chevy Chase, MD 20015

[268] Gannon, William, 321 West San Francisco, Santa Fe, NM 87501

[269] Gardner, Sydney Mike, 1604 East Turin Avenue, Anaheim, CA 92805

[270] Gartman Foundation, The, c/o F. L. Watts, P. O. Box 5581, Arlington, TX 76011

[271] Gaunt (William) and Sons, Incorporated, 3011 Gulf Drive, Holmes Beach, FL 33510

[272] Gencor, Incorporated, 15 North West Temple, Salt Lake City, Utah 84103

[273] Genealogical Books in Print, 6818 Lois Drive, Springfield, VA 22150

[274] Genealogical Publishing Company, Incorporated, 521-523 St. Paul Place, Baltimore, MD 21202

[275] Genealogical Society, The, 50 East North Temple, Salt Lake City, UT 84150

[276] Genealogy Projects Committee, Winnetka Public Library, 768 Oak Street, Winnetka, IL 60093

[277] Genealogy Shoppe, Incorporated, 4218 Ben View Drive, Salt Lake City, UT 84120

[278] George, Thomas R., Route 4, Box 106, Lynchburg, VA 24503

[279] Georgia Press, University of, Athens, GA 30602

[280] Getman, Borden C., 5 Spruce Street, Sidney, NY 13838

[281] Gibbs, Mrs. Robert L., 8705 Rolando Drive, Richmond, VA 23229

[282] Gillis, Norman E., P. O. Box 9114, Shreveport, LA 71109

[283] Glacking, Col. James R., C. G., 616 Sheridan Road, Highwood, IL 60040

[284] Globe Publishers, International, 2205 Maryland Street, Baytown, TX 77520

[285] Gloucester County Historical Society, 58 North Broad Street, Box 409, Woodbury, NJ 08096

[286] Godine (David R) Publisher, 306 Dartmouth Street, Boston, MA 02116

[287] Goeller, Mrs. Mildred S., Friendship Manor North, Apartment A-3-B, Roanoke, VA 24012

[288] Gordian Press, Incorporated, 85 Tompkins Street, Staten Island, NY 10304

[289] Gordon Press Publishers, P. O. Box 459, Bowling Green Station, New York NY 10004

[290] Gott, John K., 4515 - 17th Street, North, Arlington, VA 22207

[291] Graham, Ruth M., 2427 Fort Scott Drive, Arlington, VA 22202

[292] Granite State Searcher, The, Laird C. Towle, Ph. D., 3602 Maureen Lane, Bowie, MD 20715

[293] Gray (Edgar) Publications, P. O. Box 181, Kalamazoo, MI 49005

[294] Gray, Marilyn, 87 Brantwood Drive, Scarborough, Ontario, CANADA M1H 2G7

[295] Greater Portland Landmarks, Incorporated, P. O. Box 4197, Station "A", Portland, ME 04101

[296] Greene (Stephen) Press, P. O. Box 1000, Brattleboro, VT 05301

[297] Greenwood Press, Order Processing Department, 51 Riverside Avenue, Westport, CT 06880

[298] Gregath, Ann, P. O. Box 1045, Cullman, AL 35055

[299] Gregg Press, Incorporated, 70 Lincoln Street, Boston, MA 02111

[300] Gregory, Peggy H., 7130 Evans Street, Houston, TX 77061

[301] Grossman Publishers, Incorporated, Distributed by: Viking Press, 625 Madison Avenue, New York, NY 10022

[302] Guilford Free Library, 67 Park Street, Guilford, CT 06437

[303] Gunter, Mr. Andrew, P. O. Box 26, Kentville, Nova Scotia B4N 3V9

[304] Habelman, Mrs. Robert, Route 3, Box 177A, Black River Falls, WI 54615

[305] Haessner Publishing, Incorporated, P. O. Box 89, Newfoundland, NJ 07435

[306] Hafner Press, Distributed by: Collier-MacMillan Distribution Center, Riverside, NJ 08075

[307] Hall (G.K.) and Company, 70 Lincoln Street, Boston, MA 02111

[308] Hall, Ted Byron, 1320 Jamestown Drive, Tahlequah, OK 74464

[309] Hamby, Wallace B., M.D., 3001 Northeast 47 Court, Fort Launderdale, FL 33308

[310] Hammers, Mrs. Marian G., 651 South Scott Street, Madisonville, KY 42431

[311] Hammond, Incorporated, Maplewood, NJ 07040

[312] Hammond, Ralph, Box 486, Arab, AL 35016

[313] Harbor Hill Books, Harrison, NY 10528

[314] Harcourt Brace Jovanovich, Incorporated, 757 Third Avenue, New York, NY 10017

[315] Hardy, Miss Elizabeth, Rural Route 2, Jacksonville, IL 62650

[316] Harmony, Distributed by: Crown Publishers, Incorporated, 419 Park Avenue, South, New York, NY 10016

[317] Harper and Row, Publishers, Incorporated, Scranton, PA 18512

[318] Harter, Mrs. Bert, F.A.S.G., 3812 Flagler Avenue, Key West, FL 33040

[319] Harvard University Press, 79 Garden Street, Cambridge, MA 02138

[320] Haskell House Publishers, Limited, 1533 - 60th Street, Brooklyn, NY 11219

[321] Hastings House Publishers, Incorporated, 10 East 40th Street, New York, NY 10016

[322] Hawaii, University Press of, 535 Ward Avenue, Honolulu, HI 96814

[323] Hayden Book Company, Incorporated, 50 Essex Street, Rochelle Park, NJ 07662

[324] Heath (D.C.) and Company, College Department, 125 Spring Street, Lexington, MA 02173

[325] Heineman (James H.) Incorporated, Publisher, 475 Park Avenue, New York, NY 10022

[326] Hendrix, Ge Lee Corley, 3 Acorn Court, Greenville, SC 29609

[327] Herald Press, 616 Walnut Avenue, Scottdale, PA 15683

[328] Heraldic Publishing Company, Incorporated, 305 West End Avenue, New York, NY 10023

[329] Heritage Genealogical Society, The, P. O. Box 73, Neodesha, KS 66757

[330] Heritage House, Route 1, Box 211, Thomson, IL 61285

[331] Heritage Press, Avon, CT 06001

[332] Herr, Willis E., 1419 South Saltair #2, Los Angeles, CA 90025

[333] Hill, Mrs. Ellen C., East Montpelier, VT 05651

[334] Hill (Lawrence) and Company, Incorporated, 150 Fifth Avenue, New York, NY 10011

[335] Hillary House Publishers, Limited, Divison of Humanities Press, Incorporated, Atlantic Highlands, NJ 07716

[336] Hine, Frances Julian, 2426 Silver Fox Lane, Reston, VA 22091

[337] Hippocrene Books, Incorporated, 171 Madison Avenue, New York, NY 10016

[338] Hive Publishing Company, P. O. Box 1004, Easton, PA 18042

[339] Hodge, Mrs. Robert A., 417 Pelham Street, Fredericksburg, VA 22401

[340] Hodges, Mrs. Luke, 1811 Garfield, Wichita Falls, TX 76309

[341] Holbrook Press, Incorporated, Subsidiary of Allyn and Bacon, Incorporated, Rockleigh, NJ 07647

[342] Holbrook Research Institute, 57 Locust Street, Oxford, MA 01540

[343] Holcomb, Brent, G.R.S., Drawer 889, Clinton, SC 29325

[344] Holland, Dorothy G., 7527 Oxford Drive, Saint Louis, MO 63105

[345] Holmes, Maruice, Rural Route 3, Box 249, Shelbyville, IN 46176

[346] Holmes and Meier Publishers, Incorporated, 101 Fifth Avenue, New York, NY 10003

[347] Holt Association of America, c/o Frederick B. Holt, 131 Elmwood Drive, Cheshire, CT 06410

[348] Holt, Rinehart and Winston, Incorporated, 383 Madison Avenue, New York, NY 10017

[349] Hoover Institution Press, Stanford Branch, Palo Alto, CA 94305

[350] Hopkins County Genealogical Society, P. O. Box 51, Madisonville, KY 42431

[351] Hopper, Mrs. Rosalea, Valle Lake, Route 3, DeSoto, MO 63020

[352] Horizon Press Publishers, 156 Fifth Avenue, New York, NY 10010

[353] Horizon Publishers, 55 East 300 South, Box 490, Bountiful, UT 84010

[354] Horlacher, L. J., 639 Maxwelton Court, Lexington, KY 40508

[355] Hough, Dr. Granville W., 3438-B Bahia Blanca West, Laguna Hills, CA 92653

[356] Houghton Mifflin Company, 2 Park Street, Boston, MA 02107

[357] Howell-North Books, 1050 Parker Street, Berkeley, CA 94710

[358] Hubble, Anna Joy (Munday), Route 2, Whitefish, MT 59937

[359] Huddleston, Tim, Pickett County Historian, P. O. Box 66, Ooltewah, TN 37363

[360] Hudson Family Association (South), Route 7, Del Monte Place, Longview, TX 75601

[361] Hull, Donna M., General Delivery, Frazier Park, CA 93225

[362] Humanities Press, Incorporated, Atlantic Highlands, NJ 07716

[363] Huntington (Henry E.) Library and Art Gallery, 1151 Oxford Road, San Marino, CA 91108

[364] Hutchins, Martha Sheldon, 1123 North Myers, Burbank, CA 91506

[365] Illinois Press, University of, Urbana, IL 61801

[366] Illinois State Genealogical Society, P. O. Box 2225, Springfield, IL 62705

[367] Indian Historian Press, Incorporated, 1451 Masonic Avenue, San Francisco, CA 94117

[368] Indian, Museum of the American, Heye Foundation, Broadway at 155th Street, New York, NY 10032

[369] Indiana Historical Society, 140 North Senate Avenue, Indianapolis, IN 46204

[370] Indiana University Press, Tenth and Morton Streets, Bloomington, IN 47401

[371] In-Print Book, 3812 Lafayette, Fort Worth, TX 76107

[372] International Publishers Company, Incorporated, 381 Park Avenue, South, Suite 1301, New York, NY 10016

[373] International Publications Service, 114 East 32nd Street, New York, NY 10016

[374] International Scholarly Book Service, Incorporated, P. O. Box 4347, Portland, OR 97208

[375] Interstate, 19-27 North Jackson Street, Danville, IL 61832

[376] Iowa Genealogical Society, P. O. Box 3815, Des Moines, IA 50322

[377] Iowa State University Press, Press Building, Ames, IA 50010

[378] Ireland Indexing Service, 2237 Brooke Road, Fallbrook, CA 92028

[379] Irish University Press, Incorporated, 485 Madison Avenue, New York, NY 10022

[380] Jacob, Mrs. Vashti, 2400 McCutcheon Avenue, Shreveport, LA 71108

[381] Janlen Enterprises, 2236 South 77th Street, West Allis, WI 53219

[382] Janowski, Mrs. Joseph, 149 Morningside Avenue, Gary, IN 46408

[383] Jenkins Publishing Company, P. O. Box 2085, Austin, TX 78767

[384] Jewish Publication Society of America, 222 North 15th Street, Philadelphia, PA 19102

[385] Johns Hopkins Press, Baltimore, MD 21218

[386] Johnsen Publishing Company, 1135 "R" Street, Lincoln, NE 68508

[387] Johnson County Genealogical Society, P. O. Box 8057, Shawnee Mission, KS 66208

[388] Johnson, Donald W., P. O. Box 539, Zachary, LA 70791

[389] Johnson Historical Publications, 2409 Gaboury Lane, Huntsville, AL 35811

[390] Johnson, Jesse J., Hampton Institute, Hampton, VA 23668

[391] Johnson, Lillian B., 307 Mayfield Drive, Route 2, Smyrna, TN 37167

[392] Johnson, Patricia Givens, 6905 Westchester Drive, Camp Springs, MD 20031

[393] Johnson Publishing Company, P. O. Box 317, Murfreesboro, NC 27855

[394] Johnson Reprint Corporation, 111 Fifth Avenue, New York, NY 10003

[395] Johnston, W. Wesley, 1524 South Holmes Avenue, Springfield, IL 62704

[396] Jones (Anson) Press, Salado, TX 76571

[397] Joyner, Ulysses P., Jr., R.F.D. 1, Box 62, Orange, VA 22960

[398] Judson Press, Valley Forge, PA 19481

[399] Kalamazoo Valley Genealogical Society, c/o A.H. Kerr, Chairman of Publications, 3628 Market Street, Kalamazoo, MI 49001

[400] Kellersberger Fund, Box 5847, F.I.T., Melbourne, FL 32901

[401] Kelley (Augustus M.) Publishers, 300 Fairfield Road, Fairfield, NJ 07006

[402] Kelly, Arthur C. M., Box 79A, R.D. #1, Rhinebeck, NY 12572

[403] Kelly, Thomas, 227 Midland Avenue, East Orange, NJ 07017

[404] Kennikat Press, 90 South Bayles Avenue, Port Washington, NY 11050

[405] Kent State University Press, Kent, OH 44240

[406] Kentucky Genealogical Society, P. O. Box 153, Frankfort, KY 40601

[407] Kentucky Historical Society, P. O. Box H, Frankfort, KY 40601

[408] Kentucky, University Press of, Lexington, KY 40506

[409] Kern County Genealogical Society, P. O. Box 2214, Bakersfield, CA 93303

[410] Key, Edward S., Route 2, Box 62A, Bedias, TX 77831

[411] Kitchel, Walter H., 638-B Plymouth Drive, Lakewood, NJ 08701

[412] Knopf (Alfred A.) Incorporated, 400 Hahn Road, Westminster, MD 21157

[413] Knorr, H. A., 1401 Linden Street, Pine Bluff, AR 71601

[414] Kolb, Avery, 6417 Julian Street, Springfield, VA 22150

[415] Kraus Reprint Company, Millwood, NY 10546

[416] Kregel Publications, P. O. Box 2607, Grand Rapids, MI 49501

[417] KTAV Publishing House, Incorporated, 120 East Broadway, New York, NY 10022

[418] Lacy, Ruby, P. O. Box 628, Ashland, OR 97520

[419] Lamont, Corliss, 315 West 106 Street, New York, NY 10025 (or) A.S. Barnes Company, Incorporated, Granbury, NJ 08512

[420] Landfall Press, Incorporated, 4077 East Town and Country Road, Dayton, OH 45429

[421] Larew, Karl G., West Friendship, MD 21794

[422] La Siesta Press, P. O. Box 406, Glendale, CA 91209

[423] Ledley, Wilson Vandorn, C.G., 2 Circle Drive, Meredith, NH 03253

[424] Lee, Caroljo F., R. D. 2, 317 Forsythe Road, Valencia, PA 16059

[425] Leeran Publishers, 120 North High Street, Burkesville, KY 42717

[426] Lerner Publications Company, 241 First Avenue, North, Minneapolis, MN 55401

[427] Letey, Marilyn R., 4206 Swain Court, Riverside, CA 92507

[428] Libraries Unlimited, Incorporated, c/o Colorado Bibliographic Institute, P. O. Box 263, Littleton, CO 80120

[429] Library Research Associates, Dunderberg Road, Monroe, NY 10950

[430] Licking County Genealogical Society, P. O. Box 215, Newark, OH 43055

[431] Lightfoot, Marise P., 101 Fairview Drive, Mt. Pleasant, TN 38474

[432] Lind, Ruth V., 910 East Sierra Way, Dinuba, CA 93618

[433] Linn, Jo White, P. O. Box 1948, Salisbury, NC 28144

[434] Lippincott (J.B.) Company, East Washington Square, Philadelphia, PA 19105

[435] Little, Brown and Company, 200 West Street, Waltham, MA 02154

[436] Littlefield, Adams, and Company, 81 Adams Drive, Totowa, NJ 07512

[437] Logical Products, Incorporated, P. O. Box 5654, Baltimore, MD 21210

[438] Logos Book Store, 220 M.A.C. Avenue, East Lansing, MI 48823

[439] Los Angeles Branch Genealogical Library of the Church of Jesus Christ of Latter-day Saints, 10741 Santa Monica Boulevard, Los Angeles, CA 90025

[440] Louisiana State University Press, Baton Rouge, LA 70803

[441] Lounsbury, Raymond H., R.F.D. #1, Box 264, Vergennes, VT 05491

[442] Loyola University Press, 3441 North Ashland Avenue, Chicago, IL 60657

[443] Luce (Robert B.) Incorporated, Distributed by: David Mc Kay Company, Incorporated, 750 Third Avenue, New York, NY 10017

[444] M.I.T. Press, 28 Carleton Street, Cambridge, MA 02142

[445] McBride, Nancy S., 14 Wood Ibis Road, Hilton Head, SC 29928

[446] McClain Printing Company, 212 Main Street, Parsons, WV 26287

[447] McClelland and Stewart, Limited, Distributed by: Books Canada, 33 East Tupper Street, Buffalo, NY 14203

[448] McClure Press, Verona, VA 24482

[449] McConnell, Mrs. Catherine S., P. O. Box 153, Abingdon, VA 24210

[450] McGill-Queens Univ Pr, 3458 Redpath Street, Montreal, 109 CANADA H3A 1A2

[451] McGraw-Hill Book Company, 1221 Avenue of the Americas, New York, NY 10036

[452] McKay (David) Company, Incorporated, Department GBP, 750 Third Avenue, New York, NY 10017

[453] McManus, Thelma S., G.R.S., 507 Vine Street, Doniphan, MO 63935

[454] MacMillan Publishing Company, Incorporated, Riverside, NJ 08075

[455] McMillion and Wall, P. O. Box 148, Vienna, VA 22180

[456] McMillion, Lynn C., G.R.S., P. O. Box 148, Vienna, VA 22180

[457] McNally and Loftin, Publishers, P. O. Box 1316, Santa Barbara, CA 93102

[458] McSwain, Eleanor Davis, 1164 South Jackson Springs Road, Macon, GA 31201

[459] McHaffey, Nola Egle, P. O. Box 502, Wytheville, VA 24382

[460] Maine at Orono Press, University of, 109 P.I.C.S. Building, Orono, ME 04473

[461] Management Information Services, 22929 Industrial Drive, East, Saint Clair Shores, MI 48080

[462] Manessier Publishing Company, P. O. Box 5517, Riverside, CA 92507

[463] Mariners Press, Incorporated, 755 Boylston Street, Boston, MA 02116

[464] Markham, A. B., 215 East Markham Avenue, Durham, NC 27701

[465] Marquette University Press, 1131 West Wisconsin Avenue, Milwaukee, WI 53233

[466] Marquis-Who's Who Books, 200 East Ohio Street, Chicago, IL 60611

[467] Marsh Historical Publications, 912 Shelbyview Drive, Shelbyville, TN 37160

[468] Martz, Ralph Fraley, Route #8, Box 93, Frederick, MD 21701

[469] Maryland Historical Society, The, 201 West Monument Street, Baltimore, MD 21201

[470] Mason and Lipscomb Publishers, 384 Fifth Avenue, New York, NY 10018

[471] Massachusetts Press, University of, Amherst, MA 01002

[472] Mauk, Harold E., 8607 Greenbrier Drive, Overland Park, KS 66212

[473] Maxwell, Fay, Main Post Office, Box 83, Columbus, OH 43216

[474] Mayer, Mrs. Henrietta, RFD #1, Stonington, CT 06378

[475] Mayflower Families, P.O. Box 297, Plymouth, MA 02360

[476] Memphis State University Press, Memphis, TN 38152

[477] Metro Book Company, P.O. Box 226, Falls Church, VA 22046

[478] Metro Books, Incorporated, 1500 Skokie Boulevard, Northbrook, IL 60662

[479] Meyer, Mary Keysor, Route 10, Box 138-A, Pasadena, MD 21122

[480] Miami Press, University of, Drawer 9088, Coral Gables, FL 33124

[481] Michel, James W., M.D., 777 Niagara Street, Denver, CO 80220

[482] Michigan City Historical Society, Incorporated, P. O. Box 512, Michigan City, IN 46360

[483] Michigan Genealogical Council, 11374 Stoneybrook Drive, Grand Ledge, MI 48837

[484] Michigan Press, University of, 615 East University, Ann Arbor, MI 48106

[485] Michigan State University Press, 1405 South Harrison Road, 25 Manly Miles Building, East Lansing, MI 48823

[486] Mickler House Publications, Chuluota, FL 32766

[487] Mid-Michigan Genealogical Society, c/o Michigan Unit, State Library Services, Department of Education, 735 East Michigan Avenue, Lansing, MI 48913

[488] Milford House, 85 Newbury, Boston, MA 02116

[489] Miller, Marcus, 7770 West Marlin Road, Covington, OH 45318

[490] Millman, Dorothy K., 8613 Stockton Parkway, Alexandria, VA 22308

[491] Mills, Mrs. Henry P., 1004 Avondale Drive, Jackson, MS 39216

[492] Mills, Madeline S., 4041 East 46th Street, Tulsa, OK 74135

[493] Mills, Paul, 620 Corby Street, Woodburn, OR 97071

[494] Milner, Mrs. Anita Cheek, 1511 Rincon Villa Drive, Escondido, CA 92027

[495] Miner, John A., Flagg Hill Road, Boxborough, MA 01719

[496] Minnesota Historical Society, Order Department, 1500 Mississippi Street, Saint Paul, MN 55101

[497] Minnesota Press, University of, 2037 University Avenue Southeast, Minneapolis, MN 55455

[498] Mississippi Genealogical Exchange, P. O. Box 434, Forest, MS 39074

[499] Mississippi, University Press of, 3825 Ridgewood Road, Jackson, MS 39211

[500] Missouri Press, University of, 107 Swallow Hall, Columbia, MO 65201

[501] Mixson, John Leslie, Dadeville, AL 36853

[502] Mobile Genealogical Society, P. O. Box 6224, Mobile, AL 36606

[503] Monarch Press, Divison of Simon and Schuster, Incorporated, 1 West 39th Street, New York, NY 10018

[504] Moore, Mrs. Edith Austin, 430 Bay Street, Northeast, Apartment 501, Saint Petersburg, FL 33701

[505] Morgan, Freeman, 7209 14th Avenue, Takoma Park, MD 20012

[506] Morningside Bookshop, Press of, P. O. Box 336, Forrest Park Station, Dayton, OH 45405

[507] Price, Mrs. E. O., Route #2, Box 63, Knob Noster, MO 65336

[508] Morrison, Charles, 1117 Moler Avenue, Hagerstown, MD 21740

[509] Morrison, W. Briley, 426 Virginia Avenue, Front Royal, VA 22630

[510] Morrow (William) and Company, Incorporated, 6 Henderson Drive, West Caldwell, NJ 07006

[511] Mott, James L., P. O. Box 19, Rockville, MO 64780

[512] Moulton, Joy Wade, 1303 London Drive, Columbus, OH 43221

[513] Murphy, Vice Admiral M. E., U. S. Navy, Retired, 3510 Emerson Street, San Diego, CA 92106

[514] National Genealogical Society, 1921 Sunderland Place, Northwest, Washington, DC 20036

[515] National Geographic Society, 17th & M Streets, Northwest, Washington DC 20036

[516] Natural History Press, Doubleday & Company, Incorporated, 501 Franklin Avenue, Garden City, NY 11530

[517] Naval Institute Press, Distributed by ARCO Publishing Company, 219 Park Avenue, South, New York, NY 10003

[518] Naylor Company, P.O. Box 1838, San Antonio, TX 78206

[519] Neal, Jesse H. & Mary H., Spreading Oak Farm, Route 2, Box 338C, Auburn, AL 36830

[520] Neal, Lois S., 525 Wade Avenue, #40, Raleigh, NC 27605

[521] Nebraska Press, University of, 901 North 17th Street, Lincoln, NB 68508

[522] Negro University Press, 51 Riverside Avenue, Westport, CT 06880

[523] Nelson County Historical Society, P.O. Box 254, Lovingston, VA 22949

[524] Nelson-Hall Company, 325 West Jackson Boulevard, Chicago, IL 60606

[525] Nelson (Thomas), Incorporated, 407 Seventh Avenue, South, Nashville, TN 37203

[526] Netherton, Nan, 306 North Virginia Avenue, Falls Church, VA 22046

[527] Nevada Press, University of, Reno, NE 89507

[528] Nevada Publications, P.O. Box 15444, Las Vegas NE 89114

[529] New Castle, Town of, New York (Attention: Town Clerk), 200 South Greeley Avenue, Chappaqua, NY 10514

[530] New England Historic Genealogical Society, 101 Newbury Street, Boston, MA 02116

[531] New England, The University Press of, Box 979, Hanover, NH 03755

[532] New Hampshire Publishing Company, 1 Market Street, Somersworth, NH 03878

[533] New Jersey, Genealogical Society of, P.O. Box 1291, New Brunswick, NJ 08903

[534] New Mexico Genealogical Society, Incorporated, P.O. Box 8734, Albuquerque, NM 87108

[535] New Mexico Press, University of, Albuquerque, NM 87106

[536] New York Graphic Society Limited, 11 Beacon Street, Boston, MA 02108

[537] New York Public Library, Room 50A, Fifth Avenue & 42nd Street, New York, NY 10018

[538] New York University Press, Washington Square, New York, NY 10003

[539] Newberry Library, 60 West Walton Street, Chicago IL 60610

[540] Nicholson, Susie D., 4344 Hohman Circle, Akron, OH 44319

[541] Nissen, Sibyl M., 629 Alvarado Drive, Southeast, Albuquerque, NM 87108

[542] North, Mae Belle Barrow, Pleasant Ridge Road, Summerfield, NC 27358

[543] North Carolina Division of Archives and History, Historical Publications Section, 109 East Jones Street, Raleigh, NC 27611

[544] North Carolina Press, University of, Box 2288, Chapel Hill, NC 27514

[545] Northwestern University Press, 1735 Benson Avenue, Evanston, IL 60201

[546] Norton (W.W.) & Company, Incorporated, 500 Fifth Avenue, New York, NY 10036

[547] Norwood Editions, P.O. Box 38, Norwood PA 19074

[548] Oak Hill Press, P.O. Box 425, Belmont, MA 02178

[549] Florence W. Oakes, 7200 Peninsula Drive, Traverse City, MI 49684

[550] O'Brien (F.M.) Bookseller, 34 & 36 High Street, Portland, ME 04101

[551] Oceana Publications, Dobbs Ferry, NY 10522

[552] Octagon Books, 19 Union Square West, New York, NY 10003

[553] Odom, Dorothy Collins, Herndon Road, Route 3, Waynesboro, GA 30830

[554] Ohio Genealogical Society, P.O. Box 2625, Mansfield, OH 44906

[555] Ohio State University Press, Hitchcock Hall, Room 316, 2070 Neil Avenue, Columbus, OH 43210

[556] Oklahoma Press, University of, 1005 Asp Avenue, Norman, OK 73069

[557] Old West Publishing Company, 1228 East Colfax Avenue, Denver, CO 80218

[558] O'Nan, James Frederick, 3890 Isabella Avenue, Cincinnati, OH 45209

[559] Orange County California Genealogical Society, Box 1587, Orange, CA 92668

[560] Oregon Historical Society, 1230 Southwest Park Avenue, Portland, OR 97205

[561] Oregon State University Press, P.O. Box 689, Corvallis, OR 97330

[562] Oriole Editions, 19 West 44th Street, New York, NY 10036

[563] Ostendorf, Paul J., Campus Box 1441, St. Mary's College, Winona, MN 55987

[564] Otto, Rhea C., 8816 Ferguson Avenue, Savannah, GA 31406

[565] Owings, A.D., Route 1, Box 5, Terry, MS 39170

[566] Oxford University Press, Incorporated, 16-00 Pollitt Drive, Fair Lawn, NJ 07410

[567] Oxmoor House, Incorporated, Box C-59, Birmingham, AL 35283

[568] Ozer (Jerome S.) Publisher, Incorporated, 475 Fifth Avenue, New York, NY 10017

[569] Pace, G. Randle, 114 Robinson Place, Shreveport, LA 71104

[570] Pageant-Poseidon, 644 Pacific Street, Brooklyn, NY 11217

[571] Paisano Press, Incorporated, P.O. Box 85, Balboa Island, CA 92662

[572] Pankey, George E., P.O. Box 84, Ruston, LA 71270

[573] Parker, Anna V., Ghent, KY 41045

[574] Parker, Miss Frances E., 4112 Walnut Grove Avenue, Rosemead, CA 91770

[575] Parkinson, Preston W., 2069 Yale Avenue, Salt Lake City, UT 84108

[576] Parshall, Frank N., 1500 Pierre, Manhattan, KS 66502

[577] Patrie, Lois M., 207 Pawling Avenue, Troy, NY 12180

[578] Peabody Museum of Salem, 161 Essex Street, Salem, MA 01970

[579] Velton Peabody, 50 Williamstowne Court Apartment 3, Cheektowaga NY 14227

[580] Peake, Cyrus H., 923 West Bonita Avenue, Claremont, CA 91711

[581] Pearlman, Agnes Branch, 2001 North Westwood Avenue, Santa Ana, CA 92706

[582] Pegasus, 4300 West 62nd Street, Indianapolis, IN 42668

[583] Pelican Publishing House, 630 Burmaster Street, Gretna, LA 70053

[584] Pendergraft, Allen, P.O. Box 1079, Sedona, AZ 86336

[585] Pendle Hill Publications, 338 Plush Mill Road, Wallingford, PA 19086

[586] Penguin Books, Incorporated, 7110 Ambassador Road, Baltimore, MD 21207

[587] Pennsylvania Historical and Museum Commission, P.O. Box 1026, Harrisburg, PA 17120

[588] Pennsylvania, Historical Society of, 1300 Locust Street, Philadelphia, PA 19107

[589] Pennsylvania State University Press, The, 215 Wagner Building, University Park, PA 16802

[590] Pequot Press, Old Chester Road, Chester, CT 06412

[591] Pergamon Press, Incorporated, Maxwell House, Fairview Park, Elmsford, NY 10523

[592] Perry, Max, 2000 Harvard Street, Midland, TX 79701

[593] Petty, Gerald, 48 Chatham Road, Columbus, OH 43214

[594] Peyton Society of Virginia, c/o Mrs. P.M. Larsen, 2001 Lorraine Avenue, McLean, VA 22101

[595] Phillips County Genealogical Society, P.O. Box 114, Phillipsburg, KS 67661

[596] Phillips, Oma Dee, Box 615, Lamesa, TX 79331

[597] Phoenix Publishing, Woodstock, VT 05091

[598] Pierpont Morgan Library, 29 East 36th Street, New York, NY 10016

[599] Pike County Historical Society, College Box 2, Pikeville, KY 41501

[600] Ping, Donald Harper, 317 North Wayne Street, Warren, IN 46792

[601] Pioneers, 702 West Locust Street, Princeton, KY 42445

[602] Pitman Publishing Corporation, 6 East 43rd Street, New York, NY 10017

[603] Pittsburgh Press, University of, 127 North Bellefield Avenue, Pittsburgh, PA 15213

[604] Pixley, George G., 9339 Grove Avenue, Norfolk, VA 23503

[605] Ploughshare Press, P.O. Box 123, Sea Bright, NJ 07760

[606] Polish Institute of Arts & Sciences In America, 59 East 66th Street, New York NY 10021

[607] Pollard, Robert A., 8429 Merriweather Drive, Springfield, VA 22150

[608] Polyanthos, Drawer 51359, New Orleans, LA 70151

[609] Polynesian Dynamics, Incorporated, P.O. Box 8387, Honolulu, HI 96815

[610] Pope County Genealogy Society, Mrs. Freddy Fields, Secretary, Route 5, Box 249A, Russellville, AR 72801

[611] Poplar Creek Genealogical Society, 63 Golf View Lane, Carpentersville, IL 60110

[612] Porcupine Press, Incorporated, 1317 Filbert Street, Philadelphia, PA 19107

[613] Potomac Books, Incorporated, Publishers, 4832 MacArthur Boulevard, Northwest, Washington, DC 20005

[614] Potter (Clarkson N.) Incorporated, Distributed by Crown Publishers, 419 Park Avenue, South, New York, NY 10016

[615] Potter, Dorothy Williams, 804 Westwood Drive, Tullahoma, TN 37388

[616] Praeger Publishers, 111 Fourth Avenue, New York, NY 10003

[617] Pratt, Rupert C., 115 Spring Road, Scotia, NY 12302

[618] Prentice-Hall, Incorporated, Englewood Cliffs, NJ 07632

[619] Presley, Mrs. Leister E., 1708 West Center, Searcy, AR 72143

[620] Prince George's County Genealogical Society, P.O. Box 819C, Bowie, MD 20715

[621] Princeton University Press, Princeton, NJ 08540

[622] Pruett, Dr. Haskell, 155 South Redwood Drive, Stillwater, OK 74074

[623] Pruett Publishing Company, P.O. Box 1560J, Boulder, CO 80302

[624] Publication Committee, Municipal Building, 319 North Main Street, Chase City, VA 23924

[625] Publishing Center for Cultural Resources, Incorporated, 27 West 53rd Street, New York, NY 10019

[626] Pulling, Mrs. M. Boddie, 333 Old Mill Road, No. 294, Santa Barbara, CA 93110

[627] Putnam's (G.P.) Sons, 200 Madison Avenue, New York, NY 10016

[628] Pyne Press, Distributed by C. Scribner's Sons, Vreeland Avenue, Totowa, NJ 07512

[629] Quadrangle/The New York Times Company, 10 East 53rd Street, New York, NY 10022

[630] Quarterman Publications, Incorporated, 5 South Union Street, Lawrence, MA 01843

[631] R & E Research Associates, Publishers, 4843 Mission Street, San Francisco, CA 94112

[632] Ramfre Press, 1206 North Henderson, Cape Girardeau, MO 63701

[633] Rand McNally & Company, P.O. Box 7600, Chicago, IL 60680

[634] Random House, Incorporated, Orders to Order Department, 457 Hahn Road, Westminster, MD 21157

[635] Readex Books, 101 Fifth Avenue, New York, NY 10003

[636] Reese, Lee Fleming, M.A., 4872 Old Cliffs Road, San Diego, CA 92120

[637] Register, Alvaretta K., C.G., 307 A College Boulevard, Statesboro, GA 30458

[638] Reprint Company, The, P.O. Box 5401, Spartanburg, SC 29304

[639] Revisionist Press, P.O. Box 2009, Brooklyn, NY 11202

[640] R.I. Mayflower Descendants -- Department GB, 128 Massasoit Drive, Warwick, RI 02888

[641] Richardson Heritage Society, 944 South G. Street, Broken Bow, NE 68822

[642] Richardson, Ruth E., 408 Capital Manor, Box 5000, Salem, OR 97304

[643] Ridge, Bradley B., Ph.D., 301 East 69, 6L, New York, NY 10021

[644] Rio Grande Press, Incorporated, Glorieta, NM 87535

[645] Ritchie (Ward) Press, 474 South Arroyo Parkway, Pasadena, CA 91105

[646] Riverside, Genealogical Society of, P.O. Box 2557, Riverside, CA 92506

[647] Roberts, Mrs. William E., 1740 Azteca Drive, Fort Worth, TX 76112

[648] Robichaux, Albert J., Jr., 532 Manhattan Boulevard, Harvey, LA 70058

[649] Robinett, James M., 4875 Regina Lane, Beaumont, TX 77706

[650] Robinson, Richard D., 353 East Lake Road, Palm Springs, FL 33461

[651] Rockwell, Ross R., 5 Pleasant Court, Sunrise Terrace, Binghamton, NY 13905

[652] Rohrbaugh, Lewis Bunker, C.G., Sea Street, Rockport, ME 04856

[653] Rollings, Virginia H., Genealogy Instructor, Thomas Nelson Community College, Box 9407, Briarfield Station, Hampton, VA 23670

[654] Ronald Press Company, 79 Madison Avenue, New York, NY 10016

[655] Rose Publishing Company, Incorporated, 301 Louisiana, Little Rock 72201

[656] Ross & Haines, Incorporated, 3021 Nicollet Avenue, Minneapolis, MN 55408

[657] Ross County Genealogical Society, Box 395, Chillicothe, OH 45601

[658] Rothman (Fred B.) & Company, 57 Leuning Street, South Hackensack, NJ 07606

[659] Routh, BrigGen Ross H., USA-Ret., 2405 McKinley, Apartment 20, El Paso, TX 79930

[660] Routledge & Kegan (Paul) Limited, 9 Park Street, Boston, MA 02108

[661] Rowman and Littlefield, 81 Adams Drive, Totowa, NJ 07512

[662] Russell & Russell, Publishers, 122 East 42nd Street, New York, NY 10017

[663] Russell, George Ely, C.G., Route 3, Box 157, Middletown, MD 21769

[664] Russell, Marie, Box 34057, Houston, TX 77034

[665] Rutgers University Press, 30 College Avenue, New Brunswick, NJ 08903

[666] Saginaw Genealogical Society, c/o Gertrude Peabody, Correspondence Secretary, 1268 Coolidge Street, Saginaw, MI 48603

[667] St. Martin's Press, Incorporated, 175 Fifth Avenue, New York, NY 10010

[668] San Francisco Historic Records, 1204 Nimitz Drive, Colma, CA 94015

[669] Sandlapper Store, Incorporated, P.O. Box 841, Lexington, SC 29072

[670] Scarecrow Press, Incorporated, 52 Liberty Street, Box 656, Metuchen, NJ 08840

[671] Schempp, George C., 164 Oakwood Lane, Ithaca, NY 14850

[672] Schocken Books, Incorporated, 200 Madison Avenue, New York, NY 10016

[673] Scholarly Press, 22929 Industrial Drive, East, Saint Clair Shores, MI 48080

[674] Scholarly Resources, Incorporated, 1508 Pennsylvania Avenue, Wilmington, DE 19806

[675] Schreiner-Yantis, Netti, 6818 Lois Drive, Springfield, VA 22150

[676] Schuster, Katherine Fassett, 456 Chenango Street, Binghamton, NY 13901

[677] Scribner's (Charles) Sons, Orders to Shipping & Service Center, Vreeland Avenue, Totowa, NJ 07512

[678] Sealman, Edith Dirks, 402 - 4th Street, Grundy Center, IA 50638

[679] Seeman (E.A.) Publishing, Incorporated, P.O. Box K, Miami, FL 33156

[680] Seminary Press, P.O. Box 2218, University Station, Enid, OK 73701

[681] Shaw, Aurora C., 2525 Oak Street, Jacksonville, FL 32204

[682] Shelby, Charles E., P.O. Box 6734, Savannah, GA 31405

[683] Shipp, Ralph D., 850 - 8th Street, Boulder, CO 80302

[684] Shirey, Clarence R.,R.D. #2 - Box 305, Shippenville, PA 16254

[685] Shoe String Press, Incorporated, 995 Sherman Avenue, Hamden, CT 06514

[686] Shoemaker, Benjamin H., 3rd, 515 Locust Avenue, Germantown, Philadelphia, PA 19144

[687] Shorey Publications, 815 Third Avenue, Seattle, WA 98104

[688] Shumway, George, R.D. 7, York, PA 17402

[689] Simmons Historical Publications, Melber, KY 42069

[690] Simmons, Mrs. Walter, Natchez Trace Village, Madison, MS 39110

[691] Sistler (Byron) & Associates, 1626 Washington Street, Evanston, IL 60202

[692] Sleepy Hollow Restorations, Incorporated, 150 White Plains Road, Tarrytown, NY 10591

[693] Slinger, Mr. & Mrs. Phillip J., 301 Roselawn Boulevard, Green Bay, WI 54301

[694] Smith (B.D.), Printers, Box 449, Pulaski, VA 24301

[695] Smith, Earl Davis, 406 East Methvin Street, Longview, TX 75601

[696] Smith, Mrs. Kern, 702 Lakeside Drive, Carlsbad, NM 88220

[697] Smith, Leonard H., Jr., 1660 Harmony Drive, Clearwater, FL 33516

[698] Smith (Patterson) Publishing Corporation, 23 Prospect Terrace, Montclair, NJ 07042

[699] Smith (Peter) Publisher, Incorporated, 6 Lexington Avenue, Gloucester, MA 01930

[700] Smithsonian Institution Press, Distributed by George Braziller, Incorporated, 1 Park Avenue, New York, NY 10016

[701] Smythe-Wood, Patrick, F.S.G., Clare Park, 63, Clare Road, Ballycastle, County Antrim, Northern Ireland

[702] Somerset Publishers, 200 Park Avenue, Suite 303 East, New York, NY 10017

[703] South Carolina Press, University of, Columbia, SC 29208

[704] South Dakota Press, University of, Vermillion, SD 57069

[705] South-Western Publishing Company, 5101 Madison Road, Cincinnati, OH 45227

[706] Southern Genealogists Exchange Quarterly, The, Nancy L. Parker, editor, 4305 Coquina Drive, South, Jacksonville Beach, FL 32250

[707] Southern Genealogists Exchange Society, Incorporated, P.O. Box 2801, Jacksonville, FL 32203

[708] Southern Illinois University Press, Box 3697, Carbondale, IL 62901

[709] Southwest Pennsylvania Genealogical Services, P.O. Box 253-B, Laughlintown, PA 15655

[710] Sowell, Carolyn E., 2910 West Michigan, Apartment 104, Midland, TX 79701

[711] Special Libraries Association, 235 Park Avenue, South, New York, NY 10003

[712] Spicer, Mrs. Lindsay W., Route 1, Box 164, Lovingston, VA 22949

[713] Stackpole Books, Cameron & Keller Streets, Harrisburg, PA 17105

[714] Stanford University Press, Stanford, CA 94305

[715] Stanley, Donald W., 134 Stanley Drive, Kernersville, NC 27284

[716] Stark County Chapter, O.G.S., c/o Clifford T. Wig, 7300 Woodcrest Street, Northeast, North Canton, OH 44721

[717] State Printing Company, 1305 Sumter Street, Columbia, SC 29201

[718] Stay Away Joe Publishers, 1500 Fourth Avenue, Great Falls, MT 59401

[719] Steesy, Walter W., R.D. 1, Box 150, Interlaken, NY 14847

[720] Stein, Nancy Hawlick, 631 Central Avenue, Wilmette, IL 60091

[721] Stephens, Gertrude J., 2 Lee Circle, Spanish Fort, AL 36527

[722] Sterling Publishing Company, Incorporated, 419 Park Avenue, South, New York, NY 10016

[723] Stewart, C. R., P.O. Box 3011, Long Beach, CA 90803

[724] Stickney, Fernald S., RFD #2 Marlboro, Ellsworth, ME 04605

[725] Stiens, Robert E., Route 1, Box 148, Shelley, ID 83274

[726] Stilley, Van A., J.D., 718 9th Street, Southeast, Washington, DC 20003

[727] Stone, Kathryn Crossley, 3044 8th Street, Boulder, CO 80302

[728] Strieby, Beatrice, 6786 Sunset Terrace, DesMoines, IA 50311

[729] Strode Publishers, The, Incorporated, 7917 Charlotte Drive, Southwest, Huntsville, AL 35802

[730] Sullwold (William S.) Publishing, 18 Pearl Street, Taunton, MA 02780

[731] Sully Foundation, Limited, 3401 Sully Road, Chantilly, VA 22021

[732] Summit Press, The, Limited, P.O. Box 219, Falls Church, VA 22046

[733] Summit Publications, P.O. Box 222, Munroe Falls, OH 44262

[734] Superior Publishing Company, 708 Sixth Avenue, Box 170, Seattle, WN 98111

[735] Swallow Press, 1139 South Wabash Avenue, Chicago, IL 60605

[736] Swanson Publishing Company, P.O. Box 334, Moline, IL 61265

[737] Swanton, Mrs. John R., Jr., 27 George Street, Newton, MA 02158

[738] Swartz, B. K., Jr., Department of Anthropology, Ball State University, Muncie, IN 47306

[739] Syfrit, M.A. Brandi, 116 Dewey Avenue, Lewes, DE 19958

[740] Syracuse University Press, P.O. Box 8, University Station, Syracuse, NY 13210

[741] Tackitt, Jim W., 1830 Johnson Drive, Concord, CA 94520

[742] Talisman Press, P.O. Box 455, Georgetown, CA 95634

[743] Tallmadge (Mary Floyd) Chapter, DAR, c/o Mrs. Thomas Francis, RFD #1, Litchfield, CT 06759

[744] Taplinger Publishing Company, Incorporated, 200 Park Avenue, South, New York, NY 10003

[745] Taylor (R.J., Jr.) Foundation, P.O. Box 38176, Atlanta, GA 30334

[746] Temple University Press, Philadelphia, PA 19122

[747] Tennessee Press, University of, Communications Building, Knoxville, TN 37916

[748]   Tennessee Veterinary Medical Association, 3926 Nolensville Road, Nashville,
        TN 37211

[749]   Texas Press, University of, P. O. Box 7819, University Station, Austin,
        TX 78712

[750]   Texas State Historical Association, Richardson Hall, 2/306 University Station,
        Austin, TX 78712

[751]   Texas Western Press, University of Texas, El Paso, TX 79999

[752]   Texian Press, 1301 Jefferson, Waco, TX 76703

[753]   Textile Book Service, 1447 East Second Street, Box 907, Plainfield, NJ 07060

[754]   Thomas (Charles C.) Publishers, 301-327 East Lawrence Avenue, Springfield,
        IL 62703

[755]   Thompson, Martha McDaniel, 3782 Alma Avenue, Redding, CA 96001

[756]   Thompson, Shirley J., 3505 Washingtonian Street, Jacksonville, FL 32205

[757]   Thompson, Stephen J., RFD #4, Crawfordsville, IN 47933

[758]   Tidewater Genealogical Society, c/o Thomas Nelson Community College,
        P. O. Box 9407, Hampton, VA 23670

[759]   Tilson Family, The, c/o Mrs. Melvin G. Hurd, Hurd Road, Clintondale,
        NY 12515

[760]   Tinney-Green(e) Family Genealogical Organization, 453 North 400 East,
        Colonial Gardens, Apartment #14-A, Bountiful, UT 84010

[761]   Tipton, The Reverend Ervin Charles, 25 Sunset Way, San Rafael, CA 94901

[762]   Topeka Genealogical Society, The, P. O. Box 4048, Topeka, KS 66604

[763]   Toronto Press, University of, 33 East Tupper Street, Buffalo, NY 14208

[764]   Towne, Harold G., 58 South Street, Westboro, MA 01581

[765]   Trans-Anglo Books, P. O. Box 38, Corona Del Mar, CA 92625

[766]   Transatlantic Arts, Incorporated, North Village Green, Levittown, NY 11756

[767]   Travis, Julia M., Route 3, Box 137, Beford, IA 50833

[768]   Tri-City Genealogical Society, Route 1, Box 191, Richland, WA 99352

[769]   Trinity University Press, 715 Stadium Drive, San Antonio, TX 78284

[770]   Tudor Publishing Company, Distributed by Harlem Book Company, 221 Park
        Avenue, South, New York, NY 10003

[771]   Turk, Mrs. Edward J., 5811 Kenneth Avenue, Parma, OH 44129

[772]   Tuttle (Charles E.) Company, Incorporated, Drawer F, Rutland, VT 05701

[773]   Twayne Publishers, Distributed by G. K. Hall & Company, 70 Lincoln Street,
        Boston, MA 02111

[774]   Two Continents Publishing Group, Incorporated, Attention Larry Conti,
        5 South Union Street, Lawrence, MA 01843

[775]   Ungar (Frederick) Publishing Company, Incorporated, 250 Park Avenue,
        South, New York, NY 10003

[776]   Unipub, Incorporated, P. O. Box 433, Murray Hill Station, New York,
        NY 10016

[777] University Microfilms International, Dissertation Publishing
P.O. Box 1764, Ann Arbor, MI 48106

All publications having the vendor #777 are doctoral dissertations. Paper copies of these are made available to you by reproducing them xerographically at about 2/3 the original size. They are perfectbound and covered in paper. Clothbound copies are available at an additional charge of $3.00, with author and title stamped in gold on the spine. Unless you specify "cloth binding" (and on prepaid orders include the additional $3.00) on your order, you will be shipped the paper cover.

Pages are printed in numerical sequence by xerography; but, since printing is on one side of a continuous web, the finished copy has printing on the righthand pages only.

Prices for Paper Copies		U. S.	Canada/Mexico	Elsewhere
Academic	This includes libraries, departments, faculty, staff, and students, of all universities, colleges, and high schools.	15.00 ea.	16.50 ea.	23.00 ea.
Other		20.00 ea.	22.00 ea.	23.00 ea.

Prices for Microfilm Copies [35mm]			
Academic	7.50 ea.	8.25 ea.	11.50 ea.
Other	10.00 ea.	11.00 ea.	11.50 ea.

When ordering, please supply the order number, author's last name, complete dissertation title, format and type of binding wanted, billing name and address (on institutional orders only), and shipping name and address. Individuals must send a check or money order with their order. Orders are shipped within 2 to 4 weeks after they are received.

[778] University Microfilms International, Out-of-Print On Demand Local Histories
300 North Zeeb Road, Ann Arbor, MI 48106 U.S.A.

Publications having the vendor #778 are out-of-print genealogical or local history works, made available to you by reproducing them xerographically from microfilm masters. The prices of these books vary according to the number of pages. They are available on paper (with either a cloth or paper cover), or on 35mm microfilm. To inquire about the price of a book, please provide the order number, name of author (if given), full title, volume number (if any), and number of pages.

[779] University Microfilms International, On Demand Genealogies & Family Histories
300 North Zeeb Road, Ann Arbor, MI 48106 U.S.A.

Publications listed under vendor #779 are family genealogies or histories. They are primarily rare out-of-print works which are made available to you by reproducing them xerographically from microfilm masters. University Microfilm International's publication GENEALOGIES AND FAMILY HISTORIES: A CATALOG OF DEMAND REPRINTS [$1.00 from the above address] will provide you with the titles and authors of the books now available.

[780] University Stores, Inc., P.O. Box 7756, Austin, TX 78712

[781] Upton, Mrs. R. C., 1402 Robert Drive, Jackson, MS 39211

[782] Utah Press, University of, Building 513, Salt Lake City, UT 84112

[783] Utah State University Press, Department of English & Journalism, Logan, UT 84321

[784] Utt, Mrs. Albert, 909 East 9th, Winfield, KS 67156

[785] VKM Publishing Company, P.O. Box 11102, Fort Worth, TX 76109

[786] Valley Publishers, 1759 Fulton Street, Fresno, CA 93721

[787] Van Meter, Mrs. Oather E., 7710 Grensted Lane, Lawton, OK 73501

[788] Van Nostrand Reinhold Company, 300 Pike Street, Cincinnati, OH 45202

[789] Vanderbilt University Press, Nashville, TN 37235

[790] Vanous (Arthur) Company, Richard Court, Riveredge, NJ 07661

[791] Vantage Press, Incorporated, 516 West 34th Street, New York, NY 10001

[792] Vawter, Henry A., 217 Mountain View Boulevard, Maryville, TN 37801

[793] Vedder, Edwin H., 225 Getzville Road, Amherst, NY 14226

[794] Ventnor Publishers, P.O. Box 2078, Ventnor, NJ 08406

[795] Verry (Lawrence) Incorporated, 16 Holmes Street, Mystic, CT 06355

[796] Versailles, Elizabeth S., Route 1, #61, Williamsburg, MA 01096

[797] Viking Press, Incorporated, 625 Madison Avenue, New York, NY 10022

[798] Vineyard, Mrs. John, Route 2, Box 141D, Ozark, MO 65721

[799] Virginia Book Company, Berryville, VA 22611

[800] Virginia State Library, 12th & Capitol Streets, Richmond, VA 23219

[801] Virginia, University Press of, P.O. Box 3608, University Station, Charlottesville, VA 22903

[802] Vogt, Helen, 121 Blaine Avenue, Brownsville, PA 15417

[803] Vorpagel, Will C., 165 South Downing Street, Denver, CO 80209

[804] Vought, Lelah Ridgway, 390C Northampton Road, Amherst, MA 01002

[805] Wadsworth Publishing Company, Inc., 10 Davis Drive, Belmont, CA 94002

[806] Walker & Company, 720 Fifth Avenue, New York, NY 10019

[807] Walker, Randall M., Jr., P.O. Box 227, Jesup, GA 31545

[808] Wall, Jane Kirkpatrick, P.O. Box 148, Vienna, VA 22180

[809] Wallace, William H., 3237 Third Street, Oceanside, NY 11572

[810] Walsworth Publishing Company, Inc., 306 North Kansas Avenue, Marceline,
MO 64658

[811] Walter, Alice Granbery, 116 B Pinewood Road, Virginia Beach, VA 23451

[812] Walters, Judith Allison, P.O. Box 129, Bothell, WA 98011

[813] Wardell, Bernice, P.O. Box 246, Laurens, NY 13796

[814] Washington Press, University of, Seattle, WA 98105

[815] Washington Square Press, Inc., c/o Simon & Schuster, Inc., 701 Seneca Street,
Buffalo, NY 14210

[816] Washington State Historical Society, 315 North Stadium Way, Tacoma, WA 98403

[817] Watts (Franklin) Incorporated, 845 Third Avenue, New York, NY 10022

[818] Way, Mrs. D. Herbert, Friends Drive, Woodstown, NJ 08079

[819] Wayne State University Press, 5980 Cass Avenue, Detroit, MI 48202

[820] Weisiger, Benjamin B. III, 8 Glenbrooke Circle, East; Richmond, VA 23229

[821] Welsheimer, Edith L., 335 West Van Patten, Las Cruces, NM 88001

[822] Wesleyan University Press, 365 Washington Street, Middletown, CT 06457

[823] West, Mrs. Howard E., Shamrock Cottage, Cherokee Road, Asheville, NC 28801

[824]   West, Richard, Box 6404, Philadelphia, PA 19145

[825]   West Texas Museum Association, P. O. Box 4499, Lubbock, TX 79409

[826]   Western Epics Publishing Company, 254 South Main Street, Salt Lake City, UT 84101

[827]   Western Heraldry, Box 19281, Denver, CO 80219

[828]   Western New York Genealogical Society, 209 Nassau Avenue, Kenmore, NY 14217

[829]   Westernlore Press Publications, 5117 Eagle Rock Boulevard, Los Angeles, CA 90041

[830]   The Westminster Press, 905 Witherspoon Building, Philadelphia, PA 19107

[831]   Whatcom Genealogical Society, Supply Chairman, P. O. Box 1493, Bellingham, WA 98225

[832]   Wheatfield Press, Box 205, St. James P. O., Winnipeg, Manitoba, Canada R3J 3R4

[833]   Wheelwright Bond Company, Porter's Landing, Freeport, ME 04032

[834]   Whipple, Henry, 909 North Hamilton, High Point, NC 27262

[835]   Whitston Publishing Company, P. O. Box 322, Troy, NY 12181

[836]   Whitten, Mrs. Herbert O., 7022 Marguerite Court, Annandale, VA 22003

[837]   Wilder, W. M., 1124 Dawson Road, Albany, GA 31707

[838]   Wilderness Press, 2440 Bancroft Way, Berkeley, CA 94704

[839]   Wiley (John) and Sons, Incorporated, 605 Third Avenue, New York, NY 10016

[840]   Wilkey, Hubert Weldon, 2312 Clark Avenue, Bradenton, FL 33507

[841]   Williams, Richard T. and Mildred C. Williams, P. O. Box 307, Danboro, PA 18916

[842]   Willprecht, Mrs. Al, Rt. 3, Box 151, Frazee, MN 56544

[843]   Wilson, Mrs. Albert L., 2012 Wilkening Drive, Alton, IL 62002

[844]   Wilson and Glover Publishing Company, 571 Headden Drive, Ridgely, TN 38080

[845]   Wilson, Barr, Toll Gate, WV 26442

[846]   Wilson, Donald L., 6437 Livingston Road, Apartment 203, Oxon Hill, MD 20021

[847]   Wilson, H. W., 950 University Avenue, Bronx, NY 10452

[848]   Winona County Historical Society, 160 Johnson Street, Winona, MN 55987

[849]   Wisconsin Press, University of, P. O. Box 1379, Madison, WI 53701

[850]   Wisconsin, State Historical Society of, 816 State Street, Madison, WI 53706

[851]   Witherell, Peter C., 1 Highland Drive, Hamilton, IL 62341 - OR - Witherell, Edwin R., 710 Cedar Village Drive, York, PA 17402

[852]   Woodruff, Mrs. Howard W., 1824 South Harvard, Independence, MO 64052

[853]   World Wide Publications, 1313 Hennepin Avenue, Minneapolis, MN 55403

[854]   Worley, Ramona Cameron, 27 Clover Drive, Belleville, IL 62221

[855]   Wright, Mrs. James T., 722 South 22nd, Arkadelphia, AR 71923

[856] Wright, Mildred S., 140 Briggs, Beaumont, TX 77707

[857] Yale University Press, 92A Yale Station, New Haven, CT 06520

[858] Yankee Peddler Book Company, 38 Hampton Road, Drawer O, Southampton, NY 11968

[859] Yates, William A., P. O. Box 1687, Rifle, CO 81650

[860] Ye Galleon Press, P. O. Box 400, Fairfield, WN 99012

[861] Yesteryears Magazine, Box 52, Dixon Road, Aurora, NY 13026

[862] Zook, Lois Ann, 2176-H Lincoln Highway East, Lancaster, PA 17602

LATE ADDITIONS:

[863] Meynard, Virginia G., 5866 Woodvine Road, Columbia, SC 29206

[864] Beacon Press, Incorporated, 25 Beacon Street, Boston, MA 02108

[865] Schuyler County Historical Society, Box 188, Lancaster, MO 63548

[866] Sutter House, P. O. Box 146, Lititz, PA 17543

[867] Randall House, P. O. Box 17306, Nashville, TN 37217

[868] Westland Publications Company, 594 West Lincoln Highway, DeKalb, IL 60115

[869] Kintz, Mrs. Lorraine, Route 1, Richland Center, WI 53581

[870] Bell and Howell, MicroPhoto Division, Old Mansfield Road, Wooster, OH 44691

[871] San Joaquin Genealogical Society, P. O. Box 4817, Stockton, CA 95204

[872] Society of Ohio Archivists, Bowling Green State University Library, Bowling Green, OH 43402

[873] Smith, Dorothy Davis, 1916 North Signal Hills Drive, Kirkwood, MO 63122

[874] Utah Genealogical Association, P.O. Box 1144, Salt Lake City, UT 84110

[875] Sangamon County Genealogical Society, P.O. Box 1829, Springfield, IL 62705

[876] Lee Publishing Company, P.O. Box 44, Washington, DC 20044

[877] Donna Hotaling, Agent for The Institute of Heraldic and Genealogical Studies, 2255 Cedar Lane, Vienna, VA 22180

[878] Mrs. Randolph Norris Shreve, 715 Northridge Drive, West Lafayette, IN 47906

General Reference

Periodicals of National Scope

	Cloth	Paper	Vendor *

National Genealogical Society. National Genealogical Society
Quarterly. 1912–
Material included consists primarily of compiled
genealogies of pre-1800 families, research techniques,
source records, scholarly articles and book reviews.
Included in membership to the society. Institutions
may subscribe – $17 per year. 320pp/yr. Membership: $20/yr (514)

Utah Genealogical Association. Genealogical Journal. 178pp/yr.
Material included consists primarily of research
techniques and procedures, reports of special collections, articles of regional emphasis throughout the
world, description of original records, genealogical
publication and reporting, book reviews and scholarly
articles. Included in membership to the Association. $8/yr (874)

Textbooks, Manuals & Handbooks

Bremer, Ronald A., ed. Compendium of American Historical
Sources. 1976. 500+pp.
This monumental work attempts to describe all the
federal, state, county, church, fraternal, etc. records
in America.   100.00   ..... (272)

Burns, Nuncie. Family Tree – An Adventure in Genealogy.   4.75   ..... (766)

Clark, G. Kitson. Guide for Research Students. 1958.   1.75   ..... (114)

"Constructive Imagination in Family Research." Illinois State
Genealogical Society Quarterly, Vol. 7, No. 2. 1975. 7pp. 2.00 (366)

Creigh, Dorothy Weyer. A Primer for Local Historical Societies.
1976. 224pp. 6.50 (18)

Doane, Gilbert H. Searching for Your Ancestors: The How and
Why of Genealogy. Repr. of 1937 ed. 212pp.
Instructional guide for both beginning and advanced
genealogists on how to trace your family antecedents. 2.45 (530)

Edmunds, Helene. Family Identification, Record and Genealogy.   2.95   ..... (791)

Emmison, F. G.   Archives and Local History. 2d ed. 1974.
111pp.   9.00   ..... (661)

Helmbold, F. Wilbur. Tracing Your Ancestry – A Step-by-Step
Guide to Retracing Your Family History. 1976. 192pp.
Included are exact procedures for planning the search
and for using records of all types.   9.95   ..... (567)

———   Tracing Your Ancestry: Logbook. 256pp.
Forms on which the researcher can chart his findings
and document progress.   3.95   ..... (567)

Hilton, Suzanne. Who Do You Think You Are? 1976.   .... (830)

Kirkham, E. Kay. Making the Genealogical Record. 85 (190)

Letey, Marilyn R., comp. 1-2-3 Three Easy Steps to Climb
the Family Tree. Repr. of 1973 ed. 214pp.
A beginning genealogy instruction book designed
especially for the beginner. 7.00 (427)

McCoy, F. N. Researching and Writing in History. 1974.   7.50   1.75 (112)

Moulton, Joy Wade. Find Your Ancestors. 1976. In Process.
A guide to the use of genealogical records and library
resources with emphasis on description, interpretation,
and clues for further research.   .... (512)

Pine, L. G. Teach Yourself Heraldry and Genealogy. Repr. of
    1957 ed. 266pp. 2.95 (452)
Poulton, Helen J. and Marguerite S. Howland. The Historian's
    Handbook. 1972.   9.95   4.95 (556)
Rollings, Virginia H. Genealogy - A Basic Course. Repr. of
    1972 ed. 126pp.
    Textbook for 10-week course in college - basic but
    not elementary. 6.50 (653)
Southern Genealogist's Exchange Society, Incorporated. A Basic
    Research Kit. Repr. of 1966 ed. 90pp.
    Divided into eight sections. May be used for classes.
    Includes suggested forms for research and recommended
    source books. For the beginner as well as more
    advanced researchers. 3.50 (707)
Wrigley, E. A. Identifying People in the Past. 1974.   12.50   ..... (602)

Texts, Manuals & Handbooks for Special Subjects

Bremer, Ronald A. Federal Forms. 1975. 22pp.
    Most of the important federal forms together with explan-
    ations. Includes BC600, M154, 6751, 7163, 7029, etc. 3.00 (272)
Cook, J. Frank. Forms Manual (for Colleges and University
    Archives. 1973. 236pp. 8.00 (17)
Draznin, Yaffa. Jewish Genealogical Research and Central
    Archives. NGS Quarterly, Vol. 63, No. 3. 1975. 5pp. 3.50 (514)
Eastern Washington Genealogical Society. German Research
    Tips. 58pp. 2.00 (212)
    _____. Scandinavian Research Tips. 24pp. 1.00 (212)
Gottschalk, Louis R., Clyde Kluckhohn and Robert Angell.
    The Use of Personal Documents in History, Anthropology,
    and Sociology, Prepared for the Committee on Appraisal
    of Research. 1945.   .....   5.00 (415)
Higham, John. Writing American History: Essays on Modern
    Scholarship. 1972.   .....   2.95 (370)
Iredale, David. Enjoying Archives: What They Are, Where to
    Find Them, How to Use Them. 1973.   12.95   ..... (181)
Ireland, Norma Olin. You're Going to "Make an Index". Part II.
    Genealogical Indexing. 4pp. 3.50 (378)
Kirkham, E. Kay. A Study in Finding Aids for American
    Genealogical. 1.25 (190)
Martinson, Tom L. Introduction to Library Research in
    Geography: An Instruction Manual and Short Bibliography.
    1972.   5.00   ..... (670)
Mode, Peter G. Source Book and Bibliographical Guide to
    American Church History. Repr. of 1921 ed. 735pp.   17.50   ..... (117)
Paetow, Louis J. A Guide to the Study of Medieval History.
    Prepared under the auspices of the Mediaeval Academy of
    America. rev. ed. 1959.   25.00   ..... (415)
Rofes, William L., ed. A Basic Glossary for Archivists,
    Manuscript Curators, and Records Managers. 1974. 18pp.
    A postage and handling charge is added to orders not
    prepaid and under $10.00. *Available at $1 each in
    quantities of 10 or more delivered to one address. *2.00 (17)
Shepperd, Walter Lee. Feudal Genealogy. 1976.   .....   5.50 (514)
Smith, Clifford Neal and Anna P-C Smith. Encyclopedia of
    German-American Genealogical Research. 1976. 273pp.
    Contains material both on the European homeland and
    on the various German settlements in the United States
    and Canada. Examines tools and methods for linking

German-Americans with their Central European heritage
and places of origin.   35.00   ..... (85)
Utah Genealogical Association. Professional Genealogy Handbook.
   Genealogical Journal, Vol. 5, Nos. 1 & 2. 1976. 84pp.
   A significant book for the professional. Answers questions
   on all phases - from acquiring clients to keeping tax records. 6.00 (874)
Wagner, Anthony. Pedigree and Progress: Essays in the
   Genealogical Interpretation of History. 1975. 333pp.   25.00   ..... (661)
Weinstein, Robert A. and Larry Booth. Collection, Use and Care
   of Historical Photographs. 1976. In Process.   .... (18)
Wood, Virginia S. A Uniform System of Citation for Lineage
   Papers. 1970. 15pp. 2.00 (154)

Manuals on Use of Libraries

Brogan, Gerald E. and Jeanne T. Buck. Using Libraries
   Effectively (Effective English Series). 1969.   ..... 2.95 (193)
Gates, Jean K. Guide to the Use of Books and Libraries.
   (McGraw-Hill Series in Library Science). 3rd ed. 1973.   6.95   3.95 (451)
Heidenreich, Fred L. "How to Obtain Genealogical Books
   Through Interlibrary Loan." Copper State Bulletin, Vol. XI,
   No. 1. 1976. 8pp. 1.50 (34)
Shove, Raymond, et al. Use of Books and Libraries. 10th ed.
   1963. illus. 1.75 (497)
Thompson, Sarah K. Interlibrary Loan Involving Academic
   Libraries, Acrl. 1970.   ..... 5.00 (22)

Filing Systems, Information Storage and Retrieval

Automated Education Center. Studies in Indexing and Cataloging. 29.00 ..... (461)
Bakewell, K. G. Classification for Information Retrieval. 1968. 4.50 ..... (685)
Benrey, Ronald. Understanding Digital Computers. 1964.
   176pp. illus. 5.70 (323)
Coan, James S. Basic BASIC: An Introduction to Computer
   Programming in BASIC Language. 1970. 256pp. illus.   9.95   7.95 (323)
Data Retrieval Without a Computer - Technical Leaflet #85.   .....   .50 (18)
Haag, James N. Comprehensive FORTRAN Programming.
   1965. 256pp. illus.
   An introduction to computer programming. This text
   may be used as a self-teaching device. No previous
   experience with computers is assumed. 7.75 (323)
Murphy, John S. Baiscs of Digital Computers Revised Second
   Edition. 3 vols. 1970. 420pp. illus.   Set: 12.95 ..... (323)
   Vols. 1-3:   Each: 4.95 (323)
Spencer, Donald D. Computers in Action: How Computers
   Work. 1974. 160pp. illus.   7.50   4.95 (323)
Weeks, Bertha M. Filing and Records Management. 1964.   7.50   ..... (654)

Care & Repair of Old Materials

AASLH. Leather - Technical Leaflet #1.   .....   .50 (18)
_____. Rare Book and Paper Repair - Technical Leaflet #14. .....   .50 (18)
Brown, Lloyd A. Notes on the Care and Cataloging of Old Maps.
   Repr. of 1941 ed.   6.25   ..... (404)
Bullock, Orin M., Jr. The Restoration Manual. 12.95 (18)
Kane, Lucile M. A Guide to the Care and Administration of
   Manuscripts. 2d ed. 1966. 74pp. 3.00 (18)
Kathpalia, Yash P. Conservation and Restoration of Archive
   Materials. 1974.   ..... 7.50 (776)

Keck, Carolina K. A Handbook on the Care of Paintings. 4.75 (18)
Langwell, William H. The Conservation of Books and Documents.
Repr. of 1957 ed. 9.00 ..... (297)
Middleton, Bernard C. Restoration of Leather Bindings. 1972. ..... 10.00 (22)

Forms and Books for Recording Data

Ancestral Chart: A Genealogical Work Sheet.
A large folding chart on which to record the essential
data of six generations - on both paternal and maternal
sides. 6 charts. 1.00 (772)
Ancestral Register Of. . .
A fan-shaped chart for recording nine generations of a
family, with room for 511 names. 1.25 (772)
Family Tree, devised by William H. Whitmore.
A set of charts for the compiling of genealogical information, so arranged that eight generations of ancestors may
be recorded in connected and simple form. 32 pages. 5.25 (772)
My Personal Memory Book, Lee Sharff, et al. 1976. 112pp.
A gift item. Especially appropriate for elderly relatives, as,
when filled out (made easy by headings which serve as guide-
lines), it provides you with their complete autobiography. 5.45 (876)

Publishing Your Own Book or Newsletter

Banister, Manly. Bookbinding as a Handcraft. 1975. 11.29 ..... (722)
Clowes, William. A Guide to Printing. Repr. of 1963 ed. 10.25 ..... (297)
Curtis, Mary Barnett. Primer for First Time Publishers.
1972. 25pp. 2.00 (371)
DeVinne, Theodore. Practice of Typography. Reprint. 20.95 ..... (320)
Felt, Thomas E. Researching, Writing, and Publishing Local
History. 1976. 192pp. 6.00 (18)
Guthrie. Alphabetic Indexing. 1964. 1.44 ..... (705)
Hollander, Annette. Bookcraft - How to Construct Note Pad
Covers, Boxes, and Other Useful Items. 1974. 101pp.
The type of hardcover illustrated in this work is simple
to make. It also shows how to make a box to hold your
book - or set of books. 9.95 ..... (788)
Horne, Hervert P. Binding of Books. Repr. of 1894 ed. 11.95 ..... (320)
Hurlburt, Allen. Publication Design: A Guide to Page Layout,
Typography, Format and Style. rev ed. 1976. 134pp.
Useful in designing pages which include photographs,
and for preparing advertising brochures. 8.95 (788)
Lasky, Joseph. Proofreading and Copy Preparation. 1941. 12.50 ..... (10)
"Pedigrees for Posterity." ISGS Quarterly, Vol. 5, No. 2.
1973. 5pp. 2.00 (366)
Rosen, Ben. Type &!.,-;?: The Designer's Type Book. 1976.
406pp.
For those who are going to have their book typeset (as
opposed to typing it themselves), this book shows the
many varieties of type styles available. 9.95 (788)
Smith, Philip. New Directions in Bookbinding. 1974. 208pp.
While this work demonstrates hard bookbinding, it is
not a beginners book. Rather, it is a superb work for
the creative who wish to prepare something special in
the way of a cover for their book. Leather is stressed,
but plastic and metal are also mentioned. A case
history of the repair and rebinding of a rare old book
is given in detail. Restoration of old books, with
details on rebinding in keeping with the original, rather
than just protecting the pages is sited. Full color plates. 25.00 ..... (788)

Stone, Bernard and Arthur Eckstein. Preparing Art for
Printing. 1965. 200pp.
A comprehensive handbook which presents the
methods and tools needed to make camera-ready copy
both for black-and-white and for color productions. .... (788)
Turabian, Kate L. Manual for the Writers of Term Papers,
Theses and Dissertations. 4th ed. 1973. 5.00 1.95 (137)
Wheatley, Henry B. Dedication of Books to Patron and Friend.
Repr. of 1887 ed. 257pp.
Covers the history of English book dedications, with
explanatory introduction. 8.50 ..... (266)

History

Bolton, Herbert E. and Thomas M. Marshall. The Colonization
of North America, 1492-1783. Repr. of 1920 ed. 17.95 ..... (306)
Boulle, Pierre Henri. The French Colonies and the Reform of
Their Administration During and Following the Seven Years'
War. 735pp. DIP-69-10257. .... (777)
Brigham, Albert P., ed. Geographic Influences in American
History. Repr. of 1903 ed. 15.00 ..... (404)
_____. Geographic Influences in American History. 1970. 16.50 ..... (248)
Campbell, John. Concise History of the Spanish America 1741.
1972. 22.50 ..... (52)
Chalmers, George. Political Annals of the Present United
Colonies, from Their Settlement to the Peace of 1763. 2 vols
in 1. Repr. of 1780 ed. 50.00 ..... (248)
Christie, Ian R. Crisis of Empire: Great Britain and the
American Colonies 1754-1783. 1967. ..... 1.75 (546)
Cobbett, William. Porcupine's Works Containing Various
Writings and Selections Exhibiting a Faithful Picture of
the United States of America. . . from the End of the War
in 1783 to the Election of the President, March 1801. 12 vols.
in 6. 1801. Set: 167.50 ..... (273)
Danzer, Gerald A. America's Roots in the Past: Historical
Publication in America to 1860. 449pp. BIP-68-03170. .... (777)
Doyle, John A. The English in America. 5 vols. Volume 1-
Puritan Colonies, Part 1, Volume 2-Puritan Colonies, Part
2, Volume 3-The Middle Colonies, Volume 4-Virginia, Mary-
land and the Carolinas, Volume 5-The Colonies Under the
House of Hanover. Repr. of 1882 ed. illus. Set: 135.00 ..... (2)
Each: 27.50 ..... (2)
Fiske, John. The Critical Period of American History: 1783-
1789. Reprint. 12.50 ..... (547)
Gipson, Lawrence H. The British Empire Before the American
Revolution. 15 vols.
Volume 1: Great Britain and Ireland, 1748-1754: The British
Isles and the American Colonies. 1958.
Volume 2: The Southern Plantations, 1748-1754: The British
Isles and the American Colonies. 1960.
Volume 3: The Northern Plantations, 1748-1754: The British
Isles and the American Colonies. 1960.
Volume 4: North America, South of the Great Lakes Region,
1748-1754.
Volume 5: The Great Lakes Frontier, Canada, the West
Indies, India, 1748-1754: Zones of International Friction.
Volume 6: The Years of Defeat, 1754-1757: The Great War
for the Empire.

Volume 7: The Victorious Years, 1758-1760: The Great War
for the Empire.
Volume 8: The Culmination, 1760-1763: The Great War for
the Empire.
Volume 9: New Responsibilities Within the Enlarged Empire,
1763-1766: The Triumphant Empire. 1956.
Volume 10: Thunder-Clouds Gather in the West, 1763-1766:
The Triumphant Empire. 1961.
Volume 11: The Rumbling of the Coming Storm, 1766-1770:
The Triumphant Empire. 1965.
Volume 12: Britain Sails into the Storm, 1770-1776: The
Triumphant Empire. 1965.
Volume 13: The Empire Beyond the Storm, 1770-1776: The
Triumphant Empire. 1967.
Volume 14: A Bibliographical Guide to the History of the
British Empire, 1748-1776. 1968.
Volume 15: A Guide to Manuscripts Relating to the History
of the British Empire, 1748-1776. 1970.

Vols. 1-13:	Each:	12.50	.....	(412)
Vols. 14 and 15:	Each:	15.00	.....	(412)

Gottschalk, Louis, et al. Foundations of the Modern World,
1300-1775. 1970. ... 20.00 ..... (317)
Greene, Evarts B. Provincial America, 1690-1740. 1964. ... 8.50 ..... (775)
Hall, Michael G. Glorious Revolution in America: Documents
on the Colonial Crisis of 1689. 1972. ... . 3.95 (546)
Hennepin, Louis. A New Discovery of a Vast Country in America.
Reprinted from the Second London Issue of 1698, with
Facsimiles of Original Title-Pages, Maps, and Illustrations,
and the Addition of Introduction, Notes and Index by Reuben
Gold Thwaites. 2 vols. in 1. 1903. ... 42.00 ..... (415)
Holmes, Abiel. The Annals of America, from the Discovery by
Columbus in the Year 1492, to the Year 1826. 2d ed. 2 vols.
1829. Set: ... 95.00 ..... (2)
Jeffery, Reginald W. History of the Thirteen Colonies of North
America, 1497-1763. Repr. of 1908 ed. ... 12.50 ..... (404)
Jernegan, Marcus W. American Colonies 1492-1750 (American
Classics Series). illus. 1.95 (775)
Kavenagh, W. Keith, ed. Foundations of Colonial America: A
Documentary History. 3 vols. Volume 1-The Northeastern
Colonies, Volume 2-The Middle Atlantic Colonies, Volume 3-
The Southern Colonies. 1973. 2639pp. Set: ... 96.00 ..... (85)
MacDonald, William, ed. Documentary Source Book of American
History 1606-1926. 3rd ed. Repr. of 1926 ed. ... 30.00 ..... (248)
Mitchell, John. Contest in America Between Great Britain and
France. Repr. of 1757 ed. ... 17.50 ..... (394)
Osgood, Herbert L. American Colonies in the Seventeenth
Century. 3 vols. Each: ... 8.50 ..... (699)
_____. American Colonies in the Eighteenth Century. 4 vols.
Each: ... 8.50 ..... (699)
Oldmixon, John. The British Empire in America. Containing
the History of the Discovery, Settlement, Progress and
State of the British Colonies on the Continent and Islands of
North America. Second edition Corrected and Amended,
with the Continuation of the History, and the Variation in
the State and Trade of Those Colonies from the Year 1710 to
the Present Time, Including Occasional Remarks and the
Most Feasible and Useful Methods for their Improvement and

Security. 2 vols. xxiv, 567; 478pp. maps.
Volume 1-Being an account of the country, soil, climate,
product and trade of Newfoundland, New-England, New-
Scotland, New-York, New-Jersey, Pennsylvania, Mary-
land, Virginia, Carolina, Hudson's Bay, Volume 2-Being
an account of the country, soil, climate, product and
trade of Barbados, St. Lucia, St. Vincents, Dominico,
Antigo, Montserrat, Nevis, St. Christophers, Barbuda,
Anguila, Jamaica, Bahama and Bermudas.   Set: 50.00   ..... (273)
Pomfret, John E. and Floyd M. Shumway. Founding the
American Colonies, 1583-1660. 1970.   8.95   ..... (317)
Rogers, Robert. Concise Account of North America. Repr. of
1765 ed.   13.25   ..... (394)
Thwaites, Ruben G. The Colonies: 1492-1750. Repr. of 1897 ed. 10.00   ..... (547)
_____. France in America, 1497-1763. Repr. of 1905 ed.   15.95   ..... (320)
Tyler, Lyon G. England in America: Fifteen Eighty to Sixteen
Fifty-Two. Repr. of 1904 ed.   7.50   ..... (159)
Ubbelohde, Carl W. American Colonies and the British Empire,
1607-1763.   .....   2.50 (171)
Vaughan, Alden T., comp. The American Colonies in the
Seventeenth Century. 1971.   5.95   2.95 (1)
West, Willis M. A Source Book in American History to 1787.
Repr. of 1913 ed.   25.00   ..... (547)
Winterbotham, William. An Historical, Geographical, Commercial,
and Philosophical View of the American United States, and of
the European Settlements in America and the West-Indies.
4 vols. 1799.   Set: 175.00   ..... (2)
Wright, James Leitch, Jr. English Spanish Rivalry in North
America, 1492-1763. 239pp. BIP-58-05550.   .... (777)

Colonial Families

American Ancestry: Giving the Name and Descent, in the Male
Line, of Americans Whose Ancestors Settled in the United States
Previous to the Declaration of Independence. eds. Thomas P.
Hughes (Vols. 1-2) and Frank Munsell (Volumes 3112). 1887-99.
    Volume 1. The City of Albany, State of New York, 1887. 130pp.
    Volume 2. (Local Series) Columbia County, State of New
            York, 1887. 194pp.
    Volumes 3-12. Embracing lineages from the whole of the
            United States. 1888. 200 to 300 pp. ea.
    B-BH 6902   .... (778)
Bolton, Charles K. The Founders: Portraits of Persons Born
Abroad Who Came to the Colonies in North America Before
the Year 1701. Repr. of 1919-26 ed. 1103pp.   38.50   ..... (274)
Colket, Meredith B., Jr. Founders of Early American Families:
Emigrants From Europe 1607-1657. 374pp.
    Identifies 3500 men who settled in what became the
    13 original Colonies.   .... (247)
Dall, Caroline Wells Healey. Genealogical Notes and Errata to
Save's Genealogical Dictionary. 187?. 24pp. B-OP 15849.   .... (778)
Emory, Mary Burke. Colonial Families and Their Descendants.
1900. 282pp. B-OP 62606.   .... (778)
Savage, James. A Genealogical Dictionary of the First Settlers
of New England. 1860-62. 4 vols. 534pp.;604pp.;670pp.;
724pp.   B-BH 6656.   .... (778)

Turk, Marion G. The Quiet Adventurers in America. 1975.
300pp.
    Genealogical data and story of settlers in the American
Colonies and in the United States, from the Channel
Islands, United Kingdom; Jersey, Guernsey, Alderney
and Sark.   12.00   10.00   (771)
Wertenbaker, Thomas J. The First Americans: 1607-1690.
Repr. of 1927 ed.   14.50   .....   (673)

Biographical Collections

American Mothers Committee, Incorporated, comp. Mothers
of Achievement in American History, 1776-1976. 1976.
636pp.
    520 women who have contributed to America's history.   14.50   .....   (772)
Austin, John Osborne. American Authors' Ancestry. 1915.
111pp.
    Including some others who have influenced life wisely -
divines, diplomats, jurists, philanthropists, reformers,
and benefactors.   6.50   .....   (530)
Brown, J. H. Lamb's Biographical Dictionary of the United
States. 7 vols.   Set: 90.00   .....   (289)
Chalmers, Alexander. General Biographical Dictionary,
Containing an Historical and Critical Account of the Lives
and Writings of the Most Eminent Persons in Every Nation.
32 vols. 1812-1817.
    The Dectionary first appeared in 1761-1767 and went
through several editions.   Set: 800.00   .....   (415)
_____, ed. The General Biographical Dictionary; Containing
an Historical and Critical Account of the Lives and Writings
of the Most Eminent Persons in Every Nation; Particularly
the British and the Irish, from the Earliest Accounts to the
Present Time. 32 vols. 1812-1817.   Set: 650.00   .....   (2)
Chicorel, Marietta, ed. Chicorel Index to Biographies, Vols.
15 and 15a. 1974.   Each: 60.00   .....   (138)
Clement, Jesse, ed. Noble Deeds of American Women; With
Biographical Sketches of Some of the More Prominent. 1851.
illus.   25.00   .....   (38)
Dargan, Marion. Guide to American Biography. 2 vols. in 1.
Repr. of 1949 ed.   18.75   .....   (297)
Ellet, Elizabeth F. The Eminent and Heroic Women of America.
1873. illus.   45.00   .....   (38)
Fink, Gary M., ed. Biographical Dictionary of American Labor
Leaders. 1974. 559pp.   25.00   .....   (297)
Flexner, James T. Doctors on Horseback: Pioneers of American
Medicine. 1969.   .....   2.50   (204)
Flint, Timothy. Indian Wars of the West, Containing Biographical
Sketches of Those Pioneers Who Headed the Western Settlers
in Repelling the Attacks of the Savages. Repr. of 1833 ed.   11.00   .....   (38)
Frost, John. Pioneer Mothers of the West; Or, Daring and Heroic
Deeds of American Women. Comprising Thrilling Examples
of Courage, Fortitude, Devotedness, and Self-Sacrifice.
1869. illus.   19.00   .....   (38)
Gnacinski, Janneyne and Christine Nowak, eds. American Bicentennial Biographical Album, 1776-1976. 1976. 417pp.
    Biographies of grass roots Americans who made our
country great, each in his own way.   16.00   .....   (381)

Historical Records Survey. Bio-bibliographical Index of Musicians
in the United States of America Since Colonial Times, comp.
Keyes Porter. Completed Under the Supervision of Dr.
Leonard. 2d ed. 1956.   20.00 ..... (2)
Kaplan, Louis, et al., eds. Bibliography of American Auto-
biographies. 1961.   22.00 ..... (849)
Karolevitz, Robert F. Doctors of the Old West. 1967.   12.95 ..... (734)
Kunitz, Stanley J. and Howard Haycraft, eds. American Authors:
1600-1900. 1938.   15.00 ..... (847)
Lanman, Charles. Biographical Annals of the Civil Government
of the United States. Repr. of 1876 ed.   27.00 ..... (266)
Leonard, John William, ed. Woman's Who's Who of America.
Repr. of 1914 ed. 961pp.   42.50 ..... (266)
Mead, Mrs. Kate Campbell (Hurd). A History of Women in
Medicine from the Earliest Times to the Beginning of the
Nineteenth Century. 1938.   49.00 ..... (2)
O'Neill, Edward Hayes. Biography by Americans, 1658-1936:
A Subject Bibliography. 1939. 480pp.
   Lists some 7500 biographies of 5000 individuals that
   were written by Americans, including some books on
   foreign individuals. Arranged alphabetically by subject
   of biography. Lists books and indexes articles from
   707 collective biographies. The list of collective
   biographies in the second part indicates some holdings
   in major libraries.   16.00 ..... (299)
Packard, Francis R. History of Medicine in the United States.
2 vols. Repr. of 1931 ed.   Set: 30.00 ..... (306)
Parton, James, et al. Eminent Women Of the Age; Being Narratives of the Lives and Deeds of the Most Prominent Women
of the Present Generation. 1869. illus.   34.00 ..... (38)
Preston, Wheeler, American Biographies. Repr. of 1940 ed.
1147pp.
   5257 bio-bibliographical sketches of American men and
   women prominent since colonial times.   34.00 ..... (266)
Reel, Jerome V., Jr. Index to Biographies of Englishmen,
1000-1485. 1974. 689pp.   30.00 ..... (297)
Thacher, James and Stephen W. Williams. American Medical
Biographies of 1828 and 1845. 2 vols. 1967.   Set: 40.00 ..... (488)
Who Was Who in America: Historical Volume 1607-1896.   44.50 ..... (466)
Who Was Who in America: Volume 1 - 1897-1942.   44.50 ..... (466)
Williams, Eugene F. Soldiers of God: The Chaplains of the
Revolutionary War. 1975. 376pp.
   History of the military chaplaincy. Biographical sketches
   of Revolutionary War chaplains.   10.95 ..... (132)
Wilson, J. G. and J. Fishe. Cyclopedia of American Biography.
7 vols.   Set: 245.00 ..... (289)

Portraits and Painters

Appleton, Marion B., ed. Index to Pacific Northwest Portraits
(Pacific Northwest Library Association, Reference Division).
1972.   7.50 ..... (814)
Balknap, Waldron P., Jr. American Colonial Painting:
Materials for a History, ed. Charles C. Sellers. 1960.   15.00 ..... (319)
Cirker, Hayward and Blanche Cirker. Dictionary of American
Portraits, ed. Dover Editorial Staff. 1967.   30.00 ..... (204)

Feigenbaum, Rita, ed. American Portraits 1800-1850: A
Catalogue of Early Portraits in the Collection of Union College.
1972.   10.95   ..... (740)
Foster, Joshua J. A Dictionary of Painters of Miniatures, 1525-
1850 with Some Account of Exhibitions, Collections, Sales,
etc., ed. Ethel M. Foster. Repr. of 1926 ed.   25.50   ..... (248)
Jackson, Russell A., comp. Additions to the Catalogue of
Portraits in the Essex Institute, Received Since 1936. 1950   .....   7.50 (223)
Sears, Clara E. Some American Primitives. Repr. of 1914 ed.   12.50   ..... (404)

Surnames, Given Names

Bardsley, Charles Wareing, M.A. English Surnames: Their
Sources and Significations. Repr. of 1873 ed. 640pp.
    Lists some 4000 names, with many varients; origins of
    names explained.   6.00   ..... (772)
_____. English Surnames. 1931.   17.50   ..... (824)
Ewen, Cecil. A Guide to the Origin of British Surnames.   29.95   ..... (289)
_____. A History of Surnames of the British Isles.   28.00   ..... (289)
Reaney, P. H. A Dictionary of British Surnames, rev. R. M.
Wilson. Repr. of 1958 ed. 464pp.   37.75   ..... (660)
_____. The Origin of English Surnames. 1967. 436pp. maps.   9.00   ..... (660)
Weekley, Ernest. The Romance of Names.   12.50   ..... (824)
_____. Surnames.   25.00   ..... (824)

Gazetteers and Place-Names

Bardsley, Charles Wareing. The Romance of the London
Directory. Repr. of 1879 ed. 162pp.
    A treatise on the origins of English surnames.   12.50   ..... (266)
Blackie, Christine. Geographical Etymology: A Dictionary of
Place-Names. 3rd ed. Repr. of 1887 ed. 243pp.
    Alphabetical list of roots of topographical designations.
    With explanatory introduction.   8.50   ..... (266)
Efvergren, Carl. Names of Places in a Transferred Sense in
English. Repr. of 1909 ed. 123pp.   8.75   ..... (266)
Holt, Alfred Hubbard. American Place Names. Repr. of 1938
ed. 222pp.
    Contains correct and variant pronunciations of about
    1700 esoteric place-names, with author's comments on
    local history and legend.   7.50   ..... (266)
Knox, Alexander. Glossary of Geographical and Topographical
Terms. Repr. of 1904 ed. 432pp.
    10,000 entries.   11.50   ..... (266)
Middleton, Lynn. Place Names of the Pacific Northwest Coast.
1970.   12.95   ..... (734)
Morse, Jedidiah. American Gazetteer (First American Frontier
Series). Repr. of 1797 ed. illus.   26.00   ..... (38)
Reaney, P. H. The Origin of English Place-Names. Repr. of
1960 ed. 288pp. maps.   12.50   ..... (660)
Room, Adrian. Place-Names of the World. 1974. 216pp.   10.00   ..... (661)
Rydjord, John. Indian Place-Names: Their Origin, Evolution
and Meanings, Collected in Kansas from the Siouan, Caddoan,
Shoshonean, Algonquin, Iroquoian, and Other Tongues. 1968.   8.95   ..... (556)
Sealock, Richard A. and Pauline A. Seely. A Bibliography of
Place-Name Literature: United States and Canada. 2d ed.
1967.   7.50   ..... (22)
Stewart, George R. American Place-Names: A Concise and
Selective Dictionary for the Continental Unites States of America.
1970   12.50   ..... (566)

Taylor, Isaac. Names and Their Histories: A Handbook of
Historical Geography and Topographical Nomenclature.
Repr. of 1898 ed. 400pp.
Fully explicates about 3700 place-names from around
the world.   13.75   ..... (266)

Maps & Atlases

Black, Jeannette D., ed. Blathwayt Atlas, Volume 1 - The
Maps. 1970.   Set: 500.00   ..... (99)
Carrington, David K., ed. Map Collections in the United States
and Canada: A Directory. 2d rev. ed. 1970.   7.00   ..... (711)
Ehrenberg, Ralph E. "Cartographic Records in the National
Archives." NGS Quarterly, Vol. 64, No. 2. 1976. 29pp. 5.00 (514)
Fite, Emerson D. and Archibald Freeman. Book of Old Maps
Delineating American History from the Earliest Days Down
to the Close of the Revolutionary War.   15.00   ..... (699)
Hammond, Incorporated. Atlas of United States History. 3.95 (311)
Klemp, Egon, ed. America in Maps: 1500-1856. 1976.   325.00   ..... (346)
Klinefelter, Walter. Lewis Evans and His Maps. 1971.   .....   2.50 (24)
Kroeber, Alfred L. Native Tribes Map of North America.
Reprint. 1pp. 95 (112)
Le Gear, Clara Egli, comp. United States Atlases. A List of
National, State, County, City, and Regional Atlases in the
Library of Congress. 1950.   18.00   ..... (38)
Lord, Clifford L. and Elizabeth S. Lord. Historical Atlas of
the United States. Repr. of 1953 ed.   21.00   ..... (394)
Paullin, Charles Oscar. Atlas of the Historical Geography of
the United States. Repr. of 1932 ed. 162pp.   85.00   ..... (297)
Rand McNally and Company. Auto Road Atlas of the United
States and Canada (1926). Repr. of 1924 ed. 96pp.   10.00   ..... (633)
_____. Contemporary United States Map. 1976.
A general purpose reference map shaded mountains,
roads, railroads. 2.50 (633)
_____. Imperial United States Map. 1976.
Update each year. 1.00 (633)
_____. Road Atlas [United States]. 1976. 132pp.
This is an annual publication revised and updated each year. 3.95 (633)
_____. United States Road Maps [Contemporary] (order by State).
1975.   Each: 75 (633)
Sanchez-Saavedra, E. M. A Description of the Country: Virginia's
Cartographers and Their Maps 1607-1881. 1975. 130+pp.
Facsimiles of nine important Virginia maps, with
accompanying booklet describing Virginia cartography. 10.00 (800)
Scott, Joseph. Atlas of the United States-1795. Repr. of
1795 ed. 25pp.
This atlas 8 1/2 x 11 reprints the maps from the Joseph Scott
Gazetteer of 1795, the first U. S. Gazetteer. Individual
maps of 20 states and territories of 1795.   12.50   ..... (74)
Stevenson, Edward L. Maps Illustrating Early Discovery and
Exploration in America 1502-30. Repr. of 1903 ed.   39.00   ..... (248)
University of Michigan. Research Catalog of Maps of America to
1860 in the William L. Clements Library. 4 vols. 1973. 240.00   ..... (307)
Wright, J. K. and E. T. Platt. Aids to Geographical Research.
Repr. of 1947 ed. 331pp.
Bibliographies, periodicals, atlases, gazetteers, and other
reference books.   14.75   ..... (297)

Transportation—Roads, Trails, Canals, Rivers, Railroads.

Ahnert, Gerald T. Retracing the Butterfield Trail in Arizona. 9.75 ..... (829)
Ambler, Charles H. History of Transportation in the Ohio
Valley. Repr. of 1932 ed. 18.25 ..... (297)
Cawley, James and Margaret Cawley. Along the Old York Road.
1965. 6.00 2.75 (665)
Daniels, Jonathan. Devil's Backbone: The Story of the Natchez
Trace. ed. A. B. Guthrie, Jr. 1962. 6.95 3.50 (451)
Dickinson, John Newton. The Canal at Sault Ste. Marie,
Michigan: Inception, Construction, Early Operation, and
the Canal Grant Lands. 1968. 350pp. BIP-68-13628. .... (777)
Duane, William J. Letters Addressed to the People of Pennsylvania
Respecting the Internal Improvement of the Commonwealth: By
Means of Roads and Canals. 1968. 12.00 ..... (248)
Duffus, R. L. Santa Fe Trail. Repr. of 1930 ed. 14.50 ..... (673)
Duffus, Robert L. The Santa Fe Trail. 1972. ..... 2.95 (535)
Gard, Wayne. Chisholm Trail. Repr. of 1954 ed. 8.95 ..... (556)
Gard, Wayne, et al. Along the Early Trails of the Southwest. 200pp.
Six of the Southwest's most noted authors write about six of
the Southwest's most noted trails in this exciting volume.
The trails are: Chisolm Trail, Old San Antonio Road, Dodge
City Trail, Santa Fe Trail, Goodnight-Loving Trail and
Butterfield Overland Mail Trail. 17.50 ..... (273)
    Special Limited Edition autographed by authors, etc. 60.00 ..... (273)
Gray, Ralph D. The National Waterway: A History of the
Chesapeake and Delaware Canal, 1769-1965. 1967. 8.95 ..... (365)
Guthrie, A. B., Jr., ed. Westward Vision: The Story of the
Oregon Trail. 1963. 8.95 3.50 (451)
Hanna, Charles Augustus. The Wilderness Trail, or the Ventures
and Adventures of the Pennsylvania Traders on the Allegheny
Path. With Some New Annals of the Old West, and the Records
of Some Strong Men and Some Bad Ones. 2 vols. 1911. Set: 42.50 ..... (2)
Hewitt, James. Eye-Witnesses to Wagon Trains West. 1974. 7.95 ..... (677)
Hindley, Georffrey. A History of Roads. 1972. 7.95 ..... (141)
Holbrook, Stewart H. Old Post Road: The Story of the Boston
Post Road. ed. A. B. Guthrie, Jr. 1962. 7.95 3.50 (451)
Hulbert, Archer Butler. Historic Highways of America. 16 vols.
1902-1905.
 1. Paths of the Mound-Building Indians and Great Game
  Animals. 1902. 12.95 ..... (2)
 2. Indian Thoroughfares. 1902. 12.95 ..... (2)
 3. Washington's Road (Nemacolin's Path). The First
  Chapter of the Old French War. 1903. 12.95 ..... (2)
 4. Braddock's Road and Three Relative Papers. 1903. 12.95 ..... (2)
 5. The Old Glade (Forbes's) Road. (Pennsylvania State
  Road). 1903. 12.95 ..... (2)
 6. Boone's Wilderness Road. 1903. 12.95 ..... (2)
 7. Portage Paths. The Keys of the Continent. 1903. 12.95 ..... (2)
 8. Military Roads of the Mississippi Basin. The Conquest
  of the Old Northwest. 1904. 12.95 ..... (2)
 9. Waterways of Westward Expansion. The Ohio River and
  Its Tributaries. 1903. 12.95 ..... (2)
 10. The Cumberland Road With Maps and Illustrations. 1904. 12.95 ..... (2)
 11. Pioneer Roads and Experiences of Travelers, Vol. 1.
  1904. 12.95 ..... (2)
 12. Pioneer Roads and Experiences of Travelers, Vol. 2.
  1904. 12.95 ..... (2)

13. The Great American Canals. Vol. 1: The Chesapeake
and Ohio Canal and the Pennsylvania Canal. 1904. 12.95 ..... (2)
14. The Great American Canals. Vol. 2: The Erie
Canal. 1904. 12.95 ..... (2)
15. The Future of Road-Making in America. A
Symposium. 1905. 12.95 ..... (2)
16. Index. 1905. 12.95 ..... (2)
Set: 200.00 ..... (2)
Jordan, Philip D. The National Road. 1948. 6.00 ..... (699)
Lightner, David Lee. Labor on the Illinois Central Railroad,
1852-1900. 1969. 427pp. BIP-70-05777. .... (777)
Ligonier Valley Observance, U. S. Bicentennial Document
Preservation Committee. The Stoystown and Greensburgh
Turnpike Road Company (Minutes 1815-1826. 1976. 100pp. 9.00 (709)
Maxwell, Fay. Ohio Indian, Revolutionary and War of 1812 Trails,
Indexes to Ohio Counties and Townships. Repr. of 1968 ed. 75pp.
Contains all maps, directives to do lineage work in Ohio,
plus erection dates of counties, index of townships, which
aids filmviewing. 3.95 (473)
Parks, Roger Neal. The Roads of New England 1790-1840. 1966.
283pp. BIP-66-14161. .... (777)
Reeder, Ray M. The Mormon Trail: A History of the Salt Lake to
Los Angeles Route to 1869. 1966. 442pp. BIP-66-10518. .... (777)
Rittenhouse, Jack D. Santa Fe Trail: A Historical Bibliography.
1971. 12.00 ..... (535)
Singley, Grover. Tracing Minnesota's Old Government Roads. 1974. ..... 3.95 (496)
Stuart, Robert. The Discovery of the Oregon Trail. Repr. 391pp.
Robert Stuart's narrative of his overland trip eastward from
Astoria in 1812-13. 17.50 ..... (273)
Swanson, Leslie C. Canals of Mid-America. 1964. ..... 3.95 (736)
Tanner, Henry S. A Description of the Canals and Railroads of
the United States Comprehending Notices of all the Works of
Internal Improvement Throughout the Several States. 1840.
272pp. Illustrated. 12.50 ..... (273)
Walzer, John F. Transportation in the Philadelphia Trading Area
1740-1775. 1968. 351pp. BIP-68-07139. .... (777)
White, Helen M. Ho! For the Gold Fields: Northern Overland
Wagon Trains of the 1860x. 1966. 8.50 ..... (496)
Wilson, George R. Early Indiana Trails and Surveys. Repr. of
1919 ed. 1.50 (369)
Winnett, Thomas and Don Denison. Tahoe-Yosemite Trail. 1970. ..... 2.95 (838)

Inns, Taverns and Stagecoaches

Bates, Alan, comp. Directory of Stage Coach Services 1836.
1969. 160pp. 11.00 ..... (273)
Carter, Katherine T. Stage Coach Inns of Texas. 10.00 ..... (752)
Cole, Harry E. Stage Coach and Tavern Tales of the Old
Northwest. ed. Louise P. Kellogg. Repr. of 1930 ed. 15.00 ..... (266)
Dallas, Sandra. No More Than Five in a Bed: Colorado Hotels
in the Old Days. 1967. 5.95 ..... (556)
Drake, Samuel A. Old Boston Taverns and Tavern Clubs.
Repr. of 1917 ed. 12.50 ..... (266)
Earle, Alice Morse. Stage Coach and Tavern Days. 1900. 449pp.
Traveling throughout colonial America, with the story of
the social life of early inns. 20.00 ..... (38)
_____. Stage-Coach and Tavern Days. Repr. of 1900 ed. 11.50 ..... (266)
_____. Stage-Coach and Tavern Days. 1970. ..... 4.00 (204)

Haas, Irvin. America's Historic Inns and Taverns. 1972.   8.95 ..... (32)
Lathrop, Elise. Early American Inns and Taverns. Repr. of
   1935 ed. 365pp.
      Social life, architecture, and history of inns from Boston
      to Kentucky.   17.50 ..... (38)
Van Hoesen, Walter H. Early Taverns and Stage Coach Days in
   New Jersey.   8.00 ..... (227)
Yoder, Paton. Taverns and Travelers: Inns of the Early
   Midwest. 1969.   7.95 ..... (370)

Postal Service and the Mail

Bennett, James D., ed. Post Offices in the United States in
   1890. Repr. of 1892 ed.
      Contains the names of all the over 55000 Postal Offices in
      44 states and 7 territories in 1890, located by state and
      county, giving 1890 population, if known, and other
      interesting facts and beliefs of the times. Also lists
      names of all American cities with over 5000 inhabitants
      in 1890.   ..... 22.50 (62)
Bowyer, Mathew J. They Carried the Mail: A Survey of Postal
   History and Hobbies. 1972.   6.95 ..... (443)
Chapman, Arthur. Pony Express. Repr. of 1932 ed.   8.50 ..... (159)
Hafen, Le Roy Reuben. The Overland Mail 1849-1869; Promoter
   of Settlement, Precursor of Railroads. 1926.   15.00 ..... (2)
Harris, Robert P. Nevada Postal History. 1973.   8.50 ..... (528)
_____. Nevada Postal History. 1973.   8.50 ..... (78)
Holmes, Oliver Wendell. Stagecoach and Mail From Colonial Days
   to 1820. 1956. 308pp. BIP-00-17059.   .... (777)
Ormsby, Waterman L. Butterfield Overland Mail. eds. Lyle H.
   Wright and Josephine M. Bynum. 1942.   8.50 ..... (363)
Rich, Wesley. History of the U. S. Post Office to 1829.   33.00 ..... (289)
Taylor, Morris F. First Mail West: Stagecoach Lines on the
   Santa Fe Trail. 1971.   10.00 ..... (535)

Fur Trade

Anson, Bert. The Fur Traders in Northern Indiana, 1796-1850.
   1953. 337pp. BIP-00-05853   .... (777)
Barnhart, Warren Lynn. The Letterbooks of Charles Gratiot, Fur
   Trader: The Nomadic Years, 1769-1797, Edited With An
   Historical Introduction. 1972. 551pp. BIP-72-23896.   .... (777)
Cleland, Robert G. This Reckless Breed of Men: The Trappers
   and Fur Traders of the Southwest. 1950.   6.95 ..... (412)
Dunham, Douglas. The French Element in the American Fur
   Trade, 1760-1816. 1950. 281pp. BIP-00-01961.   .... (777)
Gates, C. M., ed. Five Fur Traders of the Northwest: Narrative
   of Peter Pond and the Diaries of John Madonnell, et al.
   Repr. of 1965 ed.   7.25 ..... (496)
Jeffries, Ewel. A Short Biography of John Leeth, With an Account
   of His Life Among the Indians. ed. Reuben Gold Thwaites. 70pp.
      The experiences of a trader-hunter in the Indian country of
      Pennsylvania and Ohio, including his captivity and life in
      Indian camps.   5.75 ..... (38)
Johnson, Ida A. Michigan Fur Trade. Repr. of 1919 ed.   7.50 ..... (71)
Saum, Lewis O. The Fur Trader and the Indians. 1966.   12.95 3.95 (814)
Sullivan, Maurice S. Jedediah Smith, Trader and Trail Breaker.
   1936.   18.00 ..... (415)

Zimmerman, Albright Gravenor. The Indian Trade of Colonial
Pennsylvania. 1966. 471pp. BIP-57-11752. .... (777)

Currency, Commerce, Manufacturing and Artisans

Arena, Carmelo R. Philadelphia-Spanish New Orleans Trade
1789-1803. 1959. 213pp. BIP-59-04590. .... (777)
Armour, David A. The Merchants of Albany, New York 1686-1760.
1965. 314pp. BIP-65-12042. .... (777)
Bailyn, Bernard, ed. New England Merchants in the 17th Century. 2.50 (317)
Barry, Peter Ralph. The New Hampshire Merchant Interest,
1609-1725. 1971. 386pp. BIP-71-24444. .... (777)
Becker, Carl M. Mill, Shop, and Factory: The Industrial Life
of Dayton, Ohio, 1830-1900. 1971. 425pp. BIP-72-01412. .... (777)
Bigelow, Bruce Macmillan. The Commerce of Rhode Island
With the West Indies, Before the American Revolution.
Parts I and II. 1930. 452pp. BIP-60-1004. .... (777)
Bradley, Lawrence James. The Longdon/Bristol Trade Rivalry:
Conventional History, and the Colonial Office Records for the
Port of New York. 1971. 376pp. BIP-71-19078. .... (777)
Cochran, Thomas C., ed. New American State Papers (Part I,
1789-1860) Commerce. 47 vols. 2290.00 ..... (674)
Coughlin, Magdalen. Boston Merchants on the Coast, 1787-1821:
An Insight Into the American Acquisition of California. 1970.
357pp. BIP-70-25014. .... (777)
Coulter, Calvin Brewster, Jr. The Virginia Merchant. 1944.
290pp. BIP-00-02930. .... (777)
Cromwell, Giles. The Virginia Manufactory of Arms. 1974. 20.00 ..... (801)
Decker, Robert Owen. The New London Merchants: 1645-1909:
The Rise and Decline of a Connecticut Port. 1970. 412pp.
BIP-71-15973. .... (777)
Dexter, Elisabeth W. (Anthony). Colonial Women of Affairs: A
Study of Women in Business and the Professions in America
Before 1776. 2d rev. ed. 1931. 223pp. 12.50 ..... (273)
Ernst, Joseph Albert. Currency in the Era of the American Revo-
lution: A History of Colonial Paper Money Practices and
British Monetary Policies, 1704-1781. 1962. 460pp.
BIP-62-01168. .... (777)
Herndon, George Melvin. The Story of Hemp in Colonial
Virginia. 1959. 208pp. BIP-59-04229. .... (777)
Kammen, Michael. Empire and Interest: The American
Colonies and the Politics of Mercantilism. 1970. 4.95 2.95 (434)
Lahey, William C. The Influence of David Parish on the Develop-
ment of Trade and Settlement in Northern New York 1808-1822.
1958. 334pp. BIP-58-07228. .... (777)
Larsen, Grace Hutchison. Profile of a Colonial Merchant:
Thomas Clifford of Pre-Revolutionary Philadelphia.
1955. 461pp. BIP-00-15635. .... (777)
Livingood, James Weston. The History of the Commercial
Rivalry Between Philadelphia and Baltimore for the Trade of
the Susquehanna Valley 1780-1860. 1937. 301pp. BIP-00-02998. .... (777)
Mailloux, Kenneth Frank. The Boston Manufacturing Company of
Waltham, Massachusetts, 1813-1848: The First Modern Factory
in America. 1957. 239pp. BIP-00-21740. .... (777)
Manges, Frances May. Women Shopkeepers, Tavern Keepers,
and Artisans in Colonial Philadelphia. 1958. 153pp.
BIP-58-01854. .... (777)

Moss, Roger William, Jr. Master Builders: A History of the
Colonial Philadelphia Building Trades. 1972. 255pp.
BIP-72-32008.   .... (777)
Oaks, Robert Francis. Philadelphia Merchants and the American
Revolution, 1765-1776. 1970. 253pp. BIP-71-02534.   .... (777)
Olton, Charles Shaw. Philadelphia Artisans and the American
Revolution. 1967. 416pp. BIP-67-11655.   .... (777)
Pelzer, Louis. The Cattlemen's Frontier: A Record of the
Trans-Mississippi Cattle Industry from Oxen Trains to
Pooling Companies, 1850-1890. Repr. of 1936 ed. 351pp.
Appendix contains "Cattle brands owned by members of
the Wyoming Stock Growers' Association." (Chicago: 1882).   11.00 ..... (662)
Scoville, Joseph A. Old Merchants of New York City. 5 vols.
Repr. of 1870 ed.   Set: 97.50 ..... (297)
Stealey, John Edmund, III. The Salt Industry of the Great
Kanawha Valley of Virginia: A Study in Ante-Bellum
Internal Commerce. 1970. 606pp. BIP-71-04857.   .... (777)
Stumpf, Stuart Owen. The Merchants of Colonial Charleston,
1680-1756. 1971. 309pp. BIP-71-31318.   .... (777)
Tevebaugh, John Leslie. Merchant on the Western Frontier:
William Morrison of Kaskaskia, 1790-1837. 1962. 342pp.
BIP-62-02976.   .... (777)
Throckmorton, Arthur Loreston. The Frontier Merchant in the
Early Development of Oregon, 1839-1869. 1956. 438pp.
BIP-58-01164.   .... (777)
Tolles, Frederick. Meeting House and Counting House: The
Quaker Merchants of Colonial Philadelphia 1682-1763.   4.25   ..... (699)
Walker, Henry P. Wagonmasters: High Plains Freighting
From the Earliest Days of the Santa Fe Trail to 1880.
Illustrated. Repr. of 1966 ed.   8.95   ..... (556)
Wittlinger, Carlton O. Early Manufacturing in Lancaster County,
Pennsylvania, 1710-1840. 1953. 236pp. BIP-00-04959.   .... (777)

Ship Building, Shipping, Pirates/Piracy, Shipwrecks

Bailyn, Bernard and Lotte Bailyn. Massachusetts Shipping,
1697-1714: A Statistical Study. 1959.   5.00   ..... (319)
Baldwin, Leland D. Keelboat Age on Western Waters. 1960.   5.95   ..... (603)
Berman, Bruce D. Encyclopedia of American Shipwrecks. 1972. 12.50 7.95 (463)
Bowen, Dana T. Shipwrecks of the Lakes. 1952.   6.75   ..... (251)
Clayton, Lawrence Anthony. The Guayaquil Shipyards in the
Seventeenth Century: History of a Colonial Industry. 1972.
324pp. BIP-72-24399.   .... (777)
Faibusy, John Dewar. Privateering and Piracy: The Effects of
New England Raiding Upon Nova Scotia During the American
Revolution, 1775-1783. 1972. 343pp. BIP-72-18043.   .... (777)
Goldenberg, Joseph Abraham. The Shipbuilding Industry in
Colonial America. 1969. 417pp. BIP-70-10261.   .... (777)
Huntress, Keith. Narratives of Shipwrecks and Disasters, 1586-1860.
1974.   9.95   ..... (377)
Jensen, Arthur L. The Maritime Commerce of Colonial
Philadelphia. Repr. of 1963 ed.   4.75   ..... (850)
Morris, Paul. American Sailing Coasters of the North Atlantic.
1973. 224pp.
The History of the Coasting Trade of the 2-7 masted
schooners. Lists ship captains, builders, ships; basic
book in its field.   29.75 ..... (74)

Shea, John G. Perils of the Ocean and Wilderness: Or,
Narratives of Shipwreck and Indian Captivity. Repr. of
1856 ed.   7.00 ..... (100)

Exploration; Early Travels, Historic Sites and Houses

Baily, Francis. Journal of a Tour in Unsettled Parts of North
America in 1796 and 1797. ed. Jack D. Holmes. Repr. of
1856 ed. abr. ed.   15.00 ..... (708)
Berger, Max. British Traveler in America, 1836-1860. 1943.   11.50 ..... (2)
Blane, William N. Excursion Through the United States and
Canada During the Years 1822-23. Repr. of 1824 ed.   20.25 ..... (522)
Brissot de Warville, Jacques Pierre. New Travels in the
United States of America Performed in 1788. Translated from
the French. 1972. 483pp.
    Containing the latest and most accurate observations on the
    character, genius and present state of the people and govern-
    ment of that country--their agriculture, commerce, manu-
    facturers, and finances—quality and price of lands, and
    progress of settlements on the Ohio and the Mississippi—
    political and moral character of the Quakers, and a
    vindication of that excellent sect, from the misrepre-
    sentations of other travellers—state of the blacks . . .   15.00 ..... (273)
Buck, Solon J. Travel and Description, 1765-1865.
    Repr. of 1914 ed.   25.50 ..... (248)
Campbell, Patrick. Travels in the Interior Inhabited Parts of
North America in the Years 1791 and 1792. Repr. of 1937 ed.   24.00 ..... (297)
Chiappelli, Fredi. First Images of America. 2 vols.
    Vol. I-537pp; Vol. II-459pp. 1976.
    The impact of the New World on the Old--impact on the
    lives and imaginations of Europeans of the discovery of
    the New World.   Set: 75.00 ..... (112)
Cobbett, William. A Year's Residence in the United States of
America. 3 parts. 1818. 610pp.
    Treating of the face of the country, the climate, the land,
    of labour, of food, of raiment; of the expenses of house-
    keeping, and of the usual manner of living; of the manners
    and customs of the people; and of the institutions of that
    country, civil, political and religious.   17.50 ..... (273)
Collot, Georges Henri Victor. A Journey in North America,
Containing a Survey of the Countries Watered by the Mississippi,
Ohio, Missouri, and Other Affluing Rivers; with Exact Observa-
tions on the Course and Soundings of These Rivers; and on the
Towns, Villages, Hamlets and Farms of That Part of the New
World; Followed by Philosophical, Political, Military, and
Commercial Remarks and by a Projected Line of Frontiers
and General Limits, Illustrated by 36 Maps, Plans, Views
and Divers Cuts by Victor Collot. . . With an Introduction
and a Critical Index, also a Translation of the Appendix
from the French Edition, by J. Christian Bay. 3 vols. including
Atlas. 1924.   295.00 ..... (2)
Country Beautiful. America's Historic Houses: The Living Past.
1971. 194pp.
    Tours of well-known and not-so-well-known homes in
    America. 100 photos, 32 full color.   7.98 ..... (165)
Crevecoeur, Michel Guillaume J. De. Crevecoeur's Eighteenth-
Century Travels in Pennsylvania and New York. ed. and tr.
Percy G. Adams. 1961.   5.00 ..... (408)

_____. Journey into Northern Pennsylvania and the State of
New York. tr. Clarissa S. Bostelmann. 1964.   15.00   ..... (484)
Cumming, W. P., et al.   The Exploration of North America,
1630-1776. 1974.   30.00   ..... (627)
Dunbar, Seymour. A History of Travel In America. Repr. of
1915 ed. 4 vols.   81.75   ..... (297)
Fearon, Henry B. Sketches of America. 1818. 454pp. 2d ed.
A narrative of a journey of five thousand miles through
the Eastern and Western states of America; contained in
eight reports addressed to the thirty-nine English families
by whom the author was deputed, in June 1817, to ascertain
whether any, and what part of the United States would be
suitable for their residence. With remarks on Mr. Birkbeck's
"Notes" and "Letters."   15.00   ..... (273)
_____. Sketches of America. 454pp. 1818.   20.00   ..... (38)
Forman, Samuel S.   Narrative of a Journey Down the Ohio and
Mississippi in 1789-90 with a Memoir and Illustrative
Notes by Lyman C. Draper. Repr. of 1888 ed.   6.00   ..... (38)
Hamilton, Thomas.   Men and Manners in America. 2 vols in 1.
1833. With additions from the 1843 ed. 393pp; 402pp.   20.00   ..... (273)
Holmes, Isaac.   An Account of the United States of America, Derived
from Actual Observation, During a Residence of Four Years in
That Republic, Including Original Communications. 1823.   24.00   ..... (38)
Janson, William C.   Stranger in America 1793-1806: Containing
Observations Made During a Long Residence in That Country.
Repr. of 1807 ed.   25.00   ..... (248)
M'Robert, Patrick.   Tour Through Part of the North Provinces of
America. Repr. of 1776 ed.   6.50   ..... (38)
Martineau, Harriett. Retrospect of Western Travel. 2 vols. Repr. 22.95 ..... (320)
Melish, John.   Travels in the United States of America, in the
Years 1806, 1807, 1809, 1810 and 1811. Repr. of 1818 ed.   31.50   ..... (394)
Miranda, Francisco De.   New Democracy in America: Travels of
Francisco De Miranda in the United States, 1783-1784.
Volume 40. tr. Judson P. Wood. 1963.   7.95   ..... (556)
Montule, Edouard De.   Travels in America, 1816-1817; Translated
from the Original French Edition of 1821. 1950.   13.00   ..... (415)
Murray, Charles A.   Travels in North America, Including a
Summer with the Pawnees. Repr. of 1839 ed.   2d ed.   37.50   ..... (176)
Palmer, Frederick Alexander.   Westerners at Home: Comments
of French and British Travelers on Life in the West 1800-1840.
1949. 278pp. BIP-00-01557.   .... (777)
Parker, Amos Andrew.   Trip to the West and Texas. Comprising
a Journey of Eight Thousand Miles, Through New York, Michigan,
Illinois, Missouri, Louisiana and Texas, in the Autumn and
Winter of 1834-5. Interspersed with Anecdotes, Incidents
and Observations. 1835.   14.00   ..... (38)
Parkinson, Richard.   Tour in America in 1798, 1799 and 1800.
2 vols. 1805.   Set: 26.50   ..... (673)
Pope, John.   Tour Through the Southern and Western Territories
of the United States of North America, the Spanish Dominions
on the River Mississippi and the Floridas, the Countries of
the Creek Nations, and Many Uninhabited Parts. Repr. of
1792 ed.   6.00   ..... (38)
Randolph, Jerry Ralph.   British Travelers Among the Southern
Indians, 1660-1763. 1970. 292pp. BIP-71-09285.   .... (777)

Reif, Rita. Treasure Rooms of America's Mansions; Manors and
Houses. 1971. 296pp.
375 photos; 100 full color; 54 homes spanning 250 years;
detailed descriptions.   19.95   ..... (165)
Robin, Abbe. New Travels Through North-America. 1783.   5.00   ..... (38)
Royall, Mrs. Anne (Newport). Mrs. Royall's America, 1828-1831.
7 vols. in 6. 1828-1831.
    Part 1: The Black Book; or, A Continuation of Travels in
        the United States (3 vols.).
    Part 2: Mrs. Royall's Pennsylvania; or, Travels Continued
        in the United States (2 vols.).
    Part 3: Mrs. Royall's Southern Tour; or, Second Series
        of the Black Book (2 vols.).   Each Volume: 16.00   ..... (2)
                                            Set: 95.00   ..... (2)
Saint-Mery, Mederic L. E. Moreau de. Moreau De St. Mery's
American Journey, 1793-98. Translated and edited by Kenneth
and Anna M. Roberts. 1947. 394pp.   15.00   ..... (273)
Sauer, Carl Ortwin. Sixteenth Century North America. 1971. 336pp.
The land and people as seen by Europeans.   14.50   4.95 (112)
Shirreff, Patrick. A Tour Through North America; Together with
a Comprehensive View of the Canadas and United States, as
Adapted for Agricultural Emigration. 1835. 478pp.
    Describes the life, daily labor (in fields, factories, and
    shops), travel and its many hazards, towns and cities,
    and social customs of the new nation.   20.00   ..... (38)
Still, Bayrd. The West: Contemporary Records of America's
Expansion Across the Continent 1607-1890. 1961.   .....   2.75 (627)
Sturge, Joseph. A Visit to the United States in 1841. 1842. 192pp. 13.50   ..... (273)
Thomas, David. Travels Through the Western Country in the
Summer of 1816. ed. George W. White. Repr. of 1819 ed.   14.95   ..... (306)
Weld, Isaac. Travels Through the United States of North America,
and the Provinces of Upper and Lower Canada, During the
Years 1795, 1796, and 1797. 2 vols. 4th ed. 1807.
427pp; 376pp.   Set: 27.50   ..... (273)
Wilhelm, Paul. Travels in North America, 1822-1824: Paul
Wilhelm, Duke Of Wurttemburg. ed. Savoie Lottinville.
trs. from German by W. Robert Nitske, et. al. 1974.   20.00   ..... (556)

Diaries, Journals, Private Papers

Abdy, Edward S. Journal of a Residence and Tour in the United
States of North America, from April 1833, to October, 1834.
Repr.   34.50   ..... (522)
Baring-Gould, Sabine. Early Reminiscences 1834-1864. Repr.
of 1923 ed. 350pp.   7.80   ..... (266)
Billigmeier, Robert and Fred A. Picard, eds. Old Land and
the New: The Journals of Two Swiss Families in America in
the 1820's. 1965.   6.50   ..... (497)
Bougainville, Louis A. De. Adventure in the Wilderness: The
American Journals of Louis Antoine De Bourgainville, 1756-1760.
tr. Edward P. Hamilton. 1964.   9.95   ..... (556)
Bray, Martha C., ed. Journals of Joseph N. Nicollet.
tr. Andre Fertey. 1970.   16.50   ..... (496)
Cobbett, William. Year's Residence in the United States of
America. 1965.   19.50   ..... (708)
Danckaerts, Jasper and Peter Sluyter. Journal of a Voyage to
New York in 1679-80. ed. Henry C. Murphy. Repr. of
1867 ed.   28.00   ..... (299)

Davis, Reuben. Recollections of Mississippi and Mississippians. Repr. of 1889 ed. 456pp. First-person account of major events of the 1800s and an interesting insight into life in Mississippi a hundred years ago.   8.95 ..... (499)

Flint, James. Letters from America: Containing Observations on the Climate and Agriculture of the Western States, the Manners of the People and the Prospects of Emigrants. Repr. of 1822 ed.   15.50 .... (394)

Fowler, John. Journal of a Tour in the State of New York in the Year 1830. With remarks on agriculture in those parts most eligible for settlers. 1831. 333pp.   15.00 ..... (273)

Gustorf, Frederick. Uncorrupted Heart: Journal and Letters of Frederick Julius Gustorf 1800-1845. tr. Gisela Gustorf. 1969.   6.50 ..... (500)

Handlin, Oscar, ed. This Was America: Tr̃ue Accounts of People and Places, Manners and Customs, As Recorded by European Travelers to the Western Shore in the 18th, 19th and 20th Centuries. 1969.   12.50 ..... (319)

James, B. B. and J. Franklin Jameson, eds. Journal of Jasper Danckaerts, Sixteen Seventy-Nine to Sixteen Eighty. 1913. Original Narratives.   6.50 ..... (52)

Jeremy, David J. Henry Wansey and His American Journal, 1794. 1970.   7.00 ..... (24)

Jones, David. A Journal of Two Visits Made to Some Nations of Indians on the West Side of the River Ohio in the Years 1772 and 1773. 1774.   6.00 ..... (38)

Koenig, George. The Lost Death Valley Forty-Niner[:] Journal of Louis Nusbaumer. 1974.   5.00   2.25 (130)

Nuttall, Thomas. Journal of Travels into the Arkansas Territory, During the Year 1819. Repr. of 1821 ed.   7.75 ..... (778)

Raeder, Ole Munch. America in the Forties. The Letters of Ole Mucn Rader, translated and edited by Gunnar J. Malmin. 1929. 244pp.   12.50 ..... (273)

Schoolcraft. Henry Rowe. Journal of a Tour Into the Interior of Missouri and Arkansas, from Potosi, Or Mine a Burton, in Missouri Territory, in a South-West Direction, Toward the Rocky Mountains. Performed in the Years 1818 and 1819. 1821.   10.00 ..... (2)

Spear, Arthur, ed. The Journals of Hekeziah Prince, Jr., 1822-1828. 1965.   12.50 ..... (532)

Trent, William. Journal of Captain William Trent From Logstown to Pickawillany, A.D. 1752. Now Published for the First Time From a Copy in the Archives of the Western Reserve Historical Society, Cleveland, Ohio, Together With Letters of Governor Robert Dinwiddie, an Historical Notice of the Miami Confederacy of Indians; A Sketch of the English Post at Pickawillany, With a Short Biography of Captain Trent and Other Papers Never Before Published. ed. Alfred T. Goodman. 1871.
Contains details on the trade and diplomatic rivalries in the Ohio wilderness on the eve of the outbreak of the French and Indian War.   6.00 ..... (38)

Weaver, Herbert, ed. Correspondence of James K. Polk, Volume I, 1817-1832. 1969. 619pp.   15.00 ..... (789)

_____. Correspondence of James K. Polk, Volume II, 1833-1834. 1972. 645pp.   15.00 ..... (789)

_____. Correspondence of James K. Polk, Volume III, 1835-1836. 1975. 872pp.   25.00 ..... (789)

Webster, Daniel. Letters of Daniel Webster. Repr.   24.95 ..... (320)

Wright, Louis B. Collection of Early Reports by Englishmen on
the New World. 1965.   10.00   ..... (319)

Frontiers and Pioneer Life

Abernethy, Thomas P. Three Virginia Frontiers. 4.50 (699)
Brown, A. Theodore. Frontier Community, Kansas City to 1870.
1963.   9.00   ..... (500)
Canedy, Charles Roscoe, III. An Entrepreneurial History of the
New York Frontier, 1739-1776. 1967. 437pp. BIP-68-03302.   .... (777)
Danker, Donald F. Some Social Beginnings in Territorial Nebraska.
1955. 301pp. BIP-00-12745.   .... (777)
Davis, James Edward. Demographic Characteristics of the
American Frontier, 1800-1840. 1971. 270pp. BIP-72-14837.   .... (777)
Dick, Everett. Tales of the Frontier: From Lewis and Clark to
the Last Roundup. 1964.   6.00   2.75 (521)
Foley, William Edward. Territorial Politics in Frontier
Missouri: 1804-1820. 1967. 266pp. BIP-68-03606.   .... (777)
Fowler, William W. Woman on the American Frontier.
Repr. of 1878 ed.   16.50   ..... (266)
Foreman, Grant. Indians and Pioneers: The Story of the
American Southwest Before 1830. Repr. of 1936 ed.   7.95   ..... (556)
Gladstone, T. H. Englishman in Kansas, Or, Squatter Life
and Border Warfare. 1971.   10.95   3.95 (521)
Greenberg, David B. Land That Our Fathers Plowed: The
Settlement of our Country as Told by the Pioneers Themselves
and Their Contemporaries. 1969.   7.95   ..... (556)
Halsey, Francis W. The Old New York Frontier. 1902.   20.00   ..... (547)
Hecht, Irene Winchester Duckworth. The Virginia Colony,
1607-1640: A Study In Frontier Growth. 1969. 397pp.
BIP-69-20232.   .... (777)
Heilbron, Bertha L., ed. With Pen and Pencil on the Frontier in
1851: The Diary and Sketches of Frank Balckwell Mayer.
(With an Introduction and Notes by Bertha L. Heilbron). 1932. 13.00   ..... (38)
Horsman, Reginald. The Frontier in the Formative Years,
1783-1815. 1973.   7.95   4.95 (535)
Lavatelli, C. S., et al. The Northern Colonial Frontier,
1607-1763.   7.95   ..... (348)
Leach, Douglas E. The Northern Colonial Frontier, 1607-1763.
1966.   7.95   4.95 (535)
Lienhard, Heinrich. From St. Louis to Sutter's Fort, 1846.
eds. Erwin G. Gudde and Elisabeth K. Gudde. 1961.   7.95   ..... (556)
McConnel, John Ludlum. Western Characters: Or, Types of
Border Life in the Western States. 1853. Illustrated.   22.00   ..... (38)
McWhorter, Lucullus V. The Border Settlers of Northwestern
Virginia From 1768 to 1795. Repr. of 1915 ed. 509pp.   20.00   ..... (274)
Moody, Robert Earle. The Maine Frontier, 1607 to 1763.
1933. 470pp. BIP-65-07515.   .... (777)
Owen, Mary Steele. An Analysis of the Frontiersman Based
Upon the Observations of Contemporary French Travellers.
1956. 594pp. BIP-00-19472.   .... (777)
Perkins, James H. Annals of the West: Embracing a Concise
Account of States and Territories, From the Discovery of the
Mississippi Valley to the Year 1850. 2d ed. rev. 1850. 808pp. 27.50 ..... (273)
Philbrick, Francis S. Rise of the West, 1754-1830.   8.95   2.45 (317)
Rathjen, Frederick W. The Texas Panhandle Frontier. 1974. 9.50   ..... (749)
Richardson, Rupert N. Frontier of Northwest Texas, 1846-1876.
1963.   12.00   ..... (144)

Seymour, Mrs. Flora Warren (Smith). Indian Agents of the Old
Frontier. 1941.   25.00 ..... (415)
Whitaker, Arthur P. The Spanish-American Frontier, 1783-1795.   5.00   ..... (699)
Wright, J. Leitch, Jr. Britain and the American Frontier,
1783-1815. 1975.   9.50   ..... (279)

Federal Land System and Policies

Abbott, Phyllis Ruth. The Development and Operation of an
American Land System to 1800. 1959. 456pp. BIP-59-03237.   .... (777)
Carstensen, Vernon, ed. Public Lands: Studies in the History
of the Public Domain.   20.00   5.50 (849)
Circular from the General Land Office: Showing the Manner of
Proceeding to Obtain Title to Public Lands Under the Homestead,
Desert Land, and Other Laws. Repr. of 1899 ed.   14.00 ..... (38)
Conover, Milton. The General Land Office: Its History, Activities
and Organization. Repr. of 1923 ed.   18.00 ..... (2)
· Dunham, Harold H. Government Handout: A Study in the Admin-
istration of the Public Lands 1875-1891. Repr. of 1941 ed.   17.50 ..... (176)
Ford, Amelia C. Colonial Precedents of Our National Land
System As It Existed in 1800. Repr. of 1910 ed. 157pp.   10.00 ..... (273)
Hibbard, Benjamin H. History of the Public Land Policies. 1965. .....   7.50 (849)
Hitchins, Fred B. The Colonial Land and Emigration Commission.
1931. 325pp. Index.   13.50 ..... (273)
Puter, S. A. and Horace Stevens. Looters of the Public Domain:
Embracing a Complete Exposure of the Fraudulent System of
Acquiring Titles to the Public Lands of the United States.
Repr. of 1908 ed.   24.00 ..... (38)
Robbins, Roy M. Our Landed Heritage: The Public Domain,
1776-1936. 1962.   .....   2.45 (521)
Rohrbough, Malcolm Justin. The General Land Office, 1812-1826:
An Administrative Study. 1963. 270pp. BIP-63-03962.   .... (777)
Sato, S. History of the Land Question in the United States.
Repr. of 1886 ed. 14.00 (394)
Treat, Bryson J. National Land System, 1785-1820. Repr. of
1910 ed.   10.00 ..... (662)

Land: Companies, Policies for Specific Areas, Grants, Boundaries, Surveying

Ackerman, Robert Kilgo. South Carolina Colonial Land Policies.
1965. 207pp. BIP-68-05916.   .... (777)
Alden, George Henry. New Governments West of the Alleghenies
Before 1780. 1897.
    A concise but thorough examination of the schemes, intrigues,
    and politics involved in the attempts before 1780 to establish
    autonomous land grants and settlements in the West. Maps.   6.00   ..... (38)
Andrews, Christopher Columbus. Minnesota and Dacotah: In Letters
Descriptive of a Tour Through the North-West, in the Autumn
of 1856, With Information Relative to Public Lands, and a Table
of Statistics.   12.00 ..... (38)
Blawis, Patricia B. Tijerina and the Land Grants: Mexican
Americans in Struggle for Their Heritage. 1971.   6.95   2.65 (372)
Bowden, J. J. Spanish and Mexican Land Grants in the
Chihushuan Acquisition. 1971.   12.00 ..... (751)
Emmons, David Michael. The Boomers' Frontier: Land Promotion
and the Settlement of the Central Plains, 1854-1893. 1969.
510pp. BIP-69-19532.   .... (777)
Hadfield, Alice M. The Chartist Land Company. 2d ed. 1970.   8.95   ..... (181)

Hundley, Norris, Jr. Dividing the Waters: A Century of Contro-
versy Between the United States and Mexico. 1966.   10.50 ..... (112)
Livermore, Shaw. Early American Land Companies. 1968.   11.00 ..... (552)
Mason, A. H. Journal of Charles Mason and Jeremiah Dixon.
1969.
    Surveyed the Mason-Dixon Line.   5.00 ..... (24)
Royce, Charles C., comp. Indian Land Cessions in the United
States. With Introduction by Cyrus Thomas. (Bureau of
American Ethnology, 18th Annual Report, 1896-97, part 2). 1899.
    With 67 Maps.   30.00 ..... (2)
Savelle, Max. George Morgan: Colony Builder. 1932.
    Affiliated with Indiana Company.   7.00 ..... (2)
Wilson, Charles. Mapping the Frontier: Charles Wilson's Diary
of the Survey of the 49th Parallel, 1858-1862. ed. George F.
Stanley. 1971.   7.95 ..... (814)

Research Aids—Directories

Directory of Business Archives in the United States and Canada
(1975). ed. SAA Business Archives Committee. 1975. 38pp. 3.00 (17)
Directory of Census Information Sources. ed. J. Konrad.
1975. 23pp.
    An index of printed census sources and census search service. 2.00 (733)
Directory of Genealogical Societies in the United States of America
and Canada. ed. Mary Keysor Meyer. 1976.
    Also contains list of independent genealogical periodicals. 5.00 (479)
Directory of Genealogical Periodicals - 1975. ed. J. Konrad.
1975. 61pp.
    Lists genealogical periodicals in United States and worldwide. 4.00 (733)
Directory of Historical Societies and Agencies in the United States
and Canada. 10th ed. ed. AASLH. 434pp. 20.00 (18)
Directory of State and Provincial Archives (1975). ed. John M.
Kinney. 1975. 71pp. 6.00 (17)
Index of Family Associations. ed. Western New York Genealogical
Society, Inc. 1976.
    Compilation of Family Associations known, with addresses
and publication information. Indexed by Family Surname.   .... (828)
SAA Individual Membership Directory. December, 1976.   .....   8.00 (17)

Research Aids—Lineage Books; Surname Indexes; Ancestor Charts or Files

Ancestor Charts of the Arkansas Genealogical Society - Charts
1 through 66 - Volume 1.   .....   3.00 (37)
Ancestor Charts [of Members of Arkansas Genealogical
Society] - Charts 67 through 136 - Volume 2.   .....   3.00 (37)
Ancestor Charts [of Members of Arkansas Genealogical
Society] - Charts 137 through 200 - Volume 3. 1976.   .....   3.00 (37)
Daughters of the American Colonists. Lineage Book, National
Society of the Daughters of the American Colonists. 1929.
Volume I-460pp. B-BH 6998.   .... (778)
Daughters of the American Revolution. Lineage Book . . . Errata
for the Lineage Book, Volumes 1-39, Inclusive. 1890/91-
32pp. B-BH 16140.   .... (778)

_____. Mississippi Daughters and Their Ancestors. 1965.
[See ad on page 192.] 3.25 (690)
_____. Oklahoma Society Roster Supplement II, 1976,
Bicentennial Edition. comp. Mrs. Oather Edward Van Meter.
1976. 172pp.
    National Number, Name and Revolutionary ancestry
    also state of each member of Oklahoma Society DAR from
    Supplement I date, 1964 until the present. 7.50 (787)
Iowa Genealogical Society. Surname Index Volume I. 1972. 365pp.
    A listing of surnames from 1500's to 1972 as submitted by
    our members from all over United States. Cross-indexed,
    giving date and state of birth, death and marriage when known.
    Some have submitted whole pedigrees. Name and address
    of contributors included. 7.50 (376)
_____. A Surname Index Volume II. 1975. 491pp.
    A listing of surnames and given names from 1500s to 1975
    submitted by our members from all over the United States.
    Cross-indexed, giving state and year of birth, death
    and marriage when known. Many submitted whole
    pedigree lines back to Europe. Name and address of con-
    tributor included. Not a repeat of Volume I. 8.50 (376)
Kitchel, Walter H. Mayflower Descendants. New Jersey Society
Lineages, 1973. 1973. 521pp.
    Lineages of members (No. 1 to 1065) 1900 to 1973.   7.50 ..... (411)
Orange County California Genealogical Society. For King Or
Country, Volume I. 1975. 350pp.
    12000 name index; lines of descent of members from
    ancestors living during Revolutionary War. 12.50 (559)
_____. For King Or Country, Volume II. 1976. c350pp.
    Lines of descent of members from ancestors living during
    Revolutionary War.   ..... x (559)
Powers, Bee. Surname Index. 1972. 91pp.
    OCCGS members' addresses keyed to list of surnames and
    states each member is researching. 1.00 (559)
Register of Ancestors, National Society of The Colonial Dames of
America in the Commonwealth of Massachusetts. comps.
Bond and Fuller. 1975. 135pp. 10.00 (154)
Western New York Genealogical Society. Ancestor File of the
Society's Members. Volume 1. 1976.
    Ancestor information of Society members through
    April, 1976. Listed alphabetically by ancestors.   .... (828)

Research Aids—Reference Sources

Boehm, Inge P. and Alexander S. Birkos, eds. Reference Works:
History and Related Fields. 1967.   ..... .95 (20)
Bremer, Ronald A. Sources and Repositories. 1975. 36pp.
    Lists the most commonly used reference works and the
    six major genealogical centers for every state. 5.00 (272)
Channing, Edward, et al. Guide to the Study and Readings of
American History. 1912.   25.00 ..... (547)
Curtis, Mary B. Bibliography of "Compleat How To" (Magazine
of Bibliographies Series). 1976.
    Lists books that tell you how to find out books, subjects,
    locations, trades, etcs. 5.00 (371)
Genealogical Society of the Church Of Jesus Christ of Latter Day
Saints. Major Genealogical Record Sources in the United States.
8pp.   ..... .85 (275)

Harvard University Library. American History, 5 Volumes
Including: Volume 1. Classification Schedule and Classified
Listing by Class Number; Volume 2. Classified Listing by
Call Number; Volume 3. Author and Title Listing, A-L;
Volume 4. Author and Title Listing, M-Z; Volume 5. Chrono-
logical Listing. 1967.   Set: 175.00   ..... (319)
Hepworth, P. How To Find Out In History. 1966. 258pp.
   A readable guide to sources of information in history.
   English, American, French and German sources are given
   in considerable detail, and there is an unusually high
   proportion of space devoted to local history and associated
   subjects like heraldry and genealogy.   9.25   5.25 (591)
Milner, Mrs. Anita Cheek. Newspaper Genealogy Columns--A
Preliminary Checklist. 1975. 94pp.
   Over 55 columnists, appearing in 100 newspapers
   (including some periodicals), offering help in 150 counties
   and 30 states. 3.00 (494)
_____. Newspaper Indexes: A Subject and Location Guide for
Researchers. 1976/77.
   Newspaper indexes printed by individuals, and the names
   of people who have indexed newspapers and will check them
   for a fee.   .... (494)
Minto, C. S. How to Find Out in Geography. 1967. 114pp.
   A selective guide to sources of information in geography,
   which includes publications to the end of February 1965.
   A connected text makes it suitable for the general reader,
   whilst librarians are provided with a most useful book
   arranged according to the Dewey Classification.   6.25   3.00 (591)

Indexes to Periodicals

Bauer, G. Philip, comp. The American Archivist: Index to
Volumes 1-20 (1938-1957). Repr. of 1960 ed. 131pp. 10.00 (17)
Dowd, Mary Jane, comp. The American Archivist: Index to
Volumes 21-30 (1958-1967). 1974. 191pp. 10.00 (17)
GS Observer (1965-1972): A Cumulative Index. comps. Marjorie
Mahan and Adele Manwaring. 1974. 20pp.
   The GS Observer was the in-house organ of the Genealogical
   Society of the Church of Jesus Christ of Latterday Saints -
   Salt Lake City. Contains many research aids.   4.50   ..... (439)
Genealogical Index to DAR Magazine 1961-1965. 1976.   .... (212)
Genealogical Index to DAR Magazine 1966-1970. comp. Elaine
Walker. 1974. 125pp.
   Index to areas, main genealogy, family and bible records
   and queries in DAR magazines. 5.00 (212)
Genealogical Index to DAR Magazine 1971-1975. 1976.   .... (212)
Genealogical Periodical Annual Index-1974. comp. Laird C.
Towle, Ph. D. 1976. 56pp.
   Surname, locality, and topical index to 90 genealogical
   periodicals published in 1974.   .....   9.50 (292)
Guide to the American Historical Review, 1895-1945; a Subject-
Classified Explanatory Bibliography of the Articles, Notes
and Suggestions, and Documents. eds. Franklin D. Scott and
Elaine Teigler. (In American Historical Association. Annual
Report for the year 1944).   12.00   ..... (415)

Iowa Genealogical Society. Topical Index Volume I - X of Hawkeye
Heritage. 1976. 4pp.
A listing of all items published in the "Hawkeye Heritage"
1966 through 1975. Most items listed according to Iowa
Counties. Please enclose a stamped addressed 4 1/2 x 9 1/2
envelope when ordering this item separately. ..... .50 (376)
Southwestern Historical Quarterly, Cumulative Index, Volumes
1 - 40. 1950. 12.50 ..... (750)
Southwestern Historical Quarterly, Cumulative Index, Volumes
41 - 60. 1960. 17.50 ..... (750)

Indexes of Published Genealogies

The American Genealogist: Being a Catalogue of Family
Histories; A Bibliography of American Genealogy.
Repr. of 1900 ed. 406pp.
Covers from 1771 to 1900. 18.00 ..... (266)
Thomson, T. R. A Catalogue of British Family Histories. 1976.
184pp.
Third Edition (revised and updated) first edition published
in 1928; second edition 1935. Includes all individual family
histories (British Families Only). 15.00 ..... (772)

Guide to Manuscripts and Archives

Billington, Ray A. Guide to American History Manuscript
Collections in Libraries of the United States. 1.50 (699)
Confederate Memorial Literary Society, Richmond, Virginia
Southern Historical Manuscripts Commission. A Calendar of
Confederate Papers, with a Bibliography of Some Confederate
Publications; Preliminary Report of the Southern Historical
Manuscripts Commission, Prepared under the Direction of
the Confederate Memorial Library Society. comp. Douglass
Southall Freeman. 1908. 33.00 ..... (415)
Crick, Bernard R. and Miriam Alman, eds. A Guide to
Manuscripts Relating to America in Great Britain and
Ireland. 1961. 32.00 ..... (415)
Kielman, Chester Valls. The University of Texas Archives: An
Analytical Guide to the Historical Manuscripts Collections
In the University of Texas Library. 1966. 1219pp. BIP-68-16169...... ..... (777)
Manuscript Society. Manuscripts. Volumes 1-22 and General
Index 1-11. 1948/49-1970. Repr.
Contains descriptions of private and institutional collections.
These collections are most useful as a primary source for
historical information. Each: 14.00 (415)
Set: 391.00 311.00 (415)
General Index 1-11: 3.00 (415)
Massachusetts Historical Society. Catalog of Manuscripts of the
Massachusetts Historical Society, Boston, 7 Volumes. 1969. 650.00 ..... (307)
New York Public Library, Research Libraries. Dictionary
Catalog of the Manuscript Division, 2 Volumes. 1967. 110.00 ..... (307)
Parker, D. W. Guide to the Materials for United States History
in Canadian Archives. Repr. of 1913 ed. 17.00 ..... (415)
Richardson, Ernest C. A Union World Catalog of Manuscript
Books Volume 3: A List of Printed Catalogs of Manuscript
Books. ed. American Library Association Committee on Bibliog-
raphy. Repr. of 1935 ed. 19.50 ..... (248)

Source Records

Esker, Katie-Prince W. The Genealogical Department, Source
Records from the DAR Magazine, 1947-1950. Repr. of
1947-1950 ed. 693pp.   28.50   ..... (274)
Francis, Elisabeth W. and Ethel S. Moore. Lost Links, New
Recordings of Old Data From Many States. Repr. of 1947 ed.
562pp.   17.50   ..... (274)

Census and Population

Greene, Evarts B. and Virginia Harrington. American Population
Before Federal Census of 1790. 1932.   4.50   ..... (699)
Konrad, J. Directory of Census Information Sources. 1975. 23pp.
Directory of printed census sources and sources for cen-
sus search service. 2.00 (733)
Sutherland, Stella H. Population Distribution in Colonial America.
1936.   15.00   ..... (2)
United States Library of Congress Census Library Project. State
Census. Repr. of 1948 ed. 73pp. 2.50 (80)
United States Library of Congress Census Library Project.
Catalog of United States Census Publications, 1790-1945. Repr.
of 1950 ed.   18.00   ..... (248)
United States Library of Congress - Census Library Project.
Catalog of United States Census Publications, 1790-1945.
Repr. of 1950 ed.   15.75   ..... (297)

Newspapers and Printing

[Newspapers are a valuable source for genealogists. Unlike today, early newspapers
often were purchased by - and carried notices concerning - persons living hundreds of
miles from the place of publication. Many early, and practically all 20th century newspapers, are available for research on microfilm. See back cover of this book.]

Arndt, Karl, J. R. and May E. Olson. The German Language Press
of the Americas 1732-1968. History and Bibliography, Volume 2
(Die deutschsprachige Presse der Amerikas 1732-1968). 1973.
708pp. illus.   50.00   ..... (661)
Barrow, Robert Mangum. Newspaper Advertising In Colonial
America, 1704-1775. 298pp. BIP-67-17585.   .... (777)
Brigham, Clarence S. History and Bibliography of American News-
papers, 1690-1820. 2 vols. Repr. of 1947.   85.00   ..... (297)
Lathem, Edward C. Chronological Tables of American Newspapers,
1690-1820. 1972.   32.50   ..... (16)
Seidensticker, Oswald. The First Century of German Printing in
America, 1728-1830. 1893.   17.00   ..... (415)
United States Library of Congress - Periodicals Division. A
Checklist of American 18th Century Newspapers in the Library
of Congress. Repr. of 1936 ed. 401pp.   24.50   ..... (297)
Wittke, K. The German Language Press in America. Repr. of
1953 ed.   18.95   ..... (320)

Bibliographies

Besterman, Theodore. Family History (Including Genealogy and
Heraldry). A Title in the Besterman World Bibliographies.
1971. 149pp.   10.00   ..... (661)
_____. History and Geography. A Title in the Besterman World
Bibliographies. 1972. 1587pp.   60.00   ..... (661)

Cappon, Lester J. American Genealogical Periodicals: A
Bibliography with a Chronological Finding-List. 1964. ..... 1.75 (537)
Filby, P. William. American and British Genealogy and
Heraldry. 2d ed. 1976. 467pp.
    More than 5200 of the best and best-known titles in
    genealogy and heraldry are listed. Index contains more
    than 10,000 entries. 25.00 ..... (22)
Richardson, E. C. and A. E. Morse. Writings on American
History 1902. Repr. of 1904 ed. 294pp. 15.00 ..... (117)
Schreiner-Yantis, Netti, ed. Genealogical (and Local History)
Books in Print, Volume I. 311pp. 4.00 (675)
Writings on American History, 1962-1973: A Subject Bibliography
of Articles. 4 vols. 1975. Set: 275.00 ..... (415)
Writings on American History, 1973-1974: A Subject Bibliography
of Articles. 1974. 15.00 ..... (415)
Writings on American History, 1974-1975: A Subject Bibliography
of Articles. 1975. 15.00 ..... (415)

RELIGIOUS AND ETHNIC GROUPS

Research Aids

Kolb, Avery E. The Great Founding Clans of America. 1976.
    National, racial and religious groups which arrived in
    America before 1776 with indexed surnames of earliest
    families in each group. .... (414)
Mode, Peter G. Source Book and Bibliographical Guide to
American Church History. Repr. of 1921. 735pp. 17.50 ..... (117)
Allison, W. H. Inventory of Unpublished Material for American
Religious History in Protestant Church Archives and Other
Repositories. 1910. ..... 10.00 (415)

General

Baird, Robert. Religion in the United States of America. 1844. 24.00 ..... (38)
Bruce, Dickson Davies, Jr. And They All Sang Halleujah: Plain-
Folk Camp-Meeting Religion, 1800-1845. 265pp. BIP-72-06140. .... (777)
Posey, Walter B. Frontier Mission: A History of Religion West
of the Southern Appalachians to 1861. 436pp. 9.00 ..... (408)
Rupp, Israel Daniel. The Religious Denominations in the United
States: Their Past History. . . 1859. 67.50 ..... (2)
Sernett, Milton Charles. Black Religion and American Evangeli-
canism: White Protestants, Plantation Missions, and the
Independent Negro Church, 1787-1865. 416pp. BIP-72-32017. .... (777)
Sprague, William B. Annals of the American Pulpit: Or, Com-
memorative Notices of Distinguished American Clergymen of
Various Denominations, from the Early Settlement of the
Country to the Close of the Year Eighteen Hundred and Fifty
Five. With Historical Introduction. 9 vols. 1857-69. Set: 236.50 ..... (38)
Sweet, William W. Religion on the American Frontier. 4 vols.
    Repr. of 1946 ed. Set: 50.00 ..... (159)
    Volume 1-The Baptists, 1783-1830: Each: 12.50 ..... (159)
    Volume 2-The Presbyterians, 1783-1840: Each: 16.50 ..... (159)
    Volume 3-The Congregationalists, 1783-1850: Each: 10.00 ..... (159)
    Volume 4-The Methodists, 1783-1840: Each: 15.00 ..... (159)
Williams, Eugene F. Soldiers of God: The Chaplains of the
Revolutionary War. 1975. 376pp.
    History of the military chaplaincy. Biographical sketches
    of Revolutionary War chaplains. 10.95 ..... (132)

Anglican [also called Protestant Episcopal or Church of England]

Addison, James T. Episcopal Church in the United States,
1789-1931. Repr. of 1951 ed.   12.00   ..... (685)
Collins, Naomi Feldman. Oliver Cromwell's Protectorate Church
Settlement: The Commission for the Approbation of Insuf-
ficient Ministers and Schoolmasters, the Ejectors. 177pp.
BIP-71-13539.   .... (777)
Goodwin, Gerald Joseph. The Anglican Middle Way in Early
Eighteenth Century America: Anglican Religious Thought
in the American Colonies, 1702-1750. 376pp. BIP-65-05125.   .... (777)
Painter, Borden W., Jr. The Anglican Vestry in Colonial
America. 266pp. BIP-65-15095.   .... (777)
Tiffany, Charles C. History of the Protestant Episcopal Church
in the United States of America. Repr. of 1895 ed.   28.00   ..... (248)

Baptists

Davidson, William F. An Early History of the Free Will Baptists,
Volume 1. 1974.   4.95   3.95 (867)
Hiscox, Edward T. New Directory for Baptist Churches. Repr.
of 1894 ed.   5.95   ..... (416)
Newman, Albert H. History of the Baptist Churches in the United
States. Repr. of 1894 ed.   25.50   ..... (248)
Schultz, George Abram. An Indian Canaan: Isaac McCoy, Baptist
Missions, and Indian Reform. 415pp. BIP-64-03426.   .... (777)
Surname Index to Benedict's General History of the Baptist
Denomination in America, Volume II. 38pp.   6.50   ..... (439)

Catholics

"Searching in Catholic Records." ISGS Quarterly, Vol. 6, No. 2.
1974. 6pp. 2.00 (366)
Shea, John Dawson Gilmary. History of the Catholic Missions
Among the Indian Tribes of the United States, 1529-1854. 1855.   17.50   ..... (2)

Huguenots

Baird, Henry Martyn. History of the Rise of the Huguenots of
France. 2 vols. 1879.   Set: 35.00   ..... (2)
                                                        Each: 18.00   ..... (2)
Huguenot Society of London. Publications. 1887-1912.
These publications of the Sister Society of the Societe de
l'Histoire du Protestantisme francaise are an extremely
accurate and thorough record of the French and Flemish
Huguenots, also giving some information on the Dutch
refugees exiled in England. Apart from documenting
the marriages, births and deaths among the exiles, the
records relate their religious, political and occupational
activities and includes ample commentary on local events
of the period inasmuch as they concerned the Huguenots.
Including original maps, appendices and indices, these
publications are essential for the study of Huguenot
history and give a very accurate picture of life in England
and Ireland from the sixteenth century. List of individual
volumes and prices available upon request.
Vols. 1-20 and General Index 1887-1908:   Set: 586.00 536.00 (415)

Turk, Marion G. The Quiet Adventurers in America. 1975.
300pp.
Genealogical data and story of settlers in the American
Colonies and United States from the Channel Islands,
United Kingdom, where many Huguenot families settled
in 1500's and 1600's.   12.00   10.00 (771)

Jewish

Daly, C. P. Settlement of the Jews in North America.   25.00   ..... (289)
Gertstein, Arnold Aaron. The American Reform Rabbi and
the East European Jewish Immigrant, 1890-1922. 488pp.
BIP-72-20106.   .... (777)
Neuringer, Sheldon Morris. American Jewry and United States
Immigration Policy, 1881-1953. 491pp. BIP-71-16092.   .... (777)
Pollack, Herman. The German-Jewish Community: Studies
in Aspects of its Inner-Life (1648-1806). 461pp. BIP-58-02241. .... (777)
Sloan, Irving J. The Jews in America, 1621-1970: A
Chronology and Fact Book. 1971. 160pp.   6.50   ..... (551)
Wierick, Peter. History of the Jews in America from the Period
of Discovery of the New World to the Present Time. Repr. of
1931 ed.   11.50   ....   (297)

Lutheran; Reformed; Moravian [also called United Brethren];
and German Baptist Brethren [also called Dunkers]

Ankrum, Freeman. Sidelights on Brethren History. 1962.   .....   2.75   (91)
Bromiley, G. W., ed. Zwingli and Bullinger (Library of
Christian Classics, Vol. 24). 1953.   7.50   ..... (830)
Corwin, Edward T. History of the Reformed Church: Dutch,
(bound with) Dubbs' History of the Reformed Church: German,
and Hamilton's A History of the Unitas Fratrum, or Moravian
Church in the United States. 3 vols. in 1. Repr. of 1895 ed. 28.00 ..... (248)
Frantz, John B. Revivalism in the German Reformed Church
in America to 1850, with Emphasis on the Eastern Synod.
314pp. BIP-61-02031.   .... (777)
Gray, Elma E. Wilderness Christians: The Moravian Mission
to the Delaware Indians. Repr. of 1956. xiv,354pp.   22.00   ....   (662)
Heckewelder, John. A Narrative of the Mission of the United
Brethren Among the Delaware and Mohegan Indians, from
its Commencement, in the Year 1740, to the Close of the
Year 1808. 1820.   17.00   ..... (38)
Nelson, Clifford and Eugene L. Fevold. Lutheran Church Among
Norwegian Americans. 2 vols. 1960.   Set: 12.50   ..... (42)
Sachse, Julius Friedrich. German Sectarians of Pennsylvania,
1708-1800: A Critical and Legendary History of the Ephrata
Cloister and the Dunkers. 2 vols. 1899-1900.   Set: 45.00   ..... (2)
                                                Each: 24.00   ..... (2)

Mennonites [Anabaptists], and Amish

Dyck, Cornelius J. Twelve Becoming, Biographies of Mennonite
Disciples from the Sixteenth to the Twentieth Century. 1973. ..... 4.50 (228)
Estep, William R. The Anabaptist Story. rev. ed. 1975.
viii,250pp. maps, notes, bibliography, index. 3.95   (215)
Hellerbrand, H. J. Bibliography of Anabaptism 1520-1630, Vol.
10 (Taeuferakien Kommission Series). 1962.   9.00   ..... (327)

Hostetler, John A. Annotated Bibliography on he Amish. 1951.   .....   1.50 (327)
Krahn, Cornelius. Dutch Anabaptism. 1968.   15.00 ..... (327)
Schelbert, Leo. Swiss Migration To America: The Swiss
  Mennonites. 1966. 335pp. BIP-67-00807.   .... (777)
Wenger, John C. Mennonite Church in America. 1967.   8.95 ..... (327)
Zeman, Jarold. Anabaptists and the Czech Brethren in Moravia,
  1526 to 1628: A Study of Origins and Contrasts. 1962.   30.00 ..... (362)

Methodist

Buckley, James M. History of the Methodists in the United
  States (American Church History Series, Volume 5). Repr.
  of 1896 ed.   30.50 ..... (248)
Overton, Julie, tr. The Ministers and Churches of the Central
  German Conference. Repr. 84pp.
    Biographies of German Methodist ministers and history of
    churches in Ohio, South Michigan, Eastern Pennsylvania,
    Indiana, and Eastern Kentucky. 6.75 (330)

Mormon

Tagg, Melvin Salway. A History of the Church of Jesus Christ of
  Latter-Day Saints in Canada, 1830-1963. 1963. 312pp.
  BIP-63-07131.   .... (777)
Hardy, Blaine Carmon. The Mormon Colonies of Northern
  Mexico: A History 1885-1912. 205pp. BIP-68-06639.   .... (777)

Presbyterian

Carson, David Melville. A History Of The Reformed Presbyterian
  Church In America To 1871. 1964. 281pp. BIP-64-10358.   .... (777)
Miller, Guy Howard. A Contracting Community: American
  Presbyterians, Social Conflict, and Higher Education 1730-1820
  (Volumes I and II). 1970. 562pp. BIP-71-15239.   .... (777)
Records of the Presbyterian Church in the United States of America,
  1706-1788. 1904.   19.00 ..... (38)
Thompson, Robert E. History of the Presbyterian Churches in
  the United States. Repr. of 1895 ed.   22.00 ..... (248)

Shaker

Brown, Thomas. An Account of the People Called Shakers: Their
  Faith, Doctrines, and Practice, Exemplified in the Life, Con-
  versations, and Experience of the Author During the Time He
  Belonged to the Society. To Which is Affixed a History of Their
  Rise and Progress to the Present Day. 1812.   14.50 ..... (2)
Richmond, Mary B., comp. and annot. Shaker Literature: A
  Bibliography. 2 vols. 634pp. 1976.   Set: 45.00 ..... (531)

Quaker

Arthur, John. New England Quakerism 1656-1830. 1969. 247pp.
  BIP-69-18699.   .... (777)
Elliott, Errol T. Quaker Profiles from the American West.
  1972. 172pp.
    Miniature biographies of some of the strong 19th century
    Quaker personalities who have shaped the course of
    Quakers in America. 2.95 (255)
Frost, Jerry William. The Quaker Family In Colonial America:
  A Social History of the Society of Friends. 1968. 533pp.
  BIP-68-17894.   .... (777)

Smith, Joseph. A Descriptive Catalogue of Friends' Books, or
Books Written by Members of the Society of Friends, Commonly
Called Quakers, from their First Rise to the Present Time,
Interspersed with Critical Remarks and Biographical Notices.
With Supplement. 3 vols. 1867-1893.   102.00   ..... (415)
Wells, Robert Vale. A Demographic Analysis of Some Middle Colony
Quaker Families of the Eighteenth Century. 1969. 169pp.
BIP-70-14249.   .... (777)

QUAKER QUEST

Book Rentals By Mail

5207 North Delaware
Indianapolis, IN 46220

Write For List

ROBERT E. STIENS, C.G.
Rt. 1 Box 290
Shelley, Idaho 83274
*German Church records available
from Genealogical Society
Salt Lake City, Utah*

Other Religions

Dollin, Norman. The Schwenkfelders In Eighteenth Century
America. 1971. 209pp. BIP-72-01298.   .... (777)
Kovach, Michael George. The Russian Orthodox Church In
Russian America. 1957. 297pp. BIP-00-22851.   .... (777)
Neidhardt, W. S. Fenianism in North America. 1975. 184pp. 10.00   ..... (589)
Newman, Henry. Henry Newman's Salzburger Letterbooks.
ed. George F. Jones. 1966.   12.00   ..... (279)
Peters, Victor. All Things Common: The Hutterian Way Of Life.
1966.
       Sect founded 1533 - from group of Moravian Anabaptists;
       migrated to Hungary and Russia, and in 1874 to South
       Dakota.   5.75   ..... (497)
Salisbury, Neal Emerson. Conquest of the 'Savage': Puritans,
Puritan Missionaries, and Indians, 1620-1680. 1972. 309pp.
BIP-72-18141.   .... (777)
Lamech, K. Chronicon Ephratense: A History of the Community
of Seventh Day Baptists at Ephrata, Lancaster County,
Pennsylvania. tr. J. Max Hark. Repr. of 1880 ed.   18.50   ..... (248)

Law and Penal System

Blackstone, Sir William. Blackstone's Commentaries, With Notes
of reference to the Constitution and Laws of the Federal
Government of the United States and of the Commonwealth of
Virginia by St. George Tucker. With an appendix to each
Volume, Containing Short Tracts Upon Such Subjects as
Appeared Necessary to Form a Connected View of the Laws
of Virginia as a Member of the Federal Union. 5 vols. 1803.
                                            Set: 135.00   ..... (273)

Crawford, William. Report on the Penitentiaries of the United
   States. Repr. of 1835 ed.   25.00 ..... (698)
Cunliffe, Marcus. The Right to Property: A Theme in American
   History. 1.25 (362)
Franklin, Frank G. The Legislative History of Naturalization In
   the United States. From the Revolutionary War to 1861.
   1906. 309pp. Index.   12.50 ..... (273)
Franklin, Robert Jorres. The Americanization of the English
   Common Law, 1776-1835. 1972. 420pp. BIP-72-11921.   .... (777)
Henderson, Dwight Franklin. Courts For a New Nation: A History
   of the Inferior Federal Courts 1787-1801. 1966. 288pp.
   BIP-67-03295.   .... (777)
Hilliard, Francis. The Elements of Law: Being a Comprehensive
   Summary of American Civil Jurisprudence. 1835.   16.00 ..... (38)
Jones, Thomas Bard. Legacy of Change: The Panic of 1819 and
   Debtor Relief Legislation in the Western States. 1968. 222pp.
   BIP-69-05023.   .... (777)
Rowsome, Beverly Zweiben. How Blackstone Lost the Colonies:
   English Law, Colonial Lawyers, and the American Revolution.
   1971. 195pp. BIP-72-13133.   .... (777)
Society for the Prevention of Pauperism. Report on the Penitentiary
   System in the United States, Prepared Under a Resolution of the
   Society for the Prevention of Pauperism in the City of New York.
   1822.   8.00 ..... (38)
Smurr, John Welling. Territorial Constitutions: A Legal History
   of the Frontier Governments Erected by Congress in the American
   West, 1787-1900. 1960. 1005pp. BIP-60-02846.   .... (777)
Story, Joseph. Commentaries on the Conflict of Laws, Foreign
   and Domestic, in Regard to Contracts, Rights, and Remedies,
   and Especially in Regard to Marriages, Divorces, Wills,
   Successions, and Judgments. 1834.   25.00 ..... (38)

Social Problems: The Poor, the Sick, and the Insane

The Almshouse Experience: Collected Papers. 1824, 1827.   14.00 ..... (38)
Blackmon, Dora Mae E. The Care of the Mentally Ill in America,
   1604-1812, In the Thirteen Original Colonies. 1964. 226pp.
   BIP-65-05408.   .... (777)
Dain, Norman. Disordered Minds: The First Century of Eastern
   State Hospital in Williamsburg, Virginia, 1766-1866. Illustrated.
   1971.   5.95 ..... (801)
Disease and Society in Provincial Massachusetts: Collected
   Accounts 1736-1939. 1972.   9.00 ..... (38)
Harstad, Peter. Health in the Upper Mississippi River Valley,
   1820-1881. 1963. 360pp. BIP-64-00642.   .... (777)
Hazard, Thomas R. Report on the Poor and Insane in Rhode-Island.
   Repr. of 1851 ed.   8.00 ..... (38)
Lawrence, Charles. History of the Philadelphia Almshouses and
   Hospitals from the Beginning of the 18th to the Ending of the
   19th Centuries, Covering a Period of Nearly 200 Years.
   Repr. of 1905 ed.   24.00 ..... (38)
McKee, Linda Ann. Health and Medicine in Connecticut,
   1785-1810. 1971. 274pp. BIP-71-19324.   .... (777)
Miller, Genevieve. Bibliography of the History of Medicine in the
   United States and Canada, 1939-1960. 1964.   17.50 ..... (385)
Powell, John Harrey. Bring Out Your Dead: The Great Plague
   of Yellow Fever in Philadelphia in 1793. 1949.   14.00 ..... (38)

Williams, William Henry. The Pennsylvania Hospital, 1751-1801:
An Internal Examination of Anglo-America's First Hospital.
1971. 402pp. BIP-72-14517. .... (777)

IMMIGRATION, REPATRIATION, AND ETHNIC GROUPS IN AMERICA

Research Aids

Boyer, Carl, 3rd. Ship Passenger Lists. 1977. c500pp.
Lists from Lancour's Bibliography, not in print, collected
from many journals and sources, set in new type with a
common index by name, place and ship. .... (88)
Janeway, William R. Bibliography of Immigration in the United
States, Nineteen Hundred to Nineteen Thirty. 1972. ..... 6.00 (631)
Wasserman, Paul and Jean Morgan, eds. Ethnic Information
Sources of the United States. 1976. 749pp.
Covers voth live and print sources of information about
all ethnic groups in the United States, with the exception of
Blacks, American Indians, and Eskimoes. 45.00 ..... (266)

General Reference

Ander, O. F., ed. In the Trek of the Immigrants: Essays
Presented to Carl Wittke. 1964. 6.95 ..... (44)
Bicha, Karel Denis. Canadian Immigration Policy and the American
Farmer, 1896-1914. 1963. 206pp. BIP-64-07288. .... (777)
Chickering, Jesse. Immigration into the United States. Repr. of
1848 ed. 5.95 ..... (568)
Chronological Library of the Americas Series. Chronology of
American Immigrants. 1975. 35.00 ..... (673)
Hansen, M. L. Immigrant in American History. 4.50 ..... (699)
Harper, Richard Conant. The Course of the Melting-Pot Idea
To 1910. 1967. 420pp. BIP-68-02424. .... (777)
Heape, Walter. Emigration, Migration and Nomadism. 1931. 19.00 ..... (415)
Holsinger, John Calvin. A Survey of the Major Arguments Used
By English Promoters to Encourage Colonization and Interest
in America in the Early Colonial Era. 1967. 127pp.
BIP-68-14137. .... (777)
Jones, Maldwyn A. American Immigration. Illustrated. 1960. 6.50 2.45 (137)
Lagumina, Salvatore J. and Frank J. Cavaioli. The Ethnic
Dimension in American Society. 1974. ..... 5.95 (341)
Leonare, Henry Beardsell. The Open Gates: The Protest Against
the Movement To Restrict European Immigration, 1896-1924.
1967. 306pp. BIP-68-03201. .... (777)
Morse, Samuel F. Imminent Dangers to the Free Institutions of
the United States Through Foreign Immigration and the Present
State of the Naturalization Laws. Repr. of 1835 ed. 4.00 ..... (38)
Smith, Darrell Hevenor. The Bureau of Naturalization; Its
History, Activities and Organization. 1926. 12.50 ..... (2)
United States Bureau of Statistics. Emigration to the United
States. Repr. of 1904 ed. 10.00 ..... (631)

Asia

Aswad, Barbara C. Arabic Speaking Communities in American
Cities. 1974. ..... 5.95 (128)
Eubank, Nancy. Russians in America. 1973. 3.95 ..... (426)
Fukei, Budd. The Japanese American Story. 1976. 160pp.
Story of Japanese in America, treatment during World
War II, and customs and traditions of Japanese-Americans. 6.95 ..... (197)

Kayal, Philip M. and Joseph M. Kayal. The Syrians and Lebanese
in America. 1975.   12.50 ..... (773)
Wand, David H. Asian American Heritage. 1974.   ..... 1.95 (815)
Wertsman, Vladimir. The Russians in America: A Chronology and
Fact Book. (Ethnic Chronology Series, No. 24). 1976. 160pp.   6.50 ..... (551)
Zo, Kil Young. Chinese Emigration Into the United States,
1850-1880. 1971. 231pp. BIP-71-23639.   .... (777)

Britisch and Welsh

Conway, Alan, ed. Welsh in America: Letters from the Immigrants.
1961.   7.50 ..... (497)
Cowan, Helen I. British Emigration to British North America: The
First Hundred Years. 1961.   12.50 ..... (763)
Furer, Howard B. The British in America, 1578-1970: A
Chronology and Fact Book. (Ethnic Chronology Series, No. 7).
1973. 160pp.   6.50 ..... (551)
Johnson, Stanley C. History of Emigration From the United King-
dom to North America 1763-1912. 1913. 387pp. Index.   12.50 ..... (273)
Kolb, Avery E. Passengers to Ye First Colonie of Britannia In
America, 1607-1625. 2 vols. 1976.
Reconstructed earliest ship passenger lists with detailed
references to source records.   .... (414)
Rhys, John. The Welsh People. Repr. of 1906 ed.   29.95 ..... (320)
Shepperson, Wilbur S. Emigration and Disenchantment: Portraits
of Englishmen Repatriated from the United States. 1965.   8.95 ..... (556)
Todd, Arthur C. Cornish Miner in America. 1968.   10.00 ..... (144)

Dutch

Nijhoff, Martinus. The Hollanders in America. Repr. of 1925 ed.   6.00 ..... (631)
Smit, Pamela and Jacobus W. Smit. The Dtuch in America,
1609-1970: A Chronology and Fact Book. (Ethnic Chronology
Series, No. 5). 1972. 116pp.   6.50 ..... (551)

French

Baldensperger, Fernand. Mouvement Des Idees Dan l'Emigration
Francaise, 1789-1815. 2 vols. Repr. of 1924 ed. 39.00 (248)
Parkman, Francis. Pioneers in the New World. Repr. of 1865 ed.   12.50 ..... (164)
Pula, James S. The French in America, 1488-1974: A Chronology
and Fact Book. (Ethnic Chronology Series, No. 18). 1975.
150pp.   6.50 ..... (551)
Robichaux, Albert J., Jr. Acadian Marriages In France:
Department d'Ille-et-Vilaine, 1759-1776. 1976. c180pp.
Collection of marriages of Acadians in the Maritime ports
of the Department d'Ille-et-Vilaine in France. Word for
word translation of each marriage. 25.00 (648)
Thwaites, Reuben G. France in America, 1497-1763.
Repr. of 1905 ed.   12.00 ..... (297)

German

Bruncken, Ernest. German Political Refugees in the United
States 1815-1860. Repr. of 1904 ed.   5.00 ..... (631)
"Brunswick Deserter-Immigrants of the American Revolution."
Illinois State Genealogical Society Quarterly, Vol. 6, No. 2.
1974. 5pp. 2.00 (366)
Cronau, Rudolf. Three Centuries of German Life in America.   27.00 ..... (289)
Faust, Albert. The German Element in the United States. 2 vols.
1927.   34.50 ..... (673)

Frank, W. Deutchland in Amerika. Repr. of 1839 ed.   8.00 ..... (631)
Furer, Howard B. The Germans in America, 1607-1970: A
Chronology and Fact Book. (Ethnic Chronology Series,
No. 8). 1973. 160pp.   6.50 ..... (551)
Knittle, Walter A. Early Eighteenth Century Palatine Emigration.
Repr. of 1937 ed. 320pp.   12.50 ..... (274)
Meynen, Emil. Bibliography on German Settlements in Colonial
North America. Repr. of 1937 ed.   20.00 ..... (266)
Nau, John Frederick. The German People of New Orleans,
1850-1900. 1954. 283pp. BIP-00-09956.   .... (777)
Olson, Audrey Louise. St. Louis Germans, 1850-1920: The
Nature of an Immigrant Community and Its Relation to the
Assimilation Process. 1970. 355pp. BIP-70-25388.   .... (777)
Pochmann, Henry A. and Arthur R. Schultz, eds. Bibliography of
German Culture in America to 1940. 1953.   15.00 ..... (849)
Rippley, LaVern. Of German Ways. 1970. 301pp.
About German customs and life, and story of German
immigration to United States. (Heritage Books Series).   6.95 ..... (197)
Schrader, Frederick F. The Germans in the Making of America.
Repr. of 1924 ed.   13.95 ..... (320)
Smith, Clifford Neal. American Genealogical Resources in
German Archives. 1976. c300pp.
Provides basic finding and descriptive data on items per-
taining to Germans who emigrated to the United States and
Canada. Included are relevant documents in some 280 German
archives and materials photocopied for the Library of
Congress before they were destroyed in World War II.   25.00 ..... (85)
_____. Emigrants from Saxony to America 1854, 1859. 1976.   ..... 6.25 (330)
_____ and Anna P-C. Smith. Encyclopedia of German-American
Genealogical Research. 1976. 273pp.   35.00 ..... (85)
Tucker, Marlin Timothy. Political Leadership in the Illinois-
Missouri German Community, 1836-1872. 1968. 391pp.
BIP-69-10871.   .... (777)
Wittke, Carl F. Refugees of Revolution. Repr. of 1952 ed.   15.75 ..... (297)
Zucker, Adolf Eduard, ed. The Forty-Eighters: Political Refugees
of the Revolution of 1848. Repr. of 1950 ed. 379pp.
Essays in the history of the emigration from Germany and
settlement in the United States; contains a biographical
dictionary of the Forty-Eighters.   8.50 ..... (662)

Irish, Scottish, and Scotch-Irish

Adams, William F. Ireland and Irish Emigration to the New World
from 1815 to the Famine. Repr. of 1932 ed.   10.00 ..... (662)
Begley, Evelyn M. Of Scottish Ways. 1976. c250pp.
Describes Scotland and its people, and the Scottish in the
United States.   6.95 ..... (197)
Black, George F. Scotland's Mark on America. Repr. of 1921 ed.   7.00 ..... (631)
Cameron, Viola R. Emigrants from Scotland to America, 1774-1775.
Repr. of 1930 ed. 117pp. 7.50 (274)
Clark, John Dennis J. The Adjustment of Irish Immigrants to Urban
Life: The Philadelphia Experience 1840-1870. 1970. 284pp.
BIP-71-10561.   .... (777)
Delaney, Mary Murray. Of Irish Ways. Repr. of 1973 ed. 356pp.
Description of Irish land and people; and of Irish in the
United States.   6.95 ..... (197)
Ford, Henry J. The Scotch-Irish in America.   27.00 ..... (289)
_____. Scotch-Irish in America. 1966.   12.00 ..... (685)

Graham, Ian C. C. Scottish Emigration to North America, 1707-
1738. 1955. 243pp. BIP-00-13484. .... (777)
Green, Samuel S. The Scotch-Irish in America. 5.00 ..... (631)
Griffin, William D. The Irish in America: A Chronology and
Fact Book. 1973. 160pp. 6.50 ..... (551)
Kennedy, Robert E., Jr. The Irish. 1973. 254pp.
Emigration, marriage, and fertility. 10.95 3.65 (112)
Maguire, John Francis. The Irish in America. 1868. 18.50 ..... (38)
Reid, Whitelaw. The Scot in America and the Ulster Scot. 5.00 ..... (631)
Schrier, Arnold. Ireland and the American Emigration, 1850-
1900. 279pp. BIP-00-19040. .... (777)

Italians

Caroli, Betty B. Italian Repatriation from the United States,
1900-1914. 1973. ..... 4.50 (128)
Logatto, Anthony F. The Italians in America, 1492-1972: A
Chronology and Fact Book. 1972. 160pp. 6.50 ..... (551)
Lord, Eliot. Italians in America. Repr. of 1905 ed. 12.00 ..... (631)
Mondello, Salvatore Alfred. The Italian Immigrant in Urban
America, 1880-1920, as Reported in the Contemporary
Periodical Press. 266pp. BIP-60-05287. .... (777)
Schiavo, Giovanni E. The Italians in America Before the Civil
War. Reprint. 23.00 ..... (38)

Jugoslavs, Hungarians, Romanians, Cechs

Biographical Directory of Americans and Canadians of Croatian
Descent, Volume 4. ..... 10.00 (631)
Capek, Thomas. The Cechs (Bohemians) in America. 1920. 13.00 ..... (38)
Colakovic, Branko M. Yugoslav Migrations to America. 9.00 ..... (631)
Eterovich, Adam S. A Guide and Bibliography to Research on
Yugoslavs in the United States and Canada. 1975. ..... 7.00 (631)
_____. Jugoslav Immigrant Bibliography. 1968. ..... 3.00 (631)
Konnyu, Leslie. Hungarians in the United States of America, an
Immigration Study. 1967. 5.50 4.25 (21)
Lengyel, Emil. Americans from Hungary. Repr. of 1948 ed. 13.00 ..... (297)
Szeplaki, Joseph. The Hungarians in America, 1583-1974:
Chronology and Fact Book. 1975. 150pp. 6.50 ..... (551)
Wertsman, Vladimir. The Romanians in America: A Chronology
and Fact Book. 1975. 128pp. 6.50 ..... (551)

Mexicans, Filipinos, Spaniards

Bogardus, Emory S. The Mexican in the United States. Repr. of
1934 ed. 6.00 ..... (631)
Mariano, Honorante. The Filipino Immigrants in the Unites
States. Repr. of 1934 ed. Thesis. 7.00 (631)
Natella, Arthur A., Jr. The Spanish in America, 1513-1974: A
Chronology and Fact Book. 1975. 150pp. 6.50 ..... (551)
Trejo, Arnulfo D., ed. Bibliografia Chicana: A Guide to Infor-
mation Sources. 1975. 193pp.
Annotated bibliography of monographic works concerning
the Chicano life experience, from 1848 to present. 18.00 ..... (266)

Polish, Lithuanians, Estonians, Latvians, Ukrainians

Budreckis, Algirdas. The Lithuanians in America: A
Chronology and Fact Book. 1976. 174pp. 6.50 ..... (551)

Duker, Abraham Gordon. The Polish Great Emigration and the
Jews Studies in Political and Intellectual History. 723pp.
BIP-00-16277. .... (777)
Halich, Wasyl. Ukrainians in the United States. 1937. 7.50 ..... (38)
Karklis, Maruta, Liga Streips, and Laimonis Streips. The
Latvians in America: A Chronology and Fact Book. 1974.
160pp. 6.50 ..... (551)
Pennar, Jaan, et al. The Estonians in America, 1627-1975: A
Chronology and Fact Book. 1975. 150pp. 6.50 ..... (551)
Renkiewicz, Frank. The Poles in America, 1608-1972: A
Chronology and Fact Book. 1973. 144pp. 6.50 ..... (551)
Wertsman, Vladimir. The Ukrainians in America: A Chronology
and Fact Book. 1976. 160pp. 6.50 ..... (551)

Scandinavians

Billigmeier, Robert and Fred A. Picard, eds. Old Land and
the New: The Journals of Two Swiss Families in America
in the 1820's. 1965. 6.50 ..... (497)
Blegen, Theodore C. Norwegian Migration to America: 1825-
1860. 1931. 12.50 ..... (38)
Furer, Howard B. The Scandinavians in America, 986-1970:
A Chronology and Fact Book. 1972. 160pp. 6.50 ..... (551)
Hoglund, Arthur William. Paradise Rebuilt: Finnish Immigrants
and their America, 1880-1920. 333pp. BIP-00-22366. .... (777)
Larson, Esther Elisabeth. Swedish Commentators on America,
1638-1865. 1963. 139pp.
An annotated list of selected manuscript and printed
materials. 5.50 (635)
Lorenzen, Lilly. Of Swedish Ways. 1964. 276pp.
Lifestyles of people in the Old Country, and as immigrants
to the United States. 6.95 ..... (197)
MacHaffie, Ingeborg, and Margaret A. Nielsen. Of Danish Ways.
1976. 250pp.
About Denmark and its people, and the story of the
Danish in the United States. 6.95 ..... (197)
Nelson, O. N. History of Scandinavians in the United States.
2 vols. in 1. Reprint. 39.95 ..... (320)
Norlie, Olaf M. History of the Norwegian People in America.
Repr. of 1925 ed. 22.95 ..... (320)
Vanberg, Bent. Of Norwegian Ways. 1970. 221pp.
Describes Norwegian customs and traditions, and
history of Norwegians in the United States. 6.95 ..... (197)

Swiss

Metraux, Guy Serge. Social and Cultural Aspects of Swiss
Immigration into the United States in the Nineteenth Century.
369pp. BIP-64-11381. .... (777)
Von Grueningen, John P. The Swiss in the United States. 8.00 ..... (631)

MILITARY

General Research Aids

Bupuy, Colonel Trevor N. and Theodore Ropp. Guide to Research Sources in Military History. 1976. c400pp. 25.00 ..... (85)
Jacobs, James R. Beginning of the United States Army, 1783-
1812. Repr. of 1947 ed. 17.50 ..... (404)

Prucha, Francis Paul. A Guide to the Military Posts of the
United States 1789-1895. Repr. of 1964 ed.   7.50   ..... (850)
Smith, Myron J., Jr. The American Navy 1789-1860: A
Bibliography. 1974.   15.00   ..... (670)

Colonial Wars

Devine, Joseph Aloysius, Jr. The British North American
Colonies in the War of 1739-1748. 359pp. BIP-69-04015.   .... (777)
Foote, William Alfred. The American Independent Companies
of the British Army 1664-1764. 591pp. BIP-66-11906.   .... (777)
Hammelef, John Christensen. British and American Attempts
to Coordinate the Defenses of the Continental Colonies to
Meet French and Northern Indian Attacks 1643-1754. 265pp.
BIP-00-11288.   .... (777)
Parker, King Lawrence. Anglo-American Wilderness Cam-
paigning 1754-1764: Logistical and Tactical Developments.
452pp. BIP-71-17534.   .... (777)
Peckham, Howard H. Colonial Wars, Sixteen Hundred Eighty-
Nine to Seventeen Hundred Sixty-Two. 1964.   7.50   2.25 (137)
Shy, John Willard. The British Army in North America, 1760-
1775. 316pp. BIP-61-04834.   .... (777)
Taylor, Philip F. Calendar of Warrants for Land in Kentucky
for Service in French and Indian War. Repr. of 1917 ed.
84pp. 7.50 (274)

Revolutionary War - Research Aids

Cappon, Lester J. Atlas of Early American History: The
Revolutionary Era, 1760-1790. 1976. 176pp.
   286 maps, 271 reproduced in as many as six colors,
   describe all aspects of early American life from politics
   to commerce, from military history to demographic
   and cultural characteristics.   125.00   ..... (621)
Clark, David Sanders, comp. Index to Maps of the American
Revolution in Books and Periodicals. 1970. 301pp.   15.00   ..... (297)
Curtis, Mary Barnett. Bibliography of the American Revolution
Battles and Eye Witness Accounts. 1973. 24pp.
   All genealogical and historical books on subject and
   where to buy them. 5.00 (371)
_____. Bibliography of the American Revolution: General
History. 1973. 32pp. 5.00 (371)
_____. Bibliography of American Revolution Roster and Lists.
1973. 32pp. 5.00 (371)
Koenig, W. J. and S. L. Mayer. European Manuscript Sources
for the American Revolution. 1974. 328pp.   27.50   ..... (85)
National Genealogical Society. Index to Revolutionary War Pension
Applications. rev. ed. 668pp.
   Lists alphabetically Revolutionary veterans and their
   widows who applied for pensions. Included are all the
   additions and corrections uncovered by National Archives,
   in their preparation for microfilms of the actual pension
   files.   31.50   ..... (514)
Nebenzahl, Kenneth and Don Higginbotham. Atlas of the
American Revolution. 1974. 218pp.
   Contains 54 period maps and commentary.   35.00   ..... (633)

Revolutionary War - General Reference

Allen, Gardner W. Naval History of the American Revolution. 2 vols. Repr. of 1913 ed. Set:	20.00	..... (662)
Applegate, Howard Lewis. Constitutions Like Iron: The Life of the American Revolutionary War Soldiers in the Middle Department, 1775-1783. 490pp. BIP-67-07057.	.....	..... (777)
Bowman, Benjamin Allen. The Morale of Continental and Militia Troups in War of Revolution. 1941. 355pp. BIP-00-00302.	.....	..... (777)
Benton, William Allen. The Whig Loyalists: An Aspect of Political Ideology in the American Revolutionary Era. 273pp. BIP-66-04601.	.....	..... (777)
Curtis, Edward E. Organization of the British Army in the American Revolution. Repr. of 1926 ed. 223pp.	7.50	..... (661)
Edmonson, James Howard. Desertion in the American Army During the Revolutionary War. 436pp. BIP-72-17754.	.....	..... (777)
Graymont, Barbara. The Border War: The Iroquois in the American Revolution. 580pp. BIP-72-15574.	.....	..... (777)
Humphrey, William. Lieutenant William Humphrey's Journal on March to Quebec under Colonel Benedict Arnold. 1976. Day by day account of hardships, on march to Quebec - nine months as a prisoner of war - and the events daily on the march, battle at Quebec and imprisonment and release. Very detailed.	.....	..... (611)
Neuenschwander, John Alfred. The Forgotten Section: The Middle Colonies and the American Revolution, 1774-1776. 325pp. BIP-72-00083.	.....	..... (777)
Rice, Howard C., Jr. and Anne S. K. Brown. The American Campaigns of Rochambeau's Army, 1780-1783. 2 vols. 1973. 732pp. A source book on the French army in America and its campaigns from Newport, Rhode Island to Yorktown, Virginia and the Caribbean. Set:	100.00	..... (621)
Slagle, Robert Oakley. The Von Lossberg Regiment: A Chronicle of Hessian Participation in the American Revolution. 236pp. BIP-65-11378.	.....	..... (777)
Smith, Clifford Neal. Muster Rolls and Prisoner of War Lists in American Archival Collections Pertaining to German Mercenaries Who Served with the British Forces During the American Revolution. 3 parts. 1976.	.....	20.00 (330)
Solberg, Curtis Brian. As Others Saw Us: Travelers in America During the Age of the American Revolution. 351pp. BIP-70-02070.	.....	..... (777)
Stadelman, Bonnie Sue Shelton. The Amusements of the American Soldiers During the Revolution. 256pp. BIP-70-06430.	.....	..... (777)
Thwaites and Kellogg. Documentary History of Dunmore's War. Repr. of 1905 ed. 472pp. Officers' journals, soldiers' letters home, Orders of Mobilization of the Virginia Militia.	25.00	..... (124)
Treacy, Mildred Freeman. Nathanael Green and the Southern Campaign: August, 1780-April, 1781. 193pp. BIP-62-05721.	.....	..... (777)

Revolutionary War - Loyalists

Barnes, Timothy M. The Loyalist Press in the American
Revolution, 1765-1781. 312pp. BIP-71-12782. .... (777)
Brown, Wallace. The Structure of Loyalism During the American
Revolution. 405pp. BIP-64-12969. .... (777)
Einstein, Lewis D. Divided Loyalties: Americans in England
During the War of Independence. Repr. of 1933 ed. 13.50 ..... (662)
Nelson, William H. The Loyalist View of the American Revolution.
230pp. BIP-59-01493. .... (777)
Peters, Thelma Peterson. The American Loyalists and the
Plantation Period in the Bahama Islands. 203pp. BIP-60-05143. .... (777)
Smith, Paul Hubert. American Loyalists in British Military
Policy, 1775-1781. 339pp. BIP-63-01220. .... (777)

Militia

Brundage, Lyle D. The Organization, Administration, and
Training of the United States Ordinary and Volunteer Militia,
1792-1861. 466pp. BIP-59-03913. .... (777)
Rutman, Darrett Bruce. A Militant New World, 1607-1640:
America's First Generation, its Martial Spirit, its Tradition
of Arms, its Militia Organization, its Wars. 838pp.
BIP-59-04245. .... (777)
Wesley, Edgar B. Guarding the Frontier: A Study of Frontier
Defense from 1815-1825. Repr. of 1935 ed. 9.75 ..... (297)

War of 1812

Volkel, Lowell. War of 1812 Bounty Land Patents in Illinois
(Introduction by James D. Walker). Repr. of 1840 ed. 380pp.
Includes name of patentee, to whom patent was delivered,
patent date, warrant number, service and land
description. 15.00 ..... (330)

Mexican War

Los Angeles Temple Genealogical Library. Surname Index to
Tyler's History of the Mormon Battalion in the Mexican War,
1846-1847. 1974. 12pp. 2.50 ..... (439)

Civil War - Research Aids

Dornbusch, Charles E. Military Bibliographies of the Civil War,
Volume II. 1967. 270pp.
Regimental publications and personal narratives: southern,
border, and western states and territories; federal
troops, union, and Confederate biographies. 20.00 (635)
_____. Military Bibliographies of the Civil War, Volume III.
1972. 224pp.
General references, armed forces, campaign and battles. 20.00 ..... (635)
Long, E. B. and Barbara Long. Civil War Day by Day: An
Almanac, 1861-1865. 1971. 17.50 ..... (203)
Nevins, Allan, et al., eds. Civil War Books; A Critical
Bibliography. 2 vols. Set: 20.00 ..... (440)
Each: 11.50 ..... (440)

Civil War - General Reference

Confederate Soldiers and Sailors Who Died as Prisoners of War
at Camp Butler, Illinois 1862-1865, comp. Alexis A. Praus.
1972. 26pp.
    Lists the name, rank, company, regiment, date of
    death and place of burial of 766 Confederate veterans.   6.00 ..... (293)
Confederate Soldiers, Sailors and Civilians Who Died As
Prisoners of War at Camp Douglas, Illinois, 1862-1865.
1970. 55pp.
    Lists name, rank, company, regiment, date of death
    and place of burial of 4454 Confederate veterans.   6.00 ..... (293)
Donnelly, Ralph W. Service Records of Confederate States
Enlisted Marines. 1977. c120pp. In Process.
    Contains information on over 1200 enlisted men,
    basically from official records but will contain some
    personal material.   6.00 ..... (200)
Ferguson, Joseph. Life-Struggles in Rebel Prisons: A Record
of the Sufferings, Escapes, Adventures and Starvation of
the Union Prisoners. 1865. 242pp. B-BH 16788.   .... (778)
Hesseltine, William B. Civil War Prisons (Original Title: Civil
War History, Volume 8, No. 2). 1972.   6.00 1.95 (405)
Jones, Charles Colcock. A Roster of General Officers, Heads of
Departments, Senators, Representatives, Military Organiza-
tions. . . in Confederate Service During the War Between the
States. 1876. 138pp. B-BH 21436.   .... (778)
McSwain, Mrs. Eleanor Davis. Crumbling Defenses, Memoirs
of Colonel John Logan Black, C.S.A. 1960. 191pp.
    Experiences of Colonel Black in Hampton's Brigade in
    the War Between the States. Index.   6.00 ..... (458)
Murdock, Eugene E. Patriotism Limited 1862-1865: The Civil
War Draft and the Bounty System. 1967.   7.95 ..... (405)
Smart, James G., ed. A Radical View: The "Agate" Dispatches
of Whitelaw Reid, 1861-1865. 2 vols. Repr. of 1861-1865 ed.
516pp.
    Front-line Civil War reports from the New York Tribune;
    many personal glimpses.   Set: 20.00 ..... (476)
Soldiers National Cemetary Association, comp. Names of All
the Officers and Privates Who Fell in the Battle of Gettysburg.
1864. 155pp. B-OP 45832.   .... (778)
Starr, Stephen Z. Jennison's Jayhawkers: A Civil War Cavalry
Regiment and Its Commander. 1973.   12.95 ..... (440)
Wilson, LeGrand J. The Confederate Soldier. Repr. of 1902 ed.
232pp.
    Memoirs of everyday life of common soldier, by a doctor
    in a Mississippi regiment.   8.95 ..... (476)

Indians

Curtis, Mary B. Bibliography of the Five Civilized Tribes -
Cherokee, Chickasaw, Choctaw, Creek and Seminole. 1972.
56pp. 5.00 (371)
The Genealogical Society of The Church of Jesus Christ of Latter-
day Saints. Major Genealogical Record Sources of Indians in
the United States. 4pp.   ..... .85 (275)
Hodge, Frederick Webb, ed. Handbook of American Indians
North of Mexico. 2 vols. Repr. of 1907-1910 ed. Vol. 1-927pp.
Vol. 2-1221pp.   Set: 40.00 ..... (661)

Hubbard, Jeremiah. Forty Years Among the Indians. Repr. of
1913 ed. 211pp.   12.50   8.50 (80)
McKenny, Thomas L. and James Hall. Indian Tribes of North
America. 3 vols. Repr. of 1934 ed. 1255pp.   Set: 100.00 ..... (661)

Negroes

Colored American Magazine. Volumes 1-17/No. 5 (All Published).
Repr. of 1900-1909 ed.   765.00 ..... (297)
Cunard, Nancy. Negro Anthology. Repr. of 1934 ed. 854pp.   97.50 ..... (297)
Mather, Frank Lincoln, ed. Who's Who of the Colored Race.
Repr. of 1915 ed. 296pp.   28.00 ..... (266)
NAACP. Crisis: A Record of the Darker Races, Volumes 1-47.
Repr. of 1910-1940 ed.   Set: 675.00 ..... (297)
Quarles, Benjamin. The Negro in the Civil War. Repr. of 1953
ed. xvi, 379pp.   15.00 ..... (662)
Rawick, George P., ed. The American Slave: A Composite
Autobiography. 19 vols. 1972.
    2000 ex-slaves were interviewed by the Federal Writers'
    Project and Fisk University in the 1920's and 1930's.
                          Set: 450.00 ..... (297)
Siebert, Wilbur Henry. The Underground Railroad from Slavery
to Freedom. Repr. of 1898 ed. xxv, 478pp.   15.00 ..... (662)

Heraldry

Barber, Richard. The Knight and Chivalry. 2d ed. 1975. 400pp.   12.50 ..... (661)
Brault, Gerard J. Eight Thirteenth-Century Rolls of Arms in French
and Anglo-Norman Blazon. 1973. 160pp.   15.00 ..... (589)
Briggs, Geoffrey, ed. Civic and Corporate Heraldry: A Dictionary
of Impersonal Arms of England, Wales, and Northern Ireland.
1971.   32.00 ..... (266)
Clark, Hugh. An Introduction to Heraldry. 18th ed. Repr. of
1866 ed. 279pp. illus.   12.00 ..... (661)
Fairbairn, James. Fairbairn's Crests of the Families of Great
Britain and Ireland. Reprint. 800pp.   20.00 ..... (772)
Fox-Davies, A. C., comp. and ed., Armorial Families: A
Directory of Gentlemen of Coat-Armour. 2 vols. 2248pp. Set: 35.00 ..... (772)
Grant, Francis J. The Manual of Heraldry. Repr. of 1929 ed.
142pp.
    Covers fundamentals and origin of heraldry.   9.00 ..... (266)
Holden, Edward S. A Primer of Heraldry for Americans. Repr.
of 1898 ed. 105pp.   9.50 ..... (266)
Parker, James. A Glossary of Terms Used in Heraldry. 692pp.   8.25 ..... (772)
Pine, L. G. International Heraldry. 244pp.   6.00 ..... (772)
_____. The Story of Heraldry. 164pp.   5.25 ..... (772)
_____. The Story of Titles. 176pp.   4.75 ..... (772)
Wagner, Anthony. Historic Heraldry of Britain. Repr. of 1939
ed. 118pp. illus.   14.50 ..... (661)
Whitmore, William H. Elements of Heraldry. Repr. of 1866 ed.
114pp.   2.75 ..... (772)
Williams, Geoffrey. The Heraldry of the Cinque Ports. 190pp.   6.50 ..... (772)
Woodward, John and George Burnett. Woodward's Treatise on
Heraldry: British and Foreign. Reprint. 896pp.   19.95 ..... (772)

Miscellaneous

Bremer, Ronald A. Things Interesting. 1975. 30pp.
    A motivational work pertaining to history, epitaphs,
    anecdotes, inspiration, humour, censuses, parish registers. 3.00 (272)

Research Sources By Locality

Alabama

Listed below is the name of a professional genealogist willing to undertake research for a fee within the state of Alabama, in the areas specified in her ad:

Foshee, John H. Alabama Canoe Rides and Float Trips. 1975.
263pp.
The author has canoed over more than 50 Alabama
waterways, taking meticulous notes and preparing
detailed maps and drawings. 4.95 (729)
Fry, Anna M. Gayle. Memories of Old Cahaba. Repr. of 1908
ed. 128pp.
An authentic historical sketch of Alabama's first
capital.   5.00 ..... (729)
Griffith, Lucille. Alabama: A Documentary History to 1900.
1972.   15.00 ..... (11)
Smith and Deland. Northern Alabama Historical and Biographical.
Repr. of 1888 ed. 776+pp. illus.   60.00 ..... (638)
Windham, Kathryn Tucker. Exploring Alabama. 1974. 257pp.
A history of the state of Alabama written in a narrative
style.   6.60 ..... (729)
Young, Mary E. Redskins, Ruffleshirts & Rednecks: Indian
Allotments in Alabama & Mississippi, 1830-1860. 1955.
305pp. BIP-00-15442.   .... (777)

Research Aids

Dodd, Donald B. Historical Atlas of Alabama. 1975.   10.00 ..... (11)
Lineback, Neal G., ed. Atlas of Alabama. 1973.   8.75 ..... (11)
Marks, Henry S. Who Was Who In Alabama. 1972. 200pp.
Brief biographies of deceased outstanding residents
of Alabama from beginning of recorded history through
1971.   12.95 ..... (729)
Strode Publishers, ed. Rivers of Alabama. 1968. 211pp.
Alabama's inland waterway system. Maps containing
original river sketches in each chapter.   6.95 ..... (729)

Records

United States Government. Territorial Papers. Vol. 18: The
Territory of Alabama, 1817-1819. Foundation of the Territory, 1816-1817. Administration of Governor Bibb,
1817-1819. 1952. Index.   57.50 ..... (2)

Military

Martin, Bessie. Desertion of Alabama Troops from the
Confederate Army. 1932.   12.50 ..... (2)
Owen, Thomas M. Revolutionary Soldiers in Alabama.
Repr. of 1911 ed. 131pp.   9.50 ..... (274)
Sterkx, H.E. Partners in Rebellion: Alabama Women in the
Civil War. 1970.   12.00 ..... (227)

BALDWIN COUNTY

"1830 Alabama U.S. Census: Baldwin Co." (Heads of household
as enumerated.) SGE Quarterly, Vol. 5, No. 31. 1964. 2pp. 2.50 (681)

BARBOUR COUNTY

Besson, J.A.B. The History of Eufaula, Alabama, the Bluff
City of the Chattahoochee. Repr. of 1875 ed. 63pp.   7.50 ..... (638)

BIBB COUNTY

"1830 Alabama U.S. Census: Bibb Co." (Heads of household
as enumerated.) SGE Quarterly, Vol. 12, No. 57. 1971. 6pp. 2.00 (681)

Hendrix, Ge Lee Corley. The 1850 Federal Census of Bibb
    County, Alabama. 1973. 126pp.
        Transcribed from National Archives Microfilm,
        Microcopy No. 432 Roll 2, Alabama per se as to Dwelling,
        Family number, Names, etc. 10.00 (326)

BLOUNT COUNTY

"1830 Alabama U.S. Census: Blount Co." (Heads of household
    as enumerated.) SGE Quarterly, Vol. 9, No. 49. 1968. 5pp. 2.50 (681)

BUTLER COUNTY

"1830 Alabama U. S. Census: Butler County." (Heads of household
    as enumerated.) SGE Quarterly, Vol. 10, No. 49. 1969. 5pp. 2.50 (681)
"1840 Alabama Census: Butler County." (Heads of households
    as enumerated.) SGE Quarterly, Vol. 19, No. 35. 1965. 4pp. 2.50 (681)

CLARKE COUNTY

"1830 Alabama U.S. Census: Clarke County." (Heads of house-
    holds as enumerated.) SGE Quarterly, Vol. 6, No. 33. 1961. 4pp. 2.50 (681)

CONECUH COUNTY

"1830 Alabama U. S. Census: Conecuh County." (Heads of house-
    hold as enumerated.) SGE Quarterly, Vol. 14, No. 66. 1973. 5pp...... 2.50 (681)

COVINGTON COUNTY

Bryan, Gus. Chronicles of Covington County, Alabama. Aug. 1976. .... (371)
"1830 Alabama U. S. Census: Covington County." (Heads of house-
    hold as enumerated.) SGE Quarterly, Vol. 15, No. 69. 1974. 2pp. 2.50 (681)

DALE

"1830 Alabama U. S. Census: Dale County." (Heads of household
    as enumerated.) SGE Quarterly, Vol. 2, No. 11. 1959. 3pp. 2.00 (681)

DALLAS COUNTY

"1830 Alabama U. S. Census: Dallas County." (Heads of house-
    holds as enumerated.) SGE Quarterly, Vol. 6, No. 35. 1965. 6pp. 2.50 (681)

FAYETTE COUNTY

"1830 Alabama U. S. Census: Fayette County." (Heads of house-
    hold as enumerated.) SGE Quarterly, Vol. 14, No. 68. 1973. 4pp. 2.50 (681)

FRANKLIN COUNTY

"1830 Alabama U. S. Census: Franklin County." (Heads of household
    as enumerated.) SGE Quarterly, Vol. 11, No. 56. 1970. 8pp. 2.50 (681)

GREENE COUNTY

"1830 Alabama U. S. Census: Greene County." (Heads of household
    as enumerated.) SGE Quarterly, Vol. 15, No. 70. 1974. 10pp. 2.50 (681)

HENRY COUNTY

"1830 Alabama U. S. Census: Henry County." (Heads of household
    as enumerated.) SGE Quarterly, Vol. 2, No. 12. 1959. 4pp. 2.50 (681)

JACKSON COUNTY

"1830 Alabama U. S. Census: Jackson County." (Heads of household
as enumerated.) SGE Quarterly, Vol. 5, No. 32. 1964. 5pp. 2.50 (681)

JEFFERSON COUNTY

"1830 Alabama U. S. Census: Jefferson County." (Heads of household
as enumerated.) SGE Quarterly, Vol. 7, No. 36. 1966. 5pp. 2.50 (681)

Elovitz, Mark H. A Century of Jewish Life in Dixie: The Birmingham
Experience. 1974.   10.00 ..... (11)

Jackson, Dorothy Belle. The Growth of an Industrial City, Birmingham,
1800-1851. 241pp. BIP-70-02838.   .... (777)

LAUDERDALE COUNTY

"1830 Alabama U. S. Census: Lauderdale County." (Heads of household as enumerated.) SGE Quarterly, Vol. 7, No. 39. 1966. 8pp. 2.50 (681)

LAWRENCE COUNTY

"1830 Alabama Census: Lawrence County." (Heads of household
as enumerated.) SGE Quarterly, Vol. 7, No. 38. 1966. 8pp. 2.50 (681)

LIMESTONE COUNTY

"1830 Alabama Census: Limestone County." (Heads of household
as enumerated.) SGE Quarterly, Vol. 8, No. 42. 1967. 10pp. 2.50 (681)

LOWNDES COUNTY

"1830 Alabama Census: Lowndes County." (Heads of household
as enumerated.) SGE Quarterly, Vol. 13, No. 64. 1972. 6nn.   · ·· ..   2.50 (681)

MADISON COUNTY

"1830 Alabama Census: Madison County." (Heads of household
as enumerated.) SGE Quarterly, Vol. 3, No. 24. 1962. 11pp. 2.50 (681)

Huntsville Directory, 1859-60. Repr. of 1859 ed. 168pp.
Text and illustrations about community and business life
in a Southern city just before the Civil War.   6.00 ..... (729)

Johnson, Dorothy Scott. Cemeteries of Madison County, Vol. II.
Fall, 1976.
Covers northeast quarter of county including communities
of New Market, Plevna, Walnut Grove, Union Grove, Deposit,
Maysville, Brownsboro, Moontown; over 100 cemeteries.
Includes census and marriage records when available.   .... (389)

_____. Madison County, Alabama Deed Books A-3, 1810-1819.
All deeds 1810-1819; includes wills, estate settlements,
servant and minor indentures, deeds, etc. Covers 1349
instruments and 1055 family names. Fully indexed. There
is a synopsis of each instrument, much more than an abstract. 10.00 (389)

MARENGO COUNTY

"1830 Alabama Census: Marengo County." (Heads of household
as enumerated.) SGE Quarterly, Vol. 4, No. 26. 1963. 4pp. 2.50 (681)

Phillips, Oma Dee. 1830 Census. 1968. 19pp.
Indexed-Offset Printing. 3.50 (596)

MARION COUNTY

"1830 Alabama Census: Marion County." (Heads of household
as enumerated.) SGE Quarterly, Vol. 4, No. 25. 1963. 3pp. 2.50 (681)

MOBILE COUNTY

"1830 Alabama Census: Mobile County and City." (Heads of household as enumerated.) SGE Quarterly, Vol. 12, No. 58. 1971. 7pp. 2.50 (681)

Burial Records, Mobile County, Alabama 1820-1856. Vol. 1.
Repr. of 1963 ed. 10.00 (502)

Burial Records, Mobile County, Alabama, 1857-1870. Vol. 2
Repr. of 1971 ed. 10.00 (502)

MONROE COUNTY

"1830 Alabama Census: Monroe County." (Heads of households as enumerated.) SGE Quarterly, Vol. 13, No. 63. 1972. 6pp. 2.50 (681)

MONTGOMERY COUNTY

"1830 Alabama Census: Montgomery County." (Heads of households as enumerated.) SGE Quarterly, Vol. 12. No. 60. 1971. 8pp .. 2.50 (681)

MORGAN COUNTY

"1830 Alabama Census: Morgan County." (Heads of households as enumerated.) SGE Quarterly, Vol. 6, No. 35. 1965. 5pp. 2.50 (681)

PERRY COUNTY

"1830 Alabama Census: Perry County." (Heads of households as enumerated.) SGE Quarterly, Vol. 3, No. 22. 1962. 5pp. 2.50 (681)

PICKENS COUNTY

"1830 Alabama Census: Pickens County." (Heads of households as enumerated.) SGE Quarterly. Vol. 13. No. 61. 1972. 6pp. 2.50 (681)

PIKE COUNTY

"1830 Alabama Census: Pike County." (Heads of households as enumerated.) SGE Quarterly, Vol. 8, No. 41. 1967. 7pp. 2.50 (681)

ST. CLAIR COUNTY

"1830 Alabama Census: St. Clair County." (Heads of households as enumerated.) SGE Quarterly, Vol. 8, No. 43. 1967. 5pp. 2.50 (681)

Crow, Mattie Lou Teague. A History of St. Clair County (Alabama). 1973. 205pp.
A well-documented and carefully written history of St. Clair County in Alabama. 10.00 ..... (729)

SHELBY COUNTY

"1830 Alabama Census: Shelby County." (Heads of households as enumerated.) SGE Quarterly, Vol. 14, No. 62. 1972. 5pp. 2.50 (681)

TUSCALOOSA COUNTY

"1830 Alabama Census: Tuscaloosa County." (Heads of households as enumerated.) SGE Quarterly. Vol 14 No 67. 1973. 10pp..... 2.50 (681)

WALKER COUNTY

"1830 Alabama Census: Walker County." (Heads of households as enumerated.) SGE Quarterly, Vol. 7, No. 40. 1966. 2pp. 2.50 (681)

WASHINGTON COUNTY

"1830 Alabama Census: Washington County." (Heads of households
as enumerated.) SGE Quarterly, Vol. 15, No. 69. 1974. 3pp. 2.50 (681)

WILCOX COUNTY

"1830 Alabama Census: Wilcox County." (Heads of households
as enumerated.) SGE Quarterly, Vol. 14, No. 65. 1973. 6pp. 2.50 (681)

Alaska

STATEWIDE REFERENCES

Phillips, James W. Alaska-Yukon Place Names. 1973.   6.95   ..... (814)

Arizona

STATEWIDE REFERENCES

Ahnert, Gerald T., Retracing the Butterfield Trail in Arizona.   9.75   ..... (829)
Arizona State Genealogical Society. Copper State Bulletin.
  Quarterly publication. Emphasis on Arizona and the South-
  west; containing primary source material, marriage,
  cemetery, bible, naturalization, etc; articles; queries;
  social calender and news.
  (Complete set of 41 back issues, 1965-75, $45)   Subscription: $5/yr (34)
Briggs, L. Vernon. Arizona & New Mexico 1882; California
  1886; Mexico 1891. 1932.   20.00   ..... (38)
Colton, Ray Charles. The American Civil War in the Western
  Territories of New Mexico, Arizona, Colorado and Utah.
  BIP-00-11882. 323pp.   .... (777)
Dobyns, Henry F. "Spanish/Colonial Sources for Genealogical
  Research in Southern Arizona." Copper State Bulletin, Vol. X,
  No. 4. 1975. 8pp. 1.50 (34)
Eterovich, Adam S. Yugoslav Survey of California, Nevada,
  Arizona & the South, 1830-1900.   7.00   ..... (631)
Faulk, Odie B. Arizona: A Short History. 1970. illus.   4.95   2.95 (556)
Henderson, Patrick C. The Public Domain in Arizona: 1863-
  1891. BIP-66-08507. 276pp.   .... (777)
Kessell, John L. Friars, Soldiers, & Reformers: Hispanic
  Arizona & the Sonora Mission Frontier, 1767-1856.   .... (33)
Lockwood, Frank C. Pioneer Portraits. 1968.   .....   4.95 (33)
McClintock, James. Mormon Settlement in Arizona. Repr. of .
  1921 ed.   14.00   ..... (2)
Mowry, Sylvester, Arizona and Sonora: The Geography, History,
  and Resources of the Silver Region of North America. 3rd ed.   12.00   ..... (38)
Peterson, Charles S. Take Up Your Mission: Mormon Colonizing
  Along the Little Colorado River, 1870-1900. 1973.   9.50   ..... (33)

Research Aids

Bahre, Stephen. Place Names in Arizona Counties.   .... (33)
Granger, Byrd H. Arizona Place Names. 2d ed. 1960.   10.00   ..... (33)

Records

Arizona State Genealogical Society, comp. Arizona Death
Records: An Index Compiled from Mortuary, Cemetery
& Church Records. 2 vols. Fall 1976. 1500pp total.
Includes 179 cemeteries. An official Arizona
Bicentennial Project. Also available unbound & 16mm
microfilm.   Pre-publication: 38.50 ..... (34)

MARICOPA COUNTY

Buchanan, James E. Phoenix: A Chronological and Documentary
History. 1976. 160pp.   7.50 ..... (551)

PIMA COUNTY

An Index to the Parker Mortuary Records, Tucson, Arizona,
1897-1912. 50pp. 5.00 (34)
Pima County, Arizona Marriage Records, 1872-1902. 66pp. 7.00 (34)

Arkansas

STATEWIDE REFERENCES

Arkansas Historical Quarterly.
The Quarterly is regarded by researchers as a permanent
reference work on Arkansas and regional history. It has
published not only important official documents and other
source materials, but also scholarly articles treating
various aspects of the state's history which demonstrate
its relationship to national history.

Vols. 1-15 - Fayetteville, 1942-1956:	Set:	265.00	225.00 (415)
	Each:	.....	15.00 (415)
Vols. 16-27 - Fayetteville, 1957-1968:	Set:	276.00	216.00 (415)
	Each:	.....	18.00 (415)

Belser, Thomas Arvin, Jr. Military Operations in Missouri
and Arkansas, 1861-1865. BIP-58-05265. 786pp.   .... (777)
Clark, Mrs. Larry P., comp. Arkansas Pioneers and Allied
Families. Fall 1976. c600pp.
A personal history of members, including pioneer an-
cestor and their descendants.   .... (145)
Leslie, James W. Saracen's Country: Some Southeast Arkansas
History. 1974.   7.95   ..... (655)
Moore, Waddy William. Territorial Arkansas, 1819-1836.
BIP-64-01875. 391pp.   .... (777)

Listed below are the names of professional genealogists willing to undertake research for a
fee within the state of Arkansas, in the areas specified to their ads:

Nuttall, Thomas. Journal of Travels into the Arkansas Territory
During the Year 1819. Repr. of 1821 ed.   7.75   ..... (778)
"Pioneer Sketches by S.C. Turnbo." The Ridge Runners, Vol. 4.
1976. 10pp.   .... (859)
Presley, Mrs. Leister E. and Imogene Rowe. Surname List -
1870 Census.
Surname list, with family number, by county.   .... (619)
Schoolcraft, Henry Rowe. Journal of a Tour Into the Interior of
Missouri and Arkansas, from Potosi, Or Mine a Burton, in
Missouri Territory, in a South-West Direction, Toward the
Rocky Mountains, Performed in the Years 1818 and 1819.
1821.   10.00   ..... (2)
Stokes, Dewey Allen, Jr. Public Affairs in Arkansas, 1836-
1850. BIP-66-14447. 462pp.   .... (777)
United States Government. Territorial Papers. Volume 20:
The Territory of Arkansas, 1825-1829. The third administra-
tion of Acting Governor Crittenden, 1825. The two administra-
tions of Governor Izard, 1825-1828. The fourth administration
of Acting Governor Crittenden, 1828-1829. 1954. Index.   57.50   ..... (2)
Walz, Robert B. Migration into Arkansas, 1834-1880. 1958.
601pp. BIP-58-01675.   .... (777)
Yates, William A. The Ridge Runners, Vol. IV. 1976. 321pp.
Genealogy: Virginia, North Carolina, Kentucky, Tennessee,
Indiana, Illinois, Missouri, Arkansas. 10.00 (859)

BENTON COUNTY

History of Benton, Washington, Carroll, Madison, Crawford,
Franklin, and Sebastian Counties, Arkansas. 1889.
Vol. 1-244pp, Vol. 2-340pp, Vol. 3-486pp, Vol. 4 -372pp.
B-BH 2010.   .... (778)

CARROLL COUNTY

"1840 Arkansas U.S. Census: Carroll County." (Alphabetized
list of all heads of households and township names.)
SGE Quarterly, Vol. 2, No. 21. 1962. 3pp. 2.50 (681)
History of Benton, Washington, Carroll, Madison, Crawford,
Franklin, and Sebastian Counties, Arkansas. 1889.
Vol. 1-244pp, Vol. 2-340pp, Vol. 3-486pp, Vol. 4-372pp.
B-BH 2010.   .... (778)

CONWAY COUNTY

"1840 Arkansas U.S. Census: Conway County." (Alphabetized
list of all heads of households and township names.)
SGE Quarterly, Vol. 1, No. 4. 1957. 5pp. 2.00 (681)

CRAWFORD COUNTY

History of Benton, Washington, Carroll, Madison, Crawford,
Franklin, and Sebastian Counties, Arkansas. 1889.
Vol. 1-244pp, Vol. 2 -340pp, Vol. 3-486pp, Vol. 4-372pp.
B-BH 2010.   .... (778)

CROSS COUNTY

Hartness, Richard L. A Postal Directory of the Cross County
Arkansas Area. 1975. 23pp.

This is a list of all the postmasters in the Cross County, Arkansas Area from March 1, 1826 to September, 1975.   .....   2.00 (170)

FAULKNER COUNTY

Rowe, Imogene. Copper Springs Cemetery - Guy, Arkansas. 1974. 26pp. 2.00 (619)

FRANKLIN COUNTY

History of Benton, Washington, Carroll, Madison, Crawford, Franklin, and Sebastian Counties, Arkansas. 1889. Vol. 1-244pp, Vol. 2-340pp, Vol. 3-486pp, Vol. 4-372pp. B-BH 2010.   .... (778)

INDEPENDENCE COUNTY

Wolf, John Quincy. Life in the Leatherwoods. 1974. 172pp. Memoirs of growing up in backwoods Arkansas in 1860's-1880's.   8.95   3.95 (476)

MADISON COUNTY

History of Benton, Washington, Carroll, Madison, Crawford, Franklin, and Sebastian Counties, Arkansas. 1889. Vol. 1-244pp, Vol. 2-340pp, Vol. 3-486pp, Vol. 4-372pp. B-BH 2010.   .... (778)

MISSISSIPPI COUNTY

Baird, W. David, ed. Years of Discontent: Frank L. James in Arkansas, 1877-1878. 1976. 88pp. Gossipy diary with many local references. 5.00 (476)

POPE COUNTY

Pope County Genealogy Society. Cemeteries of Pope County, Arkansas, Vol. I. 1973. 145pp. Contains cemeteries Adams through Guest plus map locating each cemetery. 5.00 (610)
_____. Cemeteries of Pope County, Arkansas, Vol. II. 1973. 139pp. Contains cemeteries Hale through Owens, plus map locating each cemetery. 5.00 (610)
_____. Cemeteries of Pope County, Arkansas, Vol. III. 1973. 105pp. Contains cemeteries Pascal through Van Zandt, plus map locating each cemetery. 4.00 (610)
_____. Cemeteries of Pope County, Arkansas, Vol. IV. 1973. 140pp. Has cemeteries Walker through Zion Hill. Contains an index for all four volumes plus map locating cemeteries. 5.00 (610)
_____. United States Census of 1870 Pope County, Arkansas. 1975. 274pp. Contains a general index plus legal description and map for each township in 1870.   .....   15.00 (610)
_____. United States Census of 1880 Pope County, Arkansas. 1976. In process.   .... (610)

SEARCY COUNTY

"1840 Arkansas U.S. Census: Searcy County." (Alphabetized list of all heads of households). SGE Quarterly, Vol. 1, No. 5. 1958. 2pp. 2.00 (681)

SEBASTIAN COUNTY

History of Benton, Washington, Carroll, Madison, Crawford, Franklin, and Sebastian Counties, Arkansas. 1889. Vol. 1-244pp. Vol. 2-340pp, Vol. 3-486pp, Vol. 4-372pp. B-BH 2010.   .... (778)

STONE COUNTY

Wolf, John Quincy. Life in the Leatherwoods. 1974. 172pp. Memoirs of growing up in backwoods Arkansas in 1860's - 1880's.   8.95   3.95 (476)

VAN BUREN COUNTY

Presley, Mrs. Leister E. Surname List - Van Buren County, Arkansas, 1860. With family number. 1975. 5pp. 1.50 (619)
_____ and Imogene Rowe. Surname List - Van Buren County, Arkansas, 1870 Census. With family number. 11pp. 2.50 (619)
Rowe, Imogene. Old Salem and Holland Cemeteries. 1974. 12pp. 2.00 (619)

WASHINGTON COUNTY

"1830 Arkansas U.S. Census: Washington County." (Heads of households as enumerated.) SGE Quarterly, Vol. 7, No. 37. 1966.   ..... 2.50 (681)
History of Benton, Washington, Carroll, Madison, Crawford, Franklin, and Sebastian Counties, Arkansas. 1889. Vol. 1-244pp, Vol. 2-340pp, Vol. 3-486pp, Vol. 4-372pp. B-BH 2010.   .... (778)

WHITE COUNTY

Johnson, Claude E. The Humorous History of White County, Arkansas. 1975. 132pp.
    A combination of folkways and historical statistics. 5.00 (619)
Presley, Mrs. Leister E. Cemeteries of White County, Arkansas - Volume I. 1969. 58pp. 3.00 (619)
_____. Cemeteries of White County, Arkansas - Volume II. 1970. 71pp. 3.00 (619)
_____. Cemeteries of White County, Arkansas - Volume III. 1970. 53pp. 3.00 (619)
_____. Cemeteries of White County, Arkansas - Volume IV. 1972. 63pp. 3.00 (619)
_____. Cemeteries of White County, Arkansas - Volume V. 1975. 50pp. 3.00 (619)
_____. Cemeteries of White County, Arkansas - Volume VI. 1976. 50pp. 3.00 (619)
_____. Tax List, White County, Arkansas, 1836. 5pp. 1.50 (619)

California

STATEWIDE REFERENCES

Alvina, Rose H. Spanish & Mexican Land Grants in California. 7.00 (631)

Briggs, L. Vernon. Arizona & New Mexico 1882; California 1886;
Mexico 1891. Repr. of 1932 ed.   20.00 ..... (38)

Clavigero, Francisco J. History of Lower California. ed.
A.A. Gray. tr. Sara E. Lake. Repr. of 1937 ed.   25.00 ..... (462)

Cleland, Robert. History of California. Repr. of 1930 ed.   25.00 ..... (297)

Cronise, Titus Fey. The Natural Wealth of California.
1868. 696pp. index.
    Comprising early history, geography, typography and
    scenery; climate; agriculture and commercial products;
    geology; zoology and botany; mineralogy; mines and
    mining processes; manufactures; steamship lines, rail-
    roads, and commerce; immigration, population and
    society; educational institutions and literature; together
    with a detailed description of each county.   27.50 ..... (273)

Forbes, Alexander. California: A History of Upper and Lower
California From Their First Discovery to the Present Time.
1839.
    Comprising an account of the climate, soil, natural
    productions, agriculture, commerce etc. A full view
    of the missionary establishments and condition of the
    free and domesticated Indians.   18.00 ..... (38)

Guest, Florian Francis. Municipal Institutions in Spanish
California, 1769-1821. BIP-62-01317. 348pp.   .... (777)

Hastings, Lansford W. Emigrants Guide to Oregon & California. 2d ed. 1969.   17.50 ..... (176)

Kemble, Edward C. History of California Newspapers, 1846-
1859. ed. Helen H. Bretnor. 1962.   10.00 ..... (742)

Richey, Elinor. Remain to Be Seen. 1973. 180pp.
    112 historic California houses restored and now open to
    the public.   8.50 ..... (357)

Ross, Ivy B. The Confirmation of Spanish & Mexican Land
Grants in California: Thesis. 1974.   ..... 8.00 (631)

Royce, Josiah. California from the Conquest in 1846 to the
Second Vigilance Committee in San Francisco, 1856. A
Study of American Character. 1886.   27.50 ..... (2)

Stein, Walter Joseph. California and the Dust Bowl Migration.
BIP-70-02630. 525pp.   .... (777)

Stevenson, Robert L. From Scotland to Silverado: The Amateur
Emigrant, from the Clyde to Sandy Hook, Across the Plains,
the Silverado Squatters & Four Essays on California. ed.
James Hart. 3.95 (319)

Wyman, Walker D. California Emigrant Letters. Repr. of
1952 ed.   10.50 ..... (2)

Ethnic Groups

Beatty, Donald R. History of the Legal Status of the American
Indian, with Particular Reference to California. 1957: Thesis
History 1492-1848. Legal status during American
control 1848-1865. Post Civil War 1865-1900. Treaty
arrangements, wardship. Reorganization Act of 1934.
With bibliography. 8.00 (631)

Bunje, Emil T. Russian California: 1805-1841. 1970.   .....   7.00 (631)
California Department of Industrial Relations. Facts About
Filipino Immigration Into California. Repr. of 1930 ed.
76pp.
A rare study on the Filipino. No document will
give you as much information on this subject as
this fact book. 7.00 (631)
Dyer, Ruth C. The Indians' Land Title In California: A
Case in Federal Equity, 1851-1942. 1945.
Will be helpful for the study of law, title, and
ethnicity regarding the native Americans. 8.00 (631)
Eterovich, Adam S. Jugoslav California Marriages: 1880-
1948. 1968.   .....   3.00 (631)
_____. Jugoslav Census of Population - California 1850-
1880. 1968.   .....   3.00 (631)
_____. Yugoslav Survey of California, Nevada, Arizona &
the South. 1830-1900.   7.00   ..... (631)
Glanz, Rudolf. The Jews of California. 1960.   7.50   ..... (417)
Gudde, Erwin G. German Pioneers of Early California.
Repr. of 1927 ed. 3.00 (631)
Haiman, Mieczyslaw. Polish Pioneers of California. Repr.
of 1940 ed. 5.00 (631)
Hammon, George P. German Interest in California Before
1850: Thesis. 1921.   .....   7.00 (631)
Hatch, Flora F. The Russian Advance Into California: Thesis.
1972.   .....   7.00 (631)
Hughes, David. Welsh People of California 1849-1906.   .....   7.00 (631)
Kosberg, Milton. The Polish Colony of California, 1876-1914:
Thesis. 1952.   .....   7.00 (631)
Lopez, Charlos U. Chilenos in California: A Study of the
1850, 1852 & 1860 Censuses.   10.00   ..... (631)
Mahakian, Charles. History of Armenians in California:
Thesis. 1974.   .....   8.00 (631)
Maynard, Douglas H. British Pioneers in California: Thesis.
1974.   .....   9.00 (631)
Morefield, Richard H. The Mexican Adaptation in American
California, 1846-1875: Thesis. Reprint of 1955 ed.   9.00   ..... (631)
Prendergast, Thomas F. Forgotten Pioneers: Irish Leaders
in Early California. 1942.   13.00   ..... (81)
Schofer, Jerry P. Urban and Rural Finnish Communities in
California: 1860-1960. 1975.
Covers emigration, early settlements, occupations,
settlement centers, immigration into California.
Also covers social cohesion, churches, brotherhoods,
co-ops, saunas, names and newspapers - includes
bibliography. 8.00 (631)
Thompson, R. A. The Russian Settlement in California. 3.00 (631)

Black People

Beasley, Delialah L. Negro Trail Blazers of California.   17.25   ..... (522)
_____. The Negro Trail Blazers of California. Repr. of
1919 ed.   15.00   ..... (631)
California State Convention of Colored Citizens for 1855,
1856, & 1865. Proceedings. 1969.   8.00   ..... (631)
Goode, Kenneth G. California's Black Pioneers: A Brief
Historical Survey.   6.95   3.50 (457)

Thurman, Odell A. The Negro in California Before 1890:
Thesis. Repr. of 1945 ed.
Excellent historical coverage of early California.
Fills a void and is adequate in all respects. 7.00 (631)
Thurman, Sue. Pioneers of Negro Origin in California.
Repr. of 1952 ed. 7.00 ..... (631)

Research Aids

Beck, Warren A. and Ynez P. Haase. Historical Atlas of
California. 1975. illus. 9.95 4.95 (556)
California Historical Society. Index to California Historical
Society Quarterly, Vol. 1 to 40. 15.00 10.00 (111)
Coy, Owen C. California County Boundaries. rev. ed.
1973. illus. 15.00 ..... (786)
Gudde, Erwin G. California Place Names: The Origin &
Etymology of Current Geographical Names. 1969.
449pp. 15.75 ..... (112)
Los Angeles Temple Genealogical Library. A Catalogue of
Holdings of the Los Angeles Temple Genealogical
Library, 1976 ed. 3-5 vols. Spring 1977. .... (439)
Rocq, Margaret M., ed. California Local History: A
Bibliography & Union List of Library Holdings. 2d ed.
1970. 35.00 ..... (714)
Suzuki, June and Marjorie Pulliam. California Imprints. 1961. 15.00 ..... (742)
Weber, Francis J. A Select Bibliographical Guide to
California History. 1972. 7.50 ..... (184)

Gold Rush

Audubon, John W. and John Audubon. Western Journals of
John Woodhouse Audubon, Mexico, California, Arizona,
1849-1850. Repr. of 1906 ed. 8.00 ..... (644)
Baldwin, Joseph G. Flush Times of California. eds. Richard
E. Amacher and George W. Polhemus. 1966. ..... 3.50 (279)
Bateson, Charles. Gold Fleet for California: Forty-Niners
from Australia & New Zealand. 1964. illus. 7.50 ..... (485)
Bingham, Edwin R., ed. California Gold (Selected Source
Materials for College Research Papers). 1959. ..... 2.95 (324)
Chamberlain, Newell D. Call of Gold: True Tales on the Gold
Road to Yosemite. 5.95 ..... (786)
Doble, John. John Doble's Journal & Letters from the Mines.
ed. Charles L. Camp. 1962. 22.50 ..... (557)
Gudde, Erwin G. California Gold Camps: A Geographical &
Historical Dictionary of Camps, Towns & Localities Where
Gold Was Found & Mines & of Wayside Stations & Trading
Centers. ed. Elisabeth K. Gudde. 1975. 477pp. 19.50 ..... (112)
Levinson, Robert Edward. The Jews in the California Gold
Rush. BIP-69-06642. .... (777)
Pahner, Stanley W. Death Valley Ghost Towns. 1973. 4.95 1.95 (528)
Perkins, William. Three Years in California: Journal of
Life at Sonora, 1849-1852. 1964. 12.50 ..... (112)
Rosenberger, Francis C., ed. The Robinson-Rosenberger
Journey to the Gold Fields of California, 1849-1850: The
Diary of Zirle D. Robinson. 1966. ..... 5.00 (801)
Ryan, William R. Personal Adventures in Upper & Lower
California, in 1848-1849. Repr. of 1850 ed. 36.00 ..... (38)
Walker, Ardis M. The Rough & the Righteous of the Kern
River Diggins. 1971. 15.00 ..... (571)

. . . .

Woods, Daniel B. Sixteen Months at the Gold Diggings. 1973.   . . . . .   2.95 (645)

ALAMEDA COUNTY

Pettitt, George. Berkeley: The Town and Gown of it. 1973.
210pp
    History of the City of Berkeley, California.   9.50 . . . . . (357)
Richey, Elinor. The Ultimate Victorians. 1970. 176pp.
Architectural, social and art history of San Francisco's
East Bay Area.   7.50 . . . . . (357)

AMADOR COUNTY

Mason, Jesse D. History of Amador County, California. 1881.
352pp. B-OP 134.   . . . . (778)
Sharfman, I. Harold. Jews of Jackson, California. 1969.   10.00 . . . . . (144)

BUTTE COUNTY

Book, Susan W. The Chinese in Butte County, California, 1860-
1920. 1976.
    This study, interestingly, focuses on the settlement of the
    Chinese in a Northern California county during the Gold
    Rush period, and continues through the period of their
    complete out-migration from the area (1920). Reasons
    for their migration-to California, their lifestyle, and
    particularly the discrimination experienced by the
    Chinese in California, are all examined in this study. 8.00 (631)
Wells, Harry L. and W. I. Chambers. History of Butte County,
California. Repr. of 1882 ed. 392pp.
    Facsimile edition of a rare "mug" book with 74 engravings.   22.50 . . . . . (357)

CONTRA COSTA COUNTY

Munro-Fraser, J. P., ed. History of Contra Costa County,
California. Repr. of 1882 ed.   20.00 . . . . . (94)
Richey, Elinor. The Ultimate Victorians. 1970. 176pp.
Architectural, social and art history of San Francisco's
East Bay Area.   7.50 . . . . . (357)

FRESNO COUNTY

Fresno Genealogical Society, comp. Cemetery Records of Fresno
and Madera counties. 1977.
    Book will contain records of all burials found and made
    before 1905 when California began official records of them.   . . . . (252)

INYO COUNTY

Pahner, Stanley W. Death Valley Ghost Towns. 1973.   4.95 1.95 (528)

KERN COUNTY

Kern County Genealogical Society. Kern County Cemeteries.
    Vol. I, Pt. I (1878-1882). 1967. 17pp. 2.00 (409)
_____. Kern County Cemeteries. Vol. I, Pt. II (1883-1904).
1967. 39pp. 5.00 (409)
_____. Kern-Gen Quarterly. 1964- . 30pp. Subscription/Yr. 2.50 (409)
Walker, Ardis M. Kern River Valley Vignettes. 1975.   . . . . . 1.95 (422)

LAKE COUNTY

History of Lake County - 1881. 1974.   20.00   ..... (786)

LASSEN COUNTY

Gilbert, F. T. and H. L. Wells. History of Plumas, Lassen
  and Sierra Counties, California. Repr. of 1882 ed. 688pp.
  Facsimile edition of fine source book with introduction
  by William H. Hutchinson.   22.50   ..... (357)

LOS ANGELES COUNTY

Bond, J. Max. The Negro in Los Angeles. Dissertation.
  Repr. of 1936 ed.
    One of the most comprehensive studies ever done on the
    Southern California Negro. A superior study.   9.00   ..... (631)
Bowman, Lynn. Los Angeles: Epic of a City. 1974. 406pp.
    Definitive history of a renowned metropolis of 78 cities.   10.00   ..... (357)
Carpenter, Edwin H. Early Cemeteries of the City of Los Angeles.   10.00   ..... (184)
Eterovich, Adam S. Jugoslavs in Los Angeles: 1733-1900. 1968.   .....   3.00 (631)
Fink, Augusta. Time and the Terraced Land. 1966. 140pp.
    Palos Verdes Peninsula, Los Angeles, from Indian and
    Spanish days to present.   7.50   ..... (357)
Lederer, Lillian C. A Study of Anglo-American Settlers in
  Los Angeles County Previous to the Admission of California
  to the Union: A Thesis. 1974.   .....   8.00 (631)
Lewis, Albert Lucian. Los Angeles in the Civil War Decades:
  1850 to 1868. 1970. 399pp. BIP-70-23169.   .... (777)
Mayer, Robert. Los Angeles: A Chronological and Documentary
  History. (American Cities Chronology Series). 1976. 160pp.   7.50   ..... (551)
Oxnam, G. Mexicans in Los Angeles. 1970.   .....   3.00 (631)
Thompson, Thomas and Albert West. History of Los Angeles
  County, California. Repr. of 1880 ed. 418 pp.
    Facsimile reprint of history of Los Angeles and Orange
    counties with introduction by W. W. Robinson.   22.50   ..... (357)
Vogeth, Lamberta. Germans in Los Angeles County, 1850-1909.
  Repr. of 1933 ed.   5.00   ..... (631)
Vorspan, Max and Lloyd P. Gartner. History of the Jews of
  Los Angeles. 1970.   8.50   ..... (363)
Yeretzian, Aram S. A History of Armenian Immigration to
  America with Special Reference to Los Angeles: Thesis. 1974.   .....   8.00 (631)

MADERA COUNTY

Fresno Genealogical Society, comp. Cemetery Records of Fresno
  and Madera counties. 1977.
    Book will contain records of all burials found and made
    before 1905 when California began official records of them.   .... (252)

MARIN COUNTY

History of Marin County, California. 1880. 636pp. B-OP 26632.   .... (778)

MARIPOSA COUNTY

Sargent, Shirley. Pioneers in Petticoats: Yosemite's First
  Women, 1856-1900.   3.95   ..... (765)

MONO COUNTY

Johnson, Anne. Ghost Town of Bodie.   4.95   2.25 (130)

NEVADA COUNTY

Thompson, Thomas and Albert West. History of Nevada County,
California. Repr. of 1880 ed. 410 pp.
Facsimile edition with introduction by W. Turrentine
Jackson.   22.50   ..... (357)

ORANGE COUNTY

Orange County California Genealogical Society. Orange County
California Genealogical Society Quarterly.
Contains records of California, the West, and the United
States: Bible records, census, vital, cemetery, probate;
reviews and queries. 44pp/issue, with topical and name
index annually.   Subscription/yr. 5.00 (559)
_____. Saddleback Ancestors. 1969. 182pp.
Families of Spanish, Mexican and American immigrants who,
1769-1869, settled on ranchos in Orange Co., California. 3.50 (559)
Peer, Marian R. Tombstone Inscriptions, Vol. I, Magnolia Memo-
rial Park Cemetery, Garden Grove, California. 1969. 24pp.
Dates from 1874 to 1967 included. 2.00 (559)
Thompson, Thomas and Albert West. History of Los Angeles Co.,
California. Reprint of 1880 ed. 418pp.
Facsimile reprint of history of Los Angeles and Orange
counties with introduction by W. W. Robinson.   22.50   ..... (357)

PLUMAS COUNTY

Gilbert, F. T. and H. L. Wells. History of Plumas, Lassen
and Sierra Counties, California. Repr. of 1882 ed. 688pp.
Facsimile edition of fine source book with introduction by
William H. Hutchinson.   22.50   ..... (357)

RIVERSIDE COUNTY

Genealogical Society of Riverside. Cemetery Records, Riverside
County, Series I. 8 1/2 x 11, mimeographed. 35pp. 2.00 (646)
_____. 1880 Federal Census of Riverside County, Including
Notes on Pioneers, History, Research Sources. 55pp.
Index to births: 1893-1905; marriages, 1893-1907;
deaths, 1893-1905. 8 1/2 x 11, offset. 4.50 (646)
_____. Lifeliner. Periodical of the Riverside Genealogical Soc.
Membership in society is $7.00 for individual and $8.00 for
families. Membership includes the "Lifeliner." Subscription: 5.00 (646)
_____. Vital Records: Newspaper Abstracts of Riverside County,
California, 1878-1892. 20pp.
Indexed, 8 1/2 x 11, mimeographed. 1.50 (646)

SACRAMENTO COUNTY

Thompson, Thomas and Albert West. History of Sacramento
County, California. Repr. of 1880 ed. 532pp.
Facsimile edition with introduction by Allan R. Ottley.   25.00   ..... (357)

SAN BERNARDINO COUNTY

Ingersoll, Luther A. Ingersoll's Century Annals of San Bernardino County, 1769 to 1904. 1904. 994pp. B-BH 21415.   .... (778)
Wood, Joseph Snow. The Mormon Settlement in San Bernardino,
1851-1857. 1968. 300pp. BIP-68-11113.   .... (777)

SAN DIEGO COUNTY

Mayer, Robert. San Diego: A Chronological and Documentary
History. (American Cities Chronology Series). 1976. 160pp.   7.50   ..... (551)

SAN FRANCISCO COUNTY

Beebe, Lucius and Charles Clegg. San Francisco's Golden Era.
1960. 253pp.
 A picture story of San Francisco before the 1906 fire-quake.   6.95   ..... (357)
Dickson, Samuel. Tales of San Francisco. 1955.   8.95   ..... (714)
Eterovich, Adam S. Jugoslav Cemetery Records in San Francisco,
1849-1930. 1968.   .....   3.00 (631)
_____. Jugoslavs in San Francisco: 1870-1875. 1968.   .....   3.00 (631)
Lewis, Oscar. San Francisco: Mission to Metropolis. 1966. 280pp.
 Total history of a great exciting city. 154 illustrations.   6.95   ..... (357)
Lortie, Francis M. San Francisco Black Community, 1870-1890.
Thesis. Repr. of 1970 ed.
 The struggle for equality in early San Francisco. A
 historical document.   7.00   ..... (631)
Lotchin, Roger W. San Francisco, 1846-1856: From Hamlet to
City. Illustrated. 1974.   12.50   ..... (566)
Mayer, Robert. San Francisco: A Chronological and Documentary
History. (American Cities Chronology Series). 1974. 160 pp.   7.50   ..... (551)
Myrick, David F. San Francisco's Telegraph Hill. 1972. 220pp.
 A colorful, eventful and unique area of the hilly city.
 284 illustrations.   9.95   ..... (357)
Radin, Paul. Italians in San Francisco. 1970.   .....   10.00 (631)
Rasmussen, Louis J. San Francisco Ship Passenger Lists. 5 vols.
Vol. 1, 1850-1875. 1965.   8.75   ..... (668)
_____. San Francisco Ship Passenger Lists. 5 vols. Vol. 2,
Apr. 6, 1850-Nov. 4, 1851. Vol. 3, Nov. 7, 1851-June 17, 1852.
Vol. 4, June 17, 1852-1853. 1966, 1967, 1970, 1973. VOLUME: 9.75   ..... (668)
_____. Railway Passenger Lists of Overland Trains to San Fran-
cisco and the West. 3 vols. Vol. 2, Nov. 12, 1871-April 23, 1873.
1968.   9.75   ..... (668)
Rogers, Fred B., ed. The California Star. Repr. of 1847-48 ed.
212pp.
 Facsimile reproduction of Sam Brannan's San Francsico
 newspaper of 1847-48.   20.00   ..... (357)
Soule, Frank. The annals of San Francisco. 1855. 860pp.
B-BH 5196.   .... (778)
Wetterman, August. The History and Review of the Scandinavian
Society of San Francisco. 1970.   .....   7.00 (631)

SAN JOAQUIN COUNTY

Jan Joaquin Genealogical Society. Marriage Records of San
Joaquin County, California, 1885-1889. Vol. III. 1975. 109pp.
 Contains both Groom Index and Bride Index. 7.50 (871)
Thompson, Thomas and Albert West. History of San Joaquin
County, California. Repr. of 1879 ed. 420pp.
 Facsimile edition with introduction by Robert E. Burns.   22.50   ..... (357)

SANTA BARBARA COUNTY

Thompson, Thomas and Albert West. History of Santa Barbara
and Ventura Counties, California. Repr. of 1882 ed. 478pp.
 Facsimile edition with introduction by Walker Tompkins.   22.50   ..... (357)
Tompkins, Walker A. Santa Barbara's Royal Rancho. 1960. 300pp.
 History of Spanish land grant from prehistoric Indian times.   6.00   ..... (357)

SANTA CLARA COUNTY

Bruntz, George G. History of Los Gatos: Gem of the Foothills.
Illustrated.   10.00   ..... (786)

SANTA CRUZ COUNTY

Koch, Margaret. Santa Cruz County: Parade of the Past. 1973.   12.95   ..... (786)

SHASTA COUNTY

Giles, Rosena A. Shasta County, California. Repr. of 1949 ed.   20.00   ..... (69)
Steger, Gertrude A. Place Names of Shasta County. Rev. ed. 1966. .....   2.00 (422)

SIERRA COUNTY

Gilbert, F. T. and H. L. Wells. History of Plumas, Lassen
and Sierra Counties, California. Repr. of 1882 ed. 688pp.   22.50   ..... (357)

SUTTER COUNTY

Thompson, Thomas and Albert West. History of Sutter County,
California. Repr. of 1879 ed. 274pp.   22.50   ..... (357)

VENTURA COUNTY

Thompson, Thomas and Albert West. History of Santa Barbara
and Ventura Counties, California. Repr. of 1882 ed. 478pp.   22.50   ..... (357)

Colorado

STATEWIDE REFERENCES

Bancroft, Hubert H. History of Nevada, Colorado and Wyoming.   7.00   ..... (51)
Colton, Ray Charles. The American Civil War in the Western
Territories of New Mexico, Arizona, Colorado and Utah.
1954. 323pp. BIP-00-11882.   .... (777)
Dorset, Phyllis F. The New Eldorado: The Colorado Gold
Rush. 1970.   12.50   ..... (454)
Fossett, Frank. Colorado: Its Gold and Silver Mines, Farms
and Stock Ranges, and Health and Pleasure Resorts. Tourist's
Guide to the Rocky Mountains. 1879.   26.00   ..... (38)
Guice, John D. W. The Territorial Supreme Courts of Colorado,
Montana and Wyoming, 1861-1890. 1969. 278pp. BIP-69-19539.   .... (777)
Henderson, Junius et. al. Colorado: Short Studies of It's Past
and Present. 1927.   7.50   ..... (2)

Hollister, Ovando J. The Mines of Colorado. Repr. of 1867 ed.	21.00	..... (38)
Love, Frank. Mining Camps and Ghost Towns Along the Lower Colorado. 1974.	7.95	..... (829)
MacArthur, Mildred S. Germans in Colorado. Repr. of 1917 ed.	5.00	..... (631)

Moore, Jackson W. Bent's Old Fort: An Archeological Study.
1973. 144pp.
Describes the history and construction of this famous
trading post on the Arkansas River. Based on archeological studies conducted by the National Park Service.
Published jointly with the State Historical Society of
Colorado. Trade, 10 1/2 x 8; photographs; maps;
drawings; index.   14.95 ..... (623)

Mullan, John. Miners and Travelers' Guide to Oregon, Washington, Idaho, Montana, Wyoming, and Colorado. Via the Missouri
and Columbia Rivers. 1865.   8.00 ..... (38)

Stoher, C. Eric. Bonanza Victorian: Architecture and Society
in Colorado Mining Towns. 1975.   11.95 ..... (535)

Ubbelohde, Carl, et. al. A Colorado History: Centennial Edition.
1975.   10.95   7.50 (623)

Whitford, William C. Colorado Volunteers in Civil War: The
Battle of Glorieta Pass.   7.00 ..... (644)

ARAPAHOE COUNTY

Leonard, Stephen J. Denver's Foreign Born Immigrants:
1859-1900. 1971. 271pp. BIP-71-29641.   .... (777)

BOULDER COUNTY

Smith, Duane A. Silver Saga: The Story of Caribou, Colorado.
1974. 288pp.
The history of a small mining community in the Colorado
Rockies. Because of its silver mines, Caribou helped
bring stability to a chaotic and trackless wilderness. An
important contribution to the study of Western Urban
History. Thirty-one photographs, maps, notes; bibliography, index.   10.95   7.50 (623)

JEFFERSON COUNTY

Crain, Mary Helen. Evergreen, Colorado. 1969. 86pp.
A history of this small mountain community in Bear Creek
Canyon, west of Denver, from pioneer days to the present.
Photographs, maps, index. 2.50 (623)

LAKE COUNTY

Irey, Eugene Floyd. A Social History of Leadville, Colorado,
During the Boom Days 1877-1881. 1951. 448pp. BIP-00-03163.   .... (777)

Connecticut

STATEWIDE REFERENCES

Abbott, Katherine M. Old Paths and Legends of the New England
Border. Repr. of 1907 ed. 408pp.
Focuses on Connecticut and Western Massachusetts.   13.50 ..... (266)

Briceland, Alan Vance. Ephraim Kirby, Connecticut Jeffersonian, 1757-1804. The Origins of the Jeffersonian Republican Party in Connecticut. 1965. 40lpp. BIP-72-10872.   .... (777)

....

Cohen, Sheldon Samuel. The Connecticut Colony Government and
the Polity of the Congregational Churches, 1708-1760.
1963. 306pp. BIP-64-06455. .... (777)
Connecticut General Assembly. Minutes of the Testimony Taken
Before John Q. Wilson, Joseph Eaton, and Morris Woodruff,
Committee from the General Assembly, To Inquire into the
Condtion of Connecticut State Prison. 1834. 8.00 ..... (38)
East, Robert A. Connecticut's Loyalists. ed. Glenn Weaver. 1974. 12.00 ..... (692)
King, Harold Roger. The Settlement of the Upper Connecticut
River Valley to 1675. 1965. 310pp. BIP-65-10476. .... (777)
Koenig, Samuel. Immigrant Settlement in Connecticut: Their
Growth and Characteristics. Repr. of 1938 ed. 5.00 ..... (631)
Lee, Frank F. Negro and White in a Connecticut Town: A
Study in Race Relations. 7.50 ..... (152)
McKee, Linda Ann. Health and Medicine in Connecticut,
1785-1810. 1971. 274pp. BIP-71-19324. .... (777)
Rankin, Samuel Harrison, Jr. Conservatism and the Problem
of Change in the Congregational Churches of Connecticut,
1660-1760. 1971. 368pp. BIP-72-09279. .... (777)
Wachtell, Harvey Milton. The Conflict Between Localism and
Nationalism in Connecticut, 1783-1788. 1971. 331pp.
BIP-72-19258. .... (777)
Warfle, Richard Thomas. Connecticut's Critical Period: The
Response to the Susquehannah Affair, 1769-1774.
1972. 220pp. BIP-72-32261. .... (777)
White, David O. Connecticut's Black Soldiers: 1775-1783. 1973. ..... 2.50 (590)
Wright, Norman E. Genealogy in America, Volume 1: Massa-
chusetts, Connecticut and Maine. 3.50 ..... (190)

Research Aids

Ireland, Norma Olin and Winifred Irving. Cutter Index. 88pp.
A consolidated index of Cutter's nine genealogy sets.
Over 3,150 surnames included in this "index of indexes"
as found in 33 volumes of William Richard Cutter's series
of genealogies. States: New England, Connecticut,
Massachusetts, North New York, Central New York,
West New York, Middlesex Co. (Massachusetts), Boston
(Massachusetts). Both 1913 and 1914 editions of New England. 15.00 ..... (378)
Trumbull, J. Hammond. Indian Names of Places, Etc. in and
on the Borders of Connecticut: With Interpretations of Some
of Them. Repr. of 1881 ed. 6.00 ..... (685)

Records

Bailey, Frederick W. Early Connecticut Marriages As Found
On Ancient Church Records Prior to 1800. Repr. of
1896-1906 ed. 1000pp. 28.50 ..... (274)
Bailey, Frederic William, ed. Early Connecticut Marriages
As Found on Ancient Church Records Prior to 1800. 7 vols.
1896-1906. 1070pp. B-BH 6350. .... (778)
Connecticut Historical Society. Collections of the Connecticut
Historical Society. 20 vol. set. 1860-1920. Set: 500.00 ..... (2)
Each: 25.00 ..... (2)
Connecticut Superior Court 1772-1773. (Vol. 4 of the American
Legal Series). 29.00 24.00 (415)
Manwaring, Charles William, comp. A Digest of the Early
Connecticut Probate Records. Vol. I. 1904-06. 700pp.
B-OP 41471. .... (778)

Trumbull, Hammond, ed. The Public Records of the Colony of
Connecticut, 1636-1776. Transcribed and Published, in
Accordance with a Resolution of the General Assembly, by
Charles J. Hoadly. 15 vol. set. 1850-1890. Set: 300.00 ..... (2)
Each: 20.00 ..... (2)

Military

Fitch, Jabez. The New York Diary of Lieutenant Jabez Fitch:
Of the 17th Connecticut Regiment from August 22, 1776 to
December 15, 1777. ed. William H. Sabine. (Eyewitness
Accounts of the American Revolution Ser. 3). Repr. of 1954 ed. 12.00 ..... (38)
Marcus, Richard Henry. The Militia of Colonial Connecticut,
1639-1775: An Institutional Study. 1965. 389pp. BIP-66-03257. .... (777)

FAIRFIELD COUNTY

Hawley, Emily Carrie. Annals of Brookfield, Fairfield County,
Connecticut. 1929. 636pp. B-OP 17522. .... (778)
Jacobus, Donald Lines. History and Genealogy of the Families
of Old Fairfield. Repr. of 1930-32, 1943. 2051pp. 75.00 ..... (274)
Manwaring, Adele. Surname Index to Mead's A History of the
Town of Greenwich, Fairfield County, Connecticut. 1974. 20pp. 4.50 ..... (439)

HARTFORD COUNTY

Phelps, Richard H. History of Newgate of Connecticut, at
Simsbury, New East Granby: It's Insurrections and Massacres.
Repr. of 1860 ed. 6.50 ..... (38)
Stiles, Henry R. History of Ancient Wethersfield, Connecticut.
Vol. 2. Repr. of 1904 ed. 35.00 ..... (532)
_____. History of Ancient Windsor. Vol. 1. Repr. of 1892 ed. 35.00 ..... (532)
_____. The History and Genealogies of Ancient Windsor,
Connecticut. 2 vols. 1891-92. vol. 1-1030pp. vol. 2-1016pp.
B-BH 4367. .... (778)
Hartford Times. Newspaper. 1817 to 1920.
On microfilm. 263 rolls. Individual rolls may
be purchased; $15.00 to $30.00 per roll. Ask for roll
containing span of dates you desire. .... (870)
Timlow, Heman Rowlee. Ecclesiastical and other sketches of
Southington, Connecticut. 1875. 888pp. B-BH 19193. .... (778)

LITCHFIELD COUNTY

Cropsey, Joyce Mackenzie, comp. Register of Revolutionary
Soldiers and Patriots Buried in Litchfield County.
September, 1976. c160pp.
Lists soldiers and patriots buried in Litchfield County,
with birth and death dates, marriage dates, and the
same for wife/wives, plus parentage and issue when
are known children. Fully documented. Indexed. 10.15 ..... (743)
Grant, Charles S. A History of Kent, 1738-1796: Democracy
on Connecticut's Frontier. 1957. 385pp. BIP-00-22049. .... (777)
_____. Democracy in the Connecticut Frontier Town of Kent.
1972. ..... 2.95 (546)
_____. Democracy in the Connecticut Frontier Town of Kent.
1961. 12.50 ..... (2)

NEW HAVEN COUNTY

Steiber, Bernard Christian. A History of the Plantation of
Menunkatuck and of the Original Town of Guiford . . . .
Repr. of 1897 ed. 538pp.   13.50   ..... (302)

NEW LONDON COUNTY

Caulkins, Frances Manwaring. History of New London, Connecti-
cut. 1852. 724pp. B-BH 15540.   .... (778)
Decker, Robert Owen. The New London Merchants: 1645-1909:
The Rise and Decline of a Connecticut Port. 1970. 412pp.
BIP-71-15973.   .... (777)
Miner, John A. The Minor Diaries. 1976. 390pp.
Diaries of Thomas Minor, covering the period 1653-1684;
and of Manasseh Minor, covering the period 1696-1720.
They were residents of Stonington, Connecticut. Both
included in one volume.   20.00   ..... (495)

WINDHAM COUNTY

Willingham, William Floyd. Windham, Connecticut: Profile of
A Revolutionary Community, 1755-1818. 1972. 369pp.
BIP-72-32614.   .... (777)

Delaware

STATEWIDE REFERENCES

Anderson, Enoch and Henry H. Bellas. Personal Recollections
of Captain Enoch Anderson, an Officer of the Delaware Regi-
ments in the Revolutionary War. (Eyewitness Accounts of
the American Revolution Ser., No. 3). Repr. of 1896 ed.   6.00   ..... (38)
Barber, John P. Valley of the Delaware. Repr. of 1934 ed. 12.50   ..... (253)
Christensen, Gardell D. and Eugenia Burney. Colonial
Delaware. (Colonial Delaware Series). 1974.   5.95   ....: (525)
Garber, John P. The Valley of the Delaware: And Its Place in
American History. Repr. of 1934 ed.   12.50   ..... (404)
Hunter, Alexander. The Women of the Debatable Land.
Repr. of 1912 ed.   12.00   ..... (404)
Johnson, Amandus. Swedish Settlements on the Delaware: Their
History and Relation to the Indians, Dutch and English,
1638-1664. 2 vols. Repr. of 1911 ed.   Set: 35.00   ..... (248)
Powers, Ramon S. Wealth and Poverty: Economic Base:
Social Structure, and Attitudes in Prerevolutionary Pennsyl-
vania, New Jersey and Delaware. 1971. 389pp. BIP-71-27194. .... (777)
Rodney, Richard S. and Burton A. Kinkle. Early Relations of
Delaware and Pennsylvania. fasc. ed. Including Delaware:
A Grant Yet Not a Grant. Repr. of 1930 ed.   6.00   ..... (81)
Smith, Samuel S. Fight for the Delaware, 1777. 1970.   7.95   ..... (250)
Suorinen, John Henry. The Finns on the Delaware, 1638-1655:
An Essay in American Colonial History. 1938.   7.00   ..... (2)

Research Aid

Gannett, Henry. A Gazetteer of Maryland and Delaware.
Repr. of 1904 ed. 84pp., 15pp.   7.50   ..... (274)
Historical Society of Delaware. Delaware History.
1946-1956/57. 7 vols.
   Published semi-annually. The journal features newly-
   edited documents and articles pertinent to state history.
   Each volume contains an index and annotated bibliographies
   of both articles and books on the area.   Set: 124.00   94.00 (415)
   Vols. 1-2:   Each: 7.00 (415)
   Vols. 3-7:   Each: 16.00 (415)

Records

Delaware Public Archives Commission. Delaware Archives.
   Wilmington, 1911-1919. 5 vols.   Set: 187.50   ..... (2)
   Vols. 1-3; Revolutionary War, Index.   Each: 37.50   ..... (2)
   Vols. 4-5; War of 1812, Index.   Each: 37.50   ..... (2)
Maddux, Gerald and Dorris Maddux. 1800 Census of
   Delaware. Repr. of 1964 ed. 200pp.   12.50   ..... (274)

KENT COUNTY

Court Records of Kent County, Delaware 1680-1705. (Vol. 8 of
   American Legal Series).   29.00   24.00 !15)

NEW CASTLE COUNTY

Acrelius, Israel. A History of New Sweden: Or the Settlements
   on the River Delaware. 1874.   30.00   ..... (38)
Johnson, Amandus. Instruction for Johan Printz: Governor of
   New Sweden. Repr. of 1930 ed.   12.50   ..... (253)
Montgomery, Elizabeth. Reminiscences of Wilmington in Famil-
   iar Village Tales, Ancient and New. Repr. of 1851 ed.   13.50   ..... (404)

District of Columbia

Brown, Letitia W. Free Negroes in the District of Columbia,
   1790-1846. 1972.   7.95   ..... (566)
Furer, Howard B. Washington, D. C.: A Chronological and
   Documentary History. (American Cities Chronology Series).
   1975. 160pp.   7.50   ..... (551)

Listed below are the names of professional genealogists willing to undertake research for a
fee within the District of Columbia, in areas specified in their ads:

DONNA R. HOTALING, G.R.S.	LYNN C. McMILLION, G.R.S.
2255 Cedar Lane	208 Audrey's Court
Vienna, VA 22180	Vienna, Virginia 22180
(703) 560-4496	*National Archives, Library of Congress,*
All Records	*DAR Library, Northern Virginia Counties*

(Additional names may be found on the following page.)

| RESEARCH | CONSULTATION | PHYLLIS W. JOHNSON, B.S., G.R.S. |
| *Documented* | *Personalized* | 2830 N. Westmoreland Street |

BOYD PLUMLEY, (Certified), G.R.S.
11103 Saffold, Reston, VA 22090
(B.A., M.S. in Library Science)

PHYLLIS W. JOHNSON, B.S., G.R.S.
2830 N. Westmoreland Street
Arlington, Virginia 22213

*National Archives, Library of Congress
DAR Library, Nat'l. Genealogical Society*

ANN W. WELLHOUSE
9908 Kensington Parkway
Kensington, Maryland 20795

*Records Searching
Metropolitan Washington D. C. Area*

Green, Constance M. The Church on Lafayette Square: A History
of St. John's Church, Washington, D. C. 1815-1970. 1970. 5.00 2.00 (613)
Ingle, E. Negro in the District of Columbia. Repr. of 1893 ed. 8.50 (394)
Kerwood, John R., ed. The United States Capitol: An Annotated
Bibliography. 1972. 25.00 ..... (556)
Rosenberger, Francis C., ed. Records of the Columbia Histori-
cal Society of Washington, D. C. 1961-1973.
Vols. 1957-1959, 1960-1962, 1963-1965, 1966-1968. Each: 15.00 ..... (801)
Vols. 1969-1970, 1971-1972. Each: 20.00 ..... (801)
Wills, Mary A. The Confederate Blockade of Washington, D. C.
A Courageous and Successful Campaign of the Civil War. 7.95 ..... (58)

Florida

STATEWIDE REFERENCES

Barcia, Carballido Y. and Andres Gonzalez de Zuniga. Chronological History of the Continent of Florida: From the Year
1512, in Which Juan Ponce de Leon Discovered Florida, Until
the Year 1722. tr. Anthony Kerrigan. Repr. of 1951 ed. 34.00 ..... (297)
Barrow, Bennet Hilliard. Plantation Life in the Florida Parishes
of Louisiana, 1836-1846, as Reflected in the Diary of Bennet
H. Barrow. ed. Edwin Adams Davis. 1943. 10.00 ..... (2)
Bennett, Charles E. Settlement of Florida. 1968. 12.50 ..... (242)
Chambers, H. E. West Florida and Its Relations to the Historical Cartography of the United States. Repr. of 1898 ed. 6.25 (394)
Coxe, Daniel. A Description of the Province of Carolina, by
the Spaniards Call'd Florida. Repr. of 1722 ed. .... (242)
Dau, Frederick W. Florida Old and New. Repr. of 1934. 377pp.
Comprehensive history of Florida, with a supplementary
list of exceedingly rare books and pamphlets relating to
the history of Florida. 15.00 ..... (266)
Forbes, James G. Sketches, Historical and Topographical, of
the Floridas - 1821. ed. James Covington. 1964. 7.50 ..... (242)
Gold, Robert Leonard. The Transfer of Florida From Spanish
to British Control, 1763-1765. 1964. 343pp. BIP-64-07919. .... (777)
Held, Ray Eldred. Spanish Florida In American Historiography,
1821-1921. 1955. 374pp. BIP-00-12774. .... (777)
Martin, Sidney W. Florida During the Territorial Days.
Repr. of 1944 ed. 15.00 ..... (612)

Patrick, Rembert W. and Allen Morris. Florida Under Five
Flags. 1967.   5.00   ..... (242)
Phillips, Ulrich B. and James D. Glunt, eds. Florida Plantation
Records from Papers of George Noble Jones. Repr. of 1927 ed.   37.50   ..... (248)
Proctor, Samuel, ed. Colonial Florida and Its Borderlands.   .... (242)
Tebeau, Charlton W. A History of Florida. 1971.   12.50   ..... (480)

Research Aids

Harris, Michael H. Florida History: A Bibliography. 1972.   7.50   ..... (670)
McMullen, Edwin W., Jr. English Topographic Terms in
Florida. 1953.   .....   5.50 (242)
Marks, Henry S. Who Was Who In Florida. 1973. 276pp.
Brief biographies of deceased outstanding residents or
developers of Florida from period of initial discovery and
exploration to Nov. 30, 1972.   14.95   ..... (729)
Morris, Allen C. Florida Place Names. 1974.   5.95   ..... (480)
Raisz, Edwin J. and John R. Dunkle. Atlas of Florida. 1964.   7.50   ..... (242)
Southern Genealogist's Exchange Society, Inc. 1850 Florida
Census. 1969- .
Contains all information on original census. Each
county indexed. By counties-$3.50 to $9.50. Write for
price list.   x   (707)
_____. Index to the 1850 Florida Census. 1976.
Index for the 1850 Florida census taken from our printed
counties. Contains Surname and county in which found.   x   (707)

Military

Bittle, George Cassel. In The Defense of Florida: The Organized
Florida Militia From 1821-1920. 1965. 457pp. BIP-66-02090.   .... (777)
Brown, Wilburt S. Amphibious Campaign for West Florida and
Louisiana. 1969.   10.00   ..... (11)
Buker, George E. Swamp Sailors: Riverine Warfare in the
Everglades, 1835-1842. 1973.   .... (242)
Patrick, Rembert W. Florida Fiasco: Rampant Rebels on the
Georgia-Florida Border, 1810-1815. 1954.   6.00   ..... (279)
"Registrants, Florida Armed Occupation Act." SGE Quarterly,
Vol. 17, No. 77 and 78. 1976.   .....   3.00 (706)
Starr, Joseph Barton. Tories, Dons, and Rebels: The American
Revolution in British West Florida. 1971. 435pp. BIP-72-31253.   .... (777)

Religious

Curley, Michael Joseph. Church and State in the Spanish Floridas
(1783-1822). 1940.   16.00   ..... (2)

Listed below is the name of a professional genealogist willing to undertake research for a
fee within the state of Florida:

Cushman, Joseph D., Jr. The Episcopal Church In Florida:
1821-1892. 1962. 328pp. BIP-63-01805. .... (777)
Kirk, Cooper Clifford. A History of the Southern Presbyterian
Church In Florida: 1821-1891. 1966. 344pp. BIP-67-06471. .... (777)
Matter, Robert Allen. The Spanish Missions of Florida: The
Friars Versus the Governors in the Golden Age: 1606-1690.
1972. 439pp. BIP-72-28631. .... (777)

ALACHUA COUNTY

Hildreth, Charles Halsey. A History of Gainesville, Florida.
1954. 307pp. BIP-00-09548. .... (777)

AUTAUGA COUNTY

"1830 Alabama U. S. Census: Autauga County." SGE Quarterly,
Vol. 12, No. 59. 1971. 8pp. 2.50 (681)

BREVARD COUNTY

Hoag, Amey R. Thy Lighted Lamp. 1958. 105pp.
History of Holy Trinity Episcopal Church, Melbourne,
Florida with family and local history. 3.40 ..... (400)
Hole, Louis J. Melbourne Sketches. Repr. of 1895 ed. 18pp.
Scenes sketched by Rev. Hole of Melbourne in 1895 with
added description of where located in 1975. ..... 2.25 (400)
Kellersberger, Julia Lake. Rooted in Florida Soil. 1971. 60pp.
Interesting stories of the Florida people and Brevard Co.
from earlier times to the space race. 1.50 (400)
Kjerulff, Georgiana. Tales of Old Brevard. 1972. 121pp. 4.40 (400)

COLLIER COUNTY

Tebeau, Charlton W. Florida's Last Frontier: The History of
Collier County, rev. ed. 1966. 5.95 ..... (480)

DADE COUNTY

Buchanan, James E. Miami: A Chronological and Documentary
History. (American Cities Chronology Series). 1976. 160pp. 7.50 ..... (551)

ORANGE COUNTY

Bacon, Eve. History of Oakland, Florida. 1973. .... (486)
Blackman, William F. History of Orange County, Florida.
Repr. of 1927 ed. 22.50 ..... (486)

POLK COUNTY

Hetherington, M. F. History of Polk County, Florida.
Repr. of 1928 ed. 37.50 ..... (486)

ST. JOHNS COUNTY

Arnade, Charles W. Siege of Saint Augustine in Seventeen
Hundred Two. 1959. ..... 2.00 (242)
Fairbanks, George. History and Antiquities of St. Augustine.
(Floridiana Facsimile and Reprint Ser.) Repr. of 1858 ed. 8.50 ..... (242)
Sewall, Rufus K. Sketches of St. Augustine, with a View of Its
History and Advantages As a Resort for Invalids.
Repr. of 1848 ed. .... (242)

VOLUSIA COUNTY

Brownell, Daphne. Cemetery Records of West Volusia County,
Florida. Vol. 1. 1974. 185pp. 5.50 (400)
_____. Cemetery Records of West Volusia County, Florida.
Vol. 2. 1974. 179pp. 5.50 (400)
_____. Cemetery Records of West Volusia County, Florida.
Vol. 3. 1974. 80pp. 5.50 (400)

Georgia

STATEWIDE REFERENCES

An Index to Georgia Colonial Conveyance Books, 1750-1775. 1977. .... (745)
Avery, Isaac Wheeler. The History of the State of Georgia from
1850-1881, Embracing the Three Important Epochs; the Decade
Before the War of 1861-5; the War; the Period of Reconstruc-
tion. 1881. 38.50 ..... (2)
Bishop, Abraham. Georgia Speculation Unveiled. 2 vols.
Repr. of 1798 ed. 3.55 ..... (778)
Bright, M. C. Early Georgia Portraits, 1715-1860. 1975. 344pp. 25.00 ..... (279)
Brown, John. Slave Life in Georgia. ed. L. A. Chamerovzow.
Repr. of 1855. 13.00 ..... (81)
Burge, Dolly L. Diary of Dolly Lunt Burge. ed. James I.
Robertson. 1962. 5.00 ..... (279)
Davis, Harold Earl. A Social History of Georgia: 1733-1776.
1972. 493pp. BIP-72-25935. .... (777)
_____. The Fledgling Province. October, 1976. 320pp.
Social and cultural life in Colonial Georgia, 1733-1776. 16.95 ..... (544)
Jones, G. F, ed. Detailed Report on the Salzburger Emigrants
Who Settled in America. 4 vols.
        Volume 3: 10.00 ..... (279)
        Volume 4: 12.00 ..... (279)
Kemble, Frances A. Journal of a Residence on a Georgian
Plantation in 1838-1839, ed. John A. Scott. 1961. 6.95 ..... (412)
_____. Journal of a Residence on a Georgian Plantation in
1838-1839. Repr. of 1864 ed. 13.50 ..... (478)
Longstreet, Augustus B. Georgia Scenes. Repr. of 1847 ed. 5.00 ..... (135)
Lumpkin, Wilson. The Removal of the Cherokee Indians from
Georgia, 1827-1841. 2 vols. in 1. 1907. 369pp; 328pp. 20.00 ..... (273)
_____. The Removal of the Cherokee Indians from Georgia.
2 vols. in 1. 25.00 ..... (38)

Listed below are the names of professional genealogists willing to undertake research for a
fee within the state of Georgia, in areas specified in their ads:

Morgan, David Taft, Jr. The Great Awakening in the Carolinas
and Georgia, 1740-1775. 1968.· 288pp. BIP-69-01652. .... (777)
Sonderegger, Richard Paul. The Southern Frontier from the
Founding of Georgia to the End of King George's War.
1964. 289pp. BIP-64-12688. .... (777)
Spalding, Billups Phinizy. Georgia and South Carolina During
the Oglethorpe Period, 1732-1743. 1963. 442pp. BIP-64-01895. .... (777)

Research Aids

Otto, Rhea C. 1850 Census of Georgia. (Index to 25 counties).
1975. 46pp.
Surname index only which shows how many times each name
was listed in each county. Index includes counties of:
Burke, Camden, Dooly, Early, Effingham, Elbert,
Emanuel, Fayette, Floyd, Glynn, Gordon, Greene,
Jefferson, Laurens, Lee, Liberty, Lincoln, Lumpkin,
Macon, McIntosh, Marion, Talbot, Tattnall, Telfair
and Warren. 6.75 (564)
Sherwood, Adiel. Gazetteer of Georgia. Repr. of 1847 ed. 20.00 ..... (135)
Townsend, Brigid S. comp. Indexes to Seven State Census
Reports for Counties in Georgia, 1838-1845. 1975. 152pp. 5.00 (745)
Utley, F. L. and M. P. Hemperley. Place names of Georgia.
1975. 534pp. 16.00 ..... (279)

Military and War Eras

Austin, Aurelia. Georgia Boys with "Stonewall" Jackson. 1967. ..... 3.75 (279)
Bryan, T. Conn. Confederate Georgia. 1953. 7.50 ..... (279)
Carter, Samuel, III. Siege of Atlanta - 1864. 12.50 ..... (667)
Griffin, James David. Savannah, Georgia, During the Civil
War. 1963. 321pp. BIP-64-04448. .... (777)
Jones, Charles C., Jr. ed. The Siege of Savannah, In 1779, as
Described in Two Contemporaneous Journals of French
Officers in the Fleet of Count C'Estaing. 1874. 4.50 ..... (38)
Mitchell, Robert Gary. Loyalist Georgia. 1964. 365pp.
BIP-65-02518. .... (777)
Myers, Robert M. ed. The Children of Pride: A True Story of
Georgia and the Civil War. 1972. 25.00 ..... (857)
Patrick, Rembert W. Florida Fiasco: Rampant Rebels on the
Georgia-Florida Border, 1810-1815. 1954. 6.00 ..... (279)
Stegeman, John F. These Men She Gave: Civil War Diary of
Athens, Georgia. Illustrated. 1964. 5.50 ..... (279)

Records

Beckemeyer, Frances Howell. comp. Abstracts of Georgia
Colonial Conveyance Book C-1, 1750-1761. 1975. 430pp.
Contains records of land transfers (leases, releases,
deeds, and supporting documents, dower releases,
powers of attorney, etc.). 10.00 ..... (745)
Coleman, Kenneth and Milton Ready. The Colonial Records of
the State of Georgia. Vol. 28, Pt. 1. 1976. 496pp. 15.00 ..... (279)
"Names Changed Legally in Georgia, 1800-1856." NGS Quarterly.
Vol. 55, No. 3. 1967. 34pp. .... (514)
Walker, George Fuller. comp. Abstracts of Georgia Colonial
Book J, 1755-1762. 1977.
Contains bills of sale, deeds of gift, bonds, powers of
attorney, and other miscellaneous documents. .... (745)

Watts, Frederick L. Petition for Redress. 1976. 350pp.
  Newly discovered documents showing heritage contributions of first Germans in America - from South Carolina
  to Georgia, Mississippi, and Texas from 1735 to 1976.   17.50   12.50 (270)

BALDWIN COUNTY

LeMaster, Mrs. Vernon L. Abstracts of Georgia Marriage
  Notices from 'The Southern Recorder' 1830-1855. 1971. 108pp.
  Alphabetized groom listings and bride's index. 12.50 (559)
  _____. Abstracts of Georgia Death Notices from 'The Southern
  Recorder' 1830-1855. 1971. 113pp.
  Includes 2-page Allied Names Index. 12.50 (559)
  Georgia Marriage Notices and Georgia Death Notices Set: 23.00 (559)

BIBB COUNTY

Jenkins, William Thomas. Ante Bellum Macon and Bibb County,
  Georgia. 1966. 433pp. BIP-67-03558.   .... (777)

BRYAN COUNTY

Otto, Rhea C. "1850 Census of [Bryan Co.] Georgia. 1975. 14pp. 6.75 (564)

BULLOCH COUNTY

Register, Alvaretta K. 1860 Census of Bulloch County, Georgia. 15.00 (637)
  _____. 1870 Bulloch County, Georgia. 15.00 (637)

BURKE COUNTY

Otto, Rhea C. 1850 Census of [Burke Co.] Georgia. 1975. 69pp. 6.75 (564)
Powell, Lillian Lewis, et al. Grave Markers in Burke County,
  Georgia.   15.00   13.00 (553)

CAMDEN COUNTY

Otto, Rhea C. 1850 Census of [Camden Co.] Georgia. 1974. 27pp. 6.75 (564)

CHATHAM COUNTY

Harden, William. History of Savannah and South Georgia.
  Repr. of 1913 ed.   20.00   ..... (135)
Otto, Rhea C. 1850 Census of [Chatham Co.] Georgia. 1975. 123pp. 6.75 (564)
Perdue, Robert E. The Negro in Savannah, 1865-1900. 1973. 7.50   ..... (224)

CHATTAHOOCHEE COUNTY

Rogers, Norma Kate. History of Chattahoochee County, Georgia.
  c1933. 404pp. B-OP 66773   .... (778)

CLARKE COUNTY

Hynds, Ernest C. Antebellum Athens and Clarke County,
  Georgia. 1974.   6.50   ..... (279)

DOOLY COUNTY

Otto, Rhea C. 1850 Census of [Dooly Co.] Georgia. 1971. 77pp. 6.75 (564)
Townsend, Brigid S. comp. Indexes to Seven State Census
  Reports for Counties in Georgia. 1975. 152pp. 5.00 (745)

EARLY COUNTY

Otto, Rhea C. 1850 Census of [Early Co.] Georgia. 1975. 37pp. 6.75 (564)

EFFINGHAM COUNTY

Otto, Rhea C. 1850 Census of [Effingham Co.] Georgia. 1970. 35pp. 6.75 (564)

ELBERT COUNTY

Otto, Rhea C. 1850 Census of Elbert County, Georgia. 6.75 (564)

EMANUEL COUNTY

Otto, Rhea C. 1850 Census of [Emanuel Co.] Georgia. 1970. 55pp. 6.75 (564)

FAYETTE COUNTY

Otto, Rhea C. 1850 Census of [Fayette Co.] Georgia. 1973. 80pp. 6.75 (564)

FLOYD COUNTY

Otto, Rhea C. 1850 Census of [Floyd Co.] Georgia. 1973. 68pp. 6.75 (564)

FORSYTH COUNTY

Townsend, Brigid S, comp. Indexes to Seven State Census Reports
for Counties in Georgia. 1975. 152pp. 5.00 (745)

FULTON COUNTY

Garrett, Franklin M. Yesterday's Atlanta. 1974. 9.95 ..... (679)
Lankevich, George. Atlanta: A Chronological and Documentary
History. (American Cities Chronology Series). 1976. 160pp. 7.50 ..... (551)

GLYNN COUNTY

Otto, Rhea C. 1850 Census of [Glynn Co.] Georgia. 1973. 11pp. 6.75 (564)
Wood, Virginia Steele. ed. St. Simons Island, Georgia Brunswick
and Vicinity. Description and History Written By William W.
Hazzard, 1825. 36pp.
Illustrated with original drawing by Walter E. Channing. 2.50 (548)

GORDON COUNTY

Coulter, E. Merton. Old Petersburg and the Broad River Valley
of Georgia: Their Rise and Decline. 1965. 7.50 ..... (279)
Otto, Rhea C. 1850 Census of [Gordon Co.] Georgia. 1974. 60pp. 6.75 (564)

GREENE COUNTY

Otto, Rhea C. 1850 Census of [Greene Co.] Georgia. 1974. 61pp. 6.75 (564)

HEARD COUNTY

Eller, Lynda S. Cemetery Survey. 1977.
    Transcript of tombstone inscriptions. 130+ cemeteries. .... (216)
_____. Heard County, Georgia - A History of Its People.
1977. 1000pp
    Will contain census records 1840-1880; family genealogies,
    1830-1900; early maps; historical notes. .... (216)
_____. Heard County, Georgia 1850 Census. 1976. 60pp.
    Indexed. Mimeographed. 6.50 (216)
_____. Heard County, Georgia 1860 Census. 1976. .... (216)
_____. Heard County, Georgia 1870 Census. .... (216)
_____. Heard County, Georgia 1880 Census. 1977. .... (216)

JEFFERSON COUNTY

"Jefferson County, Georgia Jury List, 1799." NGS Quarterly,
Vol. 53, No. 3. 1965. 5pp. 3.50 (514)
Otto, Rhea C. 1850 Census of [Jefferson Co.] Georgia. 1973. 54pp. 6.75 (564)

LAURENS COUNTY

The Official History of Laurens County, Georgia, 1807-1941. 1972. 15.00 ..... (135)
Otto, Rhea C. 1850 Census of [Laurens Co.] Georgia. 1973. 46pp. 6.75 (564)
Townsend, Brigid S, comp. Indexes to Seven State Census
Reports for Counties in Georgia. 1975. 152pp. 5.00 (745)

LEE COUNTY

Otto, Rhea C. 1850 Census of [Lee Co.] Georgia. 1973. 43pp. 6.75 (564)

LIBERTY COUNTY

Otto, Rhea C. 1850 Census of [Liberty Co.] Georgia. 1971. 29pp. 6.75 (564)

LINCOLN COUNTY

Hudson, Frank Parker, comp. An 1800 Census for Lincoln
County, Georgia. 1976. .... (745)
Otto, Rhea C. 1850 Census of [Lincoln Co.] Georgia. 1971. 31pp. 6.75 (564)

LUMPKIN COUNTY

Otto, Rhea C. 1850 Census of [Lumpkin Co.] Georgia. 1973. 100pp. 6.75 (564)

McINTOSH COUNTY

Otto, Rhea C. 1850 Census of [McIntosh Co.] Georgia. 1974. 16pp. 6.75 (564)

MACON COUNTY

Otto, Rhea C. 1850 Census of [Macon Co.] Georgia. 1973. 52pp. 6.75 (564)

MARION COUNTY

Otto, Rhea C. 1850 Census of [Marion Co.] Georgia. 1974. 82pp. 6.75 (564)

MERIWETHER COUNTY

Davidson, William H. Brooks of Honey and Butter, Plantations
and People of Meriwether County, Georgia. 2 vols. 2d ed.
1971. 910pp. 37.50 ..... (182)

MITCHELL COUNTY

"Hopeful Baptist Church Cemetery." SGE Quarterly, Vol. 16,
No. 74. 1975. 7pp. 3.00 (706)

MONROE COUNTY

Otto, Rhea C. 1850 Census of [Monroe Co.] Georgia. 1975. 75pp. 6.75 (564)

MONTGOMERY COUNTY

Otto, Rhea C. 1850 Census of [Montgomery Co.] Georgia. 1975. 18pp. 6.75 (564)

NEWTON COUNTY

Townsend, Brigid S. comp. Indexes to Seven State Census Reports for Counties in Georgia. 1975. 152pp. 5.00 (745)
Robertson, James L, Jr., ed. Diary of Dolly Lunt Burge. 1962. 5.00 ..... (279)

PEACH COUNTY

History of Peach County, Georgia. 1972.   15.00   ..... (135)

PIERCE COUNTY

Walker, Randall M., Jr. "Lest We Forget. . . . " Marked
Graves in Pierce County, Georgia. 1975. 60pp. 5.00 (807)

RICHMOND COUNTY

"Richmond County, Georgia Land Court - 18 September 1784 to
6 August 1787." NGS Quarterly, Vol. 56, No. 4. 1968. 25pp.   .... (514)

SCREVEN COUNTY

Otto, Rhea C. 1850 Census of [Screven Co.] Georgia. 1975. 34pp. 6.75 (564)

STEWART COUNTY

Dixon, Sara R. and A. H. Clark. History of Stewart County,
Georgia. Vol. 2. 1200pp.
    U. S. Census Records 1830-1860; Membership Roll of
    Providence Methodist Church; Marriage Records of Stewart
    County 1828 thru 1870; Abstracts of Stewart County Will
    Book A, Nov. 1837; Abstracts of Stewart County Will Book
    B, May 1848 thru December 1890; Abstracts of Stewart
    County Bond Book A, May 2, 1831 thru January 5, 1835;
    Abstracts of Stewart County Bond Book B, September 1836
    thru September 1856; Abstracts of 1841 Tax Digest of
    Stewart County; Records of 176 cemeteries (public and
    private), Copied 1955; 193 Family Bible Records; Abstract
    Justice Inferior Court Records; 261 Family Histories and
    many other items of interest; 231 pictures including
    39 pictures of old homes and churches.   25.75   ..... (143)

TALBOT COUNTY

Otto, Rhea C. 1850 Census of [Talbot Co.] Georgia. 1974. 98pp. 6.75 (564)

TATTNALL COUNTY

Otto, Rhea C. 1850 Census of [Tattnall Co.] Georgia. 1971. 32pp. 6.75 (564)
Townsend, Brigid S. comp. Indexes to Seven State Census
Reports for Counties in Georgia. 1975. 152pp. 5.00 (745)

TELFAIR COUNTY

Otto, Rhea C. 1850 Census of [Telfair Co.] Georgia. 1970. 30pp. 6.75 (564)

THOMAS COUNTY

"1840 Georgia Census: Thomas County." (Heads of Households
as Enumerated). SGE Quarterly, Vol. 2, No. 11. 1959. 5pp. 2.00 (681)
Rogers, William W. Thomas County, Eighteen Sixty-Five - Nine-
teen Hundred. 1973.   15.00   ..... (243)

TWIGGS COUNTY

McSwain, Eleanor Davis. Abstracts of Some Documents of
Twiggs County, Georgia. 1972. 354pp.
    8 1/2" x 11"; Deeds; 1818 Tax Digest; Wills; Estate
    Records; District and Land Lot Map; Index.   15.00   ..... (458)

WARE COUNTY

"1850 Georgia Census: Ware County." (Surname Index of
Families Enumerated). SGE Quarterly, Vol. 13, No. 61.
1972. 7pp. 2.50 (681)
"Pitman Chapel Cemetery, Manor, Georgia." SGE Quarterly,
Vol. 16, No. 73. 1975. 4pp. 3.00 (706)

WARREN COUNTY

Otto, Rhea C. 1850 Census of [Warren Co.] Georgia. 1974. 78pp. 6.75 (564)
Townsend, Brigid S. comp. Indexes to Seven State Census
Reports for Counties in Georgia. 1975. 152pp. 5.00 (745)

WASHINGTON COUNTY

History of Washington County, Georgia. 1973. 5.00 ..... (135)

WILKES COUNTY

Writers' Program, Georgia. The Story of Washington-Wilkes. 1941. 9.50 ..... (2)

ᚼawaii

Research Aid
Pukui, Mary K., et al. Place Names of Hawaii. 2d ed. 1974. 9.50 ..... (322)

Idaho

STATEWIDE REFERENCES

Brooks, Juanita. The History of the Jews in Utah and Idaho,
1853-1950. 1973. 7.95 ..... (826)
Highsmith, R., Jr., ed. Atlas of the Pacific Northwest. 5th ed.
1973. 136pp.
Oregon, Washington, Idaho history, development, resources,
geography, economics, etc. 13.50 7.50 (561)
Ireland, Norma Olin and Tom Clark. Idaho Index to Joyce Owen's
"Idaho Family Trees." 10pp.
Surnames of many New England and Southern families
whose descendants came West. Many hard-to-find names. 3.50 (378)
Langford, Nathaniel Pitt. Vigilante Days and Ways; the Pioneers
of the Rockies, the Makers and Making of Montana, Idaho,
Oregon, Washington, and Wyoming. 2 vol. Each: 18.00 ..... (2)
Set: 35.00 ..... (2)

Mullan, John. Miners and Travelers' Guide to Oregon, Washington,
Idaho, Montana, Wyoming, and Colorado. Via the Missouri and
Columbia Rivers. Accompanied by a General Map of the Mineral
Region of the Northern Sections of the Rocky Mountains. 1865. 8.00 ..... (38)

OWYHEE COUNTY

Hanley, Mike and Ellis Lucia. Owyhee Trails: The West's
Forgotten Corner. 1973. 7.95 ..... (127)
History of Owyhee County, Idaho. facsimile ed. 8.50 (687)

Illinois

STATEWIDE REFERENCES

Belting, Natalia Maree. Kaskaskia Under the French Regime.
Repr. 150pp. index.
A classic reference book for the French in the
Mississippi Valley. Invaluable in locating and
identifying families living in the Illinois country
during the 18th century. Extracts from parish
registers and notes on the census of 1752. ..... 15.00 (608)

Birkbeck, Morris. Notes On A Journey in America, From the
Coast of Virginia to the Territory of Illinois. (Illinois
Sesquicentennial Ser.) Repr. of 1818 ed. 5.75 ..... (778)

Edwards, Ninian W. History of Illinois, from 1778 to 1833:
And Life and Times of Ninian Edwards. Repr. of 1870 ed. 31.00 ..... (38)

Farnham, Eliza W. Life in Prairie Land. Repr. of 1846 ed. 18.00 ..... (38)

Gates, Paul W. Illinois Central Railraod and Its Colonization
Work. Repr. of 1934 ed. 21.00 ..... (394)

Harris, Norman. History of Negro Servitude in Illinois.
Repr. of 1904 ed. 14.95 ..... (320)

_____. History of Negro Servitude in Illinois and of the Slavery
Agitations in That State, 1719-1864. 11.50 ..... (522)

Howard, Robert P. Illinois: A History of the Prairie State. 1972. 10.95 ..... (215)

Illinois State Genealogical Society. Illinois State Genealogical
Society Quarterly. 1968- . 60pp./issue.
Primary source material for Illinois. Research aids,
queries, book reviews. 2.00 (366)

_____. "The Illinois Census Project - Coding Procedure,
Code Guide, Soundex Guide (Computerized)." ISG Quarterly,
Vol. 8, No. 1. 1976. 5pp. 2.00 (366)

_____. "Illinois Ancestors in the Vicinity of Flynn's Ferry
Road." ISG Quarterly, Vol. 6, No. 3. 1974. 5pp. 2.00 (366)

_____. "Staking Claims (Land) in Illinois." ISG Quarterly,
Vol. 5, No. 3. 1973. 7pp. 2.00 (366)

Lovejoy, Joseph C. and Owen Lovejoy. Memoir of the Reverend
Elijah P. Lovejoy. Repr. of 1838 ed. 14.00 ..... (38)

Miller, Otis Louis. Indian-White Relations in the Illinois Country,
1789 to 1818. 1972. 159pp. BIP-72-23975. .... (777)

Pease, Theodore C. Story of Illinois. ed. Marguerite J. Pease.
1965. 7.95 ..... (137)

Peck, John Mason. A Guide for Emigrants: Containing Sketches
of Illinois, Missouri, and the Adjacent Parts. 1831. 19.00 ..... (38)

Schuyler, Robert Livingston. The Transition in Illinois from
British to American Government. 1909. 6.00 ..... (2)

Listed below are the names of professional genealogists willing to undertake research for a
fee within the state of Illinois, in areas specified in their ads:

Tevebaugh, John Leslie. Merchant on the Western Frontier:
William Morrison of Kaskaskia, 1790-1837. 342pp.
BIP-62-02976. .... (777)
Yates, William A. The Ridge Runners, Vol. IV. 1976. 321pp.
Genealogy: Virginia, North Carolina, Kentucky,
Tennessee, Indiana, Illinois, Missouri, Arkansas. 10.00 (859)

Research Aids

Beck, Lewis C. Gazetteer of the States of Illinois &
Missouri. Repr. of 1823 ed. 1975. 22.00 ..... (38)
_____. Gazetteer of the States of Illinois & Missouri:
Containing a General View of Each State, a General
View of Their Counties, & a Particular Description of
Their Towns, Villages, Rivers, etc. Repr. of 1823
ed. 18.00 ..... (266)
Burton, William L., ed. Descriptive Bibliography of
Civil War Manuscripts in Illinois. 1966. 12.00 ..... (545)
Clayton, John, ed. Illinois Fact Book & Historical
Almanac, 1673-1968. 1970. 12.50 3.25 (708)
Illinois Historical Records Survey. Guide to Public Vital
Statistics Records in Illinois. Repr. of 1941 ed. 137pp. 8.25 (330)
"Illinois County Histories: Adams - Douglas." ISGS
Quarterly, Vol. 1, No. 2. 1969. 6pp. 2.00 (366)
"Illinois County Histories: DuPage - Massac." ISGS Quarter-
ly, Vol. 1, No. 3. 1969. 9pp. 2.00 (366)
"Illinois County Histories: Mercer - Woodford." ISGS
Quarterly, Vol. 1, No. 4. 1969. 9pp. 2.00 (366)
Smith, Dora and Marjorie Smith. Index to 1850 Illinois Census.
1978.
Includes head of household and first member of the
household having a different surname. .... (330)

Military

Behleudof, Frederick. The History of the 13th Illinois
Cavalry Regiment, Volunteers, U.S. Army from
September 1861 to September 1865. 1888. 44pp.
B-OP 71,801. .... (778)
English, William Hayden. Conquest of the Country North-
west of the River Ohio, 1778-1783, and Life of
Gen. George Rogers Clark. With Numerous Sketches
of Men Who Served Under Clark and Full Lists of
Those Allotted Lands in Clark's Grant for Service
in the Campaigns Against the British Posts, Showing
the Exact Land Allotted Each. 2 vols. in one. 1896. 48.00 ..... (38)
Hicken, Victor. Illinois in the Civil War. 1966. 7.50 ..... (365)
Illinois Soldier's and Sailor's Home at Quincy. Admission
of Mexican War and Civil War Veterans, 1887-1898.
1975. 118pp.
Contains company regiment, county of residence,
disability for 4418 veterans. Later entries give
age, nativity and pension amount. ..... 7.25 '330)
"Illinois Territory Militia - War of 1812." ISGS Quarterly,
Vol. 5, No. 3. 1973. 8pp. 2.00 (366)
"Pensioned Widows of Revolutionary War Soldiers in
Illinois." ISGS Quarterly, Vol. 4, No. 2. 1972. 5pp. 2.00 (366)
Illinois State Genealogical Society. Soldiers of the American
Revolution Buried in Illinois. 1976. 288pp.

1,053 Revolutionary War soldiers, spouses, children,
residences, military service, pension numbers,
tombstones.   8.50   ..... (366)
Stevens, Frank Everett. The Black Hawk War, Including
a Review of Black Hawk's Life; Illustrated With
Upwards of Three Hundred Rare Interesting Portraits
and Views. 1903.   42.50   ..... (2)
Volkel, Lowell. War of 1812 Bounty Land Patents in
Illinois (Introduction by James D. Walker). Repr. of
1840 ed. 380pp.
    Includes name of patentee, to whom patent was
    delivered, patent date, warrant number, service
    and land description.   15.00   ..... (330)

Religious and Ethnic Groups

Evers, Joseph Calvin. The History of the Southern Illinois
Conference of the Methodist Church. 409pp.
BIP-62-04541.   .... (777)
Galford, Justin B. The Foreign Born & Urban Growth in the
Great Lakes, 1850-1950: A Study of Chicago, Detroit,
and Milwaukee. 1957. 388pp. BIP-00-24697.   .... (777)
Fleishaker, Oscar. The Illinois-Iowa Jewish Community on
the Banks of the Mississippi River. 450pp. BIP-63-01962.   .... (777)
McGregor, John C. The Pool & Irving Villages: A Study
of Hopewell Occupation in the Illinois River Valley. 1958.   .....   5.95 (365)
Tucker, Marlin Timothy. Political Leadership in the Illinois-
Missouri German Community, 1836-1872. 391pp.
BIP-69-10871.   .... (777)

Records

"Reports of Cases at Common Law and in Chancery. . . in
the Supreme Court of . . . Illinois." ISGS Quarterly,
Vol. 6, No. 1. 1974. 6pp. 2.00 (366)
United States Government. Territorial Papers. Volume 16:
The Territory of Illinois, 1809-1814. Foundation of
the Territory, 1809. The Administration of Acting
Governor Pope, 1809. The Administration of Governor
Edwards, 1809-1814. 1948. Index.   57.50   ..... (2)
Wormer, Maxine. Illinois 1840 Census Index, Volume 3 -
Counties Jersey Through Marshall. 1975. 85pp. 6.75 (330)
Wormer, Maxine. Illinois 1840 Census Index, Volume 4 -
Counties McDonough Through Rock Island. 1976. 87pp. 6.75 (330)
Wormer, Maxine. Illinois 1840 Census Index, Volume 5 -
Counties Sangamon Through Winnebago. 1976.   .....   6.25 (330)

ADAMS COUNTY

Portrait and Biographical Record of Adams County, Illinois.
1892. 600pp. B-BH 4799.   .... (778)
Collins, William Herzog and Cicero F. Perry. Past and Present
of the City of Quincy and Adams County, Illinois. 1905.
1126pp. B-BH 4814.   .... (778)
The History of Adams County, Illinois. 1879. 1232pp.
B-BH 3157.   .... (778)

BOND COUNTY

Portrait and Biographical Record of Montgomery and Bond
Counties, Illinois. 1892. 532pp. B-BH 4997.   .... (778)

BOONE COUNTY

The Past and Present of Boone County, Illinois. 1877. 426pp.
B-BH 11576.   .... (778)
Portrait and Biographical Record of Winnebago and Boone
Counties, Illinois. 1892. 1314pp. B-BH 4942.   .... (778)

BROWN COUNTY

Biographical Review of Cass, Schuyler and Brown Counties,
Illinois. 1892. 636pp. B-BH 4798.   .... (778)
W.R. Brink and Company. Combined History of Schuyler
and Brown Counties, Illinois. With Illustrations Descriptive
of their Scenery, and Biographical Sketches of Some of
their Prominent Men and Pioneers. 1882. 446pp.
B-BH 4925.
    Includes troop rosters from these counties in Mexican
    and Civil War.   .... (778)

BUREAU COUNTY

Biographical Record of Bureau, Marshall, Putnam & Stark
Counties, Illinois. 1897. 770pp. B-BH 11636.   .... (778)
Bradsby, Henry C., ed. History of Bureau County, Illinois.
1885. 732pp. B-BH 11634.   .... (778)
Harrington, George B. Past and Present of Bureau County,
Illinois. 1906. 1026pp. B-BH 4794.   .... (778)

CARROLL COUNTY

Portrait and Biographical Album of Jo Daviess and Carroll
Counties, Illinois. 1889. 1024pp. B-OP 46688.   .... (778)

CASS COUNTY

Biographical Review of Cass, Schuyler and Brown Counties,
Illinois. 1892. 636pp. B-BH 4798.   .... (778)

CHAMPAIGN COUNTY

Decatur Genealogical Society. United States 1840 Census,
Champaign County, Illinois. 1975. 11pp. 1.25 (187)
History of Champaign County, Illinois. 1878. 552pp. B-BH 4835.   .... (778)
Mathews, Milton W. and Lewis A. McLean. Early History
and Pioneers of Champaign County, Illinois. 1886. 170pp.
B-BH 4800.   .... (778)
Stewart, John Russell, ed. A Standard History of Champaign
County, Illinois. 1918. Vol. 1-554pp. Vol. 2-668pp.
B-BH 4811.
    Volume 2 contains biographical sketches.   .... (778)

CHRISTIAN COUNTY

Decatur Genealogical Society. United States 1840 Census,
Christian County, Illinois. 1975. 10pp. 1.25 (187)
History of Christian County, Illinois. 1880. 398pp. B-BH 4805   .... (778)

McBride, James C. Past and Present of Christian County,
Illinois. 1904. 572pp. B-BH 11612. .... (778)
Portrait & Biographical Record of Christian County, Illinois.
1893. 460pp. B-BH 4797. .... (778)

CLAY COUNTY

Biographical and Reminiscent History of Richland, Clay, and
Marion Counties, Illinois. 1909. 660pp. B-BH 11960. .... (778)
History of Wayne & Clay Counties, Illinois. 1884. Text -618pp.
Supplement - 108pp. B-BH 11995. .... (778)

CLINTON COUNTY

History of Marion and Clinton Counties, Illinois. 1881. 396pp.
B-BH 4903. .... (778)
Portrait and Biographical Record of Clinton, Washington,
Marion and Jefferson Counties, Illinois. 1894. 574pp.
B-BH 4813. .... (778)
Wickliffe, Helen Sharpe. Marriages, 1825-1856. 1976. 141pp. 7.25 (330)

COLES COUNTY

Portrait and Biographical Album of Coles County, Illinois. 1887.
574pp. B-BH 4804. .... (778)

COOK COUNTY

Andreas, Alfred T. History of Chicago: From the Earliest
Period to the Present Time. 3 vols. Repr. of 1884 ed. 200.00 ..... (38)
Bernheimer, Charles S. The Russian Jew in the United States:
Studies of Social Conditions in New York, Philadelphia &
Chicago, with a Description of Rural Settlements. Repr. of
1905 ed. 11.95 ..... (568)
Furer, Howard B. Chicago: A Chronological and Documentary
History. 1974. 160pp. 7.50 ..... (551)
Historical Records Survey. Check List of Chicago Ante-Fire
Imprints, 1851-1871. 1938. 24.00 ..... (415)
Jebsen, Harry A. A., Jr. Blue Island, Illinois: The History
of a Working Class Suburb. 335pp. BIP-72-01439. .... (777)
Nelli, Humbert S. The Italians in Chicago, 1880-1930. A Study
in Ethnic Mobility. 1973. 9.95 2.95 (566)
Schiavo, Giovanni Ermenegildo. The Italians in Chicago: A
Study in Americanization. 1928. illus. 15.00 ..... (38)

DECATUR COUNTY

Richmond, Mabel E. Centennial History of Decatur and Macon
County. 1930. 480pp. B-BH 11895. .... (778)

De KALB COUNTY

The Biographical Record of De Kalb County, Illinois. 1898.
564pp. B-BH 11610. .... (778)
Boies, Henry Lamson. History of De Kalb County, Illinois.
1868. 550pp B-BH 11617. .... (778)

Gross, Lewis M. Past and Present of De Kalb County, Illinois.
1907. Vol. 2-690pp. B-BH 11784.   .... (778)

De WITT COUNTY

Decatur Genealogical Society. United States 1840 Census,
De Witt County, Illinois. 1975. 20pp. 1.25 (187)
History of De Witt County, Illinois. 1882? 400pp. B-BH 4818.   .... (778)
History of De Witt County, Illinois with Biographical Sketches.
1910. Vol. 1-436pp. Vol. 2-412pp. B-BH 11619.   .... (778)

DOUGLAS COUNTY

County of Douglas, Illinois, Historical and Biographical. 1884.
720pp. B-BH 11616.   .... (778)
Historical and Biographical Record of Douglas County, Illinois.
1900. 304pp. B-BH 11611.   .... (778)

Du PAGE COUNTY

History of Du Page County, Illinois. 1882. 544pp. B-BH 3158.   .... (778)

EDGAR COUNTY

Portrait and Biographical Album of Vermilion & Edgar Counties.
1889. 1124pp. B-BH 4939.   .... (778)

EDWARDS COUNTY

Combined History of Edwards, Lawrence and Wabash Counties,
Illinois. 1883. 444pp. B-BH 3168.   .... (778)
Decatur Genealogical Society. Cemetery Inscriptions, Edwards
County, Illinois, Volume I. 1969. 49pp.
    Contains Bennington, Old Carmey, Old Cemetery on
    Densmore p perty, Old Greathouse, Cemetery on
    Earl Ibbotson property, Old Johnson, Macedonia,
    Cemetery on Miller property, Original Pleasant Hill,
    Samsville, Original Shiloh, and Yetke. Indexed. 4.00 (187)
_____. United States 1830 Census, Edwards County, Illinois.
1968. 8pp. 1.25 (187)
Edwards County 1850 Census. 1972. 45pp. 5.25 (330)

EFFINGHAM COUNTY

Decatur Genealogical Society. United States 1840 Census,
Effingham County, Illinois. 1975. 11pp. 1.25 (187)
Portrait & Biographical Record of Effingham, Jasper &
Richland Counties, Illinois. 1893. 602pp.
B-BH 11613.   .... (778)

FAYETTE COUNTY

Decatur Genealogical Society. Cemetery Inscriptions, Fayette
County, Illinois, Volume I. Repr. of 1969 ed. 67pp.
    Contains Blankenship, Bolt, Cearlock, Craig, Haley,
    Chapel, Halford, Harris, Hoffman (Prarie Baptist),
    Liberty, Little Hickory, Loogootee, Mr. Carmel,
    Prater, Old Casey, Pope, Seminary, Shad, Sinning
    (Isbell), Stokes, Sidener, Union, and Welch. Also added
    genealogical notes. Indexed. 5.00 (187)

Winnetka Genealogy Projects Committee. An Index to Names
of Persons Appearing in History of Fayette County. 1974.
39pp. 6.25 (330)

FORD COUNTY

Gardner, E. A. History of Ford County, Illinois. 1908.
Vol. 1-428pp. Vol. 2-442pp. B-BH 11638. .... (778)
Portrait and Biographical Record of Ford County, Illinois.
1892. 830pp. B-BH 4816. .... (778)

FRANKLIN COUNTY

Greenwood, Marie. Franklin County Cemetery Inscriptions,
Ewing Township. 1974. 122+pp. 7.75 (330)
Rademacher and Rademacher. Franklin County Marriages,
1849-1865. 120+pp. 8.25 (330)

FULTON COUNTY

Blout, H. L. Spoon River Legacy. 1969. 135pp.
Part fiction and part fact but interesting reading.
Nostalgic. 2.75 ..... (259)
Cemetery Inscriptions, Volume III, Lewistown & Lewistown
Township. 1976. 133pp.
Records of every known cemetery and private burial
plot in Lewistown Township plus death records for same. 6.00 (259)
Cemetery Inscriptions, Volume IV.
Records of all known cemeteries and burial plots in
Fairview and Joshua Townships, Fulton County, Illinois.
Complete index. .... (259)
Chapman, Charles C. History of Fulton County, Illinois (1879).
Repr. of 1879 ed. 1178pp.
Valuable reference work with new every name index
added. 23.00 ..... (259)
_____. History of Fulton County, Illinois. 1879. 1090pp.
B-BH 11605. .... (778)
Depler, John. Favorite Columns From "The Years that Were."
Pertains to the Lewistown, Illinois area. 4.50 (259)
Derry, Elsie Mae Cameron. Thru the Years in an Early
Pioneer Town, Bernadotte. 1969. 46pp.
History of the area and the people who lived there.
Pictures. 2.25 (259)
Lewis, Edward R., Jr. Reflections of Canton in a Pharmacist's
Show Globe. 1967. 256pp.
A comprehensive history of Canton, Illinois and the
important events in Fulton County. Complete index. 16.75 ..... (259)
Ross, Harvey Lee. Early Pioneers & Events of the State of
Illinois. Repr. of 1899 ed. 199pp.
A history of Illinois and Fulton County mentioning many
early residents. 8.60 ..... (259)
Swan, Alonzo M. Canton: Its Pioneers and History. Repr. of
1871 ed. 176pp.
Reprint of a rare early history of the entire area with a
new people and place name index and a section showing
changes in names of streets plus an old map. 10.80 ..... (259)
White, James K. P. Ramblin' Thru Spoon River Country.
1969. 117pp.
Interviews with pioneers published in the old "Canton

Register" during the years 1904-1910. ..... 3.00 (259)

GALLATIN COUNTY

"Gallatin County, Territory . . . and State of Illinois, Marriage
Licenses, Returns and Bonds: 1813-1821." ISGS Quarterly,
Vol. 5, No. 2. 1973. 12pp. 2.00 (366)
"Gallatin County, Territory . . . and State of Illinois, Marriage
Licenses, Returns and Bonds: 1822-1829." ISGS Quarterly,
Vol. 5, No. 4. 1973. 14pp. 2.00 (366)

GREENE COUNTY

History of Greene County, Illinois. 1879. 768pp. B-BH 11641. .... (778)
History of Greene and Jersey Counties, Illinois. 1885. 1140pp.
B-BH 11754. .... (778)

GRUNDY COUNTY

History of Grundy County, Illinois. 1882. 542pp. B-BH 11646. .... (778)

HANCOCK COUNTY

Gregg, Thomas. History of Hancock County, Illinois. 1880.
1032pp. B-BH 11604. .... (778)
Biographical Review of Hancock County, Illinois. 1907. 782pp.
B-BH 3161. .... (778)
Portrait and Biographical Record of Hancock, McDonough and
Henderson Counties, Illinois. 1894. 602pp. B-BH 11688 .... (778)
Tri-City Genealogical Society. 1850 Federal Census, Hancock
County, Illinois. 1977. indexed. .... (768)

HARDIN COUNTY

General Projects Committee, Winnetka Public Library.
Index to the Biographical Review of Johnson, Massac, Pope,
& Hardin Counties, Illinois. 111pp. 6.00 (276)

HENDERSON COUNTY

Portrait and Biographical Record of Hancock, McDonough and
Henderson Counties, Illinois. 1894. 602pp. B-BH 11688. .... (778)

HENRY COUNTY

Biographical Record of Henry County, Illinois. 1901. 722pp.
B-BH 11687. .... (778)
The History of Henry County, Illinois. 1877. 590pp. B-BH 11640. .... (778)
Middelsen, M.A. The Bishop Hill Colony: A Religious Com-
munistic Settlement in Henry County, Illinois. Repr. of 1892 ed. 10.50 ..... (612)
Portrait and Biographical Album of Henry County, Illinois.
1885. 844pp. B-BH 4815. .... (778)
Tri-City Genealogical Society. 1850 Federal Census, Henry
County, Illinois. 1976. indexed. .... (768)

IROQUOIS COUNTY

Portrait and Biographical Record of Iroquois County, Illinois.
1893. 876pp. B-BH 4817. .... (778)

JACKSON COUNTY

Portrait and Biographical Record of Randolph, Jackson, Perry
and Monroe Counties, Illinois. 1894. 868pp. B-BH 4928. .... (778)

JASPER COUNTY

Portrait and Biographical Record of Effingham, Jasper and
Richland Counties, Illinois. 1893. 602pp. B-BH 11613. .... (778)

JEFFERSON COUNTY

Portrait and Biographical Record of Clinton, Washington, Marion
and Jefferson Counties, Illinois. 1894. 574pp. B-BH 4813. .... (778)
Wall, John A. Wall's History of Jefferson County, Illinois.
1909. 646pp. B-BH 11637. .... (778)

JERSEY COUNTY

Hamilton, Oscar Brown, ed. History of Jersey County, Illinois.
1919. 782pp. B-BH 11644. .... (778)
History of Greene and Jersey Counties, Illinois. 1885. 1140pp.
B-BH 11754. .... (778)
Wormer, Maxine. Illinois 1840 Census Index, Volume 3 -
Counties Jersey Through Marshall. 1975. 85pp. 6.75 (330)

Jo DAVIESS COUNTY

The History of Jo Daviess County, Illinois. 1878. 868pp.
B-BH 11690. .... (778)
Wormer, Maxine. Illinois 1840 Census Index, Volume 3 -
Counties Jersey Through Marshall. 1975. 85pp. 6.75 (330)

JOHNSON COUNTY

Genealogy Projects Committee. Winnetka Public Library.
Index to the Biographical Review of Johnson, Massac, Pope,
& Hardin Counties, Illinois. 1975. 111pp. 6.00 (276)
Wormer, Maxine. Illinois 1840 Census Index, Volume 3 -
Counties Jersey Through Marshall. 1975. 85pp. 6.75 (330)

KANE COUNTY

Bateman, Newton and Paul Selby, eds. Historical Encyclopedia
of Illinois; and History of Kane County, ed. John S. Wilcox.
1904. 344pp. B-BH 4839. .... (778)
The Biographical Record of Kane County, Illinois. 1898. 790pp.
B-BH 11783. .... (778)
Commemorative Biographical and Historical Record of Kane
County, Illinois. 1888. 1106pp. B-BH 3164. .... (778)
The Past and Present of Kane County, Illinois. 1878. 840pp.
B-BH 11689. .... (778)
Wormer, Maxine. Illinois 1840 Census Index, Volume 3 -
Counties Jersey Through Marshall. 1975. 85pp. 6.75 (330)

KANKAKEE COUNTY

_____. Illinois 1840 Census Index, Volume 3 - Counties Jersey
Through Marshall. 1975. 85pp. 6.75 (330)

KENDALL COUNTY

Genealogical and Biographical Record of Kendall and Will
Counties, Illinois. 1901. 668pp. B-BH 3163. .... (778)
Wormer, Maxine. Illinois 1840 Census Index, Volume 3 -
Counties Jersey Through Marshall. 1975. 85pp. 6.75 (330)

KNOX COUNTY

Bateman, Newton and Paul Selby, eds. Historical Encyclopedia
of Illinois, and Knox County, ed. W. Selden Gale and George
Candee Gale. 1899. 682pp. B-BH 3159. .... (778)
Calkins, Earnest E. They Broke the Prarie: Being Some Ac-
count of the Settlement of the Upper Mississippi Valley by
Religious & Educational Pioneers, Told in Terms of One
City, Galesburg, & of One College, Knox. Repr. of 1937 ed. 19.50 ..... (297)
History of Knox County, Illinois. 1878. 720pp. B-BH 11698. .... (778)
Portrait and Biographical Album of Knox County, Illinois.
1886. 1130pp. B-BH 4841. .... (778)
Wormer, Maxine. Illinois 1840 Census Index, Volume 3 -
Counties Jersey Through Marshall. 1975. 85pp. 6.75 (330)

LAKE COUNTY

_____. Illinois 1840 Census Index, Volume 3 - Counties Jersey
Through Marshall. 1975. 85pp. 6.75 (330)

LaSALLE COUNTY

History of LaSalle County, Illinois. 1886. Vol. 1-948pp.
Vol. 2-922pp. B-BH 4822. .... (778)
The Past & Present of LaSalle County, Illinois. 1877. 654pp.
B-BH 11693. .... (778)
Wormer, Maxine. Illinois 1840 Census Index, Volume 3 -
Counties Jersey Through Marshall. 1975. 85pp. 6.75 (330)

LAWRENCE COUNTY

Combined History of Edwards, Lawrence and Wabash Counties,
Illinois. 1883. 444pp. B-BH 3168. .... (778)
Wormer, Maxine. Illinois 1840 Census Index, Volume 3 -
Counties Jersey Through Marshall. 1975. 85pp. 6.75 (330)

LEE COUNTY

History of Lee County, Together with Biographical Matter,
Statistics, etc. 1881. 896pp. B-BH 11896. .... (778)
Portrait and Biographical Record of Lee County, Illinois.
1892. 850pp. B-BH 4836. .... (778)
Recollections of the Pioneers of Lee County, Illinois. 1893.
596pp. B-BH 11699. .... (778)
Wormer, Maxine. Illinois 1840 Census Index, Volume 3 -
Counties Jersey Through Marshall. 1975. 85pp. 6.75 (330)

LIVINGSTON COUNTY

_____. Illinois 1840 Census Index, Volume 3 -
Counties Jersey Through Marshall. 1975. 85pp. 6.75 (330)

LOGAN COUNTY

Decatur Genealogical Society. Cemetery Inscriptions, Logan
County, Illinois, Volume III. 1971. 130pp.
Contains Green Hill, Bethel, Union Station, Lawn-
dale, Elkhart, Hartsburg, and Carlyle. Indexed. 6.00 (187)
_____. United States 1840 Census, Logan County, Illinois.
1975. 12pp. 1.25 (187)
History of Logan County, Illinois. 1878. 590pp. B-BH 11876. .... (778)
Stringer, Lawrence B. History of Logan County, Illinois.
1911. Vol 1-704pp. Vol. 2-408pp. B-BH 11863. .... (778)
Wormer, Maxine. Illinois 1840 Census Index, Volume 3-
Counties Jersey Through Marshall. 1975. 85pp. 6.75 (330)

McDONOUGH COUNTY

Clarke, S. J. History of McDonough County, Illinois. 1878.
Text -708pp. Index -76pp. B-BH 11872. .... (778)
History of McDonough County, Illinois. 1885. 1136pp. B-BH 4895. .... (778)
"Newspaper Abstracts from McDonough County, Illinois."
(2 parts). The Ridge Runners, Vol. 4. 1976. 20pp. .... (859)
Portrait and Biographical Record of Hancock, McDonough and
Henderson Counties, Illinois. 1894. 602pp. B-BH 11688. .... (778)
Wormer, Maxine. Illinois 1840 Census Index, Volume 3 -
Counties Jersey Through Marshall. 1975. 85pp. 6.75 (330)

McHENRY COUNTY

Biographical Directory of the Tax Payers & Voters of McHenry
County, Illinois. 1877. 370pp. B-BH 11894. .... (778)
History of McHenry County, Illinois. 1885. 1085pp. B-BH 4906. .... (778)
Wormer, Maxine. Illinois 1840 Census Index, Volume 3-
Counties Jersey Through Marshall. 1975. 85pp. 6.75 (330)

McLEAN COUNTY

The Biographical Record of McLean County, Illinois. 1899.
834pp. B-BH 11865. .... (778)
Duis, E. The Good Old Times in McLean County, Illinois.
1874. 906pp. B-BH 11875. .... (778)
Hasbrouck, Jacob Louis. History of McLean County, Illinois.
1924. Vol. 1 -768pp. Vol. 2-778pp. B-BH 11861. .... (778)
The History of McLean County, Illinois. 1879. 1090pp.
B-BH 11899. .... (778)
Portrait and Biographical Album of McLean County, Illinois.
1887. 1222pp. B-BH 4907. .... (778)
Wormer, Maxine. Illinois 1840 Census Index, Volume 3 -
Counties Jersey Through Marshall. 1975. 85pp. 6.75 (330)

MACON COUNTY

Decatur Genealogical Society. Cemetery Inscriptions, Macon
County, Illinois, Volume X. 1975. 233pp.
Contains oldest cemetery in Decatur, Greenwood
Cemetery, Illinois. Death dates beginning in 1820's.
Indexed. 8.00 (187)
_____. Cemetery Inscriptions, Macon County, Illinois, Volume
XI. 1976. 227pp.
Contains Fairlawn Cemetery, over 12,000 names with
birthdates beginning in 1830's. Indexed. 8.00 (187)

_____. Deaths & Burials, Macon County Poor Farm, Decatur,
Illinois. 1975. 22pp. 3.00 (187)
_____. Macon County, Illinois, Marriage Records, Volume VI -
1891-1900. 1976. 220pp. 8.00 (187)
_____. United States 1840 Census, Macon County, Illinois.
1975. 17pp. 1.25 (187)
Portrait & Biographical Record of Macon County, Illinois. 1893.
728pp. B-BH 4892. .... (778)
Richmond, Mabel E. Centennial History of Decatur and Macon
County. 1930. 480pp. B-BH 11895. .... (778)
Wormer, Maxine. Illinois 1840 Census Index, Volume 3 -
Counties Jersey Through Marshall. 1975. 85pp. 6.75 (330)

MACOUPIN COUNTY

Biographical Record: Biographical Sketches of Leading Citizens
of Macoupin County, Illinois. 1904. 560pp. B-BH 11859. .... (778)
History of Macoupin County, Illinois. 1879. 438pp. B-BH 4891. .... (778)
Portrait & Biographical Record of Macoupin County, Illinois.
1891. 910pp. B-BH 4893. .... (778)
Walker, Charles A. History of Macoupin County, Illinois,
Biographical and Pictorial. 1911. Vol. 1 -532pp. Vol. 2 -
730pp. B-BH 11856. .... (778)
Wormer, Maxine. Illinois 1840 Census Index, Volume 3 -
Counties Jersey Through Marshall. 1975. 85pp. 6.75 (330)

MADISON COUNTY

History of Madison County, Illinois. 1882. 688pp. B-BH 4904. .... (778)
Norton, W.T., ed. Centennial History of Madison County,
Illinois and Its People, 1812 to 1912. 1912. Vol. 1 -668pp.
Vol. 2 -808pp. B-BH 3172. .... (778)
Wormer, Maxine. Illinois 1840 Census Index, Volume 3 -
Counties Jersey Through Marshall. 1975. 85pp. 6.75 (330)
_____. Madison County 1850 Census. 1976. 126,122pp. Set: 13.25 (330)

MARION COUNTY

Biographical and Reminiscent History of Richland, Clay and
Marion Counties, Illinois. 1909. 660pp. B-BH 11960. .... (778)
History of Marion and Clinton Counties, Illinois. 1881. 396pp.
B-BH 4903. .... (778)
Portrait and Biographical Record of Clinton, Washington, Marion
and Jefferson Counties, Illinois. 1894. 574pp. B-BH 4813. .... (778)
Wormer, Maxine. Illinois 1840 Census Index, Volume 3 -
Counties Jersey Through Marshall. 1975. 85pp. 6.75 (330)

MARSHALL COUNTY

Biographical Record of Bureau, Marshall, Putnam and Stark
Counties, Illinois. 1897. 770pp. B-BH 11636. .... (778)
Ellsworth, Spencer. Records of the Olden Time: or, Fifty Years
on the Praries. 1880. 760pp. B-BH 11966.
History and biographical sketches pertaining to Putnam
and Marshall Counties, Illinois. .... (778)
Ford, Henry Allen. The History of Putnam and Marshall
Counties. 1860. 160pp. B-BH 13733. .... (778)
Wormer, Maxine. Illinois 1840 Census Index, Volume 3 -
Counties Jersey Through Marshall. 1975. 85pp. 6.75 (330)

MASON COUNTY

Cochrane, Joseph. Centennial History of Mason County.
1876. 370pp. B-BH 11874. .... (778)
Genealogy Projects Committee. Winnetka Public Library.
Index to History of Menard & Mason Counties, Illinois.
1974. ..... 6.00 (276)
Portrait and Biographical Record of Tazewell and Mason
Counties, Illinois. 1894. 704pp. B-BH 4949. .... (778)

MASSAC COUNTY

Genealogy Projects Committee. Winnetka Public Library.
Index to the Biographical Review of Johnson, Massac,
Pope and Hardin Counties, Illinois. 1975. 111pp. 6.00 (276)

MENARD COUNTY

_____. Index - History of Menard and Mason Counties, Illinois.
1974. ..... 6.00 (276)

MONROE COUNTY

Combined History of Randolph, Monroe and Perry Counties,
Illinois. 1883. 509pp. B-BH 4933. .... (778)
Hotz, Roberta Sparwasser. Marriages. 1976. 172pp. 8.25 (330)
Portrait and Biographical Record of Randolph, Jackson, Perry,
and Monroe Counties, Illinois. 1894. 868pp. B-BH 4928. .... (778)
Wormer, Maxine. 1850 Census. 1976. 97pp. 6.25 (330)

MONTGOMERY COUNTY

Portrait and Biographical Record of Montgomery and Bond
Counties, Illinois. 1892. 532pp. B-BH 4997. .... (778)

MORGAN COUNTY

Bateman, Newton and Paul Selby, eds. Historical Encyclopedia
of Illinois, and History of Morgan County, ed. William F.
Short. 1906. 613pp. B-BH 3167. .... (778)
Eames, Charles M. Historic Morgan and Classic Jacksonville,
Illinois. 1885. 372pp. B-BH 11858. .... (778)
Hardy, Elizabeth. Index of Farmers (1913). 1973. 40pp.
Index of farmers, wives (maiden names), children in
Morgan County, Illinois. From Prarie Farmer 1913
Directory. 2.00 (315)
History of Morgan County, Illinois. 1878. 788pp. B-BH 11853. .... (778)
Portrait and Biographical Album of Morgan and Scott Counties.
1889. 626pp. B-BH 4896. .... (778)

MOULTRIE COUNTY

Combined History of Shelby and Moultrie Counties, Illinois.
1881. 444pp. B-BH 4944. .... (778)

OGLE COUNTY

The Biographical Record of Ogle County, Illinois. 1899. 496pp.
B-BH 11898. .... (778)
The History of Ogle County, Illinois. 1878. 860pp. B-BH 11892. .... (778)
Portrait and Biographical Album of Ogle County, Illinois. 1886.
958pp. B-BH 4899. .... (778)

PEORIA COUNTY

The History of Peoria County, Illinois. 1880. 898pp.
B-BH 3166. .... (778)
Portrait and Biographical Album of Peoria County, Illinois.
1890. 1020pp. B-BH 4931. .... (778)

PERRY COUNTY

Combined History of Randolph, Monroe, and Perry Counties,
Illinois. 1883. 509pp. B-BH 4933. .... (778)
Portrait and Biographical Record of Randolph, Jackson, Perry
and Monroe Counties, Illinois. 1894. 868pp. B-BH 4928 .... (778)

PIKE COUNTY

History of Pike County, Illinois. 1880. 972pp. B-BH 11964. .... (778)
Portrait and Biographical Album of Pike and Calhoun Counties.
1891. 816pp. B-BH 4922. .... (778)

POPE COUNTY

Genealogy Projects Committee. Winnetka Public Library. Index
to the Biographical Review of Johnson, Massac, Pope and
Hardin Counties, Illinois. 111pp. 6.00 (276)

PULASKI COUNTY

Perrin, William Henry, ed. History of Alexander, Union and
Pulaski Counties, Illinois. 1883. 926pp. B-BH 3160. .... (778)

PUTNAM COUNTY

Biographical Record of Bureau, Marshall, Putnam and Stark
Counties, Illinois. 1897. 770pp. B-BH 11636. .... (778)
Ellsworth, Spencer. Records of the Olden Time: or, Fifty
Years on the Praries. 1880. 760pp. B-BH 11966.
History and biographical sketches pertaining to
Putnam and Marshall Counties, Illinois. .... (778)
"Records of the Clear Creek Meeting of Friends: Part II -
Marriages (Putnam County)." ISGS Quarterly, Vol. 1,
No. 4. 1969. 11pp. 2.00 (366)
"Records of the Clear Creek Meeting of Friends: Part V -
Membership, Removals (Illinois)." ISGS Quarterly, Vol. 5,
No. 2. 1973. 11pp. 2.00 (366)
Wormer, Maxine. Putnam County 1850 Census. 1975. 47pp. 5.25 (330)

RANDOLPH COUNTY

Combined History of Randolph, Monroe and Perry Counties,
Illinois. 1883. 509pp. B-BH 4933. .... (778)
Portrait and Biographical Record of Randolph, Jackson, Perry
and Monroe Counties, Illinois. 1894. 868pp. B-BH 4928. .... (778)

RICHLAND COUNTY

Biographical and Reminiscent History of Richland, Clay and
Marion Counties, Illinois. 1909. 660pp. B-BH 11960. .... (778)
Portrait and Biographical Record of Effingham, Jasper and
Richland Counties, Illinois. 1893. 602pp. B-BH 11613. .... (778)

....

ROCK ISLAND COUNTY

The Biographical Record of Rock Island County, Illinois. 1897.
462pp. B-BH 11962. .... (778)
The Past and Present of Rock Island County, Illinois. 1877.
498pp. B-BH 11967. .... (778)

ST. CLAIR COUNTY

Buecher, Robert. St. Clair County Birth and Death Records,
1843-1856. 1976. 46pp. 5.00 (330)
_____. St. Clair County 1850 Census. 1974. 94,85pp. Set: 13.50 (330)
History of St. Clair County, Illinois. 1881. 528pp. B-BH 4935. .... (778)
Portrait and Biographical Record of St. Clair County, Illinois.
1892. 680pp. B-BH 4927. .... (778)
"St. Clair County, Illinois, Marriages: 1791-1810." ISGS
Quarterly, Vol. 3, No. 4. 1971. 18pp. 2.00 (366)

SALINE COUNTY

Moore, Bernard W. Marriages, 1847-1880. 1976. 272pp. 12.75 (330)

SANGAMON COUNTY

History of Sangamon County, Illinois. 1881. 1060pp. B-BH 11963. .... (778)
History of the Early Settlers of Sangamon County, Illinois. 1876.
822pp. B-BH 11965.
   Includes a genealogical record pertaining to the county. .... (778)
Sangamon County Genealogical Society. Cemetery Names and
Locations in Sangamon County, Illinois. 1.00 (875)
_____. 1850 Census & 1850 Mortality Schedule of Sangamon County. 12.00 (875)
Temple and Thomas. Sangamon County Probate Records, 1827-
1835. 1975. 59pp. 5.75 (330)

SCHUYLER COUNTY

Biographical Review of Cass, Schuyler and Brown Counties, Illinois.
1892. 636pp. B-BH 4798. .... (778)
W. R. Brink and Company. Combined History of Schuyler and
Brown Counties, Illinois. With Illustrations Descriptive of
their Scenery, and Biographical Sketches of Some of their
Prominent Men and Pioneers. 1882. 446pp. B-BH 4925.
   Includes troop rosters from these counties in Mexican
and Civil War. .... (778)

SCOTT COUNTY

Portrait and Biographical Album of Morgan and Scott Counties.
1889. 626pp. B-BH 4896. .... (778)

SHELBY COUNTY

Combined History of Shelby and Moultrie Counties, Illinois.
1881. 444pp. B-BH 4944. .... (778)
Decatur Genealogical Society. History of Sanner Chapel,
Moweaqua, Shelby County, Illinois. 1976. 16pp.
   Church history covering 1875-1950. Lists of pastors,
teachers, Cradle Roll, etc. Also, Sanner family
biographical and genealogical information. 1.25 (187)
Historic Sketch and Biographical Album of Shelby County,
Illinois. 1900. 390pp. B-BH 12016. .... (778)

STARK COUNTY

Biographical Record of Bureau, Marshall, Putnam and Stark
Counties, Illinois. 1897. 770pp. B-BH 11636. .... (778)

STEPHENSON COUNTY

Fulwider, Addison L. History of Stephenson County, Illinois.
1910. Vol. 1 -740pp. Vol. 2 -572pp. B-BH 4996. .... (778)
The History of Stephenson County, Illinois. 1880. 734pp.
B-BH 12018. .... (778)
In the Foot-Prints of the Pioneers of Stephenson County,
Illinois; a Genealogical Record. 1900. 402pp. B-BH 3170. .... (778)
Portrait and Biographical Album of Stephenson County, Illinois.
1888. 772pp. B-BH 4951. .... (778)

TAZEWELL COUNTY

History of Tazewell County, Illinois. 1879. 812pp. B-BH 12005. .... (778)
Portrait and Biographical Record of Tazewell and Mason
Counties, Illinois. 1894. 704pp. B-BH 4949. .... (778)

UNION COUNTY

Perrin, William Henry, ed. History of Alexander, Union and
Pulaski Counties, Illinois. 1883. 926pp. B-BH 3160. .... (778)

VERMILION COUNTY

Portrait and Biographical Album of Vermilion and Edgar Counties.
1889. 1124pp. B-BH 4939. .... (778)

WABASH COUNTY

Combined History of Edwards, Lawrence and Wabash Counties,
Illinois. 1883. 444pp. B-BH 3168. .... (778)

WARREN COUNTY

The Past and Present of Warren County, Illinois. 1877. 358pp.
B-BH 11998. .... (778)
Portrait and Biographical Album of Warren County, Illinois.
1886. 810pp. B-BH 4946. .... (778)

WASHINGTON COUNTY

Portrait and Biographical Record of Clinton, Washington, Marion
and Jefferson Counties, Illinois. 1894. 574pp. B-BH 4813. .... (778)

WAYNE COUNTY

Bland, Doris Ellen Witter. Wayne County, Illinois Cemetery
Inscriptions, Volume V. 1975. 264pp.
Complete inscriptions of cemeteries in the city of
Fairfield, Illinois. 12.60 (73)
_____. Wayne County, Illinois Cemetery Inscriptions, Volume
VI. 1975. 154pp.
Complete inscriptions of 11 Wayne County, Illinois,
cemeteries. 7.35 (73)
Decatur Genealogical Society. United States 1850 Census,
Wayne County, Illinois. Repr. of 1969 ed. 136pp. 6.00 (187)
History of Wayne and Clay Counties, Illinois. 1884. Text -618pp.
Supplement -108pp. B-BH 11995. .... (778)

WHITESIDE COUNTY

Bent, Charles. History of Whiteside County, Illinois. 1877.
542pp. B-BH 12000. .... (778)
The Biographical Record of Whiteside County, Illinois. 1900.
532pp. B-BH 12013. .... (778)
Portrait and Biographical Album of Whiteside County, Illinois.
1885. 954pp. B-BH 4950. .... (778)

WILL COUNTY

Genealogical and Biographical Record of Kendall and Will
Counties, Illinois. 1901. 668pp. B-BH 3163. .... (778)
Genealogical and Biographical Record of Will County, Illinois.
1900. 640pp. B-BH 12008. .... (778)
Genealogy Projects Committee. Winnetka Public Library.
An Index to the Names of Persons Appearing in "The History
of Will County, Illinois." 1973. 101pp. 6.00 (267)
The History of Will County, Illinois. 1878. 992pp. B-BH 11969. .... (778)
Portrait and Biographical Album of Will County, Illinois. 1890.
776pp. B-BH 3169. .... (778)
Souvenir of Settlement and Progress of Will County, Illinois. 1884.
458pp. B-BH 12002. .... (778)

WINNEBAGO COUNTY

Church, Charles A. and H. H. Waldo. Past and Present of the
City of Rockford and Winnebago County, Illinois. 1905.
866pp. B-BH 4947. .... (778)
The History of Winnebago County, Illinois. 1877. 672pp.
B-BH 11996. .... (778)
Portrait and Biographical Record of Winnebago and Boone
Counties, Illinois. 1892. 1314pp. B-BH 4942. .... (778)
Swartz, Elsie R. Winnebago County Early Marriages, 1836-
1866. 1975. 161pp. 8.25 (330)

WOODFORD COUNTY

Portrait and Biographical Album of Woodford County, Illinois.
1889. 606pp. B-BH 4940. .... (778)

Indiana

STATEWIDE REFERENCES

Alley, Jean and Hartley Alley. Southern Indiana. 1965. 5.95 2.95 (370)
Anson, Bert. The Fur Traders in Northern Indiana, 1796-1850.
337pp. BIP-00-5853. .... (777)
Barnhart, John D. and Dorothy Riker. Indiana to 1816. The
Colonial Period. 1971. 520pp.
History of the state of Indiana to 1816 prior to statehood.
French, British, and early American settlement
Volume I of History of Indiana. 4.50 (369)
Bayard, Charles Judah. The Development of the Public Land
Policy, 1783-1820, with Special Reference to Indiana. 331pp.
BIP-00-17933. .... (777)
Carey, James Lester. A History of the Indiana Penitentiary
System, 1821-1933. 288pp. BIP-67-03676. .... (777)

Cox, Sandford C. Recollections of the Early Settlement of the
  Wabash Valley. 1860.   9.00   ..... (81)
Ellsworth, Henry William. Valley of the Upper Wabash,
  Indiana: With Hints on its Agricultural Advantages; Plan
  of a Dwelling, Estimates of Cultivation, and Notices of
  Labor-Saving Machines. 1838.   12.00   ..... (38)
Funk, Arville L. A Sketchbook of Indiana History. 1969.
  225pp. 3.50 (14)
Indiana University Department of History. Indiana Magazine
of History. 1905-1966
    This excellent journal, edited by various members of
    Indiana University Department of History, has main-
    tained a consistently high calibre of scholarship for
    more than fifty years. Devoted primarily to articles,
    documents, and reviews concerning the political,
    economic, social and cultural history of Indiana and the
    Middle West, it also gives attention to materials in the
    general fields of American and Canadian history, insofar
    as they are relevant to its major areas of interest.

	Set:	1165.00	885.00	(415)
Vols. 1-21 (reprint):	Each:	.....	15.00	(415)
Vols. 22-62 (original edition):	Each:	.....	12.00	(415)
General Index 1-25:	Each:	.....	12.00	(415)
General Index 26-50:	Each:	.....	18.00	(415)

Krauskopf, Frances. The French in Indiana, 1700-1760: A
  Political History. 413pp. BIP-00-05869.   .... (777)
Lewis, George E. The Indiana Company, 1763-1798: A Study
  in Eighteenth Century Frontier Land Speculation and Business
  Venture. Repr. of 1941 ed.   13.75   ..... (81)
Pence, George and Nellie C. Armstrong. Indiana Boundaries,
  Territory, State and County. 1933.   7.50   ..... (369)
Phillips, Clifton J. Indiana in Transition, 1880-1920. 1968.
  674pp.
    General history of Indiana for period 1880-1920 - Volume
    IV of History of Indiana. 4.50 (369)

Savelle, Max. George Morgan: Colony Builder. 1932.
    Affiliated with Indiana Company.   7.00   ..... (2)
Strausberg, Stephen Frederick. The Administration and Sale
    of Public Land in Indiana, 1800-1860. 452pp. BIP-70-24017.   .... (777)
Thomas, David. Travels Through the Western Country in the
    Summer of 1816, ed. George W. White. Repr. of 1819 ed.   14.95   ..... (306)
Thornbrough, Emma Lou. Indiana in the Civil War Era, 1850-
    1880. 1965. 758pp.
        General history for period 1850-1880. Volume III of
        History of Indiana. 4.50 (369)
_____. The Negro in Indiana Before 1900: A Study of a
    Minority. 1958.   6.00   ..... (369)
Wilson, George R. Early Indiana Trails and Surveys. Repr.
    of 1919 ed.   1.50   ..... (369)
Woollen, William Wesley. Biographical and Historical Sketches
    of Early Indiana. 1883. illus.   32.00   ..... (38)

Research Aids

Illustrated Historical Atlas of the State of Indiana, 1876.
    Repr. of county maps (1968). 5.00 (369)
Individual county maps: Each: 90 (369)
"Published County Records of Indiana." A bibliography.
    The Ridge Runners, Vol. 4. 1976. 17pp.   .... (859)

Military

Berlin, Calvin C. Indiana's Civilian Soldiers. 279pp.
    BIP-00-17934.   .... (777)
Funk, Arville L. Hoosiers in the Civil War. 1967. 180pp. 5.00 (14)
_____. The Morgan Raid in Indiana and Ohio (1863). 1971.
    68pp. 5.00 (14)
_____. Revolutionary War Era in Indiana. 1975. 37pp. 2.50 (14)

Religious

Elliott, Errol T. Quakers on the American Frontier. 1969.
    434pp.
        An account of Quakers who migrated from the east
        to Ohio and central Indiana during the early 1800's.   4.95   ..... (255)
Heiss, Willard, comp. Abstracts of the Records of the
    Society of Friends in Indiana, Parts I - VI. 1963-1975.
        Part One contains records of Whitewater and Chester
        monthly meetings in Wayne County and Silver Creek -
        Salem monthly meetings in Union County: 7.50 (369)
        Part Two contains records of 12 monthly meetings in
        Wayne, Randolph and Jay Counties: .....   o.p. (369)
        Part Three contains records of 15 monthly meetings in
        Grant, Howard, Huntington, Miami and Wabash
        Counties: 15.00 12.50 (369)
        Part Four contains records of 11 monthly meetings in
        Wayne, Henry and Rush Counties: 15.00 12.50 (369)
        Part Five contains records of 15 monthly meetings in
        Orange, Washington, Sullivan, Parke, Morgan,
        Montgomery, Boone, Tippecanoe, Vermillion Counties
        (and Vermilion County, Illinois):   17.50 15.00 (369)
        Part Six contains records of 18 monthly meetings in
        Hendricks, Morgan, Marion and Hamilton Counties: 17.50 15.00 (369)

Gipson, Lawrence H. The Moravian Indian Mission on
White River - Diaries and Letters, May 5, 1799 to
November 12, 1806. 1938. ..... 5.00 (369)
McNamara, William. The Catholic Church on the Northern
Indiana Frontier, 1789-1844. 1931. 6.00 ..... (2)

Records

Philbrick, Francis S., ed. The Laws of Indiana Territory,
1801-1809, Collections of the Illinois State Historical
Library, Volume XXI, Law Series. 1931. ..... 4.50 (369)
Heiss, Willard, comp. 1820 Federal Census for Indiana.
Repr. of 1966 ed.
    Information follows form of original census. 10.00 ..... (369)
Index to 1840 Federal Population Census of Indiana. 1975.
374pp.
    Names are arranged alphabetically with county in
    which they resided and page number of census. 20.00 ..... (369)
United States Government. Territorial Papers. Volume 7:
The Territory of Indiana, 1800-1810. Foundations of
Indiana Territory, 1800. The Four Administrations of
Governor Harrison, 1800-1810. 1939. Index. 57.50 ..... (2)
United States Government. Territorial Papers. Volume 8:
The Territory of Indiana, 1810-1816. The Fifth
Administration of Governor Harrison, 1810-1812. The
Administration of Acting Governor Gibson, 1812-1813.
The Administration of Governor Posey, 1813-1816. 1939.
Index. 57.50 ..... (2)

ALLEN COUNTY

Poinsatte, Charles Robert. Fort Wayne, Indiana During the
Canal Era, 1828-1855: A Study of A Western Community
During the Middle Period of American History. 1964.
412pp. BIP-64-07960. .... (777)

BARTHOLOMEW COUNTY

Gerber, Adolf, tr. The Journey of Lewis David von Schweinitz
to Goshen, Bartholomew County, in 1831. 1927. ..... 1.50 (369)
Holmes, Maurice. Early Landowners of Bartholomew County,
Indiana. 1975. 88pp.
    Original purchasers from USA and landowners from
    1822-1834. 11.00 ..... (345)

BLACKFORD COUNTY

Lewis Publishing Company. 1887 History of Blackford County,
Indiana. Repr. of 1887 ed. 9.75 ..... (80)
_____. 1887 History of Jay and Blackford Counties, Indiana.
Repr. of 1887 ed. 16.75 ..... (80)

CASS COUNTY

Kingman Brothers. Cass County, Indiana 1878 Atlas.
Repr. of 1878 ed. 23.00 14.00 (80)

DECATUR COUNTY

Beers (J. H.) and Company. 1882 Landowners Atlas Decatur
County, Indiana. Repr. of 1882 ed. 103pp. 23.00 14.00 (80)

Holmes, Maurice. Early Landowners of Decatur County,
Indiana. 1975. 90pp.
Original purchasers from USA and landowners
from 1822 to 1835.   11.00   •••• (345)

DeKALB COUNTY

Beers (J. H.) and Company. DeKalb County, Indiana, 1880
Landowner Atlas. repr. of 1880 ed. 51pp.   20.00   11.00 (80)

DUBOIS COUNTY

Poplar Creek Genealogical Society, comp. Excerpts from
"Jasper Courier" 1858-1860. 1976.
National news; local news; vital statistics, etc.   •••••   x   (611)

FAYETTE COUNTY

Holmes, Maurice. Early Landowners of Fayette County,
Indiana. 1976. 80pp.
Original purchasers from USA, landowners prior to
forming of county and from 1819 to 1833.   11.00   ••••• (345)

FOUNTAIN COUNTY

Luke, Miriam. Circuit Court Records, 1829-1849. 1976. 75pp.
Petitions to partition land, Chancery Court Records.   •••••   6.25 (330)

FRANKLIN COUNTY

Beers (J. H.) and Company. 1882 Landowners Atlas of
Franklin County, Indiana. Repr. of 1882 ed. 136pp.   24.50   15.50 (80)

FULTON COUNTY

"1857 Fair,"   Fulton County Historical Society Quarterly.
1975. Quarterly No. 20.   •••••   1.00 (260)
"Fulton Blacksmith Shop." Fulton County Historical Society
Quarterly. 1976. Quarterly No. 23.   •••••   1.00 (260)
"History of Henry Township Schools." Fulton County Historical
Society Quarterly, Vol. 6, No. 1. 1969. 23pp.   •••••   1.00 (260)
"Liberty Township Schools, Part 1." Fulton County Historical
Society Quarterly. 1975. Quarterly No. 21.   •••••   1.00 (260)
"Liberty Township Schools, Part 2." Fulton County Historical
Society Quarterly. 1975. Quarterly No. 22.   •••••   1.00 (260)
"Mt. Olive Community." Fulton County Historical Society
Quarterly. 1976. Quarterly No. 23.   •••••   1.00 (260)
"Newcastle Township Schools." Fulton County Historical
Society Quarterly. 1976. Quarterly No. 24.   •••••   1.00 (260)
"Rochester In 1936." Fulton County Historical Society
Quarterly. 1974. Quarterly No. 19.   •••••   1.00 (260)

HANCOCK COUNTY

Griffing (Gordon) and Company. Hancock County, Indiana
1887 Landowner Atlas. Repr. of 1887 ed. 44pp.   16.00   7.50 (80)
Holmes, Maurice. Early Landowners of Hancock County,
Indiana. 1974. 62pp.
Original purchasers from USA and landowners from
1828 to 1837.   11.00   8.00 (345)

HARRISON COUNTY

Funk, Arville L., ed. 1810 Census of Harrison County,
Indiana. 1976. 24pp. 2.00 (14)
_____. Harrison County in the Indiana Sesquicentennial.
1967. 80pp. 1.50 (14)
_____. Historical Almanac of Harrison County. 1974. 81pp. 2.50 (14)
_____. Revolutionary War Soldiers of Harrison County,
Indiana. 1975. 37pp. 2.00 (14)
_____. Squire Boone In Indiana. 1974. 24pp. 1.50 (14)

JAY COUNTY

Lewis Publishing Company. 1887 History of Jay and Blackford
Counties Indiana. Repr. of 1887 ed. 16.75 ..... (80)
_____. 1887 History of Jay County Indiana. Repr. of 1887 ed. 12.75 ..... (80)

JENNINGS COUNTY

Holmes, Maurice. Early Landowners of Jennings County,
Indiana. 1976. 80pp.
Original purchasers from USA and landowners from 1816
to 1830. 11.00 ..... (345)

JOHNSON COUNTY

Holmes, Maurice. Early Landowners of Johnson County,
Indiana. 1974. 41pp.
Original purchasers from USA and landowners from
1882 to 1834. 11.00 ..... (345)

KNOX COUNTY

Hodges, Malcolm Maurice. A Social History of Vincennes and
Knox County, Indiana from the Beginning to 1860.
1968. 207pp. BIP-69-01974. .... (777)

KOSCIUSKO COUNTY

Edgell, Scott A. Sketches of Lake Wawasee. 1967.
Sketches of families and their life in Wawasee area,
Kosciusko County. 2.75 ..... (369)

LaGRANGE COUNTY

LaGrange County, Indiana, Combines 1874-1893 Atlases. (new
index). Reprint. 132pp. 24.00 15.00 (80)

LaPORTE COUNTY

Harris, Mrs. William H. Abijah Bigelow - Revolutionary
Soldier. 1976. 36pp.
About Bigelow Mills; founded by his son. 2.00 (482)
Packard, Jasper. History of LaPorte County and Its Townships,
Towns and Cities. Repr. of 1876 ed. 467pp.
Reprint has been indexed (6000 entries); original was not
indexed. Lists all county soldiers who served in Civil War. 13.00 ..... (482)

MADISON COUNTY

Helm, Thomas B. History of Madison County, Indiana, with
Illustrations and Biographical Sketches of Some of its
Prominent Men and Pioneers. 1880. 128pp. B-BH 15125. .... (778)

MARION COUNTY

Bolton, Nathaniel. "Early History of Indianapolis and
Central Indiana." Indiana Historical Society Publication,
Vol. 1, No. 5. 1897. ..... 5.00 (369)

Johnson, Howard. A Home in the Woods: Oliver Johnson's
Reminiscences of Early Marion County. Repr. of 1951 ed. 2.00 (369)

Thornbrough, Gayle, ed., et al. The Diary of Calvin Fletcher.
Vols. I-IV. 1972-75. c600pp.
  Calvin Fletcher (1798-1866), b. Vermont, came to
  Indianapolis 1821; was lawyer, banker, farmer, churchman,
  railroad director and railroad president; trustee of first
  public schools, legislator. Diary chronicles events that
  took place in Indianapolis, reflecting his wide interests.

Volume I:	12.50	..... (369)
Volume II-IV:	10.00	..... (369)

MIAMI COUNTY

Ferris, Ezra. "The Early Settlement of the Miami Country."
Indiana Historical Society Publication, Vol. 1, No. 5. 1897. ..... 5.00 (369)

MONTGOMERY COUNTY

"Montgomery County, Indiana Marriage Consents." The
Ridge Runners, Vol. 4. 1976. 3pp. .... (859)

Thompson, Stephen J. The First Two Censuses of Montgomery
County, Indiana (1830 and 1840). 1975.
  Entire contents of 1830 and 1840 censuses alphabetically
  indexed. 6.00 (757)

PERRY COUNTY

O'Beirne (P.) and Company. Perry County, Indiana, 1861 Atlas.
Repr. of 1861 ed. 17.00 8.00 (80)

POSEY COUNTY

Arndt, Karl J. R., comp and ed. A Documentary History of the
Indiana Decade of the Harmony Society 1814-1819. 1975. 837pp.
  Removal of Rappites from Butler County, Pennsylvania
  to Posey County, Indiana. Describes first years in
  Indiana. Vol. I of two volume work. 17.50 8.00 (369)

RUSH COUNTY

Beers (J. H.) and Company. 1879 Atlas of Rush County,
Indiana. Repr. of 1879 ed. 82pp. 20.00 11.00 (80)

Holmes, Maurice. Early Landowners of Rush County, Indiana.
1975. 79pp.
  Original purchasers from USA and landowners from
  1820 to 1832. 11.00 8.00 (345)

Shiloh Cemetary Records. 1976. c50pp.
  Includes plot layout. $1.00/book contributed to cemetary
  care. 6.00 3.00 (160)

ST. JOSEPH COUNTY

Renkiewicz, Frank Anthony. The Polish Settlement of
St. Joseph County, Indiana: 1855-1935. 1967.
361pp. BIP-68-05104. .... (777)

SHELBY COUNTY

Holmes, Maurice. Early Landowners of Shelby County, Indiana.
1976. 84pp.
    Original purchasers from USA and landowners from
    1822 to 1834.   11.00   ..... (345)
Holmes, Maurice and Robert Gordon. Excerpts from Shelbyville,
Indiana Newspapers 1853-1859. 1973. 244pp.
    Genealogy items, marriages, deaths, tax lists, letters
    at Post Office, etc., from various Shelbyville papers.   13.50   9.00 (345)
_____. Index to 1880 Beers Atlas of Shelby County, Indiana.
1975. 57pp.
    Names of all persons listed in sketches and landowners
    in all townships.   10.00   ..... (345)

STEUBEN COUNTY

The Kalamazoo Valley Genealogical Society. The Kalamazoo
Valley Family Newsletter (Steuben County, Indiana Issue).
1975. 88pp.
    General reference of material and sources available in
    county. Pioneer and some township and community
    records. All libraries, newspapers, and cemeteries
    listed and located. 4.00 (399)

VANDERBURG COUNTY

McCutchan, Kenneth P. From Then 'Til Now. History of
McCutchanville. 1969. 259pp. 3.00 (369)

WAYNE COUNTY

Lake, D. J. Wayne County, Indiana 1874 Landowner Atlas.
Repr. of 1874 ed. 77pp.   20.00 11.00 (80)

Iowa

STATEWIDE REFERENCES

Arkansas Genealogical Society. Arkansas Family Historian.
ed. Mrs. Mario B. Cia, Sr. c200pp/yr.
    Contains cemetery records, Bible records, court and
    other primary source materials and compiled family
    genealogies.   With Membership: 6.00 ..... (37)
Cooke, Philip St. George, eds., et. al. Exploring Southwestern
Trails 1846-1854: The Journal of Philip St. George Cooke,
the Journal of William Henry Chase Whiting and the Diaries
of Francois Xavier Aubry. Repr. of 1938 ed.   20.00 ..... (612)
Jones, Robert H. Civil War in the Northwest: Nebraska,
Wisconsin, Iowa, Minnesota, and the Dakotas. Repr. of
1960 ed.   8.95 ..... (556)
Mills, George S. Rogues and Heroes from Iowa's Amazing
Past. 1972.   5.95 ..... (377)
Schwieder, Dorothy. Patterns and Perspectives in Iowa
History. 1973.   .....   7.95 (377)
Schweider, Elmer and Dorothy Schweider. A Peculiar People:
Iowa's Old Order Amish. 1975.   8.50 ..... (377)

Swierenga, Robert Peter. Pioneers and Profits: Land
Speculation on the Iowa Frontier. 1965. 433pp. BIP-65-11664. .... (777)
Ware, Eugene F. Indian War of Eighteen Sixty Four.
ed. Clyde C. Walton. 1963. ..... 2.95 (521)

Research Aids

Iowa Genealogical Society. Surname Index Volume I. 1972. 365pp.
A listing of surnames from 1500's to 1972 as submitted
by our members from all over United States. Cross-indexed
giving date and state of birth, death and marriage when
known. Some have submitted whole pedigrees. Names
and addresses of contributors included. 7.50 (376)
_____. A Surname Index Volume II. 1975. 491pp.
A listing of surnames and given names from 1500's to
1975 submitted by our members from all over the United
States. Cross-indexed, giving state and year of birth,
death and marriage when known. Many submitted whole
pedigree lines back to Europe. Names and addresses
of contributors included. Not a repeat of Vol. 1. ..... 8.50 (376)
_____. Topical Index Volume I - X of Hawkeye Heritage.
1976. 4pp.
A listing of all items published in Hawkeye Heritage
1966 through 1975. Most items listed according to Iowa
Counties. Please enclose a stamped addressed 4 1/2 x
9 1/2 envelope when ordering this item separately. ..... .50 (376)

ALLAMAKEE

Iowa Genealogical Society. 1850 Census of Allamakee County,
Iowa - Every Name. 1975. 17pp. 1.50 (376)

BENTON

Iowa Genealogical Society. Benton County, Iowa 1850 Every Name
Census Index. 1975. 16pp. 1.50 (376)

BLACK HAWK

Iowa Genealogical Society. Black Hawk County, Iowa 1850 Every
Name Census Index. 1975. 4pp. 1.00 (376)

BOONE COUNTY

Iowa Genealogical Society. Boone County, Iowa 1850 Every Name
Census Index. 1975. 16pp. 1.50 (376)

BUCHANAN COUNTY

Iowa Genealogical Society. Buchanan County, Iowa 1850 Every
Name Census Index. 1975. 9pp. 1.00 (376)

CASS COUNTY

History of Cass County, Iowa. Repr. of 1884 ed. 910pp.
County history, illustrated, 7 x 10.   24.00 ..... (810)

CLARKE COUNTY

Iowa Genealogical Society. Clarke County, Iowa 1850 Every
Name Census Index. 1975. 4pp. 1.00 (376)

DALLAS COUNTY

History of Dallas County, Iowa. Repr. of 1907 ed. 800pp.
County history, illustrated and indexed, 7 x 10.   22.00 ..... (810)
Iowa Genealogical Society. Dallas County, Iowa Every Name
Census Index 1850. 1975. 20pp. 2.00 (376)

DECATUR COUNTY

Iowa Genealogical Society. Decatur County, Iowa 1850 Every
Name Census Index. 1975. 23pp. 2.00 (376)

DES MOINES COUNTY

Boeck, George Albert. An Early Iowa Community: Aspects of
Economic, Social and Political Development in Burlington,
Iowa, 1833-1866. 1961. 296pp. BIP-61-01912.   .... (777)

DICKINSON COUNTY

Iowa Genealogical Society. Dickinson County, Iowa Marriages
1871-1884. 1975. 5pp. 1.00 (376)

DUBUQUE COUNTY

Iowa Genealogical Society. Dubuque County, Iowa 1850 Every
Name Census Index. 1975. 244pp. 13.00 (376)

FAYETTE COUNTY

History of Fayette County, Iowa. Repr. of 1910 ed. 1816 pp.
County history, 2 volume set, illustrated. 6 x 9.   41.00 ..... (810)
Iowa Genealogical Society. Fayette County, Iowa 1850 Every
Name Census Index. 1975. 22pp. 2.00 (376)

IOWA COUNTY

Iowa Genealogical Society. Iowa County, Iowa 1850 Every Name
Census Index. 1975. 18pp. 1.50 (376)
Shambaugh, Bertha. Amana That Was and Amana That Is.
1932. 502pp.
    A firsthand account of the most successful community-
    living experiment in America an extraordinary experiment
    in Utopian Communism.   18.00 ..... (38)

JACKSON COUNTY

History of Jackson County, Iowa. Repr. of 1878 ed. 280pp.
County history, illustrated, 6 x 9   13.50 ..... (810)

JASPER COUNTY

Iowa Genealogical Society. Jasper County, Iowa 1850 Every
Name Census Index. 1975. 27pp. 2.00 (376)

JONES COUNTY

Iowa Genealogical Society. Jones County, Iowa 1850 Every
Name Census Index. 1975. 75pp. 4.50 (376)

KOSSUTH COUNTY

History of Kossuth County, Iowa. Repr. of 1913 ed. 1976. 1680pp.
County history, 2 volume set, indexed, illustrated, 7 x 10.   39.00 ..... (810)

LEE COUNTY

History of Lee County, Iowa. Repr. of 1879 ed. 887pp.
County history, illustrated, indexed, 6 x 9.   22.00 ..... (810)

LOUISA COUNTY

Iowa Genealogical Society. Louisa County, Iowa 1850 Every
Name Census Index. 1975. 135pp. 7.50 (376)

LUCAS COUNTY

Iowa Genealogical Society. Lucas County, Iowa 1850 Every
Name Census Index. 1975. 12pp. 1.50 (376)

MARION COUNTY

History of Marion County, Iowa. Repr. of 1881 ed. 904pp.
County history, illustrated, indexed, 6 x 9.   20.50 ..... (810)

MARSHALL COUNTY

Iowa Genealogical Society. Marshall County, Iowa 1850 Every
Name Census Index. 1975. 11pp. 1.50 (376)

OSCEOLA COUNTY

Iowa Genealogical Society. Osceola County, Iowa Marriages
1872-1900. 1975. 25pp. 2.00 (376)

PAGE COUNTY

History of Page County, Iowa. Repr. of 1880 ed. 980pp.
County history, illustrated, indexed, 6 x 9.   23.00 ..... (810)
Iowa Genealogical Society. Page County, Iowa 1850 Every
Name Census Index. 1975. 14pp. 1.50 (376)

POWESHIEK COUNTY

Iowa Genealogical Society. Poweshiek County, Iowa 1850 Every
Name Census Index. 1975. 16pp. 1.50 (376)

SHELBY COUNTY

Iowa Genealogical Society. Shelby County, Iowa Marriages
1853-1880. 1975. 25pp. 2.00 (376)

TAYLOR COUNTY

Iowa Genealogical Society. Taylor County, Iowa 1850 Every
Name Census Index. 1975. 6pp. 1.00 (376)

UNION COUNTY

Nissen, Sibyl M. Index to C. J. Colby's 1876 Illustrated
Centennial Sketches, Map and Directory of Union
County, Iowa. 1975. 41pp. 5.50 (541)

WARREN COUNTY

The History of Warren County, Iowa. 1879. 798pp. B-OP 65025. .... (778)

WAYNE COUNTY

Iowa Genealogical Society. Wayne County, Iowa 1850 Every
Name Census Index. 1975. 8pp. 1.00 (376)

WINNESHIEK COUNTY

Iowa Genealogical Society. Winneshiek County, Iowa 1850 Every
Name Census Index. 1975. 13pp. 1.50 (376)

Kansas

STATEWIDE REFERENCES

Castel, Albert. A Frontier State at War: Kansas, 1861-1865.
1958. 12.50 ..... (163)
Colt, Miriam D. West to Kansas, Being a Thrilling Account of
an Ill-Fated Expedition. Repr. of 1862 ed. 7.75 ..... (778)
Corder, Eric. Prelude to Civil War: Kansas-Missouri 1854-
1861. 1970. ..... 4.95 (454)
Donohue, Arthur T. The History of the Early Jesuit Missions
in Kansas. 256pp. BIP-00-00160. .... (777)
Ebbutt, Percy G. Emigrant Life in Kansas. Repr. of 1886 ed. 15.00 ..... (38)
Gates, Paul W. Fifty Million Acres: Conflicts Over Kansas
Land Policy, 1854-1890. 1954. 12.50 ..... (163)
Gladstone, T. H. Englishman in Kansas, Or, Squatter Life &
Border Warfare. 1971. 10.95 3.95 (521)
The Heritage Genealogical Society. The Heritage Genealogical
Society Quarterly. 30pp.
Membership in the Society entitles one to four quarterlies
with subscriptions running from June 1 to May 31. ..... $5/yr (329)

Listed below is the name of a professional genealogist willing to undertake research for
a fee within the state of Kansas, in areas specified in her ad:

Miller, Nyle H. and Joseph W. Snell. Great Gunfighters of the
    Kansas Cowtowns, 1867-1886. 1967.   .....   2.75 (521)
The Topeka Genealogical Society, comp. Kansas Pioneers.
    1976. 400pp.
        Biographical sketches and human interest stories of
        Kansas ancestors, with photographs, complete name
        index.   16.50   ..... (762)
_____. The Topeka Genealogical Society Quarterly.
        Containing primary source material, book reviews,
        and queries.   Subscription: $4/yr (762)
Vaughn, Jesse W. Battle of Platte Bridge (Kansas Cavalry,
    11th Regiment, 1862-1865). 1963.   7.95   ..... (556)
Wilder, Daniel W. The Annals of Kansas: New Edition, 1541-
    1885. Repr. of 1886.   66.00   ..... (38)
Zornow, William F. A History of the Jayhawk State. Repr. of
    1957 ed.   7.50   ..... (556)

Research Aids

Curtis, Mary Barnett. Bibliography of Kansas: The Formative
    Years. 1972. 40pp.
        All genealogical and historical books on subject and
        where to order if in print. 5.00 (371)
Historical Records Survey. Check List of Kansas Imprints,
    1854-1876. 1939.   ..... 27.00 (415)

"Index of Kansas Vital Records Published in Kansas
    Genealogical Quarterlies." The Topeka Genealogical
    Society Quarterly, Vol. VI, No. 2. 1976. 8pp. 1.50 (762)

Records

Robertson, Clara H. Kansas Territorial Settlers of 1860
    Who Were Born in Tennessee, Virginia, North Carolina,
    and South Carolina. 1976. 187pp.   17.50   ..... (274)

BARBER COUNTY

Yost, Nellie S. Medicine Lodge: The Story of a Kansas
    Frontier Town. 1970.   6.00   2.95 (735)

FORD COUNTY

Wright, Robert Marr. Dodge City. 1913. illus.   22.00   ..... (38)

JOHNSON COUNTY

Blair, Ed. A History of Johnson County, Kansas. 1915.
    530pp.
        Also contains considerable Indian lore and genealogy,
        over 200 biographical sketches, every-name index
        added.   19.50   ..... (387)
"Cumberland Presbyterian Church, Corinth Congregation."
    Johnson County Genealogist, Vol. I, No. 4. 1973. 7pp.
        History and records 1871-1873, communicants,
        elders, baptisms and marriages. 1.50 (387)
Johnson County Genealogical Society. The Johnson County
    Genealogist. c160pp.
        A genealogical quarterly containing primary source
        material, research helps, Bible records and queries. $5/yr (387)

"New England Emigrant Aid Society Papers." Johnson County
Genealogist, Vol. II, No. 1,2,3 and 4. 1974. 102pp.
   History of settlers from New England to Kansas
   1854-1855, includes names, occupations, prior
   residences and place of settlement. 1.50 (387)
"Shawnee (Indian) Depredation Claims." Johnson County
Genealogist, Vol. III, No. 3. 1975. 6pp.
   Individual claims against the United States government
   in 1855.   ..... 1.50 (387)

LEAVENWORTH COUNTY

History of Leavenworth County, Kansas. Repr. of 1906 ed.
   County history, illustrated, indexed.   13.50 ..... (810)

PHILLIPS COUNTY

Phillips County Genealogical Society, comp. Cemetery Inscriptions
of Phillips County, Kansas. 1976. In process.
   Inscriptions from the 44 cemeteries located in the
   county.   .... (595)
_____. Settlers in Phillips County, Kansas Prior to 1900.
1976. In process.
   Brief biographies of early settlers as recorded by
   their descendants.   .... (595)

RILEY COUNTY

Parshall, Frank N., comp. Riley County Obituaries with
Index. 1976. 1500pp. 121pp. of index.
   Obituaries from area around Riley County, Kansas,
   1957-1976. Gives surnames, given name, year of
   birth, year of death and page number where
   obituary is to be found. 8550 names of deceased,
   4055 surnames all on one reel of 16mm microfilm.
   Separate index will be printed and sold for $4.00
   if there is enough demand.
   Microfilm: Roll: 15.00

SHAWNEE COUNTY

Nowak, Christine M. 1860 Shawnee County Territorial Census.
   64+pp. 5.50 (381)
Topeka Genealogical Society, comp. Index to Landowners in
1873 F.W. Beers and Company. Shawnee County Atlas.
1975.
   With township maps. 3.00 (762)
_____. Index to Probate Court Records, Books I and II,
Shawnee County, 1855-1891. 1976.   ..... 4.00 (762)
_____. Shawnee County Cemeteries - Volume I. 1973.
   Small cemeteries in the city of Topeka. 2.50 (762)

WILSON COUNTY

City Directory Neodesha, Kansas 1896-1897. Repr. 1896-
1897. 18pp. 1.25 (329)
City Directory Neodesha, Kansas 1904. Repr. 1904 ed. 25pp. 1.25 (329)
City Directory Neodesha, Kansas 1909. Repr. 1909 ed. 35pp. 1.75 (329)
City Directory Neodesha, Kansas 1913. Repr. 1913 ed. 29pp. 1.50 (329)

City Directory Neodesha, Kansas 1916. Repr. 1916 ed. 45pp.
Lists each member of the family. 1.75 (329)

WYANDOTTE COUNTY

Every-name Index to Morgan's History of Wyandotte County,
Kansas. Fall 1976. c115pp.
County history originally published in 1911 - index
covers the two volumes. 2.50 (387)

WILSON COUNTY

The Heritage Genealogical Society. 1890 Wilson County,
Kansas Personal Property Tax Index. 1976. 32pp.
Name of taxpayer and township in which he lived
only information given. 2.25 (329)
_____. Index to the 1880 Wilson County, Kansas Federal
Census. 1975. 33pp.
Indexed by head of family and those in the same
household with another name. 2.25 (329)
Ramsey, Claire. Wilson County, Kansas Marriages 1864-1900.
1973. 232pp.
Contains names of many parents not listed on marriage
license applications. 5.75 (329)

Kentucky

STATEWIDE REFERENCES

Caudill, Bernice Calmes. Pioneers of Eastern Kentucky; Their
Feuds and Settlements. 1969. 108pp. B-OP 71,103. .... (778)
Collins, Lewis. Historical Sketches of Kentucky Embracing Its
History, Antiquities and Natural Curiosities, Geographical,
Statistical and Geological Description. Repr. of 1848 ed. 24.00 ..... (38)
Curtis, Mary Barnett. Abstracts of Causes Determined by the
Late Supreme Court for the District of Kentucky and by the
Court of Appeals. Repr. of 1809 ed.
In which titles to land were in dispute, reported by
James Hughes. 7.50 (371)
_____. Abstracts of Decisions of the Court of Appeals in the
State of Kentucky. Repr. of 1869 ed.
Covers cases from March, 1801 to January, 1805. ..... 7.50 (371)
The Filson Club History Quarterly.
Contains scholarly articles on many aspects of
history of Kentucky people, places and events. $8/yr (236)
Vols. 1-49 (1926-1975): Each: 3.00 (236)
Henry, Ruby. The First West. 1972. 6.95 ..... (45)
Ireland, Robert M. The County in Kentucky History. Publication
date: November 1976. Approx. 136pp.
Counties seen as the foundation of the ever-lively political
scene of 19th-century Kentucky. 3.95 ..... (408)
Johnson, Lewis F. Famous Kentucky Trails and Tragedies:
1915 Study of Famous Trails in the 1800's. Repr. of 1915 ed. 9.95 ..... (148)
Kentucky Genealogical Society. Bluegrass Roots.
Issued four times a year. Membership includes quarterly. $5/yr (406)
Back Issues: Each: 1.55 (406)

Kentucky Historical Society. Kentucky Ancestors.
Quarterly of the Kentucky Historical Society; included with
dues to the Society. It contains vital statistics, court
records, cemetery records, Bible records, queries from
members, and other genealogical material. Attempt is
made to cover all counties. THE REGISTER is also received on a quarterly basis as part of the membership
service.   Dues: $10/yr (407)
    Back issues: Each: 2.16 (407)
Kentucky's Famous Feuds and Tragedies: Authentic History of
the World Renowned Vendettas of the Dark and Bloody Ground.
Repr. of 1917 ed.   15.00 ..... (266)
Rice, Otis K. Frontier Kentucky. 142pp.
Traces the development of the territory now known as
Kentucky and follows its history to the end of the Revolu-
tionary War in 1783.   3.95 ..... (408)
Robertson, James Rood. Petitions of the Early Inhabitants of
Kentucky to the Genearal Assembly of Virginia, 1769 to 1792.
1914.   12.00 ..... (38)
Schwarzweller, Harry K., et al. Mountain Families in
Transition: A Case Study of Appalachian Migration. 1971.
300pp.
Three decades, Beech Creek area, of the families
and patterns of behavior of those leaving the area.
Information gathered in the 1940's.   11.00 ..... (589)
Shaler, Nathaniel S. Kentucky: A Pioneer Commonwealth.
1885.   23.00 ..... (2)
Smith, Clifford Neal and Anna Piszczan-Czaja Smith. "Some
German-Speaking Immigrants in Ohio and Kentucky in 1869".
NGS Quarterly, Vol. 62, No. 1. 1974. 15pp.
Names of subscribers to a German newspaper published
in Cincinnati. Five hundred twenty-one subscribers, with
the places of their origin were listed in the end papers of
Volume 1 of the newspaper. 3.50 (514)
Talbert, Charles Gano. The Life and Times of Benjamin Logan.
1952. 543pp. BIP-60-00710.
Benjamin Logan was born about 1743 and died in 1802. .... (777)
Tischendorf, Alfred P. and Elisha P. Taylor, eds. Diary and
Journal of Richard Clough Anderson, Jr., 1814-1826. 1964. 10.75 ..... (208)

Research Aids

McMurtrie, D. C. Check List of Kentucky Imprints 1811-
1820 With Notes in Supplement to the Check List of
1787-1810, ed. A. H. Allen. 1939.   10.00 ..... (415)
Townsend, J. W., ed. Supplemental Check List of
Kentucky Imprints, 1788-1820, Including the Original
Printing of the Original Kentucky Copyright Ledger,
1800-1854. 1942.   ..... 10.00 (415)
Volkel, Lowell. Index to the 1820 Census of Kentucky:
Volume 3 - Counties Jefferson Through Nicholas.
1975. 112pp. 7.25 (330)
Volkel, Lowell. Index to the 1820 Census of Kentucky:
Volume 4 - Counties Ohio Through Woodford. 1975.
91pp. 7.25 (330)

Military

Flint, Timothy. Indian Wars of the West; Containing
Biographical Sketches of Those Pioneers Who Headed
the Western Settlers in Repelling the Attacks of the
Savages, Together With a View of the Character,
Manners, Monuments and Antiquities of the Western
Indians. Repr. of 1833 ed.
Based on the eye-witness testimony of participants
in the events described. Sketches include contem-
porary estimates of such frontier figures as Boone,
Logan, Clark, Harmar, and Wayne.   11.00   ..... (38)
Hammack, James W., Jr. Kentucky & the Second American
Revolution. 132pp.
Shows how Kentucky's citizens adjusted to difficult
conditions during the War of 1812, and how the de-
termination of state leaders aided in turning defeat
into victory for the country.   3.95   ..... (408)
Harrison, Lowell H. The Civil War in Kentucky. 1975. 128pp.
A succinct account of the war in a pivotal state, show-
ing how glamor was mingled with hardship, patriotic
ardor with private anguish, and social brillance with
personal loneliness.   3.95   ..... (408)
_____. George Rogers Clark & the War in the West. 136pp.
The exciting tale of Clark's attempts to wrest control
of the American frontier away from the British dur-
ing the American Revolution.   3.95   ..... (408)
Tarrant, Eastham. Wild Riders of the First Kentucky
Cavalry: Reprint of 1894 Union Cavalry Record. 1969.   12.50   ..... (148)

Religious and Ethnic Groups

Davidson, Robert. History of the Presbyterian Church in the
State of Kentucky: Preliminary Sketch of the Churches
in the Valley of Virginia. 1974.   7.95   ..... (41)
Haiman, Mieczyslaw. Polish Pioneers of Virginia and
Kentucky. Repr. of 1937 ed.   5.00   ..... (631)
Neal, Julia. By Their Fruits: The Story of Shakerism in
South Union, Kentucky. Repr. of 1947 ed.   13.50   ..... (612)

Newspapers

Kentucky Gazette, Lexington, October 5, 1793 - December
28, 1844.
Microfilm of original papers. Individual rolls
covering a specific time span may be ordered.
Prices vary $15 to $20 per roll.   .... (870)
Mikkelson, Dwight Lawrence. Kentucky Gazette: 1787-
1848: The Herald of a Noisy World. 338pp. BIP-69-20409. .... (777)

Record

Fulton Genealogical Society. Bible Records of Western
Kentucky and Tennessee. 1975. 100pp. 7.50 (261)
Hopkins, James F. and Mary W. M. Hargreaves, eds.
The Papers of Henry Clay. Vol. 1: 1797-1814;
Vol. 2: 1815-1820; Vol. 3: 1821-1824; Vol. 4: 1825;
Vol. 5: 1826. c1,000pp.   Each: 20.00   ..... (408)

Kentucky Genealogical Society. Wills and Ways. 1975. 100pp.
Miscellaneous Kentucky records: births, marriages,
and deaths from Bible records; also miscellaneous
courthouse records.
Members: 4.30 (406)
Non-Members: 5.50 (406)
Taylor, Philip F. Calendar of Warrants for Land in Kentucky
for Service in French and Indian War. Repr. of 1917 ed.
84pp. 7.50 (274)

ADAIR COUNTY

Burdette, Ruth Paull. Adair County, Kentucky Marriage Records
1802-1840. 1975. 167pp. 10.00 (425)
Smith, Randolph N. Civil War Abstracts of Field Reports and
Correspondence. 1975. 124pp.
  Covers area of Kentucky and Tennessee within fifty
  miles of Burkesville, Kentucky. 5.25 (425)
_____. Federal Mortality Census Schedules 1860, 1870, 1880:
Adair, Clinton, Cumberland, Metcalfe and Monroe Counties,
Kentucky. 1975. 51pp. 5.00 (425)

ANDERSON COUNTY

McKee, Lewis W. and Lydia K. Bond. A History of Anderson
County, [Kentucky] 1780-1936. Repr. of 1936 ed. 219pp. 13.50 ..... (274)

BARREN COUNTY

Smith, Randolph N. Civil War Abstracts of Field Reports and
Correspondence. 1975. 124pp.
  Covers area of Kentucky and Tennessee within fifty
  miles of Burkesville, Kentucky. 5.25 (425)

BUTLER COUNTY

Hopkins County Genealogical Society. Marriages Butler County,
Kentucky - 1810-1865. 1974. 170pp. Indexed. 13.25 (350)

CALDWELL COUNTY

Eldred, Olive and Nancy Beck. Pioneers of Caldwell County,
Kentucky, Volume I Wills and Inventories (1809-1834).
1976. 200pp.
  Complete abstracts of all entries. Includes estate
  accounts, guardian accounts, sale bills with names of
  individual purchasers listed. Full name index.   15.00 ..... (601)
_____. Pioneers of Caldwell County, Kentucky, Volume II
Military Men. 1976.
  All known information on soldiers of the American
  Revolution buried in the county and soldiers of the War
  of 1812 who served from it.   .... (601)
Hopkins County Genealogical Society. Federal Census, Caldwell
County, Kentucky 1840, Indexed. 1976.   .... (350)
Phillips, Oma Dee. 1810 Census - Indexed. 1968. 16pp.
Off-set print. 3.50 (596)

CALLOWAY COUNTY

Stilley, Van A., J.D. Calloway County, Kentucky, 1850 Census,
Taken from the Original, With Notes. 1976.   .... (726)

CLARK COUNTY

Owen, Kathryn. Old Graveyards of Clark County, Kentucky.
166pp. 10.00 (608)

CLAY COUNTY

Young, Forence Nelson and Virgil D. Young. Clay County,
Kentucky Deed Book Abstracts and Court Order Book
1806 to 1848. 1975. 500pp. 30.00 ..... (827)

CLINTON COUNTY

Smith, Randolph N. Federal Mortality Census, 1860, 1870, 1880
of Adair, Clinton, Cumberland, Metcalfe and Monroe Counties,
Kentucky. 1975. 51pp. 5.00 (425)

CRITTENDEN COUNTY

Hopkins County Genealogical Society. Federal Census Crittenden
County, Kentucky, 1850. Indexed. 1976. 124pp. 10.75 (350)

CUMBERLAND COUNTY

Smith, Randolph N. Civil War Abstracts of Field Reports and
Correspondence. 1975. 124pp.
    Covers area of Kentucky and Tennessee within fifty
    miles of Burkesville, Kentucky. 5.25 (425)
_____. Cumberland County, Kentucky Census Index and
Abstracts 1800-1850. 1975. 231pp.
    1800 Tax list, 1810, 1820, 1830, 1840, 1850 Census
    abstracts and all included in one index. 10.00 (425)
_____. 1860 Cumberland County, Kentucky Census Index and
Abstracts. 1975. 150pp. 5.25 (425)
_____. 1870 Cumberland County, Kentucky Census Index and
Abstracts. 1975. 189pp. 5.25 (425)
_____. 1880 Cumberland County, Kentucky Census Index and
Abstracts. 1975. 225pp. 6.30 (425)
_____. Federal Mortality Census Schedules, 1860, 1870, 1880
Abstract and Index: Adair, Clinton, Cumberland, Metcalfe
and Monroe Counties, Kentucky. 1975. 51pp. 5.00 (425)
Smith, R. N. and Laura Lee Butler. Cumberland County,
Kentucky Deed Records 1799-1867. 1975. 597pp. 24.95 ..... (425)
_____. Cumberland County, Kentucky Survey Records 1799-1945.
1975. 431pp. 21.95 ..... (425)

FAYETTE COUNTY

Kentucky Gazette, Lexington, October 5, 1793 - December 28, 1844.
    10 rolls - microfilm of the original papers. Individual
    rolls covering a specific time span may be ordered.
    Prices vary $15.00 to $30.00 per roll. .... (870)
Kentucky Marriages Performed 1793-1831 by the
Reverend Robert Marshall. NGS Quarterly, Vol. 56, No. 2.
1968. 12pp. 3.50 (514)
Ranck, George W. Boonesborough. Its Founding, Pioneer
Struggles, Indian Experiences, Transylvania Days, and Revolu-
tionary Annals. With Full Historical Notes and Appendix.
Illustrated. Indexed. 1901.
    The standard account of Boonesborough and the origins of
    Kentucky by a learned and dedicated Kentucky scholar.
    Noteworthy illustrations; 122 page appendix. 15.00 ..... (38)

FRANKLIN COUNTY

Kentucky Genealogical Society. Franklin County Cemeteries,
Volume 1. 1976.
Family cemeteries and church cemeteries of Franklin
County, Kentucky. ..... x (406)

FULTON COUNTY

Fulton Genealogical Society. 1846 Tax List of Fulton County,
Kentucky. 1973. 22pp.
Includes number of children 5 to 17 years of age. 2.25 (261)
_____. Fulton County, Kentucky Cemeteries, Volume 1.
1976. 74pp. 6.50 (261)

GRAVES COUNTY

Simmons, Don. Graves County, Kentucky Newspaper Genealogical Abstracts (1876-1885). 1975. 77pp. 6.50 (689)
_____. Graves County, Kentucky Tax List 1841. 1972. 32pp.
Includes acreage, watercourse, blacks, children
age 7 to 17. ..... 3.00 (689)

GREEN COUNTY

Lind, Ruth Marcum. United States Census, Green County,
Kentucky, 1850 and 1860. Indexed. 1976. ..... 16.50 (432)
Smith, Randolph N. Green County, Kentucky Land Entries,
1796-1834. 1975. 185pp. 7.50 (425)

HOPKINS COUNTY

Cox, E. M. and L. F. McCulley. Federal Census of Hopkins
County, Kentucky - 1850. Repr. of 1960 ed. 189pp. Indexed. 11.75 (350)
_____. Hopkins County Records - Minute Book - 1816-1818.
1961. 104pp. Indexed. 8.25 (350)
_____. Hopkins County Marriages - 1807-1869, Index.
Repr. of 1961 ed. 130pp.
Includes the 1807 tax list. 10.75 (350)
_____. Hopkins County Records - Deed Book II - 1816-1819.
1961. 104pp.
This book includes Commonwealth of Kentucky Land
Grants 1807 as well as including deed of 1816-1819. ..... 8.25 (350)
_____. Hopkins County Will Book - 1807-1829, Will Books
One and Two. Repr. of 1961 ed. 106pp.
Besides containing Wills, this publication contains
Court Orders of July - December, 1815. Indexed. 10.75 (350)
Hammers, Marian G. Hopkins County Marriage Index 1869-1900.
1967. 153pp. 12.85 (310)
Hopkins County Genealogical Society. Federal Census of Hopkins
County, Kentucky: 1810, 1820, 1830, 1840. 1970. 180pp.
Indexed. 11.75 (350)
_____. Federal Census of Hopkins County, Kentucky: 1870.
1973. 357pp. Indexed. 15.75 (350)
_____. Federal Census of Hopkins County, Kentucky: 1880. 2 vols.
1974. 562pp. Indexed. 23.75 (350)
_____. Hopkins County Cemeteries - Volume I. Index.
1970. 205pp.
Cemeteries covered: Old Goad, Old Salem, McIntosh,
Old Pleasant Run, Fox, New Salem, Concord, Pleasant
Hill, Stanley, Furgerson, Whitfield, Clark, Oglesby,

Laffoon, Lake Grove, Martin or Croft, Baker, Ilsley,
Hamp Hamby, Christian Priviledge, Union Temple,
Southards, Shaw, Davis - Bishop, Cane Run, New Suthards,
Woodruff, Good Hope, Oates, Hight, Miller, Clements,
and Stull. 12.75 (350)
_____. Hopkins County Cemeteries - Volume II, Index.
1970. 157pp.
Cemeteries covered: Grapevine, High Glory, Browder,
Bethelem, Hicklin, Stevens (or Stephens), Stom, Nisbet,
Old Aaron Reynolds, Cemetery on Highway 175 near
Strip Pits, Mitchell, Mercer (in Muhlenberg Co.), Sam
Green (in Muhlenberg Co.), Cemetery on L. K. Bell
farm, Cemetery off Madisonville U. S. 41 By-Pass,
Bassett, Flat Creek. 10.75 (350)
_____. Hopkins County Cemeteries - Volume III, Index.
1970. 147pp.
Cemeteries covered: Providence (West Lawn and East
Lawn), Zion Brick Church, Gooch, Emberry, Mt. Zion,
Old Ashby, Old Salem Methodist, Cemetery on hill
above Ashyburg, Nelson, Washington, Hanson (Ky.),
Brabtree, Rust, Cemetery (near High Glory Cemetery),
Brown, Adams, Oakwood (at Earlington, Ky.), Old
Richland, Cemetery in Strip Pit (off highway),
Cemetery (near Trio Mines), White School House,
Pleasant View, McDonald, Pleasant Grove, Wicks,
Fuquay, Henson, Cemetery (on Kington Lane), Gore,
Tapp, Mangum. 10.75 (350)
_____. Hopkins County Cemeteries - Volume IV, Index.
1970. 158pp.
Cemeteries covered: Arcadia Hill, Bell, Beulah,
Blue, Brooks, Brown, Carter, Coffman, Cemetery
(near Dalton), Cemetery (on George Dever Farm),
Cemetery (on Lee Menser Farm), Cemetery (at Charleston),
Cemetery (on Joe Cain Farm), Dalton, Dunn, Etheridge,
Hardison, Headley (or Holloman), Hell's Hald Acre,
High Glory, Hodge, Holloman, Homesite, Howton, Jennings
or Quinn, Johnson Island, Layfette, Lick Creek, Ligon or
Dorris, Mart Young, Menser, Menser (No. 2), McNeeley,
Nichol, New Purdy, Old Beulah, Old Kendrick, Old Purdy,
Pleasant Ridge, Prospect, Ramsey, Ray (or Rhea),
Rose Creek, Rosedale, Russell, Silent Run, Terry,
Traylor, Walnut Grove, Wilson or Rea. 10.75 (350)
_____. Hopkins County Cemeteries - Volume V, Index.
1970. 161pp.
Cemeteries covered: Arnold, Bailey, Barnhill, Barron
and Cox, Brown, Browder, Burton, Cemetery (Bert Adams
Farm), Cemetery (on S. D. Franklin Farm), Cemetery
(on Tippett's Daisy Hill Farm), Cemetery (3 mi. from
Mt. Carmel Church), Cemetery (on Ray Duncan Farm),
Cemetery (on Jewell City road), Cardwell, Compton,
Concord, Cox, Crabtree, Craig, Crow, Clayton, Old Cates,
Old Dunkerson, Durham, Faucett, Groves, Harrelson,
Hobgood, Old Jackson, Jennings, Key, Lamson I, Lamson
II, Mangum, Mills, Mitchell, Mt. Carmel, New Salem
Methodist, Oakley Home, Old Onton, Olive Branch, Owen,
Pleasant Valley, Rust, Samuels, Stanley, Old Steen,
Tapp, Trice, Utterback, Union-Nebo, Vaughan, Veazey,
Weir, Whitinghill, Winstead. 10.75 (350)

Hopkins County Genealogical Society. Hopkins County Cemeteries -
Volume VI, Index. 1970. 180pp.
    Odd Fellow Cemetery, Madisonville, Kentucky. 11.75 (350)
_____. Vital Statistics, Hopkins County, Kentucky Deaths,
1911-1920. 1975. 350pp.
    Deaths (caucasion), name of deceased, birth date, birth
    place, marital status, sex, occupation, death date and
    place of burial. Also, the name of father, and his birth
    place and mother's maiden name and her birth place. 18.25 (350)
Potter, Dorothy Williams. 1860 Federal Census of Hopkins
County, Kentucky. 1974. 144pp. 10.00 (615)

JEFFERSON COUNTY

Filson Club. An Inventory of Jefferson County Records.
Repr. of 1970 ed. 37pp. 1.00 (236)

KNOX COUNTY

Fetterman, John. Stinking Creek: The Portrait of a Small
Mountain Community in Appalachia. 1970.   .....   2.95 (210)

LIVINGSTON COUNTY

Simmons, Don. Livingston County, Kentucky Tax Lists
1800-01-02. 1975. 42pp. 3.00 (689)

McCRACKEN COUNTY

Simmons, Don. McCracken County, Kentucky Census 1840.
1973. 27pp.
    Includes tax lists 1824 and 1829.   .....   3.00 (689)

MADISON COUNTY

Hubble, Anna Joy (Munday). Madison County, Kentucky 1810
Census. 1976. 28pp. 3.50 (358)
_____. Madison County, Kentucky 1820 Census. 1976.   .... (358)
_____. Madison County, Kentucky 1830 Census. 1976.   .... (358)
_____. Madison County, Kentucky 1840 Census. 1977.   .... (358)
_____. Madison County, Kentucky 1850 Census. 1976. 227pp. 12.50 (358)
_____. Surname Index to the 1850 Census of Madison County,
Kentucky. 1976. 13pp. 2.50 (358)

MARSHALL COUNTY

Simmons, Don. Marshall County, Kentucky Birth Records,
1852-1859. 1975. 96pp. 7.50 (689)
_____. Marshall County, Kentucky Marriage Records,
1852-1859. 1972. 37pp.
    These are from Vital Stats. including birthplaces,
    residences, age, etc. Not necessarily those found in
    the court house. 3.00 (689)

MASON COUNTY

Young, Florence Nelson and Virgil D. Young. Mason County,
Kentucky Deed Book Abstracts, Volume II, 1810-1819.
1976. 500pp.
    Abstracts of deed books M-N-O-P-Q-R-S-T-V.   30.00   ..... (827)

METCALFE COUNTY

Smith, Randolph N. Civil War Abstracts of Field Reports and
Correspondence. 1975. 124pp.
Covers area of Kentucky and Tennessee within 50
miles of Burkesville, Kentucky. 5.25 (425)
_____. Federal Mortality Census Schedules, 1860, 1870,
1880 Abstract and Index of Adair, Clinton, Cumberland,
Metcalfe and Monroe Counties, Kentucky. 1975. 51pp. 5.00 (425)

MONROE COUNTY

Phillips, Oma Dee. 1830 Census. 1975. 16pp. 5.00 (596)
Smith, Randolph N. Civil War Abstracts of Field Reports and
Correspondence. 1975. 124pp.
Covers area of Kentucky and Tennessee within 50
miles of Burkesville, Kentucky. 5.25 (425)
_____. Federal Mortality Census Schedules, 1860, 1870,
1880 Abstract and Index of Adair, Clinton, Cumberland,
Metcalfe and Monroe Counties, Kentucky. 1975. 51pp. 5.00 (425)

MUHLENBERG COUNTY

Cox, E. M. and L. F. McCulley. Muhlenberg County, Kentucky
Marriage Index - 1798—1900. Repr. of 1961 ed. 274pp. index. 15.75 (350)
Hammers, Marian G. Muhlenberg County, Kentucky Cemeteries,
Volume I (first of four volumes). Late 1976. 150+pp.   .... (310)
_____. Muhlenberg County, Kentucky 1850 Federal Census
(full transcript). 1969. 136pp. index. 10.35 (310)
_____. Muhlenberg County, Kentucky Wills and Administrations,
Abstracts of: 1799—1877. 1968. 120pp. 12.85 (310)

NELSON COUNTY

Howlett, William J. Old St. Thomas' at Poplar Neck, Bardstown,
Kentucky (St. Mary's College Historical Ser. No. 1). 1971. ..... 2.95 (196)

PIKE COUNTY

McCoy, Truda Williams. The McCoys: Their Story, ed. L.
Roberts. 1976. 350pp.
Story of West Virginia-Kentucky feud, notes, bibliographies,
photos, 80 pages of genealogy including: Roberts,
Williamson, Scott, Scalf, Blankenship, Blevins, etc.   12.00 ..... (30)
Roberts, Leonard, et al. One Hundred Fifty Years Pike County,
Kentucky: 1822—1972. 2d rev. ed. Repr. of 1972 ed. 102pp.
Thirty one articles on doctors, writers, schools,
hospitals, Daniel Boone, and four genealogies: Tibbs,
Justice, Huffman, Burke. 4.00 (599)
_____. Pike County, Kentucky 1822—1976; Historical Papers
Number Two. 1976. 102pp.
Thirteen articles on first Pike County tax list, Pike
County Wills, Pike County Marriages 1822—1865, early
coal operations,16 genealogies including: Cline, Roberts,
Branham, Yost, Stump, Miller, Tibbs. 5.00 (599)

RUSSELL COUNTY

Smith, Randolph N. Civil War Abstracts of Field Reports and
Correspondence. 1975. 124pp.
Covers area of Kentucky and Tennessee within 50 miles
of Burkesville, Kentucky. 5.25 (425)

SCOTT COUNTY

"Kentucky Marriages Performed 1793-1831 by the Reverend
Robert Marshall." NGS Quarterly, Vol. 56, No. 2. 1968.
12pp. 3.50 (514)

SPENCER COUNTY

"Spencer County, Kentucky Marriages 1824-1829." The Ridge
Runners, Vol. 4. 1976. 12pp. .... (859)

TAYLOR COUNTY

Smith, Randolph N. Civil War Abstracts of Field Reports and
Correspondence. 1975. 124pp.
    Covers area of Kentucky and Tennessee within 50 miles
    of Burkesville, Kentucky. 5.25 (425)

UNION COUNTY

Hopkins County Genealogical Society. Federal Census, Union
County, Kentucky - 1850. Late 1976. index. .... (350)

WAYNE COUNTY

Smith, Randolph N. Civil War Abstracts of Field Reports and
Correspondence. 1975. 124pp.
    Covers area of Kentucky and Tennessee within 50 miles
    of Burkesville, Kentucky. 5.25 (425)

WEBSTER COUNTY

Cox, E. M. and L. F. McCulley. Webster County, Kentucky
Marraige Index - 1860-1900. Repr. of 1961 ed. 141pp. index. 10.75 (350)
Hopkins County Genealogical Society. Federal Census of
Webster County, Kentucky 1860. 1975. 145pp. index. 10.75 (350)

WOODFORD COUNTY

"Kentucky Marriages Performed 1793-1831 by the Reverend
Robert Marshall." NGS Quarterly, Vol. 56, No. 2. 1968.
12pp. 3.50 (514)

Louisiana

STATEWIDE REFERENCES

Arena, Carmelo R. Philadelphia - Spanish New Orleans Trade
1789-1803. 1959. 213pp. BIP-59-04590. .... (777)
Barron, Bill. Vaudreuil Papers: 1743-1753. 600pp.
    A calendar and definitive index to the official papers
    of Pierre de Rigaud de Vaudreuil, governor of the
    French Province of Louisiana during the years im-
    mediately preceding the French and Indian War. A
    basic research tool for all states included in the
    Mississippi Valley. Index. 25.00 ..... (608)
Barrow, Bennet Hilliard. Plantation Life in the Florida Parishes
of Louisiana, 1836-1846, as Reflected in the Diary of
Bennet H. Barrow, ed. Edwin Adams Davis. 1943. 10.00 ..... (2)

Brown, Wilburt S. Amphibious Campaign for West Florida and
Louisiana. 1969.   10.00 ..... (11)
Copeland, Fayette. Kendall of the "Picayune." Being His
Adventures in New Orleans, on the Texas Santa Fe Expedition,
in the Mexican War and in the Colonization of the Texas
Frontier. Repr. of 1943 ed.   6.95 ..... (556)
Cutler, Jervis. A Topographical Description of the State of
Ohio, Indiana Territory and Louisiana. 1812.   10.00 ..... (38)
DuPratz, Antoine S. Le Page. History of Louisiana. 1975.   10.00 ..... (440)
Farnan, William Thomas. Land Claims Problems and the
Federal Land System in the Louisiana-Missouri Territory.
279pp. BIP-72-23929.   .... (777)
DuFossat, Chevalier Guy Soniat. Synopsis of the History of
Louisiana.
     An officer of the French army who arrived in New
     Orleans in 1751. 45pp. 7.50 (608)
Gayarre, Charles Etienne Arthur. History of Louisiana. With
City and Topographical Maps of the State, Ancient and
Modern. 3rd ed. 4 vols. 1885.   Set: 100.00 ..... (2)
                                              Each: 25.00 ..... (2)
Lebreton, Marietta. A History of the Territory of Orleans,
1803-1812 - Parts I and II. 1969. 523pp. BIP-69-17118.   .... (777)
Lemieux, Donald Jile. The Office of Commissaire Ordonnateur
in French Louisiana, 1731-1763: A Study in French Colonial
Administration. 226pp. BIP-72-28360.   .... (777)
Treat, V. Hugo. Migration to Louisiana 1834-1880. 1967.
764pp. BIP-68-04351.   .... (777)
Williams, Ernest Russ, Jr. The Florida Parish Ellises and
Louisiana Politics, 1820-1918. 325pp. BIP-70-09763.   .... (777)

Research Aids

Index to the Archives of Spanish West-Florida, 1782-1810.
     A series of nineteen indices covering the area of
     Louisiana known for half-a-century as "West Florida."
     This guide reveals a massive amount of historical
     and genealogical data and was originally prepared by
     the Survey of Federal Archives. 370pp. 17.50 (608)
Rowland, Dunbar, comp. and ed. Guide to the General
     Correspondence of Louisiana: 1678-1763. 177pp. index.
     An indexed calendar to forty-three large volumes
     of transcripts in the Mississippi Department of
     Archives covering thousands of pages of official
     documents which include every aspect of public
     and private life during the French regime, with
     extensive references to genealogical sources
     such as military lists, ship lists, etc. The
     original papers are now deposited in Paris. Re-
     printed from the 5th Annual Report of the director
     of Mississippi's department of archives and history. 15.00 (608)

Military

De Ville, Winston. Louisiana Recruits: 1752-1758. 100pp.
     With an essay on the military in 18th century
     Louisiana by Rene Chartrand. Ship lists of
     military recruits from France which give full
     names, parents, birthplace and occupation. Index. 12.50 (608)

_____. Louisiana Troops 1720-1770. 1965. 136pp. 8.00 (371)
"Louisiana Troops - 1745." NGS Quarterly, Vol. 56, No. 1.
1968. 15pp. 3.50 (514)
Reilly, Robin. British at the Gates: The New Orleans
Campaign in the War of 1812. 1974. 10.00 ..... (627)

Religious and Ethnic Groups

Curley, Michael Joseph. Church and State in the Spanish
Floridas (1783-1822). 1940. 16.00 ..... (2)
Deiler, John Hanno. Settlement of the German Coast of
Louisiana, and Creoles of German Descent. Repr. of
1909 ed. 154pp. 10.00 ..... (274)
_____. The Settlement of the German Coast of Louisiana
and the Creoles of German Descent. Repr. of 1900 ed. 5.00 ..... (631)
Delanglez, Jean. The French Jesuits in Lower Louisiana
(1700-1763). 1935. 24.50 ..... (2)
Vogel, Claude. The Capuchins in French Louisiana (1722-
1766). 1928. 9.50 ..... (2)
Witcher, Robert Campbell. The Episcopal Church in
Louisiana, 1805-1861. 401pp. BIP-69-17135. .... (777)

Records

Bolton, Herbert E., ed. Athanase de Mezieres and the
Louisiana-Texas Frontier, 1768-1780; Documents
Published for the First Time, from the Original
Spanish and French Manuscripts, Chiefly in the Archives of Mexico and Spain. 2 vols. 1914. 30.00 ..... (415)
The Civil War Tax in Louisiana: 1865. Reprint. 360pp.
New introduction by John Milton Price. Based on
direct tax assessments of Louisianians by the federal
government. A finding-aid for elusive ancestors during
the late ante-bellum period and the tumultuous war
years, 1861-1865. Listed by parishes (Calcasieu is
not reported) are approximately 50,000 names of landowners and the amount of the assessment. 12.50 (808)
Historical Collections of Louisiana. Historical Collections
of Louisiana; Embracing the History of that State
(1678-1770). Compiles with Historical and Biographical
Notes. 1846-1853. 5 vols. Set: 75.00 ..... (2)
Each: 15.00 ..... (2)
Historical Collections of Louisiana and Florida. Historical
Collections of Louisiana and Florida; Including Transla-
tions of Original Manuscripts Relating to Their Dis-
covery and Settlement, with Numerous Historical and
Biographical Notes, ed. Benjamin Franklin French.
New Series: 1869, Second Series: 1875. 2 vols.
Set: 37.00 ..... (2)
Each: 18.50 ..... (2)
Massicotte, E. Z., ed. Canadian Passports, 1681-1752. 150pp.
Index by Paul Jarry. Abstracts of permits, conges,
and contracts given to early frontiersmen during the
period when expansion westward and in the Mississippi
Valley from the older settlements in Canada was
beginning. Names of hundreds of the earliest settlers
(many well-known in Colonial Louisiana). A reference
for French-Canadian research, reprinted from Rapport

de l'Archiviste de la Province de Quebec. Index. 12.50 (608)
Maduell, Charles R., Jr. Federal Land Grants in the
Territory of Orleans: The Delta Parishes. 400pp.
Alphabetical abstracts of federal land grants in
the areas of Orleans, the German and Acadian
Coasts, Iberville, La Fourche, and Pointe Coupee,
based on confirmed grants by the French crown
dating from the earliest years of the 18th century,
and by the Spanish king during the dominion of the
dons. A special feature is the addition of indices
to locate non-principal names in the documents.
Adapted from American State Papers. Index. 20.00 (608)
Robichaux, Albert J., Jr. Colonial Settlers Along Bayou
La Fourche, 1770-1798, Volume 2. 1974. 219pp.
Seven lists of settlers which were Spanish censuses
for the years 1770, 1777, 1788, 1791, 1795, 1797
and 1798. Lists all inhabitants, by age, relation-
ships, as well as an account of personal property. 17.50 (648)
United States Government. Territorial Papers. Volume 9:
The Territory of Orleans, 1803-1812. Foundations of
the Territory, 1803. The Six Administrations of
Governor Claiborne, 1803-1812. 1940. index. 57.50 ..... (2)
_____. Territorial Papers. Volume 13: The Territory
of Louisiana-Missouri, 1803-1806. Foundation of the
Territory, 1803-1804. The District of Louisiana,
1804-1805. The Administration of Governor Wilkinson,
1805-1806. 1948. index. 57.50 ..... (2)
_____. Territorial Papers. Volume 14: The Territory of
Louisiana-Missouri, 1806-1814. The Administration of
Acting Governor Browne, 1806-1807. The Administration
of Acting Governor Bates, 1807-1808. The Administration of Governor Lewis, 1808-1809. The Administration
of Acting Governor Bates, 1809-1810. The Administration of Governor Howard, 1810-1813. The First Administration of Governor Clark, 1813-1814, ed. Clarence
E. Carter. 1949. index. 57.50 ..... (2)
_____. Territorial Papers. Volume 15: The Territory
of Louisiana-Missouri, 1815-1821. The Three
Administrations of Governor Clark, 1815-1820. The
Period of Transition, 1820-1821. 1951. index. 57.50 ..... (2)

EAST FELICIANA PARISH

Johnson, Donald W. 1830 - East Feliciana Enumerated Census.
1975. 17pp. 3.50 (388)
_____. 1850 - East Feliciana Louisiana Census with Index.
1975. 156pp. 12.50 (388)

ORLEANS PARISH

Blassingame, John W. Black New Orleans, 1860-1880. 1973. 9.95 ..... (137)
Nau, John F. The German People of New Orleans 1850-1900.
1954. 283pp. BIP-00-09956. .... (777)
New Orleans Bee Newspaper, September 1827 to December 1868.
77 rolls.
Microfilm of the original newspaper. Individual rolls
covering a specific time span may be ordered. Prices
from $15 to $30 per roll. .... (870)

New Orleans Times Picayune Newspaper, January 1837 to
January 1921. 510 rolls.
    Microfilm of the original newspaper. Individual rolls
    covering a specific time span may be ordered. Prices
    from $15 to $30 per roll. .... (870)
Past as Prelude: New Orleans 1718-1968. 10.00 ..... (583)
Reinders, Robert Clemens. A Social History of New Orleans
1850-1860. 1957. 881pp. BIP-00-25174. .... (777)
United States House of Representatives. New Orleans Riots
of July 30, 1866: 39th Congress, 2nd Session, Report
Number 16. 1867. 21.00 ..... (38)

ST. HELENA PARISH

Johnson, Donald. 1830 Enumerated Census of St. Helena,
Louisiana. 1975. 15pp. 3.50 (388)
_____. 1850- St. Helena Census and Index. 1975. 96pp.
    Complete listing with index by family number. 12.50 (388)

WEST FELICIANA PARISH

Johnson, Donald. 1830 Enumerated Census of West Feliciana
Louisiana. 1976. 14pp. 3.50 (388)
_____. 1850- Census of West Feliciana Louisiana and Index.
1976. 101pp. 12.50 (388)

Maine

STATEWIDE REFERENCES

Attwood, Stanley Bearce. Length and Breadth of Maine. Repr. of
1946 ed, 322pp. 3.50 (460)
Banks, Ronald Fillmore. The Separation of Maine from
Massachusetts, 1785-1820. 673pp. BIP-67-04129. .... (777)
Bridgham, Lawrence Donald. Maine Public Lands 1781-1795:
Claims, Trespassers, and Sales. 395pp. BIP-59-03453. .... (777)
Clifford, Harold B. Maine and Her People. Repr. of 1957 ed.
360pp.
    Concise history of Maine,updated State Constitution
    included. Illustrated. Maps. 7.50 ..... (79)
Davis, Harold A. An International Community on the St. Croix
(1604-1930). Repr. of 1950 ed. 412pp.
    Covering the years 1604-1930 and the people living on
    the Maine and New Brunswick sides of the St. Croix River. 4.95 (460)

Listed below are the names of professional genealogists willing to undertake research
for a fee within the state of Louisiana, in areas specified in their ads:

Hatch, Louis C., ed. Maine: A History. 1974.	25.00	10.00	(532)
Kershaw, Gordon E. Gentlemen of Large Property and Judicious Men: The Kennebeck Proprietors, 1749-1775. 1975.	15.00	.....	(532)
_____. Kennebeck Purchase: The Fortunes of a Land Company Extraordinary, 1749-1775. 475pp. BIP-72-06178.	.....	.....	(777)
Leger, Sister Mary Celeste. The Catholic Indian Missions in Maine (1611-1820). 1929.	8.00	.....	(2)
Moody, Robert Earle. The Maine Frontier, 1607-1763. 470pp. BIP-65-07515.	.....	.....	(777)
Thayer, Henry O., ed. The Sagadahoc Colony. Comprising the Relation of a Voyage into New England. 1892. 276pp. The founding of this major colony in Maine from the departure from England to the ultimate collapse of the enterprise. Illustrated.	18.50	.....	(38)

Research Aids

Bangor Public Library. Bibliography of the State of Maine. 1962.	70.00	.....	(307)
Clark, Charles E. Maine During the Colonial Period: A Bibliographical Guide. 1974.	.....	3.00	(532)
Eckstorm, Fannie Hardy. Indian Place Names of the Penobscot Valley and the Maine Coast. Repr. of 1941 ed. 272pp.	.....	3.95	(460)
Rutherford, Philip R. The Dictionary of Maine Place-Names. 1970. 284pp. Twenty thousand names taken from National Geological Survey Maps and researched for their origin.	9.95	.....	(79)
Wright, Norman E. Genealogy in America, Volume 1: Massachusetts, Connecticut and Maine.	3.50	.....	(190)

Military

Ahlin, John Howard. New England Rubicon: A Study of Eastern Maine During the American Revolution. 339pp. BIP-62-04534.	.....	.....	(777)
Kidder, Frederic. Military Operations in Eastern Maine and Nova Scotia During the Revolution. 1867.	19.00	.....	(415)
Sloan, Robert Wesley. New Ireland: Loyalists in Eastern Maine During the American Revolution. 182pp. BIP-72-16516.	.....	.....	(777)
Small, Abner R. The Road to Richmond: The Civil War Memoirs of Major Abner R. Small of the 16th Maine Volunteers: With His Diary as a Prisoner of War, ed. Harold A. Small. 1939.	.....	1.50	(112)

Records

Sargent, William Mitchell. Maine Wills 1640-1760. 1887 966pp. B-BH 5339.	.....	.....	(778)

ANDROSCOGGIN COUNTY

Rand, John. Peoples Lewiston-Auburn Maine 1875-1975. 1975. 128pp. Chronological record, focuses on physical and economic growth of the two cities and Peoples Savings Bank during each decade of their first 100 years. Many photographs.	9.95	7.95	(79)

AROOSTOOK COUNTY

Chadbourne, Ava. Piscataquis and Aroostook Maine Place-
Names and the Peopling of its Towns. 1957. 50pp.
How Maine towns were names and settled within
Piscataquis and Aroostook counties. 1.00 (79)

CARROLL COUNTY

Merrill, George D. History of Carroll County. 1971. 50.00 ..... (532)

CUMBERLAND COUNTY

Chadbourne, Ava. Maine Place-Names and the Peopling of
its Towns: Cumberland County. 1976.
How Maine towns were settled and named. Photos,
many names. 2.25 (79)
Detmer, Josephine and Patricia Rancoast. Portland, ed.
Martin Dibner. 1972.
Collector's Edition: $25.00 15.00 6.95 (295)
Willis, William. History of Portland, Maine. 1972. 22.50 ..... (550)

HANCOCK COUNTY

Calef, John. The Seige of Penobscot by the Rebels: Containing
a Journal of the Proceedings (1781). Together with The
Proceedings of the General Assembly and of the Council,
of the State of Massachusetts-Bay, Relating to the Penobscot
Expedition. 2 vols. in one. 1780. 6.00 ..... (38)
Chadbourne, Ava. Maine Place-Names and the Peopling of its
Towns: Hancock County. 1957. 72pp.
How Maine towns were settled and named. Photos,
many names. 1.95 (79)
Hutchins, Vernal. A Maine Town in the Civil War. 114pp.
Text and photos of Deer Island, Maine during the
Civil War. 1.95 (79)

KENNEBEC COUNTY

Chadbourne, Ava. Maine Place-Names and the Peopling of its
Towns: Kennebec and Somerset Counties. 1957. 50pp.
How Maine towns in the county were settled and named. 1.00 (79)

KNOX COUNTY

Chadbourne, Ava. Maine Place-Names and the Peopling of its
Towns: Knox County. 1976.
How Maine towns were settled and named. Photos,
many names. 2.25 (79)
Eaton, Cyrus. Annals of the Town of Warren, in Knox County,
Maine, with the Early History of St. George's, Broad Bay,
and the Neighboring Settlements on the Waldo Patent. 1877.
716pp. B-BH 19188. .... (778)

LINCOLN COUNTY

Chadbourne, Ava. Maine Place-Names and the Peopling of its
Towns: Lincoln County. 1957. 72pp.
How Maine towns were settled and named. Photos,
many names. 1.95 (79)

Everson, Jennie B. Tidewater Ice of the Kennebec River, ed.
Thea Wheelwright. 1971.
    Ice industry in 19th century. Many names involved.   9.95 .... (833)
Stahl, Jasper J. History of Old Broadbay and Waldoboro.
Repr. of 1956 ed.
    History of the Waldoboro Maine area. From its
    German immigrant beginning.   35.00 .... (79)

PENOBSCOT COUNTY

Chadbourne, Ava. Maine Place-Names and the Peopling of its
Towns: Penobscot County. 1957. 50pp.
    How Maine towns were named and settled within
    Penobscot County. 1.00 (79)
Laverty, Dorothy Bowler. Millinocket: Magic City of Maine's
Wilderness. 1973. 128pp.
    A history of Mt. Katahdin area. A town that started
    with one family in 1901 and developed around the paper
    industry. 6.95 (79)

PISCATAQUIS COUNTY

Chadbourne, Ava. Piscataquis and Aroostook Maine Place-
Names and the Peopling of its Towns. 1957. 50pp.
    How Maine towns were named and settled within
    Piscataquis and Aroostook Counties. 1.00 (79)

SOMERSET COUNTY

Chadbourne, Ava. Maine Place-Names and the Peopling of its
Towns: Kennebec and Somerset Counties. 1957. 50pp.
    How Maine Towns in the county were settled and names. 1.00 (79)
Chatto, Clarence I. and Clair E. Turner, comps. The East
Somerset County Register, 1911-1912. 1912. 545pp.
B-OP 24335.   .... (778)
Gilman, Stanwood and Margaret C. Gilman. Land of the Kennebec.
1966.   7.50 .... (90)

WASHINGTON COUNTY

Atkinson, Minnie. Hinckley Township, Maine, or Grand Lake
Stream Plantation. 1920. 130pp.   8.00 .... (530)
Chadbourne, Ava. Maine Place-Names and the Peopling of its
Towns: Washington County. 1957. 80pp.
    How Maine towns were settled and named. Photos,
    many names. 1.95 (79)

YORK COUNTY

Bartlett, Ralph Sylvester. History of York County, Maine, and
a Rambling Narrative about the Town of Eliot and its Mother-
Town, Old Kittery. 1938. 21pp. 5.00 (530)
Chadbourne, Ava. Maine Place-Names and the Peopling of its
Towns: York County. 1957. 78pp.
    How Maine towns were settled and named. Photos,
    many names. 1.95 (79)
Dearborn, Jeremiah Wadleigh, ed. A History of the First
Century of the Town of Parsonsfield, Maine. 1888. 710pp.
B-BH 19160.   .... (778)

Maryland

STATEWIDE REFERENCES

Alsop, George. Character of the Province of Maryland. Repr. of 1902 ed.	7.50	..... (81)
Bell, Annie Walker Burns, comp. Maryland Genealogies and Historical Recorder. 1941. Vol. 1-128pp., Vol. 2-150pp., Vol. 3-114pp., Vol. 4-94pp., Vols. 5 and 6-166pp., Vols. 7 and 8-154pp., Vol. 9-104pp., Vol. 10-112pp., Vol. 11-114pp., Vol. 12-120pp., Vol. 13-116pp. B-BH 4971.	.....	..... (778)
Baltimore, George Calvert, 1st Baron. The Calvert Papers. 3 Vols. in one. 1889-1899.	45.00	..... (2)
Boyle, Esmeralda. Biographical Sketches of Distinguished Marylanders. 1877. 380pp. B-BH 16692.	.....	..... (778)
Browne, William Hand. Maryland, the History of a Palatinate. 1904.	20.50	..... (2)
Cassimere, Raphael, Jr. The Origins and Early Development of Slavery in Maryland, 1633 to 1715. 191pp. BIP-71-27708.	.....	..... (777)
Ellefson, Clinton Ashley. The County Courts and the Provincial Court in Maryland, 1733-1763. 678pp. BIP-64-06340.	.....	..... (777)
Hartdagen, Gerald Eugene. The Anglican Vestry in Colonial Maryland. 281pp. BIP-65-12092.	.....	..... (777)
Harvey, Katherine A. Best Dressed Miners: Life and Labor in the Maryland Coal Region, 1835-1910. 1969.	19.50	..... (163)
Jordan, David William. The Royal Period of Colonial Maryland, 1689-1715. 401pp. BIP-67-05728.	.....	..... (777)
Kinnaman, John Allen. The Internal Revenues of Colonial Maryland. 600pp. BIP-00-12835.	.....	..... (777)
Maganzin, Louis. Economic Depression in Maryland and Virginia, 1783-1787. 294pp. BIP-68-01893.	.....	..... (777)
Nead, Daniel W. The Pennsylvania-German in the Settlement of Maryland. Repr. of 1914 ed. 304pp.	15.00	..... (274)
Proceedings of the Maryland Court of Appeals 1695-1729 - Volume 1 of the American Legal Series.	43.00	38.00 (415)
Riley, Elihu S. A History of the General Assembly of Maryland, 1635-1904. Repr. of 1905 ed.	17.50	..... (404)
Robbins, Michael Warren. The Principio Company: Iron-Making in Colonial Maryland, 1720-1781. 398pp. BIP-72-25063.	.....	..... (777)
Semmes, Raphael. Crime and Punishment in Early Maryland. Repr. of 1938 ed.	12.50	..... (698)
Stockbridge, Henry. The Archives of Maryland as Illustrating the Spirit of the Times of the Early Colonists. 1886.	10.00	..... (2)

Listed below is the name of a professional genealogist willing to undertake research for a fee within the state of Maryland, in areas specified in her ad:

Wagandt, Charles L. Mighty Revolution: Negro Emancipation
in Maryland, 1862-1864. 1964.   11.00   ..... (385)
Wroth, Lawrence Counselman. A History of Printing in Colonial
Maryland, 1686-1776. 1922.   28.50   ..... (2)

Research Aids

Carothers, Bettie. Maryland Source Records. 1975. 72pp.
Census records, marriages, church records, Oaths of
Fidelity, births, list of paupers, etc. 6.25 (122)
Gannett, Henry. A Gazetteer of Maryland and Delaware.
Repr. of 1904 ed. 84, 15pp.   7.50   ..... (274)
Magruder, James M., Jr. Index of Maryland Colonial Wills,
1634-1777. Repr. of 1933 ed. 543pp.   20.00   ..... (274)
Meyer, Mary K. Genealogical Research in Maryland: A
Guide, Revised and Enlarged. 1976. 109pp. 6.00 (469)
Pedley, Avril J.M. The Manuscript Collections of the
Maryland Historical Society. 1968. 390pp.
An index to the manuscript holdings of the
Maryland Historical Society.   16.00   ..... (469)

Military

Davis, Edward Graham. Maryland and North Carolina in
the Campaign of 1780-1781, With a Preliminary Notice
of the Earlier Battles of the Revolution, in Which the
Troops of the Two States Won Distinction. 1893.   10.00   ..... (2)
De Michele, Michael David. The Glorious Revolution in
Maryland: A Study of the Provincial Revolution of
1689. 218pp. BIP-68-08679.   .... (777)
Goldsborough, W. W. The Maryland Line in the Confederate
Army, 1861-1865. 2d ed. Repr. of 1900 ed.   22.50   ..... (404)
Muster Rolls and Other Records of Service of Maryland
Troops in the American Revolution, 1775-1783. 1900.
744pp. B-BH 6329.   .... (778)
Overfield, Richard Arthur. The Loyalists of Maryland During
the American Revolution. 449pp. BIP-69-07624.   .... (777)
Van Ness, James Sanuel. The Maryland Courts in the
American Revolution: A Case Study. 369pp. BIP-68-16667.   .... (777)

Newspapers

Baltimore American and Commercial Advertiser, May 1799
to December 1902. 263 rolls.
Microfilm of original newspaper. Individual rolls
covering a specific time span may be ordered.
Prices range from $15 to $30 per roll.   .... (870)
Baltimore Maryland Sun, May 1836 to December 1920.
387 rolls.
Microfilm of the original newspaper. Individual
rolls covering a specific time span may be ordered.
Prices range from $15 to $30 per roll.   .... (870)
Barnes, Robert. Gleanings From Maryland Newspapers
1776-1785. 1975. 58pp.
Abstracts of vital records such as deaths, mar-
riages, settlement of estates, runaway wives, etc. 6.25 (122)
_____. Gleanings From Maryland Newspapers 1786-1790.
1976. 71pp.
Abstracts of vital records such as deaths, marriages,
settlement of estates, runaway wives, etc. 6.25 (122)

_____. Gleanings From Maryland Newspapers 1786-1790.
1976. 71pp.
    Abstracts of vital records such as deaths, mar-
riages, settlement of estates, runaway wives, etc.   ••••• 6.25 (122)

Records

_____. Maryland Marriages, 1634-1777. 1976. 233pp.   12.50 ••••• (274)
Bell, Annie Walker Burns, comp. Maryland Will Book,
Numbers 24-35, 38. No. 24-80pp., No. 25-218pp.,
No. 26-80pp., No. 27-188pp., No. 28-292pp., No. 29-
224pp., No. 30-part 2-88pp., No. 31-266pp., No. 32-
124pp., No. 33-34pp., No. 34-176pp., No. 35-206pp.,
No. 38-262pp. 1937-1938. B-BH 4958.   ••••• ••••• (778)
Brumbaugh, Gaius M. Maryland Records, Colonial,
Revolutionary, County and Church. 2 vols. Repr. of
1915 and 1928 eds. 513pp. and 688pp.   50.00 ••••• (274)
_____. Maryland Records, Colonial, Revolutionary,
County, and Church, From Original Sources. 2 vols.
1915. Vol. 1-536pp., Vol. 2-710pp. B-BH 6666.   ••••• ••••• (778)
Carothers, Bettie. Abstracts of Maryland Will Book 38,
Part I. Reprint. 71pp.   ••••• 6.00 (122)
_____. Abstracts of Maryland Will Book 38, Part II.
Reprint. 76pp.   ••••• 6.00 (122)
Meyer, Mary Keysor. Divorces and Names Changes in
Maryland 1634-1854. 1970. 143pp.   7.50 ••••• (479)
Streeter, Sebastian Ferris. Papers Relating to the Early
History of Maryland. 1876.   18.50 ••••• (2)
Wyand, Jeffrey and Florence Wyand. Colonial Maryland
Naturalizations. 1975. 104pp.   8.50 ••••• (274)

ANNE ARUNDEL COUNTY

Maryland Rent Rolls: Baltimore and Anne Arundel Counties,
1700-1707, 1705-1724. Repr. of 1924-1931 ed. 274pp. 15.00 ••••• (274)
Moss, James E. Providence, Ye Lost Town of Severn in
Maryland. 1976. 560pp.
    Story of the settlement of Broadneck area of Anne
Arundel County.   16.00 ••••• (469)
Newman, Harry Wright. Anne Arundel Gentry; a Genealogical
History of Twenty-Two Pioneers of Anne Arundel County,
Maryland, and Their Descendants. 1933. 686pp. B-OP 24326. ••••• ••••• (778)
Warfield, Joshua Dorsey. The Founders of Anne Arundel and
Howard Counties, Maryland. 1905. 608pp. B-BH 3453.   ••••• ••••• (778)

BALTIMORE COUNTY

Barnes, Robert. Abstracts of Baltimore County Administration
Accounts Liber 6 (1763-1769). 1976. 36pp.   ••••• 5.00 (122)
_____.Abstracts of Baltimore County Administration Accounts
Liber 7 (1769-1773). 1975. 19pp.   ••••• 5.00 (122)
_____.Abstracts of Baltimore County Administration Accounts
Liber 8 (1773-1785). 1975. 23pp.   ••••• 5.00 (122)
Livingood, James Weston. The History of the Commercial
Rivalry Between Philadelphia and Baltimore for the Trade
of the Susquehanna Valley 1780-1860. 301pp. BIP-00-02998. ••••• ••••• (777)
Maryland Rent Rolls: Baltimore and Anne Arundel Counties,
1700-1707, 1705-1724. Repr. of 1924-1931 ed. 274pp. 15.00 ••••• (274)

Obert, Rowene T., comp. Baltimore, Maryland City and County
Marriage Licenses 1777-1799. 1975. 97pp.
    Alphabetical listing of marriages both by bride and groom. 10.00 (277)
Proceedings, Maryland Historical Society, ed. Settlement of
Baltimore. 1880.
    Prepared for Baltimore 150th Celebration. 10.00 ..... (2)
Scharf, J. Thomas. The Chronicles of Baltimore: Being a
Complete History of Baltimore Town and Baltimore City
From the Earliest Period to the Present Time. Repr. of
1874 ed. 25.00 ..... (404)
Vexler, Robert I. Baltimore: A Chronological and Documentary
History. 1975. 156pp. 7.50 ..... (551)

DORCHESTER COUNTY

Huelle, Walter E. Footnotes to Dorchester History. 1970. ..... 2.00 (162)
Jones, Elias. New Revised History of Dorchester County,
Maryland. 15.00 ..... (162)

FREDERICK COUNTY

Grove, William Jarboe. History of Carrollton Manor, Frederick
County, Maryland. 1928. 511pp. B-OP 71815. .... (778)
Scharf, John Thomas. History of Western Maryland. Being
a History of Frederick, Montgomery, Carroll, Washington,
Allegany, and Garrett Counties. 2 vols. 1882. Vol. 1-908pp.,
Vol. 2-914pp. B-BH 4269. .... (778)

GARRETT COUNTY

Morrison, Charles. The Western Boundary of Maryland. 1976.
112pp.
    The history of a boundary dispute with Preston County,
    West Virginia which lasted from 1736 to 1910. ..... 4.50 (508)
Olsen, Evelyn Guard. Indian Blood. 1967. 253pp.
    Covers the early settlement of the Friendsville,
    Maryland area and the history of the early settlers of
    Western Maryland. Pictures. 7.00 ..... (273)

HOWARD COUNTY

Tyson, Martha E. A Brief Account of the Settlement of Ellicott's
Mills, with Fragments of History Therewith Connected. 1871. 7.50 ..... (2)
Warfield, Joshua Dorsey. The Founders of Anne Arundel and
Howard Counties, Maryland. 1905. 608pp. B-BH 3453. .... (778)

PRINCE GEORGES COUNTY

Court Records of Prince Georges County, Maryland. Volume
   9 of American Legal Series. 43.00 38.00 (415)
Prince Georges Genealogical Society. A Bibliography of
Published Genealogical Source Records, Prince Georges
County, Maryland. 1975. 18pp.
    Contains cemetery, census, church, court, land,
    military, probate and miscellaneous records,
    gazetters, histories, research guides and vital
    records sources. 1.50 (620)
_____. 1850 Census Prince Georges County, Maryland.
1976-1977. In Process.
    Contains complete abstraction, not just an index. .... (620)

_____. Prince Georges County Land Records, Volume A,
1696-1702. 1976. 98pp.
Deed abstractions; complete index to surnames, tracts,
occupations, etc. Tract position map included. 5.50 (620)

TALBOT COUNTY

Harrison, Samuel A. Wenlock Christison, and the Early Friends
in Talbot County, Maryland. 1878.   7.50 ..... (2)

WORCESTER COUNTY

Hudson, Millard F., comp. Inscriptions on Tombstones in
Cemeteries of Worcester County, Maryland. 224pp.
B-OP 63700.   .... (778)

Massachusetts

STATEWIDE REFERENCES

Bacon, E. M., ed. Acts and Laws, of the Commonwealth of
Massachusetts (1780-1797) with Supplements (1780-1784).
13 vols. 1890-1896.   Set: 790.00 ..... (2)
Bailyn, Bernard and Lotte Bailyn. Massachusetts Shipping,
1697-1714: A Statistical Study. 1959.   5.00 ..... (319)
Banks, Ronald. The Separation of Maine from Massachusetts,
1785-1820. 1966. 673pp. BIP-67-04129.   .... (777)
Billias, George A. The Massachusetts Land Bankers of 1740.
1959. 59pp. 1.00 (460)
Bradford, Alden. History of Massachusetts. 3 vols. 1822,
1825 and 1829.   Set: 45.00 ..... (299)
Disease and Society in Provincial Massachusetts: Collected
Accounts 1736-1939. 1972.   9.00 ..... (38)
Fortin, Roger Antonio. The Decline of Royal Authority in
Colonial Massachusetts. 276pp. BIP-70-01722.   .... (777)
Haskins, George L. Law and Authority in Early Massachusetts:
A Study in Tradition and Design. Repr. of 1960 ed.   8.50 ..... (685)
Holbrook, Stewart H. Old Post Road: The Story of the Boston
Post Road, ed. A. B. Guthrie, Jr. 1962.   7.95 3.50 (451)
Howe, Octavius T. Emigrant Companies from Massachusetts
1849-1850.   11.00 ..... (631)
Hutchinson, Thomas. Additions to Thomas Hutchinson's History
of Massachusetts Bay, ed. Catherine B. Mayo. 1949.   ..... 4.00 (415)
_____. Diary and Letters of Thomas Hutchinson, comp. Peter
O. Hutchinson. 2 vols. Repr. of 1883 ed.
Thomas Hutchinson (1711-1780). Born Boston. Tory
governor of province of Massachusetts and a historian.
Set: 47.50 ..... (248)
_____ and W. H. Whitmore. The Thomas Hutchinson Papers.
2 vols. 1967.   Set: 40.00 ..... (248)
McKirdy, Charles Robert. Lawyers in Crisis: The Massachusetts
Legal Profession, 1760-1790. 279pp. BIP-70-00117.   .... (777)
Mather, Cotton. Diary of Cotton Mather. 2 vols. Vol. 1 1681-
1708, Vol. 2 1709-1724. 1957.   20.00 ..... (775)
Moore, George H. Notes on the History of Slavery in
Massachusetts. 1866.   11.75 ..... (522)
Murrin, John M. Anglicizing an American Colony: The
Transformation of Provincial Massachusetts. 329pp.
BIP-66-13918.   .... (777)

Pope, Charles Henry. The Pioneers of Massachusetts. 1900.
550pp. B-BH 4154. .... (778)
Shirley, William. Correspondence of William Shirley,
Governor of Massachusetts and Military Commander in
America 1731-1760. 2 vols. 1912. Set: 47.50 ..... (2)
Snell, Ronald Kingman. The County Magistracy in Eighteenth-
Century Massachusetts: 1692-1750. 393pp. BIP-71-23385. .... (777)
Stoddard, Francis R. The Truth About the Pilgrims. Repr.
of 1952 ed. 206pp. 10.00 ..... (274)
Sullivan, James. The History of Land Titles in Massachusetts.
1801. 17.00 ..... (38)
Towner, Lawrence William. A Good Master Well Served:
A Social History of Servitude in Massachusetts, 1620-1750.
278pp. BIP-00-13145. .... (777)
Turk, Marion G. The Quiet Adventurers in America. 1975.
300pp.
Genealogical data and story of settlers in the American
Colonies and Unites States from the Channel Islands,
United Kingdom; Jersey, Guernsey, Alderney and Sark. 12.00 10.00 (771)
Wall, Robert Emmet, Jr. The Membership of the Massachusetts
General Court, 1634-1686. 749pp. BIP-65-09724 .... (777)
Washburn, Emory. Sketches of the Judicial History of
Massachusetts from 1630 to the Revolution in 1775. Repr. of
1840 ed. 17.50 ..... (176)

Research Aids

Bond and Fuller, comps. Register of Ancestors. National
Society of The Colonial Dames of America in the
Commonwealth of Massachusetts. 1975. 135pp. 10.00 (154)
Chedwato Service. Car-Del Scribe. 36pp.
Magazine for arm-chair genealogists; reference
articles, books, queries. Six issues per year. 4.50/yr (134)

Military

Barker, John. British in Boston: Being the Diary of
Lieutenant John Barker of the King's Own Regiment
From November 15, 1774-May 31, 1776. Repr. of
1924 ed. illus. 8.00 ..... (38)
Emilio, Louis F. History of the Fifty-Fourth Regiment
of Massachusetts Volunteer Infantry. Repr. of 1865 ed. 21.00 ..... (394)
_____. History of the Fifty-Fourth Regiment of
Massachusetts Volunteer Infantry, 1863-1865. Repr. of
1894 ed. 14.50 ..... (38)
Hambrick-Stowe, Charles E. and Donna Smerlas, eds.
Massachusetts Militia Companies and Officers of the
Lexington Alarm. 1976. c100pp. In Process.
Lists those Massachusetts officers who turned out
for the Lexington Alarm in April, 1775. The list
numbers 1,240 men and includes rank, residence,
length of service, company, and regiment. .... (530)
Kendall, Walter. The Defence of Boston in the War of
1812-1815. 1899. 42pp.
Includes a list of officers of Massachusetts Militia
engaged in the defense. 2.00 (530)
MacKenzie, Frederick. Diary of Frederick MacKenzie.
Giving a Daily Narrative of His Military Service as an

Officer of the Regiment of Royal Welch Fusiliers During
the Years 1775-1781 in Massachusetts, Rhode Island
and New York. 2 vols. 1930.   20.00   ..... (38)
Millar, David Richard. The Militia, the Army, and
Independency in Colonial Massachusetts. 325pp.
BIP-68-00668.   .... (777)
Minot, G. R. History of the Insurrections in Massachusetts
in 1786. Repr. of 1788 ed.   10.00   ..... (176)
Newcomer, Lee Nathaniel. The Embattled Farmers: A
Massachusetts Countryside in the American Revolution.
Repr. of 1953 ed. xii, 274pp.
  Studies the roots of the Revolution from the view-
  point of farmers, artisans and shopkeepers in non-
  urban areas.   14.00   ..... (662)
Radabaugh, Jack Sheldon. The Military System of Colonial
Massachusetts, 1690-1740. 609pp. BIP-65-06551.   .... (777)
Voye, Nancy S., ed. Massachusetts Officers in the French
and Indian Wars, 1748-1763. 1975. c380pp.
  An alphabetical, enumerated, listing of commissioned
  officers, with categories of rank, residence, military
  expedition, service by year, time period, and length,
  company, and regiment. 9.45 (530)

Religious and Ethnic Groups

Alliman, Kirk Gilbert. The Incorporation of Massachusetts
Congregational Churches, 1692-1833: The Preservation
of Religious Autonomy. 330pp. BIP-71-05706.   .... (777)
Donovan, George Francis. The Pre-Revolutionary Irish in
Massachusetts, 1620-1775. c1932. 166pp. B-OP 24444.   .... (778)
Federal Writers Project. The Armenians in Massachusetts.
Repr. of 1937 ed.   12.50   ..... (2)
Hallowell, Richard P. The Quaker Invasion of Massachusetts.
Repr. of 1883 ed.   11.25   ..... (81)
Scholz, Robert Francis. The Reverend Elders: Faith,
Fellowship and Politics in the Ministerial Community of
Massachusetts Bay, 1630-1710. 290pp. BIP-68-01180.   .... (777)
Sharples, Stephen P., ed. Records of the Church of Christ,
1632-1830. 1906. 579pp.
  Comprising the ministerial records of baptisms,
  marriages, deaths, admission to covenant and
  communion, dismissals and church proceedings.   8.00   ..... (530)

Newspapers

Boston Evening Transcript, January 1848 to December 1915.
328 rolls.
  Microfilm of the original newspapers. Individual
  rolls covering a specific time span may be ordered.
  Prices vary from $15 to $30 per roll.   .... (870)
Walsh, Francis Robert. The Boston Pilot: A Newspaper for
the Irish Immigrant - 1829-1908. 305pp. BIP-68-18095.   .... (777)

Records

Shurtleff, Nathaniel B. and David Pulsifer, eds. Records of
the Colony of New Plymouth, in New England. Printed
by Order of the Legislature . . . of Massachusetts.
12 vols. bound into 6. 1855-1861.   Set: 437.50 ..... (2)

Shurtleff, Nathaniel B., ed. Records of the Governor and
Company of the Massachusetts Bay in New England
(1628-1686). 5 vols. in 6. 1853-1854.   Set: 390.00   ..... (2)

Massachusetts Bay Company and Colonies

Chamberlain, Nathan Henry. Samuel Sewell and the World
He Lived In. Repr. of 1897 ed. xvi, 319pp.
A recreation of the social life of early New England,
based upon Sewall's Diary (1674-1729) and other
sources.   9.00   ..... (662)
Ellis, George E. Puritan Age and Rule in the Colony of the
Massachusetts Bay 1629-1685. Repr. of 1888 ed.   28.00   ..... (248)
Minot, George Richards. Continuation of the History of the
Province of Massachusetts Bay, From the Year 1748
to 1765. 2 vols. in 1. 1803.   43.00   ..... (2)
Rose-Troup, Frances. John White. 1930. 483pp.
The patriarch of Dorchester and the founder of
Massachusetts 1575-1648. With an account of
the early settlements in Massachusetts 1620-1630.   17.50   ..... (273)
_____. The Massachusetts Bay Company and Its Pred-
ecessors. 1930. 176pp.   10.00   ....., (273)
Sewall, Samuel. Diary of Samuel Sewall, 1674-1729. 3 vols.
Repr. of 1878 ed.   Set: 100.00   ..... (38)
Twomey, Rosemary Katherine. From Pure Church to Pure
Nation: Massachusetts Bay, 1630-1692. 299pp.
BIP-72-00777.   .... (777)
Wall, Robert E., Jr. Massachusetts Bay: The Crucial Decade,
1640-1650. 1972.   12.50   ..... (857)
Young, Alexander. Chronicles of the First Planters of the
Colony of Massachusetts Bay, 1623-1636. Repr. of
1846 ed. 571pp.   18.50   ..... (274)

BARNSTABLE COUNTY

Keene, Betsey D. History of Bourne, 1622-1937. Repr. of
1937 ed.   10.00   ..... (730)
Vital Records of Eastham, Massachusetts (Index to), comp.
Leonard H. Smith, Jr. 1976. In Process.
Index of persons in Eastham vital records as
published in 34 volumes of the Mayflower Descendant,
showing volume and page number of each entry as
found in that publication. 1675 - 1827 is approximate
time period.   .... (697)
Vital Records of Falmouth, Massachusetts to 1850, comp.
Oliver B. Brown. 1976. 272pp.   8.00   ..... (640)
Vital Records of Yarmouth, Massachusetts to 1850, comps.
R. M. Sherman and R. W. Sherman. 1975. 966pp.   20.00   ..... (640)

BERKSHIRE COUNTY

Sedgwick, Sarah C. and Christina S. Marquand. Stockbridge,
1739-1974. 1974.   .....   5.95 (64)
Simpson, Norman T. Many Faces of Stockbridge. 2.95 (64)
Vital Records of Alford to 1850. 1902. 32pp.   10.00   ..... (530)
Vital Records of Becket to 1850. 1903. 98pp.   6.00   ..... (530)
Vital Records of Dalton to 1850. 1906. 82pp.   10.00   ..... (530)
Vital Records of Great Barrington to 1850. 1904. 89pp.   10.00   ..... (530)
Vital Records of Hindsale to 1850. 1902. 98pp.   6.00   ..... (530)

Vital Records of Lee to 1850. 1903. 284pp.   10.00   ..... (530)
Vital Records of New Ashford to 1850. 1916. 43pp.   5.00   ..... (530)
Vital Records of Otis (formerly Loudon) to 1850. 1941. 159pp.   7.00   ..... (530)
Vital Records of Peru to 1850. 1902. 112pp.   7.50   ..... (530)
Vital Records of Richmond to 1850. 1913. 113pp.   7.50   ..... (530)
Vital Records of Tyringham to 1850. 1903. 108pp.   10.00   ..... (530)
Vital Records of Washington to 1850. 1904. 57pp.   6.50   ..... (530)
Vital Records of Williamstown to 1850. 1907. 173pp.   7.50   ..... (530)
Vital Records of Windsor to 1850. 1917. 153pp.   6.50   ..... (530)

BRISTOL COUNTY

Vital Records of New Bedford to 1850. 3 vols. 1932, 1941.
             Set: 20.00   ..... (530)
Vital Records of Rehoboth, 1642-1896, comp. James Newell
 Arnold. 1897. 984pp. B-BH 6993.   .... (778)
Vital Records of Westport to 1850. 1918. 296pp.   7.50   ..... (530)

DUKES COUNTY

Vital Records of Chilmark to 1850. 1904. 96pp.   10.00   ..... (530)
Vital Records of Edgartown to 1850. 1906. 276pp.   12.50   ..... (530)
Vital Records of Tisbury to 1850. 1910. 244pp   10.00   ..... (530)

ESSEX COUNTY

Adams, H. B. Village Communities of Cape Anne and Salem,
 From the Historical Collections of the Essex Institute.
 Repr. of 1883 ed. 6.25 (394)
Babson, John J. History of the Town of Gloucester, Mas-
 sachusetts Cape Ann: Including the Town of Rockport.   12.50   ..... (699)
Bentley, William. The Diary of Reverend William Bentley:
 1784-1819. 4 vols.   Set: 45.00   ..... (699)
Copeland, Melvin T. and Elliott C. Rogers. Saga of Cape
 Ann. 1966.   .....   3.50 (833)
Galloupe, Augustus A., comp. Early Records of the Town of
 Beverly. 1907. 87pp.
  Vital statistics. 6.50 (530)
Garland, Joseph E. Eastern Point: Chronicle of Gloucester's
 Outer Shield and Inner Sanctum 1606-1950. 1973. 424pp.
  Contains many family histories of Gloucester and Cape
  Ann, old and new.   12.50   ..... (56)
Gildrie, Richard P. Salem, Massachusetts 1626-1683: A
 Covenant. 1975.   8.75   ..... (801)
Perzel, Edward Spaulding. The First Generation of Settlement
 in Colonial Ipswich, Massachusetts 1633-1660. 417pp.
 BIP-67-14745.   .... (777)
Phillips, James D. Salem in the Seventeenth Century. 1933.   7.50   ..... (223)
   . Salem in the Eighteenth Century. Repr. of 1937 ed.   7.50   ..... (223)
Pynchon, William. The Diary of William Pynchon of Salem.
 A Picture of Salem Life, Social and Political, a Century
 Ago, ed. Fitch Edward Oliver. 1890.   28.50   ..... (2)
Roberts, Bruce. Old Salem in Pictures. 1968.   .....   2.95 (457)
Smith, Philip C., ed. Journals of Ashley Bowen (1728-1813)
 of Marblehead. 2 vols. 1973.   Set: 35.00   ..... (578)
Thresher, Mary G., ed. Records and Files of the Quarterly
 Courts of Essex County, Massachusetts, Volume 9, Septem-
 ber 25, 1683 - April 20, 1686. 1974.   30.00   ..... (223)

Vital Records of Danvers, Massachusetts, to the End of the
Year 1849. 2 vols.

Vol. 1 - Births 1909:	Each:	12.50	..... (223)
Vol. 2 - Marriages and Deaths 1910:	Each:	12.50	..... (223)

Vital Records of Gloucester, Massachusetts, to the End of the
Year 1849.

Vol. 2 - Marriages 1923:	Each:	15.00	..... (223)
Vol. 3 - Deaths 1924:	Each:	10.00	..... (223)

Vital Records of Lynn, Massachusetts, to the End of the Year
1849. 1905, 1906.

Vol. 1:		o.p.	..... (223)
Vol. 2 - Marriages and Deaths 1906:	Each:	15.00	..... (223)

Vital Records of Manchester, Massachusetts, to the End of the
Year 1849. 1903.   10.00   ..... (223)

Vital Records of Marblehead, Massachusetts, to the End of the
Year 1849. 2 vols. 1903, 1904.   Each: 15.00   ..... (223)

Vital Records of Newburyport, Massachusetts, to the End of the
Year 1849. 2 vols. 1911.

Vol. 1 - Births 1911:	Each:	15.00	..... (223)
Vol. 2 - Marriages and Deaths 1911:	Each:	15.00	..... (223)

Vital Records of Rockport, Massachusetts, to the End of the
Year 1849. 1924.   7.50   ..... (223)

Vital Records of Wenham, Massachusetts, to the End of the
Year 1849. 1904.   7.50   ..... (223)

Watkins, Lura W. Middleton, Massachusetts: A Cultural
History. 1970.   12.50   ..... (223)

FRANKLIN COUNTY

Patrie, Lois M. History of Colrain, Massachusetts. 1974.
573pp.
    Contains genealogies of early families. Illustrated.
    Indexed.   20.00   ..... (577)
Vital Records of Ashfield to 1850. 1942. 273pp.   10.00   ..... (530)
Vital Records of Charlemont to 1850. 1917. 166pp.   6.00   ..... (530)
Vital Records of Conway to 1850. 1943. 276pp.   7.50   ..... (530)
Vital Records of Gill to 1850. 1904. 97pp.   7.00   ..... (530)
Vital Records of Greenfield to 1850. 1915. 299pp.   8.00   ..... (530)
Vital Records of Heath to 1850. 1915. 142pp.   6.00   ..... (530)
Vital Records of Shelburne, Massachusetts, to the End of the
Year 1849. 1931.   7.50   ..... (223)

HAMPDEN COUNTY

Frisch, Michael H. Town into City: Springfield, Massachusetts
and the Meaning of Community, 1840-1880. 1972.   10.00   ..... (319)
Vital Records of Brimfield to 1850. 1921. 336pp.   10.00   ..... (530)
Vital Records of Chester to 1850. 1911. 256pp.   8.00   ..... (530)
Vital Records of Granville to 1850. 1914. 236pp.   10.00   ..... (530)
Vital Records of Montgomery to 1850. 1902. 66pp.   5.00   ..... (530)
Vital Records of Palmer to 1850. 1905. 242pp.   8.00   ..... (530)
Vital Records of West Springfield to 1850. 2 vols. 1944.
    237 and 308pp.   Set: 12.50   ..... (530)

HAMPSHIRE COUNTY

Foster, Mary Catherine. Hampshire County, Massachusetts:
1729-1754 A Covenant Society in Transition. 337pp.
BIP-67-17759.   .... (777)

Sylvester, Judd. History of Hadley, Including the Early History
of Hatfield, South Hardely, Amherst and Granby, Massachusetts.
1905. 773pp. B-OP 42399.   .... (778)
Vital Records of Middlefield to 1850. 1907. 138pp.   6.00 ..... (530)
Vital Records of Worthington to 1850. 1911. 159pp.   7.00 ..... (530)

MIDDLESEX COUNTY

Bond, Henry, M.D. Genealogies of the Families and Descendants
of the Early Settlers of Watertown, Massachusetts, In-
cluding Waltham and Weston; to Which is Appended The
Early History of the Town with Illustrations, Maps and Notes.
1860. 1094pp.   60.50 ..... (530)
Butler, Caleb. History of the Town of Groton Including Pepperell
and Shirley. 1848. 538pp. B-CD 156.   .... (778)
Gozzaldi, Mary Isabella, comp. Index to Paige's History of
Cambridge, Massachusetts, 1630-1877. 860pp.   8.00 ..... (530)
Mailloux, Kenneth Frank. The Boston Manufacturing Company
of Waltham, Massachusetts, 1813-1848: The First Modern
Factory in America. 239pp. BIP-00-21740.   .... (777)
Mansur, Ina. A New England Church. 1974. 238pp.
Growth of Bedford, Massachusetts. Congregational
Church 1680-1834. Many names.   10.95 5.95 (79)
Morse, Abner. A Genealogical Register of the Inhabitants and
History of the Towns of Sherborn and Holliston. 1856.
382pp. B-OP 65395.   .... (778)
Sanborn, Franklin B. Recollections of Seventy Years. 2 vols.
Repr. of 1909 ed.   15.60 ..... (266)
Spalding, M.E. and F.R. Rice. Colonial Records of Marl-
borough, Massachusetts. 1909. 47pp. 6.50 (530)
Vital Records of Acton to 1850. 1923. 311pp.   10.00 ..... (530)
Vital Records of Arlington (formerly West Cambridge) to 1850.
1904. 162pp.   6.00 ..... (530)
Vital Records of Bedford to 1850. 1903. 142pp.   10.00 ..... (530)
Vital Records of Burlington to 1850. 1915. 100pp.   10.00 ..... (530)
Vital Records of Dracut to 1850. 1907. 302pp.   7.00 ..... (530)
Vital Records of Holliston to 1850. 1908. 358pp.   8.00 ..... (530)
Vital Records of Hopkinton to 1850. 1911. 462pp.   10.00 ..... (530)
Vital Records of Lincoln to 1850. 1908. 179pp.   7.00 ..... (530)
Vital Records of Lowell, Massachusetts, to the End of the Year
1849. 4 vols.   Set: 40.00 ..... (223)
Vol. 1-Births, Vol. 2-Marriages, Vol. 3-Marriages,
Vol. 4-Deaths: Each: 15.00 ..... (223)
Vital Records of Medford to 1850. 1907. 469pp.   10.00 ..... (530)
Vital Records of Newton to 1850. 1905. 521pp.   15.00 ..... (530)
Vital Records of Shirley to 1850. 1918. 211pp.   8.00 ..... (530)
Vital Records of Stoneham, Massachusetts, to the End of the
Year 1849. 1918.   10.00 ..... (223)
Vital Records of Stow to 1850. 1911. 270pp.   10.00 ..... (530)
Vital Records of Tyngsboro, Massachusetts, to the End of the
Year 1849. 1912.   7.50 ..... (223)
Vital Records of Waltham to 1850. 1904. 298pp.   8.00 ..... (530)
Vital Records of Wayland (formerly East Sudbury) to 1850.
1910. 160pp.   7.00 ..... (530)
Wild, Helen Tildon. Medford in the Revolution. 1903. 68pp.
The military history of Medford, Massachusetts
1765-1783.   6.50 ..... (530)

NANTUCKET COUNTY

Godfrey, Edward K. The Island of Nantucket. 1882. 398pp.
B-BH 14589. .... (778)
Obed, Macy. The History of Nantucket. Being a Compendious
Account of the First Settlement of That Island by the
English, Together With the Rise and Progress of the Whale
Fishery. 2d ed. 1880. 313pp. map. 12.50 ..... (273)
Vital Records of Nantucket to 1850. 5 vols. 1925-1928.
Set: 30.00 ..... (530)

NORFOLK COUNTY

Adams, Charles Francis. Three Episodes of Massachusetts
History: The Settlement of Boston Bay; The Antinomian
Controversy; A Study of Church and Town Government. 2 vols.
Repr. of 1892 ed. viii, iv, 1067pp.
    A third section is the history of a typical Massachusetts
    community, Quincy, from 1639 to 1888. 25.00 ..... (662)
Ayer, Mrs. James B., ed. A Brief History of Milton, Mas-
sachusetts. 1956. 48pp. 2.00 ..... (531)
Dedham, Massachusetts: An Alphabetical Abstract of the
Record of Marriages in the Town, 1844-1890. 1896. 172pp.
B-BH 2114. .... (778)
Hamilton, Edward Pierce. A History of Milton. 1957. 291pp. 9.00 ..... (531)
Lockridge, Kenneth Alan. Dedham 1636-1736: The Anatomy
of a Puritan Utopia. 378pp. BIP-66-04595. .... (777)
Vital Records of Bellingham to 1850. 1904. 222pp. 10.00 ..... (530)
Vital Records of Dover to 1850. 1908. 107pp 6.00 ..... (530)
Vital Records of Foxborough to 1850. 1911. 249pp. 7.00 ..... (530)
Vital Records of Medfield to 1850. 1903. 243pp. 12.50 ..... (530)
Vital Records of Walpole to 1850. 1902. 216pp. 10.00 ..... (530)
Weymouth Historical Society. History of Weymouth, Mas-
sachusetts. Vol. 1-492pp., Vol. 2-512pp., Vol. 3-420pp.,
Vol. 4 -433pp. 1923. B-OP 66710. .... (778)

PLYMOUTH COUNTY

Baylies, Francis. An Historical Memoir of the Colony of New
Plymouth, From the Flight of the Pilgrims Into Holland in
the Year 1608, to the Union of That Colony with Mas-
sachusetts in 1692. 2 vols. 1866. Set: 91.00 ..... (2)
Bradford, William. Bradford's History of Plymouth Plantation,
1606-1646, ed. William T. Davis. Repr. of 1908 ed. 6.50 ..... (52)
_____. Of Plymouth Plantation 1620-1647, ed. Samuel E.
Morison. 1952. 8.95 ..... (412)
_____. Of Plymouth Plantation: The Pilgrims in America. 1962. ..... 1.95 (627)
Briggs, L. Vernon. History of Shipbuilding on North River,
Plymouth County, Massachusetts. Repr. of 1889 ed. 18.00 ..... (299)
Goodwin, John A. The Pilgrim Republic; An Historical Review
of the Colony of New Plymouth, with Sketches of the Rise of
Other New England Settlements, the History of Congregation-
alism, and the Creeds of the Period. 1920. 39.00 ..... (415)
Latham, Williams. Epitaphs in Old Bridgewater, Massachusetts.
Repr. of 1882 ed. 262pp. 17.50 ..... (7)
Lincoln, Rufus. The Papers of Captain Rufus Lincoln of Wareham,
Massachusetts, comp. James Minor Lincoln. 1904. 12.00 ..... (38)

Mourt, George. Journal of the Pilgrims at Plymouth: Mourt's
    Relation. 1962.   3.95   2.50 (161)
Shurtleff, Nathaniel B. Records of Plymouth Colony: Births,
    Marriages, Deaths and Other Records 1633-1689.
    Repr. of 1857 ed. 293pp.   13.50   ..... (274)
Smith, Leonard H., Jr. Records of the First Church of Wareham,
    Massachusetts, 1739-1891. 1974. 150pp.
        Church records believed lost for many years; they have
           never been published before; transcribed and indexed. 15.00 (697)
Vital Records of Abington to 1850. 2 vols. 1912. 251pp, 381pp.
                                  Set: 15.00   ..... (530)
Vital Records of Brockton (formerly North Bridgewater) to
    1850. 1911. 371pp.   10.00   ..... (530)
Vital Records of Duxbury to 1850. 1911. 446pp.   25.00   ..... (530)
Vital Records of East Bridgewater to 1850. 1917. 406pp.   12.50   ..... (530)
Vital Records of Hanson to 1850. 1911. 110pp.   6.00   ..... (530)
Vital Records of Rochester to 1850. 2 vols. 1914.
    318pp., 450pp.   Set: 15.00   ..... (530)
Vital Records of West Bridgewater to 1850. 1911. 222pp.   7.00   ..... (530)
Young, Alexander. Chronicles of the Pilgrim Fathers of the
    Colony of Plymouth, 1602-1625. Repr. of 1841 ed.   22.50   ..... (176)

SUFFOLK COUNTY

Coughlin, Magdalen. Boston Merchants on the Coast, 1787-1821:
    An Insight Into the American Acquisition of California.
    1970. 357pp. BIP-70-25014.   .... (777)
Drake, Samuel A. Old Boston Taverns and Tavern Clubs.
    Repr. of 1917 ed.   12.50   ..... (266)
Gravestone Inscriptions and Records of Tomb Burials in the
    Central Burying Ground, Boston Common, and Inscriptions
    in the South Burying Ground, Boston. 1917.   .....   5.00 (223)
Gravestone Inscriptions and Records of Tomb Burials in the
    Granary Burying Ground, Boston, Massachusetts. 1918.   6.00   ..... (223)
Jacobs, Donald M. A History of the Boston Negro From the
    Revolution to the Civil War. 1968. 408pp. BIP-68-18097.   .... (777)
Knights, Peter Roger. The Plain People of Boston, 1830-1860:
    A Demographic and Social Study. 1969. 22pp. BIP-70-03588. .... (777)
Lankevich, George. Boston: A Chronological and Documentary
    History. 1974. 160pp.   7.50   ..... (551)
Ross, Marjorie. Book of Boston - Colonial Period. 3.95 (321)
Rutman, Darrett B. Winthrop's Boston: Portrait of a Puritan
    Town, 1630-1649. Repr. of 1965 ed.   8.25   ..... (544)
_____. A Portrait of a Puritan Town, 1630-1649. Repr. of
    1965 ed. 3.25 (546)
Seybolt, Robert Francis. The Private Schools of Colonial Boston,
    1635-1775. 1935.   7.00   ..... (38)
_____. The Public Schools of Colonial Boston. 1935.   8.00   ..... (38)
Simonds, Thomas C. History of South Boston: Formerly
    Dorchester Neck, Now Ward XII of the City of Boston. 1857. 17.00   ..... (38)
Winslow, Anna Green. Diary of Anna Green Winslow, A Boston
    School Girl of 1771. Repr. of 1894 ed. 121pp.   7.50   ..... (266)

WORCESTER COUNTY

Mooney, James Eugene. Antislavery in Worcester County,
    Massachusetts: A Case Study. 1971. 315pp. BIP-72-03339.   .... (777)

Stearns, Ezra Scollay. History of Ashburnham, Massachusetts . . .
1734-1886. 1887. 1066pp.
    Contains a genealogical register. B-OP 70742.   .... (778)
Tolman, N. F., ed. History of Westminster, Massachusetts.
1962. 400pp.

History of Westminster - With Genealogies.	10.00	..... (56)
Vital Records of Ashburnham to 1850. 1909. 215pp.	7.00	..... (530)
Vital Records of Barre to 1850. 1903. 276pp.	10.00	..... (530)
Vital Records of Charlton to 1850. 1905. 268pp.	12.50	..... (530)
Vital Records of Douglas to 1850. 1906. 192pp.	10.00	..... (530)
Vital Records of Garner to 1850. 1907. 136pp.	10.00	..... (530)
Vital Records of Grafton to 1850. 1906. 377pp.	10.00	..... (530)
Vital Records of Holden to 1850. 1904. 236pp.	10.00	..... (530)
Vital Records of Hubbardston to 1850. 1907. 226pp.	8.00	..... (530)
Vital Records of Leicester to 1850. 1903. 284pp.	10.00	..... (530)
Vital Records of Millbury to 1850. 1903. 158pp.	7.50	..... (530)
Vital Records of Northbridge to 1850. 1916. 202pp.	7.00	..... (530)
Vital Records of Petersham to 1850. 1904. 193pp.	10.00	..... (530)
Vital Records of Phillipston to 1850. 1906. 121pp.	6.00	..... (530)
Vital Records of Princeton to 1850. 1902. 195pp.	7.50	..... (530)
Vital Records of Royalston to 1850. 1906. 196pp.	10.00	..... (530)
Vital Records of Rutland to 1850. 255pp.	10.00	..... (530)
Vital Records of Shrewsbury to 1850. 1903. 282pp.	10.00	..... (530)
Vital Records of Sturbridge to 1850. 1906. 393pp.	12.50	..... (530)
Vital Records of Sutton to 1850. 1907. 478pp.	12.50	..... (530)
Vital Records of Templeton to 1850. 1907. 212pp.	7.00	..... (530)
Vital Records of Upton to 1850. 1904. 190pp.	10.00	..... (530)
Vital Records of West Boylston to 1850. 1911. 153pp.	6.00	..... (530)
Vital Records of Westminster to 1850. 1908. 258pp.	8.00	..... (530)
Vital Records of Winchendon to 1850. 1909. 223pp.	8.00	..... (530)

Michigan

STATEWIDE REFERENCES

Cooley, Thomas McIntyre. Michigan, A History of Governments.
    With a Supplementary Chapter by Charles Moore. Rev. ed. 1905. 22.00   ..... (2)
Gilpin, Alec R. Territory of Michigan Eighteen Hundred Five -
    Eighteen Hundred Thirty-Seven. 1970.   8.00   ..... (485)
Johnson, Ida A. Michigan Fur Trade. Repr. of 1919 ed.   7.50   ..... (71)
Michigan Historical Commission. Michigan History. 20 vols.
1917-1936.
    Michigan History supplanted Pioneer Collections which was

---

Listed below are the names of professional genealogists willing to undertake research for
a fee within the state of Michigan, in the areas specified in their ad:

devoted primarily to pioneer reminiscences and county
history. When Dr. George M. Fuller assumed the editor-
ship of Michigan History in 1917, he initiated a policy of
approaching Michigan's past in the context of that of
neighboring states and provinces. As a result, the articles
on fur trade, Indian customs, the War of 1812 and emigration extend far beyond the geographical borders of Michigan.
Subjects receiving excellent coverage are: French exploration and the French regime, early cartography of the Great
Lakes region, and transportation and mining on and around
Lake Superior. An important annual feature is the Michigan
Bibliography, a checklist of books, pamphlets, periodical
articles, unpublished biographies and miscellaneous
materials on the state's history.

Volumes 1-10:	Set:	305.00	260.00	(415)
	Each:	.....	26.00	(415)
Volumes 11-20:	Set:	310.00	260.00	(415)
	Each:	.....	26.00	(415)

A Michigan Reader. 2 vols. 1974.
Volume I: Eleven Thousand B. C. to 1865 A.D. eds., George
May and Herbert Brinks. 4.95 (215)
Volume II: 1865 to Present. eds., Robert Warner and
VanderHill C. Warren. 4.95 (215)
Ringenberg, William Carey. The Protestant College on the
Michigan Frontier. 1970. 219pp. BIP-70-20522.   .... (777)
Saginaw Genealogical Society, Inc. Timbertown Log. ed., Arlene
Feller Cook. 1972-date. 32pp./issue; 128pp./yr.
A Journal of the Saginaw Genealogical Society. Original
research and unpublished sources of early Saginaw
County records.   Per issue: 1.75 (666)
                                              Subscription/yr: 7.00 (666)

Research Aids

Blois, John T. Gazetteer of the State of Michigan.
Repr. of 1838 ed.   23.00 ..... (38)
Michigan Genealogical Council. [Surname] Index to the 1850
Federal Population Census of Michigan. 1976. 480pp.   20.00 ..... (483)

Military

Borger, Henry Charles, Jr. The Role of the Army Engineers
In the Westward Movement In the Lake Huron - Lake
Michigan Basin Before the Civil War. 1954. 287pp.
BIP-00-08610.   .... (777)
Katz, Irving I. Jewish Soldier from Michigan in the
Civil War. 1962.   ..... 2.50 (819)
Kidd, James H. Personal Recollections of a Cavalryman
with Custer's Michigan Cavalry Brigade in the Civil War.
Repr. of 1908 ed.   12.00 ..... (71)

Records

U. S. Government. Territorial Papers. Vol. 10: The
Territory of Michigan, 1805-1820. Foundation of the
Territory, 1803-1805. The Three Administrations of
Governor Hull, 1803-1813. The British Occupation,
1812-1813. The Three Administrations of Governor Cass,
1813-1820. 1942. Index.   57.50 ..... (2)

_____. Territorial Papers. Vol. 11: The Territory of
Michigan, 1820-1829. The Fourth through the Sixth
Administrations of Governor Cass, 1826-1829. 1943. Index.   57.50   ..... (2)
_____. Territorial Papers. Vol. 12: The Territory of
Michigan, 1829-1837. The Seventh Administration of
Governor Cass, 1829-1831. The Administration of
Governor Porter and of Acting Governor Mason,
1831-1835. The Administration of Acting Governor
Horner, 1835-1837. 1945. Index.   57.50   ..... (2)

BERRIEN COUNTY

The Kalamazoo Valley Genealogical Society. The Kalamazoo
Valley Family Newsletter - Berrien County Issue. 1976-1977.   .... (399)

CASS COUNTY

The Kalamazoo Valley Genealogical Society. The Kalamazoo Valley
Family Newsletter - Cass County Issue. 1977.   .... (399)

CHIPPEWA COUNTY

Dickinson, John Newton. The Canal at Sault Ste. Marie,
Michigan: Inception, Construction, Early Operation, and
the Canal Grant Lands. 1968. 350pp. BIP-68-13628.   .... (777)

EATON COUNTY

"Cemetery Inscriptions and Records of Carmel Township,
Eaton County, Michigan." Mid-Michigan Genealogical
Society Occasional Paper, No. 8. 1976.   .....   3.40 (487)
"Cemetery Inscriptions and Records of Windsor Township,
Eaton County, Michigan." Mid-Michigan Genealogical
Society Occasional Paper, No. 7. 1976.   .....   3.40 (487)

GENESEE COUNTY

Ellis, Franklin, ed. History of Genesee County, Michigan.
Repr. of 1879 ed. 500pp.
    Includes City of Flint and individual township histories,
    Civil War military lists, biographies and a complete
    index of persons.   24.00   ..... (241)

HOUGHTON COUNTY

The Kalamazoo Valley Genealogical Society. The Kalamazoo
Valley Family Newsletter (Houghton County, Michigan Issue).
1976. 60pp.
    Township maps, early settlers, officers, church records,
    libraries, newspapers, cemeteries, early history of
    each government in county. 3.00 (399)

INGHAM COUNTY

Edmonds, J. P. Early Lansing History [with] Index of Persons . . .
1944. 181pp. B-OP 911.   .... (778)
The Kalamazoo Valley Genealogical Society. The Kalamazoo
Valley Family Newsletter - Ingham County Issue. 1977.   .... (399)

IONIA COUNTY

The Kalamazoo Valley Genealogical Society. The Kalamazoo
Valley Family Newsletter (Ionia County, Michigan Issue).
1975. 92pp.
Township maps and early settlers and officers. Lists
of libraries, newspapers, cemeteries. Complete County
Directory of 1872.   ..... 4.00 (399)

LAPEER COUNTY

History of Lapeer County, Michigan. 1884. 300pp. B-OP 30120. .... (778)

LIVINGSTON COUNTY

The Kalamazoo Valley Genealogical Society. The Kalamazoo
Valley Family Newsletter - Livingston County Issue. 1978.   .... (399)

MACOMB COUNTY

The Kalamazoo Valley Genealogical Society. The Kalamazoo
Valley Family Newsletter - Macomb County Issue. 1977.   .... (399)

MASON COUNTY

The Kalamazoo Valley Genealogical Society. The Kalamazoo
Valley Family Newsletter - Mason County Issue. 1978.   .... (399)

MECOSTA COUNTY

The Kalamazoo Valley Genealogical Society. The Kalamazoo
Valley Family Newsletter - Mecosta County Issue. 1978.   .... (399)

MIDLAND COUNTY

Chapman Bros. Portrait and Biographical Album, Midland
County, Michigan. Repr. of 1884 ed. 450pp.
    Includes: Newly indexed - every name.   24.00 ..... (666)
_____. Portrait and Biographical Album. Repr. of 1884 ed.
Bound with Imperial Publisher's Directory of Midland
County, 1897. Repr. of 1897 ed. 600pp.
    Album newly indexed with every name from biographical
    sketches. Directory gives name, section, township, and
    post office of all people in Midland County in 1897,
    including cities, villages, and townships, with
    alphabetical arrangement.   36.50 ..... (666)
Haigh, Ellen Rambo, comp. Marriages, Midland County,
1855-1871. ed. Arlene Feller Cook. 1976. 20pp.
    From earliest Record Book of Midland County. 2.25 (666)
Imperial Publishing Company. Directory of Midland County,
Michigan, 1897. Repr. of 1897 ed. 144pp.
    Name, Section, Township and Post Office.   15.50 ..... (666)

MONTCALM COUNTY

The Kalamazoo Valley Genealogical Society. The Kalamazoo
Valley Family Newsletter - Montcalm County Issue. 1977.   .... (399)

MUSKEGON COUNTY

History of Muskegon County, Michigan [with History of
Ottawa County, Michigan]. 1882. 352pp. B-OP 64487.   .... (778)

NEWAYGO COUNTY

The Kalamazoo Valley Genealogical Society. The Kalamazoo
Valley Family Newsletter - Newaygo County Issue. 1976.
60pp (?).   .... (399)

OAKLAND COUNTY

_____. The Kalamazoo Valley Family Newsletter (Oakland
County, Michigan Issue). 1976. 100pp.
Township maps, early settlers, officer. Lists of
libraries, newspapers, cemeteries. Early history
of each governmental sub-division. 4.00 (399)

OCEANA COUNTY

_____. The Kalamazoo Valley Family Newsletter - Oceana
County Issue. 1978-1979.   .... (399)

MUSKEGON COUNTY

History of Muskegon County, Michigan with History of Ottowa
County, Michigan. 1882. 352pp. B-OP 64487.   .... (778)

OTTAWA COUNTY

History of Muskegon County, Michigan with History of Ottowa
County, Michigan. 1882, 352pp. B-OP 64487.   .... (778)
The Kalamazoo Valley Genealogical Society. The Kalamazoo
Valley Family Newsletter (Ottowa County, Michigan Issue)
1975. 96pp.
General reference for county. Contains lists of
libraries, newspapers, cemeteries, civil war veterans,
pioneer society members, etc. 4.00 (399)
Kirk, Gordon William, Jr. The Promise of American Life:
Social Mobility in a Nineteenth Century Immigrant Com-
munity, Holland, Michigan, 1847-1894. 299pp.
BIP-71-11892.   .... (777)

SAGINAW COUNTY

Beers & Company, Imperial Publisher, & Ogle & Company,
Atlas of Saginaw County, Michigan, 1877, 1896, and 1916.
Repr. of 1877, 1896, 1916 eds. 475pp.
Three atlases indexed separately and combined in
one volume.   20.00 ..... (666)
"Bridgeport Township - St. Mary's Cemetery." TL Quarterly,
Vol. IV, No. 2. 1976. 6pp. 1.75 (666)
Chapman, Charles C. History of Saginaw County, Michigan.
Repr. of 1881 ed. 1074pp.
114 page index added.   21.00 ..... (666)
"Early Saginaw County Marriages. (From 1835 and Continuing)."
TL Quarterly, Serial article: Vols. I, Nos. 1-4. II, Nos. 1,4.
III and IV, Nos. 1-4. 1972-1976. 46pp. to date. 1.75 (666)
"1840 Federal Census of Saginaw County, Michigan. (Saginaw
Township and Part of Tuscola Township, 1840, Comprising
Area That is Now Saginaw County)." TL Quarterly, Vol. IV,
No. 4. 1976. 5pp. 1.75 (666)

"First Catholic Baptisms, St. Andrew Church, Saginaw: 1862-
1869. (Includes Names of Both Parents)." TL Quarterly,
Serial article: Vols. II, Nos. 1,4, III and IV, Nos. 1-4.
1973-1976. 22pp. 1.75 (666)

"First Congregational Church, Chronological Catalogue of
Members, 1857-1873." TL Quarterly, Serial article:
Vol. III, Nos. 2,3,4. 1975. 16pp. 1.75 (666)

"First Congregational Church of East Saginaw - Transfers of
Members 1857-1880." TL Quarterly, Serial article: Vol. IV,
Nos. 1-4. 1975-1976. ..... 1.75 (666)

"First Presbyterian Church - Early Funerals 1842-1857 (City
of Saginaw)." TL Quarterly, Vol. II, No. 4. 1974. 2 1/2pp. 1.75 (666)

Fox, Truman B. History of Saginaw County, From Year 1819
Down to Present (1858). Repr. of 1858 ed. 88pp.
A facsimile reprint, with slip-in index, added, by
Leland R. Watrous, 1975. ..... 5.25 (666)

"Hammond Cemetery, (Birch Run Township,) Saginaw County."
TL Quarterly, Vol. IV, No. 4. 1976. 4pp. 1.75 (666)

"Index to 'History of Saginaw County, Michigan,' by Truman B.
Fox, 1858." TL Quarterly, Vol. IV, No. 3. 1976. 6pp. 1.75 (666)

"Index to Saginaw Photographers, 1865-1971." TL Quarterly,
Serial article: Vol. II, Nos. 1,4. 1973-1974. 8pp. 1.75 (666)

"Index to Timbertown Log, Volume I." TL Quarterly, Vol. II,
No. 2. 1974. 20pp.
Contains approximately 2,200 names. 1.75 (666)

"Index to Timbertown Log, Volume II." TL Quarterly, Vol. II,
No. 5. 1974. 21pp.
Contains approximately 3,500 names from early
Saginaw records. 2.00 (666)

"Index to Timbertown Log, Volume III." TL Quarterly, Vol. III,
No. 5. 1975. 28pp.
Contains approximately 4,500 names from early Saginaw
records. 2.00 (666)

"Maple Grove Township Cemetery." TL Quarterly, Vol. I, No.
3. 1973. 3 1/2pp. 1.75 (666)

"Oakgrove Cemetery, Bridgeport, Saginaw County, Michigan."
TL Quarterly, Vol. II, No. 3. 1974. 31pp. 1.75 (666)

"Original Land Records - Saginaw County, Michigan. TL
Quarterly, Vol. I-IV. 1972-1976. 65pp.
Chapin Township, Vol. I, Nos. 1-4, 6+pp.
Marion Township, Vol. I, No. 4, 5pp.
Lakefield Township, Vol. I, No. 4, 1pp. Vol. II, No. 1, 2pp.
Jonesfield Township, Vol. II, No. 1, 3pp.
Brady Township, Vol. II, No. 4, 5pp.
Brant Township, Vol. III, No. 1, 6+pp.
Fremont Township, Vol. III, No. 2, 6pp.
Richland Township, Vol. III, No. 3, 5pp.
Chesaning Township, Vol. III, No. 4, 6pp.
St. Charles Township, Vol. IV, No. 1, 5pp.
Swan Creek Township, Vol. IV, No. 2, 4pp.
Thomas Township, Vol. IV, No. 3, 5pp. (includes map).
Tittabawassee Township, Vol. IV, No. 4, 6pp.
(One township or more per issue until entire county has
been recorded in the TL Quarterly.) Issue: 1.75 (666)

WAYNE COUNTY

Katzman, David M. Before the Ghetto: Black Detroit in the Nineteenth Century. 1973.	10.00	..... (365)
Koerner, Alberta G. Joseph Gaspard Chaussegros De Lery and His Maps of Detroit, New Edition. 1975.	24.75	..... (374)
Mason, Philip P. Detroit, Fort Lernoult, and the American Revolution. 1964.	2.50	..... (819)
Rockaway, Robert Allen. From Americanization to Jewish Americanism: The Jews of Detroit, 1850-1914. 258pp. BIP-70-21777.	.....	..... (777)
Woodford, Arthur M. and Frank B. Woodford. All Our Yesterdays: A History of Detroit. 1969.	8.95	4.50 (819)

Minnesota

STATEWIDE REFERENCES

Andrews, Christopher Columbus. Minnesota and Dacotah: In Letters Descriptive of a Tour Through the North-West, in the Autumn of 1856. With Information Relative to Public Lands, and a Table of Statistics.	12.00	..... (38)
Blegen, Theodore C. Minnesota: A History of the State. 1963.	9.50	..... (497)
_____ and Theodore L. Nydahl. Minnesota History: A Guide to Reading and Study. 1960.	6.50	..... (497)
Bray, Martha C., ed. Journals of Joseph N. Nicollet, trans. Andre Fertey. 1970.	16.50	..... (496)
Folwell, William Watts. Minnesota, the North Star State. 1908.	20.50	..... (2)
Gluek, Alvin C., Jr. Minnesota and the Manifest Destiny of the Canadian Northwest: A Study in Canadian-American Relations. 1965.	12.50	..... (763)
Hage, George S. Newspapers on the Minnesota Frontier, 1849-1860. 1967.	.....	4.50 (496)
Massmann, John C. German Immigration to Minnesota 1850-1890. 1966. 270pp. BIP-68-01178.	.....	..... (777)
Neill, Edward D. History of Minnesota: From the Earliest French Explorations to the Present Time. Repr. of 1858 ed.	35.00	..... (38)
Parker, Nathan Howe. The Minnesota Handbook, for 1856-1857. 1857.	9.00	..... (38)
Ristuben, Peter J. Minnesota and the Competition for Immigrants. 1964. 305pp. BIP-64-04731.	.....	..... (777)
Singley, Grover. Tracing Minnesota's Old Government Roads. 1974.	.....	3.95 (496)

Spanglen, Earl. A History of the Negro in Minnesota. 1961.
240pp. BIP-61-02722. .... (777)

Research Aids

Andreas, A. I. An Illustrated Historical Atlas of the State
of Minnesota. Repr. of 1874 ed. 394pp.
Contains maps, plats, illustrations, portraits,
biographical sketches, histories of the state
and counties, statistics, and patrons' directory. .... (848)
Taylor, David Vassar, comp. Blacks in Minnesota: A
Preliminary Guide to Historical Sources. 1976. 33pp.
A bibliography of published material, manuscript
collections, photographs, and oral interviews
relating to Black citizens of Minnesota from the
1850's to 1970's. 1.75 (496)

Military

Carley, Kenneth. Minnesota in the Civil War. 3.95 ..... (656)
Hansen, Marcus. Old Fort Snelling. 10.00 ..... (656)
Imholte, John Q. First Volunteers. 6.75 ..... (656)
Jones, Robert H. Civil War in the Northwest: Nebraska,
Wisconsin, Iowa, Minnesota, and the Dakotas.
Repr. of 1960 ed. 8.95 ..... (556)
Pederson, Kern O. Story of Fort Snelling. 1966. ..... 1.50 (496)
Ziebarth, Marilyn F. and Alan Ominsky. Fort Snelling:
Anchor Post of the Northwest. 1970. ..... 2.00 (496)

Religious and Ethnic Groups

Lettermann, Edward J. From Whole Log to No Log. 1969.
291pp.
History of Indian tribes who lived in present site
of Minneapolis-St. Paul. 8.50 ..... (197)
The Mexican in Minnesota. 5.00 ..... (631)
Writers' Program. The Bohemian Flats. 1941. 6.00 ..... (2)

FILLMORE COUNTY

Willprecht, Mrs. Al. Early Settlers of Fillmore County,
Minnesota. Repr. of 1882 ed. 27pp.
Settler, birthplace, birthdate, spouse, and marriage
date, when given. 4.00 (842)

HENNEPIN COUNTY

Bonkrude, Hardean L. Crime and Its Treatment in Minneapolis
and St. Anthony to 1880. 1970. 491pp. BIP-71-18861. .... (777)
Kane, Lucile M. Waterfall That Built a City: The Falls of
St. Anthony in Minneapolis. 1966. 5.00 ..... (496)

OTTERTAIL COUNTY

Gibbons, Trieglaff, Willprecht. Cemetery Inscriptions of
Perham Township - Ottertail County, Minnesota. 1975. 29pp. 4.00 (842)

Mississippi

STATEWIDE REFERENCES

Brandfon, Robert L. Cotton Kingdom of the New South: A
History of the Yazoo Mississippi Delta from Reconstruction
to the Twentieth Century. 1967.   6.95 ..... (319)
Davis. Reuben. Recollections of Mississippi and Mississippians.
Repr. of 1889 ed. 456pp.
  First-person account of major events of the 1800's and
  an interesting insight into life in Mississippi a hundred
  years ago.   8.95 ..... (499)
Federal Writers' Project. Mississippi Gulf Coast, Yesterday
and Today, 1699-1939. 1939.   14.00 ..... (2)
Gillis, Norman E. and Irene S. Gillis. Abstract of Goodspeed's
Mississippi Memoirs. 1962. 685pp.   30.00 ..... (282)
Lowry, Robert and William H. McCardle. A History of
Mississippi, From the Discovery of the Great River by
Hernando De Soto; Including the Earliest Settlement Made
by the French, Under Iberville to the Death of Jefferson
Davis, 1541-1889. 1891.   37.50 ..... (2)
McLemore, R. A., ed. A History of Mississippi. 2 vols.
1973. 1354pp.
  A comprehensive account of Mississippi's heritage from
  prehistoric times to the present.   Set: 25.00 ..... (499)
Mississippi Genealogical Exchange, eds. Richard S. Lackey
and Etoile Loper Hopkins. 1922. 40pp. per issue.
  A quarterly publication covering all areas of
  Mississippi. Emphasis is on primary source material,
  book reviews, queries. 8.50 (498)
Mississippi Genealogy and Local History, eds. Norman E.
Gillis and Irene S. Gillis. 1969-1970, 1974-1976. 160pp./yr.
  Quarterly magazine issued in March, June, September,
  and December relating to Mississippi genealogy. $8/yr (282)
Rowland, Dunbar. Encyclopedia of Mississippi History.
Comprising Sketches of Counties, Towns, Events, In-
stitutions and Persons. 2 vols. 1907.   Set: 137.50 ..... (2)
_____. Mississippi . . . Arranged in Cyclopedic Form
(Cyclopedia of Mississippi). 4 vols. Repr. of 1907 ed.
3500+ pp.   Set: 150.00 ..... (638)
Vol. 1 (A-K) Historical: Each: 36.00 ..... (638)
Vol. 2 (L-Z) Historical: Each: 36.00 ..... (638)
Vol. 3 Biography: Each: 48.00 ..... (638)
Vol. 4 Supplemental Biography: Each: 30.00 ..... (638)

Research Aids

Cross, Ralph D., et al., eds. Atlas of Mississippi, 1974.
187pp.
  Geographic analysis of Mississippi.   15.00 ..... (499)
Mississippi Daughters (of the American Revolution) and
  Their Ancestors. 1965. [See space ad on page 192]. 3.25 (690)

Military

Dinkins, James. James Dinkins: 1861-1865, by an Old
Johnnie. Personal Recollections. 280pp.

"The Little Confederate" served in the East under
Barksdale and in the West under Forrest. The
author, a graduate of a military school, was one
of the South's finest writers. James Dinkins followed D. H. Hill in the first days of the war,
then transferred to a Mississippi regiment. Then
in 1863 back west under James R. Chalmers as
a staff officer. In January 1864 Chalmers' com-
mand became part of Forrest Cavalry.   15.00   ..... (506)
Mississippi in the Confederacy. 2 vols. in one. 1961. illus.
This comprehensive anthology of source material
forms an enduring record of Mississippi's Confederacy
period. In order to differentiate between contemporary views and reminiscenses, the material is
separated into two volumes. Volume 1: As They
Saw It, edited by John K. Bettersworth, contains
statements made by people during the war; and Volume 2: As Seen in Retrospect, edited by James W.
Silver, is comprised of what was said about the
conflict in the years after. Through the words of
the Southerners themselves, gleaned from letters,
diaries, and newspapers, historians can gain a
better understanding of Mississippi's attitude towards
the Civil War, and the extent of her participation.   36.00   ..... (415)
Rietti, J. C. Military Annals of Mississippi. 1976. 244pp.
Rolls of Mississippi units in the Confederate armies. 15.00   ..... (638)

Religious and Ethnic Groups

Curley, Michael Joseph. Church and State in the Spanish
Floridas (1783-1822). 1940.   16.00   ..... (2)
Derosier, Arthur H., Jr. The Removal of the Choctaw In-
dians from Mississippi. 1959. 270pp. BIP-59-03489.   .... (777)
Reddix, Jacob L. A Voice Crying in the Wilderness: The
Memoirs of Jacob L. Reddix. 1974. 238pp.
Memoirs of prominent Black educator. Includes
valuable information on tracing genealogy of
Blacks.   10.95   ..... (499)
Wallace, Jesse T. History of the Negroes of Mississippi
From 1865 to 1890. Repr. of 1927 ed.   7.75   ..... (394)
Watts, Frederick L. Petition for Redress. 1976. 350pp.
Newly discovered documents showing heritage
contributions of first Germans in America - from
South Carolina to Georgia, Mississippi and Texas
from 1735 to 1976.   17.50   12.50 (270)
Young, Mary E. Redskins, Ruffleshirts and Rednecks:
Indian Allotments in Alabama and Mississippi, 1830-
1860. 1955. 305pp. BIP-00-15442.   .... (777)

Records

Gillis, Irene S. Mississippi 1850 Mortality Schedules. 1973.
59pp.   11.00   8.00   (282)
_____ and Norman E. Gillis. Mississippi 1820 Census.
1963. 147pp.
Alphabetical listing of family heads in United States
1820 Census of Mississippi - with family composition
by sex and age group.   13.00   10.00 (282)

_____. Mississippi 1830 Census. 1965. 236pp.
Alphabetical listing of family heads in United States
1830 census of Mississippi - with family composition
by sex and age group.   16.00   13.00 (282)
_____. Mississippi 1850 Census Surname Index. 1972.
521pp.   60.00   ..... (282)
_____. Mississippi Genealogical Notes. 1965. 116pp.
Genealogical data relating to Mississippi officials
as recorded in the 'Mississippi Official and
Statistical Register of 1917'.   8.00   5.00 (282)
Gillis, Norman E. Early Inhabitants of the Natchez District.
152pp.
1792 Spanish Census of the Natchez District, 1805
and 1810 census of counties formed in the Natchez
District and 1816 census or tax list.   11.00   8.00 (282)
United States Government. Territorial Papers. Volume 5:
The Territory of Mississippi, 1798-1817. Foundation
of the Territory. The Administrations of Governor
Sargent and Acting Governor Steele, 1798-1802. The
Administrations of Governor Claiborne and Acting
Governor West, 1802-1805. The Administrations of
Governor Williams, 1805-1809. 1937. index.   57.50   ..... (2)
United States Government. Territorial Papers. Volume 6:
The Territory of Mississippi, 1809-1817. The First
Administration of Governor Holmes, 1809-1811. The
Administration of Acting Governor Daingerfield, 1811-
1812. The Second and Third Administrations of
Governor Holmes, 1812-1817. 1938. index.   57.50   ..... (2)

ADAMS COUNTY

Gillis, Irene S. and Norman E. Gillis. Adams County, Mis-
sissippi Marriages 1802-1859. 1976. 92pp.   18.00   15.00 (282)
James, Dorris Clayton. Ante-Bellum Natchez. 433pp.
BIP-64-11804.   .... (777)
James, Dorris Clayton. Antebellum Natchez. 1968.   10.00   ..... (440)

BOLIVAR COUNTY

Sillers, Florence W. History of Bolivar County, Mississippi.
Repr. of 1948 ed. 673pp. illus.   17.50   ..... (638)

KEMPER COUNTY

Dennis, Frank Allen. Kemper County Rebel: The Civil War
Diary of Robert Masten Holmes, C.S.A. 1973. 115pp.   4.95   ..... (499)
Lynch, James D. Kemper County Vindicated and a Peep at
Radical Rule in Mississippi. Repr. of 1879 ed.   16.00   ..... (522)
Wells, James M. Chisolm Massacre: A Picture of Home Rule
in Mississippi. Repr. of 1877 ed.   12.00   ..... (522)

LAWRENCE COUNTY

Gillis, Norman E. and Maxie H. Brake. Lawrence County,
Mississippi, Marriages 1818-1879. 1970. 81pp.   14.00   11.00 (282)

YAZOO COUNTY

Morgan, Albert T. Yazoo, Or, on the Picket Line of Freedom
in the South: A Personal Narrative. Repr. of 1884 ed.   13.50   ..... (662)

Missouri

STATEWIDE REFERENCES

Davis, Walter Bickford and Daniel Steele Durrie. An
Illustrated History of Missouri, Comprising Its Early
Record, and Civil, Political, and Military History From
the First Exploration to the Present Time Including. . .
Biographical Sketches of Prominent Citizens. 1876. 776pp.
B-BH 2376.   .... (778)
Douglass. History of Southeast Missouri. 1961.   20.00 ..... (632)
Farnan, William Thomas. Land Claims Problems and the
Federal Land System in the Louisiana-Missouri Territory.
279pp. BIP-72-23929.   .... (777)
Foley, William Edward. A History of Missouri, Volume I:
1673 to 1820. 1971. 256pp.
    A good general history.   9.50 ..... (500)
_____. Territorial Politics in Frontier Missouri: 1804-1820.
266pp. BIP-68-03606.   .... (777)
Goodspeed. History of Southeast Missouri. index.   4.00 ..... (632)
Harris, James Griffith. The Background and Development of
Early Missouri Trial Courts. 301pp. BIP-00-01468. .... (777)
McCandless, Perry. A History of Missouri, Volume II:
1820 to 1860. 1972. 326pp.
    Contains maps, index, and source essay. Describes
    Missouri's struggle for statehood, including descriptions
    of its people, their culture, and formation of social
    institutions.   9.50 ..... (500)
Ogilvie, Leon Parker. The Development of the Southeast
Missouri Lowlands. 539pp. BIP-67-13887.   .... (777)
Parrish, William E. A History of Missouri, Volume III: 1860
to 1875. 1973. 344pp.
    The Civil War and Reconstruction in Missouri.   9.50 ..... (500)
Peck, John Mason. A Guide for Emigrants: Containing Sketches
of Illinois, Missouri, and the Adjacent Parts. 1831. 19.00 ..... (38)

Listed below are the names of professional genealogists willing to undertake research for
a fee within the state of Missouri, in areas specified in their ads:

Sauer, Carl Ortwin. The Geography of the Ozark Highland
  of Missouri. 1920.   12.50   ..... (2)
Schoolcraft, Henry Rowe. Journal of a Tour Into the Interior of
  Missouri and Arkansas, from Potosi, Or Mine a Burton, in
  Missouri Territory, in a South-West Direction, Toward the
  Rocky Mountains, Performed in the Years 1818 and 1819.
  1821.   10.00   ..... (2)
Shoemaker, Floyd Calvin. Missouri's Struggle for Statehood,
  1804-1821. Repr. of 1916 ed. 383pp.
    Political and constitutional history.   12.50   ..... (662)
Stephens, Frank F. A History of the University of Missouri.
  1962. 661pp.
    Illustrated, with maps, index and bibliography of early
    founders of state university system.   9.00   ..... (500)
Switzler, William F. Switzler's Illustrated History of Missouri,
  From 1541 to 1877. 1879.   36.00   ..... (38)
Taft, William H. Missouri Newspapers. 1964.   10.00   ..... (500)

Research Aids

Beck, Lewis Caleb. Gazetter of the States of Illinois and
  Missouri. Repr. of 1823 ed.   22.00   ..... (38)
_____. Gazetteer of the States of Illinois and Missouri:
  Containing a General View of Each State, a General View
  of Their Counties, and a Particular Description of Their
  Towns, Villages, Rivers, Etc. Repr. of 1823 ed.   18.00   ..... (266)
Ramsay, Robert L. Our Storehouse of Missouri Place Names.
  1952. 160pp.
    With index; annotated listing of nearly 2000 place
    names and origins. 3.00 (500)
Wetmore, Alphonso, comp. Gazetteer of the State of Missouri.
  Repr. of 1837 ed.   21.00   ..... (38)

Military

Belser, Thomas Arvin, Jr. Military Operations in Missouri
  and Arkansas, 1861-1865. 1958. 786pp. BIP-58-05265.   .... (777)
Brownlee, Richard S. Gray Ghosts of the Confederacy:
  Guerrilla Warfare in the West, 1861-65. 1958.   10.00 6.95 (440)
_____. Guerrila Warfare in Missouri, 1861-1865.
  1955. 319pp. BIP-00-14598.   .... (777)
Lienhard, Heinrich. From St. Louis to Sutter's Fort, 1846.
  eds. Erwin G. Gudde and Elisabeth K. Gudde. 1961.   7.95   ..... (556)
"List of Survivors of the First and Second Missouri Confed-
  erate Brigades." Missouri Miscellany, Vol. II.
  1976. 32pp. 5.00 (852)
Westover, John G. The Evolution of the Missouri Militia,
  1840-1919. 1948. 300pp. BIP-00-01135.   .... (777)

Religious and Ethnic Groups

Mihanovich, C. S. Americanization of the Croats in Saint
  Louis, Missouri During the Past Thirty Years.   7.00   ..... (631)
Olson, Audrey Louise. St. Louis Germans, 1850-1920: The
  Nature of an Immigrant Community and Its Relation to the
  Assimilation Process. 1970. 355pp. BIP-70-25388.   .... (777)
Schiavo, Giovanni. The Italians in Missouri. 1929.   14.00   ..... (38)

Records

"Louisiana (Missouri) Territory - Petition to Land Commis-
sioners in Year 1810 (986 names)." Missouri Miscellany,
Vol. I. 1976. 10pp. 5.00 (852)
"Marriage Announcements - From the St. Louis Christian
Advocate, M. E. Church, South, 1880-1881. Missouri
Miscellany, Vol. I. 1976. 51pp. 5.00 (852)
Nelson, Frances R. and Gwen Brouse. 1840 Missouri Census-
State-Wide Index. 3 vols. 1976. c600pp.
Alphabetical listing of all heads-of-household - with
reference to county of residence. In process. ..... 35.00? (26)

[The following fourteen volumes - The Missouri Census of 1840 - are printed books. The
reel # referred to is the National Archives reel from which they are transcribed.]

_____. Reel #220 - The Missouri Census of 1840 - Audrain
through Buchanan Counties. Indexed. 1975. 165pp. 9.50 (26)
_____. Reel #221 - The Missouri Census of 1840 - Caldwell
through Clarke Counties. Indexed. 1975. 167pp. 9.50 (26)
_____. Reel #222 - The Missouri Census of 1840 - Clay
through Cooper Counties. Indexed. 1975. 139pp. 9.50 (26)
_____. Reel #223 - The Missouri Census of 1840 - Crawford
through Greene Counties. Indexed. 1975. 129pp. 9.50 (26)
_____. Reel #224 - The Missouri Census of 1840 - Howard
through Lafayette Counties. Indexed. 1976. 168pp. 9.50 (26)
_____. Reel #225 - The Missouri Census of 1840 - Lewis
through Livingston Counties. Indexed. 1976. 109pp. 7.50 (26)
_____. Reel #226 - The Missouri Census of 1840 - Macon
through Monroe Counties. Indexed. 1976. 161pp. 9.50 (26)
_____. Reel #227 - The Missouri Census of 1840 - Morgan
through Newton Counties. Indexed. 1976. 90pp. 6.50 (26)
_____. Reel #228 - The Missouri Census of 1840 - Perry
through Polk Counties. Indexed. 1976. 200pp. 11.50 (26)
_____. Reel #229 - The Missouri Census of 1840 - Pulaski
through Rives Counties. Indexed. 1976. 200pp. 11.50 (26)
_____. Reel #230 - The Missouri Census of 1840 - St. Charles
through Ste. Genevieve Counties. Indexed. 1976. 80pp. 6.00 (26)
_____. Reel #231 - The Missouri Census of 1840 - City and
County of St. Louis. Indexed. 1976. 180pp. 10.50 (26)
_____. Reel #232 - The Missouri Census of 1840 - Stoddard
through Van Buren Counties. Indexed. 1976. 150pp. 9.50 (26)
_____. Reel #233 - The Missouri Census of 1840 - Washington
through Wayne Counties. Indexed. 1976. 80pp. 6.00 (26)
"Selected Obituaries (200) From Northwest Missouri, 1885-1895.
Missouri Miscellany, Vol. II. 1976. 31pp. 5.00 (852)
Woodruff, Mrs. Howard W. Missouri Miscellany. 2 vols.
1976. Vol. I-126pp. Vol. II-126pp.
New series specializing in statewide records; each
book complete in itself. Indexed. 5.00 (852)
Woodruff, Mrs. Howard W. and Hodges. Missouri Obituaries,
1880, 1881 and 1882. Repr. of 1966 ed. 115pp.
From the St. Louis Christian Advocate, M. E. Church,
South. 5.00 (852)
U. S. Government. Missouri Land Claims. Reprint. 450pp.
A reprint of the report of the General Land Office,
published in 1835. Reveals the final reports for ad-
justments in land ownership in the state. Included in
the scope of the investigation were all unconfirmed
lands issued by grant from France and Spain prior to
1804, with over 1000 names included. Map. Index. 17.50 (608)

ADAIR COUNTY

History of Ada.ı, Sullivan, Putnam and Schuyler Counties, Missouri. Repr. of 1888 ed. 1225pp.
Contains 473 pages of biographical sketches.   20.00   ..... (865)

ANDREW COUNTY

History of Andrew and DeKalb Counties, Missouri. 1888. 788pp.
B-BH 3382.   .... (778)
Woodruff, Mrs. Howard W.   Andrew County, Missouri - Marriage
Book A, 1841-1856 (by Hodges). Repr. of 1967 ed. 65pp. 4.00 (852)

AUDRAIN COUNTY

Nelson, Frances R. and Gwen Brouse. 1840 Missouri Census.
1975-1976.   .... (26)

BARRY COUNTY

Nelson, Frances and Gwen Brouse. 1840 Census - Barry County,
Missouri. Indexed. 1975. 26pp. 2.50 (26)

BATES COUNTY

The History of Cass and Bates Counties, Missouri. 1883. 1456pp.
B-BH 5004.   .... (778)

BENTON COUNTY

History of Cole, Moniteau, Morgan, Benton, Miller, Maries and
Osage Counties, Missouri. 2 vols. 1889. Vol. 1-638pp.
Vol. 2-550pp. B-BH 6762.   .... (778)
Nelson, Frances and Gwen Brouse. 1840 Census - Benton
County, Missouri. Indexed. 1975. 26pp. 2.50 (26)

BOONE COUNTY

Elwang, William W. The Negroes of Columbia, Missouri: A
Concrete Study of the Race Problem. Repr. of 1904 ed.   9.00   ..... (478)
History of Boone County, Missouri. 1882. 1180pp. B-BH 3378.   .... (778)
Nelson, Frances and Gwen Brouse. 1840 Census - Boone County,
Missouri. Indexed. 1975. 68pp. 5.00 (26)
Petty, Gerald. Index of the 1830, 1840 and 1850 United States
Censuses of Boone County, Missouri. 1950. 73pp.
        One alphabetical list. About 13,500 name page entries. 15.00 (593)
Ramsay, R. L. The Place Names of Boone County, Missouri.
1952.   .....   1.50 (11)

BUCHANAN COUNTY

The History of Buchanan County, Missouri. 1881. 1072 pp.
B-BH 3383.   .... (778)
Nelson, Frances and Gwen Brouse. 1840 Census - Buchanan
County, Missouri (With Index). 1975. 38pp. 3.00 (26)
Thompson, Martha McDaniel. Buchanan County, Missouri
Cemetery Records. All known cemeteries.
        Part I. Center and Crawford Townships. 1973. 70pp. 4.50 (755)
        Part II. Bloomington, Rush and Wayne Townships. 1973. 72pp. 4.50 (755)
        Part III. Agency, Jackson, Platte and Tremont Townships.
        1974. 70pp. 4.50 (755)
        Part IV. Marion and Part of Washington Townships. 1974. 58pp. 4.50 (755)
        _____. Mt. Mora Cemetery, St. Joseph, Missouri. 1975. 128pp.
        Over 13,500 names listed. 9.00 (755)

CALDWELL COUNTY

Nelson, Frances and Gwen Brouse. 1840 Census - Caldwell
County, Missouri. Indexed. 1975. 10pp. 1.00 (26)

CALLAWAY COUNTY

History of Callaway County, Missouri. 1884. 970pp. B-BH 3377. .... (778)
Nelson, Frances and Gwen Brouse. 1840 Census - Callaway County,
Missouri. Indexed. 1975. 48pp. 3.50 (26)

CAPE GIRARDEAU COUNTY

Nelson, Frances and Gwen Brouse. 1840 Census - Cape Girardeau
County, Missouri. Indexed. 1975. 52pp. 4.00 (26)
Woodruff, Mrs. Howard W. Cape Girardeau County, Missouri -
Marriage Book B, 1839-1854. 1975. 90pp. 5.00 (852)

CARROLL COUNTY

Nelson, Frances and Gwen Brouse. 1840 Census - Carroll
County, Missouri. Indexed. 1975. 16pp. 2.00 (26)

CASS COUNTY

The History of Cass and Bates Counties, Missouri. 1883. 1456pp.
B-BH 5004. .... (778)

CHARITON COUNTY

Nelson, Frances and Gwen Brouse. 1840 Census - Chariton
County, Missouri. Indexed. 1975. 23pp. 2.00 (26)

CLARK COUNTY

History of Lewis, Clark, Knox, and Scotland Counties, Missouri.
1887. 1292pp. B-BH 2369. .... (778)
Nelson, Frances and Gwen Brouse. 1840 Census - Clark County,
Missouri. Indexed. 1975. 16pp. 2.00 (26)

CLAY COUNTY

Nelson, Frances R. and Gwen Brouse. 1840 Missouri Census -
Clay County (with Index). 1975. 38pp.
House-to-house enumeration. 3.00 (26)
St. Louis National Historical Co. History of Clay and Platte
Counties, Missouri. Repr. of 1885 ed. 1121pp.
Included name index, Withers' Map of historical sites in
Clay County and old map of Platte County. 30.50 ..... (147)
Woodruff, Mrs. Howard W. and Hodges. Genealogical Notes
From the "Liberty Tribune" 1846-1885. 5 vols.
Vol. I - 1846-1858. Repr. of 1967 ed. 132pp. 6.00 (852)
Vol. II-1858-1868. 1976. 132pp. 6.00 (852)
Vol. III-1868-1874. 1976. 132pp. 6.00 (852)
Vol. IV-1874-1880. 1976. 132pp. 6.00 (852)
Vol. V - 1880-1885. 1976. 132pp. 6.00 (852)

COLE COUNTY

History of Cole, Moniteau, Morgan, Benton, Miller, Maries and
Osage Counties, Missouri. 2 vols. 1889. V1-638pp.
V-2-550pp. B-BH 6762. .... (778)
Nelson, Frances R. and Gwen Brouse. 1840 Census - Cole County,
Missouri. Indexed. 1975. 45pp. 3.50 (26)

COOPER COUNTY

Catalogue of the Kemper Family School for Boys and Young Men,
Boonville, Missouri, Together With A Sketch of Its Location,
History, Principles and Methods Prepared With Special Refer-
ence to the Centennial Year. Repr. of 1876 ed. 23pp.
    Also includes pupil's names and their home towns. 5.00 (785)
Cordry, Eugene Allen. Descendants of Virginia, Kentucky
and Missouri Pioneers. 1973. 434pp.
    Emphasizes ancestors and descendants of Cooper County
    Pioneer Families. 15,000 names indexed. 29.00 ..... (785)
_____. History of New Lebanon, Cooper County, Missouri. 1976.
303pp.
    Historic as the site of the first seminary west of the Missis-
    sippi River, this volume emphasizes southwestern Cooper
    County and contains over 1200 surnames in the index. 29.00 ..... (785)
Ewing. Aunt Peggy: Being A Memoir of Mrs. Margaret Davidson
Ewing, Wife of the Late Rev. Finis Ewing by One of Her Sons.
Repr. of 1876 ed. 224pp.
    Rev. Finis Ewing, co-founder of the Cumberland Presby-
    terian denomination, and his wife were early (1820) Cooper
    County pioneers. The life of Mrs. Ewing from birth in
    North Carolina, through marriage and life in Tennessee and
    Kentucky, to pioneering in Cooper County, Missouri (1820-32)
    and later to Lafayette County, Missouri. Brief sketches of
    some 20 early Cumberland Presbyterian preachers of Mis-
    souri are included. 5.95 ..... (785)
History of Howard and Cooper Counties, Missouri. 1883. 1188pp.
B-BH 16798. .... (778)
St. Louis Atlas Publishing Company. Illustrated Atlas Map of
Cooper County, Missouri. Repr. of 1877 ed. 60pp.
    Contains township and city and village maps, brief
    history of Cooper County and of Townships, patron's
    directory and biographical sketches. 15.00 ..... (785)

CRAWFORD COUNTY

Breuer. Crawford County and Cuba, Missouri. 10.00 ..... (632)
Goodspeed. History of Franklin, Jefferson, Washington,
Crawford and Gasconade Counties, Missouri. Repr. of 1888 ed. 15.00 ..... (632)
Nelson, Frances R. and Gwen Brouse. 1840 Census of Missouri -
Crawford County (with Index). 1976. 22pp.
    House-to-house enumeration. 2.00 (26)

DADE COUNTY

Dade County, Missouri Historical Society. Collins Cemetery
Booklet. 1975. 18pp.
    Cemetery copied in rows with lots of family history added.
    Indexed. Located Dade Co., Missouri, Ernest Township,
    4 miles North Lockwood, Missouri. County township
    map included. 2.00 (177)
_____. King's Point Cemetery Booklet. 1975. 18pp.
    Cemetery copied in rows with additional family history.
    Indexed. Location of cemetery, Dade's Co., South
    Township near Lawrence Co. line. County township
    map included. 2.00 (177)

Dade County, Missouri Historical Society. Marriage Book B,
Dade County, Missouri - 10 January 1881 - 20 July 1886.
1976.
    Copied from Court Record Book; with Index.   x   (177)
_____. Pleasant Grove Cemetery and Other Small Cemeteries.
1976. 50pp.
    History of church and cemetery. Additional family history.
    Copied in rows with Index. These cemeteries located in
  Dade Co., Missouri in North and Center Township. County
    Township map included. 5.00 (177)

DAVIES COUNTY

Nelson, Frances R. and Gwen Brouse. 1840 Census - Davies
County, Missouri. Indexed. 1975. 17pp. 1.50 (26)

DeKALB COUNTY

History of Andrew and DeKalb Counties, Missouri. 1888. 788pp.
B-BH 3382. .... (778)

FRANKLIN COUNTY

Goodspeed. History of Franklin, Jefferson, Washington,
Crawford and Gasconade Counties, Missouri.
Repr. of 1888 ed. 15.00   ..... (632)
Nelson, Frances R. and Gwen Brouse. 1840 Census - Franklin
County, Missouri. Indexed. 1975. 40pp. 3.00 (26)
Ramsay, Robert L. The Place Names of Franklin County,
Missouri. 1954. 56pp.
    Includes bibliography and index. 2.50 (500)

GASCONADE COUNTY

Goodspeed. History of Franklin, Jefferson, Washington,
Crawford and Gasconade Counties, Missouri. Repr. of 1888 ed. 15.00   ..... (632)
Nelson, Frances R. and Gwen Brouse. 1840 Census - Gasconade
County, Missouri. Indexed. 1975. 32pp. 2.50 (26)

GREENE COUNTY

History of Greene County, Missouri. 1883. 938pp. B-BH 3625. .... (778)

HARRISON COUNTY

History of Harrison and Mercer Counties, Missouri.
1888. 764pp. B-BH 3384. .... (778)

HOWARD COUNTY

History of Howard and Cooper Counties, Missouri. 1883.
1188pp. B-BH 16798. .... (778)
Nelson, Frances R. and Gwen Brouse. 1840 Census of
Missouri - Howard County (with Index). 1976. 49pp.
    House-to-house enumeration. 3.50 (26)

JACKSON COUNTY

"Abstracts of Deed Books A and B, 1828-1833." Missouri
Miscellany, Vol. I. 1976. 22pp. 5.00 (852)
Brown, A. Theodore. Frontier Community, Kansas City
to 1870. 1963. 9.00   ..... (500)

....

Jennings, Warren A. Zion Is Fled: The Expulsion of the Mormons
  From Jackson County, Missouri. 1962. 364pp. BIP-62-06532.   .... (777)
Nelson, Frances R. and Gwen Brouse. 1840 Census - Jackson
  County, Missouri. Indexed. 1976. 35pp. 3.00 (26)
Vineyard, Mrs. John, comp. Marriage Records of Jackson
  County, Missouri - 1827-1850. 1967. 75pp.
    From original county records with many added genealogical
    notes. 5.00 (798)
_____. Marriage Records of Jackson County, Missouri -
  1851-1865. 1970. 159pp.
    Taken from original records with 24 pages genealogical
    data and bibliography added. 5.00 (798)
_____. Original Land Entries of Jackson County, Missouri.
  1971. 66pp. 5.00 (798)

JEFFERSON COUNTY

Goodspeed. History of Franklin, Jefferson, Washington,
  Crawford and Gasconade Counties, Missouri. Repr. of 1888 ed.   15.00   ..... (632)
Hopper, Rosalea, comp. Cemetery Records. 3 vols.
  1976. c55pp./vol.   Each Volume: 5.00 (351)
Nelson, Frances R. and Gwen Brouse. 1840 Census - Jefferson
  County, Missouri. Indexed. 1976. 25pp. 2.50 (26)

KNOX COUNTY

History of Lewis, Clark, Knox, and Scotland Counties, Missouri.
  1887. 1292pp. B-BH 2369.   .... (778)

LACLEDE COUNTY

"Abstract of Wills 1849-1883 and Admrs., 1849-1869."
  Missouri Miscellany, Vol. II. 1976. 22pp. 5.00 (852)

LAFAYETTE COUNTY

History of Lafayette County, Missouri. 1881. 706pp. B-BH 3376.   .... (778)
Nelson, Frances R. and Gwen Brouse. 1840 Census - Lafayette
  County, Missouri. Indexed. 1976. 31pp. 2.50 (26)

LAWRENCE COUNTY

Pace, G. Randle. Index to the 1888 Goodspeed's History of
  Lawrence County, Missouri. 1975. 102pp.
    Index can be used for the Lawrence County section of
    original edition of Goodspeed's 1888 History of Newton,
    Lawrence, Barry and McDonald Counties, Missouri as
    well as the 1973 reprint of the Lawrence County section
    by Litho Printers, Cassville, Missouri 65625.   .....   5.50 (569)

LEWIS COUNTY

History of Lewis, Clark, Knox, and Scotland Counties, Missouri.
  1887. 1292pp. B-BH 2369.   .... (778)
Nelson, Frances R. and Gwen Brouse. 1840 Missouri Census -
  Lewis County (with Index). 1976. 32pp.
    House-to-house enumeration. 2.50 (26)

LINCOLN COUNTY

Nelson, Frances R. and Gwen Brouse. 1840 Census - Lincoln
  County, Missouri. Indexed. 1976. 33pp. 2.50 (26)

LINN COUNTY

Nelson, Frances R. and Gwen Brouse. 1840 Census - Linn
County, Missouri. Indexed. 1976. 15pp. 1.50 (26)

LIVINGSTON COUNTY

Nelson, Frances R. and Gwen Brouse. 1840 Census - Livingston
County, Missouri. Indexed. 1976. 20pp. 2.00 (26)

MACON COUNTY

Nelson, Frances R. and Gwen Brouse. 1840 Missouri Census -
Macon County (with Index). 1976. 36pp.
House-to-house enumeration. 3.00 (26)
Petty, Gerald. Composite Index of the 1840 and 1850 United
States Censuses of Macon County, Missouri. 1969. 32pp.
One alphabetical list. About 7200 name-page entries. 10.00 (593)

MADISON COUNTY

Nelson, Frances R. and Gwen Brouse. 1840 Census - Madison
County, Missouri. Indexed. 1976. 20pp. 2.00 (26)

MARIES COUNTY

History of Cole, Moniteau, Morgan, Benton, Miller, Maries
and Osage Counties, Missouri. 2 vols. 1889.
Vol. I-638pp. Vol. 2-550PP. B-BH 6762. .... (778)

MARION COUNTY

Nelson, Frances R. and Gwen Brouse. 1840 Census - Marion
County, Missouri. Indexed. 1976. 46pp. 3.50 (26)

MERCER COUNTY

History of Harrison and Mercer Counties, Missouri. 1888.
764pp. B-BH 3384. .... (778)

MILLER COUNTY

Nelson, Frances R. and Gwen Brouse. 1840 Census - Miller
County, Missouri. Indexed. 1976. 16pp. 2.00 (26)
History of Cole, Moniteau, Morgan, Benton, Miller, Maries and
Osage Counties, Missouri. 2 vols. 1889. Vol. 1-638pp.
Vol. 2-550pp. B-BH 6762. .... (778)

MONITEAU COUNTY

History of Cole, Moniteau, Morgan, Benton, Miller, Maries
and Osage Counties, Missouri. 2 vols. 1889.
Vol. 1-638pp. Vol. 2-550pp. B-BH 6762. .... (778)

MONROE COUNTY

History of Monroe and Shelby Counties, Missouri. 1884.
1192pp. B-BH 3374. .... (778)
Nelson, Frances R. and Gwen Brouse. 1840 Census - Monroe
County, Missouri. Indexed. 1976. 42pp. 3.50 (26)

MONTGOMERY COUNTY

Nelson, Frances R. and Gwen Brouse. 1840 Census - Montgomery
County, Missouri. Indexed. 1976. .... (26)

....

MORGAN COUNTY

History of Cole, Moniteau, Morgan, Benton, Miller, Maries
and Osage Counties, Missouri. 2 vols. 1889.
Vol. 1-638pp. Vol. 2-550pp. B-BH 6762.   •••••   ••••• (778)
Nelson, Frances R. and Gwen Brouse. 1840 Missouri Census -
Morgan County (with Index). 1976.
House-to-house enumeration.   •••••   ••••• (26)

NEW MADRID COUNTY

Nelson, Frances R. and Gwen Brouse. 1840 Census - New
Madrid County, Missouri. Indexed. 1976.   •••••   ••••• (26)

NEWTON COUNTY

Nelson, Frances R. and Gwen Brouse. 1840 Census - Newton
County, Missouri. Indexed. 1976.   •••••   ••••• (26)

OSAGE COUNTY

History of Cole, Moniteau, Morgan, Benton, Miller, Maries
and Osage Counties, Missouri. 2 vols. 1889.
Vol. 1-638pp. Vol. 2-550pp. B-BH 6762.   •••••   ••••• (778)

PERRY COUNTY

Nelson, Frances R. and Gwen Brouse. 1840 Missouri
Census - Perry County (with Index). 1976.
House-to-house enumeration.   •••••   ••••• (26)

PETTIS COUNTY

History of Pettis County, Missouri. Repr. of 1882 ed. 1108pp.
Every-name index. Includes many biographical
sketches of persons in Pettis County, Missouri.   26.50   ••••• (507)
The History of Pettis County, Missouri. 1882. 1118pp. B-BH 5005   •••••   ••••• (778)
Nelson, Frances R. and Gwen Brouse. 1840 Census -
Pettis County, Missouri. Indexed. 1976.   •••••   ••••• (26)

PIKE COUNTY

"Adiel Cemetery, Pike County, Missouri." SGE Quarterly,
Vol. XVI, No. 76. 1975. 3pp.   •••••   3.00 (706)
Nelson, Frances R. and Gwen Brouse. 1840 Census - Pike
County, Missouri. Indexed. 1976.   •••••   ••••• (26)
"Pleasant Hill Cemetery, Pike County, Missouri." SGE Quarterly,
Vol. XVI, No. 75. 1975. 4pp.   •••••   3.00 (706)
"Spencerburg Cemetery, Pike County, Missouri." SGE Quarterly,
Vol. XVI, Nos.74 and 75. 1975. 9pp.   •••••   3.00 (706)

PLATTE COUNTY

Nelson, Frances R. and Gwen Brouse. 1840 Census - Platte
County, Missouri. Indexed.
Not for sale as separate book. This work is part of our
Reel Book #228; copyrited by Mrs. Gene Carter and
used with her permission.   •••••   ••••• (26)
Paxton, William M. Annals of Platte County, Missouri.   13.50   ••••• (632)
St. Louis National Historical Co. History of Clay and Platte
Counties, Missouri. Repr. of 1885 ed. 1121pp.
Included name index, Withers' Map of historical sites
in Clay County and old map of Platte County.   30.50   ••••• (147)

POLK COUNTY

Nelson, Frances R. and Gwen Brouse. 1840 Census - Polk County, Missouri. Indexed. 1976. .... (26)

PULASKI COUNTY

Nelson, Frances R. and Gwen Brouse. 1840 Missouri Census - Pulaski County (with Index). 1976.
House-to-house enumeration. .... (26)

PUTNAM COUNTY

History of Adair, Sullivan, Putnam and Schuyler Counties, Missouri. Repr. of 1888 ed. 1225pp.
Contains 473 pages of biographical sketches. 20.00 ..... (865)

RALLS COUNTY

Nelson, Frances R. and Gwen Brouse. 1840 Census - Ralls County, Missouri. Indexed. 1976. .... (26)

RANDOLPH COUNTY

"Death Records, 1883-1889." Missouri Miscellany, Vol. I. 1976. 10pp. 5.00 (852)
Nelson, Frances R. and Gwen Brouse. 1840 Census - Randolph County, Missouri. Indexed. 1976. .... (26)
Petty, Gerald. Composite Index of the 1830, 1840, 1850, 1860, 1870, and 1880 United States Censuses of Randolph County, Missouri. 1970. 138pp.
One alphabetical list. About 57,000 name-page entries. 30.00 ..... (593)

RAY COUNTY

Nelson, Frances R. and Gwen Brouse. 1840 Census - Ray County, Missouri. Indexed. 1976. .... (26)

RIPLEY COUNTY

McManus, Thelma S., G.R.S. Ripley County (Missouri) Cemetery Listings, Part II. 1976.
A continuation of listings of Ripley County cemeteries; especially those no longer in use. .... (453)

RIVES COUNTY

Nelson, Frances R. and Gwen Brouse. 1840 Census - Rives County, Missouri. Indexed. 1976. .... (26)

ST. CHARLES COUNTY

Nelson, Frances R. and Gwen Brouse. 1840 Census of Missouri - St. Charles County (with Index). 1976.
House-to-house enumeration. .... (26)
Oliver, Lilian Hays. Crow's Nest. 1969. 196pp. 10.00 (134)

ST. FRANCOIS COUNTY

Hopper, Rosalea. Cemetery Records. 2 vols. 1976. 60pp./volume. Each Volume: 5.00 (351)
Nelson, Frances R. and Gwen Brouse. 1840 Census - St. Francois County, Missouri. Indexed. 1976. .... (26)

STE. GENEVIEVE COUNTY

Nelson, Frances R. and Gwen Brouse. 1840 Census -
Ste. Genevieve County, Missouri. Indexed. 1976. .... (26)

ST. LOUIS COUNTY

Billon, Frederic L. Annals of St. Louis in Its Early Days Under
the French and Spanish Dominations. 1886. Index.
Abundant documentary detail, such as wills, inventories,
marriage contracts, bills of sale, etc. are combined in
this book to recreate an almost complete picture of what
life was like in early St. Louis. Also included are many
of the official documents involved in the repeated changes
of sovereignty; biographical sketches of all the important
pioneers are also given. Map. 22.00 ..... (38)
_____. Annals of St. Louis in its Early Days Under the French
and Spanish Dominations. 1886. 554pp. B-BH 13561. .... (778)
_____. Annals of St. Louis in Its Territorial Days From
1804 to 1821: Being a Continuation of the Author's Previous
Work, the Annals of the French and Spanish Period.
Index. 1888. 20.00 ..... (38)
Darby, John Fletcher. Personal Recollections of Many Prominent
People Whom I Have Known: And of Events - Especially of
Those Relating to the History of St. Louis - During the First
Half of the Present Century. 1880. 27.00 ..... (38)
_____. Personal Recollections of Many Prominent People
Whom I Have Known, and of Events . . . Especially of Those
Relating to the History of St. Louis During the First Half of
the Present Century. 1880. 484pp. B-BH 3370. .... (778)
Kennerly, William C. Persimmon Hill: A Narrative of Old
St. Louis and the Far West. ed. Elizabeth Russell.
Repr. of 1948 ed. 5.95 ..... (556)
Nelson, Frances R. and Gwen Brouse. 1840 Missouri Census -
St. Louis County (with Index). 1976.
House-to-house enumeration. .... (26)
Vexler, Robert I. St. Louis: A Chronological and Documentary
History. (American Cities Chronology Series). 1974. 160pp. 7.50 ..... (551)
Wells, Eugene Tate. St. Louis and Cities West: 1820-1880:
A Study In History and Geography. 1951. 624pp. BIP-00-02786 .... (777)

SALINE COUNTY

Nelson, Frances R. and Gwen Brouse. 1840 Census - Saline
County, Missouri. Indexed. 1976. .... (26)

SCHUYLER COUNTY

Caywood, Richard. History of Schuyler County, Missouri.
Repr. of 1878 ed. 30pp.
Contains list of some residents, including occupation,
place of birth, and year of arrival in county. 1.50 (865)
History of Adair, Sullivan, Putnam and Schuyler Counties,
Missouri. Repr. of 1888 ed. 1225pp.
Contains 473 pages of biographical sketches. 20.00 ..... (865)
Swanson and Ford. History of Schuyler County. Repr. of 1911 ed.
391pp.
Contains 215 biographical sketches with over 2000
individuals named. 6.00 ..... (865)

SCOTLAND COUNTY

History of Lewis, Clark, Knox, and Scotland Counties,
Missouri. 1887. 1292pp. B-BH 2369. .... (778)

SCOTT COUNTY

Nelson, Frances R. and Gwen Brouse. 1840 Census - Scott
County, Missouri. Indexed. 1976. .... (26)

SHELBY COUNTY

History of Monroe and Shelby Counties, Missouri. 1884.
1192pp. B-BH 3374. .... (778)
Nelson, Frances R. and Gwen Brouse. 1840 Census - Shelby
County, Missouri. Indexed. 1976. .... (26)

STODDARD COUNTY

Nelson, Frances R. and Gwen Brouse. 1840 Missouri Census -
Stoddard County (with Index). 1976.
House-to-house enumeration. .... (26)

SULLIVAN COUNTY

History of Adair, Sullivan, Putman and Schuyler Counties,
Missouri. Repr. of 1888 ed. 1225pp.
Contains 473 pages of biographical sketches. 20.00 ..... (865)

TANEY COUNTY

Nelson, Frances R. and Gwen Brouse. 1840 Census - Taney
County, Missouri. Indexed. 1976. .... (26)

VAN BUREN COUNTY

Nelson, Frances R. and Gwen Brouse. 1840 Census - Van Buren
County, Missouri. Indexed. 1976. .... (26)

WARREN COUNTY

Nelson, Frances R. and Gwen Brouse. 1840 Census - Warren
County, Missouri. Indexed. 1976. .... (26)

WASHINGTON COUNTY

"Death Records, 1883-1886." Missouri Miscellany, Vol. II.
1976. 6pp. 5.00 (852)
Goodspeed. History of Franklin, Jefferson, Washington,
Crawford and Gasconade Counties, Missouri. Repr. of 1888 ed. 15.00 ..... (632)
Nelson, Frances R. and Gwen Brouse. 1840 Missouri Census -
Washington County (with Index). 1976.
House-to-house enumeration. .... (26)

WAYNE COUNTY

Cramer, Rose F. Wayne County, Missouri. 1972. 11.00 ..... (632)
Nelson, Frances R. and Gwen Brouse. 1840 Census - Wayne
County, Missouri. Indexed. 1976. .... (26)

Montana

STATEWIDE REFERENCES

Bancroft, Hubert H. History of Washington, Idaho and Montana.   7.00   ..... (51)
Country Beautiful, ed. Montana. 1976. 160pp.
    140 full color photos.   19.95   ..... (165)
Cushman, Dan. Montana - The Gold Frontier.   8.95   ..... (718)
Howard, Joseph K. Montana: High, Wide and Handsome, New
    Edition. 1959.   15.00   ..... (857)
Langford, Nathaniel Pitt. Vigilante Days and Ways; the Pioneers
of the Rockies, the Makers and Making of Montana, Idaho,
Oregon, Washington, and Wyoming. 2 vols. 1890.
                          Set: 35.00   ..... (2)
                        Each: 18.00   ..... (2)
Mullan, John. Miners and Travelers' Guide to Oregon,
Washington, Idaho, Montana, Wyoming, and Colorado. Via
the Missouri and Columbia Rivers. Accompanied by a
General Map of the Mineral Region of the Northern Sections
of the Rocky Mountains. 1865.   8.00   ..... (38)
Thane, James L., Jr. Montana Territory: The Formative
Years 1862-1870. 1972. 323pp. BIP-72-26749.   .... (777)
Toole, K. Ross. Montana: An Uncommon Land. Repr. of 1959
ed.   5.95   ..... (556)
_____. Twentieth-Century Montana: A State of Extremes. Repr.
of 1972 ed.   7.95   ..... (556)
Wolle, Muriel S. Montana Pay Dirt: A Guide to the Mining
Camps of the Treasure State.   15.00   ..... (735)

SILVER BOW COUNTY

Writers' Program. Copper Camp; Stories of the World's
Greatest Mining Town, Butte, Montana. 1943.   16.00   ..... (2)

Nebraska

STATEWIDE REFERENCES

Coulter, Thomas Chalmer. A History of Woman Suffrage in
Nebraska 1856-1920. 1967. 212pp. BIP-68-08813.   .... (777)
Danker, Donald F. Some Social Beginnings in Territorial
Nebraska. 1955. 301pp. BIP-00-12745.   .... (777)

Listed below is the name of a professional genealogist willing to undertake research for
a fee within the state of Nebraska, in areas specified in her ad:

Eastern Nebraska Genealogical Society. Eastern Nebraska
Genealogical Society Quarterly.
Contains all kinds of records - cemetery, wills,
general Nebraska information, etc. $5/yr (211)
Holmes, Louis A. Fort McPherson, Nebraska Territory. 1963. 7.50 ..... (386)
Johnson, Harrison. Johnson's History of Nebraska. 1880. 32.00 ..... (38)
Jones, Robert H. Civil War in the Northwest: Nebraska,
Wisconsin, Iowa, Minnesota, and the Dakotas. Repr. of
1960 ed. 8.95 ..... (556)
Woolworth, James M. Nebraska in Eighteen Fifty-Seven.
1967. 12.00 ..... (386)

Research Aids

Eastern Nebraska Genealogical Society. Index to Vols. I and
III of the History of Czechs In Nebraska. 5.00 (211)
_____. Index to Vol. II (Servicemen) of the History of
Czechs in Nebraska. 3.00 (211)
Everts and Kirk. Official Atlas of Nebraska. Repr. of
1885 ed. 400+pp.
New every-name index included. 20.00 ..... (211)
Historical Records Survey: Check List of Nebraska Non-
Documentary Imprints, 1847-1876. 1942. ..... 8.50 (415)

Religious and Ethnic Groups

Dowie, James I. Lutheran Academy, 1883-1903; A Facet of
Swedish Pioneer Life in Nebraska. 1957. 384pp.
BIP-59-03777. .... (777)
Luebke, Frederick C. Immigrants and Politics: The
Germans of Nebraska, 1880-1900. 1969. 8.95 ..... (521)
Martin, Sister Aquinata. The Catholic Church on the
Nebraska Frontier (1854-1885). 1937. 8.50 ..... (2)
Rosicky, Rose. History of Czechs in Nebraska. Repr. of
1928 ed. 500pp.
New every-name index included. 17.00 ..... (211)

Nevada

STATEWIDE REFERENCES

Angel, Myron, ed. History of Nevada. Repr. of 1881 ed. 50.00 ..... (38)
Bancroft, Hubert H. History of Nevada, Colorado and Wyoming. 7.00 ..... (51)
Harris, Robert P. Nevada Postal History. 1973. 8.50 ..... (78)
_____. Nevada Postal History. 1973. 8.50 ..... (528)
Paher, Stanley W. Nevada Ghost Towns and Mining Camps.
1970. 500pp.
Covers over 575 towns whose fortunes depended on
presence of ore. 650 illustrations. 17.50 ..... (357)
Thompson, Thomas and Albert West. History of Nevada (State),
ed. Myron Angel. Repr. of 1881 ed. 900pp. 25.00 ..... (357)
Index to above, comp. Helen J. Poulton. 4.00 (527)

Research Aids

Averett, Walter R. Southern Nevada Place Names. 1963. 5.00 ..... (144)

Power, Stanley W. Nevada Books and Authors: A
Descriptive Bibliography. 1974.   36.00 ..... (528)

Religious and Ethnic Groups

BeDunnah, Gary P. A History of the Chinese in Nevada,
1855-1904. Repr. of 1966 ed.
The first study of a very important minority and
their contribution to mining and railroading. 7.00 (631)
Eterovich, Adam S. Yugoslav Survey of California, Nevada,
Arizona and the South, 1830-1900.   7.00 ..... (631)
_____. Yugoslavs in Nevada, 1859-1900.   .....   7.00 (631)
Shepperson, Wilbur S. Restless Strangers: Nevada's Im-
migrants and Their Interpreters. 1970.   7.00 ..... (527)

LINCOLN COUNTY

Hulse, James W. Lincoln County, Nevada, 1864-1909: History
of a Mining Region. 1971.   .....   3.00 (527)

WOSHOE COUNTY

Ingalls, J. W. History of Washoe County, Nevada. 1968.   .....   5.00 (687)

New Hampshire

STATEWIDE REFERENCES

Barry, Peter Ralph. The New Hampshire Merchant Interest,
1609-1725. 386pp. BIP-71-24444.   .... (777)
Belknap, Jeremy. History of New Hampshire. 2 vols. Repr.
of 1831 ed.   Set: 49.00 ..... (394)
Bishop, Alicia. My Little New Hampshire Book. 1975. 47pp.
History and contributors of New Hampshire.   4.50 ..... (224)
Fry, William Henry. New Hampshire as a Royal Province. 1908.   20.00 ..... (2)
Hill, Ralph N. Yankee Kingdom: Vermont and New Hampshire,
Enlarged Edition. 1973.   8.95 ..... (317)
New Hampshire Historical Society. Historical New Hampshire.
7 vols. 1944-1951.
Historical New Hampshire, a successor to the earliest
Collections and Proceedings of the New Hampshire
Historical Society, carries on a long tradition of
significant writings in the field of New Hampshire history
and related subjects which began with the founding of the
Society in 1823. It is exemplary for the diversity of its
coverage, made possible by the rich resources of the
Society's museum treasures on which contributors are
able to draw, manuscripts and documents collections
(embracing diaries, letters, account books, records
and miscellaneous memorabilia) and the historical
library which contains many rare editions of New Hampshire incunabula, genealogies, town and county histories,
bank records and early newspapers and maps.
7 volumes in 1.   33.00 28.00 (415)
    Each: 4.00 (415)
Page, Elwin L. Judicial Beginnings in New Hampshire, 1640-
1793. 1959. 278pp.   5.00 ..... (531)

Squires, J. Duane. The Granite State of the United States.
1974.   25.00   10.00 (532)
Turk, Marion G. The Quiet Adventurers in America. 1975.
300pp.
    Genealogical data and story of settlers in American
    Colonies and United States, from the Channel Islands,
    United Kingdom; Jersey, Guernsey, Alderney and Sark.   12.00   10.00 (771)
Writers' Program. Hands That Built New Hampshire; the Story
of Granite State Craftsmen Past and Present. 1940.   15.00   ..... (2)

Research Aids

Bent, Allen H. Bibliography of the White Mountains, Revised
Edition, ed. Jack Hanrahan. 1972.   8.00 (532)
Close, Virginia L., comp. Historical New Hampshire: Index
to Volumes 1-25 (1944-1970). 1974. 203pp. 10.00 (531)
Hunt, Elmer Munson. New Hampshire Town Names and Whence
They Came. 1970. 282pp.
    Contains much family history of early families
    plus local lorex of 235 New Hampshire towns.   5.95   ..... (56)

Military

Cleveland, Mather. New Hampshire Fights the Civil War.
1969. 230pp.   20.00   ..... (531)
Upton, Richard F. Revolutionary New Hampshire. Repr. of
1936 ed.   11.00   ..... (404)
_____. Revolutionary New Hampshire. 1970.   11.50   ..... (552)

CHESHIRE COUNTY

Armstrong, John B. Factory Under the Elms: A History of
Harrisville, New Hampshire, 1774-1969. 1969.   12.50   ..... (444)
_____. Factory Under the Elms: A History of Harrisville,
New Hampshire, 1774-1969. 1970.   17.50   ..... (753)
_____. Harrisville, A New Hampshire Mill Town in the 19th
Century. 1962. 392pp. BIP-62-04529.   .... (777)

COOS COUNTY

Burt, F. Allen. Story of Mount Washington. 1960. 315pp.   10.00   ..... (531)
Crawford, Lucy. Lucy Crawford's History of the White
Mountains, ed. Stearns Morse. Repr. of 1845 ed. 305pp.   8.50   ..... (531)
Fergusson, W. A. The History of Coos County New Hampshire.
1972.   35.00   ..... (532)

GRAFTON COUNTY

Cawley, James and Margaret Cawley. Tales of Old Grafton.
1974.   5.95   1.95 (53)
Child, Hamilton. Grafton County Gazetter and Directory. 1974.   25.00   ..... (532)

HILLSBORO COUNTY

Blood, Henry Ames. The History of Temple, New Hampshire.
1860. 440pp. B-BH 19158.   .... (778)
Cochrane, Warren Robert. History of the Town of Antrim,
New Hampshire. 1880. 918pp. B-OP 66895.
    With a brief genealogical record of all the Antrim
    families.   .... (778)

Farmer, John. An Historical Sketch of the Town of Amherst.
Repr. of 1837 ed.   10.00   ..... (532)
Haddix, J. and A. Lunt, eds. Temple, New Hampshire,
History of. 1976. 928pp.
    History of town 1758-1976, including many family
    histories.   22.50   ..... (56)
Little, Henry Gilman. Hollis, New Hampshire Seventy Years
Ago. 1894. 266pp. B-BH 2117.   .... (778)
Morison, G. A. and E. M. Smith. Peterborough, New Hamp-
shire, History of. 2 vols. 1954. 1340pp.
    History of town, plus genealogy of families.   18.50   ..... (56)

MERRIMACK COUNTY

Cogswell, Leander W. History of the Town of Henniker. Repr.
of 1880 ed.   30.00   ..... (532)

ROCKINGHAM COUNTY

Chase, John Carroll. History of Chester, New Hampshire,
Including Auburn of Old Chester (A Supplement to the
History Published 1869). 1926. 551pp.   18.00   ..... (530)
Morrison, L. A. History of Windham in New Hampshire, 1719-
1883, Volume I, Including Rural Oasis: History of Windham,
New Hampshire, 1883-1975. 1975.   .... (597)
Oedel, Howard T. Portsmouth, New Hampshire and the Role
of the Provincial Capital in the Development of the Colony,
1700-1775. 1960. 1003pp. BIP-60-03473.   .... (777)
Parker, Edward Lutwyche. The History of Londonberry,
Comprising the Towns of Derry and Londonderry, New
Hampshire. 1851. 440pp. B-BH 19053.   .... (778)

STRAFFORD COUNTY

McDuffee, Franklin. History of the Town of Rochester, New
Hampshire. 1892. Vol. 1-428pp, Vol. 2-360pp. B-BH 19072.   .... (778)
Stackpole, Everett S., et al. History of the Town of Durham,
New Hampshire. Repr. of 1913 ed.   25.00   ..... (532)

SULLIVAN COUNTY

Child, William H. History of the Town of Cornish, New Hamp-
shire, With Genealogical Record 1763-1910. 2 vols in 1.
Repr. of 1911 ed. 879pp.   30.00   ..... (638)
Tracy, Stephen P. and Dwight Wood. A Brief History of
Cornish, 1763-1974. 208pp.
    Contains a genealogical section with information on
    154 families.   15.00   ..... (531)

New Jersey

STATEWIDE REFERENCES

Barber, John Warner and Henry Howe. Historical Collections
of the State of New Jersey. 1844. 536pp. B-BH 6824.   .... (778)
Barnes, Harry E. History of the Penal, Reformatory and
Correctional Institutions of the State of New Jersey;
Analytical and Documentary. Repr. of 1918 ed.   37.00   ..... (38)

Beck, Henry C. Forgotten Towns of Southern New Jersey. 1962. ..... 2.75 (665)
_____. More Forgotten Towns of Southern New Jersey. 1963. ..... 2.75 (665)
_____. Roads of Home: Lanes and Legends of New Jersey 1956. 6.00 2.75 (665)
Budd, Thomas. Good Order Established in Pennsylvania and
New Jersey. Repr. of 1685 ed. 17.00 ..... (248)
Fisher, Edgar Jacob. New Jersey as a Royal Province, 1738 to
1776. 1911. 12.50 ..... (2)
Gerlach, Larry Reuben. Revolution or Independence? New
Jersey, 1760-1776. 816pp. BIP-69-07540. .... (777)
Horowitz, Gary S. New Jersey Land Riots, 1745-1755. 1966.
229pp. BIP-67-02460. .... (777)
Littell, John. Family Records, Or Genealogies of the First
Settlers of Passaic Valley. Repr. of 1852 ed. 512pp. 15.00 ..... (274)
_____. Family Records; Or Genealogies of the First Settlers
of Passaic Valley (and Vicinity), Above Chatham, with
Their Ancestors and Descendants. 1851. 511pp. B-OP 66538. .... (778)
McCloy, James F. and Ray Miller, Jr. The Jersey Devil.
1976. 121pp.
First book-length treatment of a mysterious creature
who has endured for over over two centuries. 8.00 ..... (285)
McCormick, Richard P. New Jersey From Colony to State,
1609-1789. 2d ed. 1970. 6.00 2.75 (665)
McCreary, John Roger. Ambition, Interest and Faction:
Politics in New Jersey, 1702-1738. 410pp. BIP-71-19502. .... (777)
Menzies, Elizabeth G. Millstone Valley. 1969. 17.50 ..... (665)
New Jersey Historical Society. Proceedings. 1845/46-1851/53.
The first series of the Proceedings contains reports of
all meetings of the Society from 1845 to 1853, as well
as excerpts from papers read before the Society and
from other articles on New Jersey. Topics range from
the "Hollanders in New Jersey" to "Criminal Statistics
of Essex County, 1838-1845."
Series 1: Vols. 1-6: Set: 87.00 72.00 (415)
Each: 12.00 (415)
Patterson, William. Glimpses of Colonial Society and the
Life at Princeton College, 1766-1773, ed. William W.
Brickman. Repr. of 1903 ed. 15.00 ..... (547)
_____. Glimpses of Colonial Society and Life at Princeton
College, 1766-1773, by One of the Class of 1763, ed. W.
Jay Mills. Repr. of 1903 ed. 13.00 ..... (266)
Pierce, Arthur D. Iron in the Pines: The Story of New Jersey's
Ghost Towns and Bog Iron. 1957. ..... 2.75 (665)
_____. Smugglers' Woods: Jaunts and Journeys in Colonial
and Revolutionary New Jersey. 1960. ..... 2.75 (665)
Pomfret, John E. A Colonial History of New Jersey 1973. 10.00 ..... (677)

Listed below are the names of professional genealogists willing to undertake research for
a fee within the state of New Jersey, in areas specified in their ads:

Powers, Ramon S. Wealth and Poverty: Economic Base:
Social Structure, and Attitudes in Pre-Revolutionary
Pennsylvania, New Jersey and Delaware. 389pp. BIP-71-27194. .... (777)
Smith, Samuel. The History of the Colony of Nova-Caesaria,
Or New-Jersey. . .to the Year 1721. 1765. 36.00 ..... (38)
Stewart, Frank. Indians of Southern New Jersey. Repr. of 1932
ed. 94pp. 3.25 (285)
Tanner, Edwin Platt. The Province of New Jersey, 1664-1738.
1908. 20.00 ..... (2)
Van Hoesen, Walter H. Early Taverns and Stage Coach Days in
New Jersey. 8.00 ..... (227)

Research Aids

Humphrey, Constance H. Check-List of New Jersey Im-
prints to the End of the Revolution. (In The Papers
of the Bibliographical Society of America.) 1930. 6.00 ..... (415)
Kitchel, Walter H. Mayflower Descendants, New Jersey
Society Lineages, 1973. 1973. XVIII, 521pp.
Lineages of members (no. 1 to 1065) 1900 to 1973. 7.50 ..... (411)

Military

Bernstein, David Alan. New Jersey in the American Revolution: The Establishment of a Government Amid Civil
and Military Disorder, 1770-1781. 498pp. BIP-70-16924. .... (777)
Bill, A. H. Campaign of Princeton, Seventeen Seventy-Six
to Seventeen Seventy-Seven. 1948. 7.00 ..... (621)
Collins, Varnum L., ed. Brief Narrative of the Ravages of
the British and Hessians at Princeton in 1776-1777.
Repr. of 1906 ed. 6.00 ..... (38)
Keesey, Ruth. Loyalty and Reprisal: The Loyalists of
Bergen County, New Jersey and Their Estates. 1957.
323pp. BIP-00-21119. .... (777)
Larrabee, Edward Conyers. New Jersey and the Fortified
Frontier System of the 1750's. 385pp. BIP-71-06208. .... (777)
Lundin, Leonard. Cockpit of Revolution: The War for
Independence in New Jersey. Repr. of 1940 ed. 15.25 ..... (552)
Smith, Samuel S. The Battle of Monmouth. 1964. 5.95 ..... (250)
_____. Battle of Trenton. 1965. 5.95 ..... (250)
_____. Fight for the Delaware. 1970. 52pp. 8.45 ..... (285)
Stewart, Frank. Foraging for Valley Force by General
Anthony Wayne in Salem and Gloucester Counties,
New Jersey with Associated Happenings. Repr. of
1929 ed. 32pp. 3.25 (285)
Stryker, William S. Battle of Monmouth. Repr. of 1927 ed. 11.50 ..... (404)

Religious and Ethnic Groups

Bailey, Rosalie F. Pre-Revolutionary Dutch Houses and
Families in Northern New Jersey and Southern New
Jersey. 1968. ..... 5.00 (204)
Chambers, Theodore Frelinghuysen. The Early Germans
of New Jersey. 1895. 806pp. B-OP 13081. .... (778)
Federal Writers' Project. The Swedes and Finns in
New Jersey. 1938. 10.00 ..... (2)
Jamison, Wallace N. Religion in New Jersey: A Brief
History. 1964. 6.00 ..... (665)

Woody, Thomas. Quaker Education in the Colony and State
of New Jersey. 1923.   25.00   •••• (38)

Records

Burlington Court Book of West Jersey 1680-1702 (Volume
5 of the American Legal Series).   29.00   24.00 (415)
Index of Wills, Inventories, etc. in the Office of the New
Jersey Secretary of State Prior to 1901. Vol. 1:
Atlantic County to Essex County -516pp., Vol 2:
Gloucester County to Monmouth County - 500pp., Vol. 3:
Morris County to Warren County. Unrecorded Wills.
Prerogative Wills. Addends -440pp. 1912-1913.
B-BH 4282.   •••••   ••••• (778)
Nelson, William. Patents and Deeds and Other Early
Records of New Jersey, 1664-1703. Repr. of 1899 ed.
770pp.   25.00   ••••• (274)

ATLANTIC COUNTY

Funnell, Charles E. By the Beautiful Sea: The Rise and High
Times of That Great American Resort, Atlantic City. 1975.   12.50   ••••• (412)
Stewart, Frank H. Letters and Papers of Richard Somers.
1942. 36pp.
Includes documents pertaining to United States Navy in
early 19th Century and lists of seamen on various
United States vessels.   •••••   1.65 (285)
Reminiscenses of Old Gloucester, Or Incidents in the History
of the Counties of Gloucester, Atlantic and Camden, New
Jersey. Repr. of 1845 ed. 170pp.   8.50   5.50 (285)

BERGEN COUNTY

Keesey, Ruth. Loyalty and Reprisal: The Loyalists of Bergen
County, New Jersey and Their Estates. 1957. 323pp.
BIP-00-21119.   •••••   ••••• (777)
Lenk, Richard W., Jr. Hackensack, New Jersey From
Settlement to Suburb 1686 - 1804. 1968. 250pp.
BIP-69-21261.   •••••   ••••• (777)
Rankin and Randolph. Paramus Dutch Reformed Church Records.
1935. 225pp.   5.00   ••••• (533)
Writers' Program. Bergen County Panorama. 1941.   18.50   ••••• (2)

BURLINGTON COUNTY

Obert, Rowene T. and Eldon H. Walker. Chesterfield Township, Burlington County New Jersey Births 1770-1785.
1973. 32pp.   •••••   2.50 (277)

CAMDEN COUNTY

Mickle, Isaac. Reminiscenses of Old Gloucester, Or Incidents
in the History of the Counties of Gloucester, Atlantic and
Camden, New Jersey. Repr. of 1845 ed. 170pp.   8.50   5.50 (285)

CUMBERLAND COUNTY

Cushing, Thomas, M.D. and Charles Sheppard. History of
Gloucester, Salem and Cumberland Counties, New Jersey.
Repr. of 1883 ed. 728pp.   20.95   ••••• (285)

Sinclair, Donald A., comp. Index to the Cushing and Sheppard
History of Gloucester, Salem and Cumberland Counties,
New Jersey. 272pp.
Totaling over 27,000 names and subjects. Parts of
Camden and Atlantic Counties are included in the scope
of this index.   17.50   ..... (608)

ESSEX COUNTY

Rice, Arnold S. Newark: A Chronological and Documentary
History. 1976. 160pp.   7.50   ..... (551)
Writers' Program. Livingston: the Story of a Community. 1939.   10.00   ..... (2)

GLOUCESTER COUNTY

Craig, H. Stanley. Gloucester County New Jersey Marriages.
Repr. of 1930 ed. 309pp.
Contains marriages from county and church records.   .... (285)
Cushing, Thomas, M.D. and Charles E. Sheppard. History
of the Counties of Gloucester, Salem and Cumberland,
New Jersey. Repr. of 1883 ed. 728pp.   20.95   ..... (285)

Index to above, compiled by Donald A. Sinclair. 272pp.
Totaling 27,000 names and subjects. Parts of Camden and
Atlantic Counties are included in the scope of this index.   17.50   ..... (608)
Everts and Stewart. Atlas of Salem and Gloucester Counties,
New Jersey. Repr. of 1876 ed. 123pp. 12.75 (285)
Gibson, G. and F. Residents of Gloucester County 1850.
1971. 335pp.
1850 Census for Gloucester County. 8.25 (285)
History and Records of St. Peter's Episcopal Church, Berkeley
and Clarksboro, New Jersey. 1974. 186pp.
Vital statistics for over 200 years, 1765-1973.   .....   6.50 (285)
Jago, Frederick West. The 12th New Jersey Volunteers,
1862-1865. Repr. of 1967 ed. 32pp. 1.15 (285)
McGeorge, Isabella. Ann C. Whitall, the Heroine of Red
Bank - The Battle of Gloucester - Lost Towns and
Hamlets in Old Gloucester County. Repr. of 1917 ed.
22pp.
Three booklets in one pertaining to people and
events in Old Gloucester County, New Jersey. 1.15 (285)
Mickle, Isaac. Reminiscenses of Old Gloucester Or Incidents
in the History of the Counties of Gloucester, Atlantic
and Camden, New Jersey. Repr. of 1845 ed. 170pp.   8.50   5.50 (285)
Minotty, Paul. History and Records of Trinity Episcopal
Church, Swedesboro, New Jersey 1785-1973. 1977.
A continuation of 'The Records of the Raccoon and
Penns Neck Swedish Lutheran Churches' as printed
by the W.P.A. in 1938.   .... (285)
_____. Records of the Moravian Church at Oldman's Creek,
Gloucester County, New Jersey. 1968.
Vital statistics for this old South Jersey Church,
1742-1810.   .... (285)
Simpson, Mrs. Walter A., comp. John Cawman Eastlack
Diary. 1952. 103pp.
Eastlacks diary covers years 1854-1887 and is full of
vital statistics, as well as everyday happenings of
these years. 3.25 (285)

....

Smith, Samuel Stelle. Fight for the Delaware. 1970. 52pp.
    Gloucester County in Revolution.   8.45   ..... (285)
Stewart, Frank. Foraging for Valley Forge by General Anthony
    Wayne in Salem and Gloucester Counties, New Jersey with
    Associated Happenings. Repr. of 1929 ed. 32pp. 3.25 (285)
_____. Gloucester County in the Civil War, Volume I.
    1941. 272pp.   6.50   ..... (285)
_____. Gloucester County Under the Proprietors. Repr. of
    1942 ed. 46pp.   1.65 (285)
_____. Historical Data. Repr. of 1933 ed. 30pp.
    Miscellaneous data on the Revolution, Indians, etc. 1.40 (285)
_____. History of the Battle of Red Bank. Repr. of 1927 ed.
    29pp.
    The complete history of South Jersey's battle during
    the Revolutionary War. 2.25 (285)
_____. Indians of Southern New Jersey. Repr. of 1932 ed.
    94pp. 3.25 (285)
_____. Letters and Papers of Richard Somers. 1942.
    36pp.
    Includes documents pertaining to United States Navy
    in early 19th Century and lists of seamen on various
    United States vessels. 1.65 (285)
_____. Mark Newby, the First Banker in New Jersey and
    His Patrick Halfpence. Repr. of 1947 ed. 30pp.
    Historical miscellany of data on Revolution, early
    coins, Indians, etc. 2.25 (285)
_____. Organization and Minutes of the Gloucester County
    Court, 1686-1687. 1930. 46pp. 1.65 (285)
_____. Stewart's Genealogical and Historical Miscellany,
    Number 1. Repr. of 1918 ed. 44pp.
    Records of Newton and Haddonfield Meetings; marriages
    by John Ladd 1731-1760, etc. 1.65 (285)

HUNTERDON COUNTY

Hammond, D. Stanton. Hunterdon County Map Series. 1965.
    6pp.
    Five area maps showing early land holdings; one
    sheet index map.   Set: 9.50   ..... (533)

HUDSON COUNTY

Versteeg, Dingman and Thomas Vermilye, Jr. Bergen
    Records: Records of the Reformed Protestant Dutch
    Church of Bergen in New Jersey, 1666 to 1788. Repr. of
    1913-1915 ed. 300pp.   15.00   ..... (274)

MIDDLESEX COUNTY

Krogh, Albert C. Historic Perth Amboy and a Story of Odd
    Fellowship.   5.95   ..... (791)
Miers, Earl S. Where the Raritan Flows. 1964.   6.00   ..... (665)

MONMOUTH COUNTY

Beekman, George Crawford. Early Dutch Settlers of Mon-
    mouth County, New Jersey. 1900. 200pp. B-BH 15815.   .... (778)
Moss, George H., Jr. Double Exposure: Early Stereographic
    Views of Historic Monmouth County, New Jersey and Their
    Relationship to Pioneer Photography. 1971.   12.95   ..... (605)

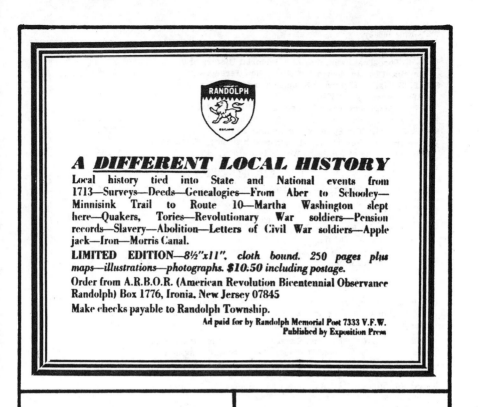

....

_____. Steamboat to the Shore: A Pictorial History of the
Steamboat Era in Monmouth County, New Jersey. 1972.   10.95   ..... (605)
Salter, Edwin. A History of Monmouth and Ocean Counties.
1890. 546pp. OP-65276.
Includes genealogical record of earliest settlers and
their descendants.   .... (778)
Smith, Samuel. The Battle of Monmouth. 1964.   5.95   ..... (250)
Van Benthuysen, Robert F., ed. Monmouth County, New Jersey:
A Bibliography of Published Works 1676-1973. 1974.   11.95   ..... (605)

MORRIS COUNTY

A History of Randolph Township. 1976. 200pp. (See ad, page 207)   10.50   ..... (3)

OCEAN COUNTY

Salter, Edwin. A History of Monmouth and Ocean Counties.
1890. 546pp. OP-65276.
Includes genealogical record of earliest settlers and
their descendants.   .... (778)

SALEM COUNTY

Cushing, Thomas, M.D. and Charles Sheppard. History of
the Counties of Gloucester, Salem and Cumberland, New
Jersey. Repr. of 1883 ed. 728pp.   20.95   ..... (285)

Index to above Cushing and Sheppard's History of Gloucester,
Salem, and Cumberland Counties, New Jersey. Compiled by
Donald A. Sinclair. 272pp.
Totals over 27,000 names and subjects.   17.50   ..... (608)
Everts and Stewart. Atlas of Salem and Gloucester Counties,
New Jersey. Repr. of 1876 ed. 123pp. 12.75 (285)
Shourds, Thomas. History and Genealogy of Fenwick's Colony.
Repr. of 1876 ed. 581pp.   17.50   ..... (274)
Stewart, Frank. Foraging for Valley Forge by General Antnony
Wayne in Salem and Gloucester Counties, New Jersey with
Associated Happenings. Repr. of 1929 ed. 32pp. 3.25 (285)
_____. Salem A Century Ago. 1934. 45pp.
Newspaper extracts from 1830 to 1834.   .....   1.15 (285)
_____. Salem More Than A Century Ago. Repr. of 1935 ed.
24pp.
Newspaper extracts from 1819 to 1822.   .....   1.15 (285)
_____. Sketches of Salem, New Jersey and Vicinity 1823-1826.
Repr. of 1933 ed. 27pp.
Newspaper extracts from Salem County papers. 1.15 (285)

SOMERSET COUNTY

Mellick, Andrew D., Jr. Old Farm, ed. Hubert G. Smith. 1961.   .....   2.75 (665)

UNION COUNTY

Silfen, Paul. New Jersey: Some Dimensions of Local History.
1976. 32pp.
History of a professor's home town - Fanwood, New Jer-
sey - a bicentennial salute to a tercentenary town.   4.50   ..... (224)

New Mexico

STATEWIDE REFERENCES

Beck, Warren A. New Mexico, A History of Four Centuries. Repr. of 1962 ed.	6.95	.....	(556)
Blawis, Patricia B. Tijerina and the Land Grants: Mexican Americans in Struggle for Their Heritage. 1971.	6.95	2.65	(372)
Briggs, L. Vernon. Arizona and New Mexico 1882; California 1886; Mexico 1891. Repr. of 1932 ed.	20.00	.....	(38)
Duffus, R. L. Santa Fe Trail. Repr. of 1931 ed. illus.	14.50	.....	( )
_____. The Santa Fe Trail. 1972.		2.95	(535)
Graham, Robert, ed. New Mexico Genealogist Quarterly. 100pp.	.....	5.00	(534)
Gregg, Kate L. Road to Santa Fe: The Journal and Diaries of George Champlin Sibley. 1968.	6.00	2.45	(535)
Historic Santa Fe Foundation. Old Santa Fe Today. 2d ed. 1972.	.....	4.95	(535)
Inman, Henry. Old Santa Fe Trail. 1897.	10.00	.....	(656)
Loomis, Noel M. Texan-Santa Fe Pioneers. 1958.	8.95	.....	(556)
Minge, Ward Alan. Frontier Problems in New Mexico Preceding the Mexican War 1840-1846. 378pp. BIP-66-04448.	.....	.....	(777)
Rittenhouse, Jack. Santa Fe Trail: A Historical Bibliography. 1971.	12.00	.....	(535)
Stocking, Hobart. Road to Santa Fe.	9.95	.....	(321)
Stratton, Porter Andrew. The Territorial Press of New Mexico 1834-1912. 585pp. BIP-13434.	.....	.....	(777)
Taylor, Morris F. First Mail West: Stagecoach Lines on the Santa Fe Trail. 1971.	10.00	.....	(535)
Tyler, Daniel. New Mexico in the 1820's - The First Administration of Manuel Armijo. 321pp. BIP-71-12799.	.....	.....	(777)
Webb, James J., ed. Adventures in the Santa Fe Trade 1844-1847. Repr. of 1931 ed.	17.50	.....	(612)
Westphall, Victor. The Public Domain in New Mexico, 1854-1891. 344pp. BIP-00-17685.	.....	.....	(777)

Research Aids

Beck, Warren A. and Ynez D. Haase. Historical Atlas of New Mexico. 1969.	4.95	2.95	(556)
Pearce, T. M. New Mexico Place Names: A Geographical Dictionary. 1965.	7.50	2.45	(535)
Shelton, Wilma Loy. Checklist of New Mexico Publications, 1850-1893. 1954.	.....	3.50	(535)

Military

Emmett, Chris. Fort Union and the Winning of the Southwest. 1965.	8.50	.....	(556)
Parker, William T. Annals of Old Fort Commings, New Mexico, 1867-1868. 1968.	3.50	2.00	(257)
Rogan, Francis Edward. Military History of New Mexico Territory During the Civil War. 1961. 589pp. BIP-61-06234.	.....	.....	(777)

Records

Chavez, Angelico. Archives of the Archdiocese of Santa Fe (New Mexico) 1678-1900. 1958.	7.50	.....	(5)
Hackett, Charles W., ed. Historical Documents Relating to New Mexico, Nueva Vizcaya and Approaches Thereto, to 1773, Collected by Adolph F. A. Bandelier and Fanny R. Bandelier; Spanish Texts and English Translations, Edited with Introductions and Annotations. 3 vols. 1923-1937. Set:	72.00	.....	(415)
Olmsted, Virginia L., G.R.S., tr. and comp., New Mexico Spanish and Mexican Colonial Censuses, 1790, 1823, 1845. 1975. 303pp.	.....	12.50	(534)
Twitchell, Ralph Emerson. The Spanish Archives of New Mexico. Compiled and Chronologically Arranged with Historical, Genealogical, Geographical, and Other Annotations, by Authority of the State of New Mexico. 2 vols. 1914. Set:	75.00	.....	(2)

BERNALILLO COUNTY

Windham, Margaret L., ed. New Mexico 1850 Territorial Census, Volume IV - Bernalillo and Santa Fe Counties. 1976. c200pp.	.....	10.50	(534)

RIO ARRIBA COUNTY

_____. New Mexico 1850 Territorial Census, Volume II - Rio Arriba and Santa Ana Counties. 1976. c200pp.	.....	10.50	(534)

SAN MIGUEL COUNTY

_____. New Mexico 1850 Territorial Census, Volume III - Taos and San Miguel Counties. c215pp.	.....	10.50	(534)

SANTA ANA COUNTY

_____. New Mexico 1850 Territorial Census, Volume II - Rio Arriba and Santa Ana Counties. 1976. c200pp.	.....	10.50	(534)

SANTA FE COUNTY

Horgan, Paul. Centuries of Santa Fe. 1956. illus.	.....	2.25	(210)
La Farge, Oliver and Arthur N. Morgan. Santa Fe: The Autobiography of a Southwestern Town. 1959. illus.	9.95	.....	(556)
Windham, Margaret L., ed. New Mexico 1850 Territorial Census, Volume IV - Bernalillo and Santa Fe Counties. 1976. c200pp.	.....	10.50	(534)

TAOS COUNTY

_____. New Mexico 1850 Territorial Census, Volume III - Taos
and San Miguel Counties. 1976. c215pp. 10.50 (534)

VALENCIA COUNTY

_____. New Mexico 1850 Territorial Census, Volume I -
Valencia County. 1976. 176pp. 10.50 (534)

ꓵew York

STATEWIDE REFERENCES

Barber, John W. and Henry Howe. Historical Collections of the
State of New York. 1841.   27.50   ..... (404)
Beauchamp, William Martin. A History of the New York
Iroquois, Now Commonly Called the Six Nations. 1905.   21.50   ..... (2)
Bradley, Lawrence James. The Longdon/Bristol Trade
Rivalry: Conventional History, and the Colonial Office
Records for the Port of New Yori. 1971. 376pp. BIP-71-19078. .... (777)
Canedy, Charles Roscoe, III. An Entrepreneurial History of the
New York Frontier, 1739-1776. 1967. 437pp. BIP-68-03302.   .... (777)
Countryman, Edward Francis. Legislative Government in
Revolutionary New York, 1777-1778. 1971. 400pp.
BIP-71-22972.   .... (777)
Crevecoeur, Michel-Guillanme St. J. De. Journey Into
Northern Pennsylvania and the State of New York.
tr. Clarissa S. Bostelmann. 1964.   15.00   ..... (484)
_____. Crevecoeur's Eighteenth-Century Travels In
Pennsylvania and New York. tr. and ed. Percy G. Adams.
1961.   5.00   ..... (408)
Danckaerts, Jasper and Peter Sluyter. Journal of a Voyage to
New York in 1679-80. ed. Henry C. Murphy. Repr. of
1867 ed.   28.00   ..... (299)

Listed below are the names of professional genealogists willing to undertake research for a
fee within the state of New York, in areas specified in their ads:

Dunlap, William. History of the New Netherlands, Province
of New York, and State of New York, to the Adoption of the
Federal Constitution. 2 vols. Repr. of 1839 ed.   Set: 40.00   ..... (248)
Ellis, David M., et al. History of New York State.
Rev. ed.   Each: 15.00   ..... (163)
_____. Landlords and Farmers in the Hudson-Mohawk Region
1790-1850. 1967.   12.50   ..... (552)
Flick, Alexander C., ed. History of the State of New York.
10 vols. in 5. 1933-1937.   124.50   ..... (253)
Fowler, John. Journal of a Tour in the State of New York
In the Year 1830. With remarks on agriculture in those
parts most eligible for settlers. 1831. 333pp.   15.00   ..... (273)
Halsey, Francis W. The Old New York Frontier. 1902.   20.00   ..... (547)
Hamilton, Milton W. Country Printer: New York State,
1785-1830. 2d ed. 1936.   6.00   ..... (253)
Higgins, Ruth L. Expansion in New York: With Especial
Reference to the Eighteenth Century. Repr. of 1931 ed.   12.50   ..... (612)
Historic Chronicles of New Amsterdam, Colonial New York,
and Early Long Island: First Series. 1968.   7.00   ..... (404)
Howe, Herbert Barber. Jedediah Barber, 1787-1876;
a Footnote to the History of the Military Tract of Central
New York. 1939.   10.00   ..... (2)
Innes, J. H. New Amsterdam and Its People. 1902.   20.00   ..... (547)
_____. New Amsterdam and Its People: Studies Social and
Topographical, of the Town Under Dutch and Early English
Rule. 2 vols. Repr. of 1902 ed.   Set: 10.00   ..... (253)
Irving, Washington. History of New York. ed. Edwin T. Bowden.
1964.   7.50   3.45 (152)
_____. A History of New York from the Beginning of the World
to the End of the Dutch Dynasty. 2 vols. 1809.   39.50   ..... (702)
_____. Knickerbocker's History of New York.
ed. Anne C. Moore. 1959.   9.50   ..... (775)
James, B. B. and J. Franklin Jameson, eds. Journal of
Jasper Danckaerts, Sixteen Seventy-Nine to Sixteen Eighty. 1913.
Original Narratives.   6.50   ..... (52)
Kapp, Fiedrich. Immigration, and the Commissioners of
Emigration of the State of New York. 1870.   7.50   ..... (38)
Lahey, William C. The Influence of David Parish on the
Development of Trade and Settlement in Northern
New York 1808-1822. 1958. 334pp. BIP-58-07228.   .... (777)
Leamon, James Shenstone. War, Finance, and Faction in Colonial
New York: The Administration of Governor York: The Admin-
istration of Governor Benjamin Fletcher, 1692-1698. 1961.
305pp. BIP-63-01442.   .... (777)
Lossing, Benson J. The Hudson: From the Wilderness to
the Sea. Repr. of 1866 ed.   17.50   ..... (404)
_____. The Hudson, From the Wilderness to the Sea.
Repr. of 1866 ed.   12.50   ..... (532)
McKee, Samuel. Labor in Colonial New York, 1664-1776. 1934. 6.00   ..... (253)
Morrison, Wayne E., Sr. Annals of Western New York.
1974. 72pp.
From settlement to 1860; 44 illustrations. 3.50 (719)
Severance, Frank H. An Old Frontier of France: The Niagara
Region and Adjacent Lakes Under French Control. 1917.   42.00   ..... (38)
Seybolt, Robert Francis. Apprenticeship and Apprenticeship
Education in Colonial New England and New York. 1917.   4.50   ..... (2)

Seybolt, Robert Francis. Apprenticeship and Apprenticeship
    Education in Colonial New England and New York. 1917.   9.00   ..... (38)
Smith, William, Jr. History of the Province of New York.
    ed. Michael Kammen. 2 vols. 1972.   25.00   ..... (319)
Sylvester, Nathaniel B. Historical Sketches of Northern New
    York and the Adirondack Wilderness: Including Traditions
    of the Indians, Early Explorers, Pioneer Settlers, Hermit
    Hunters. Repr. of 1877 ed.   12.50   ..... (313)
Taft, Pauline D. Happy Valley: The Elegant Eighties in
    Upstate New York. 1965.   7.95   ..... (740)
Van Every, Edward. Sins of New York. 1930. 316pp.
    A running narrative of crime and criminals as reported
    in the yellow pages of the original Police Gazette (1845)
    and the Richard K. Fox Gazette (1876).   17.50   ..... (38)
Vanderhoof, Elisha Woodward. Historical Sketches of Western
    New York: The Seneca Indians; Phelps and Gorham Purchase;
    Morris Reserve and Holland Purchase; Mary Jemison;
    Jemima Wilkinson; Joseph Smith, Jr. and Mormonism;
    Morgan and Anti-Masonry; the Fox Sisters and Rochester
    Knockings. 1907.   11.50   ..... (2)
Walsh, James Joseph. History of Medicine in New York:
    Three Centuries of Medical Progress. 5 vols. 1919.
    Vol. 1-3: History and index; Vol. 4 and 5: Short
    biographies in medicine and index.   Set: 125.00   ..... (2)
Western New York Genealogical Society. Western New York
    Genealogical Society Journal. 1974-
    Membership in the Society includes the WNYGS Journal
    which aids research in the eight western New York Coun-
    ties: Cattaraugus, Chautauqua, Erie, Allegany, Genesee,
    Niagara, Orleans, and Wyoming.   Membership/yr: 10.00 (828)
Wissler, Clark, ed. The Indians of Greater New York and the
    Lower Hudson. 1909.   17.50   ..... (2)
Wraxall, Peter. An Abridgement of the Indian Affairs Contained
    In Four Folio Volumes Transacted in the Colony of New York
    from the Year 1687 to 1751. ed. Charles Howard McIllwain.
    1915/1967. 368pp.
    Early economic relationships between Indians and
    settlers. It also contains a new index.   18.00   ..... (38)

Research Aids

Asher, G. M. A Bibliographical and Historical Essay on the
    Dutch Books and Pamphlets Relating to New Netherland and
    to the Dutch West-India Company, and to Its Possessions.
    Repr. of 1854-67 ed.   12.60   ..... (306)
Cutts, Dorothy Remington. Aid to Place Names: New York
    State Townships and Counties. Repr. of 1967 ed. 16pp. 2.00 (559)
Hemlow, Joyce. A Catalog of the Burney Family Correspond-
    ence 1749-1878. 1971. 487pp.   20.00   ..... (635)
Los Angeles Temple Genealogical Library. Surname Index to
    Foley's Early Settler's of New York State Magazine.
    Volumes 4-8. 1977.   .... (439)
Nestler, Harold. A Bibliography of New York State Communi-
    ties, Counties, Towns, Villages. 1968.   6.00   ..... (404)
Plum, Dorothy A., ed. Adirondack Bibliography. 1958.   15.00   ..... (740)

Western New York Genealogical Society. Ancestor File of
Western New York Genealogical Society Members.
Vol. 1. 1976.
    Ancestor information of Society members through
    April, 1976. Listed alphabetically by ancestors.   .... (828)
_____. Index of Locations in Western New York Counties. 1976.
    Includes towns and locations, both present and obso-
    lete in the eight Western New York Counties of
    Allegany, Cattaraugus, Chautauqua, Erie, Genesee,
    Niagara, Orleans and Wyoming. 5.00 (828)

Military

Abbott, W. C. New York in the American Revolution.
    Repr. of 1929 ed.   12.95 ..... (320)
Bennett, Clarence. Advance and Retreat to Saratoga.
    ed. George Billias. 2 vols. in 1. Repr. of 1927 ed.   12.00 ..... (299)
Byrd, Martha. Battle of Saratoga. 1973.   6.95 ..... (470)
Clark, R. D. and V. Lynch. The New York Volunteers in
    the Mexican War, 1846-1848. 2 vols. in 1.   10.00 ..... (644)
Dornbusch, Charles E. Communities of New York and the
    Civil War: The Recruiting Areas of the New York Civil
    War Regiments. 1962.   ..... 1.50 (537)
East, Robert A. and Jacob Judd, eds. The Loyalist Americans:
    A Focus on Greater New York. 1975.   12.00 ..... (692)
Flick, Alexander C. Loyalism in New York During the
    American Revolution. Repr. of 1901 ed.   10.00 ..... (38)
Gerlach, Don Ralph. Philip Schuyler: The Origins of a
    Conservative Patriot, 1733-1777, a Study in Provincial
    Politics and the American Revolution in New York. 1961.
    446pp. BIP-61-05374.   .... (777)
Hoyle, Martha B. Saratoga: Turning Point in the American
    Revolution. 1973.   6.95 ..... (470)
Jones, Thomas. History of New York During the Revolutionary
    War, and of the Leading Events in the Other Colonies at
    That Period. ed. Edward F. DeLancey. Repr. of 1879 ed.   20.00 ..... (38)
Kirk, Hyland Clare. Heavy Guns and Light: A History of the
    Fourth New York Heavy Artillery. 1890. 674pp. B-BH 11260. .... (778)
Lankevich, George John. The Grand Army of the Republic
    in New York State 1865-1898. 1967. 340pp. BIP-67-15497.   .... (777)
Mason, Bernard. Organization of the Revolutionary Move-
    ment In New York State 1775-1777. 1958. 255pp.
    BIP-58-02599.   .... (777)
Morhous, Henry C. Reminiscences of the 123d Regiment,
    New York Volunteer, Giving a Complete History of Its
    Three Years Service In the War. To Which is Added an
    Appendix, Containing the Name, Company, Date of
    Enlistment, and Discharge of Each Man in the
    Regiment. 1879. 224pp. B-BH 17357.   .... (778)
O'Flaherty, Patrick D. The History of the 69th Regiment
    of the New York State Militia 1852-1861. 1963.
    325pp. BIP-64-02415.   .... (777)
Riedesel, Fredericka. Letters and Journals Relating to the
    Capture of the German Troops at Saratoga.
    Repr. of 1867 ed.   10.00 ..... (38)

Religious and Ethnic Groups

Bernheimer, Charles S. The Russian Jew in the United
States: Studies of Social Conditions in New York,
Philadelphia, and Chicago, with a Description of
Rural Settlements. Repr. of 1905 ed.   11.95   ..... (568)
Corwin, E. T., ed. Ecclesiastical Record of the State of
New York. 7 vols. 1901-1916.   Each: 63.00   ..... (2)
                                           Set: 440.00   ..... (2)
Dolan, Jay P. The Immigrant Church: New York's Irish
and German Catholics, 1815-1865. 1975.   10.00   ..... (385)
Doyle, Richard David. The Pre-Revolutionary Irish in
New York (1643-1775). 1932. 287pp. BIP-00-00169.   .... (777)
Elting, I. Dutch Village Communities on the Hudson River.
Repr. of 1886 ed. 6.25 (394)
Fingerhut, Eugene R. Assimilation of Immigrants on the
Frontier of New York, 1764-1776. 1962. 348pp.
BIP-62-05172.   .... (777)
Grinstein, Hyman B. The Rise of the Jewish Community
of New York, 1654-1860. Repr. of 1945 ed.   20.00   ..... (612)
Haiman, Mieczyslaw. Poles in New York in the Seventeenth and
Eighteenth Centuries. Repr. of 1938 ed.   5.00   ..... (631)
Janvier, Thomas A. The Dutch Founding of New York.
Repr. of 1903 ed.   6.00   ..... (404)
Kreider, Harry Julius. Lutheranism in Colonial New York.
1942.   9.00   ..... (38)
Landesman, Alter E. Brownsville: The Birth, Development
& Passing of a Jewish Community in New York. 1969.   7.95   ..... (75)
Netherland Chamber of Commerce. Dutch in New Netherland,
1609-1909. and the United States. Repr. of 1909 ed. 5.00 (631)
Ottley, Roi and William J. Weatherby, eds. The Negro in
New York. 1967. 328pp.
An informal social history. From the manuscripts
in the Schomburg Collection.   7.50   ..... (635)
Pool, David de Sola. Portraits Etched in Stone; Early
Jewish Settlers, 1682-1831. 1952. 691pp.
Refers to New York City. B-OP 72477.   .... (778)
Reynolds, Helen W. Dutch Houses in the Hudson Valley
Before 1776. 1965.   .....   5.00 (204)
Singleton, Esther. Dutch New York. 1909. 360pp.
Daily life in the Dutch colony, with a record of how
social life and business were actually conducted.   16.00   ..... (38)
Zwierlein, Frederick K. Religion in the New Netherland,
1623-1664. Repr. of 1910 ed.   15.00   ..... (176)

Records

Albany County Board. Minutes of the Commissioners for
Detecting and Defeating Conspiracies in the State of
New York. ed. Victor H. Paltsits. 2 vols.
Repr. of 1909 ed.   45.00   ..... (176)
Bachman, Van Cleaf. Peltries or Plantations? The Economic
Policies of the Dutch West India Company in New Nether-
land, 1623-1639. 1965. 298pp. BIP-65-10257.   .... (777)
Fernow, Berthold. The Records of New Amsterdam From
1653 to 1674 Anno Domini. Repr. of 1897 ed. 2743pp.   125.00   ..... (274)
Goodwin, Maud W., et al.,eds. Historic New York: The
Half Moon Papers. Series 1 and 2. Repr. of 1898 ed.
4 vols.   Set: 25.00   ..... (253)

New York Colony. The Colonial Laws of New York From
the Year 1664 to the Revolution, Including the Charters to
the Duke of York, the Commissions and Instructions to
Colonial Governors, the Duke's Laws, the Laws of the
Dongan and Leisler Assemblies, the Charters of
Albany and New York and the Acts of the Colonial
Legislatures from 1691 to 1775 Inclusive. 5 vols.

1894-1896.	Each:	78.00	..... (2)
	Set:	390.00	..... (2)

_____. Documents Relative to the Colonial History of the
State of New York: Procured in Holland, England, and
France. . . All in English. John Romeyn Brodhead, et al.,

eds. 15 vols. 1853-1887.	Each:	85.00	..... (2)
	Set:	1275.00	..... (2)

_____. Journal of the Legislative Council of the Colony
of New York. Began the 9th Day of April, 1691 and
Ended the [3rd of April, 1775]. Published by Order
of the Senate of the State of New York. 2 vols. 1861. Set: 125.00 ..... (2)

_____. Journals of the Provincial Congress, Provincial
Convention, Committee of Safety, and Council of Safety
of the State of New York. 2 vols. 1842. Set: 190.00 ..... (2)

_____. Minutes of the Executive Council of the Province
of New York [with] Collateral and Illustrative Documents.
ed. Victor Hugo Paltsits. 2 vols. 1910. Set: 75.00 ..... (2)

_____. Names of Persons For Whom Marriage Licenses
Were Issued By the Secretary of the Province of
New York, Previous to 1784. 1860. 492pp. B-BH 6363. .... (778)

New York Historical Society. Collections of the New York
Historical Society. First Series: Volumes 1-5,
1809-1829. 5 vols. in 4. 1811-1829.

Vols. 1-3	Each:	30.00	..... (2)
Vols. 4/5	Each:	40.00	..... (2)
	Set:	130.00	..... (2)

"New York Inventories, 1666-1775." NGS Quarterly,
Vol. 54, No. 4. 1966. 14pp. 3.50 (514)

New York State. Military Minutes of the Council of Appointment
of the State of New York, 1783-1821.
comps. and eds. Hugh Hastings and Henry Harmon Noble.
4 vols. 1901-1902. Set: 348.50 ..... (2)

O'Callaghan, Edmund B. Calendar of British Historical
Manuscripts in the Office of the Secretary of State,
Albany, New York 1664-1776. Repr. of 1865 ed. 52.00 ..... (299)

_____. Calendar of Dutch Historical Manuscripts in the
Office of the Secretary of State, Albany, New York
1630-1664. Repr. of 1865 ed. 26.00 ..... (299)

_____, tr. The Minutes of the Orphanmasters of New
Amsterdam, 1663-1668. 1976. 29pp. 3.00 (274)

Scott, Kenneth and Kenn Stryker-Rodda. Denizations,
Naturalizations, and Oaths of Allegiance in Colonial
New York. 1975. 120pp. 12.00 ..... (274)

Stevens, John A. Colonial Records with Historical and
Biographical Sketches, 1768-1784, Including Colonial
New York: Sketches, Biographical and Historical,
1768-1784. 2 vols. in 1. Repr. of 1867 ed. 32.50 ..... (248)

"Wills of Colonial New York, 1736-1775." NGS Quarterly,
Vol. 54, No. 2. 1966. 27pp. 3.50 (514)

Western New York Genealogical Society. 1865 Census -
New York State - Eight Western New York Counties.
Indexed. 1977.
  Index of Census. Counties of Allegany, Cattaraugus,
  Chautauqua, Erie, Genesee, Niagara, Orleans,
  Wyoming.   .... (828)
Wilson, Edmund. Upstate: Records and Recollections of
Northern New York. 1971.   8.95 ..... (230)

ALBANY COUNTY

Albany Evening Journal, March 22, 1830 to 1873. 88 rolls.
  Microfilm of the original newspapers. Individual
  rolls covering a specific time span may be ordered.
  Prices vary from $15 to $30 per roll.   .... (870)
Albany Argus, January 26, 1813 to December 31, 1865.
91 rolls.
  Microfilm of the original newspapers. Individual
  rolls covering a specific time span may be ordered.
  Prices vary from $15 to $30 per roll.   .... (870)
Armour, David A. The Merchants of Albany, New York
1686-1760. 1965. 314pp. BIP-65-12042.   .... (777)
Kenney, Alice Patricia. The Gansevoorts of Albany and
Anglo-Dutch Relations in the Upper Hudson Valley, 1664-1790.
1961. 248pp. BIP-61-03445.   .... (777)
Munsell, Joel, ed. Collections on the History of Albany, From
Its Discovery to the Present Time. 4 vols. 1865-71.
  Vol. 1-564pp. Vol. 2-619pp. Vol. 3-544pp. Vol. 4-588pp.
  B-BH 832.   .... (778)
Scott, Kenneth. New York: State Census of Albany County
Towns in 1790. 1975. 68pp. 6.50 (274)

ALLEGANY COUNTY

Beers' History of Allegany County. Repr. of 1879 ed. 464pp.
  With added name index.   24.00 ..... (719)
Western New York Genealogical Society. Western New York
Genealogical Society Journal. 1974-
  Membership includes WNYGS Journal, an aid to research
  in Allegany County.   Subscription/yr: 10.00 (828)

CATTARAUGUS COUNTY

Western New York Genealogical Society. Western New York
Genealogical Society Journal. 1974-
  Membership includes WNYGS Journal, an aid to research
  in Cattaraugus County.   Subscription/yr: 10.00 (828)

CHAUTAUQUA COUNTY

Child, Hamilton and Wayne Morrison, Sr. Chautauqua County,
  New York. 1969. 96pp.   7.50 ..... (719)
Hazeltine. Personal Name Index, History of Ellicott,
  New York (1887). 1976. 18pp.
  Personal Name Index only. 3.00 (828)
Ton and Morrison. History of Clymer, New York. 1970. 80pp. 5.50 (719)
Warren, Emory F. Chautauqua County, New York.
  Repr. of 1846 ed. 159pp. Illustrations.   6.50 ..... (719)

Western New York Genealogical Society. Western New York
Genealogical Society Journal. 1974-
    Membership includes WNYGS Journal, an aid to research
    in Chautauqua County.   Subscription/yr: •••••   10.00 (828)
Young, Andrew White. History of Chautauqua County,
New York. 1875. 932pp. B-BH 2131.   •••••   ••••• (778)

CHEMUNG COUNTY

Peirce, H. B. and D. H. Hurd. History of Chemung County.
Repr. of 1879 ed. 288pp.
    Taken from the Four County History.   21.00   ••••• (719)

COLUMBIA COUNTY

Kelly, Arthur, comp. Settlers and Residents, Volume 2, Part 1,
Town of Clermont, 1756-1899. 1975. 407pp.
    R. R. Livingston's Diary, 1761-1766; Grist Mill Records,
    1781-1787; Dr. Wilson's Day Book, 1787-1813; School
    District Students, 1796-1800; Road Records; Cemetery
    Inscriptions; Death Records; many maps; indexed.   28.50   •••• (402)
_____. Settlers and Residents, Volume 2, Part 2, Town of
Clermont, 1790-1875. 1975. 214pp.
    Federal Census of 1790, 1800, 1810, 1820, 1830, 1840,
    1850, 1860, 1870; State Census of 1855, 1865, and
    1875; indexed.   17.50   ••••• (402)
_____. Settlers and Residents, Volume 3, Part 2, Town of
Livingston, 1790-1875. 1976. 449pp.
    Federal Census of 1790, 1800, 1810, 1820, 1830, 1840,
    1850, 1860, 1870; State Census 1855, 1865, and 1875;
    indexed.   31.50   ••••• (402)

DELAWARE COUNTY

History of Delaware County, New York. 1880. 441pp. B-OP 67747   •••••   ••••• (778)

DUTCHESS COUNTY

Buys, Barbara Smith, comp. Records of the Reformed Dutch
Church of Beacon, New York (Formerly Fishkill-on-Hudson).
Repr. of 1930 ed. c100pp.
    Baptisms, 1819-1876; Marriages,1823-1900; Funerals,
    1847-1899; Membership list, 1819-1904; indexed.   •••••   15.00 (110)
Federal Writers' Project. Dutchess County. 1937.   12.00   ••••• (2)

ERIE COUNTY

Anderson, Doris. History of Eden, Volume I. 1974. 72pp.
    Covers first settlers, businesses and industry to about
    1900. History of some of oldest houses.   •••••   2.25 (29)
_____. History of Eden, Volumw II. 1975. 88pp.
    Business and industry, 20th century, history of all
    churches, fire department, library, utilities, history
    of some of oldest houses.   •••••   2.25 (29)
_____. History of Eden, Volume III. 1976.
    Eden Schools, civic, social and all town wide organi-
    zation, Eden physicians and dentists, 1808-1976.   •••••   ••••• (29)
Ketchum, William. Authentic and Comprehensive History
of Buffalo. 2 vols. 1864-65.   Set: 24.50   ••••• (673)

Smith, H. Perry. History of the City of Buffalo and Erie
County. Repr. of 1884 ed. 1600pp.
A reprint of the two volume set with the addition of a
complete name index by Ridgway McNallie.   33.00   ..... (828)
Western New York Genealogical Society. 1865 Census - City of
Buffalo and Erie County. Indexed. 1977.
Indexed by families, with cross reference for additional
surnames within a family. Includes age, relationship,
birthplace, of each person.   .... (828)
_____. Historical and Genealogical Records of Freewill
Baptist Church of Hamburg, New York (years 1827-1886).
1975. 20pp.
Transcription of original records. 3.00 (828)
_____. Western New York Genealogical Society Journal.
Vol. I-1974-
Membership includes WNYGS Journal, an aid to research
in Erie County.   Subscription/yr: 10.00 (828)

FULTON COUNTY

Frothingham, Washington. History of Fulton County.
1892. 877pp. B-OP 61499.   .... (778)

GENESEE COUNTY

Western New York Genealogical Society. Western New York
Genealogical Society Journal. 1974-
Membership includes WNYGS Journal, an aid to research
in Genesee County.   Subscription/yr: 10.00 (828)

GREENE COUNTY

Kelly, Arthur, comp. Baptism Record of Reformed Church,
Coxsackie, 1738-1899. 1976. 202pp.
Transcribed baptisms with index of parents and sponsors. 34.75   ..... (402)

JEFFERSON COUNTY

Hough, Franklin B. History of Jefferson County. Repr. of
1854 ed. 601pp.   25.00   ..... (719)
Oakes, Rensselaer Allston, ed. Genealogical and Family
History of the County of Jefferson, New York. 2 vols.
1905. Vol. 1-816pp. Vol. 2-820pp. B-BH 21434   .... (778)

KINGS COUNTY

Weld, Ralph Foster. Brooklyn Village, 1816-1834. 1938. 10.00   ..... (2)

MADISON COUNTY

Estlake, Allan. The Oneida Community: a Record of an
Attempt to Carry Out the Principles of Christian Unselfishness
and Scientific Race-improvement. 1900.   9.50   ..... (2)
Fogarty, Robert S. The Oneida Community, 1848-1880: A
Study in Conservative Christian Utopianism. 1968. 355pp.
BIP-69-07008.   .... (777)
Jackson, Harry F. and Thomas F. O'Donnell. Back Home
in Oneida: Hermon Clarke and His Letters. 1965.   6.00   ..... (740)
Meyer, Mary Keysor and Joyce Clark Scott. Cemetery Inscrip-
tions of Madison County, New York. Volume 1 (Towns of
Fenner and Nelson). 1960. 88pp. 5.50 (479)

Oneida Community. Hand-book of the Oneida Community: with a
Sketch of Its Founder, and an Outline of Its Constitution and
Doctrines; [bound with] Hand-book of the Oneida Community;
Containing a Brief Sketch of Its Present Condition, Internal
Economy and Leading Principles, No. 2; [and] Mutual Criticism.
3 vols. in 1. 1867, 1871, and 1876.   12.50   ..... (2)
Robertson, Constance N., ed. Oneida Community: An
Autobiography, 1851-1876. 1970.   11.50   ..... (740)
Sobel, May Louise. An Experiment in Perfectionism: The
Religious Life of the Putney and Oneida Communities. 1968.
280pp. BIP-68-18087.   .... (777)

MONROE COUNTY

Everts, Ensign and Everts. History of Monroe County 1788-1877.
Repr. of 1877. 460pp.
    Edited by Professor W. H. McIntosh. Illustrations and
    maps. Index available.   21.00   ..... (719)
Federal Writers' Project. Rochester and Monroe County. 1937. 25.00   ..... (2)
Malo, Paul. Landmarks of Rochester and Monroe County: A
Guide to Neighborhoods and Villages. 1974.   15.00   6.00 (740)

NEW YORK CITY

American Map Company. Atlas of New York City, No. 1445
[Current Maps]. 1974.   .....   1.20 (23)
Black, George Ashton. The History of Municipal Ownership of
Land on Manhattan Island to the Beginning of Sales by the
Commissioner of the Sinking Fund in 1844. CSSS#3. 1891.   7.50   ..... (2)
Bolton, Reginald P. Indian Life of Long Ago in the City of
New York. 1972.   4.95   2.95 (316)
Dawson, H. B. New York City During the American Revolution. 29.95   ..... (289)
Freeman, Rhoda G. The Free Negro In New York City In the Era
Before the Civil War. 1966. 504pp. BIP-69-15545   .... (777)
Furer, Howard B. New York: A Chronological and Documentary
History. 1974. 160pp.   7.50   ..... (551)
Humphrey, David Churchill. King's College in the City of
New York, 1754-1776. 1968. 669pp. BIP-69-01852.   .... (777)
The Italians of New York City. 1938.   14.50   ..... (702)
Jacobs, Julius. Bronx Cheers. 1976.   .....   3.00 (429)
Mohl, Raymond A. Poverty in New York, 1783-1825. 1971.   8.50   ..... (566)
New York Herald, August, 1835 to 1919. 852 rolls.
    Microfilm of the original newspapers. Individual
    rolls covering a specific time span may be ordered.
    Prices vary from $15 to $30 per roll.   .... (870)
New York Tribune, April 10, 1841 to December, 1923. 530 rolls.
    Microfilm of the original newspapers. Individual
    rolls covering a specific time span may be ordered.
    Prices vary from $15 to $30 per roll.   .... (870)
New York as an Eighteenth Century Municipality, 2 Volumes
In 1, Including Arthur E. Peterson - Prior to 1731 - and
George W. Edwards - 1731 to 1776. 1917.   12.00   ..... (404)
Peterson, Arthur Everett and George William Edwards.
New York as an Eighteenth Century Municipality, Prior to
1731. 2 vols.
    Part 1 by A. E. Peterson; New York as an Eighteenth
    Century Municipality, 1731-1776.
    Part II by G. W. Edwards. 1917.   Each: 12.50   ..... (2)
                                             Set: 25.00   ..... (2)

Schaukirk, Ewald Gustav. Occupation of New York by the
British. [Reprinted from "The Pennsylvania Magazine of
History and Biography," January, 1887]. 1887.   4.00   ..... (38)
Scheiner, Seth M. Negro Mecca: A History of the Negro in
New York City, 1865-1920. 1965.   8.50   2.75 (538)
Scoville, Joseph A. Old Merchants of New York City. 5 vols.
Repr. of 1870 ed.   Set: 97.50 ..... (297)
Select Cases of the Mayor's Court of New York City,
1674-1784 [Volume 2 of the American Legal Series].   43.00 38.00 (415)
Shepherd, William R. Story of New Amsterdam. Repr. of
1926 ed.   6.50   ..... (253)
Ullmann, Albert. A Landmark History of New York: Also the
Origin of Street Names. Repr. of 1901 ed.   7.00   ..... (404)
Van Rensselaer, Mrs. John King. The Goede Vrouw of
Mana-Ha-Ta [Manhattan]: At Home and in Society 1609-1760.
1898.   18.00 ..... (38)
Van Rensselaer, Mariana (Griswold). History of the City of
New York in the Seventeenth Century. 2 vols. 1909. Set: 75.00 ..... (2)
Wertenbaker, Thomas J. Father Knickerbocker Rebels:
New York City During the Revolution. Repr. of 1948 ed.   12.50 ..... (159)
Wilson, James Grant, ed. The Memorial History of the City
of the Year 1892. With Over 1,200 illustrations, plates,
and maps. 4 vols. 1892-1893.   Each: 60.00 ..... (2)
                                                Set: 235.00 ..... (2)

NIAGARA COUNTY

Sanford and Company. Illustrated History of Niagara County.
Repr. of 1878 ed. 480pp.   21.00 ..... (719)
Western New York Genealogical Society. Western New York
Genealogical Society Journal. Vol. I-1974. Vol. III-1976.
Membership includes WNYGS Journal, an aid to research
in Niagara County.   Subscription/Yr. 10.00 (828)

ONEIDA COUNTY

Schiro, George. Americans by Choice: History of the Italians
in Utica, New York. 1940. Illustrated.   11.00 ..... (38)

ONONDAGA COUNTY

Clark, Joshua V. H. Onondaga: or, Reminiscences of Earlier
and Later Times; Being a Series of Historical Sketches
Relative to Onondaga; with Notes on the Several Towns
in the County, and Oswego. 2 vols. 1849.   36.00 ..... (415)
Munson, Lillian S. Syracuse, the City That Salt Built.   6.95   ..... (570)
Rudolph, G. B. From a Minyan to a Community: History of
the Jews of Syracuse. 1970.   7.50   ..... (740)

ONTARIO COUNTY

Everts, Ensign and Everts. History of Ontario County,
1788-1876. Repr. of 1876 ed. 330pp.
Illustrations and maps.   21.00 ..... (719)

ORANGE COUNTY

Brooks, Thomas B. The Augusta Tract: Map and Manual, 1858.
1972.   8.95   ..... (429)
Nutt, John J., comp. Newburgh; her Institutions, Industries and
Leading Citizens. 1891. 340pp. B-OP 69335.   .... (778)

Predmore, Helen R. First Presbyterian Church, Chester,
New York: 1799-1950. 1974.
    Contains marriages, baptisms, burials.   9.45 ..... (429)

ORLEANS COUNTY

Manwaring, Adele, comp. The Records of Horace Hibbard (of
New York and Illinois). 1975. 50pp.
    Part I-Marriages of Murray, Orleans County, 1826-1837.
    Part II-Family records of Horace Hibbard and Fanny Perry.
    Part III-Journal of Horace Hibbard.   8.50 ..... (439)
Sanford and Company. Illustrated History of Orleans County.
    Repr. of 1879 ed. 360pp.   21.00 ..... (719)
Western New York Genealogical Society. Western New York
Genealogical Society Journal. Vol. I-1974. Vol. III-1976.
    Membership includes WNYGS Journal, an aid to research
    in Orleans County.   Subscription/Yr. 10.00 (828)

OSWEGO COUNTY

Cooper, Johnston Gaylord. Oswego in the French-English
Struggle in North America 1720-1760. 1961. 378pp.
BIP-62-01095.   .... (777)

OTSEGO COUNTY

Biographical Review. This volume contains biographical sketches
of the leading citizens of Otsego County, New York. 1893.
859pp. B-OP 67739.   .... (778)
Wardell, Bernice. The History of Laurens Township. 1975. 184pp.
    Indexed, photos, covers from 1769 to 1975, maps,
    appendix. Lists: Quakers, Revolutionary and Civil
    War Vets, etc. 6.00 (813)

PUTNAM COUNTY

Pelletreau, William S. History of Putnam County, New York.
    Repr. of 1886 ed.   16.00 ..... (625)

QUEENS COUNTY

Bunker, Mary P. Long Island Genealogies. Repr. of 1895 ed.
350pp.   15.00 ..... (274)
Onderdonk, Henry, Jr. Revolutionary Incidents of Queens
County, New York. Reprint. 90pp. Index.
    New index and foreword by Harriet Mott Stryker-Rodda.
    A collection of important historical facts and references
    to Revolutionary New York families, particularly of
    Long Island, from 1775 to 1784, supplementing the
    author's earlier work. 10.00 (608)
Thompson, Benjamin Franklin. History of Long Island From
Its Discovery and Settlement to the Present Time. 4 vols.
1918. Vol. 1-486pp. Vol. 2-484pp. Vol. 3-676pp.
Vol. 4-510pp. B-OP 15509.   .... (778)
Waller, Henry D. History of Town of Flushing, Long Island. 1899. 12.50 ..... (313)

SCHENECTADY COUNTY

Pearson, Jonathan. Contributions for the genealogies of the
Descendants of the First Settlers of the Patent and City of
Schenectady, from 1662 to 1800. 1873. 334pp. B-OP 35200   .... (778)

SCHOHARIE COUNTY

Roscoe, William E. Seventeen Hundred Thirteen. History
of Schoharie County, New York. With Illustrations and
and Biographical Sketches. 1882. 532pp. B-OP 70698. .... (778)
Warner, George H., comp. Military Records of Schoharie
County Veterans of Four Wars. 1891. 430pp. B-OP 67210. .... (778)

SCHUYLER COUNTY

Peirce, H. B. and D. H. Hurd. History of Schuyler County -
1854-1879. Repr. of 1879 ed. 226pp.
Taken from the Four County History. 21.00 ..... (719)

SENECA COUNTY

Everts, Ensign and Everts. History of Seneca County 1786-1876.
Repr. of 1876 ed. 280pp.
    Illustrations. Maps. Separate index included. 21.00 ..... (719)
_____. Ovid, Seneca County, New York. Repr. of 1876 ed. 80pp. 6.50 ..... (719)
French, J. H. Ovid - Plat Book. Repr. of 1858 ed. 8.00 (719)
_____. Seneca Falls - Plat Book. Repr. of 1856 ed. 8.00 (719)
_____. Waterloo - Plat Book. Repr. of 1855 ed. 8.00 (719)
Noyes, Dr. J. O. Lakes and Legends of Central New York.
Repr. of 1857 ed. 84pp.
    25 illustrations; reprinted from 'The National Magazine.' 3.50 (719)
Pomeroy, Whitman and Company. Covert and Lodi - Plat Book.
Repr. of 1874 ed. 8.00 (719)
_____. 1874 Atlas of Seneca County. Repr. of 1874 ed. 25pp. 25.00 ..... (719)
_____. Romulus and Varick - Plat Book. Repr. of 1874 ed. 8.00 (719)
Spafford, H. G. Seneca County, New York. Repr. of 1813 ed.
20pp.
    Taken from Spafford's Gazatteer of New York State. 3.00 (719)

SUFFOLK COUNTY

Howell, N. R. Know Suffolk. 1952. 4.00 ..... (858)
McDermott, Charles J. Suffolk County, New York. 1966. 4.95 ..... (325)

TIOGA COUNTY

Peirce, H. B. and D. H. Hurd. History of Tioga County.
Repr. of 1879 ed. 224pp.
Taken from the Four County History. 21.00 ..... (719)

TOMPKINS COUNTY

_____. History of Tompkins County. Repr. of 1879 ed. 288pp.
Taken from the Four County History. 21.00 ..... (719)

ULSTER COUNTY

Commemorative Biographical Record of Ulster County, New
York. 1896. 1338pp. B-OP 66997. .... (778)
Kelly, Arthur, comp., Baptism Record St. Paul's Lutheran
Church, Westcamp, 1708-1899. 1975. 105pp.
    Transcribed baptisms with index of parents and
    sponsors. 19.50 ..... (402)
Scott, Kenneth. "Ulster County, New York, County Records,
1693-1775." NGS Quarterly, Vol. 61, No. 4. 1973. 9pp. 3.50 (514)
Sylvester, Nathaniel Bartlett. History of Ulster County, New
York. 1880. Parts 1 and 2 -805pp. B-OP 69221. .... (778)

Versteeg, Dingman, tr., Kingston Papers: Kingston Court Records, 1661-1675 and Secretary's Papers, 1664-1675. 1976. 849pp.   40.00 ..... (274)

WARREN COUNTY

Writers' Program. Warren County; a History and Guide. 1942.   20.00 ..... (2)

WAYNE COUNTY

Everts, Ensign and Everts. History of Wayne County 1789-1877. Repr. of 1877 ed. 310pp.
Illustrations. Maps.   21.00 ..... (719)
Morrison, Wayne E., Sr. History of Clyde, New York. 1969. 116pp.   5.50 ..... (719)

WESTCHESTER COUNTY

Baird, Charles W. Chronicle of a Border Town: History of Rye, Westchester County, New York, 1660-1870. Repr. of 1871 ed.   27.50 ..... (313)
Barr, Lockwood. Ancient Town of Pelham, Westchester County, New York. 1946.   5.00 ..... (195)
Hufeland, Otto. Westchester County During the American Revolution, 1775-1783. Repr. of 1926 ed.   15.00 ..... (313)
Lee, Frances Cook. Historical Records: North Castle - New Castle. 336pp.
   Colonial history and minutes of town meetings, 1736-1791. Maps. Patents. Census lists. 5.60 (529)
Walker, Eldon H. Genealogical Record Sources for Westchester County, New York. In Process.   .... (277)

WYOMING COUNTY

Beers' History of Wyoming County. Repr. of 1880 ed. 384pp. With added name index.   21.00 ..... (719)
Western New York Genealogical Society. Western New York Genealogical Society Journal. 1974-
   Membership includes Western New York Genealogical Society Journal - an aid to research in Wyoming County.
   Subscription/yr: 10.00 (828)

North Carolina

STATEWIDE REFERENCES

Baker, Gloria Beth. Dissenters in Colonial North Carolina. 1970. 227pp. BIP-71-11668.   .... (777)
Bassett, John Spencer. Slavery in the State of North Carolina. 1899.   5.00 ..... (2)
Boyd, William K. History of North Carolina, the Federal Period. Repr. of 1919 ed. 415pp.   18.00 ..... (638)
Butler, Lindley Smith. The Coming of the Revolution in North Carolina, 1763-1776. 1971. 311pp.   .... (777)
Connor, R. D. W. History of North Carolina, the Colonial and Revolutionary Periods. Repr. of 1919 ed. 528pp.   21.00 ..... (638)
_____. North Carolina, Rebuilding an Ancient Commonwealth, 2 vols. Repr. of 1929 ed. 1370pp.
   Set: 48.00 ..... (638)
   Each: 24.00 ..... (638)

Cutten, George B. Silversmiths of North Carolina. Rev. ed.
1948. xxvi, 140pp.
    Contains 207 sketches, over 90 illustrations, and 34
    silversmiths' marks.   15.00   ..... (543)
Fagg, Daniel Webster, Jr. Carolina, 1663-1683: The Founding
of a Proprietary. 363pp. BIP-70-22882.   .... (777)
Ginns, Patsy and J.L. Osborne, Jr. Rough Weather Makes
Good Timber. 1977. 240pp.
    Old-timers tell about life in the old days - taped inter-
    views, edited and transcribed.   9.50   ..... (544)
Hamilton, J.G. deRoulhac. History of North Carolina Since
1860. Repr. of 1919 ed. 440pp.   18.00   ..... (638)
Hoyt, William Henry. The Mecklenburg Declaration of
Independence. Repr. of 1907 ed.   12.95   ..... (176)
Johnson, F. Roy. Tales from Old Carolina. 1965.   5.95   ..... (393)
Kay, Marvin Lawrence Michael. The Institutional Background
to the Regulation in Colonial North Carolina. 622pp.
BIP-64-04080.   .... (777)
Koesy, Sheldon Fred. Continuity and Change in North Carolina,
1775-1789. 313pp. BIP-63-07828.   .... (777)
Leach, Douglas E. The Northern Colonial Frontier, 1607-
1763. 1973. illus.   7.95   ..... (535)
McCain, Paul M. The County Court in North Carolina Before
1750. 1954.   7.50   ..... (2)
Paschal, Herbert Richard, Jr. Proprietary North Carolina:
A Study in Colonial Government. 655pp. BIP-61-03180.   .... (777)
Powell, William S. The Proprietors of Carolina. Repr. of
1963 ed. 70pp. illus.
    Reasons given for the granting of the Charter of the
    Proprietors, and descent of the title outlined. Sketches
    of the eight original Lords Proprietors; also
    biographical sketches of forty-one later owners. 50 (543)
Schmidt, William John. The North Carolina Delegates in the
Continental Congress, 1774-1781. 401pp. BIP-69-01674.   .... (777)
Williams, Samuel C. History of the Lost State of Franklin.
Rev. ed. Repr. of 1933 ed.
    Franklin included southwestern Virginia, a portion of
    present day northwestern North Carolina and north-
    eastern Tennessee.   17.50   ..... (612)

Research Aids

Clay, Orr and Stuart, eds. North Carolina Atlas: Portrait
of a Changing Southern State. 1975. 350pp.   17.95   ..... (544)
Jones, Houston Gwynne. The Public Archives of North
Carolina, 1663-1903. 439pp. BIP-65-04862.   .... (777)

Listed below are the names of professional genealogists willing to undertake research for
a fee within the state of North Carolina, in areas specified in their ads:

McGrew, Ellen Z. North Carolina Census Records, 1784-1900 (Archives Information Circular 2). 15pp. Brief description of background and history of state census of 1784-1787 and federal decennial censuses of 1790-1900. Various types of information included in each census are described. ..... .25 (543)

Neal, Lois S., comp. Genealogical Index to D. H. Hill's 'North Carolina; Vol. 4 of Confederate . . . Over. . .' 1975. 65pp. Military rank, civil titles used only to distinguish between two given names; women indexed by maiden and married names when given. 5.50 (520)

Powell, William. North Carolina Gazetteer. Repr. of 1968 ed. 578pp. 5.50 (544)

"Published County Records of North Carolina (a Bibliography)" The Ridge Runners, Vol. 4. 1976. 13pp. .... (859)

Military

Barrett, John G. Sherman's March Through the Carolinas. 1956. 6.95 ..... (544)

Becker, Donald Eugene. North Carolina, 1754-1763: An Economic,Political and Military History of North Carolina During the Great War for the Empire. 297pp. BIP-71-20954. .... (777)

Davis, Curtis Carroll. Revolution's Godchild: Birth, Death and Regeneration of Society of Cincinnati in North Carolina. 240pp. 18.95 ..... (544)

DeForest, Bartholomew S. Random Sketches and Wandering Thoughts; Or, What I Saw in Camp, On the March, the Bivouac, the Battlefield and Hospital, While with the Army in Virginia, North and South, Carolina, During the Late Rebellion. 1866. B-BH 16108 .... (778)

Fanning, Nathaniel. Fanning's Narrative, Being the Memoirs of Nathaniel Fanning, an Officer of the Revolutionary Navy, 1778-1783, ed. John S. Barnes. 1912. 10.00 ..... (38)

Ganyard, Robert L. North Carolina During the American Revolution, the First Phase 1774-1777. 1963. 473pp. BIP-63-06996. .... (777)

Iobst, Richard William. North Carolina Mobilizes: Nine Crucial Months December 1860 - August 1861. 1968. 757pp. BIP-69-10171. .... (777)

Jordan, Weymouth T., Jr., ed. North Carolina Troops, 1861-1865, Vol. V - Infantry. 1975. xvii, 678pp. index. Thousands of names of North Carolinians who served in artillery and cavalry units and in the first three infantry regiments as well as several miscellaneous infantry units. 20.00 ..... (543)

Lemmon, Sarah M. Frustrated Patriots: North Carolina and the War of 1812. 1973. 10.50 ..... (544)

Rankin, Hugh F. North Carolina in the American Revolution. 1975. viii, 75pp. illus. 1.00 (543)

Troxler, George Wesley. The Homefront in Revolutionary North Carolina. 1970. 268pp. BIP-71-03607. .... (777)

Waugh, Betty Linney. The Upper Yadkin Valley in the American Revolution: Benjamin Cleveland, Symbol of Continuity. 176pp. BIP-72-13777. .... (777)

Wheeler, Earl Milton. The Role of the North Carolina Militia
in the Beginning of the American Revolution. 1969. 237pp.
BIP-69-20510.   .... (777)
Whitaker, Bessie L. Provincial Council and Committee of
Safety in North Carolina (James Sprunt Study in History
and Political Science). 1.25 (544)

Religious and Ethnic Groups

Franklin, John Hope. The Free Negro in North Carolina,
1790-1860. Repr. of 1943 ed. x, 271pp.   10.00 ..... (662)
_____. Free Negro in North Carolina, 1790-1860. 1971.   ..... 2.25 (546)
Hilty, Hiram Horace. North Carolina Quakers and Slavery.
381pp. BIP-69-16757.   .... (777)
McKiever, Charles F. Slavery and Emigration of North
Carolina Friends. 1970.   4.95 ..... (393)
Meyer, Duane Gilbert. The Scottish Highlanders in North
Carolina, 1733-1776. 1956. 297pp. BIP-00-16125.   .... (777)
Morgan, David Taft, Jr. The Great Awakening in the
Carolinas and Georgia, 1740-1775. 288pp. BIP-69-01652.   .... (777)
Smith, Cortland Victor. Church Organization as an Agency
of Social Control. Church Discipline in North Carolina,
1800-1860. 361pp. BIP-68-02235.   .... (777)
Stephens, Alonzo Theodore. An Account of the Attempts at
Establishing a Religious Hegemony in Colonial North
Carolina 1663-1773. 1955. 299pp. BIP-00-15118.   ,.... ..... (777)
Stokes, Durward Turrentine. The Clergy of the Carolinas
and the American Revolution. 352pp. BIP-69-01684.   .... (777)

Records

Broughton, Carrie L. Marriage and Death Notices in
Raleigh Register, North Carolina Gazette 1846-1847.
Repr. of 1949-1950 ed. 207pp.   10.00 ..... (274)
Curtis, Mary Barnett. Abstracts of Reports by Francis
X. Martin . . . in the Superior Courts of Law and
Equity. Repr. of 1843 ed.
      Covers period from 1797 to 1806.   ..... 7.50 (371)
Newsome, A. R., ed. Records of Emigrants From England
and Scotland to North Carolina, 1774-1775. 1976.   ..... 1.00 (543)
North Carolina. (Colony and State). The Colonial Records
of North Carolina (1662-1776). 10 vols. 1886-1890.
Vols. 1-10:   Set: 675.00 ..... (2)
                                                Each: 67.50 ..... (2)
North Carolina. (Colony and State). The State Records
of North Carolina (1777-1790). 16 vols. 1895-1905.
Vols. 11-26:   Set: 1160.00 ..... (2)
                                                Each: 72.50 ..... (2)
North Carolina. (Colony and State). Index to Colonial and
State Records of North Carolina (1622-1790). 4 vols.
1909-1914.   Set: 270.00 ..... (2)
Vols. 27-30:   Each: 67.50 ..... (2)
"North Carolina Deaths, Marriages, and Legal Notices."
The Ridge Runners, Vol. 4. 1976. 22pp.   .... (859)
Petty, Gerald. Index of the 1840 Federal Census of North
Carolina. 1974. vi+273pp.
      One alphabetical list. About 95,000 name-page
      entries, about 2,000 surname cross-references.   70.00 ..... (593)

....

Robertson, Clara H. Kansas Territorial Settlers of 1860 Who
Were Born in Tennessee, Virginia, North Carolina and
South Carolina. 1976. 187pp.   17.50   ..... (274)
Smith, Dora Wilson. 1810 Census Index. 1977. In Process.   .... (330)

ANSON COUNTY

Holcomb, Brent, G.R.S. Anson County, North Carolina Deed
Abstracts, Volume II - 1757-1766. 1975. 65pp. index. 13.00 (343)
_____. Anson County, North Carolina Wills and Estates, 1749-
1795. 1975. 29pp. index. 8.50 (343)
Johnson, William Perry and Dorothy W. Potter. 1800 Federal
Census of North Carolina - Anson County. 1975. 76pp. 7.25 (615)

ASHE COUNTY

_____. 1800 Federal Census of North Carolina - Ashe County.
1975. 31pp. 3.25 (615)

BEAUFORT COUNTY

_____. 1800 Federal Census of North Carolina - Beaufort
County. 1976. 56pp. 5.25 (615)

BERTIE COUNTY

_____. 1800 Federal Census of North Carolina - Bertie County.
1975. 66pp. 6.25 (615)

BLADEN COUNTY

_____. 1800 Federal Census of North Carolina - Bladen County.
1976. 58pp. 6.25 (615)

BRUNSWICK COUNTY

_____. 1800 Federal Census of North Carolina - Brunswick
County. 1975. 32pp. 3.25 (615)

BUNCOMBE COUNTY

"Buncombe County, North Carolina, First Term of Court, 1792
(Minutes)." The Ridge Runners, Vol. 4. 1976. 4pp.   .... (859)
Johnson, William Perry and Dorothy W. Potter. 1800 Federal
Census of North Carolina - Buncombe County. 1975. 60pp. 6.25 (615)

BURKE COUNTY

_____. 1800 Federal Census of North Carolina - Burke County.
1976. 99pp. 9.25 (615)

CABARRUS COUNTY

_____. 1800 Federal Census of North Carolina - Cabarrus
County. 1976. In Process.   .... (615)

CAMDEN COUNTY

_____. 1800 Federal Census of North Carolina - Camden
County. 1976. In Process.   .... (615)

CARTERET COUNTY

_____. 1800 Federal Census of North Carolina.- Carteret
County. 1976. 47pp. 4.25 (615)

CASWELL COUNTY

_____. 1800 Federal Census of North Carolina - Caswell
County. 1976. In Process.   .... (615)

CHATHAM COUNTY

_____. 1800 Federal Census of North Carolina - Chatham
County. 1976. In Process.   .... (615)

CHOWAN COUNTY

_____. 1800 Federal Census of North Carolina - Chowan
County. 1976. In Process.   .... (615)

COLUMBUS COUNTY

"1850 Federal Census, Columbus County, North Carolina."
SGE Quarterly, Vol. XVI, all issues. 1975. 48pp. 3.00 (706)

CRAVEN COUNTY

Johnson, William Perry and Dorothy W. Potter. 1800 Federal
Census of North Carolina - Craven County. 1976. In Process. .... (615)

CUMBERLAND COUNTY

_____. 1800 Federal Census of North Carolina - Cumberland
County. 1976. In Process.   .... (615)

CURRITUCK COUNTY

_____. 1800 Federal Census of North Carolina - Currituck
County. 1976. In Process.   .... (615)

DARE COUNTY

Stick, David. Dare County: A History. 1975. x, 64pp. illus.
Brief history which began with earliest English attempts
at colonization in the 1580's. Information on the Lost
Colony and the Wright Brothers' first flight.   ..... .50 (543)

DAVIE COUNTY

Wall, James W. Davie County: A Brief History. 1976.   ..... 1.50 (543)

FORSYTH COUNTY

Hendricks, J. Edwin and Adelzide Fries. Forsyth, History of
a County on the March. 368pp.   6.95 ..... (544)
James, Hunter. The Quiet People of the Land: Story of North
Carolina Moravians. Fall 1976. 160pp.
    Revolutionary era - study of North Carolina Moravians. 7.95 ..... (544)
Stanley, D. W., A.E. Sheek and H.R. Hartman. Forsyth County,
North Carolina Cemetery Records, Volume I. 1976. 240pp.
    All cemeteries in Abbotts Creek, Belews Creek, Bethania,
    and Broadbay Townships. 9.00 (715)
_____. Forsyth County, North Carolina Cemetery Records,
Volume II. 1976.
    All cemeteries in Clemmonsville, Kernersville, Lewisville,
    Middle Fork, and Old Richmond Townships.   .... (715)
_____. Forsyth County, North Carolina Cemetery Records, Volume
III. 1976.
    All cemeteries in Old Town and Salem Chapel Townships. .... (715)

_____. Forsyth County, North Carolina Cemetery Records,
Volume IV. 1977. In Process.
    All cemeteries in South Fork and Vienna Townships.   ••••• ••••• (715)
_____. Forsyth County, North Carolina Cemetery Records,
Volume V. 1977. In Process.
    All cemeteries in Winston-Salem.   ••••• ••••• (715)

GRANVILLE COUNTY

Mathis, Harry R. Along the Border. A History of Virgilina,
Virginia, and the Surrounding Area in Halifax and Mecklenburg Counties in Virginia and Person and Granville Counties
in North Carolina. 1964. 344pp.
    General information about the area; histories of
    churches and organizations; many names included,
    making book of interest to genealogists.   15.00 •••• (477)

GUILFORD COUNTY

Stein, Nancy Hawlick. Court Minutes of Guilford - Insolvents,
Guardianships, etc. 1781-1790 (?). 1977. In Process.   ••••• ••••• (720)

HAYWOOD COUNTY

Neal, Lois S., comp. Genealogical Index to W. C. Allen's
Annals of Haywood County, North Carolina 1935. 1976.
    4,000 surnames; frequently specific about in/out
    migration.   ••••• ••••• (520)

HENDERSON COUNTY

Patton, Sadie S. The Story of Henderson County. Repr. of
1947 ed. 310pp. illus.   16.00 ••••• (638)

LENOIR COUNTY

Powell, William S. Annals of Progress: The Story of Lenoir
County and Kinston, North Carolina. 1963. 107pp.   ••••• .50 (543)

MECKLENBURG COUNTY

Holcomb, Brent, G.R.S. Mecklenburg County, North Carolina
Deed Abstract, Volume I: 1763-1768. 1976. 86pp. index.   ••••• 17.50 (343)

NASH COUNTY

Watson, Joseph W. Abstracts of Early Deeds of Nash County,
North Carolina Books 1-6, 1778-1813. 1966. 299pp.   15.00 •••• (371)

NEW HANOVER COUNTY

Lennon, Donald R. and Ida Brooks Kellam, eds. The Wilmington
Town Book, 1743-1778. 1973. xliii,266pp. illus. index.
    Journal of colonial town includes information on consumer
    protection, price controls, maintenance of roads, fire
    protection, etc.   10.00 ••••• (543)

ORANGE COUNTY

Markham, A.B. Land Grants to Early Settlers in Old Orange
County, North Carolina. 1973.   ••••• 10.40 (464)

PERSON COUNTY

Mathis, Harry R. Along the Border. A History of Virgilina,
Virginia, and the Surrounding Area in Halifax and Mecklenburg Counties in Virginia and Person and Granville Counties,
in North Carolina. 1964. 344pp.
General information about the area; histories of
churches and organizations; many names included,
making book of interest to genealogists.   15.00 ..... (477)

POLK COUNTY

Patton, Sadie S. Sketches of Polk County History. Repr. of
1950 ed. 175pp.   12.00 ..... (638)

ROWAN COUNTY

Brawley, James S. Rowan County: A Brief History. 1974.
xiv,177pp. illus.
Rowan, populous Piedmont county created in 1753,
has had a colorful, exciting part to play in the
history of North Carolina. 1.50 (543)

WAKE COUNTY

Markham, A.B. Land Grants to Early Settlers in Present
Wake County. 1973.   ..... 10.40 (464)

norfh Dakota

STATEWIDE REFERENCES

Milligan, Edward. Dakota Twilight. 1976. 190pp.
History of Standing Rock Sioux Indian Reservation -
affects of Custer defeat on Indian history.   8.50   ..... (224)
North Dakota Historical Society of Germans from Russia.
Heritage Review. Volumes 1-14. 1971-1976. 40-56pp.
per issue. 2.50 (55)
Sallet, Richard. Russian-German Settlements in the United
States, tr. LaVern Rippley and Armand Bauer. Repr. of
1931 ed. 207pp.
Geographical distribution of Black Sea and Volga
Germans, maps, pictures, place-names of former
German colonies in Russia, biographical sketches,
index.   9.50   ..... (55)

Ohio

STATEWIDE REFERENCES

Chaddock, Robert Emmet. Ohio Before 1850; A Study of the
Early Influence of Pennsylvania and Southern Population in
Ohio. 1908.   10.00 ..... (2)
Craig, Neville B., ed. The Olden Time; A Monthly Publication
Devoted to the Preservation of Documents and Other Authentic
Information in Relation to the Early Explorations and Settle-

ment and Improvement of the Country Around the Head of the
Ohio. 2 vols. Repr. of the periodical issued January 1846-
December 1847. 1876.   55.00   ..... (415)
Frary, L. T. Early Homes of Ohio.   6.00   ..... (699)
Griffiths, D. Two Years' Residence in the New Settlements of
Ohio. Repr. of 1835.   6.75   ..... (778)
Jeffries, Ewel. A Short Biography of John Leeth, With an Account
of His Life Among the Indians, ed. Reuben Gold Thwaites.
70pp.
    The experiences of a trader-hunter in the Indian country
    of Pennsylvania and Ohio, including his captivity and
    life in Indian camps.   5.75   ..... (38)
Jones, David. A Journal of Two Visits Made to Some Nations of
Indians on the West Side of the River Ohio in the Years 1772
and 1773. 1774.   6.00   ..... (38)
King, Rufus. Ohio: First Fruits of the Ordinance of 1787. New
ed. with a Supplementary Chapter by Theodore Clarke Smith.
1903.   23.00   ..... (2)
Maxwell, Fay. Ohio Genealogical Helper. 1975. 64pp.
    A quarterly magazine to make public research data on
    location of materials today, know how of research, many
    aids, begins with Franklin County, Volume 1 and 2,
    Volume 3 aids to genealogy research before 1800, other
    aids; Volume 4 is on Washington County, Ohio, then
    runs alphabetically. 4.95 (473)
Ohio Genealogical Society. The Report (quarterly); Newsletters
(monthly). 1976.
    Bible records, county records, member's Five-Generation
    Charts, family records, etc; indexed at end of each year's
    publication. 10.00 (554)
Petty, Gerald. Ohio 1810 Tax Duplicate. 1977. 230(?)pp.
    One alphabetical list of taxpayer, acreage, surveyor's
    description, county, tax: sometimes township, original
    entrant, watercourse, type of title, etc. About 26,000
    land parcels. In process.   .... (593)
Siedel, Frank. The Ohio Story. 1973   6.95   3.95 (420)

Listed below are the names of professional genealogists willing to undertake research for
a fee within the state of Ohio, in areas specified in their ads:

Stewart, Eliza Daniel. Memories of the Crusade: A Thrilling Account
of the Great Uprising of the Women of Ohio in 1873, Against the
Liquor Crime, by Mother Stewart. 2d ed. 1889.   24.00   ..... (38)

Research Aids

Larson, David R., et al, eds. Guide to Manuscripts Collections
and Institutional Records in Ohio. 1974. 315pp.
This guide lists the many manuscripts to be found in
public, college, and historical society libraries and
museums. Included are the large holdings of the Cincinnati, Oberlin College, Kent State University, Hiram
College and Northwest Ohio-Great Lakes Research Center in Bowling Green, Ohio; archives of the Ohio Synod
of the Lutheran Church of America at Wittenberg University; and the Quaker collection at Wilmington College.
There are an outstanding number of churches represented, eighty in Franklin County, and forty in Mont-
gomery County. End maps, notes, index.   8.00   ..... (872)
Maxwell, Fay. Ohio Indian, Revolutionary and War of 1812
Trails, Indexes to Ohio Counties and Townships.
Repr. of 1968 ed. 75pp.
Contains all maps, directives to do lineage work in
Ohio, plus erection dates of counties, index of
townships which aids filmviewing. 8 1/2 x 11.   .....   3.95 (473)
_____. Index and Excerpts for Cutter's History of Ordinance
of 1787, Ohio's First Law. 1974. 20pp.
Lists 258 signers, rank, state of birth, service.
Ordinance of 1787 covered Ohio, Indiana, Illinois,
Michigan, Wisconsin, part of Minnesota. 8 1/2 x 11.   .....   2.00 (473)
_____. Index to Charles Galbreath's History of 1900 Ohio
Leaders. 1974. 20pp.   8 1/2 x 11.   .....   2.00 (473)
Smith, Clifford Neal. Federal Land Series Volume 1 1788-1810.
1972. 369pp.
A calendar of archival materials on the Land Patents
issued by the United States Government with Subject,
Tract, and Name Indexes.   20.00   ..... (22)
_____. Federal Land Series: A Calendar of Archival Materials
on the Land Patents Issued by the U. S. Government. With
Subject, Tract, and Name Indexes. 2 vols. Vol. 2-416pp.
1973.
Revolutionary War Bounty-Land Warrants of the Federal
Government, covering counties of Coshocton, Delaware,
Franklin, Guernsey, Holmes, Knox, Licking, Marion,
Morrow, Muskingum, Tuscarawas. It tells to whom
land was issued.   20.00   ..... (22)
Walling, H. F. Ohio Atlas 1868. Repr. 68pp.   15.00   6.00 (80)

Military

Clark, Peter. Cincinnati Black Brigade: Being a Report of
Its Labors and a Muster-Roll of Its Members; Together
with Various Orders, Speeches, Etc. Relating to It.
Repr. of 1864 ed. 4.50 (38)
Garner, Grace. Index to Roster of Ohio Soldiers War of
1812. 1974. 119pp.
Indexes a reprint of the Roster of Ohio Soldiers of
War of 1812 by Genealogical Publishing Company,
Boston 1967.   .....   6.50 (212)

De Rosenthal, Gustavus. Journal of a Volunteer Expedition to
Sandusky, from May 24 to June 13, 1782. (Reprinted from
The Pennsylvania Magazine of History and Biography,
Vol. XVIII, No. 2.) 1894.   5.00   ..... (38)

Religious and Ethnic Groups

Clossman, Richard Hunter. A History of the Organization
and Development of the Baptist Churches in Ohio From
1789 to 1907, With Particular Reference to the Ohio
Baptist Convention. 1971. 352pp. BIP-71-27448.   ....⋅.. (777)
Elliott, Errol T. Quakers on the American Frontier.
1969. 434pp.
An account of Quakers who migrated from the
East to Ohio and central Indiana during the early
1800's.   4.95   ..... (255)
Fielding, Robert Kent. The Growth of the Mormon Church
in Kirtland, Ohio. 1957. 321pp. BIP-00-22685.   .... (777)
Hayden, Amos S. Early History of the Disciples in the
Western Reserve, Ohio: With Biographical Sketches of
the Principal Agents in their Religous Movement. 1875.   22.00   ..... (38)
Hickok, Charles Thomas. The Negro in Ohio, 1802-1870. 1896.   14.50   ..... (2)
Lupold, Harry Forrest. The Forgotten People: The Woodland
Erie. 69pp.
History of now extinct Indian tribe of the Ohio Valley.   6.00   3.00 (224)
MacLean. Shakers of Ohio. Repr. of 1907 ed.   17.50   ..... (612)
Overton, Julie, tr. The Ministers and Churches of the Central
German Conference. Repr. 84pp.
Biographies of German Methodist Ministers and
History of churches in Ohio, South Michigan, East
Pennsylvania, Indiana, and East Kentucky. 6.75 (330)
Smith, Clifford Neal and Anna Piszczan-Czaja Smith. "Some
German Speaking Immigrants in Ohio and Kentucky, 1869."
NGS Quarterly, Vol. 62, No. 1. 1974. 16pp. 3.50 (514)

Newspapers

History of Ohio Journalism, 1793-1933. Repr. of 1933 ed.   10.50   ..... (394)
Ohio State Journal. Published in Columbus. Dec. 1841 - Dec.
1920. [A few issues missing.] 350 rolls.
Microfilm of the original papers. Individual rolls
covering a specific time span may be ordered.
Prices vary $15 to $30 per roll.   .... (870)

Records

Flavell, Carol Willsey, C. G. Steubenville (Ohio) Federal Land
Office Records. 1976. c150pp.
Covers land patents for Eastern Ohio counties; includes
place of prior residence of purchaser. Indexed.   .... (239)
Maxwell, Fay. Census of 1800 Northwest Territory, Before
Ohio's Statehood; Marriages 1791-1802 Index. 1974. 24pp.
Index of census plus marriages index for 1791-1802,
Washington County, before Ohio's statehood,
southeast quarter of state, plus cemetery data
of early burials. 8 1/2 x 11.   .....   5.95 (473)

Mitchener, ed. Ohio Annals, Tuscarawas and Muskingum Valleys
(5 counties), Plus Index, 1750-1850, Land Offices.
[Fay Maxwell, author, Index]. Repr. of 1876 ed. 400+pp.
Work was edited by C. H. Mitchener of New Philadelphia,
Ohio, covers eastern part of state up to the Greenville
Treaty Line. Set: 13.00 (473)
Maxwell, Fay. Index to Ohio Annals, Tuscarawas and
Muskingum Valleys Plus Maps. Repr. of 1875 ed. 30pp. 5.95 (473)
Riegel, Mayburt Stephenson. Early Ohioans' Residences from
the Land Grant Records. 1976. 62pp.
Earliest land records of Land Offices originally located
in Steubenville, Cincinnati, Refugee Tract, Chillicothe,
Canton-Wooster, Zanesville and Donation Tract Lands
searched for names of first land owners whose place
of residence was given, location of land, date of
purchase. 7.00 (554)
Smith, Marjorie, ed. Ohio Marriages Extracted From the
Old Northwest Genealogical Quarterly. Repr. of
1898-1913 eds. 356pp.
Marriages for Franklin County (1803-1830),
Jackson County (1816-1826), Licking County
(1808-1820), Marion County (1824-1825),
Pickaway County (1810-1815), Ross County
(1803-1806), Trumbull County (1800-1803),
Washington County (1789-1822). 15.00 ..... (330)

ASHTABULA COUNTY

The Ashtabula County Genealogical Society. Ancestor Hunt
Volume I. 1974. 44pp.
Society Quarterly featuring family and Bible records,
local newspaper articles, cemetery and vital
statistics, queries. 3.00 (39)
_____. Ancestor Hunt Volume II. 1975. 129pp.
Society Quarterly featuring family and Bible records,
local newspaper articles, cemetery and vital statistics,
queries. 5.00 (39)
_____. Index to Ancestor Hunt, Volumes I and II. 1976. 56pp. 1.75 (39)
_____. Ancestor Hunt Volume III. 1977. 120pp.
Society Quarterly featuring family and Bible
records, local newspaper articles, cemetery and
vital statistics, queries. 6.00 (39)
_____. "History of Colebrook, Ohio to 1876, From a
Handwritten Account Found in a Scrapbook. A Continuing
Article, not yet complete." Ancestor Hunt, Vol. II,
Nos. 2,3,4. 3pp. 1.25 (39)
_____. Surname Directory. 1976. 50pp.
Listing of member's interests by family surname,
locale and approximate dates. 1.75 (39)
_____. Union List of Materials on Genealogy and Local
History in the Libraries of Ashtabula County, Ohio.
1974. 102pp. 2.75 (39)
Fox, Carol Thomas. "Andover Area 'Round Robin,' Turn of the
Century Schoolmates Who Corresponded. Listing of Correspond
ents." Ancestor Hunt, Vols. I,II, Nos. 1,3. 1974, 1975.
Volume I Each: 1.00 (39)
Volume II Each: 1.25 (39)

•••

Legeza, Louise Passmore. "Justice of the Peace, Aaron
   Wright, Docket 1813-1817 at Salem, now Conneaut, Ohio.
   Some Abstracts." Ancestor Hunt, Vol. II, Nos. 3,4. 1975.   ..... 1.25 (39)
Lewis, Helen. Dead Soldiers of Ashtabula County."
   Ancestor Hunt, Vol. I, No. 3; Vol. II, Nos. 1,2,3. 1974, 1975.
   A continuing article, not completed.
      Volume I   Each: 1.00 (39)
      Volume II, Nos. 1,2,3.   Each: 1.25 (39)
Magons, Judith Smith. "Military Pensioners Living in
   Ashtabula County, Ohio, in 1840." Ancestor Hunt,
   Vol. II, Nos. 1,2,3. 1975.   ..... 1.25 (39)
Peet, The Reverand Stephen D. The Ashtabula Disaster.
   Repr. of 1877 ed. 208pp.
      Narrative of tragic bridge collapse on the Lake Shore
      and Michigan Southern Railroad at Ashtabula, Ohio,
      over 85 perished.   10.50 ..... (39)
Sargent, Martin P. Pioneer Sketches: Scenes and Incidents
   of Former Days. Repr. of 1891 ed. 512pp.
      Humorous account of biographical sketches and
      poems dealing primarily with life in the 1800's in
      Ashtabula County, Ohio, Erie and Crawford Counties,
      Pennsylvania. New index added.   13.00 ..... (39)
Williams Brothers. The History of Ashtabula County, Ohio,
   1798-1878. Repr. of 1878 ed. 370pp.
      Vast amounts of original source material on all
      phases of county's history, includes War of 1812 and
      Civil War Rosters, new comprehensive index added. 23.00 ..... (39)

ATHENS COUNTY

Maxwell, Fay. Athens County, Trimble Township History,
   About 200 pages, 1797-1960. Repr. of 1965 ed. 200pp.
      Athens County, Ohio, Trimble Township history,
      entire family lineage (not all included) but excellent
      source. 8 1/2 x 11, about 2000 names added, plus
      index and maps. 15.00 (473)

BELMONT COUNTY

Caldwell, J. A. History of Belmont and Jefferson Counties,
   Ohio. Repr. of 1880 ed. 642pp.
      22,000 every name index added (additional 125 page index). 25.00 ..... (716)

BUTLER COUNTY

McBride, James. Pioneer Biography. Sketches of the Lives
   of Some of the Early Settlers of Butler County, Ohio.
   2 vols. 1869-1871. Vol. 1-378pp. Vol. 2-294pp. B-BH 16814. .... (778)

CHAMPAIGN COUNTY

Maxwell, Fay. Index to Urbana and Champaign History,
   Plus Excerpts of 1812 History. 1974. 12pp.
      1812 armies mobilized here. 8 1/2 x 11.   ..... 1.50 (473)

COSHOCTON COUNTY

Smith, Clifford Neal. Federal Land Series, Volume 2: 1799-1835.
1973. 416pp.
Land bounty warrants telling to whom the land in the
Military District of Ohio, of which Coshocton County
was a part, was originally issued.   20.00   ..... (22)

CUYAHOGA COUNTY

Barton, Josef. Peasants and Strangers: Italians, Rumanians,
and Slovaks in an American City 1890-1950. 1975.   12.00   ..... (319)
Ferroni, Charles D. The Italians in Cleveland: A Study in
Assimilation. 292pp. BIP-70-11339.   .... (777)
MacCabe, Julius P. Bolivar. A Directory of the Cities of
Cleveland and Ohio, for the Years 1837-1838. 1837. 192pp.
B-BH 5249.   .... (778)

DELAWARE COUNTY

History of Delaware County and Ohio. 1880. 814pp. B-OP 66456.   .... (778)
Smith, Clifford Neal. Federal Land Series, Volume 2: 1799-1835.
1973. 416pp.
Land bounty warrants telling to whom the land in the
Military District of Ohio, of which Delaware County
was a part, was originally issued.   20.00   ..... (22)

FAIRFIELD COUNTY

Maxwell, Fay and Richard Bischoff. Index to Hervey Scott's
Fairfield County History. 1976. 115pp.
1787-1887. Over 7,500 names. 9.00 (473)
Maxwell, Fay. Index to Wiseman's History of Fairfield County.
1973. 34pp.
Includes 1806 taxpayer list. 5.00 (473)

FAYETTE COUNTY

Rankin and Robinson. Fayette County Chancery and Common Pleas   *
Court Records, 1828-1878. 1957. 186pp. 9.35 (330)

FRANKLIN COUNTY

Babics, Walter V. Assimilation of Yugoslavs in Franklin County,
Ohio. Repr. of 1964 ed.   7.00   ..... (631)
Maxwell, Fay. Living in a Landmark. Ohio - Franklin County -
Pictorial History of German Homes. 1973. 40pp.
Book covers early German homes, some history of
living in German Village landmark. 3.00 (473)
_____. Ohio: Franklin County German Village Abstract History,
a First, Landgrants Data to 1900. 1976. 200pp.
Data taken from abstracts of owners of homes in German
Village. Continuation of Volume I - Irish History. 15.00 (473)
_____. Ohio, Franklin County, German Village and Brewery
History. 1971. 44pp. index.
Some original data here. 2.50 (473)
_____. Ohio: Franklin County, Irish Refugee Tract and Irish
History. Entire Tract and Nova Scotia History. 1973. c200pp.
Begins with Irish landgrants up to 1840, but takes Irish
history back to Nova Scotia and Ireland. Includes refugees
of Iowa and New York. 15.00 (473)

Smith, Clifford Neal. Federal Land Series, Volume 2: 1799-1835.
1973. 416pp.
Land bounty warrants telling to whom the land in the
Military District of Ohio, of which Franklin County
was a part, was originally issued.   20.00   ..... (22)
Smith, Marjorie, ed. Ohio Marriages Extracted From the
Old Northwest Genealogical Quarterly. Repr. of
1898-1913 ed. 356pp.
Marriages for Franklin County (1803-1830), Jackson
County (1816-1826), Licking County (1808-1820),
Marion County (1824-1825), Pickaway County (1810-1815),
Ross County (1803-1806), Trumbull County (1800-1803),
Washington County (1789-1822).   15.00   ..... (330)

FULTON COUNTY

Geitgey, Frances. Index to 1860 Federal Census of Fulton
County, Ohio. 1975. 36pp.   .... (439)

GREENE COUNTY

Santmyer, Helen H. Ohio Town. 1963.   5.75   ..... (555)

GUERNSEY COUNTY

Smith, Clifford Neal. Federal Land Series, Volume 2: 1799-1835.
1973. 416pp.
Land bounty warrants telling to whom the land in the
Military District of Ohio, of which Guernsey County
was a part, was originally issued.   20.00   ..... (22)
Turk, Marion G. The Quiet Adventurers in America. 1975. 300pp.
Genealogical data and the story of settlers in American
Colonies and in the United States, from the Channel Islands,
United Kingdom, Jersey, Guernsey, Alderney and Sark.   12.00   10.00 (771)

HAMILTON COUNTY

Dabney, Wendell P. Cincinnati's Colored Citizens: Historical,
Sociological and Biographical. 1867.   19.00   ..... (522)
_____. Cincinnati's Colored Citizens: Historical, Sociological
and Biographical. Repr. of 1925 ed.   19.00   ..... (394)
Farrell, Richard Terrence. Cincinnati in the Early Jackson Era,
1816-1834: An Economic and Political Study. 1967. 260pp.
BIP-68-07249.   .... (777)
Feck, Luke. Yesterday's Cincinnati. 1975.   9.95   ..... (679)
Foote, John P. The Schools of Cincinnati and Its Vicinity. 1855. 10.00   ..... (38)
Glazer, Walter Stix. Cincinnati in 1840: A Community Profile.
321pp. BIP-69-12107.   .... (777)
Hall, James. West: Its Commerce and Navigation.
Repr. of 1848 ed.   17.00   ..... (248)
Mansfield, Edward Deering. Memoirs of the Life and Services
of Daniel Drake, M.D., Physician, Professor, and Author:
With Notices of the Early Settlement of Cincinnati, and
Some of its Pioneer Citizens. 1855.   23.00   ..... (38)
Vexler, Robert I. Cincinnati: A Chronological and Documentary
History. 1975. 160pp.   7.50   ..... (551)

HOLMES COUNTY

Smith, Clifford Neal. Federal Land Series, Volume 2: 1799-1835.
1973. 416pp.
Land bounty warrants telling to whom the land in the
Military District of Ohio, of which Franklin County
was a part, was originally issued.   20.00   ..... (22)

JACKSON COUNTY

Clark, Neva Sturgill, comp. Jackson County, Ohio - Miscellaneous
Information. 1976. 5pp.
Available records, marriages, births, deaths, and bits
and pieces gathered while researching my family in
Jackson County. 3.00 (146)
Maxwell, Fay. Index to Romaine Aten Jones Jackson County
History, 1960's. Repr. of 1960 ed. 20pp.
Index to history of Jackson County, Ohio by wife of
Judge Brenner Jones.   3.00   ..... (473)
Smith, Marjorie, ed. Ohio Marriages Extracted From the
Old Northwest Genealogical Quarterly. Repr. from
1898-1913 ed. 356pp.
Marriages for Franklin County (1803-1830), Jackson County,
(1816-1826), Licking County (1808-1820), Marion County
(1824-1825), Pickaway County (1810-1815), Ross County
(1803-1806), Trumbull County (1800-1803), Washington
County (1789-1822).   15.00   ..... (330)

JEFFERSON COUNTY

Caldwell, J. A. History of Belmont and Jefferson Counties,
Ohio. Repr. of 1880 ed. 642pp.
22,000 every name index added (additional 125 page index).   25.00   ..... (716)

KNOX COUNTY

Smith, Clifford Neal. Federal Land Series, Volume 2: 1799-1835.
1973. 416pp.
Land bounty warrants telling to whom the land in the
Military District of Ohio, of which Knox County was
a part, was originally issued.   20.00   ..... (22)

LAKE COUNTY

Clark, Mrs. Neva Sturgill, comp. 1840 Lawrence and Lake
County Ohio Census and Index. 1976. 90pp.
Sex and age groups; black families included. Name
of head of family, sex and age of wife and children,
black families included. 7.50 (146)
Maxwell, Fay. Index to Lake County History. 1975. 20pp.
Index to history compiled by WPA 1941. 8 1/2 x 11.   .....   1.50 (473)

LAWRENCE COUNTY

Clark, Mrs. Neva Sturgill, comp. 1840 Lawrence and Lake
County Ohio Census and Index. 1976. 90pp.
Sex and age groups; black families included. Name
of head of family, sex and age of wife and children,
black families included. 7.50 (146)

_____. Lawrence County, Ohio - Miscellaneous Information.
1976. 5pp.
Available records, marriages, births, deaths, bits
and pieces gathered while researching my family in
Lawrence County, Ohio. 2.00 (146)

LICKING COUNTY

Everts, Major L. H. Licking County, Ohio 1875 History and
Atlas. Repr. 196pp. 10.00 ..... (80)
Licking County Genealogical Society. "The Licking Lantern (A
Look Into the Past). Licking County Quarterly, February Issue.
1976. c10pp./issue.
Types of materials included: court records, membership
list, library materials, querries, newsletter.
Subscription included with membership. Subscription/Yr. 6.00 (430)
Licking County, Ohio Probate Records 1828-1904 (Abstract of
17 volumes: Administration, Executive, Guardianships).
1975. 174pp. 15.00 ..... (430)
Maxwell, Fay. Index to Isaac Smucker's 1874 History.
1974. 15pp. 8 1/2 x 11. ..... 2.50 (473)
_____. Ohio: Franklin County, Irish Refugee Tract and
Tract History; Entire Tract and Nova Scotia History.
1973. c200pp.
Begins with Irish landgrants up to 1840, but takes Irish
History back to Nova Scotia and Ireland; includes refugees
of Louisiana and New York. 15.00 (473)
Smith, Clifford Neal. Federal Land Series, Volume 2: 1799-1835.
1973. 416pp.
Land bounty warrants telling to whom the land in the
Military District of Ohio, of which Licking County was
a part, was originally issued. 20.00 ..... (22)
Smith, Marjorie, ed. Ohio Marriages Extracted From the Old
Northwest Genealogical Quarterly. Repr. of 1898-1913 ed. 356pp.
Marriages for Franklin County (1803-1830), Jackson
County (1816-1826), Licking County (1808-1820),
Marion County (1824-1825), Pickaway County
(1810-1815), Ross County (1803-1806), Trumbull
County (1800-1803), Washington County (1789-1822). 15.00 ..... (330)

MARION COUNTY

Smith, Clifford Neal. Federal Land Series, Volume 2: 1799-1835.
1973. 416pp.
Land bounty warrants telling to whom the land in the
Military District of Ohio, of which Marion County was
a part, was originally issued. 20.00 ..... (22)

MIAMI COUNTY

Miller, Marcus. Roots By the River. 1973. 255pp.
History, doctrine and practice of the Old German
Baptist Brethren (Dunkers) in Miami County, Ohio.
Biographies of 75 ministers 1816-1973; genealogical
sketches. 5.25 ..... (489)

MONTGOMERY COUNTY

Becker, Carl M. Mill, Shop, and Factory: The Industrial
Life of Dayton, Ohio, 1830-1900. 1971. 425pp. BIP-72-01412. .... (777)

Conover, Charlotte R. Dayton, Ohio: An Intimate History. 1971.   13.95   8.95 (420)
The History of Montgomery County, Ohio. 1882. 1220pp.
B-BH 21433.   .... (778)

MORGAN COUNTY

Robertson, Charles. History of Morgan County, Ohio. 1886.
644pp. B-BH 17532.   .... (778)

MORROW COUNTY

Smith, Clifford Neal. Federal Land Series, Volume 2: 1799-1835.
1973. 416pp.
    Land bounty warrants telling to whom the land in the
    Military District of Ohio, of which Morrow County was
    a part, was originally issued.   20.00   ..... (22)

MUSKINGUM COUNTY

Maxwell, Fay. Muskingum and Perry County Pottery History
to 1900. 1965. 26pp.
    History covers potteries of Roseville and Crooksville
    from Indian Mounds in county, up to 1900. 8 1/2 x 11.   .....   1.50 (473)
Smith, Clifford Neal. Federal Land Series, Volume 2: 1799-1835.
1973. 416pp.
    Land bounty warrants telling to whom the land in the
    Military District of Ohio, of which Muskingum County
    was a part, was originally issued.   20.00   ..... (22)

OTTAWA COUNTY

Durr, Eleanor. Lakeside, Ohio: First 100 Years.   5.95   ..... (118)

PERRY COUNTY

Maxwell, Fay. Muskingum and Perry County Pottery History
to 1900. 1965. 26pp.
    History covers potteries of Roseville and Crooksville
    from Indian Mounds in county, up to 1900. 8 1/2 x 11.   .....   1.50 (473)

PICKAWAY COUNTY

Smith, Marjorie, ed. Ohio Marriages Extracted From the
Old Northwest Genealogical Quarterly. Repr. of 1898-1913 ed.
356pp.
    Marriages for Franklin County (1803-1830), Jackson
    County (1816-1826), Licking County (1808-1820),
    Marion County (1824-1825), Pickaway County (1810-1815),
    Ross County (1803-1806), Trumbull County (1800-1803),
    Washington County (1789-1822).   15.00   ..... (330)

PREBLE COUNTY

Brubaker, J. B. Index to 1858 Landowners Map of Preble
County, Ohio. 1976. 40pp.
    Shows name, township, section and acres owned. 6.00 (102)
Preble County Genealogical Club. Preble County Cemetery
Inscriptions Volume I. 1976. 80pp. 8.00 (102)
Preble County, Ohio 1871 Atlas. Repr. of 1871 ed. 14pp.
    Reduced to 8 1/2 x 11 - loose leaf in folders. 5.00 (102)
Preble County, Ohio 1915 Atlas. Repr. of 1915 ed. 23pp.
    Reduced to 8 1/2 x 11 - loose leaf in folder. 10.00 (102)

ROSS COUNTY

Ross County Genealogical Society, comp. Ross County, Ohio,
Families - Bicentennial Edition. 1976. c800pp.
Compiled from family sheets and ancestor charts
submitted by members and others. In Process.   .... (657)

SUMMIT COUNTY

Nichols, Kenneth. Yesterday's Akron. 1975.   9.95 ..... (679)

TRUMBULL COUNTY

Braden, James A. "A Greene Township Directory." Ancestor
Hunt, Vol. II, No. 2. 1975. 2pp.
A 1916 poem listing many surnames of turn of century
residents. 1.25 (39)

TUSCARAWAS COUNTY

The History of Tuscarawas County, Ohio. 1884. 908pp.
B-BH 17531.   .... (778)
Smith, Clifford Neal. Federal Land Series, Volume 2:
1799-1835. 1973. 416pp.
Land bounty warrants telling to whom the land in the
Military District of Ohio, of which Tuscarawas County
was a part, was originally issued.   20.00 ..... (22)

WARREN COUNTY

The History of Warren County, Ohio 1882. 1058рp.   B-BH 21432.   .... (778)

WASHINGTON COUNTY

Maxwell, Fay. Index to Thomas Summers History of Marietta,
Washington County, Ohio (1903). 1973. 18pp. 8 1/2 x 11.   ..... 3.95 (473)
_____. Washangton County Marriages 1803-1823. 20pp. Index. 5.95 (473)
Smith, Marjorie, ed. Ohio Marriages Extracted From the Old
Northwest Genealogical Quarterly. Repr. of 1898-1913 ed. 356pp.
Marriages for Franklin County (1803-1830), Jackson
County (1816-1826), Licking County (1808-1820),
Marion County (1824-1825), Pickaway County (1810-1815),
Ross County (1803-1806), Trumbull County (1800-1803),
Washington County (1789-1822).   15.00 ..... (330)

WAYNE COUNTY

Geitgey, Frances. Index to 1860 Federal Census of Wayne County,
Ohio. Spring, 1977. In Process.   .... (439)

WILLIAMS COUNTY

The Kalamazoo Valley Genealogical Society. The Kalamazoo
Valley Family Newsletter (Williams County, Ohio Issue).
1975. 60pp.
General reference for county. Contains lists of all
libraries, newspapers, and cemeteries in county.
Township maps, and voter lists, and early settlers
and office holders. 3.00 (399)

WYANDOT COUNTY

The History of Wyandot County, Ohio. 1884. 1068pp.
B-BH 21431. .... (778)

Oklahoma

STATEWIDE REFERENCES

Savange, William W., Jr. The Cherokee Strip Live Stock
Association: Federal Regulation and the Cattlemen's Last
Frontier. 1973. 152pp.
  Federal government's dealings with cattlemen and
  Indians during a period of settlement of the west.
  Bibliography, illustrated.   8.50   ..... (500)
Thiel, Sidney. The Oklahoma Land Rush. 1973.   3.95   ..... (301)

Research Aids

Brown, Jean. Oklahoma Research - The Twin Territories.
  1975. 36pp. 5.00 (97)
Morris, John W. and Edwin C. McReynolds. Historical
  Stlas of Oklahoma. 1971.   4.95   2.95 (556)
Shirk, George H. Oklahoma Place Names. 2d ed. 1974.   5.95   ..... (556)

Military

Nye, Wilbur S. Carbine and Lance. The Story of Old
  Fort Sill. Revised Centennial Ed. 1969.   6.95   ..... (556)
Van Meter, Mrs. Oather Edward, comp. Oklahoma Society,
  National Society Daughters of the American Revolution
  Roster Supplement II, 1976, Bicentennial Edition. 1976.
  172pp.
    National number, name and Revolutionary ancestor.
    Also state of each member of Oklahoma Society
    from Supplement I date, 1964 until the present. 7.50 (787)

Religious and Ethnic Groups

Botkin, Samuel Lee. The Protestant Episcopal Church in
  Oklahoma, 1835-1941. 1958. 341pp. BIP-58-01951.   .... (777)
Paul, George H. The Religious Frontier in Oklahoma:
  Dan T. Muse and the and the Pentecostal Holiness Church.
  1965. 307pp. BIP-65-11693.   .... (777)
Thomas, M. Ursula. The Catholic Church on the Oklahoma
  Frontier 1824-1907. 1938. 392pp. BIP-00-00205.   .... (777)

Listed below are the names of professional genealogists willing to undertake research for
a fee within the state of Oklahoma, in areas specified in their ads:

Records

Mills, Madeline S. and Helen R. Mullenax. Relocated
Cemeteries in Oklahoma and Parts of Arkansas-
Kansas-Texas. 1974. 247+pp.
Original burial sites and reinterment sites covering
30 counties, 318 cemeteries and approximately
10,000 burials.   17.50   .....   (492)

CHEROKEE COUNTY

Hall, Ted Byron. Oklahoma Indian Territory. 1971. c758pp.
Early Eastern Oklahoma-historical biographical,
genealogical; 12000 names indexed of settlers, doctors,
lawyers, lawmen, merchants, and soldiers. Contains
more than 110 family genealogies.   30.00   .....   (308)

CREEK COUNTY

Brown, Jean. Creek County Burials - Volume I - Old Sapulpa
Cemetery (to 1917). 1975. 72pp.
Contains funeral, city and cemetery listings. 12.50   (97)
_____. Creek County Burials - Volume II - Old Sapulpa Cemetery
1917-1975. 1976. 153pp.
Contains funeral, city and cemetery information. 17.50   (97)

HASKELL COUNTY

Hall, Ted Byron. Oklahoma Indian Territory. 1971. c758pp.
Early Eastern Oklahoma - historical, biographical,
genealogical - 12000 names indexed of settlers, doctors,
lawyers, lawmen, merchants, and soldiers. Contains
more than 110 family genealogies.   30.00   .....   (308)

LATIMER COUNTY

Hall, Ted Byron. Oklahoma Indian Territory. 1971. c758pp.
Early Eastern Oklahoma - historical, biographical,
genealogical - 12000 names indexed of settlers, doctors,
lawyers, lawmen, merchants and soldiers. Contains more
than 110 family genealogies.   30.00   .....   (308)

LeFLORE COUNTY

Hall, Ted Byron. Oklahoma Indian Territory. 1971. c758pp.
Early Eastern Oklahoma - historical, biographical,
genealogical - 12000 names indexed of settlers, doctors,
lawyers, lawmen, merchants and soldiers. Contains
more than 110 family genealogies.   30.00   .....   (308)

McINTOSH COUNTY

Hall, Ted Byron. Oklahoma Indian Territory. 1971. c758pp.
Early Eastern Oklahoma - historical, biographical,
genealogical - 12000 names indexed of settlers, doctors,
lawyers, lawmen, merchants, and soldiers. Contains more
than 110 family genealogies.   30.00   .....   (308)

MUSKOGEE COUNTY

Hall, Ted Byron. Oklahoma Indian Territory. 1971. c758pp.
Early Eastern Oklahoma - historical, biographical,
genealogical; 12000 names indexed of settlers, doctors,
lawyers, lawmen, merchants, and soldiers. Contains
more than 110 family genealogies.   30.00   ..... (308)

PITTSBURG COUNTY

Hall, Ted Byron. Oklahoma Indian Territory. 1971. c758pp.
Early Eastern Oklahoma; historical, biographical,
genealogical; 12000 names indexed of settlers, doctors,
lawyers, lawmen, merchants and soldiers. Contains
more than 110 family genealogies.   30.00   ..... (308)

SEQUOYAH COUNTY

Hall, Ted Byron. Oklahoma Indian Territory. 1971. c758pp.
Early Eastern Oklahoma - historical, biographical,
genealogical; 12000 names indexed of settlers, doctors,
lawyers, lawmen, merchants, and soldiers. Contains
more than 110 family genealogies.   30.00   ..... (308)

WOODS COUNTY

Cherokee Strip Volunteer League, ed. Pioneer Footprints
Across Woods County, Oklahoma (1893-1939). 1976. 740pp. 26.50   ..... (136)

Oregon

STATEWIDE REFERENCES

Anderson, Sylvia F. and Jacob Korg, eds. Westward to Oregon.
1958.   .....   2.25 (324)
Hastings, Lansford W. Emigrants Guide to Oregon and
California. 2d ed. 1969.   17.50 ..... (176)
Husband, Michael B. To Oregon in 1843: The Backgrounds
and Organization of the Great Migration. 1970. 274pp.
BIP-71-09278.   .... (777)
Nash, Wallis. Oregon: There and Back in 1877.
Repr. of 1877 ed.
Account of Nash's journey from London to Oregon
in 1877. Foreword and notes by J. K. Munford.   10.00   5.75 (561)

Listed below is the name of a professional genealogist willing to undertake research for a
fee within the state of Oregon, in areas specified in her ad:

Nelson and Onstad, eds. A Webfoot Volunteer: The Diary of
William Hilleary 1864-1866. 1965. 248pp.
Diary of a citizen soldier volunteer serving in Oregon
in the Civil War.   6.00   ..... (561)
Ross, Alexander. Adventures of the First Settlers on the
Oregon or Columbia River. Repr. of 1849 ed.   7.75   ..... (778)
Throckmorton, Arthur Loreston. The Frontier Merchant
In the Early Development of Oregon, 1839-1869. 1956.
438pp. BIP-58-01164.   .... (777)

Research Aids

Brandt, P. and N. Guilford, eds. Oregon Biography Index.
1976. 144pp.
Bibliographic index to biographies of Oregon
pioneers included in 47 early state histories. 3.75 (561)
Highsmith, R., Jr., ed. Atlas of the Pacific Northwest.
5th ed. 1973. 136pp.
Oregon, Washington, Idaho history, development,
resources, geography, economics, etc.   13.50   7.50 (561)
McArthur, Lewis A. Oregon Geographic Names.
3rd ed. 1973.   17.50   ..... (560)

Records

Lacy, Ruby and Erma Lee Brown. Oregon 1860 Census
Index of Surnames. 1976. c100pp. 7.50 (418)

CLATSOP COUNTY

Franchere, Gabriel. Adventure at Astoria, 1810-1814.
tr. Hoyt C. Franchere. 1967.   7.95   ..... (556)
Irving, Washington. Astoria, or Anecdotes of an Enterprise
Beyond the Rocky Mountains. ed. Edgeley Todd. 1964.   12.50   4.95 (556)

DOUGLAS COUNTY

Minter, Harold A. Umpqua Valley, Oregon, and Its Pioneers. 1967. 6.50   ..... (68)

HARNEY COUNTY

Adams, Golden V., et al. Harney County, Oregon Cemetery
Records. 1975. 239pp.
Contains 99 pages of cemetery records from Harney
County, Oregon; 6 pages from Lake County, Oregon;
10 pages from Malheur County, Oregon; 74 pages obits;
an every name index.   25.00   ..... (8)

JACKSON COUNTY

Lacy, Ruby. Jackson County, Oregon Marriages, Volume III,
1888-1900. 1976. c100pp.
This is in the process; will be fully indexed. 5.00 (418)

JOSEPHINE COUNTY

Lacy, Ruby, comp. 1880 Census Josephine County, Oregon.
1975. 60pp.
As it appears on Census; fully indexed. 5.00 (418)
_____. Josephine County Marriages. March, 1977. c50pp. 5.00 (418)

LAKE COUNTY

Adams, Golden V., Jr. and LaRue P. Leslie. Harney County,
Oregon Cemetery Records. 1975. 239pp.
Contains 99 pages of cemetery records from Harney
County, 6 pages from Lake County, 10 pages from
Malheur County, 74 pages of obituaries and an every-
name index.   25.00   ..... (8)

LANE COUNTY

Olson, John Alden. The Danish Settlement of Junction City,
Oregon. 1975.
A collection of historical and cultural events that
added a great deal to the history of Oregon.   8.00   ..... (631)

MALHEUR COUNTY

Adams, Golden V., Jr. and LaRue P. Leslie. Harney County,
Oregon Cemetery Records. 1975. 239pp.
Contains 99 pages of cemetery records from Harney
County, 6 pages from Lake County, 10 pages from
Malheur County, 74 pages of obituaries and an every-
name index.   25.00   ..... (8)

Pennsylvania

STATEWIDE REFERENCES

Anderson, James Laverne. The Governors' Council of Colonial
America. A Study of Pennsylvania and Virginia 1660-1776.
377pp. BIP-68-03103.   .... (777)
Arbuckle, Robert D. John Nicholson, 1757 - 1800: Pennsylvania
Land Speculator, Financier and Entrepeneur. 1975. 276pp.
Covers speculation in District of Columbia, Maryland
and Pennsylvania.   14.50   ..... (589)

Listed below are the names of professional genealogists willing to undertake research
for a fee within the state of Pennsylvania, in areas specified in their ads:

Beers, Paul B. Profiles from the Susquehanna Valley: Past
and Present Vignettes of Its People, Times and Towns.
1973.
   Susquehanna mostly is in Pennsylvania - mouth is in
   Maryland. Covers half of Pennsylvania.   8.95   ..... (713)
Bliss, William Henry. English Influence on Common Law
Development in Colonial Pennsylvania. 194pp. BIP-59-06541.   .... (777)
Campanius Holm, Tomas. Description of the Province of
New Sweden. Now Called, by the English, Pennsylvania,
in America. Compiles from the Relations and Writings
of Persons Worthy of Credit, and Adorned with Maps and
Plates. Translated from the Swedish, for the Historical
Society of Pennsylvania. With Notes, tr. Peter S. Du Ponceau.
1834.   13.00   ..... (415)
Cawley, James and Margaret Cawley. Along the Old York
Road. 1965.   6.00   2.75 (665)
Chapman, Isaac. The History of Wyoming Valley in Pennsylvania.
Reprint. 209pp.
   The appendix is a gazetter of the townships of the period,
   with population data included and the topography described. 10.00   ..... (608)
De Crevecoeur, Michel-Guillanme St. J. Journey Into Northern
Pennsylvania and the State of New York, tr. Clarissa S.
Bostelmann. 1964.   15.00   ..... (484)
Fisher, Sydney G. Making of Pennsylvania. 2d ed. Repr. of
1906 ed.   10.00   ..... (253)
_____. The Making of Pennsylvania. 1896.   15.00   ..... (547)
Hanna, Charles Augustus. The Wilderness Trail, Or the
Ventures and Adventures of the Pennsylvania Traders on
the Allegheny Path. With Some New Annals of the Old
West, and the Records of Some Strong Men and Some Bad
Ones. . .With 80 Maps and Illustrations. 2 vols. 1911.
                                 Set: 42.50   ..... (2)
Hazard, Samuel. Annals of Pennsylvania: From the Discovery
of the Delaware. Repr. of 1850 ed.   27.50   ..... (404)
Historical Register: Notes and Queries, Historical and
Genealogical Relating to Interior Pennsylvania. 1883-1884.
Vol. 2-778pp. B-BH 13943.   .... (778)
Hotchkin, S. F. Country Clergy of Pennsylvania.   10.00   ..... (245)
Jensen, Arthur L. The Maritime Commerce of Colonial
Philadelphia. Repr. of 1963 ed.   4.75   ..... (850)
Keith, Charles P. Chronicles of Pennsylvania: From the
English Revolution to the Peace of Aix-la-Chapelle, 1688-
1748. 3 vols. Repr. of 1917 ed.   Set: 34.50   ..... (404)
Klein, Philip S. and Ari Hoogenboom. A History of Pennsylvania.
1973.   14.50 10.95 (451)
Lemon, James T. Best Poor Man's Country: A Geographical
Study of Early Southeastern Pennsylvania. 1972.   14.00   ..... (385)
Love, John Barry. The Colonial Surveyor in Pennsylvania.
297pp. BIP-71-19253.   .... (777)
McCadden, Joseph J. Education in Pennsylvania, 1801-1835, and
Its Debt to Robert Vaux. 1937.   13.00   ..... (38)
Meehan, Thomas Richard. The Pennsylvania Supreme Court in
the Law and Politics of the Commonwealth 1776-1790. 628pp.
BIP-60-05768.   .... (777)
Myers, Charles Bennett. Public Secondary Schools in Pennsylvania
During the American Revolution Era, 1760-1800. 281pp.
BIP-68-16347.   .... (777)

Nelson, Russell Sage, Jr. Backcountry Pennsylvania (1709 to
1774): The Ideals of William Penn in Practice. 370pp.
BIP-68-16012. ••••• ••••• (777)
Penn, William. A Collection of the Works of William Penn to
Which is Prefixed a Journal of His Life. With Many
Original Letters and Papers Not Before Published. And to
Which is Appended an Index of the Works Compiled in 1730
by Henry Portsmouth, ed. Joseph Besse. 2 vols. Set: 325.00 ••••• (2)
_____ and James Logan. Correspondence Between William
Penn and James Logan and Others, 1700-1750. From the
Original Letters in Possession of the Logan Family.
With Notes by Deborah Logan, ed. Edward Armstrong.
2 vols. 1870-1872. Set: 40.00 ••••• (2)
Pennsylvania Historical Society. Memoirs of the Historical
Society of Pennsylvania. 14 vols. 1826-1895. Set: 400.00 ••••• (2)
Each: 30.00 ••••• (2)
Rodney, Richard S. and Burton A. Kinkle. Early Relations
of Delaware and Pennsylvania. Including Delaware: A
Grant Yet Not a Grant. Repr. of 1930 ed. 6.00 ••••• (81)
Root, Winfred Trexler. The Relations of Pennsylvania With the
British Government, 1696-1765. 1912. 12.50 ••••• (2)
Secor, Robert A., ed. Pennsylvania 1776. 1975. 352pp. 15.00 ••••• (589)
Shepherd, William Robert. History of Proprietary Government in
Pennsylvania. 1896. 12.50 ••••• (2)
Smith, Edward Owen, Jr. Thomas Penn, Chief Proprietor of
Pennsylvania: A Study of His Public Governmental Activities
From 1763 to 1775. 558pp. BIP-67-04879. ••••• ••••• (777)
Trent, William. Journal of Captain William Trent From Logstown
to Pickawillany, A.D. 1752. Now Published for the First
Time From a Copy in the Archives of the Western Reserve
Historical Society, Cleveland, Ohio, Together With Letters
of Governor Robert Dinwiddie, an Historical Notice of the
Miami Confederacy of Indians; A Sketch of the English Post
at Pickawillany, With a Short Biography of Captain Trent
and Other Papers Never Before Published, ed. Alfred T.
Goodman. Repr. of 1871 ed.
Contains details on the trade and diplomatic rivalries in
the Ohio wilderness on the eve of the outbreak of the
French and Indian War. 6.00 ••••• (38)
Volwiler, Albert Tangeman. George Croghan and the Westward
Movement, 1741 - 1782. 1926. 11.50 ••••• (2)
Wallace, Paul A. Conrad Weiser, 1696-1760: Friend of Colonist
and Mohawk. 1945. 27.50 ••••• (824)
Wilkinson, Norman B. Land Policy and Speculation in Pennsylvania
1779-1800. 375pp. BIP-58-03382. ••••• ••••• (777)
Williams, William Henry. The Pennsylvania Hospital, 1751-1801:
An Internal Examination of Anglo-America's First Hospital.
402pp. BIP-72-14517. ••••• ••••• (777)
Wollenweber, Ludwig A. Mountain Mary: An Historical Tale of
Early Pennsylvania. Original Title: Die Berg-Maria: eine
Geschichtliche Erzalung aus Pennsylvanien, tr. John J. Stoudt.
1973. ••••• 4.00 (688)

Research Aids

Espenshade, Abraham H. Pennsylvania Place Names. Repr.
of 1925 ed. 14.50 ••••• (266)

Gordon, Thomas F. Gazetteer of Pennsylvania. Repr. of
1832 ed. 500pp. Map.
Includes a list of all post offices in the state in
1832.   20.00   ..... (608)
Kay, John L. and Chester M. Smith, Jr. Pennsylvania
Postal History. 1976.
Listing and cross index of all Pennsylvania post
offices and postmasters for 200 years.   25.00   ..... (630)
Lartigue, Carrie L. Index to Some Philadelphia Marriages
1745-1806. 1974. 146pp.
Index to some Philadelphia marriages at St. Michaels
and Zion Lutheran and St. Paul's Churches to be used
in conjunction with Series 2, Vol. 9 Pennsylvania
Archives 1895 Addition. 6.50 (212)
Simonetti, Martha L., comp. Descriptive List of the Map
Collection in the Pennsylvania State Archives. 1976.
200pp.
Lists 714 items and special map groups, some of
them copies.   8.50   ..... (587)
Wall, Carol. Supplement to the Bibliography of Pennsylvania
History. 1976. 265pp.
Continues bibliography (q.v.) through mid-1960's.   7.00   ..... (587)
Whipkey, Harry E. Guide to the Manuscript Groups in the
Pennsylvania State Archives. 1976. 200pp.
Guide to manuscripts but not the public records.   8.50   ..... (587)

Military

Aldrich, James Mott. The Revolutionary Legislature in
Pennsylvania: A Roll Call Analysis. 191pp.
BIP-70-01765.   .... (777)
Brunhouse, Robert L. Counter-Revolution in Pennsylvania,
1776-1790. Reprint.   12.00   ..... (552)
Feltman, William. The Journal of Lieut. William Feltman,
of the First Pennsylvania Regiment, 1781-1782. 1853.   4.50   ..... (38)
Huston, John Wilson. Fort Pitt, 1758-1772. 336pp.
BIP-00-22849.   .... (777)
Jackson, John W. The Pennsylvania Navy, 1775-1781: The
Defense of the Delaware. 1974.   12.50   ..... (665)
Keut, Donald H. The French Invasion of Western Pennsylvania.
1954. 91pp.   2.00   .75 (587)
Neuenschwander, John A. Middle Colonies and the Coming of
the American Revolution. 1974.   12.50   ..... (404)
Ousterhout, Anne McCabe. The Forgotten Antagonists:
Pennsylvania Loyalists. 322pp. BIP-72-30024.   .... (777)
The Papers of Henry Bouquet, Volume I (December 1755 -
May 1758), ed. S.K. Stevens, Donald H. Kent, and
Autumn L. Leonard. 1972. 470pp.
Papers of commander of frontier campaigns
against the French and Indians in western
Pennsylvania and Ohio. This volume covers
duty in South Carolina and Pennsylvania.   12.00   ..... (587)
The Papers of Henry Bouquet, Volume II, The Forbes
Expedition (1758), ed. S.K. Stevens, Donald H. Kent,
and Autumn L. Leonard. 1951. 736pp.
Papers of commander of frontier campaigns against
the French and Indians in western Pennsylvania
and Ohio. This volume covers the Forbes Expedition.   12.00   ..... (587)

The Papers of Henry Bouquet, Volume III (January - August
1759), ed. Donald H. Kent, Louis M. Waddell, and
Autumn L. Leonard. 1976. 700pp.
Papers of commander of frontier campaigns
against the French and Indians in western
Pennsylvania and Ohio.   20.00   ..... (587)
Philadelphia Brigade Association. Reunion of the Blue and
Gray: Philadelphia Brigade and Pickett's Division,
July 2,3,4, 1887 and September 15,16,17, 1906. 1906.
120pp. B-OP 53319.   .... (778)
Reed, John F. Valley Forge, Crucible of Victory. 1969. 10.95   ..... (250)
Rowell, John W. Yankee Cavalrymen: Through the Civil
War with the Ninth Pennsylvania Cavalry. 1971.   8.50   ..... (747)
Sargent, Winthrop, ed. A History of an Expedition Against
Fort DuQuesne in 1755. 1855.   20.00   ..... (38)
Sipe, C. Hale. The Indian Wars of Pennsylvania. 1929.   40.00   ..... (38)
Stille, Charles J. Major-General Anthony Wayne and the
Pennsylvania Line of the Continental Army. Repr. of
1893 ed.   15.00   ..... (404)
Trussell, John B.B., Jr. Birthplace of an Army: A Study
of the Valley Forge Encampment. 1976. 150pp.   4.50   3.00 (587)
_____. The Pennsylvania Line: Regimental Organization
and Operations, 1775-1783. 1976. 350pp.   8.50   ..... (587)
Watson, William. Letters of a Civil War Surgeon, ed.
Paul Fatout. 1961.   .....   2.25 (627)
Weedon, George. Valley Forge Orderly Book of General
George Weedon, of the Continental Army Under Command
of General George Washington. In the Campaign of
1777-1778. 1902.   13.00   ..... (38)
Woodward, Evan Morrison. History of the Third Pennsylvania
Reserve: Being a Complete Record of the Regiment, with
Incidents of the Camp, Marches. . . and Battles. To-
gether with the Personal Record of Every Officer and
Man During His Term of Service. 1883. 334pp.
B-BH 21102.   .... (778)

Religious and Ethnic Groups

Bodnar, John E. Ethnic History in Pennsylvania: A Sketch
Bibliography. 1974. 47pp. 1.00 (587)
_____, ed. The Ethnic Experience in Pennsylvania. 1973. 12.00   ..... (104)
Buxbaum, Melvin H. Benjamin Franklin and the Zealous
Presbyterians. 1975. 276pp.   14.50   ..... (589)
Egle, William Henry. Pennsylvania Genealogies; Scotch-
Irish and German. 1886. 736pp. B-BH 6365.   .... (778)
Gollin, Gillian L. Moravians in Two Worlds: A Study of
Changing Communities. 1967.   13.50   ..... (155)
Haiman, Mieczyslaw. Polish Pioneers of Pennsylvania.
Repr. of 1941 ed.   5.00   ..... (631)
Kuhns, Oscar. German and Swiss Settlements of Colonial
Pennsylvania. Repr. of 1901 ed.   8.75   ..... (266)
Johnson, Charles B. Letters from the British Settlement in
Pennsylvania. Repr. of 1819 ed.   9.50   ..... (702)
Sachse, Julius Friedrich. German Sectarians of Pennsylvania,
1708-1800: A Critical and Legendary History of the
Ephrata Cloister and the Dunkers. 2 vols. 1899-1900.
                                            Set: 45.00   ..... (2)
                                            Each: 24.00   ..... (2)

Turner, Edward Raymond. The Negro in Pennsylvania:
Slavery-Servitude-Freedom 1639-1861. 1911.   10.00   ..... (38)
Woody, Thomas. Early Quakers Education in Pennsylvania.
1920.   17.50   ..... (2)

Indians

Heckewelder, John. History, Manners, and Customs of the
Indian Nations Who Once Inhabited Pennsylvania and
the Neighboring States. Repr. of 1819 ed.   19.00   ..... (38)
Kent, Barry C., Ira F. Smith, and Catherine McCann, eds.
Foundations of Pennsylvania Prehistory. 1971. 615pp.
Most notable published articles republished.   10.00   ..... (587)
Wallace, Paul A. Indians in Pennsylvania. Repr. of 1961
ed. 194pp.
Indians who met the European settlers.   3.00   1.75 (587)
Zimmerman, Albright Gravenor. The Indian Trade of
Colonial Pennsylvania. 47lpp. BIP-57-11752.   .... (777)

Newspapers

Checklist of Pennsylvania Newspapers: Philadelphia
County. 1944. 325pp.   2.00   ..... (587)
Gazette of the United States. Published in Philadelphia.
July 1794 - June 1843. [Some years missing.] 58 rolls.
Microfilm of the original papers. Individual
rolls covering a specific time span may be
ordered although some spans of years are
not available. Prices vary from $15 to $30
per roll.   .... (870)
Philadelphia Public Ledger, March 25, 1836 - December
1933. 471 rolls.
Microfilm of the original papers. Individual
rolls covering a specific time span may be
ordered. Prices vary from $15 to $30 per roll.   .... (870)
Pittsburgh Gazette, July 29, 1786 - August 31, 1927.
466 rolls.
Microfilm of the original papers. Individual
rolls covering a specific time span may be
ordered. Prices vary from $15 to $30 per roll.   .... (870)

Records

Egle, William H. Early Pennsylvania Land Records, Minutes
of the Board of Property of the Province of Pennsylvania.
Repr. of 1893. 787pp.   25.00   ..... (274)
_____. Names of Foreigners Who Took the Oath of
Allegiance to the Province and State of Pennsylvania,
1727-1775. Repr. of 1890. 787pp.
Also included are foreign arrivals, 1786-1808.   25.00   ..... (274)
Fisher, Charles A. Early Pennsylvania Births, 1675-1875.
Repr. of 1947 ed. 107pp. 7.50 (274)

[Following are entries for the "Pennsylvania Archives." Although listed previously in
the first volume of this book, their treatment in it was not one which especially defined
their true importance to genealogists researching in this field. It is a highly recommended
source. Therefore, they have been re-entered here with more appropriate commentary
on what is contained in each. This further information was obtained from the

Pennsylvania Historical and Museum Commission, Division of Public Records, "Guide to the Published Archives of Pennsylvania." 1949]

Pennsylvania Archives. 1852-1935. Series 1-9 in 121 vols. Set: 6100.00   ..... (2)

Colonial Records.
A total of sixteen volumes containing the minutes of the
Provincial Council, 1683-1775, in Volumes I-X; those
of the Council of Safety (and of the Committee of Safety),
1775-1777, in X and XI; and those of the Supreme
Executive Council, 1777-1790, in XI-XVI.   Set: 520.00   ..... (2)
                                                  Each: 32.50   ..... (2)

First Series.
These twelve volumes reproduce papers selected chiefly
from the files at the office of the Secretary of the Commonwealth, printed in chronological order to parallel and
supplement Colonial Records. The earliest materials
are dated 1664 and the latest 1790.   Set: 570.00   ..... (2)
                                             Each: 47.50   ..... (2)

Second Series.
In its nineteen volumes this series contains varied and
diverse materials; militia rolls and church records are
prominent, but there are as well the minutes of the
Board of War and those of the Navy Board, both of 1777,
and much on the Wyoming Controversy with Connecticut
and on the Whiskey Insurrection.   Set: 902.50   ..... (2)
                                          Each: 47.50   ..... (2)

Third Series.
The first twenty-six volumes of this series resemble
closely those of the Second Series, while the last four
volumes consist of an index to the sixteen volumes im-
mediately preceding. Filled for the most part with
militia rolls and lists of land warrantees and taxables,
this series does contain some materials of a more
general nature, such as a discussion of Virginia's claims
to western Pennsylvania, and an account of the Donation
Lands.   Set: 1472.50   ..... (2)
                Each: 47.50   ..... (2)

Fourth Series.
In twelve volumes, this series collects the addresses,
messages, proclamations, and a very few other Papers
of Pennsylvania's Governors, 1681-1902, with brief
biographies and portraits but with a minimum of documentation.   Set: 660.00   ..... (2)
                    Each: 55.00   ..... (2)

Fifth Series.
This series fills eight volumes with muster rolls and
other military lists, chiefly of the provincial and
revolutionary period, some reprinted with greater ac-
curacy and neatness from the Second and Third Series,
and certain of the others taken from cources outside
official custody.   Set: 440.00   ..... (2)
                           Each: 55.00   ..... (2)

Sixth Series.
For fourteen volumes this series continues the printing
of military rolls, covering chiefly the period from the
Revolution to the War of 1812, including militia rolls
for the years of peace, with some material as late as
the Mexican War. There are also a few orderly books,
military accounts for the 1812 period, and some papers
non-military in nature, notably church records of
marriages and baptisms, inventories of estates con-
fiscated during the Revolution, and scattering eighteenth
century election returns. The final volume, XV,
bound in two thick parts, contains an index to the Fifth

Series.	Set:	880.00	..... (2)
	Each:	55.00	..... (2)

Seventh Series.
The five volumes of this series consist exclusively of
an index to the more than one million names found in

the first fourteen volumes of the Sixth Series.	Set:	237.50	..... (2)
	Each:	47.50	..... (2)

Eighth Series.
In eight volumes, this series reprints the eighteenth
century edition of Votes and Proceedings of the House
of Representatives of the Province of Pennsylvania,

1682-1776.	Set:	440.00	..... (2)
	Each:	55.00	..... (2)

Ninth Series.
In ten volumes, this series prints the contents of
fifteen manuscript volumes preserved in the Division
of Public Records. These are Executive Minutes, a
journal of official actions of Pennsylvania's Governors
for the period 1790-1838. This series continues
Colonial Records and supplements the Fourth Series for

the effective period of the Constitution of 1790.	Set:	550.00	..... (2)
	Each:	55.00	..... (2)

Guide to the above series of Colonial Records and Archives, eds.
Henry Eddy and Martha Simonette. Repr. of 1949 ed. 101pp.
Key to the voluminous amount of information contained in the
138 volumes. Tells which volumes contain data on specific
counties, and the type, such as: tax lists, surveys, deeds,
marriages, baptisms, militia lists, petitions, etc. 2.00 (587)

Scott, Kenneth. Abstracts (Mainly Deaths) From the Pennsylvania Gazette, 1775-1783. 1976. 58pp. 5.00 (274)
Tepper, Michael, ed. Emigrants to Pennsylvania, Ship
Passenger Lists from Pennsylvania Magazine of History
and Biographies. Repr. of 1877-1934 ed. 292pp.   15.00 ..... (274)

Western and Southwestern Pennsylvania

Harper, Robert Eugene. The Class Structure of Western
Pennsylvania in the Late Eighteenth Century. 335pp.
BIP-70-14831.   .... (777)
Vogt, Helen. Westward of Ye Laurall Hills (A History 1750-
1850). 1976. 472pp. maps. 128 drawings. photos.
Also includes some Virginia and West Virginia data.
References to hundreds of names in southwest Pa.   20.00 ..... (802)

Walker, Joseph E., ed. Pleasure and Business in Western
Pennsylvania: The Journal of Joshua Gilpin, 1809.
1975. 156pp.
    Detailed observations Philadelphia to Pittsburgh
    to Indiana County.   6.00   ..... (587)
Wright, John E. With Rifle and Plow: Stories of the
Western Pennsylvania Frontier. Repr. of 1938 ed.   8.00   ..... (404)

ALLEGHENY COUNTY

Cushing, Thomas, et al. A Genealogical and Biographical
History of Allegheny County, Pennsylvania. Repr. of 1889
ed. 578pp.   20.00   ..... (274)
Vexler, Robert I. Pittsburgh: A Chronological and Documentary
History. 1976. 160pp.   7.50   .... (551)

BEAVER COUNTY

Williams, Aaron. The Harmony Society, at Economy,
Pennsylvania. Founded by George Rapp, A.D. 1805. With
an Appendix. 1866.   10.00   ..... (2)
_____. The Harmony Society at Economy, Pennsylvania,
Founded by George Rapp, A.D. 1805. With an Appendix.
With two appendices. Thoughts on the Destiny of Man. . .
by the Harmony Society of Indiana (1824) and The
Harmony Society in Pennsylvania (1937). 182/96/48pp.
Illustrations.   16.50   ..... (273)

BERKS COUNTY

Bentley, Elizabeth Petty. Index to the 1850 Census of Pennsylvania:
Berks County. 1976. 106pp. 7.50 (274)

BUCKS COUNTY

_____. Index to the 1850 Census of Pennsylvania: Bucks County.
1976. 88pp. 7.50 (274)
Flake, Raymond, ed. Index of Papers Read Before the Bucks
County Historical Society, Volumes 1-8. 1972.   .....   12.50 (105)
MacReynolds, George. Place Names in Bucks County,
Pennsylvania: Historical Narratives. 1955.   .....   8.00 (105)
Morgan, William. Bucks County.   12.95   ..... (352)
Records of the Courts of Quarter Sessions and Common Pleas of
Bucks County, Pennsylvania, 1684-1700. 1943. 456pp.
B-OP 65312.   .... (778)
Reeder, Eastburn. Early Settlers of Solebury Pennsylvania,
rev. ed. 1971.   ..... 15.00 (105)
Siskind, Aaron. Bucks County Photographs of Early Architecture.
1974.   12.95   ..... (105)
Williams, Richard T. and Mildred C. Williams. Soldiers of
the American Revolution - Bucks County, Pennsylvania.
Repr. of 1874/1906 ed. 368pp.
    Transcribed and arranged alphabetically from the
    Pennsylvania Archives.   17.50   ..... (841)

BUTLER COUNTY

Lee, Caroljo F. Merrie Olde Middlesex. 1976. 360pp.
Ancestors and descendants of Middlesex Township,
southern Butler County, Pennsylvania. Census,
tax lists, early church records, and a guide to
general Butler County research.   15.00   ..... (424)

CENTRE COUNTY

Linn, John Blair. Annals of Buffalo Valley, Pennsylvania,
1755-1855. Reprint. 625pp.
Includes assessment lists beginning in 1755, quotes
from Committee of Safety minutes, and muster rolls.
Extensive lists of early inhabitants, as well as marriages and deaths. Map.   17.50   ..... (608)

CRAWFORD COUNTY

Miller, Miriam Larsen. "Tombstone Tales, Inscriptions in
Steamburgh Cemetery, Conneaut Township." Ancestor
Hunt, Vols. I and II, Nos. 1-3. 1974-1975. 3pp.
Vol. I, No. 3 - 1974: 1.00 (39)
Vol. II, Nos. 1-2 - 1975: 1.25 (39)
Sargent, Martin P. Pioneer Sketches: Scenes and Incidents of
Former Days. Repr. of 1891 ed. 512pp.
Humorous account of biographical sketches and poems
dealing primarily with life in the 1800's in Ashtabula
County, Ohio, Erie and Crawford Counties, Pennsylvania.
New index added.   13.00   ..... (39)

DELAWARE COUNTY

Smedley, R.C. History of the Underground Railroad in Chester
and the Neighboring Counties of Pennsylvania. 1883.   14.00   ..... (38)

ERIE COUNTY

Allds, Jean Miller. "Index to Henry Miller's Journal, Lockport
(Now Platea), Pennsylvania." Ancestor Hunt, Vol. II, Nos.
1-2. 1975. 2 pp. 1.25 (39)
_____. "Tombstone Tales From Miller Corner's Cemetery,
Platea, Pennsylvania." Ancestor Hunt, Vol. I, No. 2.
1974. 2pp. 1.00 (39)
Federal Writers' Project. Erie; a Guide to the City and County.
1938.   8.50   ..... (2)
Tarlton, Charlotte Dibble. "Those, Really, Were The Days.
Description of Life in Elk Creek Township." Ancestor Hunt,
Vol. I, No. 3 - 1974, Vol. II, Nos. 1-4 - 1975. 5 pp.
Vol. I, No. 3 - 1974: 1.00 (39)
Vol. II, Nos. 1-4 - 1975: 1.25 (39)

FAYETTE COUNTY

Gresham, John M., ed. Biographical and Portrait Cyclopedia
of Fayette County, Pennsylvania. 1889. 612pp. B-BH 1709.   .... (778)

GREENE COUNTY

Bates, Samuel P. A Biographical History of Greene County,
Pennsylvania. Repr. of 1888 ed. 338pp.   15.00   ..... (274)

LACKAWANNA COUNTY

History of Luzerne, Lackawanna and Wyoming Counties,
Pennsylvania. 1880. 878pp. B-BH 521. .... (778)
Hollister, H. History of the Lackawanna Valley. 2d ed.
1869. 422pp. illus. 15.00 ..... (273)

LANCASTER COUNTY

Bentley, Elizabeth P. Index to the 1850 Census of Pennsylvania:
Lancaster County. 1975. 156pp. 10.00 (274)
Everts & Stewart. 1875 Landowner Atlas Lancaster County,
Pennsylvania. Repr. of 1875 ed. 138pp. 25.50 16.50 (80)
Wittlinger, Carlton O. Early Manufacturing in Lancaster
County, Pennsylvania, 1710-1840. 236pp. BIP-00-04959. .... (777)
Wood, Jerome Herman, Jr. Conestoga Crossroads: The Rise
of Lancaster, Pennsylvania, 1730-1789. 538pp. BIP-70-08812. .... (777)
Zerfass, Samuel Grant. Souvenir Book of the Ephrata Cloister;
Complete History from its Settlement in 1728 to the Present
Time. Included is the Organization of Ephrata Borough and
Other Information of Ephrata Connected with the Cloister.
1921. 12.50 ..... (2)

LUZERNE COUNTY

History of Luzerne, Lackawanna and Wyoming Counties,
Pennsylvania. 1880. 878pp. B-BH 521. .... (778)
Kulp, George Brubaker. Families of the Wyoming Valley:
Biographical, Genealogical and Historical. 1885-1890.
Vol. 3-400pp. B-BH 15539. .... (778)

LYCOMING COUNTY

Linn, John Blair. Annals of Buffalo Valley, Pennsylvania,
1755-1855. Reprint. 625pp.
Includes assessment lists beginning in 1755, quotes
from Committee of Safety minutes, and muster rolls,
Extensive lists of early inhabitants, as well as
marriages and deaths. Map. 17.50 ..... (608)

NORTHAMPTON COUNTY

Clyde, John Cunningham. Genealogies, Necrology, and
Reminiscences of the 'Irish Settlement,' Or A Record
of those Scotch-Irish Presbyterian Families Who Were
the First Settlers in the 'Forks of Delaware.' Now
Northampton County, Pennsylvania. 1879. 440pp
B-BH 15514. .... (778)
History of Northampton County, Pennsylvania. 1877. 400pp.
B-BH 15824. .... (778)
Levering, Joseph Mortimer. A History of Bethlehem,
Pennsylvania, 1741-1892, With Some Account of Its
Founders and Their Early Activity in America. 1903. 35.00 ..... (2)
Martin, John H. Historical Sketch of Bethlehem in Pennsylvania.
Reprint. 8.00 ..... (2)
Trachtenberg, Joshua. Consider the Years: The Story of
the Jewish Community of Easton, 1752-1942. Repr. of 1944
ed. 17.50 ..... (338)

Williams, Richard T. and Mildred C. Williams. Soldiers of
the American Revolution - Northampton County, Pennsylvania.
Repr. of 1874/1906 ed. In process.
Including present Lehigh County. Transcribed and
arranged alphabetically from the Pennsylvania Archives. .... (841)

PHILADELPHIA COUNTY

Arena, Carmelo R. Philadelphia - Spanish New Orleans Trade
1789-1803. 1959. 213pp. BIP-59-04590. .... (777)
Armes, Ethel, ed. Nancy Shippen: Her Journal. 1935. 394pp.
The diary, kept from 1777 to 1800, of a fashionable
Philadelphia belle, with a 130-page introduction about
her life and times. 18.00 ..... (38)
Carey, Mathew. A Short Account of the Malignant Fever,
Lately Prevalent in Philadelphia. 1794. 7.00 ..... (38)
Claypoole, James. James Claypoole's Letter Book: London
and Philadelphia, 1681-1684, ed. Marion Balderston. 1967. 8.50 ..... (363)
Fisher, Sidney G. Philadelphia Perspective: The Diary of
Sidney George Fisher, ed. Nicholas Wainwright. 1967. 12.50 ..... (588)
Ford, W. C., ed. Defenses of Philadelphia in 1777. Repr.
of 1897 ed. 15.00 ..... (176)
Galloway, Grace Growden. Diary of Grace Growden Galloway:
Keep at Philadelphia, June 17, 1778 to September 30, 1779
(Reprinted from 'The Pennsylvania Magazine of History
and Biography.') With an Introduction and Notes by Raymond
C. Werner. 1931/1934. 10.00 ..... (38)
Geib, George Winthrop. A History of Philadelphia 1776 - 1789.
1969. 346pp. BIP-69-22386. .... (777)
Golab, Carol Ann. The Polish Communities of Philadelphia,
1870-1920: Immigrant Distribution and Adaptation in Urban
America. 480pp. BIP-71-26014. .... (777)
Kelley, Joseph J., Jr. Life and Times in Colonial Philadelphia.
1973. 8.95 ..... (713)
Larsen, Grace Hutchison. Profile of a Colonial Merchant:
Thomas Clifford of Pre-Revolutionary Philadelphia. 461pp.
BIP-00-15635. .... (777)
Lawrence, Charles. History of Philadelphia Almshouses and
Hospitals From the Beginning of the 18th to the Ending of
the 19th Centuries, Covering a Period of Nearly 200 Years.
Repr. of 1905 ed. 24.00 ..... (38)
Livingood, James Weston. The History of the Commercial
Rivalry Between Philadelphia and Baltimore for the Trade
of the Susquehanna Valley 1780-1860. 301pp. BIP-00-02998. .... (777)
Manges, Frances May. Women Shopkeepers, Tavern Keepers
and Artisans in Colonial Philadelphia. 1958. 153pp.
BIP-58-01854. .... (777)
Marshall, Christopher. Extracts From the Diary of Christopher
Marshall, Kept in Philadelphia and Lancaster, During the
American Revolution, 1774-1781, ed. William Duane. Repr.
of 1877 ed. 11.00 ..... (38)
Mease, James. The Picture of Philadelphia. 1811. 15.00 ..... (38)
Moss, Roger William, Jr. Master Builders: A History of the
Colonial Philadelphia Building Trades. 255pp. BIP-72-32008. .... (777)
Oaks, Robert Francis. Philadelphia Merchants and the American
Revolution, 1765-1776. 253pp. BIP-71-02534. .... (777)
Olton, Charles Shaw. Philadelphia Artisans and the American
Revolution. 416pp. BIP-67-11655. .... (777)

Pennypacker, Samuel Whitaker. The Settlement of Germantown,
Pennsylvania, and the Beginning of German Emigration to
North America. 1899. 310pp.
  Not just regional history, but a study of emigration
  to America.   15.00   ..... (38)
Peterson, Charles E., ed. Carpenters' Company of the City
and County of Philadelphia 1786 Rule Book. 1971.   9.95   5.95 (625)
Powell, John Harrey. Bring Out Your Dead: The Great
Plague of Yellow Fever in Philadelphia in 1793. 1949.   14.00   ..... (38)
Rogers, William. A Register of Baptisms, Marriages, and
Deaths, 1772-1822. 1865. 78pp. B-BH 19167.   .... (778)
Scharf, John Thomas and Thompson Westcott. History of
Philadelphia, 1609-1884. 3 vols. 1884.   Set: 450.00 ..... (2)
Tinkcom, Harry M., et al. Historic Germantown. 1955.   5.00   ..... (24)
Tolles, Frederick. Meeting House and Counting House: The
Quaker Merchants of Colonial Philadelphia 1682-1763   4.25   ..... (699)
Williams, Richard T. and Mildred C. Williams. Soldiers of
the American Revolution, Philadelphia City, Pennsylvania.
Repr. of 1874/1906 ed. c775pp.   25.00   ..... (841)
_____. Soldiers of the American Revolution - Philadelphia
County, Pennsylvania. Repr. of 1874/1906 ed. In process.
  Included is present day Montgomery County.   .... (841)
Wolf, Edwin and Maxwell Whiteman. History of the Jews of
Philadelphia From Colonial Times to the Age of Jackson.
1975.   8.50   ..... (384)
Wood, William. Old Drury of Philadelphia: A History of the
Philadelphia State, 1800-1835. Repr. of 1932 ed.   24.75   ..... (297)

SCHUYLKILL COUNTY

Rupp, Israel Daniel. History of Northampton, Lehigh, Monroe,
Carbon, and Schuylkill Counties: Containing a Brief History
of the First Settlers, Topography of Townships, Notices of
Leading Events, Incidents, and Interesting Facts in the
Early History of These Counties: With an Appendix Containing Matters of Deep Interest. 1845. illus.
  Rupp deals with the various and contrasting national
  attributes of the German, Swedish, Welsh and Irish
  immigrants who settled Pennsylvania's first
  frontier. Documentation includes the journals of
  James Young, John Van Etten and James Burd.   24.00   ..... (38)

SNYDER COUNTY

Linn, John Blair. Annals of Buffalo Valley, Pennsylvania
1755-1855. Reprint. 625pp.
  Includes assessment lists beginning in 1755, quotes
  from Committee Safety minutes, and muster rolls.
  Extensive lists of early inhabitants, as well as
  marriages and deaths. Map.   17.50   ..... (608)

SOMERSET COUNTY

Document Preservation Committee. Ligonier Valley Observance
United States Bicentennial. The Stoystown and Greensburgh
Turnpike Road Company (Minutes 1815-1826). 1976. 100pp.
  Transcribed from the original minutes, these previously
  unknown turnpike records present an informative account
  of the formation, and first ten years of operation, of this

local segment of the Pittsburgh/Philadelphia Turnpike,
which passed through Stoystown, Laughlintown, Ligonier,
Youngstown, and Greensburg. Map. Every-name index. 9.00 (709)

SULLIVAN COUNTY

Ingham, Thomas J. History of Sullivan County, Pennsylvania.
1899. Part 1-2-260pp. B-BH 519. .... (778)

UNION COUNTY

Linn, John Blair. Annals of Buffalo Valley, Pennsylvania.
1755-1855. Reprint. 625pp.
Includes assessment lists beginning in 1755, quotes
from Committee of Safety minutes, and muster rolls.
Extensive lists of early inhabitants, as well as
marriages and deaths. Map. 17.50 ..... (608)

WASHINGTON COUNTY

Bell, Raymond. "Settlement Dates, Washington County,
Pennsylvania. (Names of Some of the Earliest Pioneers,
With Dates of Their Settlement.)" NGS Quarterly,
Vol. 54, No. 3. 1966. 3pp. 3.50 (514)

WAYNE COUNTY

History of Wayne County Pennsylvania. Repr. of 1902 ed. 178pp.
County history, illustrated, indexed. 22.00 ..... (810)

WESTMORELAND COUNTY

Iscrupe, William L. Ligonier Valley Cemeteries - Volume I
(Ligonier Township - 22 Churches, Public, Abandoned
Cemeteries). 1976.
The first of a series. A comprehensive list of
tombstone inscriptions from Volume 1: 22 church,
public, and abandoned cemeteries, including histories,
maps, and directions thereto. Alphabetically arranged. 16.00 (709)
_____. Ligonier Valley Cemeteries - Volume II (Ligonier
Valley Cemetery - Ligonier Township). 1976. 200pp.
A comprehensive list of tombstone inscriptions from
Volume II: Ligonier Valley Cemetery. Inscriptions
from this cemetery comprise the entire volume.
Alphabetically arranged. 20.00 (709)
Document Preservation Committee. Ligonier Valley Observance,
United States Bicentennial. The Stoystown and Greensburgh
Turnpike Road Company (Minutes 1815-1825). 1976. 100pp.
Transcribed from the original minutes, these previously
unknown turnpike records present an informative ac-
count of the formation, and first ten years of operation,
of this local segment of the Pittsburgh/Philadelphia
Turnpike, which passed through Stoystown, Laughlin-
town, Ligonier, Youngstown, and Greensburg. Map.
Every-name index. 9.00 (709)

WYOMING COUNTY

History of Luzerne, Lackawanna and Wyoming Counties,
Pennsylvania. 1880. 878pp. B-BH 521. .... (778)

YORK COUNTY

Carter, W.C. and A.J. Glossbrenner. History of York County
From Its Erection to the Present Time (1729-1834). Repr.
of 1930 ed. 221pp.   12.50   ..... (274)
Gibson, John. A Biographical History of York County,
Pennsylvania. Repr. of 1886 ed. 207pp.   12.50   ..... (274)

Rhode Island

STATEWIDE REFERENCES

Austin, John Osborne. Ancestry of Thirty-three Rhode Islanders
(born in the eighteenth century): Also Twenty-seven Charts
of Roger Williams' descendants to the Fifth Generation.
1889. 148pp. B-BH 17193.   .... (778)
_____. The Genealogical Dictionary of Rhode Island. 1887.
452pp. B-BH 1957.   .... (778)
_____. One Hundred and Sixty Allied Families. 1893.
323pp. B-OP 66108.   .... (778)
Bigelow, Bruce Macmillan. The Commerce of Rhode Island
With the West Indies, Before the American Revolution.
(Parts I and II). 1930. 452pp. BIP-60-1004.   .... (777)
Bridenbaugh, Carl. Fat Mutton and Liberty of Conscience:
Society in Rhode Island, 1636-1690. 1974.   8.00   ..... (99)
Chapin, Howard Millar. Documentary History of Rhode Island.
2 vols. 1916-1919.   Set: 49.50   ..... (2)
Coleman, Peter J. Transformation of Rhode Island,
1790-1860. Repr. of 1963 ed.   10.00   ..... (99)
Hazard, Thomas R. Report on the Poor and Insane in Rhode-
Island. Repr. of 1851 ed.   8.00   ..... (38)
Hedges, James B. Browns of Providence Plantations,
Volume 2, The Nineteenth Century. 1968.   10.00   ..... (99)
Lowther, Lawrence Leland. Rhode Island Colonial Government,
1732-. 1964. 250pp. BIP-65-01885.   .... (777)

Military

Angell, Israel. Diary of Colonel Israel Angell Commanding
the Second Rhode Island Continental Regiment During
the AmericanRevolution, 1778-1781. ed. Edward Field.
Repr. of 1899 ed.   7.00   ..... (38)

Listed below are the names of professional genealogists willing to undertake research for a
fee within the state of Rhode Island, in areas specified in their ads:

Chenery, William H. Fourteenth Regiment Rhode Island
Heavy Artillery, Colored in the War to Preserve the
Union, 1861-1865. Repr. of 1898 ed.   18.75   ..... (522)
Cohen, Joel Alden. Rhode Island and the American
Revolution: A Selective Socio-Political Analysis.
1967. 231pp. BIP-68-01329.   .... (777)
David, Ebenezer. Rhode Island Chaplain in the Revolution.
Repr. of 1949 ed.   7.50   ..... (404)
Sabre, Gilbert E. Nineteen Months a Prisoner of War.
Narrative of Lieutenant G. E. Sabre, Second Rhode
Island Cavalry, of His Experience in the War Prisons
and Stockades of Morton, Mobile, Atlanta, Libby,
Belle Island, Andersonville, Macon, Charleston, and
Columbia. 1865. 216pp. B-BH 17418.   .... (778)

Records

Arnold, James Newell. Vital Records of Rhode Island.
1636-1850. 1891. 21 vols. c349pp to c734pp. each.
B-OP 65966.   .... (778)
Records of the Vice Admiralty Court of Rhode Island
1716-1752. (Vol. 3 of the American Legal Series.)   43.00   38.00 (415)

BRISTOL COUNTY

Bicknell, Thomas Williams. A History of Barrington,
Rhode Island. 1898. 746pp. B-OP 15534.   .... (778)

NEWPORT COUNTY

Livermore, Samuel Truesdale. A History of Block Island
From its Discovery, in 1514, to the Present Time, 1876.
1877. 381pp. B-OP 27398.   .... (778)

WASHINGTON COUNTY

Beaman, Alden Gamaliel. North Kingstown, South Kingstown,
Exeter and Richmond, Rhode Island Marriages from Probate
Records. 1975. 101pp.
           Contains only about 25% duplication of J. N. Arnold's
           Vital Record Rhode Island, Vol. 5; 75% of the
           entries are not published elsewhere. 15.00 (57)
_____. Washington County, Rhode Island Births and Marriages
from the Gravestone Records. 1977. In process.
           It is anticipated that the duplication of J. N. Arnold's
           Vital Record Rhode Island, Vol. 5, will be very low. .... (57)
_____. Washington County, Rhode Island Births 1770 to
1850 Not In Arnold's Volume 5. 1976. 185pp.
           Contains nearly 6000 birth entries not in J. N. Arnold's
           Vital Record Rhode Island, Volume 5; increases the
           number of Washington County birth entries by about 50%. 15.00   ..... (57)
Hazard, Thomas Benjamin. Nalier Tom's Diary; Otherwise, The
Journal of Thomas B. Hazard of Kingstown, Rhode Island,
1778 to 1840, Which Includes Observations on the Weather,
Records of Births, Marriages and Deaths, Transactions by
Barter and Money of Varying Value, Preaching Friends and
Neighborhood Gossip. Printed as Written and Introduced by
Caroline Hazard. 1930.   67.50   ..... (2)

Hinckley, Anita W. Wickford Memories. Original Title:
Tales of Old Wickford, Rhode Island. 1973.   6.95   ..... (90)

South Carolina

STATEWIDE REFERENCES

Ackerman, Robert Kilgo. South Carolina Colonial Land
Policies. 1965. 207pp. BIP-68-05916.   .... (777)
Duncan, John Donald. Servitude and Slavery in Colonial
South Carolina 1670-1776. 1972. 878pp. BIP-72-20766.   .... (777)
Frakes, George Edward. The Origin and Development of the
South Carolina Legislative Committee System, 1719-1776.
1966. 454pp. BIP-67-11004.   .... (777)
Izard, Ralph. Correspondence of Mister Ralph Izard of
South Carolina, from the Year 1774-1804. Repr. of 1844 ed.   16.50   ..... (2)
Jones, Lewis P. South Carolina - Synoptic History for Laymen.
1971.   .....   3.95 (669)
Kenpper, David Morton. The Political Structure of Colonial
South Carolina, 1743-1776. 1971. 281pp. BIP-72-07169. .... (777)
Leiding, Hariette K. Historic Houses of South Carolina.
Repr. of 1921 ed. 435pp.   24.00   ..... (638)
McCrady, Edward. History of South Carolina 1670-1783.
4 vols. 1897-1902.
    Volume 1   Each: 17.50   ..... (2)
    Volume 2   Each: 20.00   ..... (2)
    Volume 3   Each: 20.00   ..... (2)
    Volume 4   Each: 17.50   ..... (2)
                                Set: 75.00   ..... (2)
Meriwether, Robert L. The Expansion of South Carolina 1729-1765.
Repr. of 1940 ed.   15.00   ..... (612)
Milling, Chapman J. Red Carolinians. 1969.   14.95   ..... (703)
Nadelhaft, Jerome Joshua. The Revolutionary Era in South
Carolina, 1775-1788. 1965. 344pp. BIP-65-06228.   .... (777)
O'Neall, John B. Biographical Sketches of the Bench and Bar
of South Carolina. 2 vols. Repr. of 1859 ed. 1081pp.
    Volume 1:   21.00   ..... (638)
    Volume 2:   24.00   ..... (638)
Savage, Henry, Jr. River of the Carolinas: The Santee.
Repr. of 1956 ed.   7.50   ..... (544)
Smith, Warren B. White Servitude in Colonial South Carolina. 1970.   7.95   2.25 (703)
Spalding, Billups Phinizy. Georgia and South Carolina During the
Oglethorpe Period, 1732-1743. 1963. 3317pp. BIP-64-01895.   .... (777)

Listed below is the name of a professional genealogist willing to undertake research for a
fee within the state of South Carolina, in areas specified in her ad:

Stoney, Samuel G. Plantations of the Carolina Low Country. 6th ed.
eds. Albert Simons and Samuel Lapham, Jr. 1969.   15.00   ••••• (121)
Taylor, Alrutheus Ambush. The Negro in South Carolina During
the Reconstruction. 1924.   8.75   ••••• (2)
Wallace, David D. South Carolina: A Short History, 1520-1948.
1969.   14.95   •••• (703)
Watson, Alan Douglas. The Quitrent System in Royal South
Carolina. 1971. 247pp. BIP-71-28901.   •••••   ••••• (777)
Weir, Robert McColloch. Liberty and Property, and No Stamps:
South Carolina and the Stamp Act Crisis. 1964. 548pp.
BIP-67-04626.   •••••   ••••• (777)
Williams, Jack Kenny. Crime and Punishment in South
Carolina, 1790-1860. 1953. 353pp. BIP-58-05192.   •••••   ••••• (777)

Research Aids

Easterby, J. H. A Guide to the Study and Reading of
South Carolina History. Repr. of 1950 ed. 344pp.
A reprint of the original plus a supplement of
books on South Carolina history published since 1950.   15.00   •••• (638)
Rogers, George C., Jr. A South Carolina Chronology,
1497-1970. 1973.   •••••   1.95 (703)

Military

Burton, E. Milby. Siege of Charleston, 1861-1865. 1970.   14.95   •••• (703)
Gibbes, Robert W., ed. Documentary History of the American
Revolution, Consisting of Letters and Papers Relating to
the Contest for Liberty Chiefly in South Carolina.
Repr. of 1853 ed.   38.00   ••••• (38)
Higgins, W. Robert. A Financial History of the American
Revolution in South Carolina. 1970. 313pp. BIP-71-10383.   •••••   ••••• (777)
Hilborn, Nat and Sam Hilborn. Battleground of Freedom:
South Carolina in the Revolution. 1970.   20.00   •••• (669)
McMaster, Fitzhugh. Soldiers and Uniforms: South Carolina
Military Affairs, 1670-1775. 1971.   •••••   1.95 (703)
Pugh, Robert Coplin. The Cowpens Campaign and the
American Revolution. 1951. 316pp. BIP-00-02722.   •••••   ••••• (777)
Reid, Jesse Walton. History of the Fourth Regiment of
South Carolina Volunteers from the Commencement of the
War until Lee's Surrender. Repr. of 1892 ed. 143pp.
Reid's history of the Fourth South Carolina is told in
the letters he sent home with the request that they be
saved. Reid's letters are largely focused on the
movements of the regiment, their camps, and
soldier life, interspersed with humor and his own
experiences.   12.50   •••• (506)
Uhlendorf, Bernard A., ed. The Siege of Charleston. Diaries
and Letters of Hessian Officers from the von Jungkenn
Papers in the William L. Clements Library. 1938.   10.00   ••••• (38)
Weigley, Russell F. The Partisan War: The South
Carolina Campaign of 1780-1782. 1971.   •••••   1.95 (703)
Weir, Robert M. Most Important Epocha: The Coming of
the Revolution in South Carolina. 1970.   •••••   1.95 (703)
Wheeler, Earl Milton. The Role of the North Carolina
Militia in the Beginning of the American Revolution.
1969. 237pp. BIP-69-20510.   •••••   ••••• (777)

Religious and Ethnic Groups

Hirsch, Arthur H. Huguenots of Colonial South Carolina.
Repr. of 1928 ed.   11.00   ..... (685)
Watts, Frederick L. Petition for Redress. 1976. 350pp.
Newly discovered documents showing heritage contribu-
tions of first Germans in America - from South Carolina
to Georgia, Mississippi, and Texas from 1735 to 1976.   17.50   12.50 (270)
Wikramanayake, Marina. A World in Shadow: The Free Black
in Antebellum South Carolina. 1973.   14.95   ..... (703)

Newspapers

Charleston Daily Courier, 1803-1873. 116 rolls.
Microfilm of the original papers. Individual rolls covering
a specific time span may be ordered. Prices vary from
$15 to $30 per roll.   .... (870)
Charleston Mercury, January 1822 to November 16, 1868.
79 rolls.
Microfilm of the original papers. Individual
rolls covering a specific time span may be ordered.
Prices vary $15 to $30 per roll.   .... (870)
Charleston Times, October 6, 1800 to July 24, 1821.
36 rolls.
Microfilm of the original papers. Individual rolls
covering a specific time span may be ordered.
Prices vary $15 to $30 per roll.   .... (870)

Records

Curtis, Mary Barnett. Abstracts of Reports of Cases Argued
and Determined in the Court of Chancery by the State
of South Carolina. Volume II. 1976.
Covers period from the Revolution to December, 1813.   .....   7.50 (371)
_____. Abstracts of Cases Determined in the Superior Courts
of Law and Equity of the State of South Carolina. 1802.
Reported by John Louis Taylor. 7.50 (371)
_____. Abstracts of Reports of Judicial Decisions in the
State of South Carolina. Volume I. Repr. of 1857 ed.
Covers cases from 1793 to 1815; reported by
Joseph Brevard. 7.50 (371)
Lindsay, Morn McKoy and GeLee Corley Hendrix. The Jury
List of South Carolina 1778-1779. 1975. 131pp.
May be used as a state census over ten years before
the 1790 census. Contains over 9000 names of men
eligible for jury duty.   15.00   ..... (326)
Robertson, Clara H. Kansas Territorial Settlers of 1860 Who
Were Born in Tennessee, Virginia, North Carolina,
and South Carolina. 1976. 187pp.   17.50   ..... (274)
Russell, Mrs. Marie. 1810 Census. In process.
All counties of 1810 Census will be published by
county; index to entire state will be published upon
completion of county series.   .... (664)
Salley, Alexander S. Marriage Notices in Charleston Courier,
1803-1808. Repr. of 1919 ed. 83pp. 5.00 (274)
_____. Marriage Notices in the South Carolina and American
General Gazette, 1766-81, and The Royal Gazette,
1781-82. Repr. of 1914 ed. 52pp. 5.00 (274)

South Carolina Chancery Court Records 1671-1779 (Volume
of the American Legal Series).   43.00   38.00 (415)

ANDERSON COUNTY

Reid, Jesse Walton. History of the Fourth Regiment of South
Carolina Volunteers from the Commencement of the War
Until Lee's Surrender. Repr. of 1892 ed. 143pp.   12.50   ..... (506)

ANSON COUNTY

Holcomb, Brent, G.R.S. North Carolina Land Grants in South
Carolina, Volume II: Anson and Mecklenberg Counties,
1749-1770. 1976. 89pp. index.   18.00   ..... (343)

BEAUFORT COUNTY

Graydon, Nell S. Tales of Beaufort.   6.95   ..... (59)
Hilton, Mary K. Old Homes and Churches of Beaufort County.   7.95   ..... (59)
Inglesby, Edith. Corner of Carolina: The Four Seasons in
Hilton Head Island Beaufort and Fluffton. 1969.   10.00   ..... (717)

CHARLESTON COUNTY

Stumpf, Stuart Owen. The Merchants of Colonial Charleston,
1680-1756. 309pp. BIP-71-31318.   .... (777)
Walsh, Walter Richard. Charleston's Sons of Liberty: A
Study of the Mechanics, 1760-1785. 212pp. BIP-00-08945.   .... (777)

FAIRFIELD COUNTY

Russell, Mrs. Marie. 1810 Census of Fairfield County, South
Carolina. 1976. 55pp.
  Full census readout by household order with surname
  index. 5.00 (664)

GEORGETOWN COUNTY

Pennington, Patience. Woman Rice Planter, ed. Cornelius O.
Cathey. 1961.   10.00   ..... (319)
Russell, Mrs. Marie. 1810 Census of Georgetown District,
South Carolina. 1976.
  Full census readout by household order with surname
  index. 4.00 (664)

GREENVILLE COUNTY

Reid, Jesse Walton. History of the Fourth Regiment of South
Carolina Volunteers from the Commencement of the War
Until Lee's Surrender. Repr. of 1892 ed. 143pp.   12.50   ..... (506)

MARION COUNTY

Sellers, William W. A History of Marion County, South
Carolina, From Its Earliest Times to the Present, 1901.
1902. 658pp. B-OP 55960.   .... (778)

MECKLENBERG COUNTY

Holcomb, Brent, G.R.S. North Carolina Land Grants in South
Carolina, Volume II: Anson and Mecklenberg Counties,
1749-1770. 1976. 89pp. index. 18.00 (343)

PICKENS COUNTY

Reid, Jesse Walton. History of the Fourth Regiment of South
Carolina Volunteers from the Commencement of the War
Until Lee's Surrender. Repr. of 1892 ed. 143pp.   12.50 ..... (506)

SPARTANBURG COUNTY

WPA Writers' Program, Spartanburg Unit. A History of
Spartanburg County. Repr. of 1940 ed. 304pp. illus.   16.00 ..... (638)

South Dakota

STATEWIDE REFERENCES

Brown, Jesse and A.M. Willard. The Black Hills Trails: A
History of the Struggles of the Pioneers in the Winning of
the Black Hills, ed. John T. Milek. 1924. illus.   33.00 ..... (38)
Jones, Robert H. Civil War in the Northwest: Nebraska,
Wisconsin, Iowa, Minnesota, and the Dakotas. Repr. of
1960 ed.   8.95   ..... (556)
Peters, Victor. All Things Common: The Hutterian Way of
Life. 1971.   ..... 2.75 (317)
Schell, Herbert S. History of South Dakota. 3rd rev. ed. 1975. 11.95 6.50 (521)
Tallent, Annie D. The Black Hills: Or, The Last Hunting Ground
of the Dakotahs. 1899. illus.   47.00 ..... (38)

Tennessee

STATEWIDE REFERENCES

Abernathy, Thomas P. From Frontier to Plantation in Tennessee.
3rd ed. 1967.   7.50   ..... (11)
Alderson, William T. and Robert M. McBride, eds. Landmarks
of Tennessee History. 1965.   7.95   ..... (747)
Allison, John, ed. Notable Men of Tennessee. Personal and
Genealogical. 1905. Vol. 1-336pp, Vol. 2-326pp. B-OP 22852.   .... (778)
Bullard, Hellen. Crafts and Craftsmen of the Tennessee Mountains.
1976. 224pp.
          History of east Tennessee traditional and designer
          craftsmen from 1937 to the present. Index. Illustrated. 15.95 7.95 (732)
Clark, Blanche H. The Tennessee Yeomen, 1840-1860. Repr. of
of 1942 ed.   11.00 ..... (552)

Listed below is the name of a professional genealogist whose firm is willing to undertake
research for a fee within the state of Tennessee:

Dykeman, Wilma. French Broad. 1966.   5.50   ..... (747)

Folmsbee, Stanley J., et al. Tennessee, a Short History. 1969.   15.00   8.95 (747)

Henderson, Archibald. The Conquest of the Old Southwest.
Repr. of 1920 ed. 419pp.
The story of the westward expansion into Tennessee
and Kentucky from the Carolinas and Virginia.   18.00   ..... (638)

Kirkeminde, Patricia B. Veterinary Medicine in Tennessee,
A History. 1976. c500pp.
History of veterinary medicine in Tennessee, including
pictures and biographies, lists of blacksmiths and
farriers from the War of 1812, Civil War, World War
I. Fully documented. Numbered and signed.   20.50   ..... (748)

Lacy, Eric Russell, Sr. Sectionalism in East Tennessee, 1796-
1861. 333pp. BIP-64-04450.   .... (777)

Matthews, Elmora M. Neighbor and Kin: Life in a Tennessee
Ridge Community. 1966.   5.00   ..... (789)

Sevier, John. Commission Book of Governor John Sevier,
1796-1801, ed. Tennessee Historical Commission. 1957.   4.95   ..... (747)

Shepperson, Wilbur S. Samuel Roberts: A Welsh Colonizer
in Civil War Tennessee. 1961.   7.50   ..... (747)

Stewart, Guy Harry. History and Bibliography of Middle Tennessee Newspapers 1799-1876. 1957. 288pp. BIP-00-25291.   .... (777)

Three Pioneer Tennessee Documents: Donelson's Journal,
Cumberland Compact, Minutes of Cumberland Court. 1964.   3.95   ..... (747)

Military

Armstrong, Zella. Some Tennessee Heroes of the Revolution,
Compiled from Pension Statements. Repr. of 1933 ed.
162pp.   10.00   ..... (274)

Connelly, Thomas L. Autumn of Glory: The Army of
Tennessee, 1862-1865. 1971.   15.00   ..... (440)

Horn, Stanley F. Army of Tennessee. Repr. of 1953 ed.   9.95   ..... (556)

_____, ed. Tennessee's War, 1861-1865: Described by
Participants. 1965.   9.95   ..... (747)

McKee, Jenny S. Throb of Drums in Tennessee: 1862-1865.
1973.   6.95   ..... (202)

Murfree, Mary N. Story of Old Fort Loudon. Repr. of
1899 ed.   14.00   ..... (299)

Tennessee During the Revolutionary War. 1974.   8.75   ..... (747)

Records

Curtis, Mary Barnett. Abstracts of Reports of Cases Argued
and Determined in the Highest Court of Law and Equity
of the State of Tennessee, Volume I. Repr. of 1870 ed.
Reported by Samuel F. Cooper. 7.50 (371)

_____. Abstracts of Tennessee Reports by John Overton
Volume II. 1976.   .....   7.50 (371)

_____. Early East Tennessee Tax Lists. 1964. 200pp.
22 East Tennessee County tax lists for which there
are no census records till 1830.   .....   15.00 (371)

Fulton Genealogical Society. Bible Records of Western
Kentucky and Tennessee. 1975. 100pp. 7.50 (261)

Potter, Dorothy Williams. Tennessee Passports. 1976-1977.
Heretofore unpublished early documents showing the
travels and migrations of many individuals and
families. A brief history of the circumstances sur-
rounding the different types of passports for Tennessee.   .... (615)

BYRON SISTLER BARBARA SISTLER

Byron Sistler & Associates
TENNESSEE RECORDS

1625 WASHINGTON ST., EVANSTON, IL 60202

Ramsey, J. G. Annals of Tennessee to the End of the 18th
Century. 1853.   31.00 ..... (38)
Robertson, Clara H. Kansas Territorial Settlers of 1860
Who Were Born in Tennessee, Virginia, North Carolina,
and South Carolina. 1976. 187pp.   17.50 ..... (274)
Sistler, Byron. 1830 Census - East Tennessee. Repr. of
1969 ed. 276pp.
   Single index for the 24 easternmost counties,
   with statistical detail as per original schedules.   23.00 ..... (691)
_____. 1830 Census - Middle Tennessee. Repr. of 1971
ed. 294pp.
   Single index for 14 middle Tennessee counties,
   with statistical detail as per original schedules.   27.50 ..... (691)
_____. 1830 Census - West Tennessee. 1971. 213pp.
   Single index for 24 westernmost counties with
   statistical detail as per original schedules.   23.00 ..... (691)
_____ and Barbara Sistler. 1850 Census, Tennessee,
Volume 1, Aaron through Childress. 1974. 316pp.
   A single index for the entire state, including
   names and ages of all persons except slaves.   27.50 ..... (691)
_____. 1850 Census, Tennessee, Volume 2, Childs
through Gary. 1974. 312pp.
   A single index for the entire state, including
   names and ages of all persons except slaves.   27.50 ..... (691)
_____. 1850 Census, Tennessee, Volume 3, Gaskell
through Jonas. 1975. 300pp.
   A single index for the entire state, including
   names and ages of all persons except slaves.   27.50 ..... (691)
_____. 1850 Census, Tennessee, Volume 4, Jones through
Murley. 1975. 323pp.
   A single index for the entire state, including
   names and ages of all persons except slaves.   27.50 ..... (691)
_____. 1850 Census, Tennessee, Volume 5, Murpha through
Rudd. 1975. 253pp.
   A single index for the entire state, including
   names and ages of all persons except slaves.   27.50 ..... (691)
_____. 1850 Census, Tennessee, Volume 6, Ruddel through
Wallace. 1976. 292pp.
   A single index for the entire state, including
   names and ages of all persons except slaves.   27.50 ..... (691)
_____. 1850 Census, Tennessee, Volume 7, Walland
through G of Cross Index. 1976. In Process.
   A single index for the entire state, including
   names and ages of all persons except slaves.
   Contains the beginning of a cross index of persons whose surname differed from that of house-
   hold head.   27.50 ..... (691)
_____. 1850 Census, Tennessee, Volume 8, H through
Z of Cross Index. 1976. In Process.
   A single index for the entire state, including
   names and ages of all persons except slaves.
   Completes the series and the cross index begun
   in Volume 7.   27.50 ..... (691)

ANDERSON COUNTY

"1830 Tennessee United States Census: Anderson County Heads
of Household as Enumerated." SGE Quarterly, Vol. 1, No. 9.
1958. 3pp. 2.00 (681)

BEDFORD COUNTY

"1830 Tennessee United States Census: Bedford County Heads
of Household as Enumerated." SGE Quarterly, Vol. 10,
No. 51. 1969. 18pp. 2.50 (681)

Maesh, Timothy R. and Helen C. Maesh. Cemetery Records of
Bedford County, Tennessee (All of County). 1976. In Process.
c400pp. .... (467)

BLEDSOE COUNTY

"1830 Tennessee United States Census: Bledsoe County Heads
of Household as Enumerated." SGE Quarterly, Vol. 2, No. 11.
1959. 7pp. 2.00 (681)

BLOUNT COUNTY

"1830 Tennessee United States Census: Blount County Heads of
Household as Enumerated." SGE Quarterly, Vol. 2, No. 14.
1960. 11pp. 2.00 (681)

BRADLEY COUNTY

"1840 Tennessee Census: Bradley County Heads of Households
as Enumerated." SGE Quarterly, Vol. 6, No. 34. 1965. 3pp. 2.50 (681)

CAMPBELL COUNTY

"1830 Tennessee United States Census: Campbell County Heads
of Household as Enumerated." SGE Quarterly, Vol. 2, No. 13.
1960. 7pp. 2.00 (681)

CARROLL COUNTY

"1830 Tennessee United States Census: Carroll County Heads
of Household as Enumerated." SGE Quarterly, Vol. 11, No. 54.
1970. 9pp. 2.50 (681)

CARTER COUNTY

"1830 Tennessee United States Census: Carter County Heads of
Household as Enumerated." SGE Quarterly, Vol. 2, No. 15.
1960. 8pp. 2.00 (681)

CLAIBORNE COUNTY

"1830 Tennessee United States Census: Claiborne County Heads
of Household as Enumerated." SGE Quarterly, Vol. 2, No. 16.
1960. 11pp. 2.00 (681)

COCKE COUNTY

"1830 Tennessee United States Census: Cocke County Heads of
Household as Enumerated." SGE Quarterly, Vol. 3, No. 18.
1961. 8pp. 2.00 (681)

COFFEE COUNTY

Potter, Dorothy W. and Betty M. Majors. 1840 Federal Census
of Coffee County, Tennessee. 1970. 81pp. 5.25 (615)
Potter, Dorothy W. Original Surveyor's Record Book, 1836-1887.
1976. 375pp.
Includes entries made in Franklin, Bedford, Rutherford,
and Warren Counties in the area that later became
Coffee County. 15.00 (615)
_____. Wills, Intestates, Estates, Widow's Provisions and
Guardianships, 1836-1866 of Coffee County, Tennessee. 1976. .... (615)

DAVIDSON COUNTY

"1830 Tennessee U. S. Census: Davidson County and Nashville
City." Heads of household as enumerated. SGE Quarterly,
Vol. 11, Nos. 55, 56. 1970. 18pp. 5.00 (681)
Waller, William, ed. Nashville in the 1890's. 1970. 342pp.
The editor has culled informa tion from court records,
archives, newspapers, and personal recollections of
elderly citizens. 10.00 ..... (789)
_____. Nashville, 1900 to 1910. 1972. 390pp.
A sequel to the earlier volume Nashville In 1890's,
employing information from newspapers, recollections,
etc. 15.00 ..... (789)
Whitfield, Sara M. and June C. Williams. Index to Clayton's
Davidson County. 6.95 ..... (76)

DICKSON COUNTY

"1830 Tennessee U. S. Census: Dickson County." Heads of
household as enumerated. SGE Quarterly, Vol. 12, No. 57.
1971. 7pp. 2.50 (681)

DYER COUNTY

"1830 Tennessee U. S. Census: Dyer County." Heads of
household as enumerated. SGE Quarterly, Vol. 12, No. 58.
1971. 3pp. 2.50 (681)

FAYETTE COUNTY

"1830 Tennessee U. S. Census: Fayette County." Heads of
household as enumerated. SGE Quarterly, Vol. 10, No. 49.
1969. 6pp. 2.50 (681)

FENTRESS COUNTY

"1830 Tennessee U. S. Census: Fentress County." Heads of
household as enumerated. SGE Quarterly, Vol. 6, No. 33.
1965. 3pp. 2.50 (681)
Smith, Randolph N. Civil War Abstracts of Field Reports and
Correspondence. 1975. 124pp.
Covers area of Kentucky and Tennessee within
50 miles of Burkesville, Kentucky. 5.25 (425)

FRANKLIN COUNTY

"1830 Tennessee U. S. Census: Franklin County." Heads of
household as enumerated. SGE Quarterly, Vol. 10, No. 52.
1969. 14pp. 2.50 (681)

GIBSON COUNTY

"1830 Tennessee U. S. Census: Gibson County." Heads of
household as enumerated. SGE Quarterly, Vol. 10, No. 50.
1969. 5pp. 2.50 (681)

GILES COUNTY

"1830 Tennessee U. S. Census: Giles County." Heads of
household as enumerated. SGE Quarterly, Vol. 11, No. 56.
1970. 14pp. 2.50 (681)

GRAINGER COUNTY

"1830 Tennessee U. S. Census: Grainer County." Heads of
household as enume rated. SGE Quarterly, Vol. 3, No. 20.
1961. 13pp. 2.50 (681)

GREENE COUNTY

"1830 Tennessee U. S. Census: Greene County." Heads of
household as enumerated. SGE Quarterly, Vol. 3, No. 21.
1962. 12pp. 2.50 (681)

HAMILTON COUNTY

Armstrong, Zella. The History of Hamilton County and
Chattanooga, Tennessee. 2 vols. c1931. Vol. 1-628pp.
Vol. 2-477pp. B-OP 70068. .... (778)
"1830 Tennessee U. S. Census: Hamilton County." Heads of
household as enumerated. SGE Quarterly, Vol. 3, No. 22
1962. 4pp. 2.50 (681)

HARDEMAN COUNTY

"1830 Tennessee U. S. Census: Hardeman County." Heads of
household as enumerated. SGE Quarterly, Vol. 13, No. 61.
1972. 7pp. 2.50 (681)

HARDIN COUNTY

Curtis, Janet Austin. Hardin County, Tennessee Cemetery
Records. 1977. In Process.
    Cemeteries of southern half of the county east of
    the Tennessee River. .... (175)
_____. Hardin County, Tennessee 1820-1830-1840 Census. 1977.
    Not just an index; age catagories included. 8.00 (175)
_____. Hardin County, Tennessee Marriage Records. 1976.
    Some unrecorded marriages from private sources,
    plus loose records and first two books in County Court. 8.00 (175)
"1830 Tennessee U. S. Census: Hardin County." Heads of
household as enumerated. SGE Quarterly, Vol. 12, No. 60.
1971. 4pp. 2.50 (681)

HAWKINS COUNTY

"1830 Tennessee U. S. Census: Hawkins County." Heads of
household as enumerated. SGE Quarterly, Vol. 3, No. 22
1962. 11pp. 2.50 (681)

HAYWOOD COUNTY

"1830 Tennessee U. S. Census: Haywood County." Heads of
household as enumerated. SGE Quarterly, Vol. 13, No. 62.
1972. 5pp. 2.50 (681)

HENRY COUNTY

"1830 Tennessee U. S. Census: Henry County." Heads of
household as enumerated. SGE Quarterly, Vol. 13, No. 64.
1972. 11pp. 2.50 (681)
Inman, W. O. Pen Sketches of Henry County, Volume I.
1976. 87pp.
    Sixty articles depicting areas (people and places) of
historical record as written some years ago and published
as installment articles in the Paris Post-Intelligencer,
a newspaper publication sponsored by Henry County
Historical Society. 3.50 (254)
_____, comp. Henry County, Tennessee Marriages, Volume
II, 1853-1867. 1974. 133pp.
    Arranged alphabetical by surname. Cross indexed.
Legible print, easy to read format. 7.00 (254)
_____. Henry County, Tennessee Marriages, Volume III,
1868-1880. 1975. 168pp.
    Arranged alphabetical by surname. Cross indexed. 10.00 (254)
_____. Henry County, Tennessee Marriages, Volume IV,
1881-1899? 1976. .... (254)

HICKMAN COUNTY

"1830 Tennessee U. S. Census: Hickman County." Heads of
household as enumerated. SGE Quarterly, Vol. 15, No. 70.
1974. 8pp. 2.50 (681)

HUMPHREYS COUNTY

"1830 Tennessee U. S. Census: Humphreys County." Heads of
household as enumerated. SGE Quarterly, Vol. 12, No. 59.
1971. 7pp. 2.50 (681)

JACKSON COUNTY

"1830 Tennessee U. S. Census: Jackson County." Heads of
household as enumerated. SGE Quarterly, Vol. 8, No. 41.
1967. 8pp. 2.50 (681)

JEFFERSON COUNTY

"1830 Tennessee U. S. Census: Jefferson County." Heads of
household as enumerated. SGE Quarterly, Vol. 3, No. 23.
1962. 9pp. 2.50 (681)

KNOX COUNTY

"1830 Tennessee Census: Knox County." Heads of household
as enumerated. SGE Quarterly, Vol. 3, No. 24. 1962. 10pp. 2.50 (681)
Tennessee Historical Records Survey. Minutes of the County
Court of Knox County, 1792-1795. Repr. of 1941 ed. 300pp. 12.50 (330)

LAWRENCE COUNTY

"1830 Tennessee Census: Lawrence County." Heads of
household as enumerated. SGE Quarterly, Vol. 15, No. 72.
1974. 6pp. 2.50 (681)

LINCOLN COUNTY

"1830 Tennessee Census: Lincoln County." Heads of
household as enumerated. SGE Quarterly, Vol. 14, No. 68.
1973. 11pp. 2.50 (681)
Marsh, Timothy R. and Helen C. Marsh. Lincoln County,
Tennessee Official Marriage Records 1838-1880. 311pp. 12.50 (467)

McMINN COUNTY

"1830 Tennessee Census: McMinn County." Heads of
household as enumerated. SGE Quarterly, Vol. 4, No. 27.
1963. 11pp. 2.50 (681)

MARION COUNTY

"1830 Tennessee Census: Marion County." Heads of
households as enumerated. SGE Quarterly, Vol. 4, No. 25.
1963. 5pp. 2.50 (681)

MAURY COUNTY

"1830 Tennessee Census: Maury County." Heads of household
as enumerated. SGE Quarterly, Vol. 13, Nos. 62, 63.
1972. 18pp. 5.00 (681)
Lightfoot, Marise P. Let the Drums Roll. 1976. 235pp.
Biographical sketches of 192 veterans and patriots of
the Revolutionary War who settled in Maury County,
Tennessee, including methods and materials. 11.25 ..... (431)

MEIGS COUNTY

"1840 Tennessee Census: Meigs County." Heads of households
as enumerated. SGE Quarterly, Vol. 6, No. 35. 1965. 4pp. 2.50 (681)

MONROE COUNTY

"1830 Tennessee Census: Monroe County." Heads of households
as enumerated. SGE Quarterly, Vol. 4, No. 28. 1963. 11pp. 2.50 (681)
Lenoir, William B. History of Sweetwater Valley, Tennessee.
Repr. of 1916 ed. 419pp. 17.50 ..... (274)

MONTGOMERY COUNTY

"1830 Tennessee Census: Montgomery County." Heads of
households as enumerated. SGE Quarterly, Vol. 15, No. 71.
1974. 11pp. 2.50 (681)

MOORE COUNTY

Marsh, Timothy R. and Helen C. Marsh. Cemetery Records
of Moore County, Tennessee (Complete County). 167pp. 10.00 (467)

MORGAN COUNTY

DeBruyn, John R., ed. Dissipations at Uffington House:
Letters of Emmy Hughes, 1881-1887. 1976. 92pp.
Letters from an English girl describing life in
Tennessee. 5.00 (476)
"1830 Tennessee Census: Morgan County." Heads of households as enumerated. SGE Quarterly, Vol. 4, No. 26.
1963. 10pp. 2.50 (681)

OBION COUNTY

Vanderwood, Paul J. Night Riders of Reelfoot Lake. 1969. 172pp.
Detailed history of a violent land-use controversy in
Northwest Tennessee in 1908.   6.50   ••••   (476)

OVERTON COUNTY

"1830 Tennessee Census: Overton County." Heads of
households as enumerated. SGE Quarterly, Vol. 7, No. 39.
1966. 6pp.   ••••   2.50 (681)
Phillips, Oma Dee. Overton County, Tennessee Marriages.
Index. 1973. 40pp.
Marriage book and page listed. Not dated.   ••••   5.00 (596)
Smith, Randolph N. Civil War Abstracts of Field Reports
and Correspondence. 1975. 124pp.
Covers area of Kentucky and Tennessee within
50 miles of Burkesville, Kentucky.   ••••   5.25 (425)

PICKETT COUNTY

Huddleston, Tim. History of Pickett County, Tennessee.
1973. 300+pp. 8 1/2 x 11.   10.50   ••••   (359)

POLK COUNTY

"1840 Tennessee Census: Polk County." Heads of households
as enumerated. SGE Quarterly, Vol. 7, No. 37. 1966. 5pp.   ••••   2.50 (681)

RHEA COUNTY

"1830 Tennessee Census: Rhea County." Heads of households as
enumerated. SGE Quarterly, Vol. 5, No. 29. 1964. 7pp.   ••••   2.50 (681)

ROANE COUNTY

"1830 Tennessee Census: Roane County." Heads of households
as enumerated. SGE Quarterly, Vol. 5, No. 30. 1964. 10pp.   ••••   2.50 (681)
Wells, Emma M. The History of Roane County, Tennessee,
1801-1870. Repr. of 1927 ed. 352pp.   16.50   ••••   (274)

RUTHERFORD COUNTY

McBride, Robert M. "Rutherford County, Tennessee, Petitioners,
1803." NGS Quarterly, Vol. 61, No. 4. 1973. 4pp.   ••••   3.50 (514)
Phillips, Oma Dee. 1860 Census. 1968. 367pp.
Indexed-from new, enlarged microfilm.   ••••   20.00 (596)

SHELBY COUNTY

Baird, W. David, ed. Years of Discontent: Frank L. James in
Arkansas, 1877-1878. 1976. 88pp.
Gossipy diary with many local references.   ••••   5.00 (476)
"1830 Tennessee Census: Shelby County." Heads of households
as enumerated. SGE Quarterly, Vol. 14, No. 66. 1973. 4pp.   ••••   2.50 (681)
Tucker, David M. Lieutenant Lee of Beale Street. 1971. 217pp.
Depicts black society in Memphis over the past fifty years.   7.95   ••••   (789)

SEVIER COUNTY

"1830 Tennessee Census: Sevier County." Heads of households
as enumerated. SGE Quarterly, Vol. 5, No. 31. 1964. 4pp.   ••••   2.50 (681)

SMITH COUNTY

"1830 Census, Smith County, Tennessee." SGE Quarterly,
Vol. XVI, No. 73. 1975. 17pp. 3.00 (706)

STEWART COUNTY

"1830 Census, Stewart County, Tennessee." SGE Quarterly,
Vol. XVI, No. 75. 1975. 7pp. 3.00 (706)

SULLIVAN COUNTY

"1830 Tennessee Census: Sullivan County." Heads of households
as enumerated. SGE Quarterly, Vol. 5, No. 31. 1964. 8pp. 2.50 (681)

TIPTON COUNTY

"1830 Census, Tipton County, Tennessee." SGE Quarterly,
Vol. XVI, No. 74. 1975. 6pp. 3.00 (706)

WARREN COUNTY

"1830 Tennessee Census: Warren County." Heads of households
as enumerated. SGE Quarterly, Vo. 14, No. 65. 1973. 14pp. 2.50 (681)

WASHINGTON COUNTY

"1830 Tennessee Census: Washington County." Heads of
households as enumerated. SGE Quarterly, Vol. 5, No. 32.
1964. 8pp. 2.50 (681)

WAYNE COUNTY

"1830 Tennessee Census: Wayne County." Heads of households
as enumerated. SGE Quarterly, Vol. 9, No. 47. 1968. 7pp. 2.50 (681)

WEAKLEY COUNTY

"1830 Tennessee Census: Weakley County." Heads of households
as enumerated. SGE Quarterly, Vol. 9, No. 48. 1968. 5pp. 2.50 (681)

WHITE COUNTY

"1830 Tennessee Census: White County." Heads of households
as enumerated. SGE Quarterly, Vol. 9, No. 46. 1968. 10pp. 2.50 (681)

WILLIAMSON COUNTY

"1830 Tennessee Census: Williamson County." Heads of households as enumerated. SGE Quarterly, Vol. 9, No. 48.
1968. 19pp. 2.50 (681)

WILSON COUNTY

"1830 Tennessee Census: Wilson County." Heads of households
as enumerated. SGE Quarterly, Vol. 9, No. 46. 1968. 12pp. 2.50 (681)

Texas

STATEWIDE REFERENCES

Austin, Stephen F. Establishing Austin's Colony: The First
Book Printed in Texas, With the Laws, Orders and
Contracts of Colonization. ed. David B. Gracy, II.
 This is Stephen F. Austin's own contemporary account
 of the establishment of the first Anglo-American
 settlement in Texas.   8.50 ..... (273)
Baker, DeWitt Clinton, comp. A Texas Scrap-book. Made
Up of the History, Biography and Miscellany of Texas and
Its People. 1875. 706pp. B-BH 6083.   .... (778)
Bancroft, Hubert H. History of the North Mexican States and
Texas. 2 vols.   Set: 15.00 ..... (51)
Barker, Eugene Campbell. The Life of Stephen F. Austin, Founder
of Texas, 1793-1836. A Chapter in the Westward Movement of
the Anglo-American People. 1925.   14.75 ..... (2)
_____. Life of Stephen F. Austin, Founder of Texas, 1793-1836,
A Chapter in the Westward Movement of the Anglo-American
People. 1949.   10.00 ..... (750)
_____. Life of Stephen F. Austin: Founder of Texas, 1793-1866.
1969.   ..... 3.25 (749)
Bartholomew, Ed. Eight Hundred Texas Ghost Towns. 2d ed. 1974. ..... 3.50 (257)
Bolton, H. E., ed. Athanase de Mezieres and the Louisiana-
Texas Frontier, 1768-1780. 2 vols. in 1. 1914.
 Documents published for the first time, from the original
 Spanish and French manuscripts, chiefly in the archieves
 of Mexico and Spain; translated into English, ed. and
 annotated.   30.00 ..... (415)
Bolton, Herbert E. Texas in the Middle Eighteenth Century:
Studies in Spanish Colonial History and Administration. Repr.   8.50 3.75 (749)
Bowden, J. J. Spanish and Mexican Land Grants in the
Chihushuan Acquisition. 1971.   12.00 ..... (751)
Brown, John Henry. History of Texas, From 1685 to 1892.
2 vols. 1223pp.
 This history of Texas emphasizes American colonization,
 the Texas Revolution and Republic and Indian wars. Set: 25.00 ..... (273)
Brunson, Billy Ray. The Texas Land and Development Company.
1960. 382pp. BIP-60-05518.   .... (777)
Carter, Katherine T. State Coach Inns of Texas.   10.00 ..... (752)
Clark, Robert C. The Beginnings of Texas, 1684-1718.
Repr. of 1907 ed.   9.00 ..... (612)

Listed below are the names of professional genealogists willing to undertake research for a
fee within the state of Texas, in areas specified in their ads:

Copeland, Fayette. Kendall of the "Picayune." Being His
Adventures in New Orleans, on the Texas Santa Fe Expedition,
in the Mexican War and in the Colonization of the Texas
Frontier. Repr. of 1943 ed.   6.95   ..... (556)
Ericson, Joe E. Banks and Bankers in Early Texas: 1835-1875.
200pp. Index.
    Parts II and III list the directories of state, national,
    and private firms, with brief biographical sketches
    of over 700 early bankers, many being well-known
    Texas pioneers. 15.00 (608)
Freund, Max, ed. Gustav Dresel's Houston Journal:
Adventures in North America and Texas, 1837-1841. 1954.   6.50   ..... (749)
Garrett, Dr. Julia Kathryn. Green Flag Over Texas. 275pp.
    The story of the first war of independence in Texas and
    the last years of Spanish rule is magnificently told in
    this book. Maps, notes, index.   9.50   ..... (273)
Garrison, George Pierce. Texas: a Conquest of Civilizations.
AC#15. 1903.   18.00   ..... (2)
Hunt, Richard S. and Jesse F. Randel. A New Guide To Texas.
Repr. of 1845 ed.
    Deals with the history of Texas, its settlement, and
    the colonization and land laws. Included is a copy
    of Hunt and Randel's famous map of Texas.   6.95   ..... (273)
Jones, Anson. Republic of Texas: Its History and Annexation.   25.00   ..... (644)
Kennedy, William. Texas, The Rise, Progress and Prospects of
the Republic of Texas. 2d ed. 2 vols in 1. Repr. of 1841 ed.
939pp. Maps.   27.50   ..... (273)
Lathrop, Barnes F. Migration Into East Texas, 1835-1860: A
Study from the United States Census. 1949.   .....   3.50 (750)
Leonard, Glen Milton. Western Boundary Making, Texas, and
The Mexican Cession 1844-1850. 1970. 466pp. BIP-70-23060.   .... (777)
Lowrie, Samuel Harman. Culture Conflict in Texas, 1821-1835.
1932.   7.50   ..... (2)
Lukes, Edward Albert. The DeWitt Colony of Texas, 1825-1836.
1971. 296pp. BIP-71-22742.   .... (777)
Lundy, Benjamin. The Life, Travels and Opinions of Benjamin
Lundy. Including His Journeys to Texas. comp. Thomas
Earle. [With the addition of The War in Texas, 1836.]
1847. 372pp.   15.00   ..... (273)
Miller, Thomas L. Bounty and Donation Land Grants of
Texas, 1835-1888. 1967.   25.00   ..... (749)
Pickrell, Anne Doom. Pioneer Women In Texas. 474pp.
    Includes seventy-seven separate biographies, compiled
    from official records and embellished with anecdotes
    and recollections acquired from descendants.   12.50   ..... (273)
Rathjen, Frederick W. The Texas Panhandle Frontier. 1974.   9.50   ..... (749)
Richardson, Rupert N. Frontier of Northwest Texas,
1846-1876. 1963.   12.00   ..... (144)
Sowell, Andrew J. Early Settlers and Indian Fighters of
Southwest Texas. 2 vols. 1900.   27.50   ..... (36)
_____. Rangers and Pioneers of Texas. Repr. of 1884 ed.   15.00   ..... (36)
Ward, Forrest Elmer. The Lower Brazos Region of Texas,
1820-1845. 1962. 573pp. BIP-62-02572.   .... (777)
Welch, June R. People and Places in the Texas Past. 1974.   12.95   ..... (263)

Research Aids

Day, James M., comp. Maps of Texas, 1527-1900: The
Map Collection of the Texas State Archives.
A guide to the largest collection of maps on
the Southwest in the world today. Each map
is described physically and discussed
historically. Winner of the national Hammond Award.
178pp.   12.50   ..... (273)
Pool, William C. Historical Atlas of Texas. 1974.   15.00   ..... (218)

Military

Ashcraft, Allan Coleman. Texas: 1860-1866, the Lone Star
State in the Civil War. 339pp. BIP-60-05822.   .... (777)
Barton, Henry W. Texas Volunteers in the Mexican War. 6.95   ..... (752)
Bierschwale, Margaret. Fort McKavett, Texas.   10.00   ..... (396)
Conger, Roger N., et al. Frontier Forts of Texas.   10.00   ..... (752)
Corning, Leavitt, Jr. Baronial Forts of the Big Bend.
1969. illus. 4.00 (769)
DeBray, X.B. A Sketch of the History of DeBray's 26th
Regiment of Texas Cavalry. 6.00 (284)
Everett, Donald E., ed. Chaplin Davis and Hood's Texas
Brigade. 1962.   6.00   ..... (769)
Houston, Sam. The Battle of San Jacinto.
     Written a few days after the battle, while the
     events of the fight were still vividly fresh,
     General Houston's account is supplemented
     by his roster of the seven hundred participants
     in his command. 3.50 (273)
Jenkins, John H., ed. Papers of the Texas Revolution,
1835-1836. 10 vols.
     The largest single compilation of original source
     materials ever published in Texas. It includes
     over 4,000 letters,over 4,000 footnotes and totals
     over 5,000 pages. 102 page index, bibliography.
                                             Set: 115.00   ..... (273)
Lane, General Walter P. The Adventures and Recollections
of Walter P. Lane, A San Jacinto Veteran, Containing
Sketches of the Texas, Mexican, and Civil Wars With
Several Indian Fights Thrown In. 180pp. illus.   12.50   ..... (273)
Pierce, Gerald Swetnam. The Army of the Texas Republic,
1836-1845. 371pp. BIP-64-04127.   .... (777)
Reid, Samuel C., Jr. Scouting Expeditions of McCulloch's
Texas Rangers: Or, the Summer and Fall Campaign of
the Army of the United States in Mexico 1846. 1847.   9.75   ..... (81)
Simpson, Harold Brown. The History of Hood's Texas
Brigade, 1861-1865. 534pp. BIP-70-01993.   .... (777)
Webb, Walter Prescott. Texas Rangers in the Mexican War.
110pp. maps. index.   9.95   ..... (273)
Special Limited Edition: 25.00   ..... (273)

Religious and Ethnic Groups

Barr, Alwyn. Black Texans: A History of Negroes in Texas,
1528-1971. 259pp.
     Blacks have helped explore, settle, and create the
     Texas of today. This work comprehensively covers
     their history, with emphasis on their contributions

to Texan culture, as well as their struggles from
slavery through the civil rights movements. Index.　8.50　..... (273)
Benjamin, Gilbert G. The Germans in Texas: A Study in
Immigration. Repr. of 1909 ed.　8.00　..... (631)
Berlandier, Jean L. Indians of Texas in Eighteen Thirty,
ed. John C. Ewers, tr. Patricia R. Leclercq. 1969.　10.00　..... (700)
Brewer, J. Mason. Negro Legislators of Texas: And Their
Descendants. Repr. of 1935 ed.　7.00　..... (631)
Connell, Earl M. The Mexican Population of Austin, Texas.
1972.　.....　7.00 (631)
Downs, Fane. The History of Mexicans in Texas, 1830-
1845. 297pp. BIP-71-09632.　.....　..... (777)
Dworaczyk, Edward J. The First Polish Colonies of Americans
in Texas. Repr. of 1936 ed.　10.00　..... (631)
Hasdorff, James Curtis. Four Indian Tribes in Texas, 1758-
1858: A Reevaluation of Historical Sources. 211pp.
BIP-72-04805.　.....　..... (777)
Jordon, Terry G. German Seed in Texas Soil: Immigrant
Farmers in Nineteenth-Century Texas. 1966.　7.50　..... (749)
King, Irene M. John O. Meusebach: German Colonizer in
Texas. 1966.　6.50　..... (749)
Lowrie, Samuel H. Culture Conflict in Texas, 1821-1835.　7.50　..... (2)
Mason, Zane. Frontiersmen of the Faith: A History of
Baptist Pioneer Work in Texas 1865-1885. 1970.　7.95　..... (518)
Paschal, George H., Jr. and Judith A. Brenner. One
Hundred Years of Challenge and Change: A History of
the Synod of Texas of the United Presbyterian Church
in the United States of America. 1968.　4.00　..... (769)
Sheridan, Mary Benignus. Bishop Odin and the New Era of
the Catholic Church in Texas, 1840-1860. 419pp.
BIP-00-00204.　.....　..... (777)
Tyler, Ron C. and Larry Murphy. The Slave Narratives of
Texas. 1973.　7.50　..... (218)
Watts, Frederick L. Petition for Redress. 1976. 350pp.
Newly discovered documents showing heritage
contributions of first Germans in America - from
South Carolina to Georgia, Mississippi and Texas
from 1735 to 1976.　17.50　12.50 (270)

Records

An Abstract of the Original Titles of Record in the General
Land Office of Texas. 200pp.
Originally published in 1838 in Houston, this work
contains a listing by colony, alphabetically, of
every settler granted land in Texas between 1791
and 1836. Upon this list all land titles in Texas
were based, and land ownership established.
Following the names of the grantees, there are
columns giving date of titles, quantity of land
received, location of the land, and remarks.　15.00　..... (273)
Bolton, Herbert E., ed. Athanase de Mezieres and the
Louisiana-Texas Frontier, 1768-1780; Documents
Published for the First Time, from the Original Spanish
and French Manuscripts, Chiefly in the Archives of
Mexico and Spain, Translated into English. 2 vols. 1914.　30.00　..... (415)

Gray, R.D. and Mrs. R. D. Gray. Gray's Cemetery Records.
1968. 126pp. 5.00 (371)

Ray, Worth S. Austin Colony Pioneers. 378pp. illus. index.
Comprising history, biography, genealogy, and
research material, this reference work includes
five of the major counties - Bastrop, Fayette,
Grimes, Montgomery, and Washington - of Central
Texas. Almost all of the material is from the
original records, plus letters, diaries, and other
sources. 12.50 ..... (273)

ANGELINA COUNTY

Haltom, R.W. Angelina County, Texas. 102pp. 7.50 ..... (273)

AUSTIN COUNTY

"Naturalization Records of Austin, Guadalupe and Washington
Counties, Texas, from Circa 1856 to Circa 1870."
Copper State Bulletin. 24pp. .....` 3.00 (34)

BASTROP COUNTY

Ray, Worth S. Austin Colony Pioneers. 378pp. illus. index.
Comprising history, biography, genealogy, and research
material, this reference work includes five of the major
counties - Bastrop, Fayette, Grimes, Montgomery,
and Washington - of Central Texas. Almost all of the
material is from the original records, plus letters,
diaries, and other sources. 12.50 ``... (273)

BOWIE COUNTY

Jennings, Nancy W. and Elizabeth E. Varner. Bowie County,
Texas Historical Handbook. 1976. 60+pp.
Wordings of Historical Markers; 1830 Wavell Colony
Census; 1846 Mexican War Veterans; Householders,
1850 Census; 1865 War Between the States Unit; 1882
Directory and Town Histories; Bowie County Officers,
1841-1976; Maps, etc. 3.00 (84)
_____ and Mary Lou S. Phillips. Texarkana Centennial History,
1873-1973. 1973. 74pp.
Area history; town and railroad history; churches;
town officials, 1873-1973; black history and Scott Joplin
Area Builders; high schools and Texarkana Community
College, maps, pictures, etc. 3.00 (84)

CASS COUNTY

Bowman, Mrs. Myreline. 1886 - 1940 Church Records. 1976.
Church records from original records - no other
records churchnot there anymore. 15.00 12.00 (86)
_____. Obituaries of Cass County. 1976.
Obituaries gathered from newspapers and people -
some 1924 to 1976. 25.00 22.00 (86)
_____. People of Cass County. 1973. 236pp.
Church records, newspaper, school records, personal
information from different people of this area, death
dates, marriages, reunions and golden weddings. 10.00 (86)

_____. The Spirit of '76 - Queen City, Texas 1876-1976 (With Index). 1976. 178pp.
How Queen City was formed, people of this area from 1876 to 1976, where they came from, roads and how they were formed and by whom, down to who lives there now.   15.00   12.00 (86)

Cass County Genealogical Society. Cass County Cemeteries. 1976.
Every cemetery in Cass County named, people buried in each cemetery and kinship if possible.   25.00   22.00 (86)

_____. Cass County Texas Pedigrees. 1976. 119pp.
List of Genealogical Society members, pedigrees (105 pages). Index. 10.00 (86)

_____. Recipes of Pioneer Women of Cass County. 1974. 150pp.
Old timey recipes and brief sketch of people, pictures, and kinship. 5.00 (86)

CHAMBERS COUNTY

Wright, Mrs. Mildred S., G.R.S. Chambers County, Texas Cemeteries. 1975-1976. 89pp.
53 sites located, inventories, maps, illustrations, index.   12.95   9.95 (856)

CLAY COUNTY

Taylor, William Charles. 200pp. Index.   9.50   ..... (273)

COLLIN COUNTY

Stambaugh, J. Lee and Lillian J. Stambaugh. History of Collin County, Texas. 1958.   7.50   ..... (750)

COOKE COUNTY

Acheson, Sam and Julie O'Connell. George Washington Diamond's Account of the Great Hanging at Gainesville. 1862. 1963.   5.00   3.50 (750)
Phillips, Oma Dee. Cooke County, Texas Marriages 1849-1879. 45pp. Index. 8.50 (596)

DALLAS COUNTY

Memorial and Biographical History of Dallas County, Texas. 1892. 1105pp. B-OP 4613.   .... (778)

FAYETTE COUNTY

Ray, Worth S. Austin Colony Pioneers. 378pp. illus. index.
Comprising history, biography, genealogy, and research material, this reference work includes five of the major counties - Bastrop, Fayette, Grimes, Montgomery, and Washington - of Central Texas. Almost all of the material is from the original records, plus letters, diaries, and other sources.   12.50   ..... (273)

FISHER COUNTY

Baird, Delila and Josie Baird, comp. Early Fisher County Families, A Bibliographical History. 1976. c300pp.
Also tax lists, original land grants, news notes on citizens of county - 1888 from a non-extant paper, many early photographs of people at work, portraits.   .... (47)

GALVESTON COUNTY

Gregory, Mrs. Peggy H. Sexton's Records of Galveston,
1859-1873. 1976. c400pp. In Process.
Never before published death records of Galveston,
Texas 1859-1873. .... (300)

Hayes, Charles W. Galveston: History of the Island and the
City. 2 vols. 1044pp. index.   Set: 37.50 ..... (273)

GREGG COUNTY

History of Gregg County, Texas. Repr. of 1959 ed. 312pp.
County history, illustrated, indexed.   22.00 ..... (810)

GRIMES COUNTY

Ray, Worth S. Austin Colony Pioneers. 378pp. illus. index.
Comprising history, biography, genealogy, and research
material, this reference work includes five of the major
counties - Bastrop, Fayette, Grimes, Montgomery,
and Washington - of Central Texas. Almost all of the
material is from the original records, plus letters,
diaries, and other sources.   12.50 ..... (273)

GUADALUPE COUNTY

"Naturalization Records of Austin, Guadalupe, and Washington
Counties, Texas from Circa 1856 to Circa 1870." Copper
State Bulletin. 24pp. 3.00 (34)

HARRIS COUNTY

Buchanan, James E. Houston: A Chronological and Documentary
History, 1519-1970. (American Cities Chronology Series).
1975. 153pp.   7.50 ..... (551)

HENDERSON COUNTY

History of Henderson County, Texas. Repr. of 1904/1927/1929
ed. 666pp.
County history, three volumes in one cover, illustrated.   21.00 ..... (810)

JASPER COUNTY

Wright, Mildred S. Jasper County, Texas Cemeteries. 1976.   .... (856)

KARNES COUNTY

Didear, Hedwig K., comp. A History of Karnes County and
Old Helena. 220pp. index.   9.50 ..... (273)

LAMAR COUNTY

Lombard, Charles M. Lamartine. 1973.   6.95 ..... (773)

LIBERTY COUNTY

Partlow, Miriam. Liberty, Liberty County, and the Atascosito
District. 369pp. 878 footnotes. index.   14.95 ..... (273)

LUBBOCK COUNTY

Graves, Lawrence L., ed. History of Lubbock. 1962.   10.00 ..... (825)

McLENNAN COUNTY

Barnes, Lavonia J. Early Homes of Waco.   9.95 ..... (752)
Conger, Roger. Pictorial History of Waco.   7.50 ..... (752)

MASON COUNTY

Polk, Stella. Mason and Mason County, Texas: A History.
119pp. index.   9.50 ..... (273)

MONTGOMERY COUNTY

Montgomery, Robin. The History of Montgomery County.
345pp. 3 maps. index.   12.50 ..... (273)
Ray, Worth S. Austin Colony Pioneers. 378pp. illus. index.
Comprising history, biography, genealogy, and
research material, this reference work includes five of
the major counties - Bastrop, Fayette, Grimes,
Montgomery, and Washington - of Central Texas. Almost all of the material is from the original records,
plus letters, diaries, and other sources.   12.50 ..... (273)

NACOGDOCHES COUNTY

Ericson, Carolyn Reeves. 1847 Census Nacogdoches County,
Texas. 25pp.
State census taken after Texas joined the Union.
Given names of heads of households, numbers of
qualified electors, males over 18 and under 45;
females under 18 and over 45; number of females;
number of slaves. 2.00 (222)
_____. Fires and Firemen (of Nacogdoches, Texas).
A history of the Fire Department with a roster of the
men who served, together with accounts of selected
fires from 1840 to 1974.   ..... 12.50 (222)
_____. Nacogdoches County Cemetery Records - Volume II.
186pp.
Contains inscriptions from Oak Grove, North Church
and Sunset Memorial Park. Dates from 1837 to 1973.
Several pictures of Oak Grove. Index. 10.00 (222)
_____. Nacogdoches County Cemetery Records - Volume III.
138pp.
Full surname index. Inscriptions from Finley, Whitaker,
Douglass, White, Redland, Looneyville, Nat, Banks,
Friendship, Brewer, Mahl Baptist Church, Mahl, Rock
Springs, Union Springs, Holly Grove, Linn Flat, Barnes,
Pine Grove, Owens #1, Old Chapel, Cushing, McKnight,
Pirtle, Akin, Owens #2, Cornelius, Fenton, Russell,
Fuller. 10.00 (222)
_____. Nacogdoches - Gateway to Texas. 275pp.
A Biographical Directory from 1773-1849. Illustrations,
index, maps, bibliography, photographs. The Directory
portion includes some 5,000 names of settlers from the
petitions of 1773 to deed and other records in 1849. It
includes the complete documents of the petition of 1773;
Criminal Code of 1783 and various immigration laws
and decrees. This also includes data abstracted from
Spanish census records of 1792-1809; Mexican Census of
1828-1835; and the state census of 1847; tax lists of
1837, 1839, 1840, 1845; marriage records; Board of Land

Commissioner's Minutes for 1838; citizenship applications;
Masonic Roster for Milam Lodge #2; Muster Rolls for
San Jacinto; the militia and index to deeds from 1836-
1849 from Nacogdoches County. 20.00 (222)
_____. Nocogdoches Texas Centennial 1716-1936. Repr. of
1936 ed. 24pp.
Reprint of booklet done for Texas Centennial in 1936.
History of the area; well illustrated. 1.50 (222)
Haltom, Richard W. The History of Nacogdoches County, Texas. 7.50 ..... (273)

NEWTON COUNTY

Wright, Mildred S. Newton County, Texas Cemeteries. 1975-
1976. 215pp.
69 cemetery sites located, inventories, maps, illustrated,
indexed. 14.75 (856)

NUECES COUNTY

Taylor, Paul S. American-Mexican Frontier: Nueces County,
Texas. Repr. of 1934 ed. 15.00 ..... (662)

OLDHAM COUNTY

McCarty, John L. Maverick Town: The Story of Old Tascosa.
rev. ed. 1968. 5.95 ..... (556)

PANOLA COUNTY

Phillips, Oma Dee. Index to Deed Book "A" - 1845-1857.
Panola County, Texas. 1970. 44pp. index. 7.50 (596)

SAN SABA COUNTY

Hamrick. Alma Ward. The Call of San Saba: A History of San
Saba County. 331+25pp.
An account covering the period from 1756 to the present. 10.00 ..... (273)

TRAVIS COUNTY

Hart, Katherine. Austin and Travis County: A Pictorial History,
1839-1939. 1975. 12.50 ..... (218)

WASHINGTON COUNTY

"Naturalization Records of Austin, Guadalupe and Washington
Counties, Texas from Circa 1856 to Circa 1870." Copper
State Bulletin. 24pp. 3.00 (34)
Ray, Worth S. Austin Colony Pioneers. 378pp. illus. index.
Comprising history, biography, genealogy, and research
material, this reference work includes five of the
major counties - Bastrop, Fayette, Grimes, Montgomery,
and Washington - of Central Texas. Almost all of the
material is from the original records, plus letters,
diaries, and other sources. 12.50 ..... (273)

WICHITA COUNTY

Hodges, Mrs. Luke. Wichita County, Texas Wills, 1882-1927. ..... 7.50 (340)

Utah

STATEWIDE REFERENCES

Burton, Sir Richard Frances. The City of the Saints; and, Across the Rocky Mountains to California. With illustrations. 1862. 25.00 ..... (2)
Carr, Stephen L. The Historical Guide to Utah Ghost Towns. 1972. 7.95 4.95 (826)
Esshom, Frank, et al. Pioneers and Prominent Men of Utah, 1847-1869. 1966. 35.00 ..... (826)
Noall, Clair. Guardians of the Hearth: Utah's Pioneer Women Midwives and Doctors. 1974. 4.95 ..... (353)
Pederson, Lyman Clarence, Jr. History of Fort Douglas, Utah. 1967. 482pp. BIP-67-11755. .... (777)
Piercy, Frederick. Route From Liverpool to the Great Salt Lake Valley, ed. Fawn M. Brodie. 1962. 8.50 ..... (319)

Religious and Ethnic Groups

Brooks, Juanita. The History of the Jews in Utah and Idaho, 1853-1950. 1973. 7.95 ..... (826)
Turk, Marion G. The Quiet Adventurers in America. 1975. 300pp. Genealogical data and story of settlers in the American Colonies and in the United States, from the Channel Islands, United Kingdom; Jersey, Guernsey, Alderney and Sark. 12.00 10.00 (771)

SAN JUAN COUNTY

Miller, David E. Hole in the Rock: An Epic in the Colonization of the Great American West. 1959. 7.95 ..... (782)

Vermont

STATEWIDE REFERENCES

Bassett, T.D., ed. Outsiders Inside Vermont: Travellers' Tales of 358 Years. 1967. 4.95 ..... (296)
Bearse, Ray, ed. Vermont: A Guide to the Green Mountain State. 3rd ed. 1968. 7.95 ..... (356)
Congdon, Herbert Wheaton. Old Vermont Houses, 1763-1850. Reprint. 192pp. Contains stories of old houses and the Vermont families who lived in them. 4.95 (56)
Hill, Ralph N. Yankee Kingdom: Vermont and New Hampshire. 1973. 8.95 ..... (317)
Robinson, Rowland E. Vermont: A Study of Independence. Reprint. 400pp. Vermont's history from days as an unsettled wilderness through the Civil War. 4.95 (772)
United States. Census Office. Heads of Families at the Second Census of the United States Taken in the Year 1800: Vermont. 1938. 239pp. B-OP 43283. .... (778)
Wood, Frederick Augustus. History of Taxation in Vermont. 1894. 12.50 ..... (2)
Woodard, Florence M. Town Proprietors in Vermont. 12.50 ..... (2)

ESSEX COUNTY

Benton, Everett Chamberlin. A History of Guildhall, Vermont.
1886. 276pp.. B-BH 19163. .... (778)

RUTLAND COUNTY

Herald. June 1792 to December 1820. 4 rolls. December 1830
to December 1920. 147 rolls.
Microfilm of the original papers. Individual rolls
covering a specific time span may be ordered. Prices
vary from $15 to $30 per roll. .... (870)

WASHINGTON COUNTY

Hill, Ellen C. Revolutionary War Soldiers of East Montpelier.
109pp.
History of 34 soldiers and their families to present.
Pictures and maps. 4.25 (333)

WINDHAM COUNTY

Beers, F.W. Atlas of Windham County, Vermont. 20.00 ..... (296)

WINDSOR COUNTY

Aldrich, Lewis Cass, ed. History of Windsor County, Vermont.
1891. 1190pp. B-OP 71033. .... (778)
Steele, Zadock. The Indian Captive: Or, A Narrative of the
Captivity and Sufferings of Zadock Steele. 1908. 180pp.
Steele recounts the destruction by the British and
their Indian allies of Royalton, Vermont (October 16,
1780), and his capture by Indians. 13.50 ..... (38)

Virginia

STATEWIDE REFERENCES

Abernethy, Thomas P. Three Virginia Frontiers. 4.50 (699)
de Bellet, Louise Pecquet. Some Prominent Virginia Families.
Repr. of 1907 ed. 1715pp. 50.00 ..... (274)
Benson, Dale E. Wealth and Power in Virginia, 1774-1776:
A Study of the Organization of Revolt. 1970. 427pp.
BIP-71-20267. .... (777)
Beverley, Robert. History and Present State of Virginia, ed.
David F. Hawke. 1971. 7.50 2.95 (77)
_____. History and Present State of Virginia, ed. Louis B.
Wright. Repr. of 1947 ed. 7.50 ..... (544)
_____. History and Present State of Virginia, ed. Louis B.
Wright. 1968. illus. 3.75 (801)
Blanton, Wyndham B. Medicine in Virginia in the Seventeenth
Century. Repr. of 1930 ed. 354pp. 18.00 ..... (638)
Boogher, William F. Gleanings of Virginia History, An
Historical and Genealogical Collection. Repr. of 1903 ed. 443pp. 16.00 ..... (274)
Brock, Robert Alonzo, ed. Miscellaneous Papers, 1672-1865,
Now First Printed from the Manuscript in the Collections of
the Virginia Historical Society; Comprising Charter of the
Royal African Company, 1672; Report on the Huguenot Set-
tlement, 1700; Papers of George Gilmer, of "Pen Park,"

1775-1778; Orderly Book of Captain George Stubblefield, 1776;
Career of the Iron-Clad Virginia, 1862; Memorial of Johnson's
Island, 1862-1864; Beales' Cavalry Brigade Parole, 1865. 1887.   27.50   ..... (2)
_____. The Official Letters of Alexander Spotswood, Lieutenant-
Governor of the Colony of Virginia, 1710-1722, Now First
Printed from the Manuscript in the Collections of the Virginia
Historical Society. 2 vols. in 1. 1882-1885.   27.50   ..... (2)
Brown, Alexander, ed. The Genesis of the United States: A
Narrative of the Movement in England, 1605-1616, Which Re-
sulted in the Plantation of North America by Englishmen.
2 vols. Repr. of 1890 ed. xl, 1151pp.   Set: 40.00   ..... (662)
Burk, John Daly. The History of Virginia, From its First Set-
tlement to the Commencement of the Revolution. 4 vols.
1804-1816.   Set: 142.00   ..... (2)
Byrd, William. Histories of the Dividing Line Betwixt Virginia
and North Carolina.   5.00   ..... (699)
Caldwell, John E. Tour Through Part of Virginia in the Summer
of 1808, ed. William M. Rachal. 1951.   2.00   ..... (195)
Callahan, James Morton. History of West Virginia. . . and West
Virginia Biography. 1923. Vol. 1-752pp, Vol. 2-1176pp,
Vol. 3-1236pp. B-OP 72002.   .... (778)

Listed below are the names of professional genealogists willing to undertake research for
a fee within the state of Virginia, in areas specified in their ads:

Cooke, John E. The Virginia Comedians: Or, Old Days in the
Old Dominion. 2 vols. Reprint.   14.50   ..... (702)
Coulter, Calvin Brewster, Jr. The Virginia Merchant. 290pp.
BIP-00-02930.   .... (777)
Cromwell, Giles. The Virginia Manufactory of Arms. 1974.   20.00   ..... (801)
Curtis, George Martin III. The Virginia Courts During the
Revolution. 226pp. BIP-70-24740.   .... (777)
Dain, Norman. Disordered Minds: The First Century of
Eastern State Hospital in Williamsburg, Virginia. 1971.   5.95   ..... (801)
Dowdey, Clifford. The Virginia Dynasties. 1969.   10.95   ..... (435)
Farrar, Emmie F. and Emilee Hines. Old Virginia Houses:
The Northern Peninsulas.   15.00   ..... (321)
_____. Old Virginia Houses Along the Fall Line.   15.00   ..... (321)
Fithian, Philip V. Journal and Letters of Philip Vickers Fithian,
1773-1774: A Plantation Tutor of the Old Dominion, ed.
Hunter D. Farish. 1968.   3.95   2.75 (801)
Flippin, Percy Scott. The Royal Government in Virginia, 1624-
1775. 1919.   12.50   ..... (2)
Ginther, Herman. Captain Stauntan's River. 1968.   5.00   ..... (195)
Griffith, Lucille Blanche. The Virginia House of Burgesses, 1750-
1774. 311pp. BIP-00-23437.   .... (777)
Hecht, Irene Winchester Duckworth. The Virginia Colony, 1607-
1640: A Study in Frontier Growth. 397pp. BIP-69-20232.   .... (777)
Herndon, George Melvin. The Story of Hemp in Colonial Virginia.
208pp. BIP-59-04229.   .... (777)
Howe, Henry. Historical Collections of Virginia; Containing a
Collection of the Most Interesting Facts, Traditions, Biographical
Sketches, Anecdotes, etc. 1852. 606pp. B-BH 7006.   .... (778)
Jackson, Luther Porter. Free Negro Labor and Property Holding
in Virginia, 1830-1860. Repr. of 1942 ed. xv,270pp.   13.00   ..... (662)
Johnston, James H. Race Relations in Virginia and Miscegenation
in the South 1776-1860. 1970.   15.00   ..... (471)
Jones, Joseph. Letters of Joseph Jones of Virginia, 1777-1787,
ed. Worthington Chauncey Ford. 1889.   7.00   ..... (38)
Jordan, Daniel Porter, Jr. Virginia Congressmen, 1801-1825.
479pp. BIP-70-26630.   .... (777)
Lingley, Charles Ramsdell. The Transition in Virginia from
Colony to Commonwealth. 1910.   10.00   ..... (2)
McWhorter, Lucullus V. The Border Settlers of Northwestern
Virginia from 1768 to 1795. Repr. of 1915 ed. 509pp.   20.00   ..... (274)
Maganzin, Louis. Economic Depression in Maryland and Virginia,
1783-1787. 294pp. BIP-68-01893.   .... (777)
Mahan, Terrance Leon, S.J. Virginia Reaction to British Policy,
1763-1776. 426pp. BIP-60-05767.   .... (777)
Mitchell, Peter McQuilkin. Loyalist Property and the Revolution
in Virginia. 242pp. BIP-66-03261.   .... (777)
Morrison, Charles. The Western Boundary of Maryland. 1976.
112pp.
         Maryland's western boundary, originally with Virginia,
         became the source of a bitter dispute with West Virginia
         when the latter parted from its parent. Settled in 1910
         under a decree by the Supreme Court of the United States.   4.50   ..... (508)
Phillips, Edward H. The Lower Shenandoah Valley During the
Civil War: The Impact of War Upon the Civilian Population
and Upon Civil Institutions. 442pp. BIP-59-00056.   .... (777)

Porter, Albert Ogden. County Government in Virginia; A
    Legislative History, 1607-1904. 1947.   12.50   ..... (2)
Randolph, Edmund. History of Virginia, ed. Arthur Shaffer.   12.50   ..... (801)
Robinson, W. Stitt, Jr. Mother Land: Land Grants in Virginia.
    1957.   ..... 1.25 (801)
Russell, John H. Free Negro in Virginia, 1619-1865. Repr. of
    1913 ed.   9.00   ..... (522)
_____. Free Negro in Virginia, 1619-1865.   ..... 4.75 (699)
Smith, Alan McKinley. Virginia Lawyers, 1680-1776: The Birth
    of an American Profession. 432pp. BIP-68-06578.   .... (777)
Tyler, Lyon G., ed. Narratives of Early Virginia, Sixteen Six
    to Sixteen Twenty-Five (Original Narratives). Repr. of 1907 ed.   6.50   ..... (52)
Virginia Company of London. Abstract of the Proceedings of the
    Virginia Company of London, 1619-1624. Prepared from the
    Records in the Library of Congress by Conway Robinson, ed.
    R.A.Brock. 2 vols in 1. 1888-1889.   37.50   ..... (2)
Virginia Gazette - 1775. Selected Reprints of 17 Miniature Papers
    May through December 1775. Repr. of 1775 eds.
    News of the day; includes many names of those who
    participated in the Revolution. 7.50 (74)
Virginia Historical Society. Collections of the Virginia Historical
    and Philosophical Society - Volume I. 1833.   10.00   ..... (2)
Virginia Tidewater Genealogy. 1970. c50pp.
    Genealogical material of Tidewater Virginia and surrounding
    counties published quarterly. "Tidewater" includes
    Chesapeake, Elizabeth City, Hampton City, Isle of Wight,
    James City County, Nancemond, New Kent, Newport News,
    Norfolk City, Prince Anne, Surry, Williamsburg and York. $5/yr (758)
Young, Chester Raymond. The Effects of the French and Indian
    War on Civilian Life in the Frontier Counties of Virginia,
    1754-1763. 463pp. BIP-70-05433.   .... (777)

Research Aids

Abbot, William W. Virginia Chronology, 1585-1783: To Pass
    Away the Time. 1957.   .....   1.25 (801)
Curtis, Mary Barnett. Bibliography of the Shendoah Valley
    (Magazine of Bibliographies). 1972. 32pp.
    All genealogical and historical books on subject
    and, if in print, where to order them from. 5.00 (371)
Felldin, Jeanne Robey. Index to the 1820 Census of Virginia.
    1976. 486pp.   20.00   .... (274)
Haynes, Donald, ed. Virginia in the Printed Book Collections
    of the Virginia State Library. 2 vols. 1975.
    Catalog of printed books and pamphlets about
    Virginia and Virginians or by Virginians, except
    official state publications. Author, title, subject
    indices.   100.00   ..... (800)
Sanchez-Saavedra, E.M. A Description of the Country;
    Virginia's Cartographers and Their Maps, 1607-1881.
    1975. 130pp.
    Facsimile of nine important Virginia maps, with
    accompanying booklet describing Virginia
    cartography. 10.00 (800)
Stone, Kathryn Crossley. Research Aids for the Colonial
    Period. 1976. 40-45pp. In Process.
    A dictionary and encyclopedia for genealogical
    research, abbreviations, explanations, dealing main-
    ly with research work in Virginia. 4.50 (727)

Topping, Mary. Approved Place-Names in Virginia: An Index
to Virginia Names Approved by the United States Board on
Genealogical Names Through 1969. 1971.   6.50   ..... (801)

Military

Aldridge, Fred K. Stokes. Organization and Administration of
the Militia System of Colonial Virginia. 1964. 271pp.
BIP-64-12797.   .... (777)
Allan, William. History of Campaign of General T. J. (Stonewall)
Jackson in Shenandoah Valley of Virginia, from November
4. 1861 to June 17, 1862. 175pp. maps.   15.00   ..... (506)
Davis, Burke. Campaign That Won America: The Story of
Yorktown. (Original Title: Yorktown). 1970.   8.95   ..... (192)
Dorman, John Frederick. Virginia Revolutionary Pension
Applications, Volume 21, Cole, Joseph - Connell. 1975.   .....   7.50 (201)
_____. Virginia Revolutionary Pension Applications, Volume
22, Connelly - Copeland. 1975.   .....   7.50 (201)
_____. Virginia Revolutionary Pension Applications, Volume
23, Copenhaver - Cox, James. 1975.   .....   7.50 (201)
Fleming, Thomas J. Beat the Last Drum: The Seige of York-
town, 1781. 1963.   6.95   ..... (667)
Gerrish, Theodore. The Blue and the Gray; A Graphic History
of the Army of the Potomac and That of Northern Virginia,
Including the Brilliant Engagements of these Forces from
1861 to 1865. 1884. 820pp. B-BH 11991.   .... (778)
Graves, Thomas. The Graves Papers and Other Documents
Relating to the Naval Operations of the Yorktown Campaign
July to October 1781, ed. French E. Chadwick. Repr. of
1916 ed.   10.00   ..... (38)
Hotchkiss, Jed. Virginia Expanded Volume. Confederate
Military History. 1295pp. maps.
        Shortly before his death, in 1899, Jedediah Hotchkiss
        topographical engineer and the Confederacy's foremost
        mapmaker, prepared this volume for the Confederate
        Military History. Approximately one half - over
        600 pages - of this work is composed of biographical
        sketches of officers, privates, and patriotic citizens. 32.50   ..... (506)
Howard, McHenry. Recollections of a Maryland Confederate
Soldier and Staff Officer Under Johnston, Jackson and
Lee. illus. endpaper map. index.   20.00   ..... (506)
Patrick, Rembert W. Fall of Richmond. 1960.   4.00   ..... (440)
Sellers, John Robert. The Virginia Continental Line, 1775-
1780. 397pp. BIP-69-03822.   .... (777)
Smith, Gustavus W. The Battle of Seven Pines. 202pp. maps. 15.00   ..... (506)
Taylor, Walter Herron. Adj-General Army of Northern
Virginia; General Lee, His Campaigns in Virginia, 1861-
1865, With Personal Reminiscences. 328pp. maps.
        Excellent maps.   22.50   ..... (506)
Wise, George. History of the Seventeenth Virginia Infantry
in the War Between the States. 1969.   14.95   ..... (58)

Religious and Ethnic Groups

Brock, Robert Alonzo, ed. and comp. Documents, Chiefly
Unpublished, Relating to the Huguenot Emigration to
Virginia and to the Settlement at Manakin-Town, with an
Appendix of Genealogies, Presenting the Data of the
Fontaine, Maury, Dupuy, Trabue, Marye, Chastain, Cocke
and Other Families. 1886.   17.50   ..... (2)

Brown, Katherine Lowe. The Role of Presbyterian Dissent
in Colonial and Revolutionary Virginia, 1740-1785.
437pp. BIP-69-13488. .... (777)
Fontaine, John. Journal of John Fontaine: An Irish Huguenot
Son in Spain and Virginia, 1710-1719 (Williamsburg
Eyewitness to History Series), ed. Edward P. Alexander.
1972. 4.95 ..... (801)
Gunderson, Joan. The Anglican Ministry in Virginia 1723-
1776: A Study of Social Class. 1972. 336pp. BIP-72-26805. .... (777)
Haiman, Mieczyslaw. Polish Pioneers of Virginia and
Kentucky. Repr. of 1937 ed. 5.00 ..... (631)
Lohrenz, Otto. The Virginia Clergy and the American
Revolution, 1774-1799. 436pp. BIP-70-25370. .... (777)
Meade, William. Old Churches, Ministers and Families of
Virginia. 1857. Vol. 1-498pp, Vol. 2-618pp. B-BH 6629. .... (778)
Thom, W.T. Struggle for Religious Freedom in Virginia:
The Baptists. Repr. of 1900 ed. 9.00 (394)
Wells, Guy Fred. Parish Education in Colonial Virginia.
1923. 7.00 ..... (38)
Young, Chester Raymond. The Effects of the French and
Indian War on Civilian Life in the Frontier Counties of
Virginia, 1754-1763. 463pp. BIP-70-05433. .... (777)

Records

"Delinquent Taxpayers, 1787-1790." The Virginia Genealogist,
Vol. 19, Nos. 3,4, Vol. 20, Nos. 1-4. ..... 3.00 (201)
Johnston, Frederick, comp. Memorials of Old Virginia Clerks,
Arranged Alphabetically by Counties, with Complete Index
of Names, and Dates of Service from 1634 to the Present
Time. 1888. 438pp. B-BH 6887. .... (778)
Robertson, Clara H. Kansas Territorial Settlers of 1860 Who
Were Born in Tennessee, Virginia, North Carolina and
South Carolina. 1976. 187pp. 17.50 ..... (274)
Smith, Annie L. W. The Quit Rents of Virginia, 1704. Repr.
of 1957 ed. 114pp. 6.50 (274)
Wilson, Donald L. Virginia in 1750. 1978. In Process.
A census of inhabitants, taken from surviving records,
showing county of residence. .... (846)

Southwestern Virginia

English, William Hayden. Conquest of the Country Northwest
of the River Ohio, 1778-1783, and Life of General Rogers
Clark. With Numerous Sketches of Men Who Served
Under Clark and Full List of Those Allotted Lands in
Clark's Grant for Service in the Campaigns Against the
British Posts, Showing the Exact Land Allotted Each.
2 vols. in 1. 1896. 48.00 ..... (38)
Johnson, Patricia Givens. William Preston and the Allegheny
Patriots. 1976. 325pp.
Fully documented account of Revolutionary activities
of Virginia's mountain Patriots and Tories and a New
River regional study interwoven with a biography of
Preston. 9.25 ..... (392)
Twaites, Reuben G. and Louise P. Kellogg, eds. Frontier
Defense on the Upper Ohio, 1777-1778. 16.00 ..... (415)

Wilson, Dr. Howard M. Great Valley Patriots. 1976. 250pp.
The story of western and southwestern Virginia in the
American Revolution. 15.00 12.00 (448)
Worrell, Anne L. Over the Mountain Men, Their Early Court
Records in Southwest Virginia. Repr. of 1934 ed. 69pp. 5.00 (274)

ACCOMACK COUNTY

County Court Records of Accomack-Northampton Virginia, 1632-
1640. (Volume 7 of the American Legal Series). 23.00 18.00 (415)

ALBEMARLE COUNTY

Woods, Reverend Edgar. History of Albemarle County Virginia.
Repr. of 1901 ed. 412pp.
Brief historical sketches on some of the early families
along with a history of the county. 12.50 ..... (124)

AMHERST COUNTY

Marmon, Lee. History of Amherst-Nelson Counties, Virginia
to 1807. 1976. 300pp. 8.00 7.00 (523)

AUGUSTA COUNTY

Bushman, Katherine G. "Augusta County, Virginia in 1775."
Augusta Historical Bulletin, Vol. 11, No. 2. 1975. 8pp. 3.00 (43)
Eisenberg, William E. "North Augusta Street As it Was".
Augusta Historical Bulletin, Vol. 11, No. 2. 1975. 8pp. 3.00 (43)
Hale, John S. "Beverley Manor - Landmark in the Colonial
Frontier." Augusta Historical Bulletin, Vol. 10, No. 2.
1974. 11pp. 3.00 (43)
Henkel, Brownie Williams. "History of Civil War Hereto Un-
recorded." Augusta Historical Bulletin, Vol. 11, No. 2.
1975. 3pp. 3.00 (43)
Joyner, Peggy Shomo. "St. John's Church, 1779-1839."
Augusta Historical Bulletin, Vol. 10, No. 2. 1974. 14pp. 3.00 (43)
Kaylor, Peter C. Abstract of Land Grant Surveys of Augusta
and Rockingham Counties, Virginia, 1761-1791. Repr. of
1938 ed. 150pp. 10.00 ..... (274)
Maxwell, Fay. Augusta County, Virginia Baptismal Records of
Reverend John Craig, D.D. 1740-1749. 1974. 20pp. 2.50 (473)
Lisle, Carroll. "John Colter: Discoverer of Yellowstone."
Augusta Historical Bulletin, Vol. 10, No. 2. 1974. 5pp. 3.00 (43)
Moody, Elizabeth F. "A British Officer's Account of the Battle
of Point Pleasant." Augusta Historical Bulletin, Vol. 12,
No. 1. 1976. 4pp. 3.00 (43)
Peyton, J. Lewis. History of Augusta County, Virginia. Repr.
of 1953 ed. 428pp. 15.00 ..... (124)
Rupe, Alice Henkel. "Augusta County, Virginia Marriages,
1792-1798." Augusta Historical Bulletin, Vol. 12, No. 1.
1976. 2pp. 3.00 (43)
Shields, Randolph T., Jr., M.D. "Early Augusta County Doctors."
Augusta Historical Bulletin, Vol. 12, No. 1. 1976. 9pp. 3.00 (43)

Waddell, Joseph A. Annals of Augusta County (1726-1871). Repr.
of 1902 ed. 545pp.
Historical data on Augusta County, Virginia which
originally comprised several states. Valuable in-
formation on emigrants and emigration.   17.50   ..... (124)

BEDFORD COUNTY

Ackerly, Mary Denham, Mrs. Lula Parker and Jeter Eastman.
"Our Kin"; the Genealogies of Some of the Early Families
Who Made History in the Founding and Development of
Bedford County, Virginia. c1930. 912pp. B-OP 70064.   .... (778)
Gibbs, Mrs. Robert L. 1850 Bedford County Census. 1977. .... (281)

BOTETOURT COUNTY

Burton, Charles T. Botetourt County, Virginia, Its Men 1780-
1786. 1975. 54pp.
Information from tithable and land tax lists showing
location within the county, and their eligibility for
the military draft. 5.00 (107)
Niederer, Frances J. Town of Fincastle, Virginia. 1965. 4.50   ..... (801)

BRUNSWICK COUNTY

Fothergill, Augusta B. Marriage Records of Brunswick County,
Virginia, 1730-1852. Repr. of 1953 ed. 153pp.   10.00   ..... (274)
Knorr, Mrs. H.A. Marriages of Brunswick County, Virginia,
1750-1810. 1953.   .....   5.00 (413)
Neale, Gay Weeks. Brunswick County, Virginia 1720-1975.
1975. 502pp.
A history of Brunswick, a southside Virginia county,
with notes and appendices, pp. 301-481, including
land grants and patents, marriages, colonial militia,
register of free blacks, etc.   14.00   ..... (103)
Simmons, Don. Brunswick County, Virginia Census 1830.
1976. 24pp. 2.00 (689)

CAROLINE COUNTY

Campbell, T.E. Colonial Caroline: A History of Caroline
County, Virginia. Reprint.   15.00   ..... (195)
Wingfield, Marshall. A History of Caroline County, Virginia
from Its Formation in 1727 to 1924. Repr. of 1924 ed. 528pp. 17.50 ..... (274)

CHARLES CITY COUNTY

Byrd, William. Writings of Colonel William Byrd, ed. J.S.
Bassett. Repr. of 1901 ed.   28.00   ..... (248)

CHARLOTTE COUNTY

Knorr, Mrs. H.A. Marriages of Charlotte County, Virginia,
1764-1815. 1951.   .....   5.00 (413)

CHESTERFIELD COUNTY

_____. Marriages of Chesterfield County, Virginia, 1771-1815.
1958.   .....   5.00 (413)

CULPEPER COUNTY

Dorman, John Frederick. Culpeper County, Virginia, Deeds.
Volume 1, 1749-1755. 1975. ..... 7.50 (201)
Green, Raleigh Travers. Genealogical and Historical Notes on
Culpeper County, Virginia. 1900. 336pp. B-BH 11790. .... (778)

DINWIDDIE COUNTY

"Dinwiddie County: 1800 Tax List." The Virginia Genealogist,
Vol. 18, Nos. 1-4. All: 10.00 (201)
Gibbs, Mrs. Robert L. 1850 Census of Dinwiddie County,
Virginia. 1977. In Process.
Northern and southern districts of Dinwiddie County,
with index. .... (281)
Jarratt, Devereux. The Life of the Reverend Devereux Jarratt,
Rector of Bath Parish, Dinwiddee County, Virginia. 1806. 10.00 ..... (38)

ELIZABETH CITY COUNTY

Bentley, Right Reverend John B. Gravestone Inscriptions from
St. John's Episcopal Church. 1975. 251pp.
Cemetery inscriptions from 1697 to 1972. Over 3,500. ..... 9.50 (758)
"Elizabeth City County 1800 Tax List." The Virginia Genealogist,
Vol. 19, No. 1. ..... 3.00 (201)
Engs, Robert Francis. The Development of Black Culture and
Community in the Emancipation Era: Hampton Roads,
Virginia, 1861-1870. 255pp. BIP-72-29541. .... (777)

ESSEX COUNTY

"Essex County 1800 Tax List." The Virginia Genealogist, Vol.
19, Nos. 2,3. All: 6.00 (201)
Wilkerson, Eva Eubank. Index to Marriages of Old Rappahannock and Essex Counties, Virginia 1655-1900. Repr. of
1953 ed. 256pp. 12.50 ..... (274)

FAIRFAX COUNTY

Bacco, Thomas V.D. Moorefield. 1971. vi,52pp. illus.
Home, lands, biography of Jeremiah Moore, baptist
preacher, and others. 1.50 (226)
Cliver, E. Blaine and Tony P. Wrenn. The Dranesville Tavern:
An Architectural Analysis. 1970. illus.
History, biography and preservation proposals of an 1820
driver's rest. 1.50 (226)
Cooling, B.F. Historical Highlights of Bull Run Regional Park.
Repr. of 1971 ed. viii,96pp. illus. maps.
Civil war, biography, parks preservation. 1.50 (226)
"Fairfax County 1800 Tax List." The Virginia Genealogist, Vol.
19, No. 4, Vol. 20, Nos. 1,2. Each: 3.00 (201)
Fairfax Office of Comprehensive Planning. Fairfax County,
Virginia: A History. 1977. In Process.
Preliminary draft of 1,013 typescript pages. Illustrations.
Maps. Index. .... (226)
_____. Historic Preservation for Fairfax County. Repr. of
1967 ed. illus.
Descriptions of historic sites and legal methods for
preservation. 2.00 (226)

Gamble, Robert S. Sully: The Biography of a House.
1973. 228+pp.
  Includes history of a Lee family plantation on the early
  Northern Virginia frontier and follows history of
  subsequent owners and region, up to building of
  Dulles Airport. Illustrated, maps, index.   7.50   ..... (731)
Kilmer, Kenton and Donald Sweig. The Fairfax Family
in Fairfax County. Repr. of 1976 ed. 119+pp.
  Northern Neck (Fairfax) Proprietary, land grants,
  historic houses, biography, illustrations, maps. 3.00 (226)
McMillion, Lynn C. and Jane K. Wall. Fairfax County,
Virginia 1820 Federal Census and Schedule of Manufacturers.
1976. 76pp.
  Transcribed from original, indexed, fully enumerated
  including slaves and free colored. 3.50 (455)
Name Index Fairfax County, Virginia Court Records 1749-1774
(Microfiche). 1976.
  This index includes references to George Washington,
  George Mason; the area includes Alexandria, Arlington,
  Falls Church. 52,000 entries. (Includes fiche file.)   Microfiche: 225.00 (74)
Netherton, Ross D. The Colvin Run Mill. 1976. 64pp.
  Milling in Northern Virginia; biography, historic
  reconstruction and preservation. Illustrations; maps. 2.50 (226)
Netherton, Ross D. and Ruby Waldeck. The Fairfax County
Courthouse. 1976.
  History of three county courthouses courts in Virginia;
  Justices and Judges. Illustrations. 4.00 (226)
Netherton, Ross and Nan Netherton. Green Spring Farm.
Repr. of 1970 ed. 82+pp.
  Study of a political, religious and cultural center and
  200 years of history and biography. Now headquarters
  of county's countil of the arts. Illustrations. 1.50 (226)
Poland, Charles P., Jr. Dunbarton, Dranesville, Virginia.
Repr. of 1974 ed. 128+pp.
  History of an old stone house and its surrounding community.
  Biography. Illustrations. 2.50 (226)
Rafuse, Diane N. Maplewood. 1970. 64+pp.
  Architectural measured drawings, French Second Empire
  Mansion built 1870, demolished 1970. Also includes
  "Strawberry Vale." Illustrations. 1.50 (226)
Smith, Eugenia B. Centreville: Its History and Architecture.
Repr. of 1973 ed. 117+pp.
  Architecture, biography, Civil War; illustrations, maps. 2.50 (226)
Spann, Barbara. Carlby. 1976. 290pp.
  Careful documentation of the moving of an 18th century
  home from Sussex County, Virginia to Fairfax.
  Biographical data on owners; illustrated, maps. 3.50 (226)
Sprouse, Edith Moore. Colchester: Colonial Port on the
Potomac. 196pp.
  Detailed history and biographical data on a "ghost" town
  and its residents. Illustrations, maps. 3.00 (226)
_____. Mount Air. Repr. of 1970 ed. 112+pp.
  Study of early grantee, his lands, his family and
  subsequent owners of Mount Air. Illustrations. 2.50 (226)

Templeman, E. L. and Nan Netherton. Northern Virginia
Heritage. Repr. of 1966 ed. 202+pp.
  From Log Cabins to Mansions: an historical view of
  Northern Virginia through its architecture and
  art and people. 440 illustrations and maps, index.   5.80   ..... (526)
Wall, Jane Kirkpatrick. Cemetery Records of Fairfax
County, Virginia. 1977. In process.   .... (808)
Wrenn, Tony P. Huntley: A Mason Family Country Home.
1971. 56+pp.
  Significant plantation complex with many surviving
  brick outbuildings. Biography, illustrations. 1.50 (226)
Wrenn, Tony, et al., eds. The Legato School: A Centennial
Souvenir. 1976. 110+pp.
  History of one-room schoolhouse, teachers, county
  public school system to 1929. Illustrations. 3.00 (226)

FAUQUIER COUNTY

Bicentennial Committee. Fauquier County 1759-1959.
1959. 335pp.
  A general history of Fauquier County: Settlement,
  growth, biographical sketches, early homes,
  chronology.   10.00   ..... (290)
Gott, John K. Fauquier County in the Revolution. 1976. 500+pp.   20.00   ..... (290)
_____. Abstracts of Fauquier County, Virginia Wills,
Inventories and Accounts, 1759-1800. 1976. 1976. 358pp.
  Contains every instrument recorded in the will books
  of Fauquier, with every name, 1759-1800. Index. 12.50 (290)
King, Junie Estelle Stewart. Wills, Administrations and
Marriages, Fauquier County, Virginia, 1759-1800.
1939. 177pp. B-OP 61111.   .... (778)
Ramey, Emily G. and John K. Gott. The Years of Anguish,
Fauquier County, Virginia, 1861-1865. 1965. 233pp.
  Diaries, letters, reminiscences, rosters.   10.00   ..... (290)

FINCASTLE COUNTY

Worrell, Anne Lowry. A Brief of Wills and Marriages in
Montgomery and Fincastle Counties, Virginia, 1773-1831.
Repr. of 1932 ed. 56pp. 5.00 (274)

FREDERICK COUNTY

Cartmell, Thomas Kemp. Shenadoah Valley Pioneers and Their
Descendants. A History of Frederick County, Virginia
(Illustrated) From Its Formation in 1738 to 1908.
1909. 636pp. B-BH 4356.   .... (778)
Hough, Dr. Walter S. Braddick's Road Through the
Virginia Colony. 1970. 77pp.
  Route in Virginia west of Blue Ridge with maps and
  pictures.   8.80   ..... (249)
Lake. Lake Atlas Map of Frederick County. Repr. of 1885 ed.
6pp.
  Title page and 5 magisterial districts in original color
  22 x 13; shows location of individual homes. 5.50 (249)
Men and Events of the Revolution in Winchester and
Frederick County, Virginia. 1975. 165pp.
  It includes the "Frederick County Resolves," June 8, 1774;
  Biographical Sketches of Local Revolutionary Personalities;
  the most complete list of original memebers of Daniel Morgan;

a reprint of Izaac Zane, "A Quaker for the Times" and of
Extracts from the Journal of Lieut. John Bell Tilden of
Stephen City, relating his experiences at the Yorktowne
surrender.   8.95   5.45 (249)
Quarles, Garland R. George Washington and Winchester,
Virginia, 1748-1758. 1974. 80pp.
George in Winchester as surveyor and as Commander
of Virginia Frontier with Winchester as his headquarters. 4.45 (249)
Russell, William Greenway. What I Know About Winchester,
Virginia. Repr. of 1953 ed. 212pp.
Recollections 1800-1875 with notes and biographies.
Basic work.   8.70   ..... (249)

FREDERICKSBURG CITY

Knorr, Mrs. H.A. Marriages of Fredericksburg, Virginia,
1782-1850.
The book includes the tombstone inscriptions from
St. George's Churchyard. 5.00 (413)

GOOCHLAND COUNTY

Foley, Louise Pledge Heath. Early Virginia Families Along the
James River - Their Deep Roots and Tangled Branches. 1974.
170pp.
Brief history, geographical explanations, land patents
up to 1732, rent roll 1704-1705.   14.00   ..... (246)
Simmons, Don. Goochland County, Virginia Census of 1820.
1975. 19pp. 1.25 (689)

GRAYSON COUNTY

Nuckolls, Benjamin F. Pioneer Settlers of Grayson County,
Virginia. Repr. of 1914 ed. 219pp.   15.00   ..... (274)

GREENSVILLE COUNTY

Knorr, Katharine. Marriages of Greensville County, 1781-
1825. 1955.   .....   5.00 (413)

HALIFAX COUNTY

_____. Marriages of Halifax County, Virginia, 1753-1800. 1957. ..... 5.00 (413)
Mathis, Harry R. Along the Border, A History of Virgilina,
Virginia and the Surrounding Area in Halifax and Mecklenburg
Counties in Virginia and Person and Granville Counties in
North Carolina. 1964. 344pp.
General information about the area; histories of churches
and organizations; many names included, making book
of interest to genealogists.   15.00   ..... (477)

HAMPTON CITY

Bentley, Right Reverend John B. and William L. Litsey. Gravestone Inscriptions from the Cemetery of St. John's Episcopal
Church, Hampton, Virginia. 1975. 251pp.
Inscriptions date from 1697 to 1972. The place of birth
frequently given. Over 3500 indexed surnames. 9.50 (758)

HANOVER COUNTY

Cocke, William Ronald. Hanover County Chancery Wills and
Notes: A Compendium of Genealogical, Bibliographical
and Historical Material as Contained in Cases of the
Chancery Suits of Hanover County, Virginia. 1940. 226pp.
B-OP 66933. .... (778)

HENRICO COUNTY

Foley, Louise Pledge Heath. Early Virginia Families Along the
James River - Their Deep Roots and Tangled Branches. 1974.
170pp.
    Brief history, geographical explanations, land patents
    up to 1732, rent roll 1704-1705. 14.00 ..... (246)
Reddy, Anne Waller and Andrew L. Riffe. Richmond City,
Virginia, Marriage Bonds, 1797-1853. Repr. of 1939 ed. 158pp. 10.00 ..... (274)
Weisiger, Benjamin B., III. Henrico County, Virginia Wills.
1977. In Process.
    Abstracts of Henrico County, Virginia wills and related
    documents beginning in 1678 and up to 1783. Will pos-
    sibly be in two volumes. .... (820)
Wilson, Donald L. Abstracts of Records, 1650-1700. 1977.
    Deeds, wills, court orders, and miscellaneous records. .... (846)

HENRY COUNTY

Dodd, Virginia Anderton. Henry County, Virginia Marriage
Bonds, 1778-1849. Repr. of 1953 ed. 132pp. 10.00 ..... (274)
_____, ed. Henry County Marriage Bonds 1778-1849. 1953.
140pp. B-OP 66936. .... (778)
Hill, Judith. A History of Henry County, Virginia. 1925. 390pp.
B-OP 66577. .... (778)
_____. A History of Henry County, Virginia. Repr. of 1925.
329pp. 15.00 ..... (274)
Pedigo, Virginia G. and Lewis Pedigo. History of Patrick and
Henry Counties, Virginia. 1933. 447pp. B-OP 66737. .... (778)
Simmons, Don. Henry County, Virginia Census 1820. 1975.
14pp. 1.25 (689)
_____. Henry County, Virginia Census of 1830. 1976. 17pp. 1.25 (689)

ISLE OF WIGHT COUNTY

Chapman, Blanche Adams. Marriages of Isle of Wight County,
Virginia, 1628-1800. Repr. of 1933 ed. 124pp. 12.50 ..... (274)
_____. Wills and Administrations of Isle of Wight County,
Virginia, 1647-1800. Repr. of 1938 ed. 370pp. 17.50 ..... (274)

JAMES CITY COUNTY

Caruther, William A. The Cavaliers of Virginia: Or, the Re-
cluse of Jamestown. 2 vols. Reprint. 14.50 ..... (702)
Hatch, Charles E., Jr. First Seventeen Years: Virginia,
1607-1624. 1957. ..... 1.25 (801)
Paine, Lauran. Captain John Smith and the Jamestown Story.
1973. 6.95 ..... (337)

KING WILLIAM COUNTY

Clarke, Peyton Neale. Old King William Homes and
Families; an Account of Some of the Old Homesteads and
Families of King William County, Virginia. 1897. 244pp.
B-BH 6330.   .... (778)

LEE COUNTY

Simmons, Don. Lee County, Virginia Census 1820. 1975. 15pp. 1.25 (689)

LOUISA COUNTY

Davis, Rosalie Edith. Louisa County, Virginia Deed Book A -
1742-1754 and Deed Book B - 1742-1759. 1976. 200pp. 10.00 (183)

LUNENBURGH COUNTY

Bell, Landon Covington. The Old Free State; A Contribution
to the History of Lunenburgh County and Southside Virginia.
2 vols. o1927. Vol. 1-634pp. Vol. 2-644pp. B-BH 6819.   .... (778)

MECKLENBURG COUNTY

Brown, Douglas Summers. Chase City and Its Environs
1765-1975. 1975. 327pp.
    History of Northwestern Mecklenburg County and
    Christiansville (now Chase City).   15.50   ..... (624)
"A Guide to the Records of Mecklenburg County." Virginia
Genealogy, Vol. 18, No. 1.   .....   3.00 (201)
Mathis, Harry R. Along the Border. A History of Virgilina,
Virginia, and the Surrounding Area in Halifax and the
Mecklenburg Counties in Virginia and Person and Granville
Counties in North Carolina. 1964. 344pp.
    General information about the area; histories of churches
    and organizations; many names included, making book of
    interest to genealogists.   15.00   ..... (477)
Simmons, Don. Mecklenburg County, Virginia Census 1820.
1976. 42pp. 3.00 (689)
_____. Mecklenburg County, Virginia Census 1830. 1975. 36pp. 3.00 (689)
_____. Mecklenburg County, Virginia Census 1840. 1975. 42pp. 3.00 (689)

MIDDLESEX COUNTY

"A Guide to the Records of Middlesex County." Virginia
Genealogy, Vol. 18, No. 2.   .....   3.00 (201)
National Society of the Colonial Dames of America. The
Parish Register of Christ Church, Middlesex County,
Virginia, from 1653 to 1812. 1897. 342pp. B-OP 65451.   .... (778)

MONTGOMERY COUNTY

Givens, Lula Porterfield. Highlights in the Early History of
Montgomery County, Virginia. 1975. 200pp.
    Authentic - discovery of New River; first settlers;
    massacres, burning Draper's Meadows, Fort Vanse;
    Point Pleasant; Fincastle Resolutions, Christian;
    Preston; Jane Buchanan Floyd, Yankee Raid. 5.15 (694)
"A Guide to the Records of Montgomery County." Virginia
Genealogy, Vol. 18, No. 4.   .....   3.00 (201)
Heavener, Ulysses S. A. German New River Settlement:
Virginia. Repr. of 1929 ed. 94pp.   7.50   ..... (274)

Worrell, Anne Lowry. A Brief of Wills and Marriages in
Montgomery and Fincastle Counties, Virginia, 1773-1831.
Repr. of 1932 ed. 56pp. 5.00 (274)

NANSEMOND COUNTY

"A Guide to the Records of Nansemond County." Virginia
Genealogy, Vol. 19, No. 1. ..... 3.00 (201)

NELSON COUNTY

"A Guide to the Records of Nelson County." Virginia
Genealogy, Vol. 19, No. 1. ..... 3.00 (201)
Marmon, Lee. History of Amherst-Nelson Counties,
Virginia to 1807. 1976. 300pp. 8.00 7.00 (523)

NEW KENT COUNTY

"A Guide to the Records of New Kent County." Virginia
Genealogy, Vol. 19, No. 1. ..... 3.00 (201)

NORFOLK COUNTY

"A Guide to the Records of Norfolk County." Virginia
Genealogy, Vol. 19, No. 2. ..... 3.00 (201)
Lower Norfolk County, Virginia, Antiquary. 5 vols. in 2. 25.00 ..... (699)
Walter, Alice Granbery, ed. Virginia Land Patents of Norfolk,
Princess Anne and Warwick Counties, Virginia. From
Patent Books "O" and "6". 1972. 75pp.
　　Name and Place Indices. Illustrations of Court Script in
　　the text. 290 abstracts of patents between 1642-1786.
　　Patent Book 6 takes up where Nugent leaves off. 10.00 (811)

NORTHAMPTON COUNTY

County Court Records of Accomack-Northampton Virginia,
1632-1640. (Volume 7 of American Legal Series). 23.00 18.00 (415)
"A Guide to the Records of Northampton County." Virginia
Genealogy, Vol. 19, No. 3. ..... 3.00 (201)

NORTHUMBERLAND COUNTY

"A Guide to the Records of Northumberland County." Virginia
Genealogy, Vol. 19, No. 3. ..... 3.00 (201)

NOTTOWAY COUNTY

"A Guide to the Records of Nottoway County." Virginia
Genealogy, Vol. 19, No. 3. ..... 3.00 (201)

ORANGE COUNTY

"A Guide to the Records of Orange County." Virginia
Genealogy, Vol. 19, No. 4. ..... 3.00 (201)
Knorr, Mrs. H. A. Marriages of Orange County, Virginia,
1747-1810. 1959. ..... 5.00 (413)

PAGE COUNTY

"A Guide to the Records of Page County." Virginia Genealogy,
Vol. 20, No. 1. ..... 3.00 (201)

Strickler, Harry M. A Short History of Page County, Virginia.
Repr. of 1952 ed. 442pp.
    A fine history of Page County, Virginia. It is believed
    that here was the first settlement of the Shenandoah
    Valley.   22.50 ..... (124)

PATRICK COUNTY

"A Guide to the Records of Patrick County." Virginia
Genealogy, Vol. 20, No. 1.   ..... 3.00 (201)
Pedigo, Virginia G. and Lewis Pedigo. History of Patrick
and Henry Counties, Virginia. 1933. 447pp. B-OP 66737.   .... (778)

PITTSYLVANIA COUNTY

"A Guide to the Records of Pittsylvania County." Virginia
Genealogy, Vol. 20, No. 2.   ..... 3.00 (201)
Knorr, Mrs. H. A. Marriages of Pittsylvania County,
Virginia, 1767-1805. 1956. 127pp. 5.00 (413)

POWHATAN COUNTY

"A Guide to the Records of Powhatan County." Virginia
Genealogy, Vol. 20, No. 3.   ..... 3.00 (201)
Knorr, Mrs. H. A. Marriages of Powhatan County, Virginia,
1777-1830. 1957.   ..... 5.00 (413)

PRINCE EDWARD COUNTY

Knorr, Mrs. H. A. Marriages of Prince Edward County,
Virginia, 1754-1810. 1950. 109pp. 5.00 (413)

PRINCE GEORGE COUNTY

Weisiger, Benjamin B., III. Prince George County, Virginia
Records 1733-1792. 1975. 227pp.
    Abstracts of remaining Will and Deed Books for this
    period as well as Order Books, Loose Wills. 10.00 (820)

PRINCE WILLIAM COUNTY

"Prince William County Order Book 1759-1761." Virginia
Genealogy, Vol. 19, Nos. 3,4; Vol. 20, Nos. 1, 2, 3, 4.
[Being continued in Vol. 21.]   Each No.: 3.00 (201)
Writers' Program. Prince William, the Story of Its People
and Its Places. Repr. of 1941 ed.   10.50 ..... (2)

PRINCESS ANN COUNTY

Lower Norfolk County, Virginia, Antiquary. 5 vols. in 2. 25.00 ..... (699)
Walter, Alice Granbery. Genealogical Abstracts of
Princess Anne County, Virginia 1739-1762. 1975. 140pp.
    All of the genealogical information contained in
    Deed and Minute Books numbers 6 and 7 of the Court
    Records of Princess Anne County, Virginia. 12.50 (811)
_____, ed. Virginia Land Patents of Norfolk, Princess Anne
and Warwick Counties, Virginia from Patent Books "O" and
"6". 1972. 75pp.
    Name and Place Indices. Illustrations of Court Script
    in the text. 290 abstracts of patents between 1642-1786.
    Patent Book 6 takes up where Nugent leaves off. 10.00 (811)

RAPPAHANNOCK COUNTY

Wilkerson, Eva Eubank. Index to Marriages of Old Rappahannock
and Essex Counties, Virginia, 1655-1900. Repr. of 1953 ed.
256pp.   12.50   ..... (274)

RICHMOND CITY

Carter, Landon. Diary of Colonel Landon Carter of Sabine
Hall, 1752-1778. ed. Jack P. Greene. 2 vols. 1965.
Virginia Historical Documents No. 4 and No. 5. Illus. Set: 25.00   ..... (801)
Richmond Dispatch, January 14, 1852 to December, 1902.
128 rolls.
Microfilm of the original papers. Individual rolls
covering a specific time span may be ordered. Prices
vary $15 to $30 per roll.   .... (870)

ROCKBRIDGE COUNTY

"Rockbridge County Tithable Lists, 1778-1779." Virginia
Genealogy, Vol. 18, No. 4; Vol. 19, Nos. 1, 2.   All: 9.00 (201)

ROCKINGHAM COUNTY

Kaylor, Peter C. Abstract of Land Grant Surveys of Augusta
and Rockingham Counties, Virginia, 1761-1791.
Repr. of 1938 ed. 150pp.   10.00   ..... (274)
Strickler, Harry M. Old Tenth Legion Marriages: Marriages
in Rockingham County, Virginia, 1778-1816. Repr. of
1928 ed. 128pp.   10.00   ..... (274)
Wayland, John W. Historic Harrisonburg (Virginia).
Repr. of 1949 ed. 419pp.
A detailed history of the founding and growth of the
County Seat of Rockingham County, Virginia.   15.00   ..... (124)
_____. History of Rockingham County, Virginia.
Repr. of 1912 ed. 467pp.
A comprehensive history of the county, in the heart
of the Shenandoah Valley of Virginia.   17.50   ..... (124)

SCOTT COUNTY

Addington, Robert Milford. History of Scott County, Virginia.
1932. 394pp. B-OP 70067.   .... (778)

SOUTHAMPTON COUNTY

Knorr, Katharine. Marriages of Southampton County, 1750-1810.
1955.   .....   5.00 (413)
Turner, Nat. The Confession, Trial and Execution of Nat
Turner, the Negro Insurrectionist; Also a List of Persons
Murdered in the Insurrection in Southampton County,
Virginia, the 21st and 22nd of August, 1831. 1881.   .....   5.00 (2)

STAFFORD COUNTY

Fitzhugh, William. William Fitzhugh and His Chesapeake
World, 1676-1701: The Fitzhugh Letters and Other
Documents. ed. Richard B. Davis. (Virginia Historical
Society.) Illustrated. 1963.   9.75   ..... (801)

SURRY COUNTY

Jones: Surry Light Artillery of Virginia. ed. Lee A. Wallace, Jr.
Repr. of 1909 ed. 425pp.
    The author served throughout the war as a private with
the Surry Light Artillery from Surry County, Virginia.
After service as infantry with the Third Regiment of
Virginia Volunteers, the company in 1862 became an
independent battery and was assigned to Lt. Col.
Charles E. Lightfoot's battalion of light artillery in the
defenses of Richmond. Includes roster and notes on
each man, indexed.   20.00   ..... (506)
Knorr, Mrs. H. A. Marriages of Surry County, Virginia,
1768-1825. 112pp. 5.00 (413)

SUSSEX COUNTY

_____. Marriages of Sussex County, Virginia, 1754-1810. 111pp. 5.00 (413)

TAZEWELL COUNTY

Bickley, G. W. L. Bickley's History of the Settlement and
Indian Wars of Tazewell County, Virginia. Repr. of 1852 ed.
c390pp.
    George W. L. Bickley was the founder of the "Knights
of the Golden Circle" a strong pro-Confederacy filibuster-
oriented organization during the Civil War. Bickley was
imprisoned and appealed directly to Abraham Lincoln in
his writing about his incarceration.   21.00   ..... (217)
Pearlman, Agnes Branch. West Virginia's Southern Counties
1850 Census Surname Index: Boone, Cabell, Fayette,
Greenbrier, Kanawha, Logan, Mercer, Monroe, Raleigh,
Wayne, Wyoming, and Tazewell County, Virginia. 1976. 80pp.
    Section I, 20 pages, contains Fayette, Mercer, Raleigh,
and Tazewell Counties. Includes counties from which
Lincoln, McDowell, Mingo and Summers were later
formed. With notes and map. Section I available separately.
                                    Section I: 2.00 (581)
                                      Set: 5.00 (581)

WARWICK COUNTY

Walter, Alice Granbery, ed. Virginia Land Patents of Norfolk,
Princess Anne and Warwick Counties, Virginia. From
Patent Books "O" and "6". 1972. 75pp.
    Name and Place Indices. Illustrations of Court Script
in the text. 290 abstracts of patents between 1642-1786
Patent Book 6 takes up where Nugent leaves off. 10.00 (811)

WASHINGTON COUNTY

McConnell, Mrs. Catherine S. High On A Windy Hill. 1968.
426pp.
    All legible names and dates in 333 cemeteries in Washing-
ton County, Virginia including maps and index of cemeteries;
illustrated and documented.   20.00   ..... (449)

WESTMORELAND COUNTY

"Westmoreland County Tithables, 1776." Virginia Genealogy,
Vol. 19, No. 3.   ..... 3.00 (201)

Nottingham, Stratton. The Marriage License Bonds of Westmoreland County, Virginia, From 1786-1850. Repr. of 1928
ed. 97pp.   8.50   ..... (274)

WYTHE COUNTY

Stilley, Van A., J. D. Wythe County, Virginia, 1820 Census
with 1821 Boye Map and Notes. 1977. In process.   .... (726)
"Wills and Other Instruments of Wythe County, Virginia Before
1800." The Ridge Runners, Vol. 4. 1976. 9pp.   .... (859)
"Wythe County, Virginia Marriages, 1790-1800."
The Ridge Runners, Vol. 4. 1976. 4pp.   .... (859)

YORK COUNTY

Charles Parish, York County, Virginia. History and Registers:
Births, 1648-1789; Deaths, 1665-1786. Repr. of 1932 ed.
285pp.   .... (800)
Dorman, John Frederick. York County, Virginia, Deeds,
Orders, Wills, Etc., Number 8, 1687-1691. Parts 1 and
2. 1974-1975.   ..... 7.50 (201)

Washington

STATEWIDE REFERENCES

Avery, Mary W. Washington: A History of the Evergreen
State. 1965.   6.95 ..... (814)
Bancroft, Hubert H. History of Washington, Idaho and
Montana.   7.00 ..... (51)
Cook, Francis. The Territory of Washington in 1879.
ed. J. Orin Oliphant. Repr. of 1925 ed. 2.50 (860)
Dahlie, Jorgen. A Social History of Scandinavian
Immigration, Washington State, 1895-1910. 1967. 194pp.
BIP-68-00690.   .... (777)
Dryden, Cecil. Dryden's History of Washington. 1968.   6.50 ..... (68)
Jones, Sylvia and Myra F. Cassady. From Cabin to Cupola:
Country Courthouses of Washington.   10.00 ..... (687)
Langford, Nathaniel Pitt. Vigilante Days and Ways; the
Pioneers of the Rockies, the Makers and Making of
Montana, Idaho, Oregon, Washington, and Wyoming.
2 vols. 1890.   Each: 18.00 ..... (2)
  Set: 35.00 ..... (2)
Meeker, E. Washington Territory. Repr. of 1870 ed. 3.00 (687)
Mullan, John. Miners and Travelers' Guide to Oregon,
Washington, Idaho, Montana, Wyoming, and Colorado. Via
the Missouri and Columbia Rivers. Accompanied by a
General Map of the Mineral Region of the Northern Sections
of the Rocky Mountains. 1865.   8.00 ..... (38)
Phillips, James W. Washington State Place Names. 1971.   6.95 ..... (814)
Prosch, Charles. Reminiscences of Washington Territory. 1969.   7.00 ..... (860)
Smith, Clareta Olmstead. End of the Trail. 1976. 290pp.
  History of Kittitas Valley Region.   10.00 ..... (224)
Swan, James G. Almost Out of the World: Scenes from
Washington Territory. ed. William A. Katz. 1971.   7.50 ..... (816)
_____. The Northwest Coast: Or, Three Years' Residence in
Washington Territory. 1972.   ..... 3.95 (814)

Yonce, Frederick Jay. Public Land Disposal in Washington.
1969. 299pp. BIP-70-08437. .... (777)

ADAMS COUNTY

Tombstone Inscriptions Adams County, Washington. 1976. .... (212)

KING COUNTY

Seattle, King County, Washington Territory. Repr. of 1884 ed. 1.50 (687)

LINCOLN COUNTY

Lartigue, Wes and Carrie Lartigue. Tombstone Inscriptions
Lincoln County, Washington. 1974. 181pp. 6.50 (212)

PEND O'REILLE COUNTY

Tombstone Inscriptions Pend O'Reille County, Washington. 1976. .... (212)

SPOKANE COUNTY

Garner, Grace and Lorena Wildman. 1880 Census Spokane
County, Washington Territory. 1973. 104pp. 5.00 (212)
Sheldon, Mary and Lorena Wildman. Will Book A, Spokane,
Washington July,1891-January, 1900. 1973. 60pp. 3.50 (212)
Wildman, Lorena and Carrie Lartigue. Early Spokane County,
Washington Territory Marriages Book A, 1880-1890.
1972. 130pp. 5.00 (212)

STEVENS COUNTY

Tombstone Inscriptions Stevens County, Washington. 1976. .... (212)
Wildman, Lorena. 1880 Census Stevens County, Washington
Territory. 1973. 35pp. 3.50 (212)

THURSTON COUNTY

Blankenship, George E. Early History of Thurston County.
Repr. of 1914 ed. 20.00 ..... (687)
Rathburn. History of Thurston County, Washington - From
Eighteen Forty-Five to Eighteen Ninety-Five. 7.50 (687)

WHATCOM COUNTY

Christenson, Earle H., comp. Cemetery Records of Whatcom
County, Volume 1. 1973. 171pp.
    Cemetery records of Greenacres and Lummi Island
    Cemeteries. 5.00 (831)
_____. Cemetery Records of Whatcom County, Volume 2.
1973. 174pp.
    Cemetery records of Bay View, Congregation Beth
    Israel, Mt. Calvary, Buchanan Cemeteries. 5.00 (831)
_____. Cemetery Records of Whatcom County, Volume 3.
1975. 191pp.
    Cemetery records of Enterprise, Haynie, Mt. View,
    Ten Mile, Woodlawn and Zion Lutheran Cemeteries. 10.00 (831)
_____. Cemetery Records of Whatcom County, Volume 4.
1975. 199pp.
    Cemetery records of Blaine Masonic, Blaine, Greenwood,
    Hillsdale, Lakeside, Lynden, Monumenta, Nooksack,
    Perry, Point Roberts, Saint Anne's, Sumas Cemeteries. 10.00 (831)

_____. Cemetery Records of Whatcom County, Volume 5.
1976. c175pp.
　Cemetery records of Bethany Lutheran, Cannon,
　Clipper (St. Joseph's), Glacier, Immanuel Lutheran,
　Kendall (Welcome), Maple Falls, Mt. Hope, Nooksack,
　Nooksack Indians (5 cemeteries), Saxon, VanZandt,
　Welcome, Wickersham Cemeteries plus unknown as to
　burial place and miscellaneous burials in the county.　　.....　10.00　(831)
Pioneers of Peace - Diamond Jubilee, Blaine, Washington,
　With Index. Repr. of 1959 ed.　　　　　　　　　　　　.....　2.50　(831)

WHITMAN COUNTY

Campbell, Alice. Short History of Rosalia, Washington. 1970.　.....　1.00　(860)
Tombstone Inscriptions Whitman County, Washington,
　Volume 1. comps.Weston Lartigue and Carrie Lartigue.
　1972. 144pp.　　　　　　　　　　　　　　　　　　　.....　5.00　(212)
Tombstone Inscriptions Whitman County, Washington, Volume 2.
　comps. Lorraine Cook White and Margie Frier Robertson.
　1973. 163pp.　　　　　　　　　　　　　　　　　　　.....　5.00　(212)
Tombstone Inscriptions Whitman County, Washington, Volume 3.
　comps. Weston Lartigue and Carrie Lartigue. 1973. 165pp.　.....　5.00　(212)

West Virginia

STATEWIDE REFERENCES

Allman, Ruth Cooper. Canaan Valley and the Black Bear.
1976. 120pp.
　A history of Canaan Valley since its early settlement to
　the present time with over 80 pictures. Also, true
　stories and pictures of the black bear, very much a
　native. The author has lived in the valley all her life.　.....　.....　(273)
Cometti, Elizabeth and Festus P. Summers. The Thirty-Fifth
State. Repr. of 1966 ed. Index.
　A documentary history of West Virginia in the vivid
　language of the men who explored and settled it and
　who witnessed its development. Includes 187 narratives.　12.00　.....　(273)
DeHass, Wills. History of the Early Settlement and Indian
Wars of Western Virginia. Repr. of 1851 ed.
　One of the better early histories of what is now
　West Virginia. Illustrated.　　　　　　　　　　　　10.00　.....　(273)
Dillon, Lacy A. They Died in the Darkness. 1976.
　A journalistic history of forty-four of West Virginia's
　worst coal mine disasters such as Monongah, Eccles,
　Bartley, and Farmington. The names of victims
　follow each chapter. Human interest stories are
　evident throughout each chapter. Illustrated.　　　　9.95　.....　(273)
Doddridge, Joseph. Notes on the Settlement and Indian Wars.
Repr. of 1824 ed.
　Reprint of third printing published by John S. Ritenour and
　William T. Lindsey in 1912. Describes the settlement
　and Indian Wars of the western parts of Virginia and
　Pennsylvania from 1763 to 1783, inclusive. Indexed.
　Annotated.　　　　　　　　　　　　　　　　　　　9.00　.....　(273)

Mockler, William E. West Virginia Surnames: The Pioneers. 1974.
Written by a West Virginian who received his doctorate at
Ohio State University. This award winning book is a survey of
family names in use on America's first English-speaking
trans-Appalachian frontier. Indexed.   10.00 ..... (273)
Nutter, T. Thomas. West Virginia, 1906. 1969.   5.00 ..... (273)
Rice, Otis K. West Virginia: The State and Its People. 1972.   7.95 ..... (273)
Stealey, John Edmund, III. The Salt Industry of the Great Kanawha
Valley of Virginia: A Study in Ante-Bellum Internal Commerce.
1970. 606pp. BIP-71-04857.   .... (777)
Stutler, Boyd B. The Kinnan Massacre Including Reprint of
the Original True Narrative of the Sufferings of Mary Kannan.
1969.
    Gives background information not included in the original
    Kinnan narrative, printed in 1795 of which only two
    copies are known to exist. 2.00 (273)
Tams, W. P., Jr. The Smokeless Coal Fields of West Virginia.
1963.
    A history of coal mining in southern West Virginia.   6.00 ..... (273)
Van Liere, Edward J., Ph. D., M.D., Litt.D. Early Teachers
in West Virginia University School of Medicine, 1869-1922. 1968.
    A series of brief biographical sketches of a number of the
    early teachers in the School of Medicine of West Virginia
    University in which is woven much of the history of the
    School of Medicine. Illustrated.   5.00 ..... (273)
_____ and Gideon S. Dodds, Ph.D. History of Medical
Education in West Virginia. 1965.
    This history covers the period from 1869 to 1962.
    Included is a list of the names of the students who have
    enrolled in the Medical School from 1902-1962.
    Picture section. Indexed.   6.00 ..... (273)
Withers, Alexander Scott. Chronicles of Border Warfare.
rev. ed. 1831. Index.
    History of the settlement of northwestern Virginia and
    of the Indian wars and massacres in that section of the
    State, edited and annotated by Reuben Gold Thwaites.   10.00 ..... (273)
Withers, Alexander Scott. Chronicles of Border Warfare: Or,
a History of the Settlement by the Whites, of Northwestern
Virginia, and of the Indian Wars and Massacres in That
Section of the State, With Reflections, Annecdotes, etc.
A New Edition, Edited and Annotated by Reuben Gold
Thwaites With the Addition of a Memoir of the Author
and Several Illustrative Notes by the Late Lyman Copeland
Draper. 1895.   19.00 ..... (38)

Military

Hornbeck, Betty. Upshur Brothers of the Blue and the Gray.
1967.
    A localized history of the Civil War based on
    personal letters, diaries and selections from
    newspaper accounts. Included in the volume is a
    roster of the 10th West Virginia Volunteer Infantry
    Regiment, 1861-1865. Annotated, illustrated, indexed.   8.00 ..... (273)
Lane, Winthrop D. Civil War in West Virginia. 2.00 (562)
Matheny, H. E. Major General Thomas Maley Harris, Including
    Roster of the 10th West Vriginia Volunteer Infantry
    Regiment, 1861-1865. 1963.   6.00 ..... (273)

Records

Pearlman, Agnes Branch. West Virginia's Southern Counties
1850 Census Surname Index; Boone, Cabell, Fayette,
Greenbrier, Kanawha, Logan, Mercer, Monroe, Raleigh,
Wayne, Wyoming, and Tazewell County, Virginia. 1976. 80pp.
Includes counties from which Lincoln, McDowell,
Mingo, and Summers were later formed. Available in
20-page sections @ $2.00 each with notes and maps:
Section I: Fayette, Mercer, Raleigh, Tazewell;
Section II: Greenbrier, Monroe;
Section III: Boone, Kanawha;
Section IV: Cabell, Logan, Wayne, Wyoming. Set: 5.00 (581)

BARBOUR COUNTY

Maxwell, Hu. History of Barbour County. Repr. of 1899 ed.
Maps, sketches, annotated, indexed. 20.00 ..... (273)

BERKELEY COUNTY

Doherty, William Thomas. Berkeley County, U.S.A.: A
Bicentennial History of a Virginia and West Virginia County,
1772-1972. 1972. 20.00 ..... (273)

BOONE COUNTY

Pearlman, Agnes Branch. West Virginia's Southern Counties
1850 Census Surname Index. 1976. 20pp.
Section III, contains Boone and Kanawha Counties.
Section III available with notes and map. 2.00 (581)

BRAXTON COUNTY

Sutton, John Davison. History of Braxton County and Central
West Virginia. Repr. of 1919 ed. 466pp. 20.00 ..... (273)

CABELL COUNTY

Pearlman, Agnes Branch. West Virginia's Southern Counties
1850 Census Surname Index. 1976. 20pp.
Section IV, contains Cabell, Logan, Wayne, and
Wyoming Counties, with notes and map. 2.00 (581)
Pratt, Rupert C., comp. 1820 Census of Cabell County,
Virginia. February, 1977. 28pp.
All of the information in the original census is included. 3.00 (617)

DODDRIDGE COUNTY

Atkinson, Mary Davis. Doddridge County, Virginia (Now West
Virginia) Marriage Book I. 1968. 73pp. 4.00 (371)

FAYETTE COUNTY

Pearlman, Agnes Branch. West Virginia's Southern Counties
1850 Census Surname Index. 1976. 20pp.
Section I, 20 pages, contains Fayette, Mercer, Raleigh,
and Tazewell Counties, with notes and map. 2.00 (581)
Peters, J. T. and H. B. Carden. History of Fayette County.
Repr. of 1926 ed.
A vivid account of the growth and development of the
county's communities. Over 225 pictures. 30.00 ..... (273)

GREENBRIER COUNTY

McMillion, Lynn C. 1840 Federal Census of Greenbrier County,
Virginia (Now West Virginia). 1976. c76pp. In process.
Transcribed from original, indexed, fully enumerated
including slaves and free colored. .... (456)
Pearlman, Agnes Branch. West Virginia's Southern Counties
1850 Census Surname Index. 1976. 20pp.
Section II, contains Greenbrier and Monroe Counties,
with notes and map. 2.00 (581)

HAMPSHIRE COUNTY

Brannon, Selden W., ed. Historic Hampshire: A Symposium
of Hampshire County and Its People, Past and Present. 1976.
300pp. 15.00 ..... (273)
Maxwell, Hu and H. L. Swisher. History of Hampshire County,
West Virginia. Repr. of 1897 ed.
Reprint contains a new index. 20.00 ..... (273)

HARDY COUNTY

Moore, Commander Alvin Edward. History of Hardy County of
the Borderland. 1963. 10.00 ..... (273)

HARRISON COUNTY

Crickard, Madeline W., comp. Index to Harrison County,
(West) Virginia Marriages, 1784-1850. 1975. 67pp. 6.00 (168)
Haymond, Henry. History of Harrison County. Repr. of
1910 ed. 483pp.
Subtitle: From the Early Days of Northwestern Virginia
to the present (1910), indexed. 20.00 ..... (273)
Poling, Lena E. A History of the City of Shinnston. 1975.
Begins with the Shinn family and their exploration of the
western wilderness. The recording of the community's
development is interspersed with thumbnail sketches of
prominent citizens. Indexed. 15.00 ..... (273)

KANAWHA COUNTY

Pearlman, Agnes Branch. West Virginia's Southern Counties
1850 Census Surname Index. 1976. 20pp.
Section III, contains Boone and Kanawha Counties,
with notes and map. 2.00 (581)
Wintz, Julia, comp. Marriages of Kanawha County, 1792-1869.
1975. 10.00 ..... (273)

LOGAN COUNTY

"Logan County, West Virginia 1824 Tax List." Virginia
Genealogy, Vol. 19, No. 4. ..... 3.00 (201)
Pearlman, Agnes Branch. 1840 Census and Index for Logan
County, Virginia (Later West Virginia). 1976. 17pp.
With notes and map. 2.00 (581)
_____. West Virginia's Southern Counties 1850 Census
Surname Index. 1976. 20pp.
Section IV, contains Cabell, Logan, Wayne, and Wyoming
Counties, with notes and map. 2.00 (581)

....

Thurmond, Walter R. The Logan Coal Field of West Virginia. 1964.
The author recorded for the reader the pattern of development of the coal industry in Logan County and information
about the men most responsible for it, their place in the
industry and the part they played. Illustrated.   4.00   ..... (273)

McDOWELL COUNTY

Friedl, Joseph, Sr. A History of Education in McDowell County,
West Virginia, 1858-1976. 1975.
The story of education in McDowell County from its
beginning to the present.   10.00   ..... (273)

MERCER COUNTY

"A Guide to the Records of Mercer County." Virginia
Genealogy, Vol. 18, No. 1.   .....   3.00 (201)
Pearlman, Agnes Branch. West Virginia's Southern Counties
1850 Census Surname Index. 1976. 20pp.
Section I, contains Fayette, Mercer, Raleigh, and
Tazewell Counties, with notes and map. 2.00 (581)

MINGO COUNTY

Donnelly, Shirley. The Hatfield-McCoy Feud Reader. Repr. of
1971 ed.
A series of stories and newspaper clippings dealing with
the famous feud along the shores of the Tug River in
Mingo County, West Virginia, and Pike County,
Kentucky, during the last quarter of the past century. 2.00 (273)

MONONGALIA COUNTY

Core, Earl L. The Monongalia Story: I. Prelude. 1974.
Contains background information in chapters on the
geology, flora, fauna, and the aborigines of the
Monongahela Country, later to be Monongalia County.
This is followed by an account of more than 1000 early
settlers who were awarded land grants. Chapters are
included on the frontier forts and the daily life of the
pioneers, and the volume ends with the establishment
of the new county by the General Assembly of Virginia
in 1776.   20.00   ..... (273)
_____. The Monongalia Story: II. The Pioneers. 1976.
The second volume of this series provides a vivid account
of pioneer life in Monongalis County, each of the fifty
chapters covering the span of one year, from 1776 to
1826. Illustrated.   25.00   ..... (273)
_____. Morgantown Disciples. 1960.
A history of the First Christian Church of Morgantown,
West Virginia. Annotated. Indexed.   4.00   ..... (273)
Crickard, Madeline W., comp. 1850 Census of Monongalia
County, (West) Virginia. 1976. 157+pp. 15.00 (168)
_____. Marriage Bonds of Monongalia County, Virginia,
1796-1850. 1976. 179pp. 15.00 (168)
"A Guide to the Records of Monongalia County." Virginia
Genealogy, Vol. 18, No. 4.   .....   3.00 (201)

MONROE COUNTY

"A Guide to the Records of Monroe County." Virginia
Genealogy, Vol. 18, No. 4.   ..... 3.00 (201)

Pearlman, Agnes Branch. West Virginia's Southern Counties
1850 Census Surname Index. 1976. 20pp.
   Section II, contains Greenbrier and Monroe Counties,
   with notes and map. 2.00 (581)

NICHOLAS COUNTY

"A Guide to the Records of Nicholas County." Virginia
Genealogy, Vol. 19, No. 2.   ..... 3.00 (201)

OHIO COUNTY

"A Guide to the Records of Ohio County." Virginia Genealogy,
Vol. 19, No. 4.   ..... 3.00 (201)

PENDLETON COUNTY

"A Guide to the Records of Pendleton County." Virginia Genealogy,
Vol. 20, No. 2.   ..... 3.00 (201)

PLEASANTS COUNTY

"A Guide to the Records of Pleasants County." Virginia Genealogy,
Vol. 20, No. 3.   ..... 3.00 (201)

POCAHONTAS COUNTY

"A Guide to the Records of Pocahontas County." Virginia Genealogy,
Vol. 20, No. 3.   ..... 3.00 (201)

Price, William T. Historical Sketches of Pocahontas County.
Repr. of 1901 ed. 633pp.
   Biographic section dealing with early settlers contains
   over 450 pages. Indexed.   20.00 ..... (273)

PRESTON COUNTY

Morrison, Charles. The Western Boundary of Maryland.
1976. 112pp.
   A history of Preston County's boundary dispute with its
   Maryland neighbor. 4.50 (508)

Wiley, S. T. and A. W. Frederick. History of Preston County.
Repr. of 1882 ed. 529pp.
   This book represented a distinctive literary achievement
   because of the destruction of public records in 1796 and
   1869 by fire. Abounds with records of names of
   individuals and families. Illustrated.   20.00 ..... (273)

Powell, Harold F. Index to S. T. Wiley's History of
Preston County. 1971.
   4500 names. [$1.50 when ordered with above history.] 3.00 (273)

RALEIGH COUNTY

Pearlman, Agnes Branch. West Virginia's Southern Counties
1850 Census Surname Index. 1976. 20pp.
   Section I, contains Fayette, Mercer, Raleigh, and
   Tazewell Counties, with notes and map. 2.00 (581)

RANDOLPH COUNTY

Bosworth, A. S. History of Randolph County (West Virginia).
    Repr. of 1916 ed. 448pp.   25.00 ..... (168)
Bosworth, Dr. Albert S. History of Randolph County, West
    Virginia (Virginia). Repr. of 1916 ed. 448pp. Index.
    This history covers the period from approximately
    1753 to 1916. Included are court, town and community
    settlement records, church histories, family histories.   25.00 ..... (273)
Holmes, Charles J. and Justin M. Kunkle, eds. and comps.
    Elkins, Its Past, Present and Future. Repr. of 1906 ed.   15.50 ..... (273)
Maxwell, Hu. History of Randolph County. Repr. of 1898 ed. 531pp.
    A history of the county from its earliest settlement to
    1898. Illustrated, indexed.   '   25.00 ..... (273)
Preble, Jack. Land of Canaan. Repr. of 1965 ed.
    A collection of intriguing, hilarious and sometimes
    tragic tales from the mountains of Tucker and
    Randolph Counties. Map of the Land of Canaan.   6.00 ..... (273)

RITCHIE COUNTY

Atkinson, Mary Davis. Ritchie County, Virginia (Now West
    Virginis) Marriages, 1843-1853. 1968. 39pp. 4.00 (371)

TUCKER COUNTY

Maxwell, Hu. History of Tucker County. Repr. of 1884 ed.
    Reprint includes an index by Mrs. Louise Morris.   20.00 ..... (273)
Nutter, T. Thomas, West Virginia, 1906. Repr.   5.00 ..... (273)
Preble, Jack. Land of Canaan. Repr. of 1965 ed.
    A collection of intriguing, hilarious and sometimes tragic
    tales from the mountains of Tucker and Randolph Counties.
    Map of the Land of Canaan.   6.00 ..... (273)
Thompson, Geo. B. and Ben Thompson. A History of the Lumber
    Business at Davis, West Virginia, 1885-1924. 1974.   .....   3.00 (273)

TYLER COUNTY

Atkinson, Mary Davis. Tyler County, Virginia Marriages,
    1815-1852 (Now West Virginia). 1968. 63pp. 4.00 (371)

UPSHUR COUNTY

Pinnell, Lois M. French Creek Presbyterian Church. 1971. 250pp.
    A memorial to its 150 years of continuous service, the
    book contains histories; organizations; influences;
    lists of ministers, elders; baptisms and members for the
    first fifty years and excerpts from early minutes. Over
    125 pictures. Indexed.   10.00 ..... (273)

WAYNE COUNTY

Morris, Byron T. A Charge to Keep. 1971.
    Subtitle - History of the First Baptist Church of Kenova,
    West Virginia. Covers 60 years (1908-1968) of the
    development and growth of The First Baptist Church of
    Kenova, West Virginia.   4.00 ..... (273)
Pearlman, Agnes Branch. West Virginia's Southern Counties
    1850 Census Surname Index. 1976. 20pp.
    Section IV, contains Cabell, Logan, Wayne, and Wyoming
    Counties, with notes and map. 2.00 (581)

WIRT COUNTY

Lee, Howard B. The Burning Springs and Other Tales of the
Little Kanawha. 1968.
Historians say that the Burning Springs petroleum deposit
was the richest shallow well oil pool the world has ever
known. Annotated, illustrated.   8.00 ..... (273)

WYOMING COUNTY

Pearlman, Agnes Branch. Genealogical Index to Bowman's
Reference Book of Wyoming County History. 1976. c100+pp.
With corrections and additions to census section. 7.00 (581)
_____. West Virginia's Southern Counties 1850 Census
Surname Index. 1976. 20pp.
Section IV, contains Cabell, Logan, Wayne and
Wyoming Counties, with notes and map. 2.00 (581)

Wisconsin

STATEWIDE REFERENCES

Kellogg, Louise T. British Regime in Wisconsin and the
Northwest. Repr.   15.00 ..... (176)
Lapham, Increase Allen. Wisconsin: Its Geography and
Topography, History, Geology, and Mineralogy. 1846.   11.00 ..... (38)
Lord, Clifford L. and Carl Ubbelohde. Clio's Servant: The
State Historical Society of Wisconsin 1846-1954. 1967.   10.00 ..... (850)
Smith, Alice E. The History of Wisconsin, Volume 1: From
Exploration to Statehood. 1973.   15.00 ..... (850)
Smith, Wm. R. Observations On the Wisconsin Territory. 1838. ..... 27.00 (38)

Research Aids

Hafstad, Margaret, ed. Guide to the McCormick Collection of
the State Historical Society of Wisconsin. 1973.   10.00 ..... (850)
Harper, Josephine L., ed. Guide to the Manuscripts of the
State Historical Society of Wisconsin. Including Supplement
Number One - 1957; Supplement Number Two - 1966.
                                                  No. 1:   5.00 ..... (850)
                                                  No. 2:   9.00 ..... (850)
Oehlerts, Donald E., ed. Guide to Wisconsin Newspapers
1833-1957. 1958.   8.00 ..... (850)

Wisconsin Magazine of History: Cumulative Index, Including:
Volume I-15 (1917-1931) Repr. of 1934 ed.;
Volume 16-25 (1932-1942) 1946; Volume 26-35 (1942-1952)
1955; Volume 36-45 (1952-1962);   Each: 3.00   ..... (850)
Volume 46-55 (1962-1972).   Each: 9.50   ..... (850)
Wisconsin State Historical Society. A Check List of Wisconsin
Imprints, 1864-1869. 1953.   ..... 12.00 (415)

Religious and Ethnic Groups

La Piana, G. The Italians in Milwaukee, Wisconsin.
Repr. of 1915 ed.   4.00   ..... (631)
Nauen, Lindsay B., ed. Guide to Wisconsin Jewish Archives.
1974.   .....   1.00 (850)

Records

Gnacinski, Janneyne and Christine Nowak. Wisconsin,
"Meeting Place of the Waters." 1976. 145pp.
Vital, Cemetery, military, church, naturalization,
and miscellaneous records from a cross section of
Wisconsin counties. 10.50 (381)
Wisconsin History Commission. Original Papers of the
Wisconsin History Commission. [All Published.]
1908-1914. Nos. 1-8 in 8 vols.   Each: 15.00   ..... (2)
Set: 120.00   ..... (2)

DANE COUNTY

Cassidy, F. G. The Place-Names of Dane County, Wisconsin. 1947. .....   7.50 (11)

EAU CLAIRE COUNTY

Peterson, Dale Arthur. Lumbering on the Chippewa: The
Eau Claire Area 1845-1885. 1970. 739pp. BIP-70-20256   .... (777)

IOWA COUNTY

Fiedler, George. Mineral Point: A History. 1973.   4.50   ..... (850)

JEFFERSON COUNTY

Gnacinski, Janneyne. Probate Notices Published in Jefferson,
Wisconsin Newspapers, 1853-1879. 1972. 29+pp. 3.00 (381)
_____. Territorial Marriages, Jefferson County, Wisconsin.
1972. 20+pp.
Marriages recorded at County Court House from 1840 to
date of Statehood, May 29, 1848.   .....   2.00 (381)

MARINETTE COUNTY

Krog, Carl Edward. Marinette: Biography of a Nineteenth Century
Lumbering Town, 1850-1910. 1971. 330pp. BIP-71-20670.   .... (777)

MILWAUKEE COUNTY

Derby, Wm. Ed. A History of the Port of Milwaukee 1835-1910.
1963. 459pp. BIP-63-05742.   .... (777)
Knoche, Carl Heinz. The German Immigrant Press in Milwaukee.
1969. 302pp. BIP-69-22159.   .... (777)
Korman, Adolf G. A Social History of Industrial Growth and
Immigrants: A Study With Particular Reference to Milwaukee
1880-1920. 1959. 500pp. BIP-59-05789.   .... (777)

Lankevich, George. Milwaukee: A Chronolgical and Documentary
History. (American Cities Chronology Series). 1976. 160pp.   7.50   ..... (551)

MONROE COUNTY

Habelman, Mrs. Robert L. Genealogical Branches From Monroe
County, Wisconsin, Volume III. 1975.
    Continuation of series. Extracts of births, marriages,
    deaths, obit. taken from county newspapers; cemeteries,
    churches and school records. Nearly 3000 surnames. 4.00 (304)
_____. Genealogical Branches From Monroe County, Wisconsin,
Volume IV. 1976.
    Continuation of Volume I, II, and III. Nearly 3000 surnames. 5.00 (304)
Monroe County Bicentennial Committee. Pictorial History of
Monroe County, Wisconsin. 1976. 420pp.
    Contains 700 pictures; gives early history of every town-
    ship, village, ghost town, early people, businesses,
    post offices, maps, some biographical sketches, settlement
    patterns, churches, schools, clubs, and organization
    history. 7.50 (304)

OUTAGAMIE COUNTY

Bubolz, George C. Father Julius and Mother Emilie. 1975. 172pp.
    A personal biography of Midwestern Pioneers. The inspiring
    account of a German pioneer family who, through faith,
    courage, and dedicated work, realized the American
    Dream in Wisconsin.   9.00   ..... (438)

RACINE COUNTY

Turk, Marion G. The Quiet Adventurers in America. 1975. 300pp.
    Genealogical data on and story of settlers in Colonial
    America and the United States from the Channel Islands,
    United Kingdom, Jersey, Guernsey, Alderney and Sark.   12.00   10.00 (771)

WAUKESHA COUNTY

Gnacinski, Janneyne. Abstracts From Obituaries Published in
Waukesha, Wisconsin Newspapers, 1863-1881. 1971. 48+pp. 3.50 (381)
_____. Marriages Published in Waukesha, Wisconsin Newspapers,
1863-1881. 1970. 50+pp. 4.00 (381)
_____. Waukesha County Births, 1846-1879. 1970. 22+pp.
Births recorded at Waukesha County Court House.
Surname index. 2.00 (381)

WOOD COUNTY

Rudolph, Robert S. Wood County Place Names. 1970.   3.95   ..... (849)

Wyoming

STATEWIDE REFERENCES

Bancroft, Hubert H. History of Nevada, Colorado, and
Wyoming.   7.00   ..... (51)
Hunton, John. Diary: Wyoming 1873-1884. 5 vols.
1956-1964.   Each: 5.00   ..... (144)

Larson, T. A. History of Wyoming. 1965.   8.95 ..... (521)
Pelzer, Louis. The Cattlemen's Frontier: A Record of the
Trans-Mississippi Cattle Industry From Oxen Trains to
Pooling Companies, 1850-1890. Repr. of 1936 ed. 351pp.
   Appendix contains cattle brands owned by members of
   the Wyoming Stock Growers' Association (Chicago, 1882). 11.00 ..... (662)
Spencer, Charles Floyd. Wyoming Homestead Heritage.
1975. 199pp.
   Homesteading in the early West - personal reminiscences. 8.00 ..... (224)
Wall, J. Tom. Life in the Shannon and Salt Creek Oil Field. 1973. 7.95 ..... (202)

FREMONT COUNTY

Chisholm, Janes. Wouth Pass, Eighteen Sixty-Eight: James
Chisholm's Journal of the Wyoming Gold Rush. ed. Lola M.
Homsher. 1960.   7.95 ..... (521)

NATRONA COUNTY

Mokler, Alfred James. History of Natrona County, Wyoming,
1888-1922. 1923.   22.50 ..... (38)

UINTA COUNTY

Gowans, Frederick Ross. A History of Fort Bridger From
1841-1858. 1972. 324pp. BIP-72-32646.   .... (777)

Regions

APPALACHIA AND TRANS-APPALACHIAN

Alden, George Henry. New Governments West of the Alleghenies
Before 1780. 1897.
   A concise but thorough examination of the schemes,
   intrigues, and politics involved in the attempts before
   1780 to establish autonomous land grants and settlements
   in the West. Maps.   6.00 ..... (38)
Shapiro, Henry D. Appalachia on Our Mind: Southern Mountains,
1870-1920. 1977. 408pp.
   Study of Appalachian Mountaineers.   15.95 ..... (544)
_____. A Strange Land and Peculiar People: The Discovery of
Appalachia, 1870-1920. 1966. 296pp. BIP-67-05281.   .... (777)
Waite, Mariella Davidson. Political Institutions in the
Trans-Appalachian West, 1770-1800. 1961. 404pp.
BIP-61-05535.   .... (777)
Winsor, Justin. Westward Movement: The Colonies and the
Republics West of the Alleghanies, 1763-1798.
Repr. of 1897 ed.   25.00 ..... (248)

MISSISSIPPI VALLEY

Baily, Francis. Journal of a Tour in Unsettled Parts of
North America in 1796 and 1797. abr. ed. ed. Jack D.
Holmes. Repr. of 1856 ed.   15.00 ..... (708)
Brown, Samuel R. Western Gazetteer: Or Emigrant's
Directory. Repr. of 1817 ed. Illustrated.   15.00 ..... (38)
Chambers, Henry E. Mississippi Valley Beginnings: An
Outline of the Early History of Earlier West. Repr. of 1922 ed. 19.00 ..... (673)

Flint, Timothy. Recollection of the Last Ten Years: Passed
in Occasional Residences and Journeyings in the Valley of the
Mississippi. Repr. of 1826 ed.   17.50 ..... (394)
_____. Recollections of the Last Ten Years in the Valley
of the Mississippi. 2d ed. 1968.   17.50 ..... (176)
_____. Recollections of the Last Ten Years in the Valley
of the Mississippi. ed. George R. Brooks. 1968.   15.00 ..... (708)
Harstad, Peter. Health in the Upper Mississippi River Valley,
1820-1881. 1963. 360pp. BIP-64-00642.   .... (777)
Ogg, Frederic A. Opening of the Mississippi: A Struggle for
Supremacy in the American Interior. Repr. of 1904 ed.   16.75 ..... (297)
Pelzer, Louis. Marches of the Dragoons in the Mississippi
Valley: An Account of Marches and Activities of the First
Regiment United States Dragoons in the Mississippi Valley
Between the Years 1833 and 1850.   .... (38)
Waller, Dr. George M. The American Revolution in the West.
1976.
    An account of the American Revolutionary Era west of
    the Appalachians in the area of the states in the Ohio and
    Mississippi Valleys, including Indiana.   10.00 ..... (524)
Whitaker, Arthur P. Spanish-American Frontier, 1783-1795:
The Westward Movement and the Spanish Retreat in the
Mississippi Valley. 1969.   ..... 1.95 (521)

NEW ENGLAND
[Includes: Maine, New Hampshire, Vermont,
Massachusetts, Connecticut and Rhode Island.]

Abbott, Katherine M. Old Paths and Legends of New England.
Repr. of 1903 ed. 484pp.   13.50 ..... (266)
Adams, James T. History of New England, 3 vols. Repr. of
1923 ed.   Each: 14.50 ..... (673)
                                       Set: 39.50 ..... (673)
_____. Revolutionary New England, Sixteen Ninety One to
Seventeen Seventy Six. Repr. of 1923 ed.   9.95 ..... (159)
Akagi, R. H. Town Proprietors of the New England Colonies.
1963.   6.50 ..... (699)
Arber, Edward, ed. The Story of the Pilgrim Fathers,
1606-1623 A.D.; As Told by Themselves, their Friends,
and their Enemies. 1897.   30.00 ..... (415)
Backus, Isaac. A History of New England. 1871.   38.00 ..... (38)
Bailyn, Bernard, ed. New England Merchants in the 17th
Century. 2.50 (317)
Baxter, James P. Pioneers of New France in New England.
1894.   22.00 ..... (248)

Listed below are the names of professional genealogists willing to undertake research for a
fee within the New England area, as specified in their ads:

Brown, John. The Pilgrim Fathers of New England and their
Puritan Successors. 4th ed. 1920.   24.00 ..... (415)
Clark, Charles E. Eastern Frontier: The Settlement of
Northern New England, 1610-1763. 1970.   10.00 ..... (412)
_____. The Eastern Parts: Northern New England, 1690-1760.
1966. 430pp. BIP-67-02225.   .... (777)
Coleman, Emma L. New England Captives Carried to Canada:
Between 1677 and 1760; During the French and Indian Wars.
2 vols. Repr. of 1926 ed.   39.50 ..... (81)
Douglas, James. New England and New France: Constrasts
and Parallels in Colonial History. Repr. of 1913 ed.   24.00 ..... (662)
Drake, Samuel Adams. Nooks and Corners of the New England
Coast. Repr. of 1875 ed. 459pp.
Recreates pioneer settlements in 17th-century New England,
with each chapter focusing on a particular location.   15.00 ..... (266)
Hill, Douglas. The English to New England.   5.95 ..... (614)
Holbrook, Stewart H. Yankee Exodus: An Account of Migration
from New England. 1968.   7.95 2.95 (814)
Hubbard, William. A General History of New England, from the
Discovery to MDCLXXX. 1815, 1848.   46.00 ..... (38)
_____. General History of New England, 1620-1680. Vols. 5, 6.
1815.   Volume 5:   28.00 ..... (394)
                                                Volume 6:   34.75 ..... (394)
Mathews, Lois K. The Expansion of New England: The Spread
of New England Settlement and Institutions to the Mississippi
River 1620-1865. Repr. of 1909 ed.   8.50 ..... (662)
Neal, Daniel. The History of New-England, Containing an
Impartial Account of the Civil and Ecclesiastical Affairs of
the Country to the Year of Our Lord, 1700. To Which is
Added the Present State of New-England. With a New and
Accurate Map of the Country. And an Appendix Containing
Their Present Charter, Their Ecclesiastical Discipline, and
Their Municipal Laws. 2d ed. 2 vols. 1747.   Set: 64.00 ..... (2)
Parks, Roger Neal. The Roads of New England, 1790-1840.
1966. 283pp. BIP-66-14161.   .... (777)
Rawlyk, George A. New England and Louisbourg, 1744-1745.
1966. 348pp. BIP-66-06865.   .... (777)
Shipton, Clifford K. New England Life in the Eighteenth
Century: Representative Biographis from Sibley's Harvard
Graduates. 1963.   15.00 ..... (319)
Small, Walter Herbert. Early New England Schools. 1914.   18.00 ..... (38)
Winthrop, John. The History of New England from 1630-1649.
1826.   50.00 ..... (38)

Research Aids
Ireland, Norma Olin and Winifred Irving. Cutter Index. 88pp.
A consolidated index of Cutter's 9 genealogy sets. Over
3150 surnames included in this "index of indexes" as
found in 33 volumes of William Richard Cutter's
o series of genealogies. States: New England, Connecti-
cut, Massachusetts, North New York, Central New York,
West New York, Middlesex County (Massachusetts),
Boston (Massachusetts). Both '13 and '14 editions of
New England. 15.00 (378)

_____. Index to Hartford Times Genealogical Gleanings,
1912-1916. 28pp.
Index to major surnames, including some long
articles. 7.50 (378)
_____. Sumner Index: Colonial Pedigrees from Edith Sumner's
Five Genealogies, and Unpublished Worksheets. 6pp.
Includes 522 family lines with many extensive pedigrees. ..... x (378)

Religious and Ethnic Groups

Bacon, Leonard. The Genesis of the New England Churches.
Repr. of 1874 ed. 23.00 ..... (38)
Baker, George Claude, Jr. An Introduction to the History
of Early New England Methodism, 1789-1839. 1941. 10.00 ..... (2)
Donnelly, Marian C. New England Meeting Houses of the
Seventeenth Century. 1968. 12.50 ..... (822)
Haller, William, Jr. The Puritan Frontier: Town Planning
in New England Colonial Development, 1630-1660. 1951. 10.00 ..... (2)
Kellaway, William. The New England Company, 1649-1776
(Company for the Propagation of the Gospel in
New England and Parts Adjacent.) Repr. of 1961 ed. 14.75 ..... (297)
King, Irving Henry. The S. P. G. In New England, 1701-1784.
1968. 324pp. BIP-68-18067. .... (777)
Levy, Babette May. Preaching in the First Half Century of
New England History. Repr. of 1945 ed. 215+pp.
Major emphasis on English-bred clergy, with some
attention given to first generation of Harvard College
trained successors. 8.50 ..... (662)
McLoughin, William G. New England Dissent, 1630-1833;
The Baptists and the Separation of Church and State.
2 vols. 1971. 40.00 ..... (319)
Taft, Donald R. Two Portuguese Communities in New England.
1923. 10.50 ..... (38)
Worrall, Arthur John. New England Quakerism 1656-1830.
1969. 247pp. BIP-69-18699. .... (777)
Zabierek, Henry Carl. Puritans and Americans: An
Inquiry Into the Nature of English Settlement in New
England. 1971. 436pp. BIP-72-08076. .... (777)

OHIO VALLEY

Ambler, Charles H. History of Transportation in the Ohio
Valley. Repr. of 1932 ed. 18.25 ..... (297)
Dunham, Douglas. The French Element in the American Fur
Trade, 1760-1816. 1950. 281pp. BIP-00-01961. .... (777)
Fernow, Berthold. Ohio Valley in Colonial Days. Repr. of
1890 ed. 17.00 ..... (248)
Finnie, W. Bruce. Topographic Terms in the Ohio Valley,
1748-1800. ..... 8.00 (11)
Henlein, Paul Charles. Cattle Kingdom in the Ohio Valley:
The Beef Cattle Industry in the Valley, 1783-1860.
1957. 364pp. BIP-00-20627. .... (777)
Waller, Dr. George M. The American Revolution in the
West. 1976.
An account of the American Revolutionary Era west of
the Appalachians in the area of the states in the Ohio and
Mississippi Valleys, including Indiana. 10.00 ..... (524)

OLD NORTHWEST
[Included: Ohio, Indiana, Michigan, Illinois and Wisconsin.]

Baldwin, James. The Conquest of the Old Northwest and Its Settlement by American. 1901.   7.50 ..... (547)

Barrett, Jay A. Evolution of the Ordinance of 1787 with an Account of the Earlier Plans for the Government of the Northwest Territory. Repr. of 1891 ed.   6.00 ..... (38)

Bond, Beverley W., Jr. Civilization of the Old Northwest: A Study of Political, Social, and Economic Development, 1788-1812. Repr.   14.00 ..... (673)

Burnet, Jacob. Notes on the Early Settlement of the North-Western Territory. 1847.   28.00 ..... (38)

Cole, Harry E. Stage Coah and Tavern Tales of the Old Northwest. ed. Louise P. Kellogg. Repr. of 1930 ed.   15.00 ..... (266)

Ernest, Joseph W. With Compass and Chain: Federal Land Surveyors in the Old Northwest, 1785-1816. 1958. 328pp. BIP-58-02612.   .... (777)

Gates, C. M., ed. Five Fur Traders of the Northwest: Narrative of Peter Pond and the Diaries of John Macdonnell, et al. Repr. of 1965 ed.   7.25 ..... (496)

Gifford, Jack Jule. The Northwest Indian War, 1784-1795. 1964. 534pp. BIP-64-06383.   .... (777)

Gilpin, Alec R. War of Eighteen-Twelve in the Old Northwest. 1958.   6.50 ..... (485)

Hinsdale, Burke Aaron. The Old Northwest: The Beginnings of Our Colonial System Revised Edition. 1899.   25.00 ..... (38)

Huber, John Parker. General Josiah Harmar's Command, Military Policy in the Old Northwest, 1784-1791. 1968. 290pp. BIP-69-12138.   .... (777)

Kellogg, Louise P., ed. Early Narratives of the Northwest, 1634-1699. Repr. of 1917 ed.   6.50 ..... (52)

Prucha, Francis P. Broadax and Bayonet: The Role of the United States Army in the Development of the Northwest, 1815-1860. 1967.   ..... 1.95 (521)

Scheiber, Harry N., ed. Old Northwest: Studies in Regional History, 1787-1910. 1969.   ..... 3.25 (521)

Unger, Robert William. Lewis Cass: Indian Superintendent of the Michigan Territory, 1813-1831, A Survey of Public Opinion as Reported by the Newspapers of the Old Northwest Territory. 1967. 209pp. BIP-68-01994.   .... (777)

NEW NORTHWEST

Briggs, Harold E. Frontiers of the Northwest: A History of the Upper Missouri Valley.   7.50 ..... (699)

Connette, Earle. Pacific Northwest Quarterly Index, Volumes 1 through 53 (1906-1962). 1964.   20.00 ..... (685)

Henry and Thompson. New Light on Early History of the Greater Northwest. 2 vols.   Set: 17.50 ..... (656)

University of Washington Library. The Dictionary Catalog of the Pacific Northwest Collection of the University of Washington Libraries, Seattle. 6 vols. 1972.   590.00 ..... (307)

Winther, Oscar O. Great Northwest: A History. 2d. ed. 1950.   8.95 ..... (412)

WEST

Burnett, Peter H. Recollections and Opinions of an Old Pioneer.
Repr. of 1880 ed.   22.50   ..... (176)
Chittenden, Hiram Martin. The American Fur Trade of the Far
West. A History of Pioneer Trading Posts and Early Fur
Companies of the Missouri Valley and Rocky Mountains and
of the Overland Commerce with Santa Fe. With an Introduction
and Notes by Stallo Vinton and Sketch of the Author by
Edward S. Meany. 2 vols. 1935. 1014pp.   Set: 37.50   ..... (273)
Denver Public Library. Catalog of the Western History
Department. 7 vols. 1970.   500.00   ..... (307)
Mugridge, Ian. The Old West in Anglo-American Relations,
1783-1803. 1969. 320pp. BIP-71-10483.   .... (777)
Storm, Colton. Catalogue of the Everett D. Graff Collection
of Western Americana. 1968.   37.50   ..... (137)
Thomson, George. The History of Penal Institutions in the
Rocky Mountain West, 1846-1900. 1965. 392pp. BIP-66-02836.   .... (777)
Yale University. Catalog of the Yale Collection of Western
Americana. 4 vols. 1961.   285.00   ..... (307)

SOUTH
[Includes: Alabama, Arkansas, Florida, Georgia,
Kentucky, Lousiana, Maryland, Mississippi, North
Carolina, Oklahoma, South Carolina, Tennessee,
Texas, Virginia, and West Virginia.]

Abernethy, Thomas P. South in the New Nation, 1789-1819.
1961.   12.50   ..... (440)
Agniel, Lucien. Late Affair Has Almost Broke My Heart: The
American Revolution in the South, 1780-1781. 1972.   7.95   2.95 (133)
Alden, John R. First South. 1971.   .....   2.45 (440)
_____. John Stuart and the Southern Colonial Frontier: A
Study of Indian Relations, War, Trade, Land Problems in
the Southern Wilderness, 1754-1775. Repr. of 1944 ed.   10.00   ..... (288)
_____. South in the Revolution, 1763-1789. 1957.   12.50   ..... (440)
Armstrong, Zella, comp. Notable Southern Families.
Volume 4. 1918-1933. 340pp. B-BH 7057.   .... (778)
Boddie, Mrs. John B. Historical Southern Families. Volume XX.
1975. 201pp.   15.00   ..... (274)
Bratten, Mary Jo Jackson. John Esten Cooke: The Young
Writer and the Old South, 1830-1861. 1969. 358pp.
BIP-70-03199.   .... (777)
Claiborne, Nathaniel H. Notes on the War in the South: With
Biographical Sketches of the Lives of Montgomery, Jackson,
Sevier, Late Governor Claiborne and Others. Repr. of 1819 ed.   6.00   ..... (38)
Eterovich, Adam S. Yugoslav Survey of California, Nevada,
Arizona, and the South, 1830-1900.   7.00   ..... (631)
Gardner, Harold Warren. The Dissenting Sects on the Southern
Colonial Frontier, 1720-1770. 1969. 341pp. BIP-70-11023.   .... (777)
Grier, Douglas Audenreid. Confederate Emigration to Brazil,
1865-1870. 1968. 209pp. BIP-69-12113.   .... (777)
Menn, Joseph Karl. The Large Slaveholders of the Deep South-
1860. 1964. 1233pp. BIP-65-04333.   .... (777)
Shingleton, Royce Gordon. Rural Life in the Old South: The
British Travelers' Image, 1820-1860. 1971. 345pp.
BIP-71-18384.   .... (777)

Sonderegger, Richard Paul. The Southern Frontier From the
Founding of Georgia to the End of King George's War.
1964. 289pp. BIP-64-12688. .... (777)
"Southern Genealogical Research." (Four parts.) The Ridge
Runners, Vol. IV. 1976. 12pp. .... (859)

NEW SOUTHWEST
[Includes: Arizona, New Mexico, Southern Colorado,
Utah, Nevada, and California.]

Cortes, Carlos E., ed. Spanish and Mexican Land Grants. 1974.   25.00 ..... (38)
Faulk, Odie B. Land of Many Frontiers: A History of the
American Southwest.   7.50 ..... (566)
Hernandez, Luis F. Aztlan: The Southwest and Its People.
History of Southwest including 5 different groups,
Indian, Spaniard, Mexican, Anglo-American, and
Mexican-American; from Pre-Columbian to modern
Chicago. Includes maps.   7.95   4.95 (323)
Olmsted, Virginia L., comp. and tr. New Mexico Spanish and
Mexican Colonial Censuses, 1790, 1823, and 1845. 1975.
303pp. 12.50 (534)
Ulibarri, Richard Onofre. American Interest in the Spanish-
American Southwest, 1803-1848. 1963. 315pp. BIP-64-03142.   .... (777)
_____. American Interest in the Spanish Southwest, 1803-1848.
1963.
A rare detailed account with good references and
information of importance in the study of the period
1803-1848.   ..... 12.00 (631)
University of California Press. Publications in History.
40 vols. 1911-1951.
Includes valuable information and research particularly
in the area of the Southwest and Spanish influence.
Individual monograph listing available upon request.   597.00 ..... (415)
Wagner, Henry R. Spanish Southwest Fifteen Forty-Two-
Seventeen Ninety-Four. 2 vols. Repr. of 1937 ed. Set: 45.00 ..... (38)

---

localities Other Than the United States

Canada

COUNTRY-WIDE REFERENCES

	Cloth	Paper	Vendor #

Bouchett, Joseph. The British Dominions in North America; or, A Topographical and Statistical Description of the Provinces of Lower and Upper Canada, New Brunswick, Nova Scotia, and the Islands of Newfoundland, Prince Edward, and Cape Breton. Including Considerations on Land Granting and Emigration, and a Topographical Dictionary of Lower Canada; to Which are Annexed, the Statistical Tables and Tables of Distances. Embellished with Views, Plans of Towns, Harbours, etc. 2 vols. 1831.
Each: 62.50 ..... (2)
Set: 125.00 ..... (2)

Brossard, J. Immigration: Les Droits and Pouvoirs Du Canada and Du Quebec. 1967. ..... 4.35 (374)

Campbell, Frank W. Canada Post Office, 1755-1895. 1972. 15.00 ..... (630)

Canadian Frontiers of Settlement. Vols. 1,2,4-9. 1934-1940. A comprehensive study of the peopling of Canada. Set: 156.00 ....., (415)

Canadian Historical Review, 1920-1968. Vols. 1-49. (Separate decennial index for 1920-29, 1930-39, 1940-49)
Each: 25.00 20.00 (763)
Set: 1170.00 1053.00 (763)

Carniff, William. The Medical Profession in Upper Canada, 1783-1850. 1894. An historical narrative, with original documents relating to the profession, including some brief biographies. 56.50 ..... (2)

Careless, J. M., ed. Colonists and Canadiens: 1760-1967. 1971. 9.95 ..... (667)

Colden, Cadwallader. The History of the Five Indian Nations of Canada Which are Dependent on the Province of New York, and Are a Barrier Between the English and the French in That Part of the World. With an Introduction, Portrait and Map. 2 vol. set. 1922. 31.50 ..... (2)

Creighton, Donald. Canada's First Century. 1970. 12.75 ..... (667)

De Charlevoix, F. X. History and General Description of New France, tr. John G. Shea. 6 vols. 1962. 30.00 ..... (442)

Donnelly, Joseph P. Thwaites' Jesuit Relations, Errata and Addenda. 1967. 6.95 ..... (442)

Du Creux, Francois. History of Canada, or New France, ed. James B. Conacher. Tr. Percy Robinson. 2 vols. Repr. of 1951 ed.
Vol. 1: 26.75 ..... (297)
Vol. 2: 25.75 ..... (297)

Eccles, W. J. The Canadian Frontier, 1534-1760. 1969. 7.95 4.95 (535)

Faillon, Etienne Michel. Histoire de la Colonie Francaise en Canada. 3 vols. 1865-1866. First full scale study of the early settlement of Canada by the French from records of various branches of the French and provincial governments along with manuscripts held by the British Museum. Eclesiastical records were particularly valuable. 107.00 ..... (415)

Guillet, Edwin C. Early Life in Upper Canada. 1963.   25.00   ..... (763)
_____. Pioneer Farmer and Backwoodsman. 2 vols. 1963.   30.00   ..... (763)
_____. Pioneer Inns and Taverns. 2 vols. 1964.   50.00   ..... (763)
_____. Story of Canadian Roads. 1966.   10.00   ..... (763)
Harris, Richard C. Seigneurial System in Early Canada. 1966.   15.00   ..... (849)
Harrisse, Henry. Notes Pour Servir a l'Historie, a la
  Bibliographie et a la Cartographie de la Nouvelle-France
  et das Pays Adjacents 1545-1700. Repr. of 1872 ed.   9.00   ..... (100)
Harvard University Library. Canadian History and Literature:
  Classified, Alphabetical and Chronological Listings. 1968.   17.50   ..... (319)
Howe, Samuel Gridley. The Refugees from Slavery in Canada
  West: Report to the Freedmen's Inquiry Commission. 1864.   3.50   ..... (38)
Ivison, Stuart and Fred Rosser. Baptists in Upper and Lower
  Canada before 1820. 1956.   10.00   ..... (763)
Kingsford, William. History of Canada, 1608-1841. 10 vols.
  1887-98.   Each: 33.00   ..... (2)
                                                        Set: 325.00   ..... (2)
Lescarbot, Marc. History of New France. 3 vols.
  Repr. of 1907 ed.   Vol. 1:   27.50   ..... (297)
                                                        Vol. 2:   37.75   ..... (297)
                                                        Vol. 3:   35.25   ..... (297)
Miller, Genevieve. Bibliography of the History of Medicine
  in the U.S. & Canada, 1939-1960. 1964.   17.50   ..... (385)
Moyles, R.G., ed. English Canadian Literature to 1900: A
  Guide to Information Sources. 1976. 346pp.
    A unique feature of this guide is the comprehensive and
    classified list of Canadian travel and descriptive
    literature, including accounts of early exploration of
    Canada.   18.00   ..... (266)
Munro, William B. Documents Relating to the Seigniorial
  Tenure in Canada, 1598-1854. Repr. of 1908 ed.   30.50   ..... (297)
Smith, Justin. Our Struggle for the Fourteenth Colony:
  Canada & American Revolution. 2 vols. Repr. of 1907 ed.   65.00   ..... (176)
Tanguay, Cyprien. Dictionnaire genealogique des familes
  canadiennes depuis la fondation de la colonie jusqu'a nos
  jours. 7 vol. set. 1871-1890.   Set: 225.00   ..... (2)
                                                        Vol. 1:   20.00   ..... (2)
                                                        Vol. 2-7:   34.50   ..... (2)
Thwaites, Reuben G. France in America: 1497-1763. Repr. of
  1905 ed.   7.95   ..... (159)
Thwaites, Reuben G., ed. The Jesuit Relations and Allied
  Documents: The Travels and Explorations of the Jesuit
  Missionaries in New France, 1610-1791. 73 vols. bound
  in 36. 1959.   Set: 400.00   ..... (661)
Trudel. The Beginnings of New France. 1973.   12.50   ..... (447)
Turk, Marion G. The Quiet Adventurers in Canada. 1977.
  Genealogical data and story of settlers in Canada from
  the Channel Islands: Jersey, Guernsey, Alderney and
  Sark, 1700's on.   .... (771)
Wood, Louis A. History of Farmers' Movements in Canada.
  1975.   17.50   5.95 (763)
Wrong, George L. Rise & Fall of New France. 2 vols. 1970
  Repr.   Set: 40.00   ..... (552)
Wrong, George M. Canada & the American Revolution: The
  Disruption of the First British Empire. 1935.   12.50   ..... (159)
Zaccano, Joseph Peter, Jr. French Colonial Administration
  in Canada to 1760. BIP-62-03410.   .... (777)

Research Aids

Abler, Tom, et. al. A Canadian Indian Bibliography, 1960-1970. 1974.	35.00	.....	(763)
Campbell, H.C. How to Find Out about Canada. 1967. 236pp. 33 illus.	.....	5.25	(591)
Canadian Road Atlas. 1975.	.....	3.95	(633)
Garigue, Philip. A Bibliographical Introduction to the Study of French Canada. 1956.	13.00	.....	(415)
Hill, Brian. Canada: A Chronology and Fact Book. 1973. 160pp.	7.50	.....	(551)
Jonasson, Eric. The Canadian Genealogical Handbook. 1976. 100pp. Complete guide to Canadian Genealogical Records. Contains description of types of Canadian records useful in genealogy, plus addresses of source agencies. Each province is dealt with separately in detail.	.....	12.50	(832)
_____, comp. Guide to Canadian Military Records. 1977. Apart from a short history of the Canadian military, will contain an extensive listing of the known militia and military records (containing militia rolls, paylists, the types of records consisting of lists which can be used in genealogical research) plus a section listing published regimental histories.	.....	.....	(832)
Lochhead, Douglas. Bibliography of Canadian Bibliographies. 2d ed. 1972.	20.00	.....	(763)
Major Genealogical Record Sources for Canada, Quebec, and Acadia. 36pp.	.....	.85	(275)
Sealock, Richard A. and Pauline A. Seely. A Bibliography of Place-Name Literature: United States & Canada. 2d ed. 1967.	7.50	.....	(22)

Trading Companies

Biggar, H.P. and B.A. Litt. The Early Trading Companies of New France. Repr. of 1901 ed.	16.50	.....	(673)
Bryce, George. Remarkable History of the Hudson's Bay Company: Including That of the French Traders of Northwestern Canada & of the Astor Fur Companies. 1968.	25.50	.....	(248)
Cline, Gloria G. Peter Skene Ogden & the Hudson's Bay Company. 1974.	8.95	.....	(556)
Hargrave, James. Hargrave Correspondence, 1821-1843, ed. G.P. Glazebrook. Repr. of 1938 ed.	32.50	.....	(297)

Hudson's Bay Record Society. Publications. 1938-1961.
Incorporated by Royal Charter in 1670, the Hudson's Bay Company was made responsible for the development of a tract of a million and a half square miles watered by the rivers which enter the sea at Hudson's Bay. The unique and exciting history of the trade, administration and legislation of this vast area has always been exceedingly interesting both to historian and layman. Its massive archives comprise over 30,000 volumes and extensive files covering every phase of activity from its organization to the present day. Initially, records dealt with the most active periods of the Company's history: 1670-1680 and 1820-1840. Title list available upon request.

Vols. 1-12:	Set:	420.00	360.00	(415)
Vols. 1-14, 16, 18, 23:	Per Vol:	.....	30.00	(415)

McLean, John. John McLean's Notes of a Twenty-Five Years'
Service in the Hudson's Bay Territory, W.S. Wallace, ed.
Repr. of 1932 ed.   29.50   ..... (297)
Morton, Arthur S. History of the Canadian West to 1870-71,
L.G. Thomas, ed. 1973.   25.00   ..... (763)
Robson, Joseph. Account of Six Years' Residence in Hudson's
Bay, 1733-1736 & 1744-1747. Repr. of 1757 ed.   12.00   ..... (394)
Thompson, David. David Thompson's Narrative of His
Explorations in Western America, 1784-1812,
J.B. Tyrrell, ed. Repr. of 1916 ed.   50.00   ..... (297)
Young, Frank G., ed. The Correspondence & Journals of
Captain Nathaniel J. Wyeth, 1831-6. Repr. of 1899 ed.   15.00   ..... (38)

Records

Canada. Public Archives. Publications. 1909-1932.
These documents are among the chief manuscript
sources of the earliest history of Canada. In
addition to papers dating back to Canada's discovery,
several volumes act as catalogues of holdings
(reports, pamphlets, maps, etc.) of the Public
Archives. These holdings comprise old records from
various government departments, transcripts made
in Europe and America, and private collections.
Vols. 1-14:   Set: 450.00   370.00 (415)

ALBERTA

Atlas of Alberta. 1970.   .....   30.00 (763)
Mann, William E. Sect, Cult & Church in Alberta. rev. ed.
1972.   10.00   3.50 (763)

BRITISH COLUMBIA

Hazlitt, William C. British Columbia & Vancouver Island.
Repr. of 1858 ed.   14.00   ..... (394)
Macfie, Matthew. Vancouver Island & British Columbia:
Their History, Resources & Prospects. Repr. of 1865 ed.   28.00   ..... (38)
Provincial Archives of British Columbia. Victoria
Provincial Archives of British Columbia. 8 vols. 1971.
                                               Set: 610.00   ..... (307)

NEWFOUNDLAND

Turk, Marion G. The Quiet Adventurers in Canada. 1977.
Genealogical data and story of settlers in Canada
from the Channel Islands: Jersey, Guernsey,
Alderney and Sark.   .... (771)

NORTHWEST TERRITORY

Kaye, Vladimir J. Early Ukranian Settlements in Canada,
1895-1900: Dr. Josef Oleskow's Role in the Settlement
of the Canadian Northwest. 1964.   17.50   ..... (763)

NOVA SCOTIA

Brebner, John B. Neutral Yankees of Nova Scotia: A
Marginal Colony During the Revolutionary Years. Repr.
of 1937 ed.
Discusses composition of population, emigration from
New England, and the causes and conditions for Nova

Scotia's neutrality in the Revolution. Covers period from
1760-1783.   15.00   ..... (662)
_____. New England's Outpost: Acadia Before the Conquest
of Canada. 1974.   17.00   ..... (248)
Bell, Winthrop P. Foreign Protestants & the Settlement of
Nova Scotia: The History of a Piece of Arrested British
Policy in the Eighteenth Century. 1961.   45.00   ..... (763)
Clark, Andrew H. Acadia: The Geography of Early Nova
Scotia to 1760. 1968. illus.   19.50   ..... (849)
Jehn, Janet B. Acadian Descendants, Vol. I. 1972. 177pp.
History of the Acadians and their migration; genealogies
of some of the pioneers and their descendants.   10.50   ..... (6)
_____. Acadian Descendants, Vol.II. 1975. 504pp.
Genealogies of Jean Gaudet, Daniel LeBlanc, Etienne
Hebert, and others of France and Acadia.   17.50   ..... (6)
Kidder, Frederic. Military Operations in Eastern Maine
and Nova Scotia during the Revolution. 1867.   19.00   ..... (415)
Rawlyk, G.A. Yankees at Louisbourg. 1967. 209pp.
Siege of Louisbourg (May 21-June 7, 1745) and the
events leading up to the siege. Carefully annotated
references to participants.   2.50 (460)
Sigogne, Father Jean-Mande. St. Mary's Bay, 1818-1829,
ed. and tr. Leonard H. Smith, Jr. 1975. 152pp.
Catalogue of families of St. Mary's Bay Roman Catholic
Parish, Clare, Digby County, Nova Scotia. French-
English Glossary.   15.00 (697)
_____. St. Mary's Bay, 1840-1844, tr. Leonard H. Smith, Jr.
1975. 201pp.
Catalogue of families of St. Mary's Bay Roman Catholic
Parish, Clare, Digby County, Nova Scotia. French-
English Glossary.   15.00 (697)
Slafter, Edmund F., ed. Sir William Alexander & American
Colonization. 1966.   17.50   ..... (248)
Smith, Leonard H., Jr. Index of Persons - Isaiah W. Wilson's
"County of Digby, Nova Scotia". 1974. 150pp.
More than 3,000 names indexed.   12.00 (697)
Stewart, Gordon and George Rawlyk. A People Highly
Favoured of God: The Nova Scotia Yankees & the
American Revolution. 1972.   13.00   ..... (685)
Uniacke, Richard J. Nova Scotia Statutes: Statutes at Large.
4 vols. 1970.   Set: 135.00 ..... (271)
White, Elizabeth Pearson. "Nova Scotia Settlers from Chatham,
Massachusetts, 1759-1769," NGS Quarterly, Vol. 62, No. 2.
1974. 22pp.   3.50 (514)

Listed below are the names pf professional genealogists willing to undertake research for
a fee within Canada, in areas specified in their ads:

ONTARIO

Cumming, Ross, ed. Beer's Historical Atlas of Ontario County.
Repr. of 1879 ed. 80pp.
Maps with names of lot holders, etc.   12.00   ..... (173)
_____. Belden's Carleton County Historical Atlas. Repr. of
1879 ed. 108pp.
Township maps with names, etc.   15.00   ..... (173)
_____. Belden's Historical Atlas of Grey & Bruce. Repr. of
1880 ed. 112pp.
Maps and directories, etc.   15.00   ..... (173)
_____. Belden's Historical Atlas of Huron County. Repr. of
1879 ed. 100pp.
Maps with names of lot holders, etc.   14.00   ..... (173)
_____. Belden's Historical Atlas of Lanark & Renfrew. Repr.
of 1880 ed. 72pp.
Maps with lot holders, etc.   12.00   ..... (173)
_____. Belden's Historical Atlas of Perth County. Repr. of
1879 ed. 76pp.
Maps with names of lot holders, etc.   12.00   ..... (173)
_____. Belden's Historical Atlas of Prescott, Russell,
Stormont, Dundas, Glengarry. Repr. of 1879 ed. 80pp.
Maps with names of lot holders, etc.   12.00   ..... (173)
_____. Belden's Historical Atlas of Simcoe County. Repr. of
1881 ed. 96pp.
Maps, directory, etc.   14.00   ..... (173)
_____. Elgin County Historical Atlas. Repr. of 1877 ed. 96pp.
Township lot holders and directory.   14.00   ..... (173)
_____. Historical Atlas of Waterloo & Wellington. Repr. of
1877 ed. 96pp.
Maps, directory, etc.   14.00   ..... (173)
_____.Historical Atlas of Oxford & Brant Counties. Repr. of
1876 ed. 96pp.
Maps with names of lot holders, etc.   14.00   ..... (173)
_____. Miles' Atlas of York County, 1878. Repr. of 1878 ed.
98pp.
Maps with names of lot holders, etc.   14.00   ,.... (173)
_____. Page's Historical Atlas of Lincoln & Welland. Repr.
of 1876 ed. 88pp.
Maps with names of lot holders, etc.   12.00   ..... (173)
_____. Page's Historical Atlas of Muskoka & Parry Sound.
Repr. of 1879 ed. 128pp.
Maps with names of lot holders, etc.   8.00   ..... (173)
_____. Walker & Miles' Historical Atlas of Halton County.
Repr. of 1877 ed. 76pp.
Maps with names of lot holders, etc.   12.00   ..... (173)
_____. Walker & Miles' Historical Atlas of Peel, 1877. Repr.
of 1877 ed. 76pp.
Maps with names of lot holders, etc.   14.00   ..... (173)
Guillet, Edwin C., ed. Valley of the Trent. 1957.   15.00   ..... (173)
Harvey, Joanne. Voters List 1879, Municipalities of
Walsingham Township, Norfolk County, Onatrio, Canada. 22pp. 2.40 (487)
Kalbfleisch, Herbert K. History of the Pioneer German
Language Press of Ontario, 1835-1918. 1969.   .....   3.75 (763)
Kingsford, William. The Early Bibliography of the Province of
Ontario, Dominion of Canada, with a Supplemental Chapter
of Canadian Archaeology. 1892.   6.50   ..... (2)

Phelps, E.C., ed. Belden's Historical Atlas of Essex-Kent.
Repr. of 1880 ed. 116pp.   15.00 ..... (173)
_____. Historical Atlas of Lambton County. Repr. of 1880 ed.
80pp.   15.00 ..... (173)
_____. Page's Historical Atlas of Haldimand & Norfolk. Repr.
of 1879 ed. 112pp.   15.00 ..... (173)
_____. Page's Historical Atlas of Middlesex County. Repr. of
1878 ed. 88pp.   14.00 ..... (173)
Robinson, Percy J. Toronto During the French Regime: A
History of the Toronto Region from Brule to Simcoe, 1615-
1793. 2d ed. 1965.   7.50   3.50 (763)
Spencer, Loraine & Susan Holland, eds. Northern Ontario:
A Bibliography. 1968.   6.00 ..... (763)
Steward, Austin. Twenty-Two Years a Slave & Forty Years a
Freeman. eds. Jane H. and William H. Pease. 1969.   .....   2.95 (9)
_____. Twenty-Two Years a Slave & Forty Years a Freeman.
1856.   14.25 ..... (522)
Tivy, Louis, ed. Your Loving Anna: Letters from the Ontario
Frontier. 1972.   7.50 ..... (763)
Turk, Marion G. The Quiet Adventurers in Canada. 1977.
Genealogical data and story of settlers in Canada from
the Channel Islands; Jersey, Guernsey, Alderney and
Sark. In process.   .... (771)

PRINCE EDWARD ISLAND

Harvey, Daniel Cobb. The French Regime in Prince Edward
Island. 1926   8.50 ..... (2)

QUEBEC

Cumming, Ross, ed. Belden's Historical Atlas of Quebec
Eastern Townships. Repr. of 1880 ed. 80pp.   14.00 ..... (173)
Dionne, Narcisse E. Inventaire Chronolgique des Ouvrages
Publies a l'Etranger en Diverses Langues sur Quebec et la
Nouvelle France. 5 vols. in 2. 1969.   41.50 ..... (248)
Grenier, Fernand, ed. Quebec (Studies in Canadian Geography)
1972.   10.00   5.00 (763)
Holbrook, Jay Mack. Ascott, Quebec, Canada 1825 Census.
1976. 14pp.
A census index and demographic profile of Ascott, Canada 5.00 (342)
_____. Shipton, Quebec, Canada 1825 Census. 1976. 15pp.
A census index and demographic profile of Shipton (now
Danville and Richmond) Canada. 5.00 (342)
Scott, Seaman Morley. Chapters in the History of the Law of
Quebec, 1764-1775. Thesis. 547pp. BIP-65-07522   .... (777)
Turk, Marion G. The Quiet Adventurers in Canada. 1977.
Genealogical data and story of settlers in Canada from
the Channel Islands; Jersey, Guernsey, Alderney and
Sark, 1700's on. In process.   .... (771)

SASKATCHEWAN

Hind, Henry Y. Narrative of the Canadian Red River Exploring
Expedition of 1857, & of the Assiniboine & Saskatchewan
Exploring Expedition of 1858. 2 vols. Repr. of 1860 ed.
     Set: 29.50 ..... (297)

England

GENERAL REFERENCES

Bebbington, Gillian. London Street Names. 1972. 367pp.	10.00	.....	(661)
Beresford, Maruice W. English Medieval Boroughs: A Handlist. 1973. 200pp.	11.50	.....	(661)
Cameron, Kenneth. English Place Names. 2d ed. 1969.	7.50	.....	(795)
Carlton, Charles Hope. The Court of Orphans: A Study in the History of Urban Institutions with Special Reference to London, Bristol, and Exeter in the Sixteenth and Seventeenth Centuries. 1970. 422pp. BIP-70-19837.	.....	.....	(777)
Collins, Arthur. Collins's Peerage of England: Genealogical, Biographical and Historical. Greatly Augmented and Continued to the Present Time by Samuel E. Brydges. 9 vols. 1812.			
Each:	28.00	.....	(2)
Set:	250.00	.....	(2)
Coxe, H. O. Catalogue of the Manuscripts in the Oxford Colleges. Volume I. Repr. of 1852 ed.	40.00	.....	(661)
Darby, H. C., ed. A New Historical Geography of England. 1973.	38.50	.....	(114)
Ekwall, Eilert. Concise Oxford Dictionary of English Place-Names. 4th ed. 1960.	12.75	.....	(566)
_____. English River Names. Repr. of 1928 ed.	18.75	.....	(566)
England and Wales Nu-Way Road Series (Contemporary).	.....	2.95	(93)
Finn, Rex Weldon. Domesday Book: A Guide. 1973. 109pp.	9.50	.....	(661)
Fullard, Harold, ed. Esso Road Atlas Great Britain and Ireland (Contemporary). 1974.	10.50	.....	(373)
Genealogical Society of LDS. English-Wales Genealogical Research Procedures--Flow Charts. 12pp.	.....	.85	(275)
_____. Major Genealogical Record Sources in England and Wales. 8pp.	.....	.85	(275)
_____. Population Movements in England and Wales by Canal and Navigable Rivers. 8pp.	.....	.85	(275)
_____. Population Movements in England and Wales During the Industrial Revolution. 17pp.	.....	.85	(275)
_____. The Social, Economic, Religious and Historical Background of England as it Affects Genealogical Research. 8pp.	.....	.85	(275)
Great Britain, Public Record Office. Guide to the Contents of the Public Record Office. 2 vols. 1963.	20.00	.....	(415)
Hardy, Thomas D. Descriptive Catalogue of Materials Relating to the History of Great Britain and Ireland, to the End of the Reign of Henry 7th, 3 Volumes in 4, 1862-71. Each:	40.00	.....	(248)
Set:	175.00	.....	(248)
Hoskins, W. G. Local History in England. 2d ed. 1972. 268pp.	10.00	.....	(661)
Humphrey-Smith, C. R. Guide to Marriage Licences and Where To Find Them.	.....	3.00	(877)
_____. Family History Journal. [3 yrs. subsc./$32.00] 1 yr. subsc.	.....	12.00	(877)
_____. Introducing Family History.	.....	2.50	(877)
_____. Genealogist's Bibliographical Guide and Glossary.	.....	8.00	(877)
_____. Palaeography and Document Reading.	.....	10.00	(877)
Kinney, Arthur F. Titled Elizabethans: A Directory of Elizabethan State and Church Officers and Knights, with Peers of England, Scotland, and Ireland. 1973.	5.00	.....	(685)
Lobel, M. D., ed. Historic Towns: Maps and Plans of Towns and Cities in the British Isles, with Historical Commentaries, from Earliest Times to 1800, Volume 2. 1975.	57.50	.....	(385)
McClure, Edmund. British Place Names in Their Historical Setting. Repr. of 1910 ed.	15.00	.....	(93)

Madge, Sidney J. Domesday of Crown Lands. A Study of the
Legislation, Surveys and Sales of Royal Estate Under the
Commonwealth. 1938. 499pp.   15.00   ..... (273)
Mason, Oliver. The Gazetteer of England: England's Cities, Towns,
Villages and Hamlets: A Comprehensive List with Basic Details
of Each. 2 vols. 1972. 760pp.   Set: 25.00   ..... (661)
Mingay, G. R. English Landed Society in the Eighteenth Century.
1963.   12.50   ..... (763)
Reaney, P. H. The Origin of English Place-Names. Repr. of
1960 ed.   10.50   ..... (660)
Saklatvala, Beram. Origins of the English People. 1970.   7.50   ..... (744)
Stephens, W. B. Sources for English Local History. 1973. 260pp. 6.50 (661)
Stubbs, William, Bishop of Oxford. Historical Introduction to the
Rolls Series. ed. Arthur Hassall. 1902.   11.50   ..... (2)
_____. Historical Introduction to the Rolls Series. Repr.   21.95   ..... (320)
U. S. Library of Congress, Processing Department. British
Manuscripts Project: A Checklist of the Microfilm Prepared
in England and Wales for the American Council of Learned
Societies 1941-1945. Repr. of 1955 ed.   18.75   ..... (297)
Upcott, William. Bibliographical Account of the Principal Works
Relating to English Topography. 3 vols. Repr. of 1818 ed.
                                                     Set: 90.00   ..... (248)
Vexler, Robert I. England: A Chronology and Fact Book. (World
Chronology Series). 1974. 160pp.   7.50   ..... (551)
Wagner, Anthony R. English Genealogy. 1972.   20.50   ..... (566)

HISTORICAL AND GEOGRAPHICAL REFERENCES
[In Chronological Order]

Camden, William. Britannia. Ora, a Chronological Description
of the Flourishing Kingdoms, of England, Scotland and Ireland,
and the Islands Adjacent; From the Earliest Antiquity. . . .
Translated from the Edition Published by the Author in 1607.
Enlarged by the Latest Discoveries, by Richard Gough. 2d ed.
4 vols. 1806.
    Contains illustrations, fold-out maps and genealogies. Set: 145.00 ..... (2)
Hume, David and George Smollett Tobias. The History of England
from the Invasion of Julius Caesar [55 B.C.] to the Revolution
in 1688, Continued to the Death of George the Second by Tobias
George Smollett. A New Edition, with Portraits and Lives of
the Authors. 13 vols. 1825.   Each: 20.00   ..... (2)
                                                     Set: 260.00   ..... (2)
Adams, George Burton. The History of England from the Norman
Conquest to the Death of John (1066 to 1216). 1905.   22.50   ..... (2)
Domesday Geography of England. [Date: 1066 Domesday] 4 vols. Incl.:
Darby, Henry C. Volume 1-Eastern England.   32.50   ..... (114)
Darby, Henry C. and I. B. Terrett. Volume 2-Midland England.   32.50   ..... (114)
Darby, Henry C. and E. M. Campbell. Volume 3-South-East
England.   32.50   ..... (114)
Darby, Henry C. and R. W. Finn. Volume 5-South-West England.   29.50   ..... (114)
Paris, Matthew. Matthew Paris's English History, From the Year
1235 to 1273. Translated from the Latin by J. A. Giles. With
General Index to Matthew Paris and Roger of Wendover. 3 vols.
1852-1854.   Each: 15.00   ..... (2)
                                                     Set: 45.00   ..... (2)
Holmes, George. The Later Middle Ages 1272-1485. (A History
of England Series No. 3). 1962. 276pp.   5.00   ..... (661)

Oman, Sir Charles William Chadwick. The History of England from
the Accession of Richard II to the Death of Richard III (1377-1485).
1906.   22.50   ..... (2)
James, Mervyn. The Tudor Age: 1485-1603. (History of England
Series No. 4). 1977.   .... (661)
Taylor, Eva G. Tudor Geography, Fourteen Eighty-Five to Fifteen
Eighty-Three. 1968.   11.50   ..... (552)
Pollard, Albert Frederick. The History of England from the
Accession of Edward VI to theDeath of Elizabeth (1547-1603).
1910.   22.50   ..... (2)
Ashley, Maurice. England in the Seventeenth Century.   4.50   ..... (268)
Gardiner, Samuel Rawson. History of England. From the Accession
of James I. to the Outbreak of the Civil War. 1603-1642.
10 vols.   Set: 175.00   ..... (2)
Ashley, Maurice. England in the Seventeenth Century: 1603-1714.   .....   1.75 (586)
Hill, Christopher. The Century of Revolution 1603-1714. (A History
of England Series No. 4). 1961. 340pp.   5.00   ..... (661)
Gardiner, Samuel Rawson. History of England, 1603-1656. 18 vols.
1884-1903.
    In Three Sections. Each of the three sections may be obtained
    separately.   Set: 315.00   ..... (2)
Montague, Francis Charles. The History of England from the
Accession of James I to the Restoration (1603-1660). 1907.   22.50   ..... (2)
Gardiner, Samuel Rawson. History of the Great Civil War.
1642-1649. 4 vols.   Set: 70.00   ..... (2)
_____. History of the Commonwealth and Protectorate.
1649-1656. 4 vols.   Set: 70.00   ..... (2)
Lodge, Sir Richard. The History of England from the Restoration
to the Death of William III (1660-1702). 1910.   22.50   ..... (2)
Macaulay, Thomas Babington Macaulay, 1st Baron. The History
of England from the Accession of James II. The Best Edition.
ed. Charles Harding Firth. 1913-1915. 6 vols.   Each: 20.00   ..... (2)
                                                 Set: 120.00   ..... (2)
Lecky, William Edward Hartpole. A History of England in the
Eighteenth Century. New Edition. 7 vols. 1892-1893. Each: 20.00   ..... (2)
                                                 Set: 140.00   ..... (2)
Selley, Walter T. England in the Eighteenth Century. 1964.   5.00   ..... (335)
Mowat, Robert B. England in the Eighteenth Century. Repr. of
1932 ed.   15.00   ..... (245)
Stanhope, Philip Henry Stanhope, 5th Earl. The History of England
from the Peace of Utrecht to the Peace of Versailles, 1713-1783.
5th ed., rev. 1858. 7 vols.   Set: 210.00   ..... (2)
Owen, John B. The Eighteenth Century 1714-1815. (History of
England Series No. 6). 1975. 365pp.   12.50   ..... (661)
Hunt, William. The History of England from the Accession of
George III to the Close of Pitt's First Administration (1760-1801).
1905.   22.50   ..... (2)
Brodrick, George Charles and John Knight Fotheringham. The
History of England from Addington's Administration to the Close
of William IV's Reign (1801-1837). 1906.   22.50   ..... (2)
Low, Sir Sidney James Mark and Lloyd Charles Sanders. The
History of England during the Reign of Victoria (1837-1901).
1907.   22.50   ..... (2)

Religious and Ethnic Groups

Collins, Naomi F. Oliver Cromwell's Protectorate Church
Settlement: The Commission for the Approbation of
Publique Preachers, the Triers, and the Commission
for the Ejecting of Scandalous, Ignorant and Insufficient
Ministers and Schoolmasters: The Ejectors. 1970.
177pp. BIP-71-13539. .... (777)

Cooper, William D. List of Foreign Protestants, and Aliens,
Resident in England, 1618-1688. 1862. 14.00 ..... (394)

Cox, J. Charles. Parish Registers of England, 1910.
Repr. of 1910 ed. 290pp. 12.50 ..... (661)

Hale, William H., ed. Domesday of St. Paul's of the Year
Twelve Twenty-Two. Repr. of 1858 ed. 20.00 ..... (2)

Stratford-Upon-Avon. The Vestry Minute Book of the Parish of
Stratford-on-Avon, . . . from 1617 to 1699 A.D.
ed. George Arbuthnot. 1899. 6.50 ..... (2)

Norwich England Diocese. Visitations of the Diocese of
Norwich, A.D. 1492-1532. ed. A. Jessopp. 1888. 22.75 ..... (394)

Simpson, W. S., ed. Visitations of Churches Belonging to
St. Paul's Cathedral (London) in 1297 & 1458. Repr. of
1895 ed. 20.25 ..... (394)

Visitations and Memorials of Southwell Minster. ed. Arthur F.
Leach. 1891. 20.25 ..... (394)

Records

Appleton, William S. Index to the Testators in Henry F. Waters,
Genealogical Gleanings in England. Repr. of 1898 ed. 20pp. 3.50 (530)

Bateman, John. The Great Landowners of Great Britain and
Ireland. 4th ed., revised. Repr. of 1883 ed. 533pp.
A list of all owners of three thousand acres and upwards
. . . also, one thousand three hundred owners of two
thousand acres and upwards in England, Scotland, Ireland,
and Wales, their acreage and income from land, culled
from the modern Domesday Book. 17.50 ..... (273)

British Record Society. Index Library. 75 vols. 1888-1953.
Walford II p. 378. The Index Library contains calendars
and indexes of chancery proceedings and wills proved in
various British courts, abstracts of inquisitiones post
mortem, records of marriage licenses, etc. It is a
prime source for the study of British genealogy and local
history. List of individual volumes available upon request.
Volumes 1-50. 1888-1920. 975.00 810.00 (415)
Volumes 51-75. 1920-1953. 570.00 470.00 (415)

Bury St. Edmunds, Commissary Court. Wills and Inventories.
From the Registers of the Commissary of Burty St. Edmund's
and the Archdeacon of Sudbury. ed. Samuel Tymms. 1850. 20.00 ..... (2)

Cambridge University Press. Alumni Cantabrigienses. comps.
J. and J. A. Venn. 10 vols. 1922-1954.
A biographical list of all known students, graduates,
and holders of office at the University of Cambridge, from
the earliest times to 1900. 310.00 ..... (415)

Cooper, William Durrant, ed. Lists of Foreign Protestants,
and Aliens, Resident in England 1618-1688. From Returns
in the State Paper Office. 1862. 10.00 ..... (2)

Maps

Parish maps of all the counties of England and Wales (showing (877)
probate jurisdictions, boundaries, dates of registers. Each: 2.50 (877)

G.R.O. Map 1837-1851 - shows census and registration 3.75 (877)

GREAT BRITAIN'S PRIMARY RECORDS

[These are transcripts of the early British Archives located in the Great
Britain Public Record Office and are of great value to historians, genealogists and other scholars. Guides, finding aids and indexes added to the
primary source material facilitate research in this massive amount of
records.]

Great Britain. Public Record Office. Calendar of Charter
Rolls. 6 vols. 1903-1927.
The royal charter was the solemn instrument whereby
the Sovereign made original and confirmatory grants
in perpetuity of lands, liberties, privileges, etc., to
both corporations and individuals. The full Latin texts
of numerous charters are given in all volumes.

Vols. 1-6 covering years 1226-1516:	Set:	234.00	204.00 (415)
	Each:	.....	34.00 (415)

_____. Calendar of Patent Rolls. 1891-1966.
Patent rolls fall within the category of Chancery Records.
Both before and after the emergence of the equity
jurisdiction of the court of Chancery, the medieval
Chancellor, custodian, like the present-day Lord
Chancellor, of the Sovereign's Great Seal, combined
the duties of all the modern Secretaries of State.
Letters patent, announced royal acts of the most diverse
kinds, including grants and leases of land, appointments
to offices, licenses and pardons, denizations of aliens,
and presentations to ecclesiastical benefices. From
1516 the sort of royal grant which had hitherto been
made by charter took the form of letters patent.

Henry III (1216-1272). 6 vols.	Set:	253.50	223.50 (415)
Vols. 1-3:	Each:	.....	34.00 (415)
Vols. 4-6:	Each:	.....	40.50 (415)
Vols. 1-2 contain the full Latin text and have the title Patent Rolls.			
Edward I (1272-1307). 4 vols.	Set:	156.00	136.00 (415)
	Each:	.....	34.00 (415)
Edward II (1307-1327) 5 vols.	Set:	228.00	203.00 (415)
Vols. 1 and 3:	Each:	.....	40.50 (415)
Vol. 2:	Each:	.....	54.00 (415)
Vols. 4-5:	Each:	.....	34.00 (415)
Edward III (1327-1377). 16 vols.	Set:	624.00	544.00 (415)
	Each:	.....	34.00 (415)
Richard II (1377-1399). 6 vols.	Set:	273.50	243.50 (415)
Vols. 1-2, 6:	Each:	.....	40.50 (415)
Vols. 3-4:	Each:	.....	34.00 (415)
Vol. 5:	Each:	.....	54.00 (415)
Henry IV (1399-1413). 4 vols.	Set:	156.00	136.00 (415)
	Each:	.....	34.00 (415)
Henry V (1413-1422). 2 vols.	Set:	78.00	68.00 (415)
	Each:	.....	34.00 (415)
Henry VI (1422-1461). 6 vols.	Set:	273.00	243.00 (415)
	Each:	.....	40.50 (415)
Edward IV (1461-1467). 1 vol.	Each:	39.00	34.00 (415)
Edward IV-Henry VI (1467-1477). 1 vol.	Each:	45.50	40.50 (415)
Edward IV-Edward V-Richard III (1476-1485). 1 vol.	Each:	39.00	34.00 (415)
Henry VII (1485-1509). 2 vols.	Set:	84.50	74.50 (415)
Vol. 1:	Each:	.....	34.00 (415)

Vol. 2:	Each:	..... 40.50	(415)

Henry VIII (1509-1547).
Patent Rolls are included in "Letters and Papers"
which are listed under "State Papers".

Edward VI (1547-1553). 6 vols.	Set:	193.00	163.00	(415)
Vols. 1-5:	Each:	.....	24.50	(415)
Vol. 6 (Index):	Each:	.....	40.50	(415)
Philip and Mary (1553-1558). 4 vols.	Set:	155.50	135.50	(415)
Vols. 1 and 4:	Each:	.....	34.00	(415)
Vol. 2:	Each:	.....	27.00	(415)
Vol. 3:	Each:	.....	40.50	(415)
Elizabeth I (1558-1572). 5 vols.	Set:	201.50	176.50	(415)
Vols. 1, 3-5:	Each:	.....	34.00	(415)
Vol. 2:	Each:	.....	40.50	(415)

_____. Calendar of Close Rolls. 1892-1947.
The Close Rolls also fall in the category of Chancery
Records. Until Tudor times the Close Rolls contain
royal instructions for the performance of multifarious
acts; the observance of treaties, the levying of subsidies,
the repair of buildings, the payment of salaries, the
provision of household requirements, the delivery of
their landed inheritances to heirs and the assignment
of dower to widows, and so forth. Private deeds enrolled for safe custody on the back of the Close Rolls
are especially numerous from 1382, and from 1532-3
such deeds form the entire content of the roll.

Henry III (1227-1272). 14 vols.	Set:	546.00	476.00	(415)
	Each:	.....	34.00	(415)
Edward I (1272-1307). 5 vols.	Set:	195.00	170.00	(415)
	Each:	.....	34.00	(415)
Edward II (1307-1327). 4 vols.	Set:	182.00	162.00	(415)
	Each:	.....	40.50	(415)
Edward III (1327-1377). 14 vols.	Set:	637.00	567.00	(415)
	Each:	.....	40.50	(415)
Richard II (1377-1399). 6 vols.	Set:	273.00	243.00	(415)
	Each:	.....	40.50	(415)
Henry IV (1399-1413). 5 vols.	Set:	192.50	167.50	(415)
Vols. 1-4:	Each:	.....	30.00	(415)
Vol. 5 (Index):	Each:	.....	47.50	(415)
Henry V (1413-1422). 2 vols.	Set:	70.00	60.00	(415)
	Each:	.....	30.00	(415)
Henry VI (1422-1461). 6 vols.	Set:	234.00	204.00	(415)
	Each:	.....	34.00	(415)

_____. Calendar of Fine Rolls.
The "fines," from which the Fine Rolls take their name
were payments made for writs, grants, licences, pardons,
etc., of various kinds, most of them under the Great
Seal, relating to matters in which the Crown had a financial interest. The documents enrolled include writs to
inquire post mortem, writs to the Barons of the
Exchequer to assign terms for the payment of debts due
to the Crown and to cause fines to be taken from
prisoners for their release, licences to marry, appointments of sheriffs and other royal officers who would
be required to account at the Exchequer, writs to remove
causes from inferior tribunals into the King's courts, etc.

Vols. 1-13 covering years 1272-1413:	Set:	451.50	386.50 (415)

Vols. 1, 4, 5:	Each:	.....	38.00	(415)
Vols. 2, 7-10:	Each:	.....	27.00	(415)
Vol. 3:	Each:	.....	30.00	(415)
Vol. 6:	Each:	.....	34.00	(415)
Vols. 11-13:	Each:	.....	24.50	(415)

_____. Treaty Rolls, etc., Diplomatic Documents, ed. Pierre Chaplais. 1964.
Included in this work are the Diplomatic Documents of the Chancery and Exchequer as well as items from Ancient Correspondence consisting mainly of the diplomatic correspondence sent from abroad.

Vol. 1 covering years 1101-1272:		26.50	21.50 (415)

_____. Calendar of Chancery Rolls, Various. 1912.

Vol. 1 covering years 1277-1326:		36.00	31.00 (415)

_____. Calendar of Inquisitions Post Mortem. 1904-1938.

Vols. 1-12 (Henry III-43 Edward III) covering years 1227-1370:	Set:	516.00	456.00 (415)
	Each:	.....	38.00 (415)

_____. Inquisitions Post Mortem, (Henry VII). 2d series. 1898-1915.
Upon the death of any land-holder presumed to have been a tenant of the king in chief, sworn inquiry was held to establish of what lands etc. he was seised at the time of his death, their value, by what rents or services they were held, and the name and age of his next heir. The "proofs of age" returned when minor heirs came of age and filed with the Inquisitions post mortem.

Vols. 1-2 covering years 1485-1505:	Set:	98.00	88.00 (415)
	Each:	.....	44.00 (415)

_____. Calendar of Miscellaneous Inquisitions. 1916-1937.
After the formation of the classes of Inquisitions post mortem, Inquisitions ad quod damnum, and Criminal Inquisitions, there remained a number of inquisitions returned in the Chancery, of too varied a nature to allow of further classification, which are calendared in this series.

Vols. 1-3 (Henry III-51 Edward III):	Set:	142.50	127.50 (415)
Vol. 1:	Each:	.....	46.00 (415)
Vol. 2:	Each:	.....	43.50 (415)
Vol. 3:	Each:	.....	38.00 (415)

Exchequer and Judicial Records

_____. Liber Feodorum, The Book of Fees. Commonly called "Testa de Nevill", reformed from the earliest Manuscripts. 1921-1931.
The two manuscript volumes known as the "Testa de Nevill" or Book of Fees contain copies, entered about 1307, of a number of returns and lists preserved in the Exchequer, of which some survived and were used for this edition. The Book of Fees is an important source of information about the holdings of feudal tenants. Vol. 3 contains the index.

3 vols. covering years 1198-1293:	Set:	126.00	111.00 (415)
	Each:	.....	37.00 (415)

_____. Feudal Aids. 1899-1920.
Inquisitions and Assessments relating to Feudal Aids.
This work, based on various accounts, returns, surveys,
etc., among the Exchequer records, is of considerable
topographical value as illustrating the succession of
holders of land in England between the thirteenth century
and the fifteenth.

6 vols. covering years 1284-1431:	Set:	252.00	222.00 (415)
	Each:	.....	37.00 (415)

_____. Curia Regis Rolls. 1923-1949.
The rolls of which the Latin text is transcribed in this
series record proceedings in the Bench (later known as
the court of Common Pleas) and in the court "coram rege."
Apart from their value for the study of medieval English
law, these rolls reflect the social and economic life of
all classes of contemporary English society.

Vols. 1-10 covering years Richard I-1222:	Set:	317.00	267.00 (415)
Vol. 1:	Each:	.....	34.00 (415)
Vols. 2-5:	Each:	.....	24.50 (415)
Vols. 6-10:	Each:	.....	27.00 (415)

State Papers - State Papers, Domestic

_____. Letters and Papers, Foreign and Domestic, of the Reign
of Henry VIII. Preserved in the Public Record Office, the
British Museum, and elsewhere. ed. J.S. Brewer, et. al.
21 vols. in 35 parts and 1 vol. Addenda in 2 parts, together
37 parts. 1862-1932.

Henry VIII (1509-1547):	Set:	1484.50 1299.50 (415)	

_____. Calendar of State Papers, Domestic Series, of the
Reigns of Edward VI, Mary, Elizabeth and James I. eds.
R. Lemon and Mrs. Everett Green. 12 vols. 1856-1872.

Edward VI, Mary, Elizabeth I, James I (1547-1625):	Set:	468.00	408.00 (415)
	Each:	.....	34.00 (415)

_____. Calendar of State Papers, Domestic Series, of the
Reign of Charles I. Preserved in the State Paper Department
of Her Majesty's Public Record Office. eds. J. Bruce and
Mrs. S.C. Lomas. 23 vols. 1858-1897.

Charles I (1625-1649):	Set:	828.00	713.00 (415)
	Each:	.....	31.00 (415)

_____. Calendar of State Papers, Domestic Series (of the
Commonwealth). Preserved in the State Paper Department
of Her Majesty's Public Record Office. ed. Mrs. Everett
Green. 13 vols. 1875-1886.

The Commonwealth (1649-1660):	Set:	507.00	442.00 (415)
	Each:	.....	34.00 (415)

_____. Calendar of the Proceedings of the Committee for
Advance of Money. Preserved in the State Paper Department
of Her Majesty's Public Record Office. ed. Mrs. Everett
Green. 3 vols. 1888.

Covering years 1642-1656:	Set:	88.50	73.50 (415)
	Each:	.....	24.50 (415)

_____. Calendar of the Proceedings of the Committee for
Compounding with Delinquents. Preserved in the State Paper
Department of Her Majesty's Public Record Office. ed. Mrs.
Everett Green. 5 vols. 1889-1893.

Covering years 1643-1659:	Set:	195.00	170.00 (415)
	Each:	.....	34.00 (415)

_____. Calendar of State Papers, Domestic Series, of the
Reign of Charles II. Preserved in the State Paper Department
of Her Majesty's Public Record Office. ed. Mary Anne
Everett Green, et. al. 28 vols. 1860-1939.

Charles II (1661-1685):	Set:	1108.50	968.50 (415)
Vols. 1-23:	Each:	.....	37.00 (415)
Vols. 24-28:	Each:	.....	23.50 (415)

_____. Calendar of State Papers Domestic Series, of the Reign
of William and Mary. Preserved in the Public Record Office.
eds.William John Hardy and Edward Bateson. 11 vols.
1896-1937.

William III (1689-1702):	Set:	379.50	324.50 (415)
Vols. 1-5, 7-11	Each:	.....	30.00 (415)
Vol. 6	Each:	.....	24.50 (415)

_____. Calendar of State Papers, Domestic Series, of the
Reign of Anne. Preserved in the Public Record Office.
ed. Robert Pentland Mahaffy. 2 vols. 1916-1924.

Anne (1702-1704):	Set:	75.00	65.00 (415)
	Each:	.....	32.50 (415)

_____. Calendar of Home Office Papers of the Reign of
George III. Preserved in Her Majesty's Public Record
Office. eds.J. Redington and R. A. Roberts.
4 vols. 1878-1899.

George III (1760-1775):	Set:	156.00	136.00 (415)
	Each:	.....	34.00 (415)

State Papers, Foreign

_____. Calendar of State Papers, Foreign Series, of the
Reign of Mary. Preserved in the State Paper Department
of Her Majesty's Public Record Office. ed. W. B. Turnbull.
1861.

Mary (1553-1558):	Each:	29.50	24.50 (415)

_____. Calendar of State Papers, Foreign Series, of the
Reign of Elizabeth. Preserved in the State Paper Department
of Her Majesty's Public Record Office. eds. J. Stevenson,
et al. 25 vols. 1863-1950.

Elizabeth I (1558-1588): Vols. 1-22.	Set:	1050.00	925.00 (415)
Vols. 1-20, 22:	Each:	.....	37.00 (415)
Vol. 21 in 4 parts:	Each part:	.....	37.00 (415)

Colonial Records

[This series is particulary important for the study of American history.
In the volumes entitled "America and the West Indies" there are, chrono-
logically arranged, extensive summaries of documents, correspondence
and acts of various kinds relating to the Colonies. The period covered as
far as America is concerned, begins with the year 1575 and is brought up
to the year 1738 with Volume 44, which has just come off the press. The
series is being continued and further volumes can be expected within the
next few years. This series is a prime source for the study of Colonial
times in America. Each volume has an extensive preface by its editor,
and these prefaces form individual chapters in Colonial history. A general index of persons and places at the end of the volumes facilitates their
use.]

_____. Calendar of State Papers. Colonial Series.
eds. W. N. Sainsbury, et. al. 40 vols. 1860-1939.

Vols. 1-40:	Set:	1720.00	1520.00 (415)
	Each:	.....	38.00 (415)

Supplement to Vol. 14 (addenda 1688-1696). Nendelyn,
Lichtenstein. 1970:   Each: 11.75   6.75 (415)
_____. Journal of the Board of Trade and Plantations.
14 vols. 1920-1938.
Vols. 1-14 covering years 1704-1782:   Set: 357.00   287.00 (415)
                                                Each: 20.50 (415)

Treasury Books and Papers

[The "Papers" are the original correspondence of the Treasury Board be-
tween 1557 and 1745, with occasional minutes, reports, etc. "Treasury
Books" comprise a number of classes or records, including the Board's
Minutes and several series of entry books of Warrants, etc.]
_____. Calendar of Treasury Papers. 1868-1889.
Vols. 1-6 covering years 1557-1728:   Set: 249.00   219.00 (415)
                                                Each: 36.50 (415)
_____. Calendar of Treasury Books and Papers. ed. W.A.
Shaw. 1898-1903.
Vols. 1-5 covering years 1729-1745:   Set: 247.50   222.50 (415)
                                                Each: 44.50 (415)

Ireland

_____. Calendar of Documents Relating to Ireland. ed. H.S.
Sweetman. 1875-1886.
Vols. 1-5 covering years 1171-1307:   Set: 188.50   163.50 (415)
Vols. 1-3:   Each: 36.50 (415)
Vols. 4-5:   Each: 27.00 (415)
_____. Calendar of State Papers Relating to Ireland. ed. H.C.
Hamilton. 1806-1912.
Vols. 1-11 covering years 1509-1603:   Set: 473.00   418.00 (415)
                                                Each: 38.00 (415)
_____. James I. eds. C.W. Russell and J-P Prendergast.
1872-1880.
Vols. 1-5 covering years 1603-1625:   Set: 235.00   210.00 (415)
                                                Each: 42.00 (415)
_____. Calendar of Carew Papers in the Lambeth Library.
eds. J.S. Brewer and W. Bullen. 1867-1873.
Vols. 1-6 covering years 1515-1624:   Set: 240.00   210.00 (415)
                                                Each: 35.00 (415)

Researches in Foreign Archives

_____. France. Calendar of Documents preserved in France
illustrative of the history of Great Britain and Ireland. ed.
J.H. Round. 1899.
Vol. 1 covering years 918-1206:   Each: 39.00   34.00 (415)
_____. Spain. Letters, Despatches and State Papers relating
to the Negotiations between England and Spain preserved in
the Archives at Vienna, Brussels, Simancas, and elsewhere.
1862-1916.
    This calendar was compiled mainly from the originals
    or from transcripts in the Public Record Office. For
    the most part the work deals with affairs during the
    reign of Henry VIII (vols. 2-8). The supplement to
    vols. 1-2 contains papers relating to Queen Katherine,
    and to the intended marriage of Henry VII with Queen
    Joanna.

Vols. 1-11 (in 17 parts) covering years 1485-1553:   Set: 796.50 711.50 (415)
Vols. 1,5 pt. I, 5 pt. II, 7-11:   Each: 34.00 (415)
Vols. 2,3 pt. I, 4 pt. II: Each: 54.00 (415)
Vols. 3 pt. II, 4 pt. I: Each: 61.00 (415)
Vol. 4 pt. II - cont.   Each: 47.50 (415)
Vol. 6 pt. I, 6 pt. II: Each: 40.50 (415)
Supplement to Vols. 1-2:   Each: 27.00 (415)

_____. Letters and State Papers relating to English Affairs.
Preserved principally in the Archives of Simancas. ed.
M.A.S. Hume. 1892-1899.
    This calendar was compiled mainly from transcripts in
    the British Museum and from printed sources.

Vols. 1-4 covering years of Elizabeth I (1558-1603):   Set: 182.00 162.00 (415)
               Each: 40.50 (415)

_____. Italy. Entries in Papal Registers relating to Great
Britain and Ireland: Papal Letters. 1894-1933.

Vols. 1-12 covering years 1198-1471:   Set: 565.00 505.00 (415)
Vols. 1-5, 7, 9:   Each: 38.50 (415)
Vol. 6:   Each: 33.50 (415)
Vols. 8, 10-12:   Each: 50.50 (415)

_____. Petitions to the Pope. 1897.

Vol. 1 covering years 1342-1419:   45.50 40.50 (415)

_____. State Papers and Manuscripts Relating to English
Affairs. Existing in the Archives and Collections of Venice,
and in other Libraries of Northern Italy. 1864-1939.

Vols. 1-37 covering years 1202-1672:   Set: 1566.50 1371.50 (415)
Vols. 1-5, 7-24:   Each: 40.50 (415)
Vols. 25-37:   Each: 24.50 (415)
Vol. 6 (3 parts):   Each: 121.50 (415)

_____. Lists and Indexes. 1892-1936.
    The "Lists and Indexes" of the Public Record Office,
    London, was begun in 1892 to present historians with
    guides, finding aids and indexes to the massive amount
    of records contained in the British National Archives.
    These series deal with state documents in the various
    branches of administration, dating from approximately
    1500 to our time: Chancery Proceedings, Court of
    Requests Proceedings, Inquisitions ad quod damnum,
    Inquisitions post mortem, Star Chamber Proceedings
    and records of the Exchequer, Admiralty, War Office,
    Foreign Office, Colonial Office, Treasury, etc.
    Detailed price list of single volumes available upon
    request.

Vols. 1-55 (all published; without volumes 3 and 41).   2610.00 ..... (415)
Supplemental Series. Series I-XV in 59 vols.(as far as
published to date). 1963-1975.   2437.00 ..... (415)

Lists and Indexes. Supplementary Series

_____. No. 1 List of Rolls and Writs of the Court Coram Rege,
Henry III. List of Bench (Common Pleas) Plea and Essoin
Rolls, Henry III. List of Common Pleas Essoin Rolls, Edw. I -
George III. Revised List of Gaol Delivery Rolls and Files.
1970.
    The present publication amplifies and brings up to date, in
    the light of recent study, some of the information con-
    tained in "Public Record Office Lists and Indexes, Vol. 4,
    List of Plea Rolls of Various Courts." Each of the lists

of five categories of common-law records (Bench Plea
Rolls, Henry III; Bench Essoin Rolls, Henry III; Rolls
and Writs of the Court "Coram Rege", Henry III; Gaol
Delivery Rolls and Files, 1271-1476; and Common
Pleas Essoin Rolls, Edward I - George III) is here
provided with an Introduction, and with such other
material by way of commentary and explanation as the
reader may need in order to make the best use of the
records themselves. Supplement to vol. 4.   45.00   40.00 (415)

_____. No. II. List of Ministers' Accounts. Edward VI-18th
Century, and Analogous Documents. 1967.

The original printed series of "Lists and Indexes" contain particulars, for the period from 1216-1547, of the
accounts rendered by the ministers and receivers of
lands belonging to the Crown or temporarily in its
hands. (Some of the documents listed in vol. 34 are
abstracted in greater detail in No. III of the Supplementary Series.) In the present volume the listing of the
record class specifically entitled 'Ministers' and
'Receivers' account is continued and completed. Although a few of the documents in this class are of the
eighteenth, and even of the nineteenth, century, for
most counties it contains no accounts later than the
reign of Charles II (1685). The Appendix consists of a
list of the class of records from the office of the Auditors
of Land Revenue entitled 'Receivers'-Accounts, Series
III, which consists of forty-three bundles of ministers'
and receivers' accounts extending in date from the reign
of Henry VIII to 1832. The pre-Mary accounts in this
class were originally records of the Court of
Augmentations. Supplement to vols. 5, 8, 34.   42.00   37.00 (415)

_____. No. III. List of the Lands of Dissolved Religious
Houses. 7 vols. 1963-1964.

This "List of the Lands of Dissolved Religious Houses"
expands one category of entries in the "Lists of Ministers'
Accounts," Part II, Henry VII and Henry VIII. In the
printed list, the accounts of royal ministers for the
possessions of dissolved monasteries are briefly noted
under the counties in which the monasteries lay. In this
Supplementary List the lands named in the earliest
surviving post-dissolution account for each monastery's
possessions are listed in detail as they occur in the
original manuscripts. There is an exhaustive index of
places, in which cross-reference is used to identify
obsolete forms of place names with those on the modern
map. Supplement to Lists and Indexes vol. 34.   Set: 211.00 176.00 (415)

_____. No. IV. Index to Proceedings in the Court of Star
Chamber. 1966-1969.

The printed list of Proceedings in the Court of Star
Chamber for the period 1485-1558 provides, in respect
of each suit, particulars of the names of the parties, the
subject of the litigation (often involving reference to a
named place) and the name of the county concerned. No
attempt was made by the original compilers of the list
to arrange the suits in any order. It was accordingly
decided to compile the exhaustive indexes, which con-
stitute this "Supplementary List", by the names of persons

and places mentioned in the printed list.
Vol. 1 - 1485-1558 (Index to Persons and Places):   Each: 45.00   40.00   (415)
Vol. 2 - Elizabeth I (A-C):   Each: 45.00   40.00   (415)
Vol. 3 - Elizabeth I (D-K):   Each: 45.00   40.00   (415)
Vol. 4 - Elizabeth I (L-R):   Each: 45.00   40.00   (415)
Vol. 5 - Elizabeth I (S-Z):   Each: 41.00   36.00   (415)
_____. No. V.   Supplementary List of Records, Duchy of
Lancaster. 3 vols. 1964-1965.
    Vol. 1 is primarily a continuation of "Lists & Indexes",
    vol. 14. The lists of additions to the Duchy of Lancaster
    classes of Court Rolls and of Rentals and Surveys sup-
    plement information contained in "Lists & Indexes",
    vols. 6 and 25. Vol. 2 contains a detailed list of the
    class of Duchy of Lancaster Royal Charters which is
    summarily described on page 97 of "Lists & Indexes",
    vol. 14. The documents listed herein range from the
    reigns of William II to George II. The class includes
    not only charters but also letters, patent and close,
    which passed the Great Seal, exemplifications under
    the Exchequer Seal and Privy Seals. Most of the later
    documents were issued under either the Palatinate or
    Duchy seals, or both. The provenance of the family
    and other collections among the Duchy charters has been
    outlined in the Introduction to the "List of Cartae Miscel-
    laneae. Vol. 3". The printed "List of Records of the
    Duchy of Lancaster, Lists and Indexes", vol. 14,
    provides no particulars of the Duchy of Lancaster class
    of "Cartae Miscellaneae" beyond the statement that it
    consists of three volumes into which deeds and charters
    which had lost their seals have been collected and bound.
    Vol. 3 is a fully indexed descriptive list of all the deeds
    and other documents comprised in the three volumes of
    "Cartae Miscellaneae".   Set: 81.00   66.00   (415)
_____. No. VI.   List of Admiralty Records (to 1913). 5 vols.
1967-1975.
    Besides continuing to 1913 (so far as individual series
    reach that date) the lists begun in "Lists and Indexes",
    vol 18, this Supplementary List deals with a number of
    classes of much earlier date which were not represented
    in that work, either because they were deliberately ex-
    cluded from its scope, or because they were transferred
    to the custody of the Public Record Office after its
    publication.
Vol. 1 - Accounting Department — Dockyard Records: 39.00   34.00   (415)
Vol. 2 - Greenwich Hospital — Transport Department: 39.00   34.00   (415)
Vol. 3 - Various Classes — 1914-1945:   51.00   46.00   (415)
Vol. 4 - Admiralty and Secretariat Cases —1914-1945:   41.00   36.00   (415)
Vol. 5 - Admiralty and Secretariat Papers.—1914-1941:   67.00   62.00   (415)
_____. No. VII.   Indexes to Proceedings in the Court of
Requests. 4 vols. 1963-1972.
    The printed calendar of the first 136 bundles of Requests
    Proceedings provides, in respect of each document
    calendared, particulars of the names of the parties, the
    subject of the litigation (which may be land in a named
    place) and the county concerned. Though the earlier
    bundles belong in general to the earlier part of the
    period covered, the documents are in no particular order

that facilitates research. This Supplementary List forms
an exhaustive index of the names of persons and places
and of subjects mentioned in the printed calendar. Although it is in principle an index to the printed text, the
information it contains has regularly been verified by
reference to the original manuscripts.   220.00   200.00 (415)
_____. No. VIII. List of War Office Records. 1969.
The scope of this volume is determined not by an attempt
to catalogue the relevant classes down to a specified date
but by the extent of the Public Record Office's holding at
the beginning of 1967 of War Office records now accessible
to the public. For this reason no general terminal date
is suggested on the title-page; in practice it will be
found that many of the classes here treated are listed
down to about 1922 but that there are also many that fall
short of that date or are continued beyond it.   51.00   46.00 (415)
_____. No. IX. Exchequer Records. 1964-1969.
The class of records known as Warrants for Issues consists of original instruments conveying authority for
payments out of the royal Exchequer. The objects of
this official expenditure being broadly those reflected in
the class of Exchequer Accounts Various, the present
analytical index to the Warrants for Issues supplements,
for the years between 1399 and 1485, the contents of the
printed "List of Exchequer Accounts, Various (Lists
and Indexes, vol. 35)".
Vol. 1 - Lists of Accounts, various
Vol. 2 - List and Index of Warrants for Issues 1399-1485.
With an Appendix: Indentures of War, 1297-1527.
Supplement to Lists and Indexes vols. 35.   Set: 57.00   47.00 (415)
_____. No. X. Supplementary List of State Papers, Foreign
and Domestic, and List of State Papers, Miscellaneous, etc.
1970.
The volumes in the printed series of Public Record Office, "Lists and Indexes" which are supplemented by the
present publication are No. 43, "List of State Papers,
Domestic, 1547-1792", and No. 19 "List of State Papers,
Foreign, 1577-1781". Of the classes of State Papers
here listed two, State Papers Miscellaneous (S.P. 9)
and Commonwealth Exchequer Papers (S.P. 28), are
described in introductions prefixed to the lists. Of the
third (S.P. 110) it is perhaps sufficient to say that it
is composed for the most part of archives of British
legations for the 17th and 18th centuries.   30.00   25.00 (415)
_____. No. XI. List of Board of Trade Records to 1913. 1964.
The original edition of "Lists and Indexes", vol. 46 contained lists of Board of Trade documents up to 1837.
These lists dealt with such a very small part of the
Board of Trade records now available for consultation
in the Public Record Office that it was decided to omit
them from the reprint of "Lists and Indexes", vol. 46
and to unite them with other material to provide a class
list, as nearly comprehensive as possible, of all of the
Board of Trade records up to the year 1913 in the
Public Record Office. The present Supplementary List
is the result. The only important classes of pre-1914
records excluded from it are those of the Companies

Registration Office and of the Patent Office and Industrial
Property Department. Supplement to vol. 46.   37.00   32.00 (415)
_____. No. XII. List of Treasury Records, 1838-1938. 1970.
The present publication brings down to the year 1938 the
listing of the Treasury records in the Public Record Office which was begun in Public Record Office Lists and
Indexes, vol 46, "List of Records of the Treasury . . .
Prior to 1837". It will be realized that the boundary
dates specified on the title-page do not necessarily apply
to each individual class here listed; but in principle the
"List" cited above and this continuation of it comprehend
almost all the Treasury records which had been transferred to the Public Record Office and were open to public
inspection at the time when this Supplementary List went
to press. Supplement to Lists and Indexes vol. 46.   45.00   40.00 (415)
_____. No. XIII. List of Foreign Office Records. 23 vols.
1964-1975.
This series continues the Foreign Office General Correspondence and the Embassy and Consular Archives
begun in "Lists and Indexes", No. 52. It also supplements
the newly released "Index to Foreign Office Correspondence
1920-1938". Supplement to vol. 52.   Set: 962.00   847.00 (415)
Vols. 1-4, 7-8:   Each: 37.00   32.00 (415)
Vols. 5, 9, 12, 14:   Each: 45.00   40.00 (415)
Vol. 6:   Each: 39.00   34.00 (415)
Vols. 10-11:   Each: 51.00   46.00 (415)
Vol. 13:   Each: 30.00   25.00 (415)
Vols. 15-16, 21:   Each: 41.00   36.00 (415)
Vols. 17, 20:   Each: 29.00   24.00 (415)
Vols. 18-19, 22:   Each: 47.00   42.00 (415)
Vol. 23:   Each: 67.00   62.00 (415)
_____. No. XIV. List of Rentals and Surveys. Addenda and
Index. 1969.
The present publication consists of addenda to "Lists
and Indexes", vol. 25, in the preface of which will be
found an account of the nature and scope of the documents,
drawn from different record classes, which qualify for
the description of rentals and surveys. The index of
places (distributed under counties) which appears in this
volume covers both the original printed list and this
supplement to it. Supplement to Lists and Indexes vol. 25.   27.00   22.00 (415)
_____. No. XV. List of Ancient Correspondence of the
Chancery and the Exchequer. Indices. 2 vols. 1969.
The present publication is a comprehensive index of
persons and places to the Public Record Office class of
Ancient Correspondence. This class is calendared in
Public Record Office "Lists and Indexes", vol. 15; but
since the index is to the full text of the original documents
it will be found to contain references to persons and
places not mentioned in the condensed entries forming
the calendar. Supplement to revised vol. 25.   Set: 122.00   112.00 (415)
_____. Acts of the Privy Council of England. ed. J.R. Dasent,
et. al. 1890-1938.
Vols. 1-42 covering years 1542-1627:   Set: 1487.00   1277.00 (415)
Vols. 1-27, 31-32, 35-42:   Each: 28.50 (415)
Vols. 28-30, 33-34:   Each: 44.50 (415)

_____. Acts of the Privy Council of England. Colonial Series.
6 vols. 1908-1912.
    Transcript. Vols. 2-5 have appendices of commissions
    and instructions to colonial governors, nominations, etc.
    to colonial councils, extracts from the Plantation Register
    and colonial acts confirmed or disallowed by the Privy
    Council. In addition, vols. 4 and 5 have appendices on
    grants of lands in the American colonies.
    Vols. 1-6 covering years 1613-1783:   Set: 213.00 183.00 (415)
    Each: 30.50 (415)

_____. Guide to the Contents of the Public Record Office.
2 vols. Orig. ed. London, 1963.   20.00 ..... (415)

[This completes the GREAT BRITAIN'S PRIMARY RECORDS Section]

The Irish University Press Series of the British Parliamentary
    Papers: Emigration. 28 vols. 1971.   1930.00 ..... (379)
Nichols, John, ed. A Collection of All the Wills, Now Known to
    be Extant, of the Kings and Queens of England, Princes and
    Princesses of Wales, and Every Branch of the Blood Royal,
    from the Reign of William the Conqueror to that of Henry the
    Seventh, exclusive, with explanatory notes and a glossary.
    1780.   22.00 ..... (415)
Oxford University. Alumni Oxonienses 1887-1892. comp. J. Foster.
    8 vols. in 4.
    The members of the University of Oxford, 1500-1886,
    their parentage, birthplace and year of birth, with a
    record of their degrees.   132.00 ..... (415)
Pipe Roll Society, London. Publications.
    The Pipe Rolls are the ancient records of the crown revenue
    and expenditures of England. The oldest pipe roll dates
    from 1131 and from 1156 they are almost completely intact.
    Prices for single volumes vary; a list of single volumes,
    with contents, available upon request.
    S. 1: Vols. 1-38 (all publ.). London, 1884-1925.   638.00 ..... (415)
    S. 2: Vols. 1-11. London, 1925-1933.   304.00 ..... (415)
    S. 2: Vols. 12-36. London, 1934-1962.   637.00 ..... (415)

BEDFORDSHIRE

Genealogical Society of the LDS. Pre-1858 English Probate
    Jurisdictions -- Bedfordshire. 5pp.   ..... .85 (275)

BERKSHIRE

_____. Pre-1858 English Probate Jurisdictions--Berkshire. 6pp. ..... .85 (275)

BUCKINGHAMSHIRE

Dickson, R. Bruce, comp. Parish Register of Stewkeley,
    Buckinghamshire, England, 1545-1653. 1897. 88pp. 6.50 (530)
Genealogical Society of LDS. Pre-1858 English Probate
    Jurisdictions--Buckinghamshire. 6pp.   ..... .85 (275)

CAMBRIDGESHIRE

Genealogical Society of the LDS. Pre-1858 English Probate
    Jurisdictions--Cambridgeshire. 5pp.   ..... .85 (275)

CHESHIRE

Genealogical Society of the LDS. Pre-1858 English Probate
Jurisdictions--Cheshire. 7pp. ..... .85 (275)

CORNWALL

_____. Pre-1858 English Probate Jurisdictions--Cornwall. 6pp. ..... .85 (275)

CUMBERLAND

Hughes, Edward. North Country Life in the Eighteenth Century,
2 Volumes Including Volume 1: The North-East 1700-1750;
Volume 2: Cumberland and Westmoreland 1700-1830.
1952 and 1965. Each: 12.00 ..... (566)
Hutchinson, William. The History of the County of Cumberland.
1794-97. 2 vols. Repr. Set: 115.00 ..... (661)
Genealogical Society of the LDS. Pre-1858 English Probate
Jurisdictions--Cumberland. 6pp. ..... .85 (275)

DERBYSHIRE

_____. Pre-1858 English Probate Jurisdictions--Derbyshire. 6pp. ..... .85 (275)

DEVONSHIRE

_____. Pre-1858 English Probate Jurisdictions--Devonshire. 8pp. ..... .85 (275)
MacGaffrey, Wallace. Exeter, 1540-1640: The Growth of an
English Country Town. 2d ed. 5.50 ..... (319)

DORSET

Hutchins, John. The History and Antiquities of the County of
Dorset. eds. W. Shipp and J. M. Hodson. 3rd ed. 1861-70.
2500pp. 4 vols. Set: 285.00 ..... (661)
Genealogical Society of the LDS. Pre-1858 English Probate
Jurisdictions--Dorset. 8pp. ..... .85 (275)

DURHAM

Hughes, Edward. North Country Life in the Eighteenth Century,
2 Volumes Including: Volume 1 - The North-East 1700-1750;
Volume 2 - Cumberland and Westmoreland 1700-1830.
1952 and 1965. Each: 12.00 ..... (566)
Genealogical Society of the LDS. Pre-1858 English Probate
Jurisdictions--Durham. 7pp. ..... .85 (275)
Surtees, Robert. The History and Antiquities of the County
Palatine of Durham. 1816-40. Repr. 4 vols. Set: 150.00 ..... (661)

ESSEX

Andrews, W. Bygone Essex. Repr. of 1892 ed. 10.50 ..... (93)
Genealogical Society of the LDS. Pre-1858 English Probate
Jurisdictions--Essex. 8pp. ..... .85 (275)

GLOSTERSHIRE

Atkyns, Robert. Ancient and Present State of Glostershire.
Repr. of 1712 ed. 866pp. 157 plates. 2 parts. 90.00 ..... (661)

GLOUCESTERSHIRE

Genealogical Society of the LDS. Pre-1858 English Probate
Jurisdictions--Gloucestershire. 7pp. ..... .85 (275)

HAMPSHIRE

Jowitt, R. L. History, People and Places in Hampshire. 1975.	12.50	.....	(373)
Willis, Arthur J. Hampshire Marriage Licenses 1607-1640, from Records in the Diocesan Registry, Winchester.	9.00	.....	(41)
Genealogical Society of the LDS Pre-1858 English Probate Jurisdictions--Hampshire. 7pp.	.....	.85	(275)

HEREFORDSHIRE

_____. Pre-1858 English Probate Jurisdictions--Herefordshire. 7pp.	.....	.85	(275)

HERTFORDSHIRE

Cussans, John Edwin. The History of Hertfordshire. Repr. of 1870-81 ed. 3 vols. Set:	165.00	.....	(661)
Genealogical Society of the LDS. Pre-1858 English Probate Jurisdiction--Hertfordshire. 6pp.	.....	.85	(275)

HUNTINGDONSHIRE

Charles, Nicholas. The Visitation of the County of Huntingdon, Under the Authority of William Camden . . . by His Deputy, Nicholas Charles . . . A.D. 1613. ed. Sir Henry Ellis. 1849.	10.00	.....	(2)
Genealogical Society of the LDS. Pre-1858 English Probate Jurisdictions--Huntingdonshire. 6pp.	.....	.85	(275)

KENT

Hasted, Edward. The History and Topographical Survey of the County of Kent. 2d ed. Repr. of 1797-1801 ed. 7000pp. 12 vols. Set:	265.00	.....	(661)
Genealogical Society of the LDS. Pre-1858 English Probate Jurisdictions--Kent. 5pp.	.....	.85	(275)

LANCASHIRE

Bagley, John J. History of Lancashire. 1961. rev. ed.	7.95	.....	(207)
Baines, Edward. Lancashire: History, Directory and Gazetteer of the County Palatine of Lancaster. 2 vols. 1824-25. 668pp; 656pp. Set:	27.50	.....	(273)
Bamford, Samuel. Walks in South Lancashire and on Its Borders. With letters, descriptions, narratives and observations, current and incidental. 1844. 288pp.	12.50	.....	(273)
Ekwall, E. The Place-Names of Lancashire. Repr. of 1922 ed.	12.50	.....	(93)
Genealogical Society of the LDS. Pre-1858 English Probate Jurisdictions--Lancashire. 8pp.	.....	.85	(275)
Walker, Frank. Historical Geography of Southwest Lancashire Before the Industrial Revolution. Reprint.	12.00	.....	(394)
Whitaker, Harold. Descriptive List of the Printed Maps of Lancashire, 1577-1900. Repr. of 1938 ed.	17.50	.....	(394)

LEICESTERSHIRE

Genealogical Society of the LDS. Pre-1858 English Probate Jurisdictions--Leicestershire. 7pp.	.....	.85	(275)
Nichols, John. The History and Antiquities of the County of Leicester. Repr. of 1795-1815 ed. 4500pp. 4 vols (8 part). Set:	325.00	.....	(661)

LINCOLNSHIRE

Genealogical Society of the LDS. Pre-1858 English Probate
Jurisdictions--Lincolnshire. 6pp.   ..... .85 (275)
White, William. History, Gazetteer and Directory of Lincolnshire,
and the City and Diocese of Lincoln. 2d ed. 1856. 900pp.
Comprising, under a lucid arrangement of subjects, a
general survey of the county, and separate historical,
statistical and topographical descriptions of all the
wapentakes, hundreds, sokes, boroughs, towns, ports,
parishes, townships, chapelries, villages, hamlets,
manors, and unions showing the lords of the manors and
owners of the soil and tithes.   20.00   ..... (273)

LONDON

Genealogical Society of the LDS. Pre-1858 English Probate
Jurisdictions--London. 6pp.   ..... .85 (275)
London County Council. Survey of London. ed. F. W. H. Sheppard,
et al. 36 vols. 1900-1970.
   1. Ashbee, C. R., ed.: The Parish of Bromley-By-Bow.
      1900.   57.50   ..... (2)
   2. Godfrey, W. H., ed.: The Parish of Chelsea. Part 1.
      1909.   57.50   ..... (2)
   9. Reddan, M. and A. W. Clapham: The Parish of St.
      Helen, Bishopsgate, Part 1.   74.50   ..... (2)
  10. Cox, M. H., ed.: The Parish of St. Margaret,
      Westminster, Part 1. 1926.   57.50   ..... (2)
  11. Bodfrey, W.H.: The Parish of Chelsea. Part 4. 1927.   74.50   ..... (2)
  12. Redstone, L.J., ed.: The Parish of All Hollows Barking.
      Part 1. 1929.   57.50   ..... (2)
  13. Cox, M. and G. T. Forrest: The Parish of St. Margaret,
      Westminster. Part 2. 1930.   74.50   ..... (2)
  17. Lovell, P. W. and W. McB. Marcham, eds.: The
      Parish of St. Pancras. Part 1. 1936.   57.50   ..... (2)
  18. Gater, Sir G. H. and E. P. Wheeler, eds.: The Parish
      of St. Martin-In-The-Fields. Part 2. 1937.   57.50   ..... (2)
  19. Lovell, P. W. and W. McB. Marcham, eds.: The Parish
      of St. Pancras. Part 2. 1938.   57.50   ..... (2)
  20. Gater, Sir G. H. and F. R. Hiorns: The Parish of St.
      Martin-In-The-Fields. Part 3. 1940.   74.50   ..... (2)
  22. London County Council: Bankside. The Parishes of
      St. Saviour and Christchurch, Southwark. 1950.   57.50   ..... (2)
  24. Godfrey, W. H.: The Parish of St. Pancras. Part 4.
      1952.   74.50   ..... (2)
  26. London County Council: Survey of London. The Parish
      of St. Mary Lambeth. Part 2. Southern Area. 1956.   74.50   ..... (2)
  27. London County Council: The Parishes of Christ Church and
      All Saints . . . 1957.   74.50   ..... (2)
London, St. Paul's Cathedral. The Domesday of St. Paul's of the
Year MCCXXII. . . And Other Original Documents Relating to the
Manors and Churches Belonging to the Dean and Chapter of St.
Paul's London in the Twelfth and Thirteenth Centuries. 1858.   20.00   ..... (2)

MIDDLESEX

Genealogical Society of the LDS. Pre-1858 English Probate
Jurisdictions--Middlesex. 9pp.   ..... .85 (275)

MONMOUTHSHIRE

Genealogical Society of the LDS. Pre-1858 English Probate
Jurisdictions--South Wales and Monmouthshire. 14pp.   ..... .85 (275)
_____. Welsh Patronymics and Place Name Problems in
Wales and Monmouthshire. 10pp.   ..... .85 (275)

NORFOLK

_____. Pre-1858 English Probate Jurisdictions--Norfolk. 5pp.   ..... .85 (275)

NORTHAMPTONSHIRE

_____. Pre-1858 English Probate Jurisdictions--Northamptonshire.
6pp.   ..... .85 (275)

NORTHUMBERLAND

_____. Pre-1858 English Probate Jurisdictions--Northumberland.
7pp.   ..... .85 (275)

NOTTINGHAMSHIRE

Chambers, Jonathan D. Nottinghamshire In the Eighteenth
Century. A Study of Life and Labour Under the Squirearchy.
Reprint. 377pp.   13.50 ..... (273)
Genealogical Society of the LDS. Pre-1858 English Probate
Jurisdictions--Nottinghamshire. 8pp.   ..... .85 (275)
Thoroton, Robert. The Antiquities of Nottinghamshire. ed. John
Throsby. Repr. of 1790-6 ed. 3 vols.   Set: 90.00 ..... (661)

OXFORDSHIRE

Genealogical Society of the LDS. Pre-1858 English Probate
Jurisdictions--Oxfordshire. 6pp.   ..... .85 (275)

RUTLANDSHIRE

_____. Pre-1858 English Probate Jurisdictions--Rutlandshire. 5pp. ..... .85 (275)

SHROPSHIRE

Ludlow, England (Parish). Churchwardens' Accounts of the Town of
Ludlow in Shropshire From 1540 to the End of the Reign of Queen
Elizabeth. ed. Thomas Wright. 1869.   10.00 ..... (2)
Genealogical Society of the LDS. Pre-1858 English Probate
Jurisdictions--Shropshire. 6pp.   ..... .85 (275)

SOMERSET

_____. Pre-1858 English Probate Jurisdictions--Somerset. 9pp.   ..... .85 (275)

STAFFORDSHIRE

_____. Pre-1858 English Probate Jurisdictions--Staffordshire. 8pp. ..... .85 (275)

SUFFOLK

_____. Pre-1858 English Probate Jurisdictions--Suffolk. 6pp.   ..... .85 (275)

SURREY

_____. Pre-1858 English Probate Jurisdictions--Surrey. 7pp.   ..... .85 (275)
Manning, Owen (with William Bray). The History and Antiquities of
the County of Surrey. Repr. of 1804-1814 ed. 3 vols. Set: 240.00 ..... (661)

SUSSEX

Genealogical Society of the LDS. Pre-1858 English Probate
Jurisdictions--Sussex. 6pp.   ..... .85 (275)

WARWICKSHIRE

_____. Pre-1858 English Probate Jurisdictions--Warwickshire.
7pp.   ..... .85 (275)
Parsons, Harold. History, People and Places in Warwickshire.
1975.   12.50 ..... (373)

WESTMORLAND

Genealogical Society of the LDS. Pre-1858 English Probate
Jurisdictions--Westmorland. 7pp.   ..... .85 (275)

WILTSHIRE

_____. Pre-1858 English Probate Jurisdictions--Wiltshire. 6pp. ..... .85 (275)

WORCESTERSHIRE

_____. Pre-1858 English Probate Jurisdictions--Worcestershire.
6pp.   ..... .85 (275)

YORKSHIRE

Atthill, William Lombe, ed. Documents Relating to the Foundation
and Antiquities of the Collegiate Church of Middleham in the
County of York. With an Historical Introduction, and Incidental
Notices of the Castle, Town, and Neighbourhood. 1847.   10.00 ..... (2)
Aveling, Hugh. Northern Catholics: The Catholic Recusants of
the North Riding of Yorkshire 1558-1790. 1966.   13.75 ..... (335)
Baines, Edward. Yorkshire: History, directory and gazetteer
of the county of York. 2 vols. 654pp; 615pp.   1822-23.
    Volume I. West Riding.
    Volume II. East and North Ridings.   Set: 25.00 ..... (273)
Hunter, Joseph. South Yorkshire. 1828 and 1831. Repr.
2 vols.   Set: 115.00 ..... (661)
Genealogical Society of the LDS. Pre-1858 English Probate
Jurisdictions--Yorkshire. 13pp.   ..... .85 (275)

Wales

Clement, Mary, ed. Correspondence and Records of the
S.P.G. Relating to Wales, 1701-1750. 1973.   6.50 ..... (795)
Davies, Margaret. Wales in Maps. 2d. rev. ed.   3.50 ..... (795)
England and Wales Nu-Way Road Series (Contemporary Maps). 2.95 (93)
Fletcher, H. L. North Wales. 1972.   7.50 ..... (373)
_____. South Wales. 1972.   6.25 ..... (373)
Fraser, D. Wales In History. 2 vols. 2d ed. Vol. 1-1965.
Vol. 2-1967.
    Volume 1: The Invaders: To 1066; Volume 2: The
    Defenders: 1066-1485.   Each: 4.50 ..... (795)
Genealogical Society of the LDS Church. English-Welsh
Genealogical Research Procedures--Flow Charts. 12pp.   ..... .85 (275)
_____. Major Genealogical Record Sources in England and Wales.
8pp.   ..... .85 (275)

Genealogical Society of the LDS Church. Population Movements in
  England and Wales by Canal and Navigable Rivers. 8pp. 85 (275)
  _____. Population Movements in England and Wales During the
  Industrial Revolution. 17pp. 85 (275)
  _____. Pre-1858 English Probate Jurisdictions--North Wales.
  13pp. 85 (275)
  _____. Pre-1858 English Probate Jurisdictions--South Wales and
  Monmouthshire. 14pp. 85 (275)
  _____. Welsh Patronymics and Place Name Problems in Wales
  and Monmouthshire. 10pp. 85 (275)
Griffiths, Ralph A. The Principality of Wales in the Later Middle
  Ages: The Structure and Personnel of Government, Part 1,
  South Wales, 1277-1536. 1972.   27.50   .... (795)
Historical Society of West Wales. West Wales Historical Records,
  1912-1913. 2 vols.
    These volumes contain genealogies of Cardiganshire,
    Carmarthenshire and Pembrokeshire families. There are
    diaries, documents, reports, and other such material which
    are all important to the study of the local history of West
    Wales.   Each: 16.00 (415)
                                      Set: 38.00   32.00 (415)
History of Wales from the Earliest Times to the Edwardian
  Conquest. 2 vols. 3rd ed. 1967.   Set: 16.50   ..... (233)
Jack, R. Ian. Medieval Wales. ed. G. R. Elton. 1973.   9.75   4.50 (163)
Lloyd, H. A. Gentry of South-West Wales, 1540-1640. 1968.   11.00   ..... (795)
Pine, L. G. Princes of Wales. 208pp.
  Recounts the history of the title of Prince of Wales from
  1284 to the present day.   5.00   ..... (772)
Rees, William. Historical Atlas of Wales: From Early to Modern
  Times. Repr. of 1951 ed.   5.50   ..... (233)
Rhys, John and David B. Jones. Welsh People: Chapter on Their
  Origin, History, Laws, Language, Literature and Characteristics.
  4th ed. Repr. of 1906 ed.   23.25   ..... (297)
Savory, H. J. Geography of Wales. 1968.   3.95   ..... (114)
Welsh-English, English-Welsh Gem Pocket Dictionary.   3.95   ..... (153)

Scotland

Research Aids

Black, George F. Surnames of Scotland; Their Origin, Meaning,
  and History.   10.00   ..... (635)
Bloxham, Ben V. Key to the Parochial Registers of Scotland.
  1970. 463pp.
    Genealogical research in Scotland prior to 1854; an
    indispensable and standard reference to registers of
    over 900 parishes. 6.95 (92)
Genealogical Society of the LDS Church. The Social, Economic,
  Religious and Historical Background of Scotland As It Affects
  Genealogical Research. 8pp. 85 (275)
  _____. Major Genealogical Record Sources in Scotland. 5pp. 85 (275)
Munro, R.W., ed. The Gazetteer of Scotland. 1974.   14.95   ..... (93)

General Information

Bain, Robert. Clans and Tartans of Scotland. rev. ed.   8.95   6.95 (153)

Brown, Peter Hume. History of Scotland. 3 vols. 1900-1909.

Each:	19.00	.....	(2)
Set:	55.00	.....	(2)

Chadwick, H. M. Early Scotland: The Picts, the Scots and
the Welsh of Southern Scotland. 1972. 10.50 ..... (552)

Church of Scotland, General Assembly. Acts and Proceedings of
the General Assemblies of the Kirk of Scotland, from the
Year MDLX. Collected from the Most Authentic Manuscripts.
ed. Thomas Thomson. (Also Known as "The Booke, of the
Universall Kirk of Scotland"). 3 vols. 1839-1845. Set: 125.00 ..... (2)

Church of Scotland. Register of Ministers, Exhorters and
Readers and of Their Stipends, after the Period of the
Reformation. ed. Alexander Macdonald. 1830. 15.00 ..... (2)

Colahan, Thomas S. The Cautious Revolutionaries: The Scottish
Middle Classes In the Making of the Scottish Revolt 1637-1638.
1962. 254pp. BIP-62-04226. .... (777)

Craigie, William and A. J. Aitken, eds. Dictionary of the
Older Scottish Tongue. 4 vols. 26 pts. 1970. Each: 13.50 ..... (137)
                                               Set: 190.00 ..... (137)

_____. A Dictionary of the Older Scottish Tongue, Volume 4.
1973. 47.50 ..... (137)

Ferguson, William. Scotland: 1689 to the Present. 1968. 14.50 ..... (52)

Fullarton, John, ed. Records of the Burgh of Prestwick in the
Sheriffdom of Ayr. MCCCCLXX-MDCCLXXXII. 1834. 20.00 ..... (2)

Green, E. R., ed. Essays in Scotch-Irish History. 1969. 6.00 ..... (362)

Grimble, Ian. Scottish Clans and Tartans. 1973. 5.95 ..... (770)

Hamilton, William. Descriptions of the Sheriffdoms of Lanark
and Renfrew 1831. Repr. of 1831 ed. 34.50 ..... (2)

Johnston, James B. The Scottish Macs: Their Derivation and
Origin. Repr. of 1922 ed. 6.00 ..... (266)

Lang, Andrew. A History of Scotland; from the Roman Occupation.
rev. ed. 1903-1907. 4 vols. Each: 21.50 ..... (2)
                                  Set: 82.50 ..... (2)

Leslie, John, Bishop of Ross. The History of Scotland, from the
Death of King James I, in the Year MCCCCXXXVI to the
Year MDLXI. ed. Thomas Thomson. 1830. 42.50 ..... (2)

_____. Historie of Scotland. eds. E.G. Cody and William
Murison. tr. James Dalrymple. 2 vols. Repr. of 1888-95 eds.
Set: 64.50 ..... (394)

MacDonald, Donald F. Scotland's Shifting Population 1770-1850.
1937. 172pp. 11.00 ..... (273)

McDowall, William. History of the Burgh of Dumfries. Repr.
of 1906 ed. 31.50 ..... (93)

Mackenzie, William Cook. The Highlands and Isles of Scotland;
A Historical Survey. 1937. Description. Local History. 14.50 ..... (2)

Maclean, Fitzroy. Concise History of Scotland. 1970. 8.95 ..... (797)

Mitchison, Rosalind. History of Scotland. 1970. 12.00 6.00 (52)

Pitcairn, Robert, ed. Ancient Criminal Trials in Scotland, from
A.D. MCCCCLXXXVIII to A.D. MDCXXIV. . . Compiled
from the Original Records and Mss., with Historical Notes
and Illustrations and c. by Robert Pitcairn, Esq. 1833.
3 vols. in 4. Set: 205.00 ..... (2)

Scarlett, James D. Tartans of Scotland. 3.50 ..... (321)

Scotland, Court of Teinds. Reports on the State of Certain Parishes
in Scotland, Made to His Majesty's Commissioners for
Plantation of Kirks, & c. in Pursuance of Their Ordinance
Dated April XII. MDCXXVII. From the Originals Preserved
in His Majesty's General Register House. 1835.   24.50   ..... (2)
Selkirk, Thomas D. Observations on the Present State of the
Highlands of Scotland, with a View of the Causes and Probable
Consequences of Emigration. Repr. of 1805 ed.   14.00   ..... (394)
Watson, John. The Scot of the Eighteenth Century. 1973.   20.00   ..... (245)
Wodrow, Robert, Rev. Collections upon the Lives of the
Reformers and Most Eminent Ministers of the Church of
Scotland. 2 vols. in 3 parts. 1834-1848.   Set: 105.00   ..... (2)

Ireland

[Also see "Ireland" under ENGLAND - page 335]

Research Aids

The Genealogical Society of The Church of Jesus Christ of
Latterday Saints. Major Genealogical Record Sources in
Ireland. 7pp. 85 (275)
Joyce, P. W. Irish Names of Places. 4th ed. Repr. of 1875
ed.   25.00   ..... (93)
Kennedy, James F. Sources for the Early History of Ireland:
Ecclesiastical. 1967.   26.00   ..... (552)
Lewis, Samuel. Topographical Dictionary of Ireland. 3 vols.
Repr. of 1837 ed.   Set: 150.00   ..... (404)
Matheson, Sir Robert E. Special Report on Surnames in Ireland.
Repr. of 1901, 1905 ed. 78, 94pp.   11.00   ..... (274)
National Library of Ireland - Dublin. Manuscript Sources for
the History of Irish Civilisation. 11 vols. 1965.   Set: 880.00   ..... (307)
Smythe-Wood, Patrick, F.S.G., ed. Index to Kilmore Diocesan
Wills. 1975. 80pp.
      Comprises a) Betham copy of the Index dated to 1838,
      b) entries transcribed from the original (now fragmentary)
      Index to 1858, c) Kilmore entries extracted (1838-1858)
      from the Index to the Irish Will Registers. Surface mail: $6.   By air: 7.50 (701)
Taylor, George and Andrew Skinner. Maps of the Roads of
Ireland.   17.65   ..... (379)

General References

Black, J. Anderson. Your Irish Ancestors: An Illustrated
History of Irish Families. 1974.   14.95   ..... (774)
Carty, James, ed. Ireland. 2 vols. Volume 1 - A Documentary
Record, from the Flight of the Earls to Grattan's Parliament,
1607-1782. Volume 2 - A Documentary Record, from
Grattan's Parliament to the Great Famine, 1783-1850.
                                              Each: 4.75   ..... (207)
Davitt, Michael. The Fall of Feudalism in Ireland: Or, The
Story of the Land League Revolution. Repr. of 1904 ed. 751pp.   25.00   ..... (661)
Edwards, Dudley. An Atlas of Irish History. 1973.   11.50   5.75 (52)
_____ and T. Desmond Williams, eds. The Great Famine:
Studies in Irish History, 1845-1852. 2d ed. Repr. of 1957 ed.   27.50   ..... (662)
Falls, Cyril. The Birth of Ulster. Repr. of 1936 ed.   16.00   ..... (52)

Four Masters. Annals of the Kingdom of Ireland from the Earliest
Period to the Year 1616. Edited from Manuscripts in the
Library of the Royal Irish Academy and of Trinity College,
Dublin, With a Translation, and Copious Notes, by John
O'Donovan. 7 vols. 1854.

> The chief impetus to modern Anglo-Irish-Celtic studies
> in history and literature can be said to have been
> O'Donovan's editing, amplification and translation of
> the Annals of the Four Masters.   Set: 340.00   ..... (2)
>
>   Each: 49.50   ..... (2)

Hill, George. An Historical Account of the Plantation in
Ulster at the Commencement of the 17th Century. 1608-1620.
Repr. of 1877 ed. 624pp.   30.00   ..... (661)

Lecky, William Edward Hartpole. A History of Ireland in the
Eighteenth Century. 5 vols. 1892-1893.   Set: 57.50   ..... (2)

                                            Each: 15.00   ..... (2)

Lodge, John. The Peerage of Ireland; Or, A Genealogical
History of the Present Nobility of That Kingdom . . . Collected from Public Documents . . . Revised, Enlarged and
Continued to the Present Time by Tervyn Archdall. 7 vols.
1789.   Set: 150.00   ..... (2)

                                            Each: 22.50   ..... (2)

O'Hart, John. Irish Pedigrees, The Origin and Stem of the
Irish Nation. Repr. of 1892 ed. 896, 948pp.   50.00   ..... (274)

Percival-Maxwell, M. Scottish Migration to Ulster in the Reign
of James First. 1974.   17.25   ..... (362)

Petty, Sir William. The History of the Survey of Ireland, Commonly Called the Down Survey, ed. Thomas Larcom. 1851.
426pp. index.   17.50   ..... (273)

OTHER FOREIGN

Genealogical Society of the LDS. Major Genealogical Records in
Austria. 15pp. 85 (275)

_____. The Austro-Hungarian Empire Boundary Changes and
Their Effect Upon Genealogical Research. 7pp. 85 (275)

_____. The Social, Economic, Religious, and Historical Back-
ground of Denmark As It Affects Genealogical Research. 9pp. 85 (275)

_____. Census Records of Denmark. 14pp. 85 (275)

_____. Church Records of Denmark. 11pp. 85 (275)

_____. Military Levying Rolls of Denmark. 6pp. 85 (275)

_____. The Probate Records of Denmark. 16pp. 85 (275)

_____. Major Genealogical Record Sources in Finland. 5pp. 85 (275)

_____. Boundary Changes of the Former German Empire and
Their Effect Upon Genealogical Research. 7pp. 85 (275)

_____. Major Genealogical Record Sources in Germany. 5pp. 85 (275)

_____. The Social, Economic, Religious, and Historical Background
of Germany and Austria As It Affects Genealogical Research. 14pp. 85 (275)

_____. Major Genealogical Record Sources in Hungary. 6pp. 85 (275)

_____. Major Genealogical Record Sources in Italy. 9pp. 85 (275)

_____. The Census Records of Norway. 7pp. 85 (275)

_____. Church Records of Norway. 8pp. 85 (275)

_____. Major Genealogical Record Sources in Norway. 5pp. 85 (275)

_____. The Probate Records of Norway. 10pp. 85 (275)

_____. Church Records of Sweden. 19pp. 85 (275)

_____. Major Genealogical Record Sources in Sweden. 5pp. 85 (275)

_____. The Social, Economic, Religious, and Historical Back-
ground of Sweden As It Affects Genealogical Research. 18pp. 85 (275)

Family Genealogies

1 - SOME SOUTHERN TALBERTS by Eugene Talbert Aldridge and Alelaide
   (Martin) Aldridge, 1975.
   Talberts: Contains four Talbert lines. Sixty photos and maps. Surname index.
   Cloth-300pp-$20. 00 --- - Vendor   #13

2 - BROOKS MOON WILLINGHAM AND HIS DESCENDANTS by Chester Morse and
   Frances Sullivan Willingham, 1972.
   Willingham: Georgia-1790-1859; Texas-1859-date.
   Paper-86pp-$5. 00--- Vendor   #25

3 - WILLIAM RILEY OGDEN - HIS DESCENDANTS AND SOME ALLIED
   FAMILIES by Chester Morse Willingham and Frances Sullivan Willingham, 1973.
   Ogden: Alabama-1830-1833; Arkansas-1833-1867; Texas-1867-date. Book
   contains information pertaining to William Riley Ogden's brothers, David
   Lawrence Ogden and Frank Ogden, and their descendants.
   Paper-186pp-$10. 00--Vendor   #25

4 - HENRY CAVINIS, THE IMMIGRANT INFANT: AND SOME OF HIS DESCEND-
   ANTS by Alloa C. Anderson (Mrs.), 1971.
   Cabanis: France-1675-1700; Virginia-1700-1720; Indiana and Iowa - 1740-date.
   Caviness: North Carolina-1800-date; Texas-1840-date.
   Vestal: England-1640-1690; Pennsylvania-1690-1751; North Carolina-1751- date.
   Chamness: England-1713-1730; Maryland-1730-1777.
   Os(z)bun: England-1710-1728; Pennsylvania-1728-1752.
   Osborn: North Carolina-1752-date; Iowa-1840-date.
   Wolcott: England-1550-1630; Connecticut-1630-1800; Ohio-1800-1870.
   Descendants, immigrant son. "V" spellings - more than fifty variations.
   Paper-526pp-index-$25. 00----------------------------------- Vendor   #27

5 HISTORY AND GENEALOGY OF THE LEXINGTON, MASSACHUSETTS
   MUNROES by Richard S. Munroe, 1966.
   Munroes in all locations descended from William Munroe of Lexington, Mass.
   Cloth-468pp-$6. 50---Vendor   # 7

6 - R. P. ANDERSON, HIS ANCESTORS AND DESCENDANTS by Alloa C.
   Anderson, 1971.
   Anderson: Skane, Sweden-1860-1879; Muskegon, Michigan-1879-1900; Chicago-
   1900-1905; Port Huron, Michigan-1905-1909.
   Torgeson: Larvik, Norway-1826-1853; Muskegon, Michigan-1853-19- .
   Ferguson: Grand Rapids, Michigan-1845-1932.
   Glasius: Denmark-1833-1923; Youngstown, Ohio-1923-1930; Grosse Ile,
   Michigan-1930-date.
   Stienon: Belgium-1866-1914; London, England-1914-1940; Ann Arbor, Michigan-
   1940-date.
   Layton: London, England-1820-1925; Flint, Michigan-1925-1969.
   Oltman: Netherlands-1850-1875; Grand Rapids, Michigan-1875-date.
   Boer: Netherlands-1860-1876; Holland, Michigan-1876-date.
   Hutcheson: England-1602-1634; Salem, Massachusetts-1634-1820.
   Knappen: Wales-1750-1771; Vermont-1771-1831.
   Paper-180pp-index-$15. 00---------------------------------- Vendor   #27

7   -VASS AND ALLIED FAMILIES: THE DESCENDANTS OF VINCENT AND MARY
MARY (COSNER) VASS by Alvin L. Anderson, 1975.
Vass: North Carolina, Stokes Co.-1790(?)-1833; Indiana, Hendricks Co.-
1833-1849; Iowa, Wapello Co.-1849-date. 977 Descendants.
Paper-169+pp-Index-$5.00 -------------------------------------Vendor   #28

8   - SATURDAY'S CHILDREN: A HISTORY OF THE BABCOCK FAMILY by
C. Merton Babcock, 1974.
Babcock: Rhode Island-1640-1799; New York State-1800-1840; Wisconsin and
Minnesota-1840- date. .
A history of the Babcock family, and over thirty allied families (of Rhode
Island, Connecticut and Massachusetts) including Burdicks, Thayers, and
Masons. (Includes genealogies).
Paper-250pp-$20.00 --- Vendor   #46

9   - THE BAKER FAMILY AND THE EDGAR FAMILY OF RAHWAY, N.J. AND
NEW YORK CITY by John Milnes Baker, 1972.
Genealogy of Descendants of Jacobus Backer and Margaret (Stuyvesant)
Ba(c)ker, New Amsterdam 1653, and New Jersey 1677. Also Kentucky 1792.
Over 200 biographies and 70 spouses' genealogical charts, 75 photos, index,
three 19th century diaries, many New England lines. A valuable reference.
Cloth-466pp-$37.50 -- Vendor   #48

10   - THE BALLS OF FAIRFAX AND STAFFORD IN VIRGINIA by Bonnie S.
Ball, 1976, reprint.
Cloth-$15.00 ---Vendor   #49

11   - THE HATFIELDS AND THE McCOYS by Virgil C. Jones, 1974.
Hatfield-McCoy Feud.
Paper-$1.75 -- Vendor   #50

12   - LYON MEMORIAL BOOK IV, BICENTENNIAL ISSUE by John Smith,
Esq., ed., 1976.
Contains 5,000 names with 62 Lyon lineages. Data is included on Lyon(s)
in the Revolutionary War.
Paper-c280pp-$10.00 --- Vendor   #54

13   - PATTON EXCHANGE LETTER edited by Elaine Elliott Beebe, Jan., 1977.
Published yearly. Names and addresses of people researching Patton,
marriage, land, census records, etc. Queries free and encouraged to give
all known data.
Paper-$3.00 -- Vendor   #60

14   - SELECTED NAMES IN 1850 OHIO CENSUS by Elaine Elliott Beebe, Dec., 1976.
Full census readout on following families: Boggs, Elliott, Fairley, Ferguson,
Holiday, Kirkpatrick, McClintock, McCune, Mitchel, Morrow, Patton, Steel,
Vanneman, all spellings.
Paper-$3.00(?) -- Vendor   #60

15   - THE WOTRING-WOODRING FAMILY by Raymond Martin Bell, assisted by
Edna Jordan and the late Mabel Ghering Granquist, 1968.
Pennsylvania.
Paper-20pp-$2.00 --Vendor   #61

16   - THE BASKIN(S) FAMILY by Raymond Martin Bell, 1975.
South Carolina; Pennsylvania; with Stephens and Martin notes.
Paper-50pp-$5.00 --Vendor   #61

17   - GRANDPARENTS ARE GREAT! THE GENEALOGY AND HISTORY OF THE
     DORSEY, PALMER, MOSHER AND ADAMS FAMILIES: WITH ALLIED FAM-
     ILIES by Lois Colette Dorsey Bennington, Fall, 1976.
     Dorsey: Maryland, Ann Arundel Co.-1650-1850; Kentucky, Jefferson Co.-
     1810-1875; Indiana, Dearborn Co.-1811-1860; Nebraska, Johnson, Nance Co.-
     1857-1939.
     Palmer: Plymouth Colony, Mass.-1637-1661; New York, Dutchess Co.-1740-1812.
     Mosher: Dartmouth, Bristol Co., Mass.-1633-1770; Sarotoga Co., New
     York-1770-1875.
     Adams: Watertown, Mass.-1645-1699; Simsbury, Conn., Windsor, Conn.-
     1700-1850.
     Included in the "Allied Section," the relationship of the Dorsey family to
     Wallis Warfield Simpson; the James Brothers, Frank and Jesse; Abraham
     Lincoln . . . . Other allied Lines . . . . Avery, Buttolph, Chesebrough,
     Darling, Feake, Finch, Gaylord, Greenbury, Griffith, Griswold, Hayden,
     Howard, Lindsay, Phelps, Packer, Strong, Trumbull, Todd, Walworth,
     Wells, Wyatt . . . . "Many others."
     Paper-app. 250pp+-$12.50 ------------------------------------- Vendor   #63

18   - DAVIS, JESSE BUFORD-DESCENDANTS, ANCESTORS, CONNECTING
     FAMILIES by Mrs. Betty (Davis) Berndt, 1973.
     Davis, Jesse Buford: Whitley Co., Kentucky-1845; S. Lineville, Missouri-1871;
     Mercer, Missouri-1928.
     His eleven children to date, father Melton Lewis, grandfather William (one
     armed Billie), Whitley Co., Kentucky early 1800's. Connecting families of
     Title second son.
     Paper-348pp-$15.00 -- Vendor   #65

19   - THE PETTY AND FRANCIS FAMILIES AND ALLIED LINES by Mrs. Zora
     Petty Billingsley, 1967, 1969, 1971, 1975, Index.
     Petty: Georgia-182?-184?; DeKalb Co., Alabama-184?-1877.
     Deeds, Wills, family narratives, pictures, coats of arms. Supplements con-
     tain additional research as well as current happenings of original data published
     in 1967.
     Paper-240pp-$18.00 -- Vendor   #67

20   - THE TUNIS HOOD FAMILY: ITS LINEAGE AND TRADITIONS by Dellmann
     O. Hood, 1960.
     Genealogy of the Hood family in the Carolinas, Virginia, Arkansas, and
     westward to the Pacific Coast from 1695 to the present. Author researched
     for twelve years in this country and abroad to gather and verify the voluminous
     detail in this historic record. 46 illustrations. Every-name index.
     Cloth-666pp-$17.50 ---Vendor   #68

21   - THE BIRDSALL FAMILY by George A. Birdsall, 1976.
     Contains every Birdsall author could find in U.S. and Canada from 1400 A.D.
     to the present listed by families where possible. Completely revised since
     1964.
     (In process)-300pp -- Vendor   #70

22   - BOONE PIONEER ECHOES, edited by Louis Raymond Boone, 4 issues
     per year.
     Boon, Boone: All descendants of families in United States, from England
     and Germany.
     Paper-$3.00 yr. --- Vendor   #82

23   - THE BORDNER AND BURTNER FAMILIES AND THEIR BORTNER
      ANCESTORS IN AMERICA by Howard W. Bordner, 1971, reprint of
      1967 edition.
      Genealogical data on all Bordners and Burtners and their ancestors in
      America. Also background of Pennsylvania Dutch in Pennsylvania and
      Europe. Coat-of-arms.
      Paper-362pp-$8.75 -- Vendor   #83

24   - BLALOCKS - RELATED FAMILIES - OF CASS COUNTY, TEXAS by
      Mrs. Myreline Bowman, 1976.
      Pedigrees, history of each family, pictures, indexed. Each family will go
      back as far as their records and come down to present day.
      Cloth-$25.00-Paper-$22.00-250-300pp --------------------------Vendor   #86

25   - TALLEY - LINDSEYS - RELATED FAMILIES - OF CASS COUNTY,
      TEXAS by Mrs. Myreline Bowman, 1976.
      Wills, records of all kinds, sourced records, histories, pedigrees and
      families from back years to present day records. Indexed.
      Cloth-$25.00-Paper-$22.00-250-300pp --------------------------Vendor   #86

26   - DAILEY - ADAMS - RELATED FAMILIES OF CASS COUNTY, TEXAS by
      Mrs. Myreline Bowman, 1976.
      Pictures, Pedigrees, Histories of each family, families as far back as
      their records and to present day. Indexed.
      Cloth-$20.00-Paper-$17.00-150-175pp --------------------------Vendor   #86

27   - ANCESTRAL LINES: 144 FAMILIES IN ENGLAND, GERMANY, NEW
      ENGLAND, NEW YORK, NEW JERSEY AND PENNSYLVANIA, 1975.
      Genealogy of compiler's children; families given alphabetically, mostly
      colonial including Mayflower lines, early Quakers, Pennsylvania Dutch;
      bibliography, name and place indices; information for SASE
      Cloth-487pp-$25.00 --- Vendor   #88

28   - THE BOYDS OF BOYDS TANK by Frank E. Boyd and W. Taylor Boyd, 1970.
      Boyd: Pennsylvania-16?-1700's; Virginia-17?-1800's; Georgia-17?-1800's;
      Alabama-18?-1900's.
      The Boyds of Boyds Tank covers the line of descent from Scotland to Pennsyl-
      vania, Virginia, Georgia, Alabama, Texas, the migration period about
      300 years. The Boyds moved inland. Today they are in practically every
      state. Related families included in the book are: Adams, Beall, Bruce,
      Glass, Hart, Heard, Hudson, Hunt, Lewis, Oakes, Scott, Slaton.
      Cloth-107pp-$5.00 ---Vendor   #87

29   - DESCENDANTS OF JOHANN ADAM AND ANNA MARIA BECKENBACH by
      Edwin T. and Atha Peckenpaugh Brace, 1975.
      Forty-six different spellings of Beckenbach, including Beckenbaugh, Peck-
      enpaugh, Peckinpah, Peckinpaugh, Pickenpaugh, evolved between 1751 and
      1853 as this family migrated from Maryland to California.
      Cloth-468pp-$12.50 ---Vendor   #89

30   - JOHNSTON'S CLAN HISTORIES SERIES by various authors, 1974.
      Histories of the following clans - giving tartan, etc.: Mackenzie, Mackintosh,
      Scott, Fraser, Munro, Donald, Grant, Macleod, Macgregor, Mackay, Maclean,
      Campbell, Ross, Macrae, Robertson, Morrison, Graham, Stewart.
      Paper-$2.50 for each family -----------------------------------Vendor   #93

31 - SVEN NJELLSON (NELSON)/AARSVOLL AND GRETE MARIE HANS-
DAUGHTER, THEIR DESCENDANTS IN NORTH AMERICA by Gwendolyn
Irene Brouse, 1974.
Njellson/Aarsvold: Saskatchewan, Canada-1900-date; Hyland, Norway-1500-
1900; Minnesota-1880-date; Iowa-1800-1900.
Paper-144pp-Index-$7.50 ------------------------------------ Vendor   #95

32 - THE BENJAMIN FAMIL Y IN AMERICA by Gloria Wall Bicha and Helen
Benjamin Brown, late 1976.
Benjamin: All-mainly U.S. and Canada-1632-1875.
Covers both the John[1] and Richard[1] lines from 1632 through 8 generations.
Only complete Benjamin genealogy heretofor published. Fully indexed.
Cloth-1000+pp-approx. $25.00 -------------------------------- Vendor   #96

33 - CASTEEL'S EVERYWHERE - Vol. 1 Southern Branch by Jean Casteel
Brown, 1977.
Casteel: Tennessee-1780-1900; Kentucky-1780-1900; Missouri-1820-1900;
Arkansas-1815-1900.
A reference book for Casteel's from Pennsylvania, Maryland and Virginia,
through the southern states and westward.
(In process) -- Vendor   #97

34 - GENEALOGY OF THE BROWN FAMILY AND ALLIED FAMILIES: CHAPIN,
MURRAY, ALLEN by Dorothy E. Brown, 1975.
Brown: Pennsylvania, Luzerne Co.-1780-1820; New York State-1820;
Michigan-1873.
Paper-70pp-$7.95 ---Vendor   #98

35 - ANCESTORS AND DESCENDANTS OF JUSTUS H. AKIN OF RENSSELAER
COUNTY, NEW YORK by Daphne M. Brownell, 1971.
Akin: Dartmouth, Massachusetts-1662-1742; Dutchess Co., New York-1742-
1800; Rensselaer Co., New York-1800-1971; Throughout United States-1850-1971.
Kroydon-flex morocco cover-256pp-$10.50 ----------------------Vendor   #101

36 - KILGORE'S TREE, Editor-JoAnn Burgess, Volume I-May,1975-Feb.,1976.
Devoted to all Kilgore families in U.S. Includes copied records, biographical
sketches, maternal lines, queries. Back issues $1.00 each, queries $1.00
each, free to subscribers.
Quarterly-16 pages per issue-$4.00 year--------------------------Vendor   #106

37 - THE DARDEN FAMILY HISTORY by Newton Jasper Darden, Leroy W.
Tilton, ed., 1971, reprint of 1957 ed.
Darden Ancestry and allied Families: Washington, Lanier, Burch, Strozier,
Dodson, Pyles, McNair, Burnett in Virginia, Georgia, Tennessee, Alabama,
Mississippi, Texas.
Paper-190pp-$22.00 --Vendor   #108

38 - PETER GRANT, SCOTCH EXILE, BERWICK, ME. HIS STORY by
Leola Grant Bushman, 1971.
His adventures in the Colonies, following some of the family through the
Civil War. Some genealogy.
Paper-180pp-$12.50 -- Vendor   #109

39 - PETER GRANT (1631-1721) GENEALOGY by Leola Grant Bushman, 1976.
Descendants of Peter Grant, Scotch Exile, who came as prisoner of Oliver
Cromwell, sold into bondage, when freed settled at Berwick, Maine, ca 1652.
Velo Hard-$24.50-Paper-$15.00-258pp------------------------Vendor   #109

40   - THE GENEALOGY OF FRANCIS WEEKS OF OYSTER BAY, LONG ISLAND
        TOGETHER WITH NOTES ON POSSIBLE FAMILY TIES AND DESCENDANTS
        compiled by Charles Edwin Weeks (1920), edited (from carbon-typed copy) by
        B. S. Buys, 1967.
        Charles Edwin Weeks own research. Edited from his original notebooks.
        Emphasis on Fishkill family and descendants, but Long Island and Westchester
        data, too.
        Paper-54pp-$15.00 --- Vendor   #110

41   THE CALLAWAY JOURNAL, published by The Callaway Family Assoc., Inc.
        Callaway Records. Virginia Tax Lists - 1782 to 1800; North Carolina -
        Onslow and Carteret counties, 18th century; England - 17th century.
        Paper-abt. 55pp-$6.00 --- Vendor   #113

42   - THE HOUNSHELL FAMILY OF SOUTHWEST VIRGINIA by Clifford R.
        Canfield, 1973.
        Hounshell: Wythe County, Virginia-1760's-1973.
        Paper-527pp-$15.00 ---Vendor   #116

43   - CARMAN CHRONICLES, Vol. I by Clarice Eland Carman, 1976.
        Carman and Allied Families: England-1066-1600; New England-1600; North
        Carolina-1700; Kentucky-1800.
        Paper-abt. 100pp-$5.95   -------------------------------------Vendor   #119

44   - DESCENDANTS OF TIMOTHY CARPENTER OF RENSSELAER CO.,
        NEW YORK, compiled by Rear Admiral Charles L. Carpenter, c1976.
        Genealogical carry down known descendants of Timothy Carpenter who
        settled in Pittstown, Rensselaer County, New York in 1775, having re-
        moved there from Dutchess County.
        Paper-200+pp-$12.50 ---Vendor   #123

45   - THE BOWMANS, A PIONEERING FAMILY IN VIRGINIA, KENTUCKY AND
        THE NORTHWEST TERRITORY by John W. Wayland, 1974, reprint of 1943 ed.
        some genealogy and exploits of four brothers, grandsons of Jost Hite,
        pioneer. All four brothers were officers in the American Revolution.
        Cloth-192pp-$11.50 ---Vendor   #124

46   - OUR KIN by Mary Denham Ackerly and Lula Eastman Jeter Parker, 1976,
        reprint of 1930 ed.
        The genealogies of some of the early families who made history in the
        founding and development of Bedford County, Virginia.
        Cloth-845pp-$37.50 --- Vendor   #124

47   - VIRGINIA COUSINS by G. Brown Goode, 1974, reprint of 1887 ed.
        The ancestry of John Goode of Whitby, a Virginia Colonist. A history of
        the English name Gode, Goad, Goode, and Good from 1148 to 1887.
        Cloth-562pp-$20.00 --- Vendor   #124

48   - SETTLERS BY THE LONG GREY TRAIL by J. Houston Harrison, 1975,
        reprint of 1935 ed.
        Some Pioneer families of Old Augusta County, Virginia and their descendants
        of the family of Harrison and allied lines. Present day Rockingham County,
        Virginia families.
        Cloth-665pp-$25.00 ---Vendor   #124

49   - GENEALOGY OF THE PAGE FAMILY IN VIRGINIA by Richard Channing
Moore Page, 1972, reprint of 1893 ed.
Containing a condensed account of the Nelson, Walker, Pendleton and
Randolph families. References to Bland, Byrd, Cary, Duke, Rives,
Washington and others.
Cloth-288pp-$12.50 ---Vendor   #124

50   - THE DESCENDANTS OF CAPT. THOMAS CARTER OF "BARFORD,"
LANCASTER COUNTY, VIRGINIA by Joseph Lyon Miller, Dr., 1972,
reprint of 1912 ed.
A thorough documentation of the Carter family, 1652-1912. The descendants
of the sons of Capt. Thomas Carter, divided into sections in this book.
Cloth-388pp-$17.50 -- Vendor   #124

51   - A CARTWRIGHT ODYSSEY OR THREE REBELS FROM SHARON by
Lloyd J. Cartwright, 1976, reprint of 1975 ed.
Family history from Edward of Isles of Shoals (1670) and three Revolutionary
soldiers from Sharon, Conn. Maps, pedigree charts, photos. Indexed.
Over 1300 names.
Cloth-220pp-$10.50 ---Vendor   #125

52   - THE CASON QUARTERLY by The Cason Family Assn., Wm. R. Cason, Ed.
Four issues/yr. Approximately 16 pp /issue. Back issues available $1.50 per.
Complete file of back issues (3 yrs.)/$15.00. All of Cason-Caison-Cayson
surname invited to subscribe.
Paper-$5.00 ---Vendor   #126

53   - WYNN/WINN - DANIEL AND HIS NINE SONS, compiled by Naomi (Giles)
Chadwick.
Virginia-1750-1800; North Carolina-1800-1814; Tennessee-1814-1868.
Seventy pages of photos, illustrations, charts.
Paper Hi Tone Binder-225pp-8 1/2 x 11-$20.00 -------------------Vendor   #129

54   MEDEARIS, compiled by Naomi (Giles) Chadwick.
Descendants of Charles Medearis (will probated Guilford County, North
Carolina 1793) and Elizabeth Gregory. Ohio 1803; Kansas 1868.
Paper-90pp-$10.00 -- Vendor   #129

55   - BARDWELL/BORDWELL DESCENDANTS, Book 1 and Book 2, by Robert
Bardwell Descendants' American Ancestry Association. Edited by Portia
Chamberlain. Book 1: 1964. Book 2: 1974.
Index of names, 177 pages. Queries welcome.
Cloth-889pp-$31.00 ---Vendor   #131

56   - HUNDRED HUNTER COUSINS (GRANDCHILDREN OF BENJAMIN HUNTER)
Harriett A. Chilton, Compiler, Summer, 1976.
Hunter: Appomattox and Campbell Counties, Virginia-1760-1900.
Paper-25pp-$5.00 --Vendor   #139

57   - THE CLAGETT-CLAGGETT FAMILY AND ITS DESCENDANTS by Brice
M. Clagett, abt. 1979.
Genealogy of all Clagett-Claggett families in England, U.S. and other countries,
and of all families descended from Claggetts, no matter how remotely.
Abt. 5,000pp --- Vendor   #142

58   - COLBY CLARK CLAN by Neva Sturgill Clark, 1977.
Clark: Kentucky born-1805-1840; Clark Co., Indiana-1840-185?; Schuyler-
Sagamon Co., Illinois-186?-1865; Hancock Co., Illinois-1865.
Akers: Clark Co., Indiana born-1820-1850.
Burnette (Hosea): Kentucky-1820-1825; Saugamon-Hancock Co., Illinois-1825.
Langford: Mt. Mellmick, Queens Co., Ireland-1821-1853; Utica, Oneida Co.,
New York-1853-1856.
Jones (Thomas): Virginia-1788; Anderson Co., Tennessee-1809.
Haggard: England-1703-1720; Eastern Virginia-1720.
Tracing Colby Clark and wife Mary Hannah Akers from Kentucky and Indiana,
and descendants to Illinois.
Paper-50pp-$5.00 --- Vendor   #146

59   - STODGILLS - STOGDELLS - STURGILLS by Mrs. Neva Sturgill Clark,
1977-78.
Stodgill-Stogdell-Sturgill: Essex Co., Virginia-1650-1730; Orange Co., Virginia-
1730-1755; Orange Co., Virginia-Ashe Co., North Carolina-1755-182?;
Lawrence Co., Ohio-182?-date.
Franks: Essex Co., Virginia-1650-1720; Orange Co., Virginia-1720-1770.
Madison: Essex Co., Virginia-1690-1720; Orange Co., Virginia-1730-1765.
Hash(e): Grayson Co., Virginia-1770-1820.
King: Newport, Rhode Island-1793-1806.
Greer: Ashe Co., North Carolina-1820-1830.
Louderback: Pennsylvania-1818-1845; Lawrence-Jackson Co., Ohio-1846-1890.
Neal: Kentucky-1835-1865; Greene Co., Indiana-1865-1933.
Russell: Spencer, Owen Co., Indiana-1832-1870; Bloomfield, Greene Co.,
Indiana-1870-1940.
Rochelle: North Carolina-1900-1942.
Armstrong: Essex Co., Virginia-1720-1745.
Tracing my Sturgills through Virginia, North Carolina, Ohio, Illinois, Indiana
and Iowa.
Cloth-50pp-$5.00 --- Vendor   #146

60   - MABINOGI AN CLEM by Frederick Hedley Barker Climo and Percy
Lloyd Climo, January-1976.
Clemo-Climo-etc.: Cornwall, Great Britain-Fifth Century to Twentieth Century.
"The Story of the Children of Clem." A genealogical-historical book with
early Celtic origins and family story blended with Cornish history down through
the centuries. Maps, charts, pictures, lineages of Climo families in various
countries. Appendix, Index.
Cloth-250pp-$20.00 --- Vendor   #150

61   - JOHN MAY, JR. OF VIRGINIA: HIS DESCENDANTS AND THEIR LAND by
Ben H. Coke, 1975.
May: Petersburg, Virginia area-1720's to 20th Century; Other areas in Virginia-
1760's to 20th Century; Kentucky-1770's to 20th Century; Throughout U.S.-
1790's to 20th Century.
Cocke (Coke): Virginia-1630's-1790's; Kentucky-1790's-20th Century.
Love: Kentucky-1790's-20th Century; Missouri, Texas-1830's-20th Century.
Percefull: Kentucky-1790's-20th Century.
Joplin: Kentucky-1820's-20th Century; Missouri-1880's-20th Century.
Perrin: Botetourt-Bedford Co., Virginia-1810's-1850's; Tippecanoe-Clinton
Co., Indiana-1850's-20th Century.
Tompkins: Fayette Co., Kentucky-1790's-1840's; Missouri-1840's-20th Century.
Hobbs: Kentucky-1810's-20th Century; Arkansas, Georgia-1850's-20th Century.
Over 6000 people (with 1500 last names) who have lived in 49 states and several
foreign countries. Every-name index; 27 biographical sketches; maps; samples

of land documents and samples of handwriting; account of the May family's
extensive land holdings.
Cloth-383+-$13.00 ---Vendor   #151

62   - THINGS THAT COUNT, STORY OF THE COOKE FAMILY by Velma M.
     Cooke, 1974.
     Cooke: Rhode Island-1603-1792; North Carolina-1798-1834; Tennessee-1834-1835;
     Texas-1835-1974.
     Paper-93pp-$5.00 ---Vendor   #156

63   - MORE DESCENDANTS OF JOHN AND MARY COOLIDGE, WATERTOWN,
     MASS. 1630 by Lyle C. Coolidge, Lt. Col. USA (ret.), 1978.
     Extension of Coolidge genealogy published in 1930 for the four lines established
     by the only progenitor in America. All states.
     (Publication date about 1978) ---------------------------------Vendor   #157

64   MY ANCESTORS:LESTER, DUNCAN, DICKERSON AND SIMMONS by
     Leonard G. Lester, 1970.
     Lester, Duncan, Dickerson, and Simmons: Floyd and Montgomery Counties,
     Virginia—1752-1900. Lists Revolutionary soldiers of Lester and Duncan
     families. Census information from 1850-1880 Montgomery and Floyd County
     enumerations. Other documented information included. Simmons family
     (Surry Co. 1648, to Floyd Co. 1900). Dickerson intermarried with Duncan.
     Paper-35pp-$10.00 --Vendor   #158

65   HUDDLESTON DICTIONARY by Donald L. Cordell, 1976.
     Every Huddleston from ancient days to present times whose ancestry may
     or may not be known; with references, alphabetical by first and middle name.
     (In process) -- Vendor   #160

66   - HUDDLESTON FAMILY NEWSLETTER by Donald L. Cordell, 1976 Quarterly.
     Huddleston history, ancient and present; plus an introduction to the skills and
     arts of our present day Huddleston cousins. Data, unavailable, in Huddleston
     books.
     Paper-$3.00--Vendor   #160

67   - HUDDLESTUN FAMILY, A BRIEF HISTORY OF, 1109-1940 by Ira W.
     Huddlestun of Yale, Illinois, 1976, reprint of 1940 ed.
     Descendants of Henry Huddleston (d. 1706) of Bucks County, Pennsylvania,
     who settled in East Central Illinois about 1830.
     Cloth-$6.00-Paper-$3.00-64pp ----------------------------- Vendor   #160

68   - HUDDLESTON-HUDDLESON-HUDELSON FAMILIES OF NORTH AMERICA
     by Donald L. Cordell, 6+volumes, 1976.
     An expansion of the original HUDDLESTON FAMILY TABLES in six (or more
     volumes) covers many immigrant lines heretofore unrecognized in original
     work.
     (In process)---Vendor   #160

69   - HUDDLESTON FAMILY TABLES by Congressman George Huddleston
     (1869-1960), reprint of 1933 ed.
     Represents 75 years of work by Sam'l B. Huddleston and other contributors,
     plus many years of loving labor by the author, with handwritten additions.
     Cloth-$18.00pp-Paper-$15.00pp-145pp(289pp) --------------------Vendor   #160

70   - COVINGTON AND KIN by Elbert E. Covington, 1975.
     Covington: Anson Co., North Carolina-1780-1854; Calhoun Co., Mississippi-
     1854-1922; Jackson Co., Illinois-1922-1976.
     Pictures, data on Bell, Tindall, Boyd, Bennett, Stewart, Dockery, Costner
     back to 1550.
     Cloth-$20.00-Paper-$17.00-202pp ----------------------------- Vendor   #166

71   - COLONEL JOSEPH HARDIN OF DAVIDSONVILLE: 1784-1826 by Marion
     Stark Craig, M.D.,1973.
     Hardin: Joseph Hardin was born 1784 in Rutherford County, North Carolina.
     This is a survey of his life, and that of his family and parents, in Rutherford
     County, and in the Western Lands of North Carolina that later became the State
     of Tennessee, and in the State of Kentucky, and in the Territories of Missouri
     and Arkansas. Joseph Hardin died August 25, 1826, at his residence in David-
     sonville, the county-seat of Lawrence County, Arkansas Territory, where he
     was Colonel of the Third Regiment of the Territorial Militia of Arkansas, and
     Sheriff. From Lawrence County have come, in whole or in part, 32 of the
     current 75 counties of the State of Arkansas. Included are the Revolutionary
     War Pension Application, and Obituary, of his father, Benjamin Hardin, a
     soldier of the Revolution and later Pensioner, who died April 2, 1848, in
     Christian Township, Independence County, Arkansas. Photocopies of numerous
     official legal instruments are included for positive documentations.
     Paper-124pp-$10.00 ---Vendor   #167

72   - McDOWELL AND RELATED FAMILIES - A GENEALOGY by John A. Crook,
     Jr., M.D., 1975.
     McDowell: Antrim, Ireland-1787; Rockbridge County-1803; Botetout County,
     Virginia-1827; Greenville, Tennessee-1865.
     McNair: Robeson, Scotland, and Richmond Counties, North Carolina-1865;
     Barbour County, Alabama-1900.
     McKay: Robeson, Scotland, and Richmond Counties, North Carolina-1865;
     Barbour County, Alabama-1927.
     Related families include Allen, Baker, Barnett, Boyes, Brown, Buie, Burkhart,
     Compton, Chronister, Crook, Dean, Delaney, Dent, Ellixon, Ely, Gage, Gillespie,
     Greer, Johnston, Lee, Levinski, Little, May, Mays, Maxwell, McBride, McDonald,
     McFarland, McGill, McKay, McNair, McRae, Moffett, Montalbano, Morgan, Pat-
     terson, Patton, Pritchard, Randall, Ramsey, Robalis, Sa unders, Singletary, Ste-
     wart, Stubbs, Sylvester, Thrush, VanPatton, Walker, Wilkerson, Williams, Wood,
     Woodley. These families are scattered over many of the 50 states. Geograph-
     ically the story involves the Shenendoah Valley of Virginia; Greeneville, Tenn.;
     Alabama; Robeson, Scotland, and Richmond Counties, N.C.; and other
     places. There's a great deal of early history of the Presbyterian Church and
     much Civil War history. It includes over 35 pictures and reproductions of
     daguerreotypes and tintypes of two Confederate soldiers in their uniforms.
     Portion of Confederate soldier's Civil War diary is included. The McDowells
     and most of the related families were Scotch-Irish immigrants.
     Cloth-$17.00-Paper-$14.00-117pp ---------------------------- Vendor   #169

73   - DOUBLEDAY FAMILIES OF AMERICA by Margaret B. Curfman, 1972.
     Doubleday: The most complete history ever published of two immigrant
     Doubleday families from England. One was in Boston 1672 and the other in
     Ohio 1833.
     Cloth-232pp-$15.00 -- Vendor   #174

74 -THE CURTIS FAMILY OF BUCKINGHAMSHIRE ENGLAND & WESTERN N.Y.
by Janet Austin Curtis, C.G., Summer 1976.
Curtis: Buckinghamshire, England—   -1880; Western New York—1881-present.
Profusely illustrated with maps, pictures, documents, charts and completely
indexed.
Paper-100+pp-$8.00-- Vendor   #175

75 -AUSTIN FAMILY OF VIRGINIA AND CAROLINA by Janet Austin Curtis, C.G.,
1980.
Austin: Southside Virginia-1740- present; North Carolina-1770-present; Georgia-
1770-present; Tennessee-1798- present.
Austins of Southside Virginia and their descendants in North Carolina, Georgia,
Tennessee and points west. Indexed.
Approximate no. of pages-400+--------------------------------- Vendor   #175

76 -DAFFT/DAFT FAMILY NEWSLETTER by P.R. Dafft, 1977.
Dafft/Daft: St. Mary's Co.,MD.-1690-1820; Ohio-1820-present; Texas-1850-
present; Virginia-1820-present.
10pages per issue-six issues per year-$5.00 per year------------- Vendor   #178

77 -BRITTAIN-BRATTAIN GLEANINGS (all spellings of name), edited by Joyce
M. Daugherty, 1975-
Brittain: Worldwide.
This is a research work. Mostly court records, census, etc. used as an aid to
help people know what has already been found on all spellings of the above names.
Not at a profit.
300 pages per year-six issues per year-$15.00 per year------------ Vendor   #180

78 -THE GARTH FAMILY by Rosalie Edith Davis, 1979.
Descendants of John Garth of Louisa Co., VA. Issue: Thomas, David, John,
Elizabeth Ross, Sarah Mousley (Mosby?), Mary Ann Lobbans 1733 to present.
(In process) --- Vendor   #183

79 -THE ANCIENT FAMILIES OF DEE AND DAY OF WALES, ENGLAND &
IRELAND by Leonard F. Day, Sr., 1972.
Day: Gloucester, Massachusetts. Many states.
Copy of and additions to the Genealogical Register of Robert Day of Hartford,
Connecticut.
Cloth-380pp-$30.00-- Vendor   #185

80 -THE DESCENDANTS OF CHRISTOPHER DAY OF BUCKS COUNTY, PA. by
Leonard F. Day, Sr..
Shows those who moved from Bucks County, Pa. to the mid-west and far west.
Also, there is a SUPPLEMENT to the DEE & DAY book of information which
arrived from Wales too late to be in the first book.
Paper-136pp-$12.00---Vendor   #185

81 -THE GRINDLE FAMILY OF MAINE by Priscilla Grindle DeAngelis, 1980.
Grindle, John: Portsmouth, N.H.-1690-about 1730.
I am planning to write a history of the Grindle Family of Maine and their
English antecedents - including Archbishop of Canterbury, Edmund Grindall
(1519?-1583).
(In process)--- Vendor   #186

82   -DORNING IN ENGLAND AND AMERICA by Barbara Dennis and Jeanne Walker,
      1974.
      Dorning: Lancashire, England—1630-1844; Racine Co., Wisconsin—1844-1877;
      Washington (state)—1877-present; Nebraska—1870-1910.
      Paper-86pp-$6.00-- Vendor   #189

83   -HERITAGE OF STILLWELLS AND MITCHELLS IN ARKANSAS by Robert W.
      Dhonau, c1977.
      Stillwell: Arkansas Post, Arkansas—1798-1822.
      Michel (Mitchell): Arkansas Post, Arkansas—1804-1831.
      Listing and biographies, if available, of known descendants of Joseph Stillwell
      and Francois Michel, pioneers in Territorial Arkansas. Paper binding.
      Information accepted.
      (In process) -- Vendor   #191

84   -THE REVISED DICKSON-McEWEN AND ALLIED FAMILIES GENEALOGY
      by Austin W. Smith, 1975, partial reprint of 1945 and 1958 editions.
      Genealogy of Dickson, McEwen and McKisick families, including biography of
      General Joseph Dickson. Reprint of 1946 book and 1958 supplement, plus
      new second supplement.
      Cloth-663pp-$15.00 ---------------------------------------Vendor   #194

85   -THE BOYDSTUN-BOYDSTON FAMILY by Gladys Boydstun Domonoske, 1975,
      revision of 1971 ed.
      Boylston-Boydston: Talbot Co., Maryland—1656-1666.
      Thomas Boylston immigrant ancestor 1656 from Renfrew Co., Scotland to
      Maryland.
      William Boylston-Boydston: Prince William Co., Virginia.
      David Boydston: Maryland; Southwest Virginia.
      David Boydston, Jr.: Pennsylvania
      James Boydston: Maryland, Southwest Virginia, North Carolina, Kentucky.
      Cloth-$13.50-Paper-$12.50-440pp------------------------------ Vendor   #198

86   -MARYLAND LIVERS FAMILY AND KIN (1699 to 1976) by Sister Mary Louise
      Donnelly, c1976.
      Livers: Arnold, Sr.: Prince Georges Co., Maryland—1699-1751; Frederick Co.,
      Maryland—1734-1751.
      (In process)---Vendor   #199

87   -MARYLAND ELDER FAMILY AND KIN by Sister Mary Louise Donnelly, 1975.
      William Elder (1707-1775), Emmittsburg, Maryland ancestors and descendants -
      including Archbishop Elder of Natchez, Mississippi and Cincinnati, Ohio. Some
      lines carried to 1975.
      Cloth-331pp-$15.00--- Vendor   #199

88   -OP DYCK GENEALOGY by Charles Wilson Opdyke, 1976, reprint of 1889 ed.
      Wesel Line from 1261 and American descendants of Gysbert. Holland Line
      from 1355 and American descendants of Louris Jansen. With illustrations.
      While supply lasts.
      Cloth-499pp-$30.00---Vendor   #205

89   -THE VERNON FAMILY by Janette M. Vernon Drotts, 1974.
      Vernon: Virginia—   -1798; North Carolina—1798-1839; Indiana—1839-1880;
      Illinois—1860-1904.
      Medearis/Medaris: Ohio—c1800-1851; Illinois—1851-1900.
      Harris: Ohio—1818-1840; Illinois—1840-1886.
      Paper-123pp-$9.00--- Vendor   #206

90 -THE DESCENDANTS OF ANDREW FORD OF WEYMOUTH, MASSACHUSETTS,
PART II by Mrs. Robert L. Eastwood, about 1979.
Part II will contain 7th generation to the present. Would like information
from and about descendants.
(In process) --- Vendor   #213

91 -HENRY SHARP (c1737-1800) OF SUSSEX COUNTY, NEW JERSEY & FAYETTE
COUNTY, PENNSYLVANIA AND HIS WIFE LYDIA MORGAN AND SOME OF THEIR
DESCENDANTS INCLUDING DEPUY, CHALFANT, SILVERTHORN AND WHEATLEY
FAMILIES by E.C.S. Eastwood & H.S. Wickliffe, 1975.
Walker: Clinton Co., Illinois—1814-present; Washington Co., Illinois—c1820-
present; Rush Co., Kansas—c1888; Denver, Colorado—1900.
Cloth-276pp-$25.00---Vendor   #213

92 - DESCENDANTS OF DOSWELL ROGERS by Eleanor Rogers Edmondson, 1976.
Doswell Rogers, Revolutionary Patriot, Montgomery and Lee Counties, Virginia;
descendants in Hawkins, White, Marion, Sequatchie Counties, Tennessee;
Eastland, Tarrant, Dallas Counties, Texas.
Cloth-250pp-$15.00-- Vendor   #214

93 - THE MIDDLETON FAMILY (INCLUDING MYDDELTON AND MYDDLETON)
RECORDS FROM WALES, ENGLAND, BARBADOS AND THE SOUTHERN
UNITED STATES by Beth Bland Engel, 1972.
Received the Donald Lines Jacobus award 1974, presented by the American
Society of Genealogists. A source book for anyone interested in the Middleton
name.
Cloth-330pp-$15.45--------------------------------------- Vendor   #219

94 - JOSEPH ENGLAND AND HIS DESCENDANTS by C. Walter England, 1975.
Joseph England settled in lower Chester Co., Pennsylvania (now Cecil Co.,
Maryland) in 1723. Genealogical and biographical data on Joseph and his
descendants. 9 maps, 11 plats, 49 photographs, 20 charts.
Cloth-464pp-8 1/2 x 11-$31.00 --------------------------- Vendor   #220

95 -THE CLENDINEN FAMILY: A CHRONICLE OF THE NAME FROM SCOTLAND
TO AMERICA, WITH EMPHASIS ON THOMAS CLENDINEN, HIS DESCENDANTS AND
RELATED FAMILIES by Anita C. Clendinen Enquist.
Clendinen: Cecil Co., Maryland—1770-1775-6; York Co., South Carolina—1776-1845;
Henry Co., Alabama—1846-1966; Houston Co., Alabama—c1885-1976.
White: Brookline, Massachusetts—c1640; Chatham, Baldwin Cos., Georgia—c1790.
---Vendor   #221

96 -PETER PINE ALEXANDER FAMILY by Edythe Fader, 1975.
Alexander, Peter Pine: Broome, Co., New York—1820-1856; Iowa and Vernon Cos.,
Wisconsin—1856-1887
Paper-51pp-$5.00 -- Vendor   #225

97 -WESTERN PIONEERS: THE DESCENDANTS OF PETER PINE ALEXANDER
by Edythe Fader, c1976 or early 1977.
Alexander: Montfort, Wisconsin—1878-1883; Waterville, Washington—1883-1910;
Mount Vernon, Washington—1910-1930.
Covers the lives of the one daughter and six sons of Peter Pine and Eliza McClure
Alexander.
Paper-c400pp-about $12.50-------------------------------- Vendor   #225

98   -MARTIN FAMILY QUARTERLY edited by Michal Martin Farmer, 1975.
      Martin: Wills, Bible Records, Marriages, Rev. Soldiers, Cemetery Research
      & Documented Family Lines in the U.S. from 1650-1900. Free queries for
      subscribers.
      86 pages per year-$5.00 per year------------------------------- Vendor   #229

99   -DANIEL MEADOWS & HIS DESCENDANTS by Michal Martin Farmer, 1976.
      Meadows: Greene Co., Georgia—1800-1835; Coweta Co., Georgia—1835-1976;
      Heard & Troup Cos., Georgia—1840-1976; Claiborne Parish, Louisiana—1853-1976.
      Over 600 descendants of Daniel Meadows, born 1779, North Carolina and his
      wife, Ann Thompson, born 1783, North Carolina. Some allied families:
      Alexander, Allgood, Chapman, Cook, Daniel.
      Cloth-(In process) --Vendor   #229

100   -ONCE UPON QUOKETAUG by Rudy J. Favretti, 1974.
      Williams: Stonington, Connecticut—1712-present.
      Book in three parts: six chapters- one for each generation of family; chapter
      on house; chapter on farm; detailed genealogical information; appendix of
      wills, inventory, genealogy on branches of family. About 50 photos. Family
      descendants of Robert of Roxbury.
      Paper-171pp-$5.00--Vendor   #231

101   -WILLIAM R. KING & HIS KIN by Henry Poellniz Johnston, Sr.
      [See space ad on page 201]---- ------------------------------- Vendor   #232

102   -LEDBETTERS FROM VIRGINIA by Roy C. Ledbetter et. al., 1964.
      An indexed history of the Ledbetter who settled in Virginia before 1655 and his
      descendants.
      Cloth-369pp-$16.00--------------------------------------- Vendor   #234

103   -FEWKES FAMILY HISTORY by Dora Reid Fieber, late 1976.
      Descendants and antecedents of Joseph and Martha (Root) Fewkes, includes her
      lineage to Mayflower passengers, John Alden, Francis Cooke, and Richard
      Warren.
      (In process) --Vendor   #235

104   -NOTES ON ONE OF THE EARLY BALLARD FAMILIES OF KENTUCKY,
      INCLUDING THE BALLARD MASSACRE by Margaret M. Bridwell
      Filson Club History Quarterly, Vol. 13, No. 1, Jan. 1939.
      Ballard: Shelby Co., Kentucky—1787-1800.
      Paper-20pp-$3.00--- Vendor   #236

105   -THE COXES OF COX'S CREEK, KENTUCKY by Evelyn C. Adams
      Filson Club History Quarterly, Vol. 22, No. 2, Apr. 1948.
      Cox: Nelson Co., Kentucky—1780-1800.
      Paper, 29pp-$3.00--------------------------------------- Vendor   #236

106   -THE BEAUCHAMP FAMILY by Stith Thompson
      Filson Club History Quarterly, Vol. 28, No. 2, Apr. 1954.
      Beauchamp: England—1066-1665; Maryland—1665-1790; Kentucky—1790-1900.
      Paper-39pp-$3.00--------------------------------------- Vendor   #236

107 -DESCENDANTS OF GENL. JONATHAN CLARK 1750-1811 by John
Frederick Dorman III. Reprint from the Filson Club History Quarterly,
Vol. 23, Nos. 1, 2 & 4, 1949.
Clark: Virginia—1750-1802; Kentucky—1802-1811.
Paper-62pp-$1.00 ---Vendor   #236

108   - THE ZOI LIE TREE by Raymond E. Myers, 1964.
Life of General Felix K. Zollicoffer and the story of the battle of Mill
Springs, Kentucky. Appendix includes Zollicoffer ancestors and descendants.
Cloth-200pp-$6.50 ---Vendor   #236

109   - DESCENDANTS OF THOMAS COOKE OF PORTSMOUTH, RHODE ISLAND
by Jane Fletcher Fiske and Richard W. Cook, winter 1976/77.
Descendants of Thomas Cooke of Taunton, Massachusetts and Portsmouth,
Rhode Island (died 1677); as many male lines as possible carried through to
present. Based on primary source research.
(In process)-approx. 300pp --------------------------------------Vendor   #238

110   - THE MEANS FAMILY OF AMERICA by Elizabeth Cissel Foglesong, 1972.
Very complete documented work in four indexed sections with many wills,
deeds, court records, military records, letters and photographs. Descendants
in many states.
Cloth-1018pp-$30.00 ---Vendor   #244

111   - ANCESTRY OF MARGARET ANN (FRITCHEY) TRAHAN by Dr. John A.
Fritchey, II.
Includes the families of her great-great-grandparents: Barden, Bower,
Fritchey, Hoon, House, Hover, Jackson, Losey, Maurer, Mead, Miller,
Moore, Scheffer, Seagraves, Stucker, and Warren.
Paper-125pp-$10.00 --------------------------------------- Vendor   #256

112   - COL. JOSHUA FRY OF VIRGINIA—SOME OF HIS DESCENDANTS—ALLIED
FAMILIES by George W. Frye, 1966.
Part 1—Col. Joshua Fry; Part 2—Descendants and allied families;
Part 3—Descendants in Tennessee and allied families. Indexed-Illustrated-
Documented-Bond paper.
Cloth-750+pp=$20.60 --------------------------------------- Vendor   #258

113   - HOME FOLKS by Marguerite Miller, 1975, reprint of 1910 ed.
A series of stories of old settlers of Fulton County, Indiana, originally 2 volumes,
reprinted both together as 1 volume. Contains Civil War soldiers, history of
Rochester town bands, Knights of Pythias, Odd Fellows, family stories.
Families included are: Ward, Dawson, Troutman, Jewell, Hill, Miller,
Essick, Jackson, Mitchell, Waymire, Sibert, Myers, Perschbacher, Mow,
Dillon, Pownall, Stallard, Banta, Hickman, Barker, Sinks, Rannells, Shryock,
Hall, McNeely, Brown, Kesler, Brackett, Bitters.
Cloth-266pp-$10.00 --Vendor   #260

114   - DULANY-FURLONG AND KINDRED FAMILIES by Roland Dulany Furlong,
1975.
Dulany: Maryland—1730-1750; Connecticut—1755-1756; Pennsylvania—1776-1800.
Dennis Dulany, son of 1709 immigrant Thomas. Progenitor of surname in
western Pennsylvania, West Virginia and Ohio. John Furlong, 1816 immigrant of
Cambria County, Pennsylvania.
Cloth-544pp-$25.00--Vendor   #262

115 - A BRANCH OF THE MADISON TREE by Ruth Gadbury, 1974.
Genealogy of Mattisons in Virginia and South Carolina, spelled Madison in
Alabama and Texas. Supplements on Ware, Barley, Sample, and Rusler.
Sketches and pictures.
Cloth-138pp-$10.95 -- Vendor   #264

116 - GALBREATH FAMILY GENEALOGY by Joseph William Galbreath, 1976.
Galbreath: Wayne Co., Illinois—1850-1976; Columbiana Co., Ohio—1803-1850;
South Carolina—1799-1803; Pennsylvania—1761-1799.
Paper-63pp-$9.30 --Vendor   #265

117 - GANNETT DESCENDANTS OF MATTHEW AND HANNAH GANNETT OF
SCITUATE, MASSACHUSETTS, compiled by Michael R. Gannett, 1976.
Introductory chapters, and data on Gannett descendants and spouses from
1638. Illustrated. Family trees compiled 1770 and 1975. Sources cited.
Name index. Bibliography.
Cloth-238pp-$9.75 --- Vendor   #267

118 - THE CRECELIUS BOOKS, BOOK I: DESCENDANTS OF JOHANNES CRECELIUS
by Sydney Mike Gardner, July, 1976.
Includes Crecelius in Tennessee, Indiana, Kentucky, Missouri; Critselous in
Tennessee; Criscillis in Kentucky. Also Bartles/Bottles, Conrad, Lashbrook(s),
Meadors, Neas(e), Ottinger, Stephens, Weedman, West.
Cloth-ca 700pp-$22.00 ---Vendor   #269

119 - GEORGE FAMILY RECORD: DESCENDANTS OF COL. JOHN GEORGE OF
VIRGINIA by Thomas R. George, 1976.
Traces descendants of Col. John George of Virginia (1604-1678) through
counties of Charles City, Isle of Wight, Middlesex, Essex, Caroline and
Pittsylvania. Includes wills, letters, and other records dating from early
1600's.
Paper-Abt.150pp-$15.00 -------------------------------------- Vendor   #278

120 - THE GETMAN FAMILY GENEALOGY, 1710-1974, 1975.
Genealogy of George, Christian and Frederick, sons of Frederick and Mary
(Bierman) Getman who settled in the Mohawk Valley about 1723.
Paper-564pp-$15.00 --- Vendor   #280

121 - JOHN CAWMAN EASTLACK DIARY compiled by Mrs. Walter A. Simpson,
1952.
Eastlack: Gloucester Co., New Jersey.
1854-1887 diary of John Eastlack, his family and friends of Gloucester Co.,
New Jersey. Indexed.
Paper-103pp-$3.25 --- Vendor   #285

122 - THOMAS KNIGHT OF PENNSYI VANIA AND SOME OF HIS DESCENDANTS by
William Beckett Brown, III, 1973.
Knight: South Jersey and Pennsylvania descendants of Thomas Knight of
England from 1687 to present.
Paper-78pp-$5.50 --Vendor   #285

123 -THE WEEKS FAMILY OF SOUTHERN NEW JERSEY by Elmer Garfield Van Name.
Weeks: A detailed work on the Weeks, Wicks, Wyke families of South Jersey.
Paper-67pp-$2.20--Vendor   #285

124 -I ETTERS AND PAPERS OF RICHARD SOMERS by Frank Stewart, 1942.
Somers: Excerpts of Somers' life from his midshipman days of 1798 to 1804
in U.S. Navy. Somers was from Atlantic Co., New Jersey.
Paper-36pp-$1.65--Vendor   #285

125 -THE LEEK FAMIL Y OF SOUTHERN NEW JERSEY by Helen Leek Mack, 1975.
Leek: South Jersey descendants of Philip Leek, who came to America in 1640.
Paper-200pp-$6.50--- Vendor   #285

126 -THE EASTLACK FAMIL Y by John William Eastlack, Sr., 1971.
Eastlack: Gloucester Co., New Jersey.
Descendants of Francis Estlack of England, who settled in Old Gloucester Co.,
New Jersey in late 1600's.
Paper-138pp-$7.00--- Vendor   #285

127 -BRITTON GENEALOGY by Elmer Garfield Van Name, 1964.
Britton: Fine study of the Britton, Britaine, Britten family from England to
Staten Island, New York.
Paper-34pp-$1.15--Vendor   #285

128 -THE JOSEPH SMITH FAMILY OF GLOUCESTER AND SALEM COUNTIES -
THE JAMES DYE FAMILY OF GLOUCESTER COUNTY by Elmer Garfield Van
Name, 1976, reprint of 1964 ed.
Smith: Gloucester Co., New Jersey—1762-1841.
Dye: Salem and Gloucester Cos., New Jersey—1742-1835.
Paper-32pp-$1.15--Vendor   #285

129 -PIERRE CRESSON, THE HUGUENOT OF STATEN ISLAND, PENNSYLVANIA
AND NEW JERSEY PROGENY , 1968.
Cresson: France—1609-1657; Delaware (state)—1657-1679; Long Island—1679-
c1681.
Paper-21pp-$1.15--- Vendor   #285

130 -GENEALOGY OF JOSEPH PAULL 1657-1717 by Elmer Garfield Van Name, 1969.
Paull: England—1657-1685; Pennsylvania—1685-1717.
Paper-18pp-$1.15--- Vendor   #285

131 -THE HOUSMAN - (HUYSMAN) SIMONSON FAMILY OF STATEN ISLAND NEW
YORK by Elmer Garfield Van Name, 1955.
Housman: Staten Island, New York—1700-1850.
Paper-10pp-$1.15--- Vendor   #285

132 -ANTHONY NELSON 17th CENTURY PENNSYLVANIA AND NEW JERSEY AND
SOME OF HIS DESCENDANTS by Elmer Garfield Van Name, 1976, reprint of
1962 ed.
Nielson-Nelson: Gloucester Co., New Jersey—1652-1695.
Paper-54pp-$2.75--Vendor   #285

134 -PIERRE BILLIOU FAMILY by Elmer Garfield Van Name, 1960.
Billiou: France—1632-1661; New York (state)—1661-1699.
Paper-16pp-$1.15--Vendor   #285

135   -THE ELWELL FAMILY- 17th AND 18th CENTURY SOUTHERN NEW JERSEY
       by Elmer Garfield Van Name.
       Elwell: Concerns various branches of Elwell family in Southern New Jersey,
       founded by Thomas Elwell, born in Massachusetts in 1654.
       Paper-40pp-$2.75---Vendor   #285

136   -THE STEELES OF STEELES TAVERN, VIRGINIA AND RELATED FAMILIES
       by Mildred S. Goeller, 1974.
       Traced are descendants of David, Samuel and Andrew Steele. Also short
       histories of Moore, Moon, Calvert, Massie, Strother, Searson, Digges and
       Harris families.
       Paper-126pp-$6.50--- Vendor   #287

137   -THE DESCENDANTS OF JOHN LAKE OF FAUQUIER COUNTY, VIRGINIA
       by John K. Gott, 1977.
       Descendants of John and Susan (Savaul) Lake.
       (In process)-- Vendor   #290

138   -DESCENDANTS OF JOHN SIMMONS AND THE ALLIED FAMILIES OF HATTON,
       McGREW, SHERWOOD, LINTHICUM, AND CATHCART by Ruth Maxwell Graham,
       1975.
       Biographical genealogy of Simmons of Pennsylvania, Ohio, Indiana, Iowa, Kansas
       and Oregon. 25 illustrations. From 1734. (Genealogy Hatton, McGrew, Sher-
       wood, Linthicum, Cathcart from 1613).
       Paper-606pp-$15.00--------------------------------------- Vendor   #291

139   -THE DOWNINGS OF EUROPE AND AMERICA, 1273-1973 by Anna May
       Cochrane IV Gregath, 1976.
       A new book containing history and statistics spanning four generations of
       research and continual collection of thousands of Downing and hundreds of al-
       lied families.
       Cloth-554pp-$25.00-------------------------------------- Vendor   #298

140   -A LOCKHART FAMILY IN AMERICA by Anna May Cochrane IV Gregath, 1972.
       A branch of the Lockhart's of Lanark, Scotland to America became first
       settlers of American frontiers, their history and statistics of descendants.
       Paper-138pp-$10.00--Vendor   #298

141   -AND NOW WE ARE MANY by Marilyn Tone Gray, 1971.
       A history and genealogy of the Brohman family from 1750. Covers all
       descendants in Canada and U.S. from 1807. Unique copyrighted method of
       listing genealogical data developed for this book. 4000 names indexed.
       Numbered limited edition.
       Cloth-181pp-$15.00---------------------------------------Vendor   #294

142   -COTTEN PICKING WITH ADDENDUM, VOLUME ONE by Mrs. Peggy H.
       Gregory, 1976, reprint of 1973 ed.
       Cotten/Cotton: Edgefield Co., South Carolina—1786-1806; Christian Co.,
       Kentucky—1806-1816; Cooper & Miller Cos., Missouri—1819-1853; Texas—
       1853-1976.
       McComb: Roane Co., Tennessee—1800-1830; Miller Co., Missouri—1840-1976.
       Judd: Wilkes Co., North Carolina—1775-1825; Texas—1859-1976.
       Massive compilation of Cotten and allied families. Complete dates, places, wills,
       Bible records. Many states, south to west. Over four thousand surnames.
       Fully indexed.
       Paper-442pp-$14.00-------------------------------------- Vendor   #300

143   -DESCENDANTS OF ROBERT AND JOHN POAGE, V. 2: DESCENDANTS OF JOHN
      POAGE OF ROCKBRIDGE COUNTY by John Guy Bishop and Robert B.
      Woodworth, 1954.
      Poage, John: Rockbridge Co., Virginia.
      Cloth-247pp-$15.00--- Vendor   #302

144   -JOHN AND NANCY GUNTER OF JEMSEG, NEW BRUNSWICK, THEIR
      ANCESTORS AND DESCENDANTS by Andrew Gunter, 1969.
      Gunter: New York (state)—   -1783; New Brunswick, Canada—1783-1969.
      Paper-48pp-$2.00--- Vendor   #303

145   -HAMBYS DESCENDED FROM THOMAS OF GEORGIA by Wallace B.
      Hamby, M.D., 1976.
      Direct descendants of Thomas Hamby, d: Newton Co., Georgia, 1826.
      1000 name Index.
      Paper-58pp-$7.50--- Vendor   #309

146   -PHILLIP HAMMAN: MAN OF VALOR by Ralph Hammond, May 1976.
      Hamman: Greenbrier Co., Virginia—1772-1782; Madison Co., Kentucky—1782-
      1795; Montgomery Co., Kentucky—1796-1821; Jackson Co., Alabama—1822-1832.
      Cloth-116pp-$5.00--- Vendor   #312

147   -HENCKEL GENEALOGICAL BULLETIN by Mrs. Bert Harter, F.A.S.G., 1970-
      1976.
      Hinkle, Henkel, Henkle, etc. Additions and corrections to early (first seven)
      generations of Henckel Genealogy by Junkin, now out of print.
      Semi-Annual-40 pages per year-$3.00/yr. ---------------------- Vendor   #318

148   -THE SPRUNGER FAMILY-DESCENDANTS OF PETER SPRUNGER BORN 1757
      by Willis Herr, 1975.
      Sprungers originally from Switzerland. Emigrated to Ohio and Indiana in 1852.
      Over 8000 names listed. Includes Peter's male ancestral to Hans born 1565.
      Paper-300pp-$7.25--- Vendor   #332

149   -THE JULIAN FAMILY edited and compiled by Frances Julian Hine, 1974.
      Compilation of genealogical data from Rene St. Julien of seventeenth century
      France to Julian family descendants through 1974, including the Revolutionary
      War Period.
      Paper-92pp-$12.50--- Vendor   #336

150   -MUSSETTERS AND RELATED FAMILIES 1769-1975 by Lois (Redmond) Hodge, 1976.
      Mussetter: Frederick Co., Maryland—1786-1975; Berkeley Co., West Virginia—
      1793-1975; Greene Co., Ohio—1822-1975; throughout U.S.—1850-1975.
      Paper-184pp-$10.00--Vendor   #339

151   -NEVILLE FAMILY OF VIRGINIA by Mrs. Luke Hodges.
      Paper-$10.00--Vendor   #340

152   -THE GARESCHE, de BAUDUY AND DESCHAPELLES FAMILIES: HISTORY
      AND GENEALOGY by Dorothy Garesche Holland, 1963.
      Three French families who fled from Santo Domingo to Wilmington, Delaware
      in 1790's where Peter Bauduy became a Dupont partner. Letters, diaries,
      memoirs. Illustrations.
      Cloth-300pp-$15.00--------------------------------------- Vendor   #344

153   -THE HOLT FAMILY IN EUROPE AND AMERICA 1248-1971 by V. Holt Tatum,
       1971.
       A brief account of Holt genealogy, history and armory in England and Germany;
       also in New England and Virginia in America.
       Paper-16pp-$2.20-- Vendor   #347

154   -GENEALOGY OF THE HERBERT HOOVER FAMILY by Hulda Hoover McLean,
       1967.
       In two parts: I Ancestors of Herbert Hoover, II Descendants of Andrew Hoover
       (Andreas Huber).
       Cloth-$10.00-Paper-$8.00-485pp--------------------------------Vendor   #349

155   -WHETSTONE FAMILY OF WILKINSON COUNTY, MISSISSIPPI by Levi Jackson
       Horlacher, 1976.
       Looseleaf IBM-Plastic Cover-$10.00----------------------------Vendor   #354

156   -HOUGH AND HUFF FAMILIES OF THE U.S., VOL. VI, THE WEST, 1850-
       1900 by Granville W. Hough, 1976.
       Hough: Western States—1850-1900.
       Huff: Western States—1850-1900.
       Census and family data on families from Missouri and Texas west through the
       plains and mountains.
       Paper-200pp-$15.00-- Vendor   #355

157   -HUDSONS OF THE SOUTH IN THE 1790 CENSUS by Malcolm H. Hudson, 1976.
       Hudson: Provides data on all Hudson (Hutson) names found in 1790 census and
       reconstructed records of ten states including names of allied families and
       neighbors.
       Paper-70pp-$4.00--- Vendor   #360

158   -AND THEN THERE WERE THREE THOUSAND by Donna M. Hull, 1975.
       Akers: Roundrock, Texas—1839-1852; Fresno Co., California—1853-1976;
       Kentucky—1756-1839; Illinois—1838-   .
       McHaley: Williamson Co., Texas—1840's-1852; Fresno Co., California—1861-
       1976
       Huckaby: Little Rock, Arkansas—1838-1842; Fresno Co., California—1861-1976.
       Fike: Ralls Co., Missouri—1777-1890; Chatham Co., North Carolina—1770's-
       1777.
       Hull: Pennsylvania—1815-1837; Ohio—1837-1868.
       Miller: Kentucky—1756-1839; Arkansas—1839-1840.
       A family history and genealogy of descendants of two sisters, Delilah and Elsie
       Miller. Tells of their trek from Kentucky to California.
       Cloth-522pp-$25.00--Vendor   #361

159   -DESCENDANTS OF THOMAS OLCOTT, 1630-1874, ONE OF THE FIRST SETTLERS
       IN HARTFORD,CONNECTICUT by Nathaniel Goodwin, 1975, reprint of 1874 ed.
       Includes early history of Hartford,Connecticut. Many surnames given.
       Paper-124pp-$2.50--- Vendor   #364

160   -BRADLEY GENEALOGY (1637-1850) by Henry Olcott Sheldon and Martha Sheldon
       Hutchins, 1976.
       First part of book in H.O. Sheldon's handwriting. Second part-Indexes by M.S.
       Hutchins. Names include Bartholomew, Bird, Tillolson, and Sheldon.
       Paper-about 40pp-$7.75--------------------------------------Vendor   #364

161   -THE SCHRAMM LETTERS, WRITTEN BY JACOB SCHRAMM AND MEMBERS OF
       HIS FAMILY FROM INDIANA TO GERMANY IN THE YEAR 1836 translated and
       edited by Emma S. Vonnegut, 1935.
       $2.00-- Vendor   #369

162   -THE FAMILY HISTORY OF THOMAS MARTIN, SR. A NORTH CAROLINA
       REVOLUTIONARY SOLDIER by Jenny Martin Fagg, 1976.
       Cloth-385pp-$25.00--- Vendor   #371

163   -HOWARD FAMILIES OF SOUTH CAROLINA by Mary Barnett Curtis, 1974.
       Paper-53pp-$10.00--Vendor   #371

164   -ABSTRACTS FROM ORIGINAL RECORDS ON STRICKLANDS OF NORTH
       CAROLINA by Mary Barnett Curtis, August 1976.
       Paper-250pp-$50.00--- Vendor   #371

165   -BRADFORD ROOTS AND BRANCHES by Nancy Vashti Anthony Jacob, 1975.
       Bradford: Antrim Co., Ireland—   -1767; Kershaw Co. South Carolina—1768-
       1975; Pickens Co., Alabama—1824; throughout U.S..
       Paper-175pp-$10.00---Vendor   #380

166   -EDGECOMBE, YATES & ALLIED LINES by Frances E. Blake, 1968.
       Genealogies of descendants of Nicholas Edgecomb, Maine, 1636, John Yates,
       Cape Cod, 1650, and 76 allied New England families 1620-1880, with charts,
       index.
       Cloth-519pp-$35.00--- Vendor   #382

167   -HISTORIC CANE RIDGE AND ITS FAMILIES by Lillian B. Johnson,1972.
       Johnstone - Johnson: Tyrone, Ireland—1654-1680; North Carolina—1680-1800.
       Cannon: North Carolina—1753-1799; Williamson Co., Tennessee—1799-1972.
       Peay: Virginia—1734-1792; North Carolina—1793-1810.
       Gamble: Londondery, Ireland—   -1735; Augusta Co., Virginia—1735-1800.
       Cloth-452pp-$21.95--- Vendor   #391

168   -WILLIAM PRESTON & THE ALLEGHENY PATRIOTS by Patricia Givens Johnson,
       1976.
       Fully documented account of Revolutionary activities of Virginia's mountain
       Patriots and Tories and a New River regional study interwoven with a bio-
       graphy of Preston. Descendants of William Preston through female lines, and
       other families who are frequently mentioned in this work include: Preston, Patton,
       Buchanan, Floyd, Breckenridge, Brown, McDowell, Lewis, Peyton, Watts,
       Marshall, Randolph, Campbell, Burk, Price, Smith, Cloyd, Ingles, Fleming,
       Christian, Thompson, Russell, Crickett, & Havens.
       Cloth-325pp-$9.25--Vendor   #392

169   -JOYNER OF SOUTHAMPTON by Ulysses P. Joyner, Jr., 1975.
       A study of Thomas Joyner (1619-1694) of Isle of Wight County, Virginia and
       his descendants in Eastern Virginia and North Carolina with emphasis on the
       Joyners of Southampton County, Virginia with brief sketches of related families
       and abstracts of pertinent public records.
       Cloth-233pp-$25.00--Vendor   #397

170 - KEY AND COLLATERAL FAMILIES, 1776-1972 by Edward S. Key and
Irene T. Sevier, 1972.
Chesnutt: Sampson Co., North Carolina—1777-1853; Kemper Co., Miss-
issippi—1854; Angelina Co., Texas—1866; Bee Co., Texas—1876-1972.
Webster: McClesfield, England—1831; Boone Co., Illinois—1884.
Smith: Kemper Co., Mississippi—1869; Grimes Co., Texas—1869.
561 Surnames; 12 Charts.
Cloth-300pp-$9.50 -- Vendor   #410

171 - THE THOMAS LAMONTS IN AMERICA by seven Lamonts & four others,
edited by Corliss Lamont, 1971.
An account of the Lamont family, centering around banker Thomas W.
Lamont, with historical background going back to the Clan Lamont of
Scotland.
Cloth-255pp-$10.00 --- Vendor   #419

172 - GARRET LAREW, CIVIL WAR SOLDIER WITH AN ACCOUNT OF HIS
ANCESTORS AND OF HIS DESCENDANTS by Karl G. Larew, 1975.
17th and 18th century Larews; Abraham (Revolutionary War); Garret
(based on his Civil War diary); Indiana Larews; and allied families:
Ricketts, Denny, Goff, Rittenhouse.
Cloth-277pp-$12.00 --- Vendor   #421

173 - MERRIE OLDE MIDDLESEX by Caroljo F. Lee, Limited Edition, 1976.
Contains genealogies of the following families of Middlesex Twp., Butler
County, Pennsylvania: Hays, Harbison, Park, Brown, Bartley, Mahan,
Miller, Scott, Wigfield-Baker, Murray, McCaslin, Cooper, Croikshauk,
Ferguson, Fritz, Fulton, Kennedy, Leslie-McBride, Logan, Love, Shepard,
Steiner, Thompson, Wilson.
Cloth-360pp-$15.00 ---Vendor   #424

174 - THE GRAY FAMILY by Jo White Linn, late 1976.
Gray: Randolph Co., North Carolina—1740-date; and allied lines of Bowman.
(New Jersey; Stokes and Guilford Co., North Carolina), Lindsay (Guilford
Co., North Carolina), Wiley, Shannon, Dick, Millis, McGee, Lamar,
Peebles—all of North Carolina—from earliest ancestor found to point where
lineage connects with Gray line. Pictures, maps, charts.
(In process) -- Vendor   #433

175 - WILLIAM PULLEN - REVOLUTIONARY SOLDIER by Hester M. Smith and
Edward S. Smith, 1971.
Pullen: Bedford Co., Virginia—1757-1784; Wilkes Co., Georgia—1784-1812;
Pendelton Dist., South Carolina—1812-1822; Jefferson Co., Alabama—1822-1845.
Hickman: Pendelton Dist., So. Carolina to 1818; Jefferson Co., Ala. from 1818.
Shackelford: Georgia to 1820; Jefferson Co., Ala. from 1820.
Paper-39pp-$5.00 --Vendor   #437

176 - FATHER JULIUS AND MOTHER EMILIE by George C. Bubolz, 1975.
Bubolz: East Lansing, Michigan; Outagamie Co., Wisconsin.
A personal biography of midwestern pioneers. The inspiring account of
a German pioneer family who, through faith, courage, and dedicated work,
realized the American Dream in Wisconsin.
Cloth-172pp-$9.00 ---Vendor   #438

177   - PENNOYER BROTHERS: COLONIZATION, COMMERCE, CHARITY
      IN THE SEVENTEENTH CENTURY by Raymond H. Lounsbury, 1971.
      The surname of the Pennoyers was actually Butler. Biographical,
      Historical.
      Cloth-$5.95--- Vendor   #441

178   - LOUNSBURY - ORIGIN, MEANING AND SIGNIFICANCE, WITH EMPHASIS
      ON THE EVIDENCE AND CONCLUSIONS CONCERNING THE RELATIONSHIP
      OF THE LOUNSBURY FAMILY TO ROYALTY IN THE MIDDLE AGES
      by Raymond H. Lounsbury, 1976.
      Paper-40pp-$5.25 --- Vendor   #441

179   - PHELPS - MARSHALL KINSHIP by Nancy S. McBride, 1976.
      Phelps: Europe and England—1200-1630; New England—1630-1850;
      Southern Phelps—1654-1850.
      History and genealogy of Phelps, Marshalls and allied families.
      Cloth-abt. 350pp --- Vendor   #445

180   - GORDON KINSHIP by Nancy S. McBride, 1973.
      Gordon: France and Scotland—800-1640; Ireland—1640-1730; Virginia—1730-1820;
      Ohio—1820-1973.
      Harrison: England—1600-1632; Virginia—1632-1850.
      Conway: England and Wales—1400-1640; Virginia—1640-1812.
      Ball: England—1400-1650; Virginia—1650-1812.
      Lee: England—1200-1640; Virginia—1640-1750.
      Bryarly: England—1600-1635; Maryland and Virginia—1634-1870.
      Barrington: England and Ireland: 1200—1760; Pennsylvania—1760-1850.
      Very full account of the Gordon family from its origins to recent times, with
      chapters on the families with which they were inter-married.
      Cloth-452pp-$15.50--- Vendor   #445

181   - SANDERS SAGA by Mrs. Catherine S. McConnell, 1972.
      Sanders: Virginia
      Genealogy of an English family descending from James Sanders and
      Sarah Scrimschire, 1698. Sketches of 46 families connected by
      marriage. Fully indexed and illustrated.
      Cloth-400pp-$20.00 --- Vendor   #449

182   HOWDY, MR. MAC by Thelma S. McManus, 1978.
      McManus: Larance McManus lineage: Ireland, North Carolina (Chatham),
      Tennessee (Maury), Missouri (Cape Girardeau and Ripley), Illinois (Macoupin),
      Arkansas (Calhoun), Louisiana (St. Landry), Texas (Henderson), etc.
      (In process)--Vendor   #453

183   - SOME DESCENDANTS OF DAVID McSWAIN (1700-1770) OF ISLE OF SKYE
      by Mrs. Eleanor Davis McSwain, 1974.
      Allied families Hamrick, Washburn, McGowan, McWilliams, Wells, and
      Randle (Randolph).
      Cloth-234pp-Index-8 1/2 x 11-$21.00--------------------------Vendor   #458

184   - STYLES - FRANKLING (STILES-FRANKLIN) by Mrs. Eleanor Davis
      McSwain, 1975.
      Some descendants of Joseph Styles, attorney, New Kent Co., Virginia (1680);
      and James Frankling, planter, Henrico Co., Virginia (1643-c1704)
      Cloth-267pp-Index-$25.00-------------------------------------Vendor   #458

185 - RELATIVE-LY SPEAKING by Nola Egle Mahaffey, 1969.
Egle: Book of Egle family history, genealogy, portraits, documents,
utilizing numeric system identifying family offspring. Egles originated
Switzerland, migrated to Germany, Pennsylvania, Midwestern States.
Paper-75pp-$7.00 --Vendor   #459

186 - MARTZES OF MARYLAND by Ralph Fraley Martz, 1973.
Chapters concerning name, Coat of Arms, letters of 1880, the Delaware,
Berks, Lancaster, York, Adams, Frederick, Washington, Augusta,
Loudoun, Rockingham, Bedford, Kentucky counties, etc.
Cloth-207pp-$12.48 -- Vendor   #468

187 - REISTER'S DESIRE by Lillian B. Marks, 1975.
Reister: Reisterstown, Baltimore Co., Maryland—1750-.
Cloth-236pp-$16.00 -- Vendor   #469

188 - DESCENDANTS OF GOTTLIEB MAUK AND SONS MATHIAS AND
CORNELIUS by Harold E. Mauk, 1975.
Mauk: Colonies—1750-1820; Hocking County, Ohio; Clark County, Illinois;
Kansas; Oklahoma. Biographies, family sheets, history. Data on Mauks,
Moores, Catlins, Bruces, Goodrichs, others. Eight generations.
Paper-55pp-8 /12 x 11, 3 hole punched-$4.00-------------------- Vendor   #472

189 - MAXWELL GENEALOGY AND HISTORY by Fay Maxwell, 1974.
Bezalell Maxwell (Revolutionary War soldier) of Albemarle County, Virginia -
1751-1828. Son, John Maxwell (1775-1817) in Jefferson County, Ohio. Five
Robert Maxwells listed in Jefferson County. William Maxwell (1700-1800s),
pioneer publisher. Begins with 14th century in Ireland, 15th century
in Scotland, covers Nova Scotia, New York and Iowa. Lists Maxwell,
Maxwell-Schnebele (Snively) history, origin of Maxwells, castles, crests
in 14th century, covers Maxwells of many states including Virginia,
Pennsylvania, New Jersey, Indiana, Tennessee, but mostly in Ohio. Many
related lines, including Marshalls, Williams, Anderson, Houston-Cowan,
McCullough.
Cloth-200pp-$10.00 --Vendor   #473

190 - FIRST PORTUGUESE GENEALOGY IN UNITED STATES by Henrietta
Mello Mayer, 1976.
Silva, Sylvia: Stonington, Connecticut—1849-1976; New Bedford, Massa-
chusetts—1890-1976; New London, Connecticut—1859-1976; Berkeley,
California—1920-1976.
Joseph: New London, Connecticut—1890-1950; Medford, Massachusetts—1920-1976.
Paper-$10.00 --Vendor   #475

191 - UNCLE CHARLEY AND HIS RIFLE by Archibald L. Camp, 1960.
Camp: Covington, Georgia—1830-1867.
Cloth-112pp-$3.75 --Vendor   #481

192 - THE STEWART COUSIN REUNION RECORDS 1931-1975 WITH THE
DESCENDANTS AND ANCESTRY OF SARAH ANN (MILLS) STEWART
(1842-1925) by Stewart Cousin Reunion Records Committee, Sept., 1976.
Minutes, Historians' Reports, etc., for Hamilton/Tipton County,
Indiana, Stewarts, plus ancestors (six generations) and all known descendants
of Sarah (Mills) Stewart. Completely indexed.
Paper-150pp-$5.75 --- Vendor   #481

193 - ROOTS BY THE RIVER by Marcus Miller, 1973.
History, doctrine, and practice of the Old German Baptist Brethren
(Dunkers) in Miami Co., Ohio. Short biographies of 75 ministers
including Arnold, Bowman, Cable, Cadwallader, Cassell, Cover, Darst,
Davy, Deeter, Etter, Frantz, Hoover, Mohler, Murray, Nead, Quinter,
Risser, Shellabarger, Studebaker, Younce, 1816-1973. Genealogical Sketches.
Cloth-255pp-$5.25 --- Vendor #489

194 - THE CONLEY FAMILY - DESCENDANTS OF NICHOLAS by Jean
Alonzo Curran, M.D., 1976.
Nicholas arrived Boston, 1758. Family moved westward generally to New York,
Iowa, and Minnesota. Completely indexed - includes pictures, written family
account and lineage.
Cloth-$25.00-Paper-$15.00-320pp ----------------------------- Vendor #490

195 - HISTORY OF THE JERSEY SETTLERS OF ADAMS CO., MISSISSIPPI
edited by Frances Preston Mills, late 1976.
Swayze: Salem, Massachusetts—1629-1650; Southold, Long Island—1650-1740;
Chester, New Jersey—1740-1773; Jersey Settlement, Kingston, Adams Co.,
Mississippi—1773-date.
King: Salem, Massachusetts—1635-1650; Adams Co., Mississippi—1775-1976.
Eaton: Kingston, Mississippi—1820-1830; Illinois—1836-date.
Chronological, geographical, genealogical history of the Swayze-King families
coming to the Natchez District 1773, founding the Protestant Church in
Mississippi, Rev. Samuel Swayze, Pastor.
Cloth-250-300pp-$12.50 --Vendor #491

196 - MILLS FAMILY HISTORY - QUAKER AND OTHER EARLY ARRIVALS
by Paul Mills and Rodney Mills, 1976.
John Mills, the immigrant, born 1660 and descendants for many generations.
Also lists many other early arrivals named Mills. Indexed, 1300 names.
Paper-122pp-$6.50 ---Vendor #493

197 - THE AUTOBIOGRAPHY OF EDWIN W. MILNER, 1906-1969 edited by
Mrs. Anita Cheek Milner, 1973.
While essentially a description of childhood days in Fredonia, Kansas, in
the early 1900's, the book also contains a brief Milner history from 1700's.
Paper-100pp-$3.00 --- Vendor #494

198 - THE MINOR DIARIES edited by John A. Miner, 1976.
Diaries of Thomas Minor, covering the period 1653-1684; and of Manasseh
Minor, covering the period 1696-1720. Both included in one volume. They
were residents of Stonington, Connecticut.
Cloth-390pp-$20.00 --Vendor #495

199 - THE MIXON-MIXSON FAMILY, Vol. III by John Leslie Mixson.
Section I (265pp) contains public records, censuses, land grants,
military rosters. Section II, genealogy, etc. Included are almost
50 pictures of Mixon-Mixson and allied lines.
Cloth-450pp-$20.00--Vendor #501

200 - THE DESCENDANTS OF RICHARD AUSTIN, CHARLESTOWN,
MASSACHUSETTS, 1638 by Edith Austin Moore
Richard Austin: Charlestown, Massachusetts—1638. Branch of Austins that
goes to the Mayflower.
Paper-608pp-$25.75--Vendor #504

201   -DINWIDDIE CLAN RECORDS by Rev. Timothy H. Ball. Repr. of 1902 ed,
       with corrections. An APPENDIX and INDEX added by Freeman E. Morgan.
       1976.
       Dinwiddie/Dunwoody: Complete 144 page text (with 26 pictures) of 1902 printing
       rearranged on 36 8 1/2 x 14 pages with hard Acco cover. Scotch-Irish "Dunwoody"
       (Pennsylvania 1741, Ohio 1810, Indiana 1833 as "Dinwiddie", some to Oregon 1853).
       Thirty page APPENDIX added with family history, much of Rev. Cuthbertson's
       diary. Additional pictures, documentation and index. Lineage on 70 other
       surnames such as Turner, Wilson, Dilley/Dillie, Buchanan, Pearce, Brownell,
       LeRoy, Sweney, Smith, Bryant, McAlpin, Foster, Crooks, etc.
       Paper-$4.95-- Vendor   #505

202   -LIFE OF NATHAN BEDFORD FORREST by John Allan Wyeth, M.D., reprint
       of 1899 ed.
       Written by a Confederate veteran from personal knowledge and from
       information supplied by many who had served under Forrest, this has long been
       considered by many historians to be the most definitive work written on this
       cavalry leader who has been called the outstanding soldier produced by the
       War Between the States. It details his early life, his wartime activities, and
       his postwar years. Rare and much sought after, this is a book that should be in
       every Civil War library. Illustrated, endpaper map, maps, bound and stamped
       as the original.
       655pp-$20.00-- Vendor   #506

203   -THE MORRISON FAMILY OF WARREN COUNTY, VIRGINIA by W. Briley
       Morrison, Early 1977.
       Listing descendants of Thomas Morrison, 1753-1823, who married Polly Elless,
       daughter of Nathaniel Elless whose will is recorded in the Warrenton, Virginia
       courthouse.
       Paper-- Vendor   #509

204   -LEIMER FAMILY HISTORY by "The Committee" - James Mott, Glenn and
       Helen Leimer, Marylyn Piepmeier, 1975.
       Factual history of Anton Leimer, Goisern, Austria-Prairie City, Missouri;
       and his descendants chronologically from 1821-1975, including four fold-out
       family trees, 1000 names.
       Paper-120pp-$8.50--- Vendor   #511

205   -EARLY LESLIES IN YORK COUNTY, SOUTH CAROLINA, THEIR MIGRATIONS
       TO TENNESSEE, MISSOURI AND ARKANSAS, THEIR ANCESTRY AND DESCEND-
       ANTS (THIRD EDITION) by Vice Admiral M.E. Murphy, USN, Retired, reprint
       of 1972 ed.
       The ancestry of Samuel Leslie, born c1735, and brother George Leslie (1734-
       1775) and their descendants in South Carolina, Tennessee, Missouri and
       Arkansas and numerous other states; 4100 descendants; 1300 surnames indexed.
       Cloth-270pp-$9.50-- Vendor   #513

206   -JOHN WESLEY NEAL, DESCENDANTS & ANCESTORS, 1653-1968 by Jesse H.
       Neal and Mary H. Neal.
       Neal(e): Northumberland Co., Virginia—1653-1691; Westmoreland Co., Virginia—
       1691-1735; Fairfax Co., Virginia—1735-1790; Scott Co., Kentucky—1790-1836;
       Linn Co., Missouri—1836-1876; Osage Co., Kansas—1876-1968.
       Cloth-160pp-$10.00--------------------------------------- Vendor   #519

207   -PALMER FAMILIES IN AMERICA, VOL. III compiled and arranged by
       Horace Palmer, Palmer & Wood, eds., 1973.
       Palmer: William Palmer of Plymouth and Duxbury, Massachusetts.
       Cloth-231pp-$15.50--- Vendor   #530

208   -JONATHAN BEADLE FAMILY by Walter J. Beadle, 1973.
       Beadle: History and genealogy of descendants of Jonathan Beadle who came to
       Ovid, Seneca Co., New York about 1805 from New Jersey, probably Somerset
       Co.
       Cloth-80pp-$20.00---Vendor   #530

209   -SAMUEL BEADLE FAMILY by Walter J. Beadle, 1970.
       Beadle: History and genealogy of descendants of Samuel Beadle, planter,who
       lived in Charlestown, Massachusetts in 1656 and died in Salem, Massachusetts
       in 1664.
       Cloth-1043pp-$30.00--- Vendor   #530

210   -HOWE GENEALOGIES by Daniel Wait Howe, 1929.
       Howe: This volume contains genealogies of Abraham of Roxbury, James of
       Ipswick, Abraham of Marlborough and Edward of Lynn, Massachusetts.
       Cloth-655pp-$22.50--- Vendor   #530

211   -GREGORY STONE GENEALOGY by J. Gardner Bartlett, 1918.
       Stone: Ancestry and descendants of Dea. Gregory Stone of Cambridge, Mas-
       sachusetts 1320-1917.
       Cloth-905pp-$25.00---Vendor   #530

212   -FAMILY HISTORY OF JOHN BISHOP OF WHITBURN, SCOTLAND; ROBERT
       HAMILTON BISHOP OF OXFORD, OHIO; EBENEZER BISHOP OF McDONOUGH
       COUNTY, ILLINOIS: JOHN SCOTT OF IRELAND by Stanley R. Scott & Robert
       H. Montgomery, compilers, 1951.
       Bishop: Whitburn, Scotland.
       Cloth-148pp-$10.00--- Vendor   #530

213   -MEEKER FAMILY OF EARLY NEW JERSEY by LeRoy Meeker, 1974.
       Paper-375pp-$5.50--- Vendor   #533

214   -DAVIS. . . THE SETTLERS OF SALEM, WEST VIRGINIA by Susie Davis
       Nicholson, 1975.
       A genealogy of the Davis and related families who settled Salem, West Virginia
       with many descendants to the present generation.
       Cloth-$15.00-Paper-$10.00-320pp--------------------------- Vendor   #540

215   -THE BARROW FAMILY OF VIRGINIA 1620-1972 by Maebelle Barrow North,
       1972.
       Descendants of John and Thomas Barrow - James City, Surry, Old
       Rappahannock, Isle of Wight, Prince George, Brunswick, Dinwiddie, Sussex,
       Pulaski, Henry County 1620-1972; Rockingham, Surry and Stokes County, North
       Carolina; Clarendon County, South Carolina; Southampton County, Virginia;
       Cedar County, Missouri; Illinois; Kentucky; Tennessee and Louisiana. Maps,
       pictures and coat of arms - edition limited.
       Cloth-204pp-$16.00--- Vendor   #542

216   -THE WITTWER FAMILY by Florence W. Oakes, 1968.
       Cloth-220pp-$7.50---Vendor   #549

217   -TREASURE UP THE MEMORY by James Frederick O'Nan, 1969.
       Some genealogical notes relating to the O'Nan and allied families. Chapters
       on Lincoln, Bowles, Potts, Carrico, Looney(Luna), Robinet, Taylor,
       Malohon, Monahan, Hanley, Cook connections. Index includes over 500
       surnames, some Revolutionary War soldiers.
       Cloth-157pp-$12.50--Vendor   #558

218   -WILSON RESEARCH VOLUME II by Mrs. Fred Shaw, 1971.
       Wilson name records from Pennsylvania, Ohio, Indiana, Illinois, Iowa, Missouri
       and Kansas.
       Paper-58pp-$5.00-- Vendor   #559

219   -WILSON RESEARCH VOLUME I by Mrs. Fred Shaw, 1971.
       Wilson name records from Arkansas, Mississippi, Texas, Oklahoma, Tennessee,
       North Carolina, South Carolina, Virginia, Georgia, and Kentucky.
       Paper-54pp-$5.00-- Vendor   #559

220   -A WEDGE OF THE WEDGE FAMILY IN AMERICA by Paul J. Ostendorf, 1974.
       Thomas Wedge came to America in 1668, married Deborah Stevens, lived
       in Sudbury, Massachusetts. Descendants moved to Connecticut, then to all
       New England, etc. Descendants of Robert Winter of Foston, Lincolnshire,
       England and Ohio.
       Paper-407pp-$8.00--- Vendor   #563

221   -OWINGS AND ALLIED FAMILIES by Addison D. and Elizabeth S. Owings, 1976.
       Owings: Maryland—1685-1975; South Carolina—1757-1975; Missouri—1816-1975;
       Illinois—1820-1975.
       A genealogy of some of the descendants of Richard Owings I of Maryland, 1685-
       1975, who were in twenty additional states.
       Cloth-440pp-$13.00--- Vendor   #565

222   -JOHN PANKEY OF MANAKIN TOWN, VIRGINIA AND HIS DESCENDANTS,
       VOL. I by George Edward Pankey, 1969.
       Descendants and connections of his son, Stephen Pankey, Sr., of Lucy's Springs,
       Chesterfield Co., Virginia.
       Cloth-576pp-$12.50---Vendor   #572

223   -JOHN PANKEY OF MANAKIN TOWN, VIRGINIA AND HIS DESCENDANTS,
       VOL 2 by George Edward Pankey, 1972.
       Descendants and connections of his son, John Peter Pankey, of Manakin Town,
       now Powhatan Co., Virginia.
       (Vol. 1 & 2 sold as a set for $25.00)
       Cloth-488pp-$14.75--- Vendor   #572

224   -THE SANDERS FAMILY OF GRASS HILLS by Anna Virginia Parker.
       A history of Lewis Sanders and his family, taken from private letters, diaries,
       notes and business papers. He was born in 1781, died 1861. The book covers
       the genealogy of the Sanders family from 1728 to 1965, and includes data on
       the allied families of Carter, Nicholas, Armistead, Cary, Hawkins, Smith and
       Craig.
       Cloth-172pp-$5.25---Vendor   #573

225 -THE PARKERS OF HERTFORD CO., NORTH CAROLINA NEWS by Frances E.
Parker, compiler, four issues each year, first issue June 1976.
Parker: Old Bertie Co., (area) North Carolina—c1656-present.
It is a quarterly covering Parkers in Hertford, Bertie, Northampton, and
Gates Cos., relatives that moved elsewhere.
Paper-$6.00--Vendor   #574

226 -PARKERS OF HERTFORD CO., NORTH CAROLINA by Frances E. Parker,
Fall of 1977.
Parker: Roanoke-Chowan area—c1656-present.
It starts with Thomas, son Peter, then all descendants of Peter that have
been located. Some allied names are Boyette, Copeland, Griffith, Harrell,
Whitley.
Cloth-c500pp--------------------------------------—------------------Vendor   #574

227 -THE UTAH WOOLLEY FAMILY by Preston Woolley Parkinson, 1967.
Woolley: Chester Co., Pennsylvania—1729-1833; Columbiana Co., Ohio—1833-
1838; Nauvoo, Hancock Co., Illinois—1838-1846; Salt Lake City, Utah—1847-1976.
Cloth-1145pp-$18.00--Vendor   #575

228 -TALL BARNEY'S PEOPLE: A GENEALOGY by Velton Peabody, 1974.
Beal(e): Maine—1650-1974.
Emphasis on descendants of Barna (Tall Barney) Beal, the Maine folk hero
who lived 1835-1899. Includes Alley, Lenfestey, Chandler, Woodward,
Merchant, Faulkingham, Backman.
Cloth-183pp-$10.00-- Vendor   #579

229 -THE PEAK-PEAKE FAMILY HISTORY by Cyrus H. Peake, editor, 1975.
First installment: includes British Peak/Peake/Peaks/Peakes/Peeks and
their descendants who migrated overseas.
275pp-$11.00 unbound-$14.50 3-ring vinyl cover-------------------Vendor   #580

230 -PENDERGRASS FAMILIES OF NORTH CAROLINA by Allen Pendergraft, 1977.
Pendergrass, Pendergast: Central North Carolina—1760-1900.
Descendants of Job, John, William and David Pendergrass of Orange Co., North
Carolina and vicinity, c1760-1900, who moved west through South Carolina,
Georgia, Alabama, Tennessee, Missouri, Kentucky, Arkansas, and Iowa.
Paper-c50-$7.50-- Vendor   #584

231 -CARDWELLS OF VIRGINIA by Allen Pendergraft, enlarged edition of 1973 copy.
Cardwell: Virginia—1636-1865; Stoddard Co., Missouri—1865-1898.
Descendants of Thomas Cardwell of Lancaster and Middlesex Cos, Virginia,
whose descendants moved to Halifax and Charlotte Cos.,later to North Carolina,
Tennessee and Missouri.
Paper-c50pp-$7.50--Vendor   #584

232 -THE DESCENDANTS OF SIMPSON - ROACH FAMILIES OF SOUTH CAROLINA
by Max Perry, 1974.
Related families in Chester, York and Anderson Cos., South Carolina, including Revolutionary War service. Indexed.
Paper-258pp-$10.00-- Vendor   #592

233 -NOTES ON SOME DESCENDANTS OF DUNCAN CAMPBELL OF IRELAND
     AND SOME DESCENDANTS OF JOHN S. DARBY OF KENTUCKY by Gerald
     Petty, 1966.
     Campbell: Scotland and Ireland—1600-1750; Virginia—1726-1970; Missouri
     and U.S.—1800-1970.
     About 8000 name-page index entries. Based on the Pilcher Book, with many
     additions, and some corrections. MICROFILM.
     Microfilm-612pp-$15.00 ------------------------------------- Vendor   #593

234 -SOME DESCENDANTS OF MORDECAI McKINNEY by Petty & Ridgway, 1953.
     McKinney: New Jersey, Virginia and Pennsylvania—1710-1810; Kentucky, etc.—
     1800-1840; Missouri, Texas and U.S.—1820-1950.
     About 1800 name-page index entries.
     Cloth-v+185(+4)pp-$25.00------------------------------------- Vendor   #593

235 -PETTY, WRIGHT, RILEY AND RELATED FAMILIES by Gerald Petty, 1973.
     Petty (Pettus): England—1486-1650; Virginia—1630-1970; Kentucky, Missouri
     and U.S.—1800-1970.
     Wright: Virginia and Kentucky—1785-1850; Missouri and U.S.—1830-1970.
     Riley: Maryland and Virginia—1750-1850; Kentucky, Missouri and U.S.—1830-1970.
     Families related to Petty/Pettus: Hubbard, Douglass, Alexander, Rowland,
     Copeland. Families related to Wright: Owens, Givens. Families related to
     Riley: Dale, Paxton, Tedford, Patton, McClung. About 11,000 index entries.
     Cloth-538pp-$25.00--Vendor   #593

236 -THE PEYTONS OF VIRGINIA by The Peyton Society of Virginia, 1977.
     Peyton: Virginia—1654-1800.
     Their children, plus limited number of descendants in subsequent generations.
     Prepublication price: Cloth-$12.00- Paper-$10.00-c300pp --------- Vendor   #594

237 -SOME KIBLERS FROM THE SHENANDOAH VALLEY, 1764-1975 by Donald
     Harper Ping, 1975.
     Descendants of Adam Kibler who by 1828 lived Portage and Trumbull Cos., Ohio;
     then by 1837 Jasper Co., Illinois. Major lines lived in Illinois: Batman,
     Brooks, Cummins, Clark, Fasnacht, Foltz, Foust, Koontz, McComas, Riley,
     Rodgers, Smith, Weaver. Offset, 8 1/2 x 11.
     Paper-172pp-$8.50-Indexed-Offset-8 1/2 x 11-------------------- -Vendor   #600

238 -THE PIXLEY STORY FROM HADLEY, MASSACHUSETTS TO ILLINOIS by
     Ralph Pixley and Pauline Pixley, 1976.
     Pixley: Great Barrington and Lee, Massachusetts—1763-1797; Pompey,
     Onondada Cos., New York—1800-1811; Firelands, Ohio—1811-1867; Southern
     Illinois—1867-1942.
     Cloth-173pp-$10.00--- Vendor   #604

239 -THE VAN CLEEF FAMILY by Wilson V. Ledley, C.G., 1976.
     Descendants of Jan Van Cleef; covers branches spelling names Van Cleaf, Van
     Cleave, Van Cleft, Van Cleve, Van Clief, and Van Clift; pioneers in Kentucky
     and Tennessee, Ohio, Indiana, Iowa, and three Pacific States. Included in this
     book are Addis, Adriance, Allen, Andrews, Ayers, Bailey, Baird or Beard,
     Blackwell, Bond, Bowie, Brinley, Britain, Brooks, Burke, Carpenter, Carter,
     Chandoin, Cheadle, Clark, Clayton, Clepson, Clevemeyer, Coggins, Compton,
     Conoway, Cook, Cottrel, Crawford, Daniel Boone, Wright brothers, etc.
     Cloth-270pp-$17.50--- Vendor   #608

240   -THE FULLERTONS OF NORTH AMERICA by Gordon W. Fullerton, Jr.,
       April 1976, reprint of 1974 ed.
       Fullerton: Traces immigrant Fullertons, Fullartons, Fullontons, Fullingtons
       from 1600's to present day generations. Also background history of the
       name(s) in Great Britain since 13th century.
       Cloth-$22.50-Paper-$17.50-500pp--------------------------------Vendor   #609

241   -THE LAFFOON FAMILY AND ALLIED LINES OF MALIN, WEST, FOX, AND
       WILSON by Dorothy Williams Potter and Della D. Hinman, 1977-78.
       Laffoon, William & family: Virginia; North Carolina; South Carolina; and
       Kentucky(prior 1820).
       (In process) --- Vendor   #615

242   -THE PRUETT PRUITT FAMILY by Haskell Pruett, Ph.D., 1975.
       Marriage (1846, Alabama) of descendants of emmigrants, Henry Pruet
       (c1654-1712) and Samuel Pruitt (c1684-1760) ties two lines together with
       c2,000 names, 447 family names, over 400 years. Pictures, drawings,
       stories. Index.
       Cloth-130pp-8 1/2 x 11-$20.00 -------------------------------- Vendor   #622

243   -HISTORICAL SOUTHERN FAMILIES, VOLUME XXI by Mrs. John Bennett
       Boddie, editor, 1976.
       Newton and related families: North Carolina and Georgia.
       Foster and related families: Virginia and Mississippi.
       Nelson and related families: North Carolina, Mississippi and Georgia.
       Chisholm: South Carolina.
       Another volume in this well-known series. An authoritative contribution to
       Southern genealogy, compiled from documented evidence. Source references
       given.
       Cloth-c250pp-$11.50--Vendor   #626

244   -THE ASHBY BOOK - DESCENDANTS OF CAPT. THOMAS ASHBY OF
       VIRGINIA by Lee Fleming Reese, M.A., 1976.
       836 pp of Ashbys, 110 in-laws names of one page or more, thousands of
       other names in Virginia, Kentucky, Missouri, Ohio, Indiana, Illinois, Texas,
       Florida, California and Colorado, etc.
       Cloth-1430pp-$50.00---Vendor   #636

245   -NOTABLE SOUTHERN FAMILIES, VOL. I by Zella Armstrong, 1974, reprint 1918.
       Genealogies included: Armstrong, Banning, Blount, Brownlow, Calhoun,
       Deaderick, Gaines, Howard, Key, Luttrell, Lyle, McAdoo, McGhee, McMillan,
       Phinizy, Polk, Sevier, Shields, Stone, Turnley, and VanDyke.
       Cloth-247+pp-$12.00--- Vendor   #638

246   -NOTABLE SOUTHERN FAMILIES,VOL. 2 by Zella Armstrong, 1974, reprint 1922.
       Genealogies included: Bean, Boone, Bordon, Bryan, Carter, Davis, Donaldson,
       Hardwick, Haywood, Holliday, Hollingsworth, Houston, Johnston, Kelton, Magill,
       Rhea, Montgomery, Shelby, Vance, Wear, and Williams.
       Cloth-376pp-$15.00--- Vendor   #638

247   -NOTABLE SOUTHERN FAMILIES, VOL. 3 by Zella Armstrong, 1974, reprint 1926.
       Genealogies included: Armstrong ("Trooper"), Cockrill, Duke, Elston, Lea,
       Park, Parkes, and Tunnell.
       Cloth-369+pp-$15.00--- Vendor   #638

248 -NOTABLE SOUTHERN FAMILIES, VOL. 4 by Zella Armstrong, 1974, reprint
of 1926 ed.
Genealogy of the Sevier family.
Cloth-325pp-$15.00--- Vendor #638

249 -NOTABLE SOUTHERN FAMILIES,VOL. 5 by Janie P. C. French and Zella
Armstrong, 1974, reprint of 1928 ed.
Genealogy of the Crockett family and connecting lines.
Cloth-611+pp-$18.00---Vendor #638

250 -NOTABLE SOUTHERN FAMILIES, VOL. 6 by Janie P.C. French, 1974, reprint
of 1933 ed.
Genealogy of the Doak family.
Cloth-98pp-$10.50--- Vendor #638

251 - RICHARDSON FAMILY RESEARCHER AND HISTORICAL NEWS, edited by
Harry M. Richardson.
Richardson: Maryland—1640-1700; Virginia—1700 on.
An aid for the Richardson genealogist.
$3.00 per year-- Vendor #641

252 -RICHARDSON-ELLSWORTH-ANCESTORS AND DESCENDANTS by Ruth
Ellsworth Richardson, April 1976.
Early history of Richardson and Ellsworth families in England, Scotland,
Holland and in America in early 1600's. Ships they came in, Mayflower Pilgrims,
military service, occupations.
Cloth-792pp-$25.00---Vendor #642

253 -A BATEMAN INDEX, VOLUMES I & II by Bradley B. Ridge, 1976-77.
Bateman (Baitman, Beatman): Massachusetts—1630-1830; Connecticut—1658-
1830; New Jersey—1697-1901; New York—1680-1880.
(In process) --- Vendor #643

254 -HUGH COOPER (1720-1793) OF FISHING CREEK, SOUTH CAROLINA AND HIS
DESCENDANTS by Lesbia Word Roberts, 1976.
Hugh Cooper came from Ireland and settled on Fishing Creek in Chester Co.,
South Carolina in 1773. With him were his sons, Capt. Robert, John and James
and his daughters Jane McGaughey and Elizabeth Ferguson. All his sons and
sons-in-law fought in the Revolution. The book covers the Revolution, the
Mexican War, and the Civil War with letters and diaries of the Cooper men and
women of these periods. Family migrations from South Carolina to Tennessee,
Mississippi, Arkansas, Texas and other points. Over 2000 surnames including
allied families of Gill, Ferguson, Wherry, Patton, Anderson, Barr, Hemphill,
McGaughey, Hinkle, and Smith.
Cloth-945pp-$50.00---Vendor #647

255 -ALLEN ROBINETT AND HIS DESCENDANTS IN AMERICA by James M.
Robinett, final 1980.
Five parts including tree of descendants of Allen from 1782 to present, and
details of first four generations. Prelim issue in 1970.
1000pp---Vendor #649

256 -REPASSING AT MY SIDE . . . A STORY OF THE JUNKINS by Richard D.
Robinson and Elisabeth C. Robinson, 1976.
Junkin, Joseph: Cumberland Co., Pennsylvania—1735-1806; Mercer Co.,
Pennsylvania—1806.
Thumbnail genealogical sketches of 1229 descendants of Joseph Junkin I and
Elizabeth Wallace Junkin—1735 to present.
Paper-88pp-$3.75--Vendor   #650

257 -ROCKWELL FAMILIES FROM THE BEGINNING OF TIME AND FOREVER
by Ross R. Rockwell, 1975.
Rockwell: U.S. and Canada—1630 to present.
Covers 415 years of line of descent from John and Honor Rockwell of Fitzhead,
England in 1560. Contains authentic coat of Rockwell arms.
Cloth-160pp-$6.50---Vendor   #651

258 -ONE THOUSAND FIFTY YEARS OF CONTINUOUS ROCKWELL FAMILIES
by Ross R. Rockwell, 1976.
Shows descent from King Jarl Ragnvald of Norway, born A.D. 827; William
the Conqueror, King of England & Sir Frances Drake. Illustrated.
Cloth-42pp-$6.50--Vendor   #651

259 -ROHRBAUGH GENEALOGY, VOLUME II by Lewis Bunker Rohrbaugh, 1976-77.
Rohrbaugh: Berks and Lehigh Cos., Pennsylvania—1732 to present; elsewhere
in U.S.—1732 to present.
All Rohrbach and Rorabaugh descendants of Hans Georg Rohrbach.
Cloth-c380pp-$20.00---Vendor   #652

260 -THE ROUTH FAMILY IN AMERICA by Brig. Gen. Ross H. Routh, USA (ret.)
1976.
The first published genealogy of the Routh family in America, from 1688 to
date, 4333 names, completely indexed.
Cloth-721+viiipp-$20.00-- Vendor   #659

261 -RICHARD TAYLOR, TAILOR AND SOME OF HIS DESCENDANTS by James W.
Hawes, repr. of 1914 ed.
Taylor: Massachusetts, Connecticut, New York—1646-1914.
Paper-38pp-$4.50-- Vendor   #663

262 -DESCENDANTS OF ALEXANDER PATON, TENANT OF . . .FENWICK,
AYRSHIRE by James R. Paton, repr. of 1903 ed.
Paton: Scotland—1644-1903.
Paper-12pp-$3.50--- Vendor   #663

263 -DESCENDANTS OF JAMES PATON (1811-1853) & JACOBINA WILLS (OSBORNE)
PATON OF GALSTON, SCOTLAND, AND UTAH by Hubert A. Paton, 1959, reprint.
Paton: Scotland—1811-1855; U.S.—1855-1959.
Paper-48pp-$5.00-- Vendor   #663

264 -THE FASSETT GENEALOGY by Katherine Fassett Schuster, 1974.
Fassett, Patrick and Sarah: Charlestown, Massachusetts—1651.
The book includes the descendants of Patrick and Sarah plus material on
allied families.
Hardbound-360pp-$18.00------------------------------------- Vendor   #676

265 -HISTORY AND RECORD OF C.E. AND ANTJE DIRKS by Edith Dirks
Sealman, 1969.
Dirks: Emden, Germany—   -1870; Forreston, Illinois—1870-1875;
Grundy Co., Iowa—1875-1969.
Complete record of births, deaths, marriages as well as obituaries of the
descendants (and their spouses) of C.E. and Antje Dirks through 1969. The
history and record of C.E. and Antje Oetten Ulderks (Uilderks) Dirks con-
sists of records of descendants and includes surnames of Dieken, Kramer,
Saathoff, Asmus, Wickers, Lingelbach.
Paper-168pp-$17.50--- Vendor   #678

266 -DESCENDANTS OF EVAN SHELBY SR., THE IMMIGRANT: I. REES, SR.
by Charles E. Shelby, 1977.
All known descendants listed with biographical sketches of each family,
largely in Pennsylvania, North Carolina, South Carolina, Tennessee, Illinois,
Missouri, Ohio. Indexed.
(In process)-approx. 800pp ------------------------------------- Vendor   #682

267 -THE SHIPP FAMILY GENEALOGY by Ralph D. Shipp, 1975.
372pp-$10.00 post paid--- Vendor   #683

268 -PARENTAGE & DESCENDANTS OF JOHN SHIRY, SR. & MARY "POLLY"
SHAFFER - PIONEER SETTLERS REDBANK TWP., ARMSTRONG COUNTY,
PENNSYLVANIA - VOL. 1 by Clarence Ray Shirey, 1974.
Features parents John Shira, Sr. (Rev. War) Anna Margaret Freivogel -
highlights fourth child John Shiry, 1789-1876, wife Mary "Polly" (Shaffer)
1803-1876, Berks, Westmoreland, Butler, Armstrong Cos., Pennsylvania
(War of 1812), biographies - nine children following volumes. Presently sold
out - will reprint again if enough orders!
Paper-180pp-*$20.00 *subject to change - - - - -------------------- Vendor   #684

269 -PARENTAGE & DESCENDANTS OF JOHN SHIRY, SR. & MARY "POLLY"
SHAFFER - PIONEER SETTLERS REDBANK TWP., ARMSTRONG COUNTY,
PENNSYLVANIA - VOL. 2 by Clarence Ray Shirey, 1974.
Features eldest child, Margaret Ann (Shiry) - Peter Bloom, Sr. thirteen
children's descendants 1822-1974. Armstrong Co., Pennsylvania; Moorepark,
Michigan; Cass Co., Missouri. Photos, biographies - limited supply remains.
Paper-549pp-*$35.00 *subject to change ------------------------ Vendor   #684

270 -PARENTAGE & DESCENDANTS OF JOHN SHIRY, SR. & MARY "POLLY"
SHAFFER - PIONEER SETTLERS REDBANK TWP., ARMSTRONG COUNTY,
PENNSYLVANIA - VOL. 3 by Clarence Ray Shirey, 1974.
Features second child, Elizabeth (Shiry) - William Martz descendants. Third
child, Jonathan Shirey- Amanda Elizabeth Strome descendants. Armstrong,
Jefferson Cos., Pennsylvania. Michigan 1823-1974. Biographies. Presently
sold out - will reprint again if enough orders! ----------------------- Vendor
Paper-440pp-*$30.00 *subject to change ------------------------ Vendor   #684

271 -PARENTAGE & DESCENDANTS OF JOHN SHIRY, SR. & MARY "POLLY"
SHAFFER - PIONEER SETTLERS REDBANK TWP., ARMSTRONG COUNTY,
PENNSYLVANIA - VOL. 4 by Clarence Ray Shirey, 1974.
Features fourth child, Simon Jonas Shiry - Roseanna Haas, eleven children's
descendants. 1827-1974, Redbank Township, Armstrong Co., Pennsylvania.
Biographies, photos, detailed! Author's great-grandparents. Presently
sold out - will reprint again if enough orders!
Paper-542pp-*$35.00 *subject to change ----------------------- Vendor   #684

272 -PARENTAGE & DESCENDANTS OF JOHN SHIRY, SR. & MARY "POLLY"
SHAFFER - PIONEER SETTLERS REDBANK TWP., ARMSTRONG COUNTY,
PENNSYLVANIA - VOL. 5 by Clarence Ray Shirey, 1974.
Features succeeding children's descendants. John Shiry, Jr. - Susanna Haines;
Solomon M. Shirey - Mary M. (Alsbach), Emma (Grubber), Hannah L. (Haven)
Nettleton; William Shirey - Eliza Ann George: Polly (Shiry) - John Young
Catharine (Shiry) - Levi Dinger.
Paper-274pp-*$25.00 *subject to change------------------------Vendor   #684

273 -WHO BEGOT THEE? - DESCENDANTS OF JACOB BRUBACHER OF SNYDER
COUNTY, PENNSYLVANIA by Lois Ann Zook, 1976.
Brubacher / Brubaker: Snyder Co., Pennsylvania—1800-present; Rockton,
Pennsylvania—1839-present; Lancaster Co., Pennsylvania—1885-present;
Juniata Co., Pennsylvania—1840-present.
Paper-$5.00--Vendor   #862

274 -SHOEMAKER PIONEERS by Benjamin H. Shoemaker, 3rd, 1975.
Early history of the eighty or more Shoemaker-Schumacher families who came
to American colonies before the Revolution. Contains frontispiece (coat of
arms) in six colors. Also 79 black and white pictures. Index 45 pages. A nice
memorial to your family.
Cloth-530pp-$25.00---Vendor   #686

275 -GRANDFATHER WAS ALWAYS A VERY OLD MAN by Byron Sistler, 1972.
Sitzler (Sistler-Sitchler): Monroe Co., Tennessee—1824-1972; Pope Co., Illinois—
1853-1972; Lamar Co., Texas—1870-1972.
Gibson: Pope Co., Illinois—1840-1972; Chatauqua Co., Kansas—1870-1972.
Rexer: Pope Co., Illinois—1848-1972.
Holloway: Monroe Co., Tennessee—1821-1853; Pope Co., Illinois—1853-1972.
History of Sitzlers of East Tennessee, Sistlers & Sitchlers & Gibsons & Rexers
of Pope Co., Illinois.
Cloth-239pp-$10.00---Vendor   #691

276 -ANCESTORS AND DESCENDANTS OF JOHN DODGE 1816-1898, VOL.I
by Marilyn M. Slinger and Phillip J. Slinger, 1976.
Volume I presents the biographies of John Dodge 1816-1898, his ancestors
and descendants. Many siblings of his 24 Dodge ancestors are included. Other
general Dodge family subject matter will be presented in subsequent volumes.
Paper-130pp-$12.50---Vendor   #693

277 -MY TEN IMMIGRANTS, AND FIFTY OTHER SMITH & SKAGGS LINES OF
DESCENT by Earl Davis Smith, December 1976.
Whitfield, Matthew (born c1679): From England to Nansemond Co., Virginia.
Living in Nansemond Co. in 1779.
Kennard, Richard (born c1670): Immigrant. Born near Aberdeen, Scotland.
Came to Kent Co., Maryland on January 10th, 1671. Married Mary Pullen
Howard in 1693.
King, Michael: Immigrant. Came to Virginia c1640. In Nansemond County,
Virginia in October 1667.
Crowell, John (brother of Oliver Cromwell, "The Cruel Prime Minister of
England"): Immigrant. Died in America, 1674.
Jones, Robert Ist: Immigrant. From Wales to Virginia. Died middle
1600's.
Sargeant, James (born c1730): Immigrant. Came, presumably, to Virginia.
Schaggs, William (born c1666): Immigrant. From Londonderry, Ireland to
Kent Co., Maryland in 1686.
Avent, Col. Thomas, Sr. (born in France in 1671): Immigrant. Lived
briefly in England. Came to Sussex Co., Virginia in 1698. A Huguenot.
Gooch, Lieut. Col. Henry, Sr. (born in England c1632): Immigrant. Lived
in York Co., Virginia in 1656. Was a brother of Sir William Gooch, Gov-
enor of Virginia from 1727 to 1749.
Claiborne, Col. William (born in England c1587): Immigrant. Came to
Virginia Colony in 1621. Was the first surveyor of the Virginia Company.
Book to be made up mostly of pedigree charts, with 40 Smith and 20 Skaggs
forebear charts. *Prepublication discount: 10% on advance remittance be-
fore December 1976 - $2.70.
Paper-approx. 25-30pp-8 1/2 x 11-$3.00 after publication ------------------ #695

278 -A HISTORY OF THE JOHN ALEXANDER AND LAURA HILTON SOWELL
FAMILY by Mary Sowell Hays & Carolyn E. Sowell, 1973.
Sowell: Chowan Co., North Carolina—1703-1759; Bertie Co., North Carolina—
1759-c1800; Kershaw Co., South Carolina—c1800-1886; Madison Co., Texas—
1886 to present.
Paper-102pp-$10.00 --- Vendor   #710

279 -THE COLEMANS, FITZPATRICKS AND THEIR KIN by Reba Fitzpatrick Lea,
1954.
Genealogy and life of Coleman, Fitzpatrick, Penn, Hawes, deJarnette, Hart,
Goodwin and Witt families in Caroline, Amherst, Nelson, Albemarle, and
Louisa Counties, Virginia.
Cloth-470pp-$10.50--- Vendor   #712

280 -THE FAMILY OF JACOB & MARY OLMSTEAD by Walter W. Steesy, 1975.
A complete genealogy and history of this Olmstead family tracing them from
Lycoming Co., Pennsylvania in 1840's to the present with emphasis in McKeen
Co., Pennsylvania and Allegany Co., New York. Follows all descendants.
Paper-200pp-$10.00--- Vendor   #719

281 -OLMSTEAD'S GENEALOGY RECORDED edited by Walt Steesy, started 1976.
Tracing all genealogical information relating to Olmsted/Olmstead. Queries.
Quarterly.
$5.00 per year--- Vendor   #719

282 -THE FAMILY TREE OF JOHN "PEALICKER" JOHNSON OF CONECUH COUNTY,
ALABAMA AND WILLIAM JOHNSON by Mrs. Gertrude J. Stephens, 1973, reprint.
From census records, father of above was born c1760 in South Carolina. Some
other surnames included: King, Pressley, Bain, Gaskey, Gary, Hill, Lee
Witherington and many, many others.
Cloth-275pp-$12.50 --- Vendor   #721

283 -GENEALOGICAL CLASSIFICATION BY FAMILY-GROUP CODING by Cameron
Ralph Stewart, 1977.
McLean-Stewart: Perthshire, Scotland; Puslinch, Ontario, Canada; North
Dakota; Minnesota—18th-20th century.
McAlester-McMaster: Isle of Arran, Scotland; Puslinch, Ontario, Canada—18th
-20th century.
Sharrard-S(e)arles: Dutchess Co., New York; Ontario, Canada—18th-20th
century.
Bentl(e)y-Badg(e)ro(w): New York; Markham, Ontario, Canada—18th-20th
century.
Benkestok-Miltzow: Pomerania, DDR; Gjerde-Voss, Norway—16th-20th century.
Kvale-Sandnes: Setesdal, Norway; Minnesota—15th-20th century.
Author's known ancestors' American, Canadian, Scotch, Norwegian descendants--
genealogically classified, indexed by enciphered names, well illustrated; evidence
carefully documented with relevant dates, places, events.
(In process)-approx. 1000pp --Vendor   #723

284 -FAMILY FROM STICKNEY HILL by Fernald S. Stickney, 1973, partial reprint
of 1869 ed.
Stickney: Frampton, England—1465-1638; Rowley, Massachusetts—1639-1781;
Brownville, Maine—1809-1973; Worcester, Massachusetts—1902-1973.
Johnson: Brownville, Maine—1898-1922; Trenton, North Carolina—1958-1973.
Cloth-225pp-$10.50-- Vendor   #724

285 -A SUPPLEMENT TO A STUDY OF THE BARBEE FAMILIES OF CHATHAM,
ORANGE AND WAKE COUNTIES IN NORTH CAROLINA compiled by Kathryn
Crossley Stone, 1976.
Barbee/Barby: Middlesex Co., Virginia—1685-1720; Essex Co., Virginia—1714-
1766; Orange (Chatham/Wake) Cos., North Carolina—1752-present, many
counties, Tennessee—1809- on.
Miller: Middlesex Co., Virginia—1653-1742.
Includes corrections, additions and "A Study of the Virginia Ancestors" as well
as additional lines to present.
Paper-320pp-$12.75--- Vendor   #727

286 -A STUDY OF THE BARBEE FAMILIES OF CHATHAM, ORANGE AND WAKE
COUNTIES IN NORTH CAROLINA compiled by Ruth Herndon Shields, Belle
Lewter West, Kathryn Crossley Stone, 1976, reprint of 1971 ed.
Barbee/Barby: Middlesex Co., Virginia—1685-1720; Essex Co., Virginia—1714-
1766; Orange (Chatham/Wake) Cos., North Carolina—1752-present; many
counties, Tennessee—1809- on.
Won First Runner-up in Cooke Competition 1974, sponsored by North Carolina
Society of County and Local Historians.
Paper-260pp-$15.00--Vendor   #727

287 -FOLLMER GENEALOGY AND HISTORY by Byard B. Strieby, 1975.
Follmer/Fullmer: Pennsylvania—1738 to date; Utah—1840 to date; South
Carolina—1752- ?; Alabama—1825- ?.
Crossett: Pennsylvania—1874 to date.
H'Doubler/Hougendoubler: Illinois—1857 to date; Missouri—1925 to date.
Shreffler: Pennsylvania—1780 to date; Kansas—1869 to date.
Vollmer/Vollmar: Germany—1640-1738.
Paper-164pp-$10.00--- Vendor   #728

288   -THE SWANTON GENEALOGY by Louise M. Swanton, 1976.
      Swanton: Boston—1716; throughout U.S.—1976.
      Paper-466pp-$10.00-- Vendor   #737

289   -THE DESCENDANTS OF JOHN SWARTZ, SR. (1760?-1817) OF SAUMSVILLE,
      SHENANDOAH COUNTY, VIRGINIA by B. K. Swartz, Jr., 1970.
      Swartz: Modified Lincoln notation used. Entries include date and place of
      birth, marriage and death. Descent through female lines included.
      Unbound-106pp-No charge----------------------------------- Vendor   #738

290   -TINKLEPAUGH FAMILY NEWSLETTER by M.A. Brandi Syfrit.
      Tinklepaugh: Newsletter published in September and July. Covers annual
      reunion(s) and periodically provides various lines of all Tinklepaughs as
      they are received. Additional lines/questions invited.
      Paper-send self addressed stamped envelope for price------------ Vendor   #739

291   -THE AMERICAN PIONEER - TACKETT-TACKITT FAMILIES by Jim W.
      Tackitt, editor, quarterly published since 1964.
      Tackett-Tacket-Tackitt: Over 850 pages published to date on genealogy,
      history, biographical and source records on Tackett-Tackitt families and
      descendants.
      Paper-24pp ea-prices vary------------------------------------ Vendor   #741

292   -THE WOODBINE TWINETH by Shirley Joiner Thompson, 1972.
      Joiner (Joyner): Tattnall and Camden Cos., Georgia—1847 to present.
      Drury: East Florida—1780-1795; Camden Co., Georgia—1795 to present.
      Harrell: Wayne Co., North Carolina—prior to 1785; Camden Co., Georgia—
      1785 to present.
      Mills: East Florida—1780-1795; Camden Co., Georgia—1795 to present.
      Lane (Lean): East Florida—1780-1795; Camden Co., Georgia—after 1795.
      Copeland: Tattnall Co., Georgia—   -1847; Camden Co., Georgia—1860?
      to present.
      Early history Camden Co., Georgia especially northern Bartram Trail section.
      Includes history and genealogy Spanish East Florida during late 1700's. Pictures,
      maps, charts, indexed.
      Cloth-$7.50-Paper-$6.00-156pp------------------------------- Vendor   #756

293   -TILSON by Mercer V. Tilson, 1911, reprint.
      Tilson: Plymouth, Massachusetts—1638-1911; throughout U.S.—1650-1911.
      Descendants of Edmond Tilson and wife Joanne -, Plymouth to 1911. Traces
      migration to other states. Many allied families. Supplement in progress.
      Cloth-546pp casebound-$13.00 ------------------------------- Vendor   #759

294   -TENEY, TENNEY, TENNEYSON, TENNISON, TINEY, TINN, TINNE, TINNEY,
      TINNEYSON, TINNING, TINNISON, TINNY (AND SOME VARIATIONS) FAMILY
      RECORD KEY by Thomas Milton Tinney, 1975.
      Basic index key to census, probate, vital records, histories and genealogies,
      in Europe, British Isles and America from earliest times to the present time.
      Cloth-750+pp-$79.00------------------------------- ----------Vendor   #760

295 -WE TIPTONS AND OUR KIN by Rev. Ervin Charles Tipton, 1975.
A genealogical account of the Tipton family, from 850 A.D. at Tipton, England,
the immigrants in America and related families into which they married.
Cloth-1564pp-$35.00--Vendor   #761

296 -ANCESTRY OF MY PARENTS- REJOICE FOSTER TOWNE AND ELIZABETH
CHLOE SESSIONS by George Towne, 1975.
Towne: William, Salem and Topsfield, Massachusetts—1672; Jacob, Salem,
and Topsfield, Massachusetts—1704; John, Framingham and Oxford, Massachusetts—1740; George, Union and Stafford, S. Connecticut—1953.
83 family branches traced. Some 44 to first immigrant ancestor. Compact
radial genealogical chart shows eight generations of most lines, at a glance.
11 maps.
Cloth-$10.00-- Vendor   #764

297 -ALL IN THE FAMILY by Julia M. Travis, 1975.
Travis: Pike Co., Ohio—1809-1830; Tippecanoe Co., Indiana—1830-1871;
Southern Iowa—1852-present; throughout U.S.—1900-present.
80 photographs; indexed.
Cloth-321pp-$15.00--Vendor   #767

298 -THE McCLEERS AND THE BIRNEYS - IRISH IMMIGRANT FAMILIES -
INTO MICHIGAN AND THE CALIFORNIA GOLD FIELDS, 1820-1893 by
Robert Edward Stack.
736pp-Thesis: BIP-72-24019 --------------------------------- Vendor   #777

299 -THE VERNEY FAMILY IN THE SEVENTEENTH CENTURY by Miriam Slater.
231pp-Thesis: BIP-72-14166 --------------------------------- Vendor   #777

300 -THE MASSIES OF VIRGINIA: A DOCUMENTARY HISTORY OF A PLANTER
FAMILY by Oliver Morris Refsell.
1344pp-Thesis: BIP-59-04735 --------------------------------- Vendor   #777

301 -THE HUNTS AND MORGANS: A STUDY OF A PROMINENT KENTUCKY FAMILY
by James Alfred Ramage.
440pp-Thesis: BIP-72-29289 --------------------------------- Vendor   #777

302 -THE SAGA OF AN IRISH IMMIGRANT FAMILY: THE DESCENDANTS OF JOHN
MULLANPHY by Alice Lida Cochran.
275pp-Thesis: BIP-59-00891 --------------------------------- Vendor   #777

303 -THE MANIGAULT FAMILY OF SOUTH CAROLINA, 1685-1783 by Maurice
Alfred Crouse.
469pp-Thesis: BIP-64-12266 --------------------------------- Vendor   #777

304 -THE SHIPPEN FAMILY: A GENERATIONAL STUDY IN COLONIAL AND
REVOLUTIONARY PENNSYLVANIA by Randolph Shipley Klein.
451pp-Thesis: BIP-72-17848 --------------------------------- Vendor   #777

305 -THE FAMILY OF LOVE IN ENGLAND by Jean-Kathleen Dietz Moss.
224pp-Thesis: BIP-69-20710 --------------------------------- Vendor   #777

306 -THE OTIS FAMILY IN PROVINCIAL AND REVOLUTIONARY MASSACHUSETTS
1631-1780 by John Joseph Waters, Jr.
243pp-Thesis: BIP-69-00575 --------------------------------- Vendor   #777

307 -WILLIAM ALLEN: CHIEF JUSTICE OF PENNSYLVANIA 1704-1780 by
Norman I onny Cohen, 1966.
374pp-Thesis: BIP-66-08292 ------------------------------------- Vendor   #777

308 -BIOGRAPHY OF AN IOWA BUSINESSMAN: CHARLES MASON, 1804-1882 by
Willard Irving Toussaint.
519pp-Thesis: BIP-64-03436 ------------------------------------- Vendor   #777

309 -NEW HAMPSHIRE HISTORY AND THE PUBLIC CAREER OF MESHECH WEARE
1713-1786 by Avery John Butters.
310pp-Thesis: BIP-61-01566 ------------------------------------- Vendor   #777

310 -MAHLON DICKERSON OF NEW JERSEY, 1770-1853 by Robert Russell Beckwith.
303pp-Thesis: BIP-64-00922 ------------------------------------- Vendor   #777

311 -BRIGADIER GENERAL JOHN ADAMS, C.S.A: BIOGRAPHY OF A FRONTIER
AMERICAN (1825-1864) by Rita Grace Adams.
213pp-Thesis: BIP-64-13438 ------------------------------------- Vendor   #777

312 -JONATHAN TRUMBULL, 1710-1785: CONNECTICUT'S PURITAN PATRIOT
by David Morris Roth.
427pp-Thesis: BIP-71-23589 ------------------------------------- Vendor   #777

313 -THE BRIGHTEST ORNAMENT: A BIOGRAPHY OF NATHANIEL CHAPMAN,
M.D. 1780-1853 by Irwin Richman.
343pp-Thesis: BIP-65-13376 ------------------------------------- Vendor   #777

314 -THE LETTERBOOKS OF CHARLES GRATIOT, FUR TRADER: THE NOMADIC
YEARS, 1769-1797 by Warren Lynn Barnhart.
551pp-Thesis: BIP-72-23896 ------------------------------------- Vendor   #777

315 -CHRISTOPHER GADSDEN AND THE AMERICAN REVOLUTION by James L.
Potts.
418pp-Thesis: BIP-59-0114 ------------------------------------- Vendor   #777

316 -THE ASHURSTS: FRIENDS OF NEW ENGLAND by Philip Arthur Muth.
355pp-Thesis: BIP-67-13328 ------------------------------------- Vendor   #777

317 -THE GINNS & THEIR KIN by Mrs. R.C. Upton, 1963.
Ginn: Iancaster Co., South Carolina—   -1802; Mississippi Territory—1804-
1820.
Tracing Jeptha Ginn's descendants to date.
Paper-133pp-$10.25--- Vendor   #781

318 -BULLOCK TWIGS AND BRANCHES by Mrs. R.C. Upton, 1966.
Bullock: Sussex Co.,Virginia—1757; Robeson Co., North Carolina—1825;
Marion Co., Mississippi—1840; Lawrence Co., Mississippi—1860.
Tracing Joel Bullock's descendants to date.
Paper-133pp-$10.25--- Vendor   #781

319 -"UTT - VENTURES" by Claire Utt, 1976-77.
Progenitor - Henry Utt I, of Pennsylvania, had five sons in Revolution:
Adam, Elias, Henry, George, Jacob. Some migrated to Virginia, Ohio, Illinois,
Missouri, Kansas, Idaho, California. Includes some Ott and Utz.
(In process)--- Vendor   #784

320 - 1719 - JOHN AND ESTHER HOUSTON MONTGOMERY - 1973 by
Beulah Henry Anderson, et al., 1974.
Lines - Edmonson - Doak, Lowry, McCroskey, Newell, Colville, Vawter,
Well illustrated. From Pennsylvania to Augusta Co., Virginia - Greenbrier
Co., West Virginia - Blount Co., Tennessee and other locations.
Cloth-512pp-$20.00 -- Vendor   #792

321 - THE VEDDER FAMILY IN AMERICA, 1657-1973 by Edwin H. Vedder, 1974.
2630 descendants of Harmen Albertse Vedder, early Dutch settler 1657 in
Albany, later Schenectady. Full index 50 pages. Intermarriages include
Bancker, Banta, Bratt, Brouwer, Clute, Davis, De Graff, Fonda, Grott,
Marselis, Mebie, Newkirk, Putman, Quackenbos, Schermerhorn, Truax,
Van Antwerp, Van der Vogart, Van Eps, Van Patten, Veeder, Vrooman,
Wemple.
Cloth-258pp +50pp index-$12.00 ------------------------------Vendor   #793

322 - HATHAWAYS OF AMERICA by Elizabeth S. Versailles, 1970.
26,000 Hathaways, mostly U.S.A. A genealogy sponsored by Hathaway
Family Association. Descendants of Nicholas, Arthur, William et als.
Cloth-1426pp-$20.00 --------------------------------------Vendor   #796

323 - THE BULLETIN OF THE VORPAGEL FAMILY ASSOCIATION edited by Will
C. Vorpagel, Vols. IV & V, 1975-76.
Vorpagel: Brabant-Flanders—1320-1611; Metz, France—1630-1670;
German States—1680-1857; Walworth Co., Wisconsin—1857-date.
Vols. I-III out of print. Vols. IV-V-$15.00 set. Hintz, Radke, Belveal
lines included with family heraldry. Annual subscription $7.00 quarterly.
Cloth-60-70pp-$15.00 ------------------------------------- Vendor   #803

324 - RIDGWAY-RIDGEWAY FAMILY HISTORY by Lelah Ridgway Vought, 1973.
First documented Ridgway - Ridgeway history. 103 pages; Lists
109 sources; charts, maps, census; Revolutionary War records;
photographs; Coats of Arms; 604 names in index.
Cloth-$20.00-Paper-$10.00-103pp----------------------------- Vendor   #804

325 - GENEALOGY OF THE DeBAUN FAMILY by William H. Wallce, 1974,
revision of 1970 ed.
1665 descendants in eleven generations of Joost DeBaun, who settled in
New Utrecht, New York, in 1683. (Sixth Revision).
Cloth-193pp-$18.00 -- Vendor   #809

326 - KEELING-LOVETT-CARTWRIGHT-CORNICK - CHART OF FIVE
GENERATIONS by Alice Granbery Walter, 1975.
Keeling: Lower Norfolk Co., Virginia—1674-1691; Princess Anne Co.,
Virginia—1691-1779.
Lovett: Princess Anne Co.—1700-1817.
Cartwright: Princess Anne Co., Virginia—ca 1700-1762.
Cornick: Princess Anne Co.—1748-1804.
A continuation of the previously published Martin/Keeling Book.
Paper-folding chart-$5.00-------------------------------Vendor   #811

327 - A SEVEN GENERATION CHART OF BOUSH/NIMMO FAMILIES by
Alice Granbery Walter, 1975.
Boush: Lower Norfolk Co., Virginia—1642-1691; Princess Anne Co.,
Virginia—1691—1834; Norfolk, Virginia—1900; North Carolina—1800s.
Snayle: Lower Norfolk Co., Virginia—1640s-1700.
Bennett: Lower Norfolk Co., Virginia—1650s-1700.
Folding chart-$7.00-- Vendor   #811

328 - SET OF THREE CHARTS OF WALKE FAMILY CONNECTIONS by
Alice Granbery Walter, 1975.
Four generations of the Thomas Walke lines and five generations of the
Anthony Walke lines. A two generation chart of the four marriages of
Mary Anne Thorowgood/Thorowgood/Walke/Phripp/Hackett and their issue.
Third chart five generations of Daynes-Conner-Lawson-Thorowgood connections
to Walke. Showing intermarriages with Lawson, Bassett, Conner, Sanford,
Newton, Armistead, Clouse, Thorowgood, Moore, Sayer, Boush, Wright,
Williamson, Murdaugh, Westcott, Calvert, Willoughby, Hunter, Randolph,
Moseley, McClennan, McClenahan, Fisher, Ritson, Livingston, Massenburg,
Land, et als. Lower Norfolk Co., Virginia—1662-1691; Princess Anne Co.,
Virginia—1691-1800s.
Folding charts (3)-$12.00 ----------------------------------- Vendor   #811

329 - CHART OF THE GENESIS OF THE LOVETT FAMILY IN VIRGINIA by
Alice Granbery Walter, 1975.
Lovett: Lower Norfolk Co., Virginia—1638-1691; Princess Anne Co.,
Virginia—1691-ca 1750.
Folding chart - $5.00 ---------------------------------------Vendor   #811

330 - BRIEF BIOGRAPHIES OF TWELVE ILLINOIS MEN WHO FOUGHT IN THE
CIVIL WAR, ILLUSTRATED WITH THEIR PHOTOGRAPHS by Judith
Allison Walters, 1975.
The men oncluded in this book are Luther Andrews, Samuel Baker, Edward
Bonham, John Marshall Brown, William Denchfield, Christopher Gilbert,
Joseph Goodwin, Carlton Gossett, Thomas Gray, John Hawkes, Royal
Olmsted, and George Wilkins.
Paper-34pp-$4.50 --- Vendor   #812

331 - THE DESCENDANTS OF ROBERT AND HANNAH HICKMAN WAY OF
CHESTER COUNTY, PENNSYLVANIA by D. Herbert Way.
See space ad on page 192.
--- Vendor   #818

332 - A HISTORY OF THE WELSHEIMER FAMILY by Edith L. Welsheimer, 1969.
Johannes Philip Weltzheimer immigrant to America in 1766, his sons
Frederick and Philip, the stockingweaver, and some 1,500 descendants.
Photographs, illustrations, biographies, index.
Cloth-126pp-$10.00 -- Vendor   #821

333 - BOST FAMILIES OF NORTH CAROLINA AND SOME OF THEIR
DESCENDANTS by Mary Pegram West, late 1976-1977.
Approximately 10,000 Bost descendants of two daughters and five
Revolutionary War sons of Johannes Bast. Pennsylvania, North Carolina,
and U.S.A. 1740-1975. Documented, illustrated, indexed.
Cloth-many pp --Vendor   #823

334 - A SCOFIELD SURVEY by Harriet Scofield and Henry B. Whipple, 1972.
Daniel Scofield (d. 1669), Richard Scofield (1613-1670), and their descendants
for about six generations; Rufus Scofield (1773-1854) and descendants.
Cloth-mimeographed binder iii + 132-$7.50 ---------------------- Vendor   #834

335 - SAMUEL FOGG OF HAMPTON, NEW HAMPSHIRE (1628-1672): HIS
ANCESTORS AND DESCENDANTS by Mrs. Herbert O. Whitten, Aug., 1976.
Samuel Fogg of Hampton, New Hampshire (1628-1672): His ancestors and
descendants. Approximately 1700 pages; index - 3 columns per page, 200 pages
allied families; covers all areas. Compiled by Fogg descendant.
Cloth-abt. 1700 --- Vendor   #836

336 - WILDER AND CONNECTING (ESPECIALLY WARE) FAMILIES IN THE
SOUTHEASTERN STATES by William M. Wilder, 1969.
Traces descendants of Edward Wilder in Virginia about 1648 and Robert
Ware in Virginia about 1650 and the families of the women the Wilders married.
Cloth-1131pp-$20.00 ---Vendor   #837

337 - THE WILKIE/WILKEY FAMILY by Hubert Weldon Wilkey, 1976.
Several lines of Wilkies/Wilkeys.
Cloth-250pp-$9.00 ---Vendor   #840

338 - THE JOHN DUNHAM FAMILY by Nora (Dunham) Willprecht, 1974.
The John Dunham family of Ottertail Co., Minnesota--his ancestors and
descendants—1773-1974.
Paper-44pp-$3.25 -- Vendor   #842

339 - DESCENDANTS OF ABRAHAM FUNKHOUSER by Frieda Wilson, 1972.
Nine generations, 1750-1972, Shenandoah Co., Virginia; Beaver Co.,
Pennsylvania; Ripley Co., Indiana; westward. Includes Brodbeck, Showalter,
Freed, Foster, Main, and many others.
Paper-54pp-$3.50 ---Ve ndor   #843

340 - THE LEES AND KINGS OF VIRGINIA AND NORTH CAROLINA, 1636-1976
by Mrs. Reba S. Wilson and Mrs. Betty R. Glover, 1975.
Handsome and useful genealogy and history beautifully illustrated, some in
color; maps, migration routes, 15 generations of lineage charts; fully
documented, indexed with 30,000 names. An excellent and monumental work
receiving great acclaim.
Cloth-186pp-$25.00 --- Vendor   #844

341 - DESCENDANTS OF JOHN WILSON, 1756-1827 (BROTHER OF COLONEL
BENJAMIN) by Barr Wilson, 1975.
Lists over 3100 descendants of John Wilson plus early Wilson history. The
children of John Wilson settled in Doddridge, Ritchie and Wood counties, Virginia
(now West Virginia). Includes early history of the following related families:
Moses Wilson, II, Solomon Wilson, John and William White, Blackburn,
Joel Westfall, Warthen, Modesitt, Hudkins, Slaven, Ingram, Shinn, Cunningham,
Richards, Jones, Dotson, Bee, Prunty, Broadwater, Ellifrits, Duckworth,
Clayton and Amos. 450 pages, offset printing, indexed, cloth. Printed by
McClain Printing Co., Parsons, West Virginia. Price $20.00 postpaid.
Cloth-450pp-$20.00 ---Vendor   #845

342 - HISTORY AND GENEALOGY OF THE WITHERELL/WETHERELL/
WITHERILL FAMILY OF NEW ENGLAND by Peter C. Witherell and
Edwin R. Witherell, abt. Sept., 1976.
Descendants of Rev. William Witherell (c1600-1684) of Scituate,
Plymouth Colony, and of William Witherell (c1627-1691) of Taunton,
Plymouth Colony.
Cloth-approx. 600pp --Vendor   #851

343 - LOOK BEHIND YOUR MIRROR - DESCENDANTS OF MICHAEL RUGH
AND ALLIED FAMILIES by James C. Rugh and Ramona Cameron
Worley, 1975.
Rugh: Alsace, Lorraine—1664; Lehigh Co., Pennsylvania—1733; Westmore-
land Co., Pennsylvania—1772; Indiana Co., Pennsylvania—1916.
Cameron: Scotland—c1779; Indiana Co., Pennsylvania—1884.
Grow: Franklin Co., Pennsylvania—1792; Indiana Co., Pennsylvania—1899.
Truby: Germany—1727; Indiana Co., Pennsylvania— c1900.
Kelly: Cumberland Co., Pennsylvania— c1751; Indiana Co., Pennsylvania—1863.
Bell: Dauphin Co., Pennsylvania—1737; Indiana Co., Pennsylvania—1873.
Markle: Rhine Germany—1678; Berks Co., Pennsylvania—1728.
Pershing: Germany—1749; Indiana Co., Pennsylvania—1856.
Tombs: Ireland—1760; Indiana Co., Pennsylvania—1893.
McDonald: Scotland—1772; Indiana Co., Pennsylvania—1915.
Carnahan: Scotland—1790; Indiana Co., Pennsylvania—early.
Paper-238pp-$10.65 ---Vendor   #854

344 - THE WRIGHT BOOK: WORTHY HERITAGE, ENDURING CHALLENGE by
Pauline Williams Wright, 1974.
Subtitle: "Being the history of some of the descendants of John Wright (1745-1814),
Bedford Co., Virginia." Appendices on Schooley, Short, Grant, Tallant
families.
Cloth-251pp-$7.50 --- Vendor   #855

345 - YESTERYEARS MAGAZINE edited by Francis V. Grifone, 1974-76.
Serial article entitled "Mohawk Valley Early Families." Vol. 18, No. 69-
Ferris, Fursman, Baehler; Vol. 18, No. 70- Dyer, Robertson, Rudley;
Vol. 18, No.71 - Schaick, Smith, Walrath; Vol. 18, No. 72- Christie, Place,
Greene, and Sherrill; Vol. 19, No. 73- Zee, Doane; Vol. 19, No. 74- Van Antwerp,
Hilton, Pierson; Vol. 19, No. 75- Flack, Berry, Bauder, Miller.
Paper-$2.50 per vol., $15.00 per set --------------------------Vendor   #861

346 - MY GENEALOGY by George C. Schempp, 1974.
This family history includes ten families: Schempp, George, Page, Thrasher,
Adams, Ford, Donnison, Pickert, DeGarmo, VanderWerken. New England
and New York State.
Cloth-200pp-$16.00 --- Vendor   #671

347 - THE ADVENTURES OF MY GRANDFATHER by John Lewis Peyton, 1867.
Cloth-$12.50 --- Vendor   #38

348 - A BIOGRAPHICAL SKETCH OF THE LIFE OF THE LATE CAPTAIN
MICHAEL CRESAP by John J. Jacob, 1866.
Northwestern Maryland; Hampshire County, Virginia. 1700's.
Cloth-$7.00--- Vendor   #273

349 -FOUR YEARS IN THE ROCKIES by James B. Marsh, 1884.
The adventures of Isaac P. Rose, of Shenango Township, Lawrence Co.,
Pennsylvania, giving his experience as a hunter and trapper in that remote
region and containing numerous interesting and thrilling incidents con-
nected with his calling. Also including his skirmishes and battles with the
Indians, his capture, adoption and escape. One of the most thrilling nar-
ratives ever published.
Cloth-$13.00--- Vendor   #38

350 -DIARY OF PHILLIP HONE 1828-1851 edited by Allen Nevins, 1927.
Two volumes in one.
$34.00--- Vendor   #38

351 -SIMON KENTON, HIS LIFE AND PERIOD, 1755-1836 by Edna Kenton, 1930.
$16.00---Vendor   #38

352 -THE PERSONAL NARRATIVE OF JAMES O. PATTIE OF KENTUCKY by
James O. Patty, edited by Timothy Flint, 1831.
During an expedition from St. Louis through the vast regions between that place
and the Pacific Ocean, and thence back through the City of Mexico to Vera Cruz,
during journeyings of six years.
$15.00-- Vendor   #38

353 -PRESIDENT JAMES BUCHANAN: A BIOGRAPHY by Philip Shriver Klein, 1962.
Cloth-520pp-$12.50--Vendor   #589

354 -BIOGRAPHY OF FRANCES SLOCUM, THE LOST SISTER OF WYOMING by
John F. Meginness, 1891.
A complete narrative of her captivity and wanderings among the Indians. Il-
lustrated.
$14.00------------------------------------- ------------------Vendor   #38

355 -THE INDIAN CAPTIVE: OR, A NARRATIVE OF THE CAPTIVITY AND SUF-
FERINGS OF ZADOCK STEELE by Zadock Steele, 1908, reprint.
Cloth-$13.50 --Vendor   #38

356 -BENJAMIN BROWNE FOSTER'S DOWN EAST DIARY edited by Charles H.
Foster, 1975.
Includes information from Maine, Kansas, Virginia and Washington, D.C.
Covers 1847-1853.
Cloth-367pp-$10.95--Vendor   #460

357 -LIEUTENANT LEE OF BEALE STREET by David M. Tucker, 1971.
Early believer in black power through black capitalism.
Cloth-217pp-$7.95--Vendor   #789

358 -CHARLES MORGAN AND THE DEVELOPMENT OF SOUTHERN TRANSPORTA-
TION by James P. Baughman, 1968.
Cloth-302pp-$10.00--Vendor   #789

359 -A VICTORIAN GENTLEWOMAN IN THE FAR WEST: THE REMINISCENCES OF
MARY HALLOCK FOOTE by Mary H. Foote, edited by Paul Rodman, 1972.
Illustrated.
$8.50--- Vendor   #363

360 -THE HISTORY OF THE ANCIENT SURNAME OF BUCHANAN AND OF
ANCIENT SCOTTISH SURNAMES by William Buchanan, 1793.
366pp- B-BH 15522 --- Vendor #778

361 -HISTORY OF THE WANTON FAMILY OF NEWPORT, RHODE ISLAND by
John Russell Bartlett, 1878.
153pp- B-OP 67772 --- Vendor #778

362 -DULANYS OF MARYLAND: A BIOGRAPHICAL STUDY OF DANIEL DULANY,
THE ELDER, 1685-1753 AND DANIEL DULANY, THE YOUNGER 1722-1797-
SECOND EDITION by Aubrey C. Land, 1968.
Cloth-$11.00 --Vendor #385

363 -BUCKSKIN JOE: BEING THE UNIQUE AND VIVID MEMOIRS OF EDWARD
JONATHAN HOYT, 1840-1869 by Edward J. Hoyt, 1966.
Cloth-$5.50---Vendor #521

364 -KIT CARSON'S AUTOBIOGRAPHY by Kit Carson, 1966.
Paper-$1.75-- Vendor #521

365 -SPURR GENEALOGY BEING TEN GENERATIONS FROM ROBERT SPURR OF
DORCHESTER,MASSACHUSETTS by Evelyn Davis Fincher, 1966.
Paper-108pp-$6.00ppd--Vendor #134

366 -WILLIAM CULLEN BRYANT, HIS ANCESTORS AND WHERE THEY LIVED
by Harold Stanley Bryant, 1972.
Paper-43pp-$3.50ppd-- Vendor #134

367 -PHILADELPHIA PERSPECTIVE: THE DIARY OF SIDNEY GEORGE FISHER
by Sidney G. Fisher, edited by Nicholas Wainwright, 1967.
Cloth-$12.50--Vendor #588

368 -GEORGE MASON, GENTLEMAN REVOLUTIONARY by Helen Hill Miller, 1975.
Cloth-400pp-$18.95--Vendor #544

369 -THE PAPERS OF ZEBULON BAIRD VANCE, VOLUME I, 1843-1862, edited by
Frontis W. Johnston, 1963.
Letters to and from Civil War governor for the years 1843-1862. Biographical
sketch of Vance through Civil War years included. Sketch to be continued in
future volumes. Illustrated; indexed.
$10.00--- Vendor #543

370 -THE PETTIGREW PAPERS, VOLUME I, 1685-1818, edited by Sarah McCulloh
Lemmon, 1971.
Letters to and from Pettigrew family of eastern North Carolina. Correspondence
of Charles Pettigrew, Episcopal bishop, and his only surviving child, Ebenezer,
a successful planter. Illustrated; indexed.
$15.00--Vendor #543

371 -THE PAPERS OF JOHN WILLIS ELLIS, VOLUME I - 1841-1859, VOLUME II -
1860-1861, edited by Noble J. Tolbert, 1964.
Each volume illustrated. Index to both volumes in Volume II.
$10.00 per volume--Vendor #543

372 -THE PAPERS OF WILLIE PERSON MANGUM edited by Henry Thomas Shanks.
Volume I, 1807-1832,published 1950; Volume II, 1833-1838, published 1952;
Volume III, 1839-1843, published 1953; Volume IV, 1844-1846, published 1955;
Volume V, 1847-1894, published 1956. Each volume illustrated; indexed.
Letters to, from, and about Mangum, legislator, judge of superior court,
congressman, United States senator, leading Whig.
$10.00 per volume---Vendor   #543

373 -THE PAPERS OF WILLIAM ALEXANDER GRAHAM edited by J.G. de Roulhac
Hamilton.
Volume I, 1825-1837, published 1957; Volume II, 1838-1844, published 1959;
Volume III, 1845-1850, published 1960; Volume IV, 1851-1856, published 1961;
Volume V, 1857-1863, edited by Max R. Williams, published 1973. Volumes
I and V illustrated. Each volume indexed. Papers of William Alexander Graham,
legislator, governor, United States senator, secretary of the navy. Biographical
sketches of Graham in first volume. Additional volumes planned for future.
Volumes I-IV-$10.00 per volume, Volume V-$15.00----------------Vendor   #543

374 -LETTERS TO LAURA: LETTERS FROM JOSIAH PIERCE, JR. TO LAURA
DUNHAM, 1884-1889 by Josiah Pierce, 1975.
Cloth-$7.50--Vendor   #286

375 -HISTORY AND GENEALOGY OF THE LEXINGTON, MASSACHUSETTS
MUNROES by Richard S. Munroe, 1966.
Munroes in all locations descended from William Munroe of Lexington,
Massachusetts.
Cloth-468pp-$6.50ppd--Vendor   #7

376 -JUSTICE DANIEL DISSENTING by John P. Frank, 1964.
A biography of Peter V. Daniel, 1784-1860.
Cloth-336pp-$8.00 --- Vendor   #273

377 -WILLIAM COURTENAY: ARCHBISHOP OF CANTERBURY by Joseph Dahmus,
1966.
Cloth-349pp-$12.50---Vendor   #589

378 -MEMOIRS OF BENJAMIN VAN CLEVE from Cincinnati Historical Society
Quarterly, 1963-1965.
Paper-72pp-$4.00---Vendor   #371

379 -THE UHRBROCK FAMILY OF SCHLESWIG-HOLSTEN (1640); HANOVER,
NEW YORK: AND MARYLAND.
Article from National Genealogical Society Quarterly, Vol. 55, No. 3.
Paper-12pp-$3.50--- Vendor   #514

380 -THE UPPER YADKIN VALLEY IN THE AMERICAN REVOLUTION: BENJAMIN
CLEVELAND, SYMBOL OF CONTINUITY by Betty Linney Waugh.
176pp-Thesis: BIP-72-13777 ------------------------------- Vendor   #777

381 -McDANIEL FAMILY by Martha McDaniel Thompson, 1975.
McDaniel family - North Carolina, Kentucky, Virginia, Indiana, Missouri and
others. Most common names - Eli, John,James, Daniel, William and
others. Research date. Indexed.
Paper-56pp-$4.00--- Vendor   #755

382 - NORTON GENEALOGY (DESCENDANTS OF MERCER [Messer] NORTON) by
Erma Melton Smith., 1976.
Norton: Randolph and Burke Cos., North Carolina—1750-1799; Wayne Co.,
Kentucky—1799-1820; Hardeman and Franklin Cos., Tennessee—1805-1860;
Tippah Co., Mississippi—1836 to present; Webster Co., Missouri—1853 to
present; many Utah Counties—1850 to present.
Fully indexed, legal documented proofs, 50 pictures of early ancestors, life of
each descendant.
Paper-c500pp --- Vendor   #696

383 - DOCTOR THOMAS WALKER (1715-1794) EXPLORER, PHYSICIAN,
STATESMAN, SURVEYOR AND PLANTER OF VIRGINIA AND KENTUCKY
by Keith Ryan Nyland, 1971.
177pp- BIP-72-04596 --- Vendor   #777

384 - THE OFFICE OF COMMISSAIRE ORDONNATEUR' IN FRENCH LOUISIANA,
1731-1763: A STUDY IN FRENCH COLONIAL ADMINISTRATION by Donald
Jile Lemieux, 1972.
226pp- BIP-72-28360 --- Vendor   #777

385 -CAROLINA CAVALIER: THE LIFE OF JAMES JOHNSTON PETTIGREW by
Clyde Norman Wilson, Jr., 1971.
447pp- BIP-72-10783 --Vendor   #777

386 -WILLIAM A. GRAHAM, NORTH CAROLINA WHIG PARTY LEADER, 1804-1849
by Max Ray Williams, 1965.
282pp- BIP-66-04737---Vendor   #777

387 - WILLIAM LOWNDES: SOUTH CAROLINA NATIONALIST, 1782-1822 by
Carl Jackson Vipperman, 1966.
308pp- BIP-67-03770 --- Vendor   #777

388 - WILLIAM STITH, HISTORIAN OF COLONIAL VIRGINIA by Toshiko Tsuruta,
1957.
228pp- BIP-58-01097 --- Vendor   #777

389 - JAMES MARTIN BELL: IRONMASTER AND FINANCIER, 1799-1870 by
Samuel Nissly Stayer, 1970.
323pp- BIP-71-10427-- Vendor   #777

390 - SENATOR JOHN BROWN OF KENTUCKY, 1757-1837: A POLITICAL
BIOGRAPHY by Stuart Seely Sprague, 1972.
333pp- BIP-72-21544 --- Vendor   #777

391 - A BIOGRAPHY OF HOWELL COBB, 1815-1861 by John Eddins Simpson,
1971.
329pp- BIP-72-02544--Vendor   #777

392 - THE CAREER OF JACOB DOLSON COX, 1828-1900: SOLDIER, SCHOLAR,
STATESMAN by Eugene David Schmiel, 1969.
534pp- BIP-70-14094 --- Vendor   #777

393 - ARTHUR LEE - AMERICAN REVOLUTIONARY by Louis Watson Potts, 1970.
1740-92, born Stratford, brother of Richard Henry Lee.
483pp- BIP-71-10413 --- Vendor   #777

394 - JOHN MACPHERSON BERRIEN OF GEORGIA (1781-1856): A POLITICAL
BIOGRAPHY by Royce Coggins McCrary, Jr., 1971.
456pp- BIP-72-11004 --- Vendor   #777

395 - STEPHEN BORDLEY OF COLONIAL ANNAPOLIS by Joseph Chandler
Morton, 1964.
239pp- BIP-65-00632 --- Vendor   #777

396 - HENRY DELANO FITCH: A YANKEE TRADER IN CALIFORNIA: 1826-1849
by Ronald Lee Miller, 1972.
260pp- BIP-72-21688-- Vendor   #777

397 - OLD BOB LA FOLLETTE: CHAMPION OF THE PEOPLE by Eugene
A. Manning, 1966.
(1855-1925) born Wisconsin.
213pp- BIP-66-01295--------------------------------------- Vendor   #777

398 - JAMES ANDREW CORCORAN: EDITOR, THEOLOGIAN, SCHOLAR
(1820-1889) by Mary Marcian Lowman, 1958.
499pp- BIP-59-00907 -- Vendor   #777
399 - A BIOGRAPHY OF WILLIAM CLARK, 1770-1813 by John Louis Loos, 1953.
Lewis and Clark Expedition. born Caroline Co., Virginia; moved to
Louisville, Kentucky when 14 years old; Governor of Missouri Territory;
died 1838 in St. Louis.
1071pp- BIP-00-08982 --- Vendor   #777
400 - JOHN JAY: COLONIAL LAWYER [of New York] by Herbert Alan
Johnson, 1965.
(1745-1829) b. New York City; President of the Continental Congress;
first Chief Justice of Supreme Court.
2151pp- BIP-65-11089--Vendor   #777
401 - LANGDON CHEEVES: SOUTH CAROLIAN, 1776-1857 by Archie
Vernon Huff, Jr., 1970.
316pp- BIP-70-21991--Vendor   #777
402 - THE LIFE AND TIMES OF ISAAC SHELBY 1750-1826 by Paul W. Beasley,
1968.
Soldier of Revolution and War of 1812; first Governor of Kentucky.
305pp- BIP-69-15455--Vendor   #777
403 - THE POLITICAL POSITION AND DOMESTIC POLICY OF ROBERT CECIL,
FIRST EARL OF SALISBURY, 1603-1612 by Thomas Malcolm Coakley, 1959.
425pp- BIP-60-03551 --Vendor   #777
404 - THE HOUSEHOLD AND SECRETARIAT OF WILLIAM CECIL, LORD
BURGHLEY by Richard Chambers Barnett, 1963.
3305- BIP-64-01832 --Vendor   #777
405 - COBBLER IN CONGRESS: LIFE OF HENRY WILSON, 1812-1875 by
Richard Henry Abbott, 1965.
469pp- BIP-65-13709 -- Vendor   #777
406 - GEORGIA GENTLEMEN: THE HABERSHAMS OF EIGHTEENTH-CENTURY
SAVANNAH by Wallace Calvin Smith, 1971.
411pp -BIP-72-18452 -- Vendor   #777
407 - MASTERS OF ASHLEY HALL: A BIOGRAPHICAL STUDY OF THE BULL
FAMILY OF COLONIAL SOUTH CAROLINA, 1670-1737 by M. Eugene
Sirmans, Jr., 1959.
413pp- BIP-60-05056 -- Vendor   #777
408 - THE GHENTS: A FLEMISH FAMILY IN NORMAN ENGLAND by Richard
Mylius Sherman, 1969.
BIP-70-16210--- Vendor   #777
409 - THE MASSIES OF VIRGINIA: A DOCUMENTARY HISTORY OF A PLANTER
FAMILY by Oliver Morris Refsell, 1959.
1344pp- BIP-59-04735 -- Vendor   #777
410 - THE FAMILY OF LOVE IN ENGLAND by Jean-Kathleen Dietz Moss, 1969.
224pp- BIP-69-20710 -- Vendor   #777
411 - THE SHIPPEN FAMILY: A GENERATIONAL STUDY IN COLONIAL AND
REVOLUTIONARY PENNSYLVANIA by Randolph Shipley Klein, 1972.
451pp- BIP-72-17848--Vendor   #777
412 - A CONCEPT OF THE FAMILY IN COLONIAL AMERICA: THE PEMBERTONS
OF PHILADELPHIA by Judy Mann Distefano, 1970.
371pp- BIP-71-07434 -- Vendor   #777
413 - THE MANIGAULT FAMILY OF SOUTH CAROLINA, 1685-1783 by
Maurice Alfred Crouse, 1964.
469pp- BIP-64-12266 -- Vendor   #777
414 - HE BUILT WELL by James R. Glacking, 1975.
Translation of autobiography of Johann Konrad Daehler of Carroll County,
Illinois and genealogy of his descendants.
Paper-125pp-$10.00-- Vendor   #283

415 - JOHN BRECKINRIDGE, JEFFERSONIAN REPUBLICAN by Lowell H. Harrison, 1969.
Breckinridge (1760-1806) was a leading Kentucky politican, lawyer, planter, and businessman, U. S. Senator and Attorney General.
Cloth-243pp-$9.00 --Vendor   #236

416 - HART FAMILY HISTORY - SILAS HART, HIS ANCESTORS AND DESCENDANTS by William Lincoln Hart, Repr. of 1942 ed.
1600's--Hart, Sweet, Clark, Swift, Warren, Smith, Gilson, Truesdale, Janney, McIntosh, Peckham, Gillingham, Schmid, McPherson, Rose, Milner, Artman, Beckwith, many more. Civil War Diary.
Paper-218pp-$6.00 --Vendor   #869

417 - HAMPTON, HARRISON, EARLE FAMILIES OF VIRGINIA, SOUTH CAROLINA AND TEXAS, 1977 (in process).
History of southern migration of Hampton, Harrison, Earle families of Virginia, North Carolina, South Carolina, Alabama, Mississippi, and Texas, 1619-1900, with genealogy to 1976.
--- Vendor   #863

418 - FAMILY RECORDS AND JOURNAL OF DR. WILLIAM THOS. MEBANE 1851-1857, 1972.
Mebane: Orange Co., North Carolina—1790-1850; Cross Co., Arkansas—1851-1857.
Plantation life in early Arkansas with Bible records, only 12 copies available, privately printed. Applied names: Sutton, Graham, Allen, Campbell, Reynolds, Maget.
Cloth-60pp-$12.00---Vendor   #873

419 - DAVIS, DAVID, DAVIES, DAVY by Dorothy Davis Smith.
Data on all persons of these names who were born before 1850 or married before 1875 is being gathered for computerization. 40,000 now in program. Information solicited - and given. No fee.
--- Vendor   #873

420 - THE SCHRAMM LETTERS, WRITTEN BY JACOB SCHRAMM AND MEMBERS OF HIS FAMILY FROM INDIANA TO GERMANY IN THE YEAR 1836.
Translatted and edited by Emma S. Vonnegut, 1935.
Paper-$2.00 ---Vendor   #369

421 - MARK WHITE (1690-1758) OF ACTON, MASSACHUSETTS by Robert M. Sherman and Ruth W. Sherman.
Article in National Genealogical Society Quarterly, Vol. 61, No. 4.
Paper-6pp-$3.50 --Vendor   #514

422 - "LEVI STEVENS - ONE, TWO, OR THREE?" by Cj Stevens.
National Genealogical Society Quarterly, Vol. 59, No. 4, 1971.
Paper-6pp-$3.50 -- Vendor   #514

423 - "DESCENDANTS OF MATTHEW WATSON OF BURLINGTON COUNTY, NEW JERSEY" by Lewis D. Cook, F.A.S.G., National Genealogical Society Quarterly, Vol. 58, No. 4. 1971.
Matthew was of Scarborough, Yorkshire in England, and married Anne Maulliverer of the same parish in 1681.
Paper-11pp-$3.50 --Vendor   #514

424 - "THE DIARY OF ISAAC PARSHALL, AND PARSHALL FAMILY, (CHEMUNG, NEW YORK TO PARSHALLVILLE, LIVINGSTON CO., MICHIGAN)" Timbertown Log, Vol. III, Nos. 1,2,3,4. 1974-1975.
Paper-11pp-$1.75-- Vendor   #666

425 - THE McCOYS: THEIR STORY by Truda Williams McCoy and edited by L. Roberts, 1976.
Story of West Virginia-Kentucky Feud, notes, bibliography, photos, 80 pages genealogy; including Roberts, Williamson, Scott, Scalf, Blankenship, Bevins, etc.
Cloth- c350pp-$12.00 --Vendor   #30

426 - ANNALS OF TAZEWELL COUNTY, VIRGINIA FROM 1800-1922
by John Newton Harman, Sr., 1922.
Abstracts of all wills (1800-1924); marriages 1800-1868; soldiers of
Revoluionary, Civil and World War I. Besides transcriptions of
marriages, 1800-1853, Military Records Rev. War through World
War I, the following families treated very fully: Baldwin, Bandy,
Barnes, Bowen, Chapman, Copenhaven, Coulling, Crockett, Deskins,
Gillespie, Harrison, Johnston, Gose, Graham, Graybeal, Greeves, Hankins,
Harman, Higginbotham, Hopkins, Leece/Leech, Linkous, Litz, Lockhart,
McGuire. Maxwell, Martin, May, Mays, Moore, Moss, Mustard, Peery,
St. Clair, Stras, Sparks, Thompson, Whitley, Williams, Witten, Wohlford,
Yost, Young; new every-name index of 100 pages.
Cloth-1152pp-$27.50 --Vendor   #273

427 - MAYFLOWER FAMILIES THROUGH FIVE GENERATIONS, Volume I
edited by Lucy Mary Kellogg, 1975.
There were 23 families aboard the Mayflower known to have descendants
today. The General Society of Mayflower Descendants has undertaken what
they term the "Five Generations Project." This project entails researching
and publishing data found on each of these pilgrims from their arrival in
1620 and their descendants through five generations-approximately until the
time of the Revolutionary War. One of the objects of this project is to help
others trace their ancestry without prohibitive genealogical expense. Unlike
most genealogies, both the male and female lines are being traced. This
book is the first of the series to be published and follows the descendants of
Francis Eaton, Samuel Fuller, and William White. Surnames introduced
through marriage of the female descendants include: Alden, Allen, Bacon,
Bannister, Bassett, Bisbee, Brown, Bryant, Bumpas, Chamberlain, Cowing,
Crapo, Curtis, Cushman, Demoranville, Doggett, Eaton, Eddy, Edson,
Fairbanks, Faunce, Fuller, Gibbs, Gilbert, Goss, Hall, Hamilton, Hayward,
Holmes, Howe, Hurd, Leach, Lewis, Livermore, Phillips, Pollard, Pratt,
Prince, Ramsdell, Raymond, Rice, Rich, Rickard, Robbins, Samson, Sherman,
Smith, Snell, Soule, Sturtevant, Thompson, Tinkham, Walker, Waterman,
Wheeler, White, Wilder, Willard, Wood, Young.
Cloth-300pp-$10.00---Vendor   #475

428 - SEAMAN-HUNT-WRIGHT GENEALOGY by William M. Seaman, et al.
1957, letter press.
Seaman: New Jersey—1780; Pennsylvania—1790; Midwest, Ohio—1800;
Indiana; Ohio.
Seaman children:
   1. Mary m. Aaron Hunt of Hopewell, New Jersey 1784; to Washington,
       Pennsylvania 1789; to Warren County, Ohio 1797. 12 children.
   2. Joseph, b. 1767 m. Lydia Vaughn. D. Warren Co., Ohio 1837.
       9 children.
   3. Benjamin D. in infancy.
   4. William m. Margaret Braddock. D. Washington, Pennsylvania 1812.
   5. John D. m. Mary Braddock .
   6. Charity, b. 1777; m. John McCammant.
   7. Jonas m. Martha Forbes. In Warren Co., Ohio 1803-1809; 1819.
       Then where ?
   8. Hannah, b. 1782 m. Robert Brasher in 1798. To Vigo Co., Indiana 1818.
   9. Rachel, b. 1784 in Jew Jersey. D. 1851 in Keesauqua, Iowa, m. John
       Wright; to Monroe Co., Indiana 1819.
Information desired on 4, 5, 7, 8.
Cloth-70pp-$5.00 --- Vendor   #878

779 - GENEALOGIES AND FAMILY HISTORIES: A CATALOG OF DEMAND
REPRINTS. [Copies of these books are produced on demand from microfilm
masters. Xerographic (paper) copies are priced at a minimum of $10.00
per volume. Roll microfilm copies are also available. This catalog containing
full bibliographic information is available from the publisher for $1.00 pre-paid.
Orders for the catalog or individual books should be accompanied by the publisher's
vendor number 779. Additional information on individual books is provided free
of charge. If there is more than one book pertaining to a surname this is
indicated in parenthesis following surname. Asterisk indicates that the family
is treated in a book also discussing other names.] Books on the following
families have been added recently to the catalog:

Abbe(y), Adams (2), Alden, Aldworth, Alexander (2), Alfriend, Allen (4),
*Anderson, Andrews, Angell, *Archer, Arnold, *Atlee, Axtell, Ayres,
Babbitt, Bailey/Bayley (2), Baillie, Baker (2), Ball (2), Barber, *Barger,
Barker, Barnaby, Bartholomew, Bartlett (2), Bartow, Bascom (2), *Bass,
Bates, Bathurst, Beardsley (2), Beatty, Beede, Beers, *Belcher, Belfield,
*Bell, Bellinger, Benjamin (2), Bennett (2), *Benschoter, Benson (2),
Bentley (2), Berkey, *Bernard, *Berry, Beynes, Bird, Black, *Blackiston,
Blackman, Blakely, Blanchard, *Bland, *Bloomfield, *Bloss, *Blowers,
Boardman (2), Boevey, Bolles, *Bolling, Bolton, *Bonner, Boos(e), *Booth,
*Boreman, Botsford, *Boulter, Bowman, Boyd, Bradford, Bradley, *Branch,
*Breese, Briggs (2), Brigham, Brooks, Brockway, *Bromfield, Brown,
*Brownell, *Browning, Buchanan, Buck (2), Buckingham, Bulloch, *Burley,
Burnham, *Burritt, Burton, Butler, *Cabell, *Campbell, Carpenter, Carroll,
*Carter, *Cary, Case, *Caswell, *Catesby, *Catlett, *Cave, Chenoweth,
Chevalier, Claiborne, *Clapp, Clark(e) (3), *Clay, *Cleland, Cocke, Coddington,
Coggin, Cole(s), Collier, *Collings, *Colvard, *Cook, Coombs, Corser, Covington,
Cowles, Craig, Creekmore, *Curtiss, Dana, *Dandridge, Dann, Darrow,
David(son), Davis (2), Deacon, Dean, De Haven, De Jarnette, Dennis, De Peyster,
De Veaux, Dickinson, Dickson, Dinwiddie, *Dixon, Dodge (3), Downing, Dudley,
*Dummer, Dunster, *Douglas, Duval(1), Eames, *Eardley, Eaton, Eddy,
Egle, Elbridge, Eller, *Ellett, Ellis (3), Elwell, Emery, Ewers, Fairfax,
Fairman, *Fauntleroy, *Fellows, Fenton, Ferguson (3), Ferris, *Field,
Finch, *Fleming, *Flickinger, Folsom, Foster, Forshee, Fo(r)ster, Fowler,
Fox, Francis, Franklin, *Freeman, Fuller, Gallup/Gallop, Ganung, *Gardiner,
Gardner, Garfield, Garnier, *Gay, Gibson, Giddings, Gilman, Glattfelder/
Glattfelter, *Godfrey, *Gookin, *Gordon, Goulding, Graham (2), Grant,
Graves, Graybill, *Grayson, Griffen/Griffin (3), Grimes, Grimmesey, Grout,
Grove, Guthrie (2), Haeffner, Hallock (2), *Hambly/Hambling, Hamilton (2),
Hamley/Hamlyn, Hamlin, Handerson, *Harlow, Harmon, Harriman, Harris (3),
Harrison (3), Hartwell, Haskell, *Haskins, Hathaway, Hawkins, Hayes (2),
*Heffner, *Heley, *Henderson, Henry, *Hiatt, *Hickman, Hicks, Hildreth,
Hill (2), Hilligoss, Hoge, *Holdredge, Holbrook, Holmes, Holstein/Holsten,
Hoskins, Howard (2), *Howland, Hubard (3), Hughes, Hull (2), Humphrey,
Hunt, Hunto(o)n, H(o)uston (2), *Hyde, Jackson, Jacoby, Janney, Jarboe,
Jarvis, Jennings, Jessop/Jessup (2), Jewell, Johnson (2), Jones (2), Kane,
*Keeler, Keener, Keim, Kelley, Kellum, Kent, Kerr, Kimball, King,
Kirtland, Kissam, Kneeland (2), Knox, Lamb, Lambert, Lanier, Lasher,
Latane, Latham, Lathrop, Layton, Lee (2), Lefferts, Leisler, Levering,
Levi, Lewis (2), Linn, Livingston, *Lockwood, *Logan, Logue, Lord (2),
Lothrop, Loucks, Ludlow, Lyman, McAfee, MacClay, McClure, McCormick,
McCoy, MacDonald, McIntosh, Mack, M(a)cKenzie (2), McNeil, *McRae,
Macomber, Manning, Markham, Mason, Mead(e) (2), Meigs, Meres,
Meriwether/Merryweather (2), Merrill (2), Metcalf, Meyer, *Monson,
Morgan (3), Morr, Morse, *Muller/Mueller, Munson, *Murdock, *Murray (2),
Musser, Neel, Nesbit, Newberry, Nichols, Norris, Noyes, Olin, Orth, *Page,
Painter, Pannebacker, Parry, Parsons, Parthemore, Pearce, Pendleton,

779 Penn, Pennypacker, Penrose, Perkins (2), Peter(s), *Phelps, Philbrick/
cont. Philbrook, *Phillips, Phoenix, Pierce, Pillsbury/Pilsbery, Plumb,
Pocahontas, Porter, *Potts, Powell (2), *Poythress, Pratt, *Prescott,
Prime, Provoost, Purdy, Putman (2), *Pyldren, *Quincy, *Randolph,
Reade/Reed, Requa, Resseguie, Rexford, Reynolds, Richardson (2),
Richmond (2), *Rigby, *Rittenhouse, Roberts, Robinson, Rogers (4),
Rolfe, Ross, *Rounsevill, Rowell, Royall, Rummel/Rummell, Rundle,
Runkle, Russell (2), Rutherford/Rutherfurd, Ryder, Sackett, Salisbury,
*Sanford, *Sares, Sargent, Sater, *Saunders, Savage, Savory (2),
Sawyer, Sayward, Schell, *Schumacher, Scott, Sears (2), Severance/Severans,
Sewall (3), Sharpe, Shaw, *Sheffield, *Shelley, Shep(p)ard, Sherman,
Sherrill (2), Shipley, *Shipman, Shoemaker, *Skelton, *Skipwith, *Sleeper,
Smith (6), Southworth, Spa(u)lding, Spangler, Spare, Sparr, Speed,
Spencer (3), Spengler, Spofford, Spotswood, Spray, Springer, Stanard,
Standish, Stanton (2), Starin, Starkweather, *Stauffer, Stearns (2), Steele,
*Ster, *Stetson, Stevens, Stevenson, Stickney, Stockton, Stoker, Stone,
Stouffer, Strang(e), *Straw, *Streing, Strickler, Strong, Studwell, Sumner,
Sutherland, *Swaine, Swift/Swyft, *Taggart, Talcot(t), Tanner, Taylor (3),
*Tazewell, Teffe/Tefft, Temple, Terrell, Thackeray, Thayer (2), *Thomas,
Thompson (2), *Thorne, Thornton (2), Throckmorton, *Tifft, Tomlinson,
Townsend (2), *Tredway, Trogdon, Turner, Tuthill/Tuttle, Twining, Upton,
Valentine, Van Deu(r)sen (2), Van Horn(e), Van Noy/Vannoy, Van Sickle,
Wait(e) (3), Wakeman, Waldo, *Walke(r) (3), Wallace, *Walley, Wanton,
*Warden, Ware, *Waring, Warner, Warren (3), Washburn, Washington,
Waterman, Watson, Watts, *Weare, Weaver (2), Webb, Webster (3),
Week(e)s, Welch, Welker, *Wendel(l), Wentworth, West, Westcott, Wharton,
Wheelock, *Whitcomb, White (2), Whitney (3), Whittingham, *Whittington,
*Whittle, *Wiggin, Wilcox, Wilder, Wilkinson, Williams (6), *Wilmot,
Wilson (2), Winston, Wiswall, Witter, Wolfe, Wood (2), Woodbury, Woodford,
Woods, Woodson, Woodward, Worden, Wright (2), *Younglove, Youngman,
Zuber.

---Vendor   #779

Index to Family Genealogies & Newsletters

FAMILY SHEET

HUSBAND'S NAME _____

Date of Birth _____ Place _____

Date of Death _____ Place _____

Present Address (or) Place of Burial _____

His Father _____ His Mother's Maiden Name _____

Date of Marriage of HUSBAND and WIFE on this sheet _____ Place _____

Check here if there was another marriage: By husband ☐ By Wife ☐ Was this couple divorced? Yes ☐ No ☐ When? _____

WIFE'S MAIDEN NAME _____ (Use separate sheet for each marriage)

Date of Birth _____ Place _____

Date of Death _____ Place _____

Present Address (or) Place of Burial _____

Her Father _____ Her Mother's Maiden Name _____

Items of interest about the above couple (occupations, hobbies, achievements; social, civil, and political activities; physical descriptions—include photos if possible; military service; cause of death):

Do not write in this space   Do not write in this space   Use reverse side for additional information

Have family sheet	CHILDREN (Arrange in order of birth)	Code	Birth Information	Death Information	Marriage Information
1			ON / AT	ON / AT	ON / TO
2			ON / AT	ON / AT	ON / TO
3			ON / AT	ON / AT	ON / TO
4			ON / AT	ON / AT	ON / TO
5			ON / AT	ON / AT	ON / TO

Check here if there are additional children ☐

Footnoting. To substantiate the information recorded on this page, please use the footnotes listed below. One of these numbers should be placed in the circle provided next to each answer on the questionnaire. If you got the information from a source not listed, place that source on a vacant line and use the number next to which it has been placed as your footnote number.

Use ① only if you have filled in the blank from personal knowledge (such as the name of your brother). If you must look up his marriage date, give as the source wherever you looked it up. If you asked him, give his name as the source.

① Name and address of person filling in this sheet. _____ Date _____

② _____

③ _____

④ _____

⑤ _____

⑥ _____

⑦ _____

⑧ _____

THE MARK ✔ OF A GOOD GENEALOGIST IS CAREFUL DOCUMENTATION.
THE FORM WHICH PROVIDES SPACE FOR CAREFUL DOCUMENTATION IS ABOVE.

The continuation sheet for the above form contains space for 10 additional children; plus space for additional documentation. Ratio received with 1st order is as below. Subsequent orders may specify exact number of each sheet.

8½ x 11:	100 FORMS – 75/25 — $ 3.55		8½ x 14:	100 FORMS – 75/25 — 3.85
	250 FORMS – 200/50 — 5.95		See	250 FORMS – 200/50 — 6.25
	500 FORMS – 400/100 – 9.95		next page	500 FORMS – 400/100 – 11.25
	1000 FORMS – 800/200 – 19.95			1000 FORMS – 800/200 – 20.25

ORDER FROM: GENEALOGICAL BOOKS IN PRINT, 6818 LOIS DRIVE – SPRINGFIELD, VIRGINIA 22150

FAMILY SHEET

HUSBAND'S NAME _____

Husband's Code _____

Wife's Code _____

Date of Birth _____ Place _____

Date of Death _____ Place _____

Present Address (or) Place of Burial _____

Footnoting. To substantiate the information recorded on this page, please use the footnotes listed below. One of these numbers should be placed in the circle provided next to each answer on the questionnaire. If you got the information from a source not listed, place that source on a vacant line and use the number next to which it has been placed as your footnote number.

His Father _____

His Mother's Maiden Name _____

Date of Marriage of HUSBAND and WIFE on this sheet _____ Place _____ When? _____

(Use separate sheet for each marriage)

Check here if there was another marriage: By husband ☐ By wife ☐ Was this couple divorced? Yes ☐ No ☐

Use ① only if you have filled in the blank from personal knowledge (such as the name of your brother). If you must look up his marriage date, give as the source wherever you looked it up. If you asked him, give his name as the source.

WIFE'S MAIDEN NAME _____

Date of Birth _____ Place _____

Date of Death _____ Place _____

Present Address (or) Place of Burial _____

① Name and address of person filling in this sheet.

Her Father _____

Her Mother's Maiden Name _____

② Bible Record (in possession of): _____

Items of Interest About This Couple

Occupations; hobbies; achievements; social, civil, and political activities; physical descriptions—include photos if possible; military service; cause of death; etc.

③ Tombstone: _____

④ _____
⑤ _____
⑥ _____
⑦ _____
⑧ _____
⑨ _____
⑩ _____

[Actual size: 8 1/2 x 14]

See preceding page for prices of this form.

Use reverse side for additional information.

Have family sheet	CHILDREN (Arrange in order of birth)	Do not write in this space Code ⓒ	When Born			Where Born		Married to	When Married			When Died			Present Address (or) Where Buried:
			Day	Month	Year	Town or County	State		Day	Month	Year	Day	Month	Year	
1															
2															
3															
4															
5															
6															

(Use reverse side for additional children—check here if there are additional children ☐)

Nettie Schreiner-Yantis, 6818 Lois Drive, Springfield, Virginia 22150

© 1969

Form A-166

ORDER FROM CATALOGUE OF GENEALOGICAL BOOKS IN PRINT

Title: _____

If periodical: Vol. _____ No. _____   Enclosed: $ _____
                                                 [In-state residents, please add sales tax]

Send to: _____

_____

_____

ORDER FROM CATALOGUE OF GENEALOGICAL BOOKS IN PRINT

Title: _____

If periodical: Vol. _____ No. _____   Enclosed: $ _____
                                                 [In-state residents, please add sales tax]

Send to: _____

_____

_____

ORDER FROM CATALOGUE OF GENEALOGICAL BOOKS IN PRINT

Title: _____

If periodical: Vol. _____ No. _____   Enclosed: $ _____
                                                 [In-state residents, please add sales tax]

Send to: _____

_____

_____

ORDER FROM CATALOGUE OF GENEALOGICAL BOOKS IN PRINT

Title: _____

If periodical: Vol. _____ No. _____   Enclosed: $ _____
                                                 [In-state residents, please add sales tax]

Send to: _____

_____

_____

If your supply of order forms is depleted, please acknowledge *Genealogical Books in Print* as the source of your order when writing the vendor.